Women, Power and Autonomy

Jocelynne A. Scutt
Editor

Women, Power and Autonomy

Rights, Respect and Representation in Law and Society

palgrave
macmillan

Editor
Jocelynne A. Scutt
School of Social Sciences
University of New South Wales (UNSW)
Sydney, Australia

ISBN 978-3-031-97957-6 ISBN 978-3-031-97958-3 (eBook)
https://doi.org/10.1007/978-3-031-97958-3

This Palgrave Macmillan imprint is published by the registered company Springer Nature Switzerland AG
The registered company address is: Gewerbestrasse 11, 6330 Cham, Switzerland

I do not wish them [women] to have power over men, but over themselves.

—Mary Wollstonecraft, *A Vindication of the Rights of Woman,* 1792

Index of Cases

Akinnubi v Akinnubi (1997) 2 NWLR 144 (SC).
Amaka Ezeaku v Delphine Zikere Okonkwo and Anor (2011) LPELR-57009(CA).
Australian Capital Television Pty Ltd and New South Wales v Commonwealth and Anor [1992] HCA 45, (1992) 18 CLR 106, Australian Capital Television Pty Ltd & New South Wales v Commonwealth [1992] HCA 45; (1992) 177 CLR 106 (30 September 1992) (accessed 2 March 2025).
Australian Iron and Steel Pty Ltd v Banovic (1989) 168 CLR 165, Australian Iron & Steel Pty Ltd v Banovic [1989] HCA 56 - BarNet Jade - BarNet Jade (accessed 2 November 2024).
Australian Iron & Steel Pty Ltd v Banovic [1989] HCA 56; (1989) 168 CLR 165 (5 December 1989) (accessed 2 November 2024).
Australian Iron & Steel Pty. Ltd. v. Banovic | Women and Justice | US Law | LII / Legal Information Institute (accessed 2 November 2024).
Australian Iron & Steel Pty Ltd v Najdovska and Ors (1988) NSWLR 587, NSWLR | 12 NSWLR 587 | AUSTRALIAN IRON & STEEL PTY LTD V NAJDOVSKA AND OTHERS[EDITORIAL NOTE: An

Contents

Contributors

Wandoo Grace Aibangbee Nigeria Bar Association, Abuja (Unity) Branch, Abuja, Nigeria

Baljit Banga Institute of Policy Research, University of Bath, Bath, UK

Shabina Begum Goodman Ray Solicitors, London, UK

Patricia Branco University of Coimbra, Coimbra, Portugal

Paula Casaleiro University of Coimbra, Coimbra, Portugal

Karen Dacy Independent Scholar, Melbourne, Australia

Janne Ellen Swift Independent Scholar, Wauchope, NSW, Australia

Judy Anne Forshaw Cambridge, UK

Robin R. Joyce Independent Scholar, Canberra, Australia

Anna Kerr Feminist Legal Clinic Inc, Sydney, New South Wales, Australia

Anjana Narayan California State Polytechnic University, Pomona, CA, USA

Helen Pringle School of Social Sciences, University of New South Wales, Sydney, NSW, Australia

Bandana Purkayastha University of Connecticut, Mansfield, CT, USA

Rianka Roy Wake Forest University, Winston-Salem, NC, USA

Jocelynne A. Scutt Department of Arts, Design and Architecture, School of Social Sciences, University of New South Wales (UNSW), Sydney, Australia

Anne Thacker The University of Queensland, St Lucia, QLD, Australia

Natalie Turney University of Reading, Reading, UK

Maja von Bolton Uppsala University, Uppsala, Sweden

Simone Watson Independent Scholar, Perth, WA, Australia

Jessica K. Williams Independent Scholar and Women's Rights Advocate, Victoria, Australia

Ameena Zia Division of Humanities, Brevard College, Asheville, NC, US

List of Figures

List of Tables

1

Introduction: Autonomy, Power and Respect in Women's Rights and Representation

Jocelynne A. Scutt

Introduction

Women, Power and Autonomy—Rights, Respect and Representation in Law and Society is a companion volume to *Women, Law and Culture—Conformity, Contradiction and Conflict* (Scutt 2016). *Women, Law and Culture* comprised contributions from seventeen women writing from Canada, the United States, the United Kingdom, the Netherlands and Australia incorporating scholarship and activism with their different cultural backgrounds and lived experience. *Women, Law and Culture* illustrates the ways in which law and culture are intimately intertwined, that laws are based on and in culture, laws change with cultural change, and culture is influenced by law. The book's chapters confirm that the oppression of

J. A. Scutt (✉)
Fraser Chambers, London, UK
e-mail: j.scutt@unsw.edu.au; jocelynne.scutt@cantab.net

Department of Arts, Design and Architecture, School of Social Sciences, University of New South Wales (UNSW), Sydney, Australia

J. A. Scutt (ed.), *Women, Power and Autonomy*,
https://doi.org/10.1007/978-3-031-97958-3_1

women, and women's necessary struggle to overturn it, is not confined to any one culture or country, law or religion, society or civilisation.

Women, Power and Autonomy continues this theme through the contributions of twenty-one women from India, Australia, the United States, Nigeria, Portugal, Pakistan, Sweden and the United Kingdom, with some crossing boundaries of ethnicity, state, and citizenship. English literature and literary criticism, law, politics and political science, philosophy, history, rights campaigning, linguistics, film and film criticism are included in contributors' expertise and their chapters exploring rights, respect and representation in law and society. Weaving academic expertise with activist insights, the book explores the impact of legislative change and whether it can impact on masculinist culture; the power of women's writing through fact and fiction and film, and how it can effect advances for women through law and practice; and the continuing struggle to ensure that women's status as human is firmly fixed at the baseline of society, infused through cultural norms, and entrenched in economics, law, and politics. The potential for success of this endeavour lies at the heart of rights, respect and representation.

Part I—Rights

> Definition of "rights"
> Rights in British English
> **plural noun**
> (raɪts ⓘ)
> 1.
> those things that one is morally or legally entitled to do or have
> ...
> *You must stand up for your rights.*
> *equal rights for women*

"The personal is political" is the slogan coined by the Women's Liberation Movement (WLM) in the 1970s, and attributed often to activist, writer and campaigner Robin Morgan (1970, 1977, 1999, 2011). This was a time when women defied the split of the world into public and private, determined to ensure that the inequality and oppression women experienced in the world of paidwork and in their private lives as wives, homemakers, mothers or daughters. In this, women campaigning on and for women's rights in the workplace (both the paid and the unpaid) were following firmly in the steps of women globally who had gone before: Mary Wollstonecraft on women's right to travel independently (as she did, to Paris where she lived during the French Revolution (1790, 1792), and through Scandinavia on a fruitless attempt to recover her former lover and father of her child, Gilbert Imlay's property purloined by a ship's captain (1795); Caroline Norton on rights to child custody, the entitlement of a woman to retain ownership of her own property rather than its passing into her husband's hands, and to freedom from abusive husbands (1839, 1854, 1857)[1]; Josephine Butler on women's rights not to be subjected to exploitation and medical intrusion as prostituted women (1870a, 1870b, 1871a, 1871b, 1879; Deakin 1871; The Health Foundation nd)[2]; Frances Power Cobbe on women's (lack of) property rights (1869), denial of the right to freedom and independence from matrimony (at the time allowed only by parliamentary passage of a Bill of Divorcement or under limited provisions of the *Matrimonial*

---

[1] The *Custody of Infants Act* 1839 (UK), 1839: 2 & 3 Victoria c.54: Custody of Infants | The Statutes Project, https://statutes.org.uk/site/the-statutes/nineteenth-century/1839-2-3-victoria-c-54-custody-of-infants/ (accessed 2 March 2025) is attributed to Caroline Norton's campaigning, as is the *Matrimonial Causes Act* 1857 (UK), Matrimonial Causes Act—Oxford Reference, https://www.oxfordreference.com/display/10.1093/oi/authority.20110803100140335 (accessed 2 March 2025) which abolished ecclesiastical law in its control of marriage and associated law through the Ecclesiastical Courts, ensuring that this became subject instead to secular law under the (secular) Divorce and Matrimonial Causes Court, a hugely significant advance.

[2] Repeal of the *Contagious Diseases Act* 1864 (UK), *Contagious Diseases Act* 1866 (UK) and *Contagious Diseases Act* 1869 (UK) is attributed to Josephine Butler (Hageman nd). The British Contagious Diseases Acts (1864, 1866, and 1869) | Towards Emancipation?, https://hist259.web.unc.edu/contagious-diseases-acts-1864-1866-and-1869/ (accessed 2 March 2025); *Contagious Diseases Acts Repeal (No 2) Bill* 1886 (UK), CONTAGIOUS DISEASES ACTS REPEAL (NO. 2) BILL. (Hansard, 18 March 1886), https://api.parliament.uk/historic-hansard/commons/1886/mar/18/contagious-diseases-acts-repeal-no-2-bill (accessed 2 March 2025); The Health Foundation, *Policy Navigator—The Contagious Diseases Act*, nd, The Contagious Diseases Act | Policy Navigator, https://navigator.health.org.uk/theme/contagious-diseases-act#:~:text=The%20Contagious%20Diseases%20Act%20was%20first%20passed%20in,transmitted%20diseases%20within%20the%20British%20army%20and%20navy. (accessed 2 March 2025).

Causes Act of 1857),[3] and freedom not to be subjected to wife torture (1878).

Lawyer Anna Kerr, in Chapter 2 "A Mother of a Job—The Control and Commodification of Women's Reproduction", canvasses the subjection of women to control and denial of independence through marriage and motherhood, pregnancy, forced maternity, rights to and for children, abortion and adoption under Australian laws, and failures in justice. Reforms, she explains, are variable: advances are minimised through the exercise of judicial discretion and (mis)interpretation; then countervailing pressures on governments adhering to traditional notions of a rightful woman's place generate changes oppositional to those gained through women's campaigns. Women recommence lobbying in a seemingly endless round of advance, opposition, pressing forward ... Including reference to abortion, her contribution runs alongside Chapter 3, Patricia Branco and Paula Casaleiro's dissertation on legislative and political advances in family law and freedoms, finances and fashioning women's rights through constitutional measures and by revolutionary reform—successes, misses and failures—in "The Daughters of the Carnation Revolution: 50 Years of Women's Rights in Portugal". Together, Kerr, Branco and Casaleiro illustrate and confirm what is a global phenomenon of women's subjection to patriarchal power exercised through rights and wrongs in marriage and maternity, pregnancy and pregnancy termination, with women's rights to decide upon our bodies for ourselves, and the struggle for women's very personhood, at its heart.

[3] The *Matrimonial Causes Act* 1857 (UK), Matrimonial Causes Act—Oxford Reference, https://www.oxfordreference.com/display/10.1093/oi/authority.20110803100140335 (accessed 2 March 2025), gained through Caroline Norton's efforts was an advanced on the then existing law, but women's rights to freedom from matrimonial tyranny remained a matter for continued campaigning—the then existing law, but the *Matrimonial Causes Act* 1878 (UK), The Matrimonial Causes Act of 1878 | COVE, https://editions.covecollective.org/chronologies/matrimonial-causes-act-1878-0#:~:text=As%20a%20result%2C%20the%20Matrimonial%20Causes%20act%20of,opportunity%20to%20separate%20from%20their%20physically%20abusive%20husbands (accessed 2 March 2025); Matrimonial Causes Act—Oxford Reference, https://www.oxfordreference.com/display/10.1093/acref/9780199532988.001.0001/acref-9780199532988-e-1192 (accessed 2 March 2025), attributed to Frances Power Cobbe's campaigning was designed to enable women to escape from violent husbands, though it was criticized in the press and fiction as failing to do so. House of Commons Hansard entries provide an insight into how many separation orders were issued during particular periods (House of Commons, *Hansard*, 1895a; House of Commons, *Hansard* 1895b).

In Chapter 4 "Widows—Denial of Rights and Respect in Southern Nigeria", Wandoo Grace Aibangbee confirms the application of this principle beyond the shores and laws of Europe. For the women of Southern Nigeria, when a marriage ends by the husband's death, women continue to be controlled: this time, by the husband's family. Custody rights are absent. They are automatically conferred upon his family, not her or hers. She is denied the right to marriage until re-marriage is deemed respectable through a sufficient lapse of time (determined by laws and customs enforced by social conformity and a desire not to be humiliated or demeaned): if the widow defies this diktat, she is shamed and derided, potentially becoming a victim of abuse, mockery and ridicule, or worse. Reading this against the backdrop of Kerr, Branco and Casaleiro highlights that although the customary practices Aibangbee describes are absent from European and Australian contemplation, and the battle for mother's rights was fought and formally won by Caroline Norton and those who followed her, child custody may be resolved on the law's face, yet applying laws justly for and to women may not be so simple.

Janne Ellen Swift, Natalie Turney and Anne Thacker turn to the woman outside the home. Swift and Turney consider respectively her chances of non-traditional paidwork, of financial freedom, and company advancement, while Thacker addresses the woman who transgresses the boundaries of "female" behaviour, and her potential for maintaining a life outside prison where threatened with gaol. Swift's Chapter 5 "Forging the Right to Work with Metal—Women and the Struggle for Work in Wollongong" recounts the story from the perspective of one who was there, campaigning for women workers' rights. The women battled for jobs in the iron and steel country of New South Wales, the Australian state where the British invasion of the land, displacement and attempted genocide (Australian Human Rights Commission 1997) of First Nations or Indigenous Australians began. A grassroots campaigner, together with others Swift infiltrated Australian Iron & Steel (AI&S), defying the company's assertions that women were incapable of working in steel, that foundries were not workplaces for women, that women's bodies were not fit for the lifting required—albeit the "requirement" was manufactured

(Refshauge 1984; Mason 1990 1992). The women won, and worked, were dismissed, then won again.[4]

The fight to gain a woman's foothold is replicated in the commercial world, as recounted by Turney in Chapter 6 "Demanding the Right of Representation for Women in Corporate Structures and Policy in the United Kingdom". Incorporating personal anecdote with her company law expertise, Turney apprehends the "virulent" lack of representation of women in corporations at "decision and policy-making levels". Considering the interplay of board members' powers set beside those of directors, and the overarching role of the shareholder, Turney delivers an indictment of unconscious bias that undermines any effort to include women in the make-up of boards or senior management. Yes, (some) women may achieve the highest positions within the company, yet more than the isolated elevation is necessary to overturn years of male-rule and the notion that men alone possess board and upper management qualifications and skill. As she points out, women's inclusion leads to a corporation's greater achievements in production, research and development, so that leaving women out of the equation is poor economics.

Chapter 7, Thacker's "Criminal Court Links to a Better Lifestyle and a Better Community in Queensland, Australia" addresses the potential for positive difference as a factor in applying criminal court processes. Women, she says, appear to be more responsive to the Court Link bail policy which is designed to provide support for those granted bail and entering the program. Just as in the corporate world women are

[4] *Australian Iron and Steel Pty Ltd v Banovic* (1989) 168 CLR 165, *Australian Iron & Steel Pty Ltd v Banovic* [1989] HCA 56—BarNet Jade—BarNet Jade, https://jade.io/article/67531 (accessed 2 November 2024); *Australian Iron & Steel Pty Ltd v Banovic* [1989] HCA 56; (1989) 168 CLR 165 (5 December 1989), https://www.austlii.edu.au/cgi-bin/viewdoc/au/cases/cth/HCA/1989/56.html (accessed 2 November 2024); Australian Iron & Steel Pty. Ltd. v. Banovic | Women and Justice | US Law | LII / Legal Information Institute, https://www.law.cornell.edu/women-and-justice/resource/australian_iron_steel_pty._ltd._v._banovic (accessed 2 November 2024); Australian Iron & Steel Pty Ltd v Banovic [1989] HCA 56; (1989) 168 CLR 165 (5 December 1989), https://www.austlii.edu.au/cgi-bin/viewdoc/au/cases/cth/HCA/1989/56.html (accessed 1 November 2024); *Australian Iron & Steel Pty Ltd v Najdovska and Ors* (1988) NSWLR 587, NSWLR | 12 NSWLR 587 | AUSTRALIAN IRON & STEEL PTY LTD V NAJDOVSKA AND OTHERS[EDITORIAL NOTE: An application for special leave to appeal to the High Court from part of the judgment herein has been lodged.], https://nswlr.com.au/view/12-NSWLR-587 (accessed 2 November 2024).

noticeable (or too often unnoticed) for their general absence, in the world of crime women are far less likely to feature (Mukherjee and Scutt 1981, 2016; Carlen 2009). Yet the aims of Court Link appear to be better able to be fulfilled when women enter the system. Thacker writes as a magistrate of some 25 years and now presiding as Court Link magistrate overseeing the bail program. The aim is to buoy and sustain offenders' capacity to rehabilitate before going to prison, so that custody is avoided. Thacker posits four possibilities underpinning the outcomes for women. First, it may be that women "are more ready and open" to accept and work within the program through their adherence to "societal norms" and a responsiveness to the "more holistic approach" advanced. Secondly, the inclusion of women-focussed agencies means that women are managed by women—an improvement on a system that fails to understand that a "women only" or "women-centred" approach is a better fit. Thirdly, women may be more ready to accept "life planning" when provided by women, and in turn this may mean that the implementation of the package is better able to be adapted to the woman and society's imperatives. Finally, it may be, says Thacker, that an unconscious bias operates due to fewer women being in the program, and their successful outcomes are more likely to be recorded. Yet equally the recognition that a male prison system, designed with men in mind because there are more of them, is antithetical to the needs of woman-as-prisoner may be the reality behind the successes.

Part II—Respect

> ***Meaning of respect in English***
> **respect**
> *noun*
> uk
> **/rɪˈspekt/ us**
> **/rɪˈspekt/**
> respect *noun* (ADMIRATION)
> …

> admiration felt or shown for someone or something that you bel ieve has good ideas or qualities:
>
> I have great/the greatest respect for his ideas, although I don't agree with them.
>
> …

The elements inherent in the chapters on rights lead readily into those categorised under "respect". That the law under patriarchy has harboured no or little respect for women underlies failures in the legal system or customary law as reflected in the contributions of Aibangbee, Kerr and Branco and Casaliero. Efforts at law reform will be less likely to be resisted, and more likely to be affirmed in operation, where respect is inherent in the way parliaments, courts and society as a whole regard women and women's rights to equality. Similarly the infiltration of women into traditional male workplaces or management will meet less resistance and, indeed, would be embraced with alacrity, were women to be respected for their qualities and skills, as illustrated in Turney and Swift's chapters on corporations and company decision-making. So, too, with women in conflict with the law: the failure of the criminal justice system is well-documented when it comes to women, and the success related by Thacker in the Court Link bail system is likely due to the respect women experience when being treated as individuals, each with her own identity, responsibilities, and life circumstances.

The chapters in Part II also exhibit rights discourse, or lack of rights. This cross-over between rights refused and respect denied, with the denial of respect at the heart of the refusal of rights, is evident in Jocelynne A Scutt's Chapter 8 "When a Woman's Body is Not her Own: Regulating Women through Abortion Law", in Maja von Bolton's comprehensive and nuanced analysis in Chapter 9 of "Surrogacy: A Question of Women's Right to Self-Determination or Exploitation of Women's Bodies?" and by Simone Watson and Helen Pringle in Chapter 10 "The Prostitution System as the Wreckage of Women's Autonomy: Revising Sexual Assault Law to Undermine Structural Coercion". Decision-making about women's bodies is corralled by laws, regulations, religious diktat and dominant cultural demands that transfer power from women into the hands and minds of men. Abortion is pre-eminent in this discourse on rights and respect, for it cannot be treated as a health matter alone, so long as women are not entitled to equal rights and respect as men. As Scutt points out, even where decriminalisation of abortion has occurred, women's health and safety remain on a knife-edge, with forces assembled to threaten and undercut women's health rights by depriving her of the respect she and her decision-making warrant.

The use of women's bodies as objects to be prostituted through "sex work" or "womb work" is explored by Watson and Pringle, and Bolton through meticulous evaluation of women's right to respect and to equal rights as fully human. Consent is a key: how can it be taken seriously where parties are not equal, where opportunities are distributed differently and differentially on the basis of class, country and context, and sex. The circumstances surrounding consent and the point at which it operates are skipped over in public discussion and legislative debate. It is almost as if, when this issue is raised at the site of the prostituted woman, the principle enunciated in chief justice Matthew Hale's direction (1636) that marital rape did not exist, because the wife had given her consent to marry and that was the end of it, is applied. As political activist Rachel Moran (2015) says in *Paid For*, just where does consent arise? Is it at the point where the 15-year-old, homeless and desperate for a bed on which to sleep, "agrees" to "exchange" sexual intercourse for a roof over her head? Or is it when, responsible for the lives of her children, the single mother sees the easiest way out of her impoverished state to resort to a street corner or advertise for men to come to her home? Or does it come with demands of a male partner whom she believed was a love-match, conditioning, coercing or persuading her that his (and her) survival (and his continuing "love") are dependent upon her trading her body? Is it when, teeth gritted, she endures the foul smell of a "customer" (or "client") whilst praying to get it over with? Watson and Pringle advocate a review of consent as defined and applied in law where prostituted woman are concerned (a submission they put to the Australian Senate in its review into rape law and consent [Parliament of Australia 2023]), concluding with four proposals for addressing the prostitution industry comprehending the commerce as violence against women.

Bolton addresses issues of consent, too—this time in the context of surrogacy. She addresses commercial surrogacy and the contended differences between it and altruistic surrogacy, looking at the legal position in Sweden where both are prohibited, yet the "differences" provide a springboard for those lobbying for introduction of the practice. She progresses arguments for and against altruistic surrogacy, surveying and questioning the ethics and elements that guide proposals that Sweden adopt new surrogacy laws allowing for this type of transaction. As the title of her chapter indicates—"... Self-Determination or Exploitation ...", any conclusion one way or the other must weigh up contentions specifically addressing women's rights to bodily autonomy. This cannot be effectively nor honestly addressed without taking into account women's position in the polity, power relationships and power dynamics. Those advocating "altruistic surrogacy"—between friends, relations, or where it is simply an absence of financial inducement claimed to take the transaction out of "commercial" surrogacy—do so contending that surrogacy provides women with a "right to self-determination". This is said to be a woman's right, and this—in being an "I am entitled to do with my own body as I wish" desire—should not be taken from them. Bolton balances that position against the assertion that surrogacy constitutes exploitation of women's bodies. Having canvassed the debates swirling in this contested terrain, she advances a conclusion as to what is the answer in philosophical and real-world terms—for the rights of women whose bodies are vulnerable to this use. The discourse she painstakingly reconnoitres explodes the too easy reliance upon the notion that exploitation of women is centred alone in commercialisation. It nullifies the idea that because no monetary profit accrues, the transaction is between equals. It negates the proposition that autonomy exists where a woman's body is subjected to use by another or others, to fulfil the non-existent "right" to a child. A woman's rights lie in the entitlements accruing to all human beings, to be treated as human, as a person entire. A woman is more than the womb at the centre of surrogacy. Whether commercial or non-commercial, the equation of a woman with a womb undercuts her autonomy and denies her personhood, normalising "a view of the female body merely as a means to achieve others' goals".

For Shabina Begum, her Chapter 11 "Informed Consent and Preventing Loss of Innocence: Child and Forced Marriage in the United States" thoroughly outlines laws pertaining to child marriage and forced marriage in the United States. As the field is governed by state legislatures, she highlights action taken by the various states to direct how the law should promote the rights of children and young people (mainly girls and young women) who are subjected to, or threatened with or at risk of being married to older—often far older—men, despite their youth, their right to childhood and young womanhood, and their right to make uncoerced, adult choices in adulthood. As state law is the regulatory vehicle, variation in accordance with where a child and her family live can be considerable. As Begum observes, the impact of child and forced marriage is substantial, with education interrupted (leading to a denial of career prospects and job opportunities), sexual intercourse and pregnancy imposed upon too-young bodies, rape (which this sexual intercourse constitutes as consent cannot be real), other forms of abuse and violence, the responsibilities of motherhood clashing with the status of childhood, and all too often having their lives abruptly ended through murder whether at the hands of the husband or his family or hers, should she seek to escape. Quoting the UN Population Fund (2025), Begum affirms child marriage as "a human rights violation". She advocates adoption by all US states of the law passed by the UK Parliament, legislation she was directly involved in drafting and advocating, the *Marriage and Civil Partnership (Minimum Age) Act* 2022—where under any circumstances it is a crime to arrange for a child to marry, whether the marriage be religious or secular. The aim is to "safeguard children against child, early and forced marriage ... and protect their futures" (Dunn 2023).

Chapter 12 sees Rianka Roy, Bandana Purkayastha and Anjana Narayan advocating for attention to be paid to the conundrum confronting those existing "Between Legal and Non-Legal Terrains: Religious Nationalisms and Racialized Women Immigrants in the United States". This again raises questions of rights and respect, and the ways in which women's backgrounds, ethnic origins and ethno-religious connections can place them at a double disadvantage. Roy, Purkayastha and Narayan focus on Hindu Indian American women in a climate that has seen the rise of religious nationalism, both in India and the Indian diaspora in the US—Hindu nationalism or Hindutva, and in the US—white Christian nationalism. The latter is hostile or at least adverse or even adversarial to those adhering to Hinduism, so that women in this position are "othered" both in their status as woman and in their religious observance. Yet fundamentalism advancing through Hinduism does not treat women with equanimity, particularly where the women are seen as "their" women. The position of women in this chapter is thus precarious on account of religious belief (or renunciation of it), because of their identity as women, and through their "foreignness" in a "white" (particularly a white Christian nationalist) country.

Rights, or lack of them, are centre stage in Chapter 13 "Lobbying for Change—One Woman's Experiences of Incarceration and Male Violence". Having lived the experience herself, Jessica K Williams reflects on women outside the law and in prison because of it. Now a campaigner for woman-as-prisoner, and well-versed in research and reasons for women's transgressions, Williams considers the background conditions that result in women's detention. Facing myriad health issues (never treated properly or effectively in the outside world (Nargund 2024), never mind through imprisonment), grappling with children and family responsibilities, confronting lack of opportunities in education and employment, forced to live on less through the pay gap, the pensions gap and the superannuation gap, dealing with lack of self-esteem, physical, psychological and emotional violence, makes it almost inevitable that some women err. Coping with the lack of respect experienced by all women dwelling in the realm of second-hand citizenship and her place in the world contested, extricating herself from a world literally and figuratively behind bars may be beyond her reach.

Part III—Representation

Dictionary – Definitions
representation
/ˌrɛprɪz(ɛ)nˈteɪʃn/
noun

the action of speaking or acting on behalf of someone or the state of being so represented.

"you may qualify for free legal representation"

the description or portrayal of someone or something in a particular way.

"the representation of women in newspapers"

The chapters comprising "Part III—Representation" address the varying ways representation relates to and positions women in law and society. Women may be in parliaments or have a real opportunity, now, to be represented in them by women members, just as women may have comparatively leading roles (as well as occupying a majority of subservient ones) in religious bodies or financial institutions. As considered by Ameena Zia in Chapter 14 "Representation: Making the Absent Present", opportunities formerly (and formally (Scutt 2016)) denied to women provide avenues for entry, although as Zia reports this can be problematic. Integrating research with international declarations promoting women's inclusion, and national and local efforts to increase numbers of women and minorities in representative positions, particularly legislative bodies, she explores what constitutes democracy. In this, Zia addresses the question whether populations and communities do or can accept that incorporating women and minorities into political institutions is mandatory for true or real democracy. Achieving this goal, which bespeaks attaining "alternatives to the dominant culture", is reliant upon the existence of or creating an "inclusive civil society" consisting of "political parties, political challengers, the media, interest groups, hearings, opinion surveys, and other processes of communications ...". Referencing US examples alongside brief case studies of Pakistan's approach to women's representation, she references Hillary Clinton's campaign for the US presidency in 2016. Albeit unsuccessful, Zia concludes that Hillary Clinton's stand as a candidate, and the campaign itself, shifted perceptions of who is entitled to hold political office—or at least run for it.

The reference to "Hillary for President" and the media's role as a partner in inclusive civil society brings into sharp relief the portrayal of women as authority figures. Is there an authority gap (Sieghart 2021) that women must cross before society does regard them as equal, and equally authoritative? Control of the media by "big money" and corporate interests, yet courts' ignorance of the impact this has on democracy's reliance on an informed public, presents a challenge.[5] Some would contend that the rapidly growing role and influence of social media provides an antidote. Yet does this follow? Women members of parliaments may universally contest this. Considering former MP Julia Gillard's time as Australian prime minister (the first-ever women in the job), women can be targeted viciously. This Karen Dacy graphically recounts in Chapter 15 "'Thieving Rorters!' A Linguistic Analysis of Australian Female Politicians Construction in Public Comments in the post-Gillard Period". The media and the public, particularly when it comes to social media, can be ruthless in distorting the actions and work of women who take on high-profile posts, particularly in politics. Notwithstanding this, women in government may have some sway in making the world outside the boundaries of parliament a better place for women. The hope lying with policies aimed at increasing the number of women in leadership is that their socialisation and lived experience as women will make them more likely to press for women-centred action. Does this follow? Party political strategies, plans and pressures have an effect, and standing out against the whips can result in dis-endorsement and loss of position. That women are in a minority despite measures directed at increasing their numbers, means that they must fight in their own corner, as well as fighting to support the women outside.

One of the most serious tests is that relating to women-centred services. This arose in Part I—Rights, in Anne Thacker's Chapter 7 "Criminal Court Links to a Better Lifestyle …" relating to women in

[5] Both the Australian High Court and the United States Supreme Court have held that seeking to rein in corporate media influence is an attack on freedom of speech, despite the exclusive advantage it gives to corporate interests and media moguls, who thereby dominate broadcasting, television and print media, rendering "free speech" a commodity owned by the corporate interests and media moguls, to the detriment of public discourse. See *Citizens United v FEC* 558 US 310 (2010), Citizens United v. FEC | 558 U.S. 310 (2010) | Justia U.S. Supreme Court Center, https://supreme.justia.com/cases/federal/us/558/310/ (accessed 2 March 2025); *Australian Capital Television Pty Ltd and New South Wales v Commonwealth and Anor* [1992] HCA 45, (1992) 18 CLR 106, *Australian Capital Television Pty Ltd & New South Wales v Commonwealth* [1992] HCA 45; (1992) 177 CLR 106 (30 September 1992), https://www.austlii.edu.au/cgi-bin/viewdoc/au/cases/cth/HCA/1992/45.html (accessed 2 March 2025).

the Court Link bail program, where support is targeted to "fit" the woman's circumstances so that she can work with measures designed to help reintegrate her in society. It is addressed also in Part II—Respect, where Jessica K Williams' Chapter 13 "Lobbying for Change ..." reflects upon the importance of women prisoners being housed with women. It arises again here, in the context of funding women's services. In Chapter 16 "State Violence, Women's Safety and the Deficit in Resources and Services" Baljit Banga points out that services for women is an ever-continuing contest, particularly in relation to access for Black and minority women. In the UK, the notorious "austerity budget" of 2010 under the coalition Conservative-Liberal Democrat government was challenged in the courts by the Fawcett Society's application for judicial review. Their contention that the government erred by failing to adhere to the *Equality* Act 2010 (UK)[6] in its requirement that a gender impact assessment should be undertaken was recognised, but the budget measures were so far advanced in implementation that this superseded the action. Hence on 6 December 2010 the judicial review was refused.[7] That women were disproportionally affected, contrary to the discrimination provisions of the Equality Act, was not sufficient for the court to intervene. Then as Banga emphasises, austerity cuts were compounded by the impact of the 2019–2020COVID pandemic (The Week Staff 2022), preceded by Brexit[8] and the replacement of ring-fenced (or quarantined) grants "with service contracts under [a] commissioning and public procurement regime". This, she observes, has a major deleterious effect on service-provision addressing violence against women and girls, with "women's refuge provision ... fundamentally impacted by [a] funding policy that subjects these services to open market competition" favouring "bigger non-specialist providers operating on economies

---

[6] *Equality* Act 2010 (UK), Equality Act 2010, https://www.legislation.gov.uk/ukpga/2010/15/contents (accessed 2 March 2025).

[7] *Fawcett Society v Chancellor of the Exchequer* [2010]EWHC 3522 (Admin), Fawcett Society v Chancellor of the Exchequer—Case Law—VLEX 792,911,661, https://vlex.co.uk/vid/fawcett-society-v-chancellor-792911661 (accessed 2 March 2025).

[8] The term given to the result of the referendum held in the United Kingdom in 2016 whereby the UK severed its membership of the European Union (EU), Britain exiting the EU despite a significant sector of the population having voted to remain—simply too few as against the majority voting "leave": Government of the Netherlands (nd).

of scale". Women miss out, their right to equal provision undermined and ignored through government failure to acknowledge that "equal" must take into account the unequal realities of women's lower pay, lower pensions, greater poverty (an issue referenced by Ameena Zia earlier) and lesser representation in governments and legislatures.

Encapsulated in the claim for equal representation in these sectors is the question of women's depiction in classical literature and cinema, pornography and social media, and in stories written for the girls' and teenage market. Chapters addressing these aspects raise, too, questions of women's activism and motivators to their action. Interlinkages between Part III contributions and those earlier in this volume become clear when considering, as one example, the impact on girls of the issues at the heart of property and financial rights explored by Robin Joyce in Chapter 17, "Women and Property: An Early Literary Response", and Natalie Turney's Chapter 6 in Part I, "Demanding the Right of Representation for Women..". Were teenage girls influenced by the emphasis on wills, inheritance, and women's missing out or having to fight for these rights in books by Mary Grant Bruce, LM Montgomery, Elsie J Oxenham and Roberta Moss (Robert Moss writing under a female nom de plume as Joyce observes)? That the first book in the "Anne of Green Gables" series bears that title, and throughout the series the house Green Gables features prominently, so with the "Billabong books", outlined by Joyce:

> Billabong is described throughout the novels, demonstrating Grant Bruce's concern with the magnitude of the property surrounds as well as the rambling house, and later her emphasis on Norah's right to a Billabong homestead, if not the original.

Joyce goes on to observe on the significance of the property in content and title: *Norah of Billabong*, *Bill of Billabong*, *Mates of Billabong*, *Billabong's Daughter*, *Billabong Riders* and *Son of Billabong*. Albeit the reality is that Norah, the principal character, has no title to or in Billabong, she "is associated with the property in the [book's] titles more than any other character".

The influence of fiction may go beyond literature. As discussed by Jocelynne A Scutt in Chapter 20 "Barbie Meets a Very Poor Thing Silenced by the Lambs: Feminist Filmmaking (En)Counters Masculine Renditions of the Female", has Barbie the doll promoted young women's independence besides (or instead of) persuading them to strive after a body shape impossible for any woman or girl to secure? Do the films *Anora* and *Poor Things* as juxtaposed against the feminist implications of *Barbie* the film link graphically with the exploitative wrongs done to women as untangled by Helen Pringle in Chapter 19 "Living in a Pornographic World: Constraint on the Autonomy of Girls and Women", and Judy Forshaw in Chapter 18 "Lolita: The Mocked Female Reader".

Themes in Forshaw's "Lolita" ally with those addressed by Pringle in her "Living in a Pornographic World ..." and Scutt's reflection on the film *Poor Things* in Chapter 20. Forshaw observes that the publication in the US of Vladimir Nabakov's *Lolita* led, by reason of its "rocky reception", to an avoidance of addressing the reality of the book's central theme, namely the exploitation and sexual abuse by an adult man—Humbert Humbert—of the child Dolores (named by him "Lolita"). Scutt recognises the failure by author Alisdair Gray in the book *Poor Things*, and director Yorgos Lanthimos, production, cast and crew of *Poor Things* the film plus Academy voters bestowing on it eleven nominations and four Oscars, to acknowledge the exploitation inherent in adult sexual activity with a three-year-old (the age of Bella/Victoria's brain when Wedderburn commences his sexual relationship with her fully-grown body). These chapters address directly the question of women's autonomy—or lack of it—in living in a world where women's bodies are accepted as rightly subject to the male gaze and more, the imposition of male handling where the man has the upper-hand. In confirming that pornographic objects and practices "reflect, construct, normalise and even valorize violence and systemic inequality on the basis of sex", Pringle's chapter dovetails with the normalisation and even validation provided by the elevation of Nabakov's *Lolita* into the cannon, and *Poor Things* having transported Gray and his work into the upper reaches of Scots literature, simultaneously ensuring Lanthimos a place in cinema history, so legitimating the sexual exploitation of girl children.

This effectively raises the denial of autonomy that comes, too, with the undermining of women's identity through (re)naming. Akin with prostituted women, women in pornography are known by names that are not their own. Linda Boreman Marchiano, known as "Lovelace" through her exploitation in *Deep Throat* and other films made by her husband Chuck Traynor (Lovelace (Marchiano) and McGrady 1980) is, along with Dolores, one of the most notorious: even her autobiography is published under the name "Linda Lovelace" rather than Linda Marchiano (or Boreman). Humbert Humbert's insistence, as Forshaw pinpoints, that Dolores is "Lolita" denies her identity not only in the novel, but in the universal acceptance of his title for her in everyday language. Originally this use (in the language of everyday) attributed to Dolores responsibility for Humbert's abusive paedophilic exploitation of her, which was never recognised in that reality, those terms, as adult sexual activity imposed by an adult on a minor. Today's more ready acceptance (at least in some circles) of Humbert as the story's villain (however much Nabakov dissimulated, attempting to camouflage his character's lack of it) nevertheless continues to privilege "Lolita" over Delores.[9] Before reading Forshaw's chapter, how many even recalled that the 14-year-old girl had a real name? or recognised that "Lolita" was not it? Similarly with *Poor Things*. "Bella" is originally Victoria, this name stripped of her by her "rescuer" Godwin Baxter when he revives her dead body by inserting into it the brain of the foetus she is carrying when she jumps to her watery death. This renaming parallel's the old law of coverture, where upon marriage a woman's personhood was subsumed in that of her husband, starkly confirming the married woman's loss of identity, compounded by the loss of her name in the legal or cultural requirement that she take the name of her husband.

Nonetheless, Joyce's consideration of women's property rights (and wrongs) in Chapter 17 highlights the way in which writers can and do engage politically to advance women's claims. Albeit coverture has been abolished by women's campaigns for autonomy, the continued

[9] See for example Wood (2020). Alisson Wood's book bears a title incorporating "Lolita" with no recognition that Humbert Humbert's victim was Dolores—despite the book's expose of Wood's own subjection to coercive control in a sexually abusive and exploitative "relationship" with her teacher.

practice of the woman adopting her husband's name links these chapters back to those in Part I, relating to woman's place in family law: Chapter 2, Anna Kerr's "A Mother of a Job …", Chapter 3, Patricia Branco and Paula Casaleiro's "The Daughters of the Carnation Revolution …", and Chapter 4, Wandoo Grace Aibangbee's "Widows …", and in Part II, Chapter 11, Shabina Begum's contribution on child and forced marriage, "Informed Consent and the Prevention of Loss of Innocence". These challenges to autonomy are reflected, too, in Maja von Bolton's Chapter 9, "Surrogacy - …".

Conclusion

When rights are in issue, inevitably questions of power and autonomy surface. That women not infrequently find the embrace of power difficult can be no surprise. When "power over" has been used to control women, it is no wonder that women are reluctant to embrace power as a positive prospect. Yet as *Women, Power and Autonomy* illustrates, women must gain autonomy and claim it without demur. In so doing, women will gain the facility to take on power—both in challenging its misuse and abuse, and in adopting the stance that it is right to assert power when the purpose is to declare one's own rights and the rights of others who have similarly been denied. Attributed to the English Lord Acton (Acton Institute 2025):

> Power tends to corrupt and absolute power corrupts absolutely. Great men are almost always bad men, even when they exercise influence and not authority; still more when you superadd the tendency of the certainty of corruption by authority.

It is equally true or more so that lack of power corrupts and can corrupt absolutely. Wollstonecraft's *A Vindication of the Rights of Woman* saw this clearly. She was in no sanguine state when it came to addressing the way in which patriarchy undermined women as human, laying women vulnerable to charges of being wilful, inconsistent, unworthy of equal claims to citizenship and equal rights in the polity. Wollstonecraft wanted women to fight back. In *Women, Power and Autonomy* twenty-one women from around the globe join forces with her. In setting out the challenges that confront us all in both public and private spheres, the contributors make evident their political positioning in the world and their determination to make it a better one.

No one—no one—has a right to exercise coercive control over any woman. No one—no one—has a right to deny any woman power over herself to exercise for herself and to promote for those who are similarly disempowered. Wollstonecraft wanted woman-as-voice-of-reason to be heard and did her utmost to ensure that it was. The contributors to *Women, Power and Autonomy* are equally engaged in the endeavour to right women's wrongs through—

The Voice of Reason

The voice of reason
Is
A woman's voice
Loudly resonating
Voicing
Feminist claims
Feminist demands
Down the ages

Spoken
Voiced
Enunciated
        Heard
        Yet
        Too often not ever acknowledged
        Too often ignored
        Too often not listened to
Yet resonating
Loudly

Christine de Pizan – Not Christopher
Matilda Joslyn Gage – Not Martin Jimmy
Vida Goldstein – Not Victor
Adela Pankhurst – Not Adam

Emily Wilding Davison – Not Emmanuel Winston
Sojourner Truth – Not Samuel
Mary Wollstonecraft – Not Maurice
Mary Shelly – Not Michael
Frances Wright – Not Frank
Balaram Das – Not Benjamin
Laura Cereta – Not Laurence
Isabel de Villena – Not Ian
Lucrezia Marinella – Not Lance
Elizabeth Cady Stanton – Not Effriam
Susan B Anthony – Not Solomon B

How many more names should we celebrate?
How many more names should we know?
How many more names ought be recalled?
How many more names lost, forgotten, to be resurrected?

Today
/women
        celebrate them all – together with the celebration of self in
        power and autonomy,
        tailing on the magnificent history
        the herstory of every woman before us, who holds out
        her arms to us,
        welcoming us into the fold of the feminists of fame and sorority,
        her arms, their arms, lifting us up,
        pushing us forward,
        pressing us on,
/to keep going in strength and in fortitude

Heroines with voice, everyone of them
        \and
as Heroines of History and Herstory
we make sure that their voices are added to
        \by
        \our
        \voices

Voices today

Requiring, demanding, entreating, claiming and –
in one great chorus
Demanding
The governments
Globally
Honour the rights of women
Honour the rights of girl children
Reserve a place, for all, every one
In a global recognition of rights, humanity, personhood

The voice of reason
The voice of women
The voice of women as human
Will – Be – Heard!

Voiced at The Women's Parliament of 9 December 2024

Bibliography

Reported Cases

Australian Capital Television Pty Ltd and New South Wales v Commonwealth and Anor [1992] HCA 45, (1992) 18 CLR 106, Australian Capital Television Pty Ltd & New South Wales v Commonwealth [1992] HCA 45; (1992) 177 CLR 106 (30 September 1992), https://www.austlii.edu.au/cgi-bin/viewdoc/au/cases/cth/HCA/1992/45.html (accessed 2 March 2025).

Australian Iron and Steel Pty Ltd v Banovic (1989) 168 CLR 165, *Australian Iron & Steel Pty Ltd v Banovic* [1989] HCA 56 - BarNet Jade - BarNet Jade, https://jade.io/article/67531 (accessed 2 November 2024).

Australian Iron & Steel Pty Ltd v Banovic [1989] HCA 56; (1989) 168 CLR 165 (5 December 1989), https://www.austlii.edu.au/cgi-bin/viewdoc/au/cases/cth/HCA/1989/56.html (accessed 2 November 2024).

Australian Iron & Steel Pty. Ltd. v. Banovic | Women and Justice | US Law | LII / Legal Information Institute, https://www.law.cornell.edu/women-and-justice/resource/australian_iron_steel_pty._ltd._v._banovic (accessed 2 November 2024).

Australian Iron & Steel Pty Ltd v Banovic [1989] HCA 56; (1989) 168 CLR 165 (5 December 1989), https://www.austlii.edu.au/cgi-bin/viewdoc/au/cases/cth/HCA/1989/56.html (accessed 1 November 2024).

Australian Iron & Steel Pty Ltd v Najdovska and Ors (1988) NSWLR 587, NSWLR | 12 NSWLR 587 | AUSTRALIAN IRON & STEEL PTY LTD V NAJDOVSKA AND OTHERS[EDITORIAL NOTE: An application for special leave to appeal to the High Court from part of the judgment herein has been lodged.], https://nswlr.com.au/view/12-NSWLR-587 (accessed 2 November 2024).

Citizens United v FEC 558 US 310 (2010), *Citizens United v. FEC* | 558 U.S. 310 (2010) | Justia U.S. Supreme Court Center, https://supreme.justia.com/cases/federal/us/558/310/ (accessed 2 March 2025).

Fawcett Society v Chancellor of the Exchequer [2010]EWHC 3522 (Admin), Fawcett Society v Chancellor of the Exchequer - Case Law - VLEX 792911661, https://vlex.co.uk/vid/fawcett-society-v-chancellor-792911661 (accessed 2 March 2025).

Statutes, Conventions and Treaties

Contagious Diseases Act 1864 (UK), The Contagious Diseases Act | Policy Navigator, https://navigator.health.org.uk/theme/contagious-diseases-act#:~:text=The%20Contagious%20Diseases%20Act%20was%20first%20passed%20in,transmitted%20diseases%20within%20the%20British%20army%20and%20navy. (accessed 2 March 2025).

Contagious Diseases Act 1866 (UK), The Contagious Diseases Act | Policy Navigator, https://navigator.health.org.uk/theme/contagious-diseases-act#:~:text=The%20Contagious%20Diseases%20Act%20was%20first%20passed%20in,transmitted%20diseases%20within%20the%20British%20army%20and%20navy. (accessed 2 March 2025).

Contagious Diseases Act 1868 (UK), The Contagious Diseases Act | Policy Navigator, https://navigator.health.org.uk/theme/contagious-diseases-act#:~:text=The%20Contagious%20Diseases%20Act%20was%20first%20passed%20in,transmitted%20diseases%20within%20the%20British%20army%20and%20navy. (accessed 2 March 2025).

Contagious Diseases Act 1869 (Ireland), The Contagious Diseases Act | Policy Navigator, https://navigator.health.org.uk/theme/contagious-diseases-act#:~:text=The%20Contagious%20Diseases%20Act%20was%20first%20passed%20in,transmitted%20diseases%20within%20the%20British%20army%20and%20navy. (accessed 2 March 2025).

Custody of Infants Act 1839 (UK), 1839: 2 & 3 Victoria c.54: Custody of Infants | The Statutes Project, https://statutes.org.uk/site/the-statutes/nineteenth-century/1839-2-3-victoria-c-54-custody-of-infants/ (accessed 2 March 2025).

Equality Act 2010 (UK), Equality Act 2010, https://www.legislation.gov.uk/ukpga/2010/15/contents (accessed 2 March 2025).

Marriage and Civil Partnership (Minimum Age) Act 2022 (England and Wales), Marriage and Civil Partnership (Minimum Age) Act 2022, https://www.legislation.gov.uk/ukpga/2022/28/enacted (accessed 2 March 2025).

Married Women's Property Act 1870 (UK), 1870: 33 & 34 Victoria c.93: Married Women's Property Act | The Statutes Project, https://statutes.org.uk/site/the-statutes/nineteenth-century/1870-33-34-victoria/1870-33-34-victoria-c-93-married-womens-property-act/ (accessed 2 March 2025).

Matrimonial Causes Act 1857 (UK), Matrimonial Causes Act 1857 - UK Non-devolved - Legislation - VLEX 808408569, https://vlex.co.uk/vid/matrimonial-causes-act-1857-808408569 (accessed 2 March 2025).

Matrimonial Causes Act 1878 (UK), Matrimonial Causes Act - Oxford Reference, https://www.oxfordreference.com/display/https://doi.org/10.1093/oi/authority.20110803100140335 (accessed 2 March 2025).

Matrimonial Causes Act 1878 (UK), The Matrimonial Causes Act of 1878 | COVE, https://editions.covecollective.org/chronologies/matrimonial-causes-act-1878-0#:~:text=As%20a%20result%2C%20the%20Matrimonial%20Causes%20act%20of,opportunity%20to%20separate%20from%20their%20physically%20abusive%20husbands. (accessed 2 March 2025).

Articles and Book Chapters

Cobbe, Frances Power, "Wife-torture in England", *Contemporary Review*, vol 32, April 1878, 55–87, https://www.proquest.com/docview/6686178, https://www.proquest.com/docview/6686178 (accessed 2 March 2025).

Dunn, Madaline, "Long overdue legislation change brings an end to child marriage in England and Wales", *The Legal Journal*, 30 arch 2023, Long overdue legislation change brings an end to child marriage in England and Wales | The Legal Journal, https://legaljournal.com/long-overdue-legislation-change-brings-an-end-to-child-marriage-in-england-and-wales/#:~:text=Under%20the%20legislation%2C%20it%20is%20now%20a%20crime,and%20forced%20marriage%20%28CEFM%29%20and%20protect%20their%20futures. (accessed 2 March 2025).

Mason, Chloe, "Submission to the National Occupational Health and Safety Commission in Response to Lead: A Public Discussion Paper" in *Discrimination Against Women in the Lead Industry*, Occasional Papers from the Sex Discrimination Commissioner, No 5, Sydney, Australia, 1990.

Mason, Chloe, "Anti-discrimination Law and Occupational Health and Safety" in Doug Blackmuir, Di Fingleton and David Akers, eds, *Women's Occupational Health and Safety: The Unmet Needs*,Queensland Women's Consultative Council/School of Management, Human Resources and Industrial Relations, QUT, 1992, 63.

Morgan, Robin, "The Personal Is Still Political" *NPQ New Perspectives Quarterly*, vol 16 (4), 53–54 (Fall 1999), 1 February 2011, New Perspectives Quarterly: Vol 16, No 4, https://onlinelibrary.wiley.com/toc/15405842/1999/16/4 (accessed 22 March 2025).

Nargund, Geeta, "We need to transform women's healthcare to tackle 'medical misogyny'", *BMJ* 387:q2813, 2024, We need to transform women's healthcare to tackle "medical misogyny" | The BMJ, https://www.bmj.com/content/387/bmj.q2813 (accessed 2 March 2025).

The Week Staff, "UK's Covid timeline: key dates in the pandemic", *The Week*, 19 October 2022, UK's Covid timeline: key dates in the pandemic | The Week UK, https://theweek.com/uk-news/107044/uk-coronavirus-timeline (accessed 2 March 2025).

Books and Reports

Australian Human Rights Commission, *Bringing Them Home Report*, AHRC, Sydney, Australia, 1997, Bringing them Home Report (1997) | Australian Human Rights Commission, https://humanrights.gov.au/our-work/projects/bringing-them-home-report-1997 (accessed 2 March 2025).

Butler, Josephine, *The Constitutional Iniquity of the Contagious Diseases Acts of 1866 and 69*, The National Association for the Repeal of the Contagious Diseases Acts, London, UK, 1871a.

Butler, Josephine, *The Constitution Violated*, Edmonston and Douglas, Edinburgh, UK, 1871b.

Butler, Josephine, *Social Purity*, Morgan and Scott, London, UK, 1879.

Carlen, Pat, *Women, Crime and Poverty*, Open University Press, Berkshire, UK, 2009.

Cobbe, Frances Power, *Criminals, Idiots, Women, and Minors: is the Classification Sound? A Discussion on Laws Concerning Property of Married Women,*

A Ireland and Company, Manchester/London, UK, 1869; Nabu Press, Charleston, SC, US, 2011.
Hale, Matthew, *The History of Pleas of the Crown*, F Gyles, T Woodward, and C Davis, London, UK, 1736.
Lovelace (Marchiano), Linda and McGrady, Mike, *Ordeal*, Citadel Press, NYC, NY, 1980; reprinted Citadel Press, NYC, NY, US, 2006.
Moran, Rachel, *Paid For – My Journey Through Prostitution*, WW Norton, NYC, NY, US, 2015.
Morgan, Robin (ed), *Sisterhood is Powerful – An Anthology of of Writings from the Women's Liberation Movement*, Vintage Books, NYC, NY, US, 1970.
Morgan, Robin, *Going Too Far: The Personal Chronicle of a Feminist*, Random House, NYC, NY, US, 1977.
Norton, Caroline Elizabeth, *English Laws for Women in the Nineteenth Century*, 1854 orig. pub., reprinted Chicago Review Press Incorporated, Chicago, Il, US, 1982.
Parliament of Australia, *Report – Current and proposed sexual offence laws in Australia*, Canberra, ACT, September 2023, Current and proposed sexual consent laws in Australia – Parliament of Australia, https://www.aph.gov.au/Parliamentary_Business/Committees/Senate/Legal_and_Constitutional_Affairs/sexualcontentlaws/Report (accessed 2 March 2025).
Refshauge, Chloe, *Protective Legislation at Work. A case study of the "weight limit" on manual handling*, Report of the President of the NSW Anti-Discrimination Board, Sydney, Australia, 1984.
Scutt, Jocelynne A (ed), *Women, Law and Culture – Conformity, Contradiction, and Culture*, Palgrave Macmillan, London, UK, 2016.
Mukherjee, SK and Scutt, Jocelynne A, *Women and Crime*, Allen and Unwin, Sydney, Australia, 1981; Routledge, Oxford, UK, 2016.
Sieghart, Mary Ann, *The Authority Gap: Why women are still taken less seriously than men, and what we can do about it*, Doubleday, London, UK, 2021.
Wollstonecraft, Mary, *Letters Written During a Short Residence in Sweden, Norway and Denmark*, 1795 orig. pub., Oxford University Press, Oxford, UK, 2009.
Wollstonecraft, Mary, *A Vindication of the Rights of Men*, 1790 orig. pub., reprinted HarperTorch, NYC, NY, US, 2014.
Wollstonecraft, Mary, *A Vindication of the Rights of Woman*, 1792 orig. pub., reprinted Everyman's Library Classics, London, UK, 1992.
Wood, Allison, *being lolita – a memoir*, FlatIron Books, NYC, NY, US, 2020.

Information Documents (inc. Pamphlets) and Sources

Acton Institute, *Acton Research – Lord Acton Quote Archive*, 2025, Lord Acton Quote Archive | Acton Institute, https://www.acton.org/research/lord-acton-quote-archive (accessed 22 March 2025).

Butler, Josephine, *An Appeal to the People of England on the Recognition and Superintendence of Prostitution by Governments*, Banks, Nottingham, UK, 1870a.

Butler, Josephine, *The Duty of Women in Relation to Our Great Social Evil, and Recent Legislation Thereupon*, Hudson Scott, Carlisle, UK, 1870b.

Contagious Diseases Acts Repeal (No 2) Bill 1886 (UK), CONTAGIOUS DISEASES ACTS REPEAL (NO. 2) BILL. (Hansard, 18 March 1886), https://api.parliament.uk/historic-hansard/commons/1886/mar/18/contagious-diseases-acts-repeal-no-2-bill (accessed 2 March 2025).

Deakin, Charles Washington Shirley, *The Contagious Diseases Acts, 1864, '66, '68' (Ireland), '69, From a Sanitary and Economic Point of View*, University College, London, 30 November 1871, The Contagious Diseases Acts: the Contagious Diseases Acts, 1864, '66, '68 (Ireland), '69, from a sanitary and economic point of view: being a paper read before the Medical Society of University College, London, on Thursday, November 30th, 1871: Deakin, Charles Washington Shirley: Free Download, Borrow, and Streaming: Internet Archive, https://archive.org/details/b22298423 (accessed 2 March 2025).

Government of the Netherlands nd, What is Brexit? | Government.nl, https://www.government.nl/topics/european-union/question-and-answer/what-is-brexit (accessed 22 March 2025).

Hagemann, Karen, "The British Contagious Diseases Acts ...", nd, *Towards Emancipation* - The British Contagious Diseases Acts (1864, 1866, and 1869) | Towards Emancipation?, https://hist259.web.unc.edu/contagious-diseases-acts-1864-1866-and-1869/ (accessed 2 March 2025).

The Health Foundation, *Policy Navigator – The Contagious Diseases Act*, nd, The Contagious Diseases Act | Policy Navigator, https://navigator.health.org.uk/theme/contagious-diseases-act#:~:text=The%20Contagious%20Diseases%20Act%20was%20first%20passed%20in,transmitted%20diseases%20within%20the%20British%20army%20and%20navy. (accessed 2 March 2025).

House of Commons, *Hansard* 1895a, MATRIMONIAL CAUSES ACT, 1978 (SEPARATION ORDERS). 1, *Hansard* 31 August 1895, MATRIMONIAL CAUSES ACT, 1878 (SEPARATION ORDERS). (Hansard, 31

August 1895), https://api.parliament.uk/historic-hansard/commons/1895/aug/31/matrimonial-causes-act-1878-separation (accessed 2 March 2025).

House of Commons, *Hansard* 1895b, MATRIMONIAL CAUSES ACT, 1878 (SEPARATION ORDERS). 2, *Hansard*, 13 June 1895, MATRIMONIAL CAUSES ACT, 1878 (SEPARATION ORDERS). (Hansard, 13 June 1895), https://api.parliament.uk/historic-hansard/commons/1895/jun/13/matrimonial-causes-act-1878-separation#S4V0034P0_18950613_HOC_45 (accessed 2 March 2025).

Norton, Caroline, *A Plain Letter to the Lord Chancellor on the Infant Custody Bill by Pearce Stevenson*, 1839, Oxford University, Oxford, UK, https://archive.org/details/aplainlettertol00nortgoog (accessed 2 September 2024).

Norton, Caroline, *A Review of the Divorce Bill of 1856, with propositions for an amendment of the laws affecting married persons*, JW Parker, London, UK, 1857; National Library of Australia, ACT, https://catalogue.nla.gov.au/catalog/6350046 (accessed 2 September 2024)

REPRESENTATION definition and meaning | Collins English Dictionary, https://www.collinsdictionary.com/dictionary/english/representation (accessed 22 March 2025).

RESPECT | English meaning - Cambridge Dictionary, https://dictionary.cambridge.org/dictionary/english/respect (accessed 22 March 2025).

RIGHTS definition and meaning | Collins English Dictionary, https://www.collinsdictionary.com/dictionary/english/rights (accessed 22 March 2025).

UN Population Fund, Geneva, Switzerland, *Child marriage*, 2025, https://www.unfpa.org/child-marriage (accessed 9 July 2024).

Part I

Rights

Human rights are women's rights, and women's rights are human rights. So let us not forget that among those rights are the right to speak freely—and the right to be heard.

—Hillary Clinton, UN International Women's Conference Beijing 1995

2

A Mother of a Job: The Control and Commodification of Women's Reproduction

Anna Kerr

Introduction

Controlling women's reproduction is one of the most effective means of controlling women. The history of collusion between church, state and medical profession confirms a concerted effort to maintain this control. Although the freedom to determine the number and spacing of children has been recognised as a human right,[1] and some jurisdictions have fully decriminalised abortion, in practice women's access to contraception and abortion services continues to be subject to legislative limitations around the world, including Australia.[2] Constraints apply, too, binding women's

A. Kerr (✉)
Feminist Legal Clinic Inc, Sydney, New South Wales, Australia
e-mail: anna@feministlegal.org

[1] *Convention on the Elimination of All Forms of Discrimination Against Women* (CEDAW) Article 16.

[2] In Australia, state by state and territory abortion has been decriminalised substantially, for example NSW on 2 October 2019 with repeal of *Crimes Act* 1900 (NSW) Sections 83 and 84, and Queensland *Criminal Code* 1899 (Qld) Sections 224, 225 and 226 in October 2018

J. A. Scutt (ed.), *Women, Power and Autonomy*,
https://doi.org/10.1007/978-3-031-97958-3_2

rights to determine the circumstances in which they give birth (Hazard 2015). Perhaps of greatest concern is the failure to recognise a mother's right to retain care of her own children and to have access to adequate means of support while raising them (Kerr 2018a).

Maternal rights are not properly recognised or protected within international human rights law. Our society remains structured so that most women are forced to be at least partially reliant on their children's father to support them during childbearing years. This leaves many women susceptible to exploitation, abuse and violence within domestic relationships. Due to systemic pay and wealth inequality and inequity, few women are of sufficient means to independently support themselves. For most, the alternative is the stigma, hardship and poverty that accompanies being a sole parent reliant upon the state for support (Remeikis 2017). For those most vulnerable, there remains a risk of having their babies removed under duress and given to individuals financially better equipped to provide for the "best interests of the child" in accordance with Article 3 of the UN *Convention on the Rights of the Child*.[3]

The "best interests of the child" and a care and protection rationale has been used to justify a return to the use of adoption in Australia, despite the devastating legacy of past child removal policies and extensive evidence of the harm done to both mothers and children (Higgins 2010a, 2010b, 2010c; Australian Human Rights Commission (AHRC) 1997; Senate Community Affairs References Committee (SCARC) 2004; SCARC 2012). Furthermore, a neo-capitalist narrative increasingly condones the commodification of women's reproduction including the use of forced removals in the context of surrogacy arrangements (Kerr 2018b). Wealth is emerging as the ultimate measure of parental suitability, with contractual provisions being allowed to trump the human rights of mothers and children. Finally, a deficient family law system does nothing to ensure that women are adequately supported to

(*Termination of Pregnancy Act* 2018 (Qld), but legislative sanctions remain on late term terminations (Dahlstrom nd); and see Jocelynne A Scutt, "When a Woman's Body is Not Her Own—Regulating Women through Abortion Law", Chapter 8, this volume.

[3] General Assembly Resolution 44/25, UN *Convention on the Rights of the Child*, 20 November 1989, Convention on the Rights of the Child | OHCHR, https://www.ohchr.org/en/instruments-mechanisms/instruments/convention-rights-child (accessed 2 March 2025).

raise their children independently of abusive men. Instead, it oversees a system that actively facilitates the further control and coercion of women (Kerr 2018a).

In creating the dystopia described in her novel, *The Handmaid's Tale* (1993) Margaret Atwood claimed to be inspired by real life events. Atwood repeatedly contends that every aspect of Gilead's culture is based on what has really happened in history, somewhere in the world (White 2017). Indeed, the impositions on women today echo historical infringements of their human rights. However, the victor writes history and in the battle of the sexes men have long been triumphant. Throughout history, men have had the privilege of not only writing it, but also making the laws, and writing religious texts to keep women in their place (Stanton 1985, 7–13). This is the "phallusy of history" (Miles 1989). Accordingly, rather than an evolution of women's rights, the world witnesses a revolution only in the sense of going in a circle.

What is truly revolutionary in signalling a seismic shift are the recent innovations in medical technologies facilitating the medical profession in gaining further control over reproduction. This is apparent not only in the exponential increase in the use of gestational surrogacy arrangements but also in the rapid development of an artificial womb[4] and the prospect of womb transplants. However, it is primarily wealthy men who have more choices available through these innovations, including the option of creating a motherless family (Ekman 2017; Kerr 2018c).

Despite finally attaining the vote over 100 years ago in Australia, women have yet to effectively revolt against patriarchal authority and control. History is punctuated by periods of feminist protest, but inevitably a correction takes place and equilibrium is restored with male authority firmly re-established (Rossi 1973). This is evident in the strong global backlash against the feminist progress made in the 1970s, with a new approach to commandeering women's reproduction through the manipulation of the concepts of "choice" and "consent".

While feminism clearly represents a threat to male authority, it is currently being subsumed within a capitalist narrative. With the decline

[4] Predicted in the 1970s by Shulamith Firestone, albeit she saw this as enhancing women's rights by freeing them from pregnancy and childbirth (Firestone 1970).

in religious affiliation (ABS 2013), many misogynistic measures are instead being justified by women's "consent", without taking account of the oppressive context in which this consent is obtained. If anything, this neoliberal narrative has the potential to do even greater harm with its re-framing of prostitution and surrogacy as legitimate means of economic empowerment for women. Womanhood itself is being framed as a choice rather than a physiological reality. However, in practice most of these "choices" seem to operate to free men from constraints on their ability to control and exploit women and children. It is difficult to know which narrative, the religious or the capitalist, will ultimately prove most damaging to the lives of women. There is no doubt that together they constitute a toxic mix.

In the Beginning

To the woman he said,
"I will make your pains in childbearing very severe;
with painful labor you will give birth to children.
Your desire will be for your husband,
and he will rule over you."
Genesis 3:16

Constantine, in the fourth century being the first Roman Emperor to embrace Christianity, is also remembered for having had his wife boiled alive (Okun 1986). Despite this (if not because of it), he is venerated as a saint by the Roman Catholic Church. Henceforth the Romans stopped persecuting the Christians and the church gained an increasing stronghold. At this time much valuable knowledge of women's accomplishments was systematically destroyed (Nixey 2018).

The first recorded witch killing sanctioned by the church was the brutal mutilation and murder of Hypatia, an event some historians claim effectively marked the end of antiquity and the commencement of the Dark Ages (Soldan 1843). Hypatia was revered as the greatest mathematician and astronomer of the times and from about 400AD was head of the Platonist school in Alexandria. Carl Sagan (1980, 17.52) narrates this description of the events, beginning with the acknowledgment of the "last scientist" working in the Library as Hypatia: "a mathematician, astronomer, physicist and the head of the Neoplatonic school of philosophy-an extraordinary range of accomplishments for any individual in any age". Born in Alexandria in 370 when the "growing Christian Church was consolidating its power and attempting to eradicate pagan influence and culture", Hypatia "stood at the epicenter of these mighty social forces". Despised by Cyril, the Archbishop of Alexandria, "... because of her close friendship with the Roman governor, and because she was a symbol of learning and science, which were largely identified by the early Church with paganism", Hypatia was greatly endangered. Nevertheless she "... continued to teach and publish" then:

> ... in the year 415, on her way to work she was set upon by a fanatical mob of Cyril's parishioners. They dragged her from her chariot, tore off her clothes, and, armed with abalone shells, flayed her flesh from her bones. Her remains were burned, her works obliterated, her name forgotten. Cyril was made a saint. (Sagan 1980, 17.52)

This episode is perhaps illustrative of how the church forcibly shifted people from their "pagan" beliefs to revering the male authority of the church. In the Old Religion women's knowledge of herbs and healing was valued, and the assistance of wise women was also sought in respect of birth control, abortions and midwifery (Ehrenreich and English 1973). Women had always been healers. They were the alchemists and anatomists, as well as the abortionists, midwives and counsellors. They cultivated herbs and exchanged their secrets, and passed them onto their daughters. They had a host of remedies, tried and tested over generations, with many retaining a place in modern pharmacology. They had pain-killers, digestive aids and anti-inflammatory agents. They used ergot for the pain of labor and ergot derivatives continue in use today to hasten labor and aid in the recovery from childbirth. Belladonna, also used in medicines today, was employed by the witch-healers to inhibit uterine contractions when miscarriage threatened. The witch-healer was an empiricist who worked to relieve suffering. The church, by contrast, was deeply anti-empirical and held that the pain of labour was the Lord's just punishment for Eve's original sin (Ehrenreich and English 1973, 30–32).

Simultaneously with the witch hunting craze, the male medical profession was becoming established. Strictly controlled by the church, it was a profession from which women were actively excluded. Physicians were required to call in a priest to aid and advise them. Bleeding with use of leeches was one of their main practices, along with incantations and quasi-religious rituals. The physician to Edward II of England prescribed writing prayers on the patient's jaw as a remedy for toothache. Such was the state of medical science, at the time when witches were being persecuted for practising "magic". Meanwhile it was "witches" who developed an extensive understanding of bones and muscles, herbs and drugs (Ehrenreich and English 1973, 30–32).

The church and early medical profession worked in tandem to eradicate women's influence as healers within their communities (Morgan 2018). If something positive happened, the church claimed it as a miracle but if a woman was implicated it was denounced as black magic. Magic was paganism and forbidden and punishable. Witchcraft was declared heresy and made a key focus of the Inquisitions (Bailey 2003). Meanwhile the fledgling medical profession petitioned parliament to stop women usurping them (Bailey 2003, 35).

After the papal bull of Innocent VIII in 1484 the efforts to put wise women out of business for good intensified. Two friars, Heinrich Kramer and James Sprenger, were appointed as inquisitors and in 1486 wrote *Malleus Malificarum* (usually translated as *The Hammer of Witches*), the Guidebook for Witch Trials (Kramer and Sprenger 1971). Kramer and Sprenger reserved their greatest contempt for midwives whom they condemned as the worst heretics of all. The church had set in motion vicious machinery for the suppression of women, and now the witch-hunts escalated (Guilford 2018). Women of independent means who survived as healers and had a wealth of gynecological knowledge were the first to be hunted and murdered.

Witch trials increased dramatically in Europe over the fifteenth century and continued through the sixteenth and seventeenth centuries (Frederici 2017). The accused were almost always women who were poor peasants and could not afford a lawyer. They were often tortured into confession and it was in any case almost impossible for them to prove their innocence. Alibis were useless since it was known witches could appear in more than one place at a time. Domesticated animals were evidence of having a familiar. Lay healers had no defence since women were forbidden to practice medicine and the courts had the might of the church and medical profession behind them. A woman's success in curing anything was merely evidence of her sorcery.

The witch-hunts were orchestrated by a partnership of church, state and medical profession. Both Catholic and Protestant witch-hunters deferred to the authority of Kramer and Sprenger on how to conduct a witch hunt. The witch craze did not arise spontaneously in the peasantry. It was a calculated, ruling class terrorist campaign (Ehrenreich and English 1973, 22, 25). Women were often charged if they displayed medical or obstetrical skills. In particular, the association of the witch and the midwife was strong, with Kramer and Sprenger writing: "No one does more harm to the Catholic Church than midwives" (Ehrenreich and English 1973, 29). Throughout Europe many thousands of female healers were burned and hanged as wicked witches, including many who assisted with abortions or gave drugs to ease labour pains (Parton 2020).

Over this period, the church became firmly established and the position of women sank low. Women were legally regarded as chattels of men, their role to keep quiet and produce children. Any aggressive or subversive behaviour or signs of organisation put them at risk of being condemned as a witch. They were encouraged to be suspicious of each other. The church and the state and the emerging medical profession had successfully discredited women's role in healing and instead established a male monopoly over medicine. After several years of bloodshed, women were effectively eliminated not only as a threat to the medical profession but to male authority generally. The male medical profession in winning the right to an exclusive monopoly had destroyed an unbroken tradition of healing skills passed down among women from ancient times (Pfeffer 1993).

While men no longer burn midwives in public in Western countries, midwives are suppressed in more covert ways. The distinction between female superstition and male medicine was made so thoroughly that the woman as healer was entirely discredited, thus opening the way for male practitioners to make inroads into that last preserve of female healing, midwifery. In time, they were to assert their technical superiority with the use of obstetrical forceps. Although female midwives resisted and charged males with commercialism and dangerous misuse of forceps, it was too late—they were easily dismissed as "old wives" clinging to superstitions of the past. Today, women continue this battle against the medicalisation of birth (Alford 1984).

In modern times health care, including obstetrics and gynecology, has continued to be the realm of male professionals with nursing invented to provide women with a role suitably subservient to obstetricians and gynecologists who are, in the main (and to a significant extent due to the structure of specialist medical training that militates against women students' inclusion), male. Despite this, 50 per cent of babies were, in the United States, delivered by midwives until it was decided to outlaw the profession altogether. Even today in Australia it has become largely impossible for self-employed midwives to secure insurance. The suppression of women as healers and midwives was originally achieved through collusion of church, state and the male-dominated medical profession and this continues into the present.

Family

> *A woman should learn in quietness and full submission. I do not permit a woman to teach or to assume authority over a man; she must be quiet. For Adam was formed first, then Eve. And Adam was not the one deceived; it was the woman who was deceived and became a sinner. But women will be saved through childbearing—if they continue in faith, love and holiness with propriety.*
>
> **1 Timothy 2:11–15**

According to the traditional teachings of Christianity it is through childbearing and deference to male authority that women are to be redeemed. The institutions of marriage and family have been developed as the principal means by which this submission is achieved. It is noteworthy that the men's rights movement, actively working to oppose feminism, often conceals this under the guise of campaigning on behalf of "families". The decision by the Australian Brotherhood of Fathers (ABF) to establish a political party under the alternative name "Australian Better Families" (ABF) exemplifies this approach (AEC 2018).

It is the "family" which is hailed in human rights instruments as the "natural and fundamental group unit of society" and entitled to the protection of the State, incorporated from Article 23.1 of the *International Covenant on Civil and Political Rights*.[5] In keeping with this, the notion of the "family" underlies the Australian *Family Law Ac*t 1975 (Cth) ("the Act")[6] with the Australian Family Court established to give it "the widest possible protection and assistance". This is despite the "family" being nowhere defined. Under section 43(1)(a) of the Act the Family Court is also tasked to "preserve and protect" the "institution of marriage" that, despite its recent expansion to embrace same sex relationships, continues to operate primarily as a means of constraining maternal autonomy. The Family Court is also required under section 43(1)(c)(ca)(d) of the Act to have regard to protecting children, protecting against family violence (a later amendment) and assisting parties with reconciliation. However, there is no acknowledgement of the need to preserve the critical bond between a mother and her child (the mother-child dyad) or to specifically protect women from male violence, exploitation and control while they are raising children.[7] This

[5] General Assembly Resolution 2200A (XXI), UN *International Covenant on Civil and Political Rights*, 16 December 1966, International Covenant on Civil and Political Rights | OHCHR, https://www.ohchr.org/en/instruments-mechanisms/instruments/international-covenant-civil-and-political-rights (accessed 2 March 2025).

[6] *Family Law Act* (Cth) 1975, Federal Register of Legislation—Family Law Act 1975, https://www.legislation.gov.au/C2004A00275/latest/text (accessed 2 March 2025).

[7] Editor's Note: The dissenting judgment of Justice Lionel Murphy in Gronow v Gronow [1979] HCA 63; (1979) 144 CLR 513 (14 December 1979) (austlii.edu.au), https://www.austlii.edu.au/cgi-bin/viewdoc/au/cases/cth/HCA/1979/63.html (accessed 14 August 2024) did not concede that fathers were equally good mothers as a female parent (the position of the majority) saying that the question whether the presumption in favour of custody by mothers in a child's early years was obsolete should be tasked to the Australian Institute of Family Studies (AIFS), not overturned by the Australian High Court in the absence of research. As Australian Attorney-General (prior to his appointment to the High Court) Murphy was the architect of the *Family Law Act* 1975 (Cth) and the reference to "the family" as the basis unit of society (taken from the UN International *Covenant on Civil and Political Rights* (ICCPR)) was included to ensure the Family Law Bill's passage through the Australian Parliament. In

deficiency in domestic law mirrors its neglect in international human rights law.

Upon giving birth to a child in Australia, a woman's fundamental human rights are eroded, including her right to self-determination and freedom of movement, the right to just and favourable conditions of work, and the right to physical and moral integrity. In Australian family law there is no recognition of any specific maternal rights, and indeed mothers have been constrained until recently by a legal obligation (under section 66CC (2)(a)) to ensure a child has a "meaningful relationship" with their father. Flowing from amendments to the Act, passed in 2006 (Australian Institute of Family Studies (AIFS) 2009) and incorporating "shared parental responsibility", a mother's human rights were made effectively subject to the father of her child with whom she was presumed to share equal parental responsibility.[8] This provision extended even to children conceived as a result of rape, so that these fathers, too, had the benefit of provisions which effectively enabled a man to constrain a woman's life once having fathered her child.[9] Although provision was made for the presumption of equal shared parental responsibility to be rebutted where there was a history of child abuse or family violence, in practice this was exceedingly difficult to prove and lawyers routinely advised women against raising such concerns (Higgins 2007; Higgins 2010a, 2010b; Higgins 2010c). As a result, in many cases women were required to continue relationships with perpetrators of violence and to consult with them about a child's upbringing such as education, health care and activities. She had to consider him before travelling or moving residence. She was also required to seek his contribution to the support of the child if she wanted to claim welfare benefits. She was required to facilitate his contact with the child against her own better judgement and natural inclinations, and even when she believed this may endanger the child's safety and well-being. In the worst cases, she risked losing

abolishing fault divorce, the Bill was under extreme conservative opposition as "'an attack on the family".

[8] *Family Law Act* 1975 (Cth) s61DA.

[9] *Family Law Amendment (Shared Parental Responsibility) Act* 2006 (Cth), FAMILY LAW AMENDMENT (SHARED PARENTAL RESPONSIBILITY) ACT 2006, https://classic.austlii.edu.au/au/legis/cth/consol_act/flapra2006500/ (accessed 2 March 2025).

the child to him altogether if seen to be impeding his contact without sufficient evidence of his wrongdoing (Easteal et al. 2019).

In the absence of convictions for violence, and not infrequently even despite these, if a mother opposed the father having contact she risked being characterised as a hostile parent and losing care of her child altogether. Australian family law required that she must facilitate contact between the child and their father or she would have to fight not only him, but the state, to retain care of her own offspring. After lobbying by women's groups, amendments came into effect in 2012 requiring the need to protect the child from harm to take precedence over contact with the father.[10] However, in practice the evidentiary requirements to prove risk of harm continued to be insurmountable with the result that many women were forcibly made to facilitate contact between their child and a man they considered unsafe.

Amendments under the *Family Law Amendment Act* 2023 (Cth) have promised to make the family law system "simpler, safer and fairer for all Australian families" (Attorney-General's Department 2024). This Act has removed the presumption that it is in the best interests of children for parents to have equal shared parental responsibility. The Court is no longer compelled to consider an equal time arrangement and the word "meaningful" is no longer used to describe the required relationship of a child with its parent. Unfortunately, the presumption of equal shared parental responsibility has not been replaced by any rebuttable presumption in favour of mothers, so there is a real risk that these changes could worsen rather than improve circumstances for many women where the father has been awarded primary care of the child.

When confronted with the risks of the family law system, many women contemplate moving overseas, perhaps to return to the support of their own family of origin, only to be blocked by operation of the Hague Convention on the Civil Aspects of International Child Abduction (Australian Lawyers Alliance 2018). As highlighted by FiLiA's Hague Mother's Project (Hague Mothers 2022), although aimed at abducting fathers, this Convention is now primarily used against mothers who are

---

[10] *Family Law Legislation Amendment (Family Violence and Other Measures) Act* 2011 (Cth).

fleeing domestic violence. As a result of the operation of laws ostensibly designed for their protection, for many mothers there is simply no escape from male violence and control until their children are close to adulthood.

For others, the risk is not of violence but of domestic enslavement. The law monetises most things, the exception being unpaid domestic and care work done by mothers. The "woman's work that is never done" (Meleis and Lindgren 2022) is attributed no economic value within our free market system (Waring 1999; Scutt and Graham 1984).[11] Nor is there any attempt by the state to adequately compensate for the time taken out of the workforce by women to give birth and care for offspring or other family relatives. During this time most women are confronted with the unenviable choice of dependency on an individual man or being subjected to the stigma of welfare dependency, neither of which is guaranteed to be adequate or reliable. Men frequently evade the financial burden of supporting their offspring, particularly in the context of relationship breakdown, and the state is increasingly shying away from responsibility for bearing the economic costs of raising the next generation.

In September 2017 the National Council for Single Mothers & their Children (NCSMC) assisted a Melbourne single mother to lodge Australia's first communication with the United Nations Committee for the Convention for the Elimination of Discrimination against Women (CEDAW Committee), labelling Australia's parenting payment scheme as discrimination and a human rights abuse (Remeikus 2017). The lack of financially viable support from the state for mothers means that many women are financially trapped in abusive relationships (Kutin et al. 2017). Furthermore, the tendency by the Australian Government to increasingly outsource welfare services, including "women's services" such as women's refuges (Bonaci 2014), to religious agencies also involves

---

[11] As noted by Scutt and Graham 1984, originally the *Family Law Act* 1975 (Cth) endeavoured to set a value on unpaid domestic work and child, etc. care as equal to paidwork outside the home. This was subverted by traditional ways (held by judges and lawyers) of regarding unpaidwork in the home done by women as lacking value or absent economic worth. This is similar to the problem confronted by women in the equal pay and pay/pensions/superannuation gap where women's work in paid employment, particularly but not only in traditional women's jobs, is grossly undervalued (Scutt 2024).

putting vulnerable women and children at the mercy of those historically responsible for orchestrating their oppression (Royal Commission 1977; Royal Commission 2017b).

In *CES v Superclinics Australia Pty Ltd* [1995], where medical negligence resulted in an unwanted pregnancy continuing to birth, the three NSW Court of Appeal judges were split on the question whether the mother was entitled to compensation. Cases for wrongful life have since been largely restricted to disabled offspring—with judges opining that women have no place claiming compensation for the birth of a healthy child even if it were unplanned. This is consistent with the state's convenient approach of not attaching economic value to the care work traditionally undertaken by women (ABS 2016). On the other hand, Australia continues to have such expensive and inadequate childcare provisions that for many women returning to the workforce is simply not financially viable.

The law does not attempt to provide compensation for breaches of the "marriage contract". These promises, sealed with a kiss, are uniquely unenforceable. Parties cannot be compelled "to love and to cherish". Rather, it seems that emotional cruelty and exploitation of women are currently being facilitated by the legal system. Whereas romantic love defies legal regulation, the love and attachment between a mother and child is at the whim of legal agreements and court rulings. A misguided equality narrative results in even more mothers having to endure forced separations from their children, in addition to being left impoverished (Graycar 1994). It remains for lawyers to explain that the vows exchanged at the altar are not enforceable, their breaches not compensable.

In such a context it is wise that women should limit their losses by controlling the number and spacing of their offspring. Yet this is dependent upon access to contraception and abortion, and protection against rape, including rape in marriage. Where children were born in circumstances where a woman was not adequately supported to raise the child, she was often coerced into agreeing to adoption.

Adoption

A sword was brought, and Solomon ordered, "Cut the baby in half! That way each of you can have part of him."
"Please don't kill my son," the baby's mother screamed. "Your Majesty, I love him very much, but give him to her. Just don't kill him."
The other woman shouted, "Go ahead and cut him in half. Then neither of us will have the baby."
Solomon said, "Don't kill the baby." Then he pointed to the first woman, "She is his real mother. Give the baby to her."
1 Kings 3:16–28

The rise of formal adoption accompanied the suppression of abortion, with modern adoption laws being introduced in the United States at the end of the nineteenth century (adopted.com 2022). Prior to that these arrangements were made informally, and typically in secret, due to the high level of stigma attached to children born out of wedlock. Unmarried mothers have throughout history been compelled to give up their babies to spare them the hardship of the condition of being illegitimate or a "bastard". Relinquishing a newborn is cast as an altruistic sacrifice for the good of the child as well as an act of kindness to an infertile couple.

Women whose children are taken for adoption typically experience pressure from a variety of sources including family members, religious leaders, doctors and social workers which, when combined with financial hardship, can prove overwhelming. In modern times women have been compelled to sign binding legal documents, signalling their consent, despite often being in no condition to do so, still under the influence of sedatives and painkillers, subjected to significant duress, and given no opportunity to obtain legal advice. Examples of this practice drawn from the 1940s to the 1980s are well documented (Senate Community Affairs 2012).

Until the introduction of the Supporting Mother's Benefit by the Whitlam government in 1973, it was common in Australia for babies of unwed mothers to be adopted. Since then, the number of babies available for adoption has dropped drastically, demonstrating the link between the woman's "choice" and the financial resources available to her. Therefore, even in cases where lawyers claim the woman has made an "informed choice", it is often a Hobson's choice of the worst kind. In this manner, our legal system is facilitating a systemic reversal of the judgment of Solomon.

Sadly, despite the good intentions of these mothers, a long history exists of adopted children exploited and abused by those who have taken them in. There is no evidence to establish that this has changed. The Australian Royal Commission into Institutional Responses to Child Sexual Abuse commented on the difficulties associated with the limited data available but was able to report that rates of child sex abuse were considerably lower for children in kinship/relative care than for those placed with strangers in foster or residential care (Royal Commission 2017b).

There is a continuing tendency to disregard the traumatic impact on an infant of being removed from its natural mother, and to ignore the ongoing breach of human rights under the United Nation's *Convention on the Rights of the Child*. Children have an explicit right to be known and cared for by their parents pursuant to Article 7 and a right not to be separated under Article 9. They also have a right to have their identity preserved under Article 8. As parties to the Convention, Australia and Aotearoa/New Zealand also have an obligation to take appropriate measures to "prevent the abduction of, the sale of or traffic in children in any purpose or in any form" pursuant to Article 35.

The Australian government has issued a string of apologies to individuals subjected to forced removals in past, including the stolen generations of the Aboriginal or First Nations people, child migrants and unwed mothers and their children removed under duress. Despite this history and the increased understanding of the traumatic effects (Higgins 2010a; Verrier 1993; Riben 1988; Riben: Huffington Post 2017) of forced removals, adoption is again winning favour as a response to disadvantage. Recently, some state child protection authorities have renewed policies to remove children from their parents at an earlier stage to make them available for adoption ("Giles defends call ..." 2013; Lodewyke 2017; Ceglie 2017; Brown 2016; Moffett 2017; Sara 2009). This has the benefit for governments of reducing the numbers of children legally wards of the state, cutting the expense of having to monitor the welfare of these children, and limits government exposure to liability for failures in the system.

The continuing role of the churches as major providers of adoption services should also be noted. As a result of these policies, fashioned with direct church input, mothers who are Aboriginal, disabled, incarcerated, extremely young, in out-of-home care, or affected by substance abuse or mental health issues remain vulnerable to having their children removed. Where it is formally obtained, their "consent" is still given in a context of personal and financial crisis and under intense pressure from others.

With far fewer Australian babies available for adoption than in the past, some couples instead adopt from overseas, but here again the children may be sourced from desperate and impoverished women. Disturbing stories appear of children sold, or kidnapped and passed off as orphans, to sustain this lucrative trade (Custer 2017). The unpleasant fact is that the white middle class people making up the majority of adoptive parents fuel the exploitation of poor and oppressed women (Latty 2017). Transracial and overseas adoptions raise myriad ethical concerns, reflected in foreign countries tightening their laws and regulations (Australian Institute of Health and Welfare (AIHW) 2017). However, the restrictions on children available for adoption has seen a rise in the use of surrogacy arrangements.

Surrogacy

Now Sarai, Abram's wife, had borne him no children. But she had an Egyptian slave named Hagar; so she said to Abram, "The LORD has kept me from having children. Go, sleep with my slave; perhaps I can build a family through her."

Genesis 16

Traditional surrogacy is described in the Book of Genesis when the handmaiden Hagar acts as a surrogate for Abraham and his infertile wife Sarah. However, the advent of medical technologies has made "gestational" surrogacy a reality, with rapid growth in recent years.[12] In 1978 in the United Kingdom the first Test Tube Baby was born using in vitro fertilisation technology, and then in 1982 the first baby was born from an egg donation. The combination of these technological breakthroughs enabled the first successful gestational surrogate pregnancy in 1985 and its popularity has grown exponentially over the past 30 years (Klein 2017; Rothenberg 2021).

The theory is that a woman not genetically related to the child she carries will be more willing to part with it upon birth. Unfortunately, in practice this is not so. A woman cannot be separated entirely from the child she is carrying, even if she is not genetically related to it. She experiences intense physical and psychological impacts, and her body is directly associated with the development of the child from the time of embryo implantation. Furthermore, she cannot know in advance or control how she will feel or react. A connection exists between a baby and the woman who carries it, irrespective of a genetic relationship (Allen 2018, 774). Scientists have found DNA from male babies on their mother's brain—"potentially remaining there for life" (Allen 2018, 754). Male DNA has also been found in "mothers' bloodstreams, as long as twenty-seven years after birth" (Allen 2018, 776). The birth mother is indelibly bonded to the child after sustaining its life in her womb (Allen 2018, 774). Then, when that baby is born, the birth mother is the only mother it knows and seeks out (Allen 2018, 775). Bonding, promoted through the release of oxytocin, imprints the baby on the mother, and the mother on the baby (Allen 2018, 755). Meanwhile, the baby feels no immediate connection to the father with whom it shares its DNA.

It is archetypal that Sarah and Hagar fell out once Hagar conceived. Sarah mistreated pregnant Hagar so that she ran away until persuaded by God's angels to return. And so it continues today. In 1986 the *In re*

[12] See also Maja von Bolton, 'Surrogacy—A Matter of Women's Right to Self-Determination or Exploitation of Women's Bodies', Chapter 9 this volume.

Baby M case (1988) case[13] involved a surrogate and biological mother who refused to cede custody. But like God's angels, the court intervened and gave custody to the biological father, thus restoring patriarchal order. Again in 1990 in *Johnson v Calvert* (1993)[14] a woman classed as "gestational surrogate" refused to give up the child, but again the court awarded custody to the couple who commissioned the pregnancy. Here, Anna Johnson was hired by the Calverts to carry to term their genetic child. When Johnson instead sued for custody, the California Supreme Court ruled that she had no parental rights to the child.

Globally a new phenomenon of reproductive tourism has arisen in the form of global commercial gestational surrogacy where both eggs and the "gestational surrogates" are "procured in countries where women's economic/material conditions are most precarious" (Dworkin 1983; Cherry 2014; Rothenberg 2021). The exploitation of women for egg donation in Eastern Europe is particularly popular due to the demand for "white" egg donors by prospective parents (Cherry 2014, 261, 262). Undergoing potentially dangerous egg harvesting procedures provides an alternative to prostitution for many vulnerable women. Andrea Dworkin's predictions regarding the growth of "reproductive brothels" were treated with scepticism in 1983 yet emerged in India prior to its recent prohibition on commercial surrogacy, with hostels housing local women living under supervision while performing the function of a gestational carrier (Cherry 2014, 251, 257–258, 264).

Recent cases highlight severe ethical problems with commercial surrogacy. The Baby Gammy case involved an Australian couple hiring a Thai surrogate. In *Farnell & Anor and Chanbua* [2016], following the

---

[13] *In re Baby M* 537 A 2d 1227, 109 NJ 396 (NJ 02/03/1988), First Surrogacy Case—In re Baby M, 537 A.2d 1227, 109 N.J. 396 (N.J. 02/03/1988) (lsu.edu), https://biotech.law.lsu.edu/cases/cloning/baby_m.htm#:~:text=Compliments%20of%20Versuslaw-,First%20Surrogacy%20Case%20%2D%20In%20re%20Baby%20M%2C%20537%20A.,N.J.%2002%2F03%2F1988)&text=Decided%3A%20February%203%2C%201988.&text=On%20certification%20to%20the%20Superior,reported%20at%20217%20N.J.%20Super. (accessed 14 August 2024).

[14] *Johnson v Calvert* 19 Cal Rptr 2d 494 (1993), P2d 776 (1993), 5 Cal 4th 84 (1993), https://scocal.stanford.edu/opinion/johnson-v-calvert-31446) (accessed 13 August 2018).

birth, the biological parents returned to Australia with the twin sister, leaving the twin brother with Down Syndrome to be raised by the surrogate. It also emerged that the biological father was a convicted pedophile ("Baby Gammy ..." 2016). Another case investigated by Interpol involved a 24-year-old Japanese businessman Shigeta Mitsutoki fathering 15 children using Thai surrogates (the "Baby Factory" case) (Rawlinson 2014).[15] Despite suspicions over child exploitation and trafficking, evidence that the millionaire was breaking any laws was missing. Following widespread international condemnation of these cases, the Thai government banned foreigners travelling to Thailand from entering into commercial surrogacy arrangements. India, also banning commercial surrogacy arrangements, is facing a new challenge with fertility clinics moving mothers across international borders to circumvent the ban (Rudrappa 2017). Similar movement of pregnant mothers is occurring in Asia. These women are even more at risk of exploitation as they are completely reliant on the surrogacy agency for their basic needs whilst in the foreign country (Nilsson 2024; Rudrappa 2017).

The attack on women's reproductive rights is therefore evident not only in measures being taken to restrict access to abortion, but also in an increasing trend to commodify and commandeer women's reproductive capacities generally. While steps are afoot to limit women's access to family planning services, at the same time comes an increase their "choice" in selling their children and the use of their bodies for the gratification of others. Commercial surrogacy provides an opportunity for anyone to create a child, with a woman's reproductive capacity simply viewed as a commodity. This is facilitated by courts willing to treat a woman as a mere vessel with no rights to the child she has carried to birth.

Development of reproductive technologies and the resulting commoditisation of pregnancy have produced complicated outcomes for

[15] Sally Nicholes, "The Australian Position on Surrogacy", Paper for 6th LAWASIA Family Law & Children's Rights Conference—International Academy of Family Lawyers Symposium, June 2016, sally-nicholes-cv-wfjnxsxghkrd.docx, https://view.officeapps.live.com/op/view.aspx?src=https://www.gbea.com.au/static/uploads/files/sally-nicholes-cv-wfjnxsxghkrd.docx&wdorigin=browselink (accessed 24 July 2024).

mothers and babies, raising ethical issues as to abuse of women's reproductive rights. Reproductive technologies are essentially patriarchal in aiming to control female bodies. Like prostitution, surrogacy represents the use of women's bodies for the benefit of others without regard for their health and wellbeing (Cherry 2014, 261, 280; Waylen et al. 2013).

In Australia, commercial surrogacy is largely illegal, but some states allow altruistic surrogacy (Wilson 2017). Altruistic domestic surrogacy in Aotearoa/New Zealand is governed by the Human Assisted Reproductive Technology Act (2004)[16] making commercial surrogacy illegal but permitting altruistic surrogacy assuming the surrogate mother is paid her reasonable expenses only. However, understandably there is short supply of women willing to have a baby for someone else on a genuinely entirely altruistic basis.

Many Australians and Aotearoa/New Zealanders are entering international commercial surrogacy arrangements, creating a wealth of legal complexities. Factors including the growth in gay male couples desiring to raise a family, have generated increased demand (Everingham 2014). Australians are reportedly the largest client market for international surrogacy arrangements (Human Rights Law Centre 2015). Although it is a criminal offence in NSW, Queensland and the ACT to engage in commercial surrogacy arrangements anywhere in the world, few prosecutions are brought, with increased calls for legalisation of commercial surrogacy (Bailes 2017) and an approach by the courts largely tolerant of overseas surrogacy arrangements made in defiance of domestic laws (Everingham 2014). Regulation, rather than prohibition, is advocated as the solution to current difficulties.

Closure of foreign markets generates increased pressure to follow the lead set by various US states and to legalise commercial surrogacy arrangements in Australia. Advocates point to "freedom of contract" as a basis for the legitimacy of the transaction but fail to acknowledge that "surrogacy contracts inherently dehumanize the birth mother and child" (Allen 2018, 753). Feminists assert that "the objectification and

[16] *Human Assisted Reproductive Technology Act* 2004 (Aotearoa/New Zealand), Human Assisted Reproductive Technology Act 2004 No 92 (as at 01 July 2023), Public Act—New Zealand Legislation, https://legislation.govt.nz/act/public/2004/0092/latest/whole.html (accessed 2 March 2025).

alienation of the woman in selling gestational services are so extreme that the contract is by nature illegitimate" (Allen 2018, 781). Framed as representing autonomy and choice, surrogacy advocates ignore that for many of the women involved, there are few other options to earn an income and their "choice" results from economic desperation similar to that driving individuals to sell their organs.

International surrogacy arrangements breach many internationally recognised human rights of the child, including the right not to be separated from their parents and to have their identity preserved; they further breach the obligation not to allow any sale or trafficking in children. However, these provisions are circumvented by arguments that the best interests of the child are served by adoption by parents more affluent than the birth mother. Existing laws, including international human rights provisions, fail to protect the rights of these mothers and fail to recognise the strength of the mother-child bond and the inherent harm of trading children as commodities. In the race to commandeer women's reproductive capacities for the benefit of the wealthy and privileged, fundamental human rights are falling victim to market forces.

According to reports an artificial womb or "biobag" has successfully grown a baby sheep at a Philadelphia children's hospital (Swetlitz and Stat 2017). One scientist noted: "It was appealing to imagine a world where artificial wombs grow babies, eliminating the health risk of pregnancy" (Galloway 2017). Cambridge researchers have reportedly kept an embryo alive for 13 days outside the body, their study limited only by ethical constraints rather than technological limits. Some argue that by freeing women from the tyranny of pregnancy and childbirth, this revolutionary technology will be the final step towards gender equality (Firestone 1972). However, others question whether these technologies will simply facilitate the loss of the main (if not the only) area in which women exercise real influence, that being the raising of offspring. Certainly, an artificial womb may eventually have the advantage that male couples wishing to have and raise a family of their own will no longer rely on services of a surrogate to fulfil their dream. But have we as a society reflected sufficiently on the implications of motherless families?

Conclusion

Globally women's reproductive rights are under renewed attack, evident not only in continued restrictions on access to abortion, but also in an increasing trend to commodify and commandeer women's reproductive capacities generally. While women's access to family planning services can be limited, there are moves to increase women's "choice" in selling the use of their bodies and their children for the gratification of others. A revolution in reproductive rights has occurred in that we have gone in a circle and are back to where we started, with women at the mercy of established male authority, wealth and power.

Throughout history men have worked to control and commandeer women's reproduction. While women have traditionally developed means to influence the spacing and number of their children, the patriarchal state, church and medical profession collude to constrain this capacity. Men continue to forcibly assume control of children once they are born and, to this day, mothers' right to retain care of their offspring is not acknowledged as a fundamental human right. Commodification of reproduction is further undermining any emerging recognition of maternal rights, replacing it with a disingenuous neo-liberal narrative of choice. Women and children are increasingly up for sale.

Bibliography

Reported Cases

In re Baby M 537 A 2d 1227, 109 NJ 396 (NJ 02/03/1988), First Surrogacy Case—In re Baby M, 537 A.2d 1227, 109 N.J. 396 (N.J. 02/03/1988) (lsu.edu), https://biotech.law.lsu.edu/cases/cloning/baby_m.htm#:~:text=Compliments%20of%20Versuslaw-,First%20Surrogacy%20Case%20%2D%20In%20re%20Baby%20M%2C%20537%20A.,N.J.%2002%2F03%2F1988)&text=Decided%3A%20February%203%2C%201988.&text=On%20certification%20to%20the%20Superior,reported%20at%20217%20N.J.%20Super (accessed 14 August 2024).

CES v Superclinics (Australia Pty Ltd) [1995] NSWSC 103; (1995) 38 NSWLR 47, Court of Appeal (NSW, Australia).
Farnell & Anor and Chanbua [2016] Family Court of Western Australia 17.
Gronow v Gronow [1979] HCA 63; (1979) 144 CLR 513 (14 December 1979) (austlii.edu.au), https://www.austlii.edu.au/cgi-bin/viewdoc/au/cases/cth/HCA/1979/63.html (accessed 14 August 2024).
Johnson v Calvert 19 Cal Rptr 2d 494 (1993), P2d 776 (1993), 5 Cal 4th 84 (1993), https://scocal.stanford.edu/opinion/johnson-v-calvert-31446) (accessed 13 August 2018).

Statutes, Treaties Conventions

Convention on the Elimination of All Forms of Discrimination Against Women, (CEDAW) Article 16, https://www.ohchr.org/en/instruments-mechanisms/instruments/convention-elimination-all-forms-discrimination-against-women (accessed 2 October 2025).
Convention on the Rights of the Child, Article 3, Convention on the Rights of the Child | OHCHR, https://www.ohchr.org/en/instruments-mechanisms/instruments/convention-rights-child (accessed 14 August 2024).
Crimes Act 1900 (NSW), sections 83, 84, https://legislation.nsw.gov.au/view/html/inforce/current/act-1900-040 (accessed 2 October 2025).
Criminal Code 1899 (Qld), sections 224, 225 and 226m https://www.legislation.qld.gov.au/view/pdf/inforce/current/act-1899-009 (accessed 2 October 2025).
Family Law Act 1975 (Cth) sections 43 (1)(a), 43(1)(b), 43(1)(c)(ca)(d), 60CC(2)(a), 61DA, https://www.alrc.gov.au/publications/4.%20Purposes%20of%20Laws%20Relevant%20to%20Family%20Violence/family-law#_ftnref67 (accessed 14 August 2024).
Family Law Amendment Act 2023 (Cth), https://www.legislation.gov.au/C2023A00087/asmade/text (accessed 2 October 2025).
Family Law Amendment (Shared Parental Responsibility) Act 2006 (Cth), FAMILY LAW AMENDMENT (SHARED PARENTAL RESPONSIBILITY) ACT 2006, https://classic.austlii.edu.au/au/legis/cth/consol_act/flapra2006500/ (accessed 2 March 2025).
Family Law Legislation Amendment (Family Violence and Other Measures) Act 2011 (Cth), https://www.legislation.gov.au/C2011A00189/asmade/text (accessed 2 October 2025).

Human Assisted Reproductive Technology Act 2004 (Aotearoa/New Zealand), Human Assisted Reproductive Technology Act 2004 No 92 (as at 01 July 2023), Public Act—New Zealand Legislation, https://legislation.govt.nz/act/public/2004/0092/latest/whole.html (accessed 2 March 2025).

International Covenant on Civil and Political Rights, Article 23.1, International Covenant on Civil and Political Rights | OHCHR, https://www.ohchr.org/en/instruments-mechanisms/instruments/international-covenant-civil-and-political-rights (accessed 2 March 2025).

Termination of Pregnancy Act 2018 (Qld), https://www.legislation.qld.gov.au/view/pdf/inforce/current/act-2018-023 (accessed 2 October 2025).

Articles and Book Chapters

ABS, *Australian Social Trends*, "Pregnancy and work transitions", November 2013, http://www.abs.gov.au/ausstats/abs@.nsf/Lookup/4102.0Main+Features10Nov+2013 (accessed 24 November 2024).

ABS, "Religion", *2016 Census*, http://www.abs.gov.au/AUSSTATS/abs@.nsf/mediareleasesbyReleaseDate/7E65A144540551D7CA258148000E2B85 (accessed 24 July 2024).

AEC, "Notice of Party Registration Decision – Application Approved to Register a Non-Parliamentary Party in the Register of Political Parties – Australian Better Families", AEC, 31 August 2018, 2018-australian-better-families-statement-of-reasons.pdf (accessed 2 September 2025).

AEC, *Political Party Registration*, 29 November 2024, https://www.aec.gov.au/Parties_and_Representatives/party_registration/applications/files/2018/register-abf-wap-tsis.pdf (accessed 29 November 2024).

Allen, Adeline, "Surrogacy and Limitations to Freedom of Contract: Toward Being More Fully Human", *Harvard Journal of Law and Public Policy*, 2018, 41, 753–812.

Adopted.com, University of Oregon, 24 February 2022, https://pages.uoregon.edu/adoption/topics/adoptionhistbrief.htm (accessed 24 November 2024).

Attorney-General's Department, *Media Release*—A simpler, safer and fairer family law system, 22 August, Canberra, ACT, 2024.

Australian Lawyers Alliance, *Opinion—Hague Convention*, March 2018, https://www.lawyersalliance.com.au/opinion/hague-convention-on-the-civil-aspects-of-international-child-abduction (accessed 14 August 2024).

"Baby Gammy: Surrogacy row family cleared of abandoning child with Down syndrome in Thailand", *ABC News*, 14 April 2016, http://www.abc.net.au/news/2016-04-14/baby-gammy-twin-must-remain-with-family-wa-court-rules/7326196 (accessed 14 August 2024).

Bailes, Morry, "Time to think of the children in surrogacy cases", *In Daily*, 26 October 2017, https://indaily.com.au/opinion/2017/10/26/time-to-think-of-the-children-in-surrogacy-cases/ (accessed 14 August 2024).
von Bolton, Maja, 'Surrogacy—A Matter of Women's Right to Self-Determination or Exploitation of Women's Bodies', Chapter 9 this volume.
Bonaci, Mara, 'Women's refuges closed ...', *Green Left*, 5 September 2014, https://www.greenleft.org.au/content/womens-refuges-closed-welfare-reforms (accessed 24 November 2024).
Brown, Rachel, "NSW government tackles adoption 'bottleneck", *Sydney Morning Herald* (online), 30 March 2016, http://www.smh.com.au/nsw/nsw-government-tackles-adoption-bottleneck-20160328-gns6zf.html (accessed 14 August 2024).
de Ceglie, Anthony, "Adoption reforms: Families to be paid to welcome vulnerable youngsters into their lives", *Daily Telegraph* (online), 29 March 2017, http://www.dailytelegraph.com.au/news/nsw/adoption-reforms-families-to-be-paid-to-welcome-vulnerable-youngsters-into-their-lives/news-story/9317485588d648db74f660aefae6e81f (accessed 14 August 2024).
Cherry, April, "The Rise of the Reproductive Brothel in the Global Economy: Some Thoughts on Reproductive Tourism, Autonomy, and Justice", *University of Pennsylvania Journal of Law and Social Change* 17 (2014) 261–271, The Rise of the Reproductive Brothel in the Global Economy: Some Thoughts on Reproductive Tourism, Autonomy, and Justice (upenn.edu), https://scholarship.law.upenn.edu/cgi/viewcontent.cgi?article=1170&context=jlasc (accessed 14 August 2023).
Custer, Charlie, "Kidnapped and sold: Inside the dark world of child trafficking in China", *Special Broadcasting Service (SBS)*, 2 June 2017,
http://www.sbs.com.au/news/dateline/article/2017/06/02/kidnapped-and-sold-inside-dark-world-child-trafficking-china (accessed 14 August 2024).
Dahlstrom, Fernanda, "Abortion in Queensland", *Go to Court—Criminal Law*, Abortion in Queensland—Go To Court, https://www.gotocourt.com.au/criminal-law/qld/abortion-in-queensland/ (accessed 22 July 2024).
Easteal, Patricia, Prest, Alicia, and Thornton, Fanny, "Discounting the Mother-Child Relationship in Parenting Orders: A Snapshot in Time", *Australian Journal of Family Law*, 27 March 2019, 32(3), 221–248.
Ekman, Kajsa Ekis,"Cristiano Ronaldo, Women Are Not Your Baby Factories", 27 September 2017, http://www.stopsurrogacynow.com/cristiano-ronaldo-a-woman-is-not-a-factory/#sthash.sTU6J2V9.dpbs (accessed 24 July 2024).
Everingham, Sam, "Use of surrogacy by Australians: Implications for policy and law reform", *Australian Institute of Family Studies: Families, Policy and*

the Law, May 2014, https://aifs.gov.au/publications/families-policy-and-law/8-use-surrogacy-australians-implications-policy-and-law-reform (accessed 14 August 2024).

Galloway, Kate, "Artificial womb has many possible futures", *Eureka Street,* 9 May 2017, https://www.eurekastreet.com.au/article.aspx?aeid=51310 (accessed 14 August 2024).

Genesis 3:16 *Bible* New International Version, The New International Version (NIV) Bible—Read Online, https://www.biblestudytools.com/niv/ (accessed 24 July 2024).

"Giles defends call for Aboriginal child adoptions", *ABC News* (online), 16 May 2013, http://mobile.abc.net.au/news/2013-05-16/giles-defends-adoptions-of-neglected-aboriginal-children/4693462 (accessed 14 August 2024).

Graham, Diana, "Through Life in Pursuit of Equality" in JA Scutt, *Different Lives—Reflections on the Women's Movement and Visions of its Future,* Penguin, Melbourne, 1987, 178–187.

Graycar, Regina, "Gendered Assumptions in Family Law Decision Making", *Federal Law Review*, 1994, 22(2), 278–299.

Guilford, Gwynn, "Germany was once the witch-burning capital of the world. Here's why", *Quartz*, 25 January 2018 (https://qz.com/1183992/why-europe-was-overrun-by-witch-hunts-in-early-modern-history/) (accessed 24 July 2024).

Hague Mothers, *About the Hague Mother's Project—A Good Law Gone Bad*, 11 April 2022, https://www.hague-mothers.org.uk/about/ (accessed 24 November 2024).

Hazard, Bashi, "Human rights in childbirth and midwifery care—Joining hands to change the 21st century for any woman, anywhere", *Journal of the Australian College of Midwives,* 6 July 2015, www.midwives.org.au (accessed 22 July 2024).

Higgins, Dr Daryl J, "Cooperation and Coordination: An Evaluation of the Family Court of Australia's Magellan case management model", Family Court of Australia & Australian Institute of Family Studies, 2007, Download citation of Cooperation and coordination: An evaluation of the Family Court of Australia's Magellan case-management model, https://www.researchgate.net/publication/266404662_Cooperation_and_coordination_An_evaluation_of_the_Family_Court_of_Australia's_Magellan_case-management_model/citation/download (accessed 24 July 2024).

Higgins, Daryl, "Impact of past adoption practices: summary of key issues from Australian research (Final report, March 2010)", *Australian*

Institute of Family Studies, 2010a, Impact of past adoption practices: Summary of key issues from Australian research | Department of Social Services, https://www.dss.gov.au/forced-adoption/resource/impact-past-adoption-practices-summary-key-issues-australian-research (accessed 24 July 2024).

Higgins, Daryl, "Summary of Key Issues", 2010b, Dr Daryl Higgins, Impact of past adoption practices: Summary of key issues from Australian research (Final report, March 2010) | Towards Truth, https://www.dss.gov.au/sites/default/files/documents/pastadoptionreport.pdf, https://www.towardstruth.org.au/doc1401-dr-daryl-higgins-impact-of-past-adoption (accessed 24 July 2024).

Higgins, Dr Daryl, "Past Adoption Experiences", 2010c, Past Adoption Experiences | Department of Social Services, https://www.dss.gov.au/forced-adoption/resource/past-adoption-experiences (accessed 24 July 2024).

Huffington Post, 'Trauma of mothers …', 2017, https://www.huffingtonpost.com/mirah-riben/the-trauma-of-mothers-who-have-lost-children-to-adoption_b_6919982.html (accessed 24 July 2024).

Human Rights Law Centre, Regulatory Surrogacy, 17 April 2015, https://www.hrlc.org.au/bulletin-content/regulating-surrogacy-in-australia (accessed 14 August 2024).

Kerr, Anna, "The Hague Convention on the Civil Aspects of Child Abduction Opinion", *Opinion*, Australian Lawyers Alliance, 8 March 2018a

Kerr, Anna, "Maternal rights must be recognised for the sake of children", *Opinion*, Australian Lawyers Alliance, 5 July 2018b.

Kerr, Anna, "Women's Reproductive Rights—Spoiled for Choice?" *Precedent (Australian Lawyers Alliance)*, 122, Jan/Feb 2018c, Sydney: Australia, ISSN 1449–7719, https://classic.austlii.edu.au/au/journals/PrecedentAULA/2018/8.html (accessed 22 July 2024).

Kings 3:16–28, *Bible*, Contemporary English Version (CEV).

Kutin, Jozica, Russell, Roslyn, and Reid, Mike, "Economic Abuse Between Intimate Partners in Australia: Prevalence, Health Status, Disability and Financial Stress", *Australian and New Zealand Journal of Public Health*, 2017, 41 (3), 269–274.

Latty, Liz, "Adoption is a feminist issue, but not for the reasons you think", *The Establishment,* 19 April 2017, https://theestablishment.co/adoption-is-a-feminist-issue-but-not-for-the-reasons-you-think-93ba3824bcbb (accessed 14 August 2024).

Lodewyke, Tom, "Child protection bill creates 'terrible' dilemma: LSSA", *Lawyers Weekly* (online), 10 July 2017, https://www.lawyersweekly.com.au/wig-chamber/21448-child-protection-bill-creates-terrible-dilemma-lssa (accessed 14 August 2024).

"Margaret Atwood on How She Came to Write *The Handmaid's Tale*", *Literary Hub*, 25 April 2018 https://lithub.com/margaret-atwood-on-how-she-came-to-write-the-handmaids-tale/ (accessed 24 July 2024).

Meleis, Afaf Ibrahim and Lindgren, Teri, "Man works from sun to sun, but woman's work is never done: insights on research and policy", *Health Care Woman International*, September-November 2022 (6–7), 742–753, Man works from sun to sun, but woman's work is never done: insights on research and policy—PubMed, https://pubmed.ncbi.nlm.nih.gov/12418993/ (accessed 14 November 2024).

Moffett, Amber, "Trafficking in Children? Actually No—Why Illegal Adoption is NOT Child Trafficking", *Human Trafficking Centre,* 5 April 2017, http://humantraffickingcenter.org/trafficking-children-actually-no-illegal-adoption-not-child-trafficking/ (accessed 24 July 2024).

NIH, *National Library of Medicine*, https://www.ncbi.nlm.nih.gov/pubmed/12418993 (accessed 14 August 2024) (accessed 24 November 2024).

Nicholes, Sally, "The Australian Position on Surrogacy", Paper for 6th LAWASIA Family Law & Children's Rights Conference—International Academy of Family Lawyers Symposium, June 2016.

Nilsson, Elina, "Travelling Thai Surrogate Mothers: Required and Restricted Mobility in Transnational Surrogacy", *Medical Anthropology*, 2024, 734–747, Full article: Travelling Thai Surrogate Mothers: Required and Restricted Mobility in Transnational Surrogacy, https://www.tandfonline.com/doi/full/10.1080/01459740.2024.2424364 (accessed 12 November 2024).

Past Adoption Experiences | Department of Social Services, https://www.dss.gov.au/forced-adoption/resource/past-adoption-experiences (accessed 24 July 2024).

Pope Innocent VIII, *Summis desiderantes* (1484) Pope Innocent VIII, "Pope Innocent VIII (1484–1492) and the <i>Summis desiderantes affectib" by Maral Deyrmenjian, https://pdxscholar.library.pdx.edu/mmft_malleus/1/#:~:text=The%20papal%20bull%20%28or%20decree%29%20Summis%20desiderantes%20affectibus%2C,and%20authorized%20a%20formal%20inquisition%20into%20their%20activities. (accessed 24 July 2024).

Rawlinson, Kevin, "Interpol investigates 'baby factor' as man fathers 16 surrogate children", *Guardian*, 23 August 2014, https://www.theguardian.com/lifeandstyle/2014/aug/23/interpol-japanese-baby-factory-man-fathered-16-children (accessed 14 August 2024).

Remeikis, Amy,"Melbourne woman complains to UN, saying parenting cuts are human rights abuse", *Guardian*, 21 September 2017, https://www.theguardian.com/world/2017/sep/21/un-complaint-parenting-payment-melbourne-cuts-human-rights-abuse (accessed 24 July 2024).

Rudrappa, Sharmila, "India outlawed commercial surrogacy—clinics are finding loopholes", 23 October 2017, *The Conversation*, India outlawed commercial surrogacy—clinics are finding loopholes, https://theconversation.com/india-outlawed-commercial-surrogacy-clinics-are-finding-loopholes-81784 (accessed 14 August 2024).

Carl Sagan, "Who speaks for Earth", *Cosmos*, 13th episode, 1980, https://vimeo.com/15107421 from 17.52 (accessed 23 July 2024).

Sara, Sally, "Families Caught Up In India Adoption Scandal", *ABC News* (online), 23 February 2009, http://www.abc.net.au/news/2009-02-22/australian-families-caught-up-in-india-adoption/304668 (accessed 14 August 2024).

Scutt, Jocelynne A, "When a Woman's Body is Not Her Own—Regulating Women through Abortion Law", Chapter 8, this volume.

Swetlitz, Ike and Stat, "Brave New Wool? Artificial Womb Sustains Premature Lambs for Weeks", *Scientific American*, 25 April 2017, https://www.scientificamerican.com/article/brave-new-wool-artificial-womb-sustains-premature-lambs-for-weeks/ (accessed 14 July 2024).

Timothy 2:11–15, *Bible*, New International Version, The New International Version (NIV) Bible—Read Online, https://www.biblestudytools.com/niv/ (accessed 24 July 2024).

White, Catriona, "Dystopian Fantasy? The Handmaid's Tale is Based Entirely on Real History", *BBC*, 2 June 2017, https://www.bbc.co.uk/bbcthree/article/c7bbe6fc-f452-4015-acdb-719ff8e5d389 (accessed 24 July 2024).

Wilson, Audrey, "How Asia's surrogate mothers became a cross-border business", *South China Morning Post,* 4 June 2017, http://www.scmp.com/week-asia/society/article/2096675/how-asias-surrogate-mothers-became-cross-border-business (accessed 14 August 2024).

Books and Reports

Alford, Katrina, *Production or Reproduction: An Economic History of Women in Australia, 1788–1850,* Melbourne: Oxford University Press, 1984.

AIHW, Adoptions Australia, About—Australian Institute of Health and Welfare, https://www.aihw.gov.au/reports/adoptions/adoptions-australia/contents/about (accessed 14 August 2024).
Australian Human Rights Commission, *Bringing Them Home* (27 May 1997); https://www.humanrights.gov.au/sites/default/files/content/pdf/social_justice/bringing_them_home_report.pdf (accessed 24 July 2024).
Atwood, Margaret, *The Handmaid's Tale*, Heinemann, London, UK, 1993.
Australian Institute of Family Studies, *Evaluation of the 2006 family law reforms: Summary report, December, 2009,* https://aifs.gov.au/research/research-reports/evaluation-2006-family-law-reforms-summary-report#:~:text=In%202006%2C%20the%20Australian%20Government,and%20a%20national%20advice%20line, https://www.lavan.com.au/advice/family_lawyers_perth/navigating_change_amendments_to_the_family_law_act#:~:text=The%202006%20changes%20introduced%20the,a%20child%20or%20family%20violence (accessed 14 August 2024).
Australian Institute of Health and Welfare, *Report Adoptions Australia 2016–17*, Australian Government (13 December 2017) https://www.aihw.gov.au/reports/adoptions/adoptions-data-visualisations/contents/overview (accessed 14 August 2024).
Australian Parliament, Senate Legal and Constitutional Affairs Committee, *Report on Inquiry into the Hague Convention*, Chapter 2, https://www.aph.gov.au/Parliamentary_Business/Committees/Senate/Legal_and_Constitutional_Affairs/Completed_inquiries/2010-13/childabduction/report/c02 (accessed 22 July 2024).
Bailey, Michael D, *Battling Demons: Witchcraft, Heresy, and Reform in the Late Middle Ages.* Pennsylvania: Pennsylvania State University Press, 2003.
Dworkin, Andrea, *Right-Wing Women*, Tarcher Perigee, New York, NY, US, 1983.
Ehrenreich, Barbara and English, Deirdre, *Witches, Midwives & Nurses: A History of Women Healers,* Feminist Press, New York, 1973, https://www.marxists.org/subject/women/authors/ehrenreich-barbara/witches.htm, https://sites.evergreen.edu/plantchemeco/ergot-miracle-drug-or-death-sentence/ (accessed 24 July 2024).
Federici, Silvia, *Caliban and the Witch: Women, the Body and Primitive Accumulation*, Autonomedia, New York, 2017.
Firestone, Shulamith, *The Dialectic of Sex—The Case for Feminist Revolution*, 1970, republished Farrer, Strauss and Giroux/Macmillan, London, 2003; *The Dialectic of Sex: The Case for Feminist Revolution*, 1972 https://daily.jstor.org/reproductive-technology-motherhood/ (accessed 24 November 2024).

Klein, Renate, *Surrogacy: A Human Rights Violation*, Spinifex, Nth Melbourne, Australia, 2017.
Kramer, Heinrich and Sprenger, James, *The Malleus Malificarum*, Dover, New York, NY, 1971 edn.
Miles, Rosalind, *The Women's History of the World*, HarperPerennial, New York, NY, 1989.
Morgan, Louisa, *The Secret History of Witches -The spellbinding historical saga of love and magic*, Orbit, London, 2018.
Nixey, Catherine, *The Darkening Age: The Christian Destruction of the Classical World*, Houghton Mifflin Harcourt, London, 2018.
Okun, Lewis, *Woman Abuse: Facts Replacing Myths*, SUNY Press, New York, 1986.
Parton, Susan, *Burning Times*, A Study of Witchhunting, Autonomedia, New York, 2020
Pfeffer, Naomi, *The Stork and the Syringe: A Political History of Reproductive Medicine*, Polity Press, Cambridge, 1993.
Riben, Marsha, *Shedding Light on the Dark Side of Adoption*, Harlo Publisher, Detroit, 1988.
Rossi, Alice S, *The Feminist Papers—From Adams to de Beauvoir*, Northeastern University Press, Boston, MA, 1973.
Rothenberg, Karen H, "Gestational Surrogacy and the Health Care Provider: Put Part of the 'IVF Genie' Back into the Bottle", 29 April 2021, Cambridge University Press online, Gestational Surrogacy and the Health Care Provider: Put Part of the "IVF Genie" Back into the Bottle | Law, Medicine and Healthcare | Cambridge Core, https://www.cambridge.org/core/journals/law-medicine-and-healthcare/article/abs/gestational-surrogacy-and-the-health-care-provider-put-part-of-the-ivf-genie-back-into-the-bottle/0D47A07EFF526C904284CF15796EEDE2 (accessed 24 July 2024)
Royal Commission on Human Relationships, Final Report, Final report/Royal Commission on Human Relationships | Catalogue | National Library of Australia (accessed 2 August 2025).
Royal Commission into Institutional Responses to Child Sexual Abuse, *Final Report*, 2017a, https://www.childabuseroyalcommission.gov.au/religious-institutions (accessed 24 November 2024).
Royal Commission into Institutional Responses to Child Sexual Abuse, "Case Study 24: Out-of-home care", 2017b, https://www.childabuseroyalcommission.gov.au/case-studies/case-study-24-out-home-care (accessed 14 August 2024).

Scutt, Jocelynne A, *Wage Rage for Equal Pay—Australia's Long, Long Struggle*, Palgrave Macmillan, London, 2024.

Scutt, Jocelynne A and Graham, Di, *For Richer, For Poorer—Money, Marriage and Property Rights*, Penguin, Melbourne, Australia, 1984.

Senate Community Affairs References Committee, Parliament of Australia, *Forgotten Australians* (2004) (accessed 24 July 2024).

Senate Community Affairs Reference Committee Report, *Commonwealth Contribution to Former Forced Adoption Policies and Practices*, Parliament of Australia, February 2012 (accessed 24 July 2024).

Soldan, Wilhelm Gottlieb, History of the Witchcraft Trials, Verlag der JG Cotta'schen Buchhandlung, Stuttgart, 1843, 82.

Stanton, Elizabeth Cady, *The Woman's Bible: The Original Feminist Attack on the Bible*, 1895 (1st edn), Arno Press, New York, NY, 1985, The Woman's Bible by Elizabeth Cady Stanton | Project Gutenberg, https://www.gutenberg.org/ebooks/9880 (accessed 14 August 2024).

Verrier, Nancy, *The Primal Wound: Understanding the Adopted Child*, Gateway, 1993, http://www.originscanada.org/adoption-trauma-2/trauma_to_surrendering_mothers/adoption-trauma-the-damage-to-relinquishing-mothers/ (accessed 14 August 2024).

Waring, Marilyn, *Counting for Nothing—What Men Value and What Women are Worth*, 1988 (1st edn), Toronto Press, Ontario, 1999.

Georgina Waylen, Karen Celis, Johanna Kantola and S Laurel Weldon (eds), *The Oxford Handbook of Gender and Politics*, Oxford University Press, New York, NY, 2013.

3

The Daughters of the Carnation Revolution:50 Years of Women's Rights in Portugal

Patricia Branco and Paula Casaleiro

Introduction

The Carnation Revolution, the democratic revolution taking place in 1974 in Portugal, is the twentieth-century historical event marking the beginning of a crucial legal transformation of women's rights, harshly limited and repressed under the previous dictatorial regime. Following the democratic revolution, profound legislative changes were introduced to extend women's rights and citizenship in voting rights, divorce, and access to professions previously barred to them, including the judiciary and diplomacy (Amâncio and Santos 2021). On the fiftieth anniversary of the Carnation Revolution and at a time when conservative social movements are proposing the recognition of a "status" and subsidy for

P. Branco (✉) · P. Casaleiro
University of Coimbra, Coimbra, Portugal
e-mail: patriciab@ces.uc.pt

P. Casaleiro
e-mail: pcasaleiro@ces.uc.pt

J. A. Scutt (ed.), *Women, Power and Autonomy*,
https://doi.org/10.1007/978-3-031-97958-3_3

the "housewife",[1] a discourse that sounds old and refers to the past, two critical topics illuminate the positive change related to women's rights and autonomy in Portugal: abortion and domestic violence.

The Portuguese Republican Constitution approved in 1976 enshrined the equality principle in its article 13, stating "no one may be discriminated against on the grounds of ancestry, sex, race, language, territory of origin, religion, political or ideological convictions, education, economic situation, social condition or sexual orientation".[2] This constitutional principle led to the unconstitutionality of all inegalitarian rules and, consequently, to elimination of all express discriminations in law, even in what concerns language. However, as recalled by Monteiro and Ferreira (2012, 14), the persistent disjuncture between laws and social practices is often pointed out as an outstanding and disturbing feature of Portuguese society when addressing equality between women and men.

Discussion of women's rights and autonomy globally—and in Portugal—engages with the feminist legal theory[3] debate on the power of law and its ability to generate good for women (Smart 1989; Auchmuty and Van Marle 2012; Casaleiro 2014). Carol Smart's initial feminist

---

[1] The Ethical Action Movement (MAE—Movimento de Acção Ética) was founded on 1 January 2021 under the slogan Life, Humanism and Science. MAE is a civic initiative that aims to propose approaches, reflections, studies and contributions on current ethical issues, proposing an ethics centred on the person and on valuing human life, combating indifference and ethical relativism, hoping to contribute to a greater awareness of ethical imperatives and to an ethics of the future that is not an ethics for the future, but for today. In this context, in 2024, four founders of MAE coordinated the publication of the book *Identidade e Família—Entre a consciência da tradição e as exigências da modernidade* (Identity and Family—Between the conscience of tradition and the demands of modernity). This book brings together a series of texts on the importance of a central pillar of life in society: the family. "Of all human societies, the family is the only natural, universal and timeless one", emphasise the book's coordinators, who add: "Although society is constantly changing and scientific advances require constant updating, there is a set of ethical principles that are not negotiable, but timeless" (MAE 2024).

[2] For a complete version of the Constitution of the Portuguese Republic in English see Portugal 1976 (rev 2005), Portugal 1976 (rev. 2005) Constitution—Constitute, https://www.constituteproject.org/constitution/Portugal_2005 (accessed 2 April 2025).

[3] Feminist legal theory, like feminism itself, is not a unified discipline, and there are multiple currents and ways of categorising them, from feminism of difference, through domination theory to postmodern feminism and ecofeminism, among others (Levit and Verchick 2006). In this sense, some authors prefer to speak of feminist theories of law in the plural. Despite the differences, feminist theories of law distinguish themselves within feminism by highlighting the role of law in defining society and prescribing change, while other feminist theories relativise or even question the role of law in these areas (Levit and Verchick 2006).

critique of law and legal reform contended that the law is more likely to generate harms for women than to engender beneficial social change (Smart 1989, 81).[4] This argument is based on two forms of evidence: empirical and theoretical. First, according to Smart, the history of feminist law reform efforts reveals the law's failure to legitimise women's claims. In Rosemary Hunter's view (2012), the failure of the law to legitimise women's demands seems to be confirmed by the attempts at reform discussed by Smart in her book *Feminism and the Power of Law*, such as Catharine MacKinnon's successive efforts to revise rape law or the anti-pornography decrees in the US. However, if we consider other areas or other countries, the reforms were not necessarily a failure, as in Portugal with the revision of the Civil Code, specifically of Family Law, between 1976–1977 (Decree-Law no 496/77 of 25 November), the institutionalisation of the Commission for the Status of Women (Decree-Law no 485/77, of 17 November) and the current Commission for Citizenship and Gender Equality, or the Law on Equality in Work and Employment (Decree-Law no 392/79, of 20 September), in the period after the 1974 democratic revolution (Monteiro and Ferreira 2012). And although the effective influence of these movements has been diminishing in Portugal, the decriminalisation of abortion, with Law no 16/2007 of 17 April, and the criminalisation of domestic violence as an autonomous crime type, approved by Law no 7/2000 of 27 May, prove that the movements' efforts were not in vain (Duarte 2007, 2012; Santos and Alves 2009; Monteiro and Ferreira 2012).

It is also important to consider that the failure of the law to legitimise women's demands does not mean that feminist efforts are not useful in other (non-legal) fields and may even clear the way for future legal reforms. In Portugal, for example, on the one hand, in the revision of the Penal Code that led to Law no 59/2007 of 4 September, the demand by feminist organisations for the law to adopt the concept of gender-based

[4] *Feminism and the Power of Law*, which followed in 1989, took as its point of departure the idea that "in accepting law's terms in order to challenge law, feminism always concedes too much" (Smart 1989, 5). In this book Smart sought to "de-centre" law, to think of "non-legal strategies", and to "discourage a resort to law as if it holds the key to unlock women's oppression" (1989, 5). The book was instantly influential, becoming perhaps the best-known and most-cited book in British feminist legal studies (Auchmuty and Van Marle 2012).

violence instead of domestic violence was unsuccessful (Duarte 2012). However, the legal change and successive campaigns have helped to raise public awareness of gender-based violence and increase reporting. On the other hand, the struggle to decriminalise abortion took more than three decades, culminating only after the 2007 referendum (Santos and Alves 2009, 47). In this sense, we agree with Sandland (1995) who suggests the need to resist an excessively pessimistic reading of legal reforms. He argues that no one fails to recognise, for example, that reform has symbolic value, regardless of its "success" in achieving material change (Sandland 1995, 32–33).

The second form of evidence Smart (1989, 160) invokes to warn feminists to "avoid the siren call of law" is a theoretical one relating to legal method. That is, legal categories and frameworks limit and distort feminist agendas. Women's claims, she argues, cannot simply be fitted into existing legal constructs. However, authors such as Hunter (2012) and Ratna Kapur (2006) argue that the legal method is considerably more open and produces less determined results than Smart suggests. Smart herself maintains in a later publication that the development of law is uneven. She sees law as operating in several dimensions simultaneously. Law is not identified as a simple tool of patriarchy or capitalism. Analysing law in this way allows us to see it both as a means of "liberation" and as reproducing the oppressive social order. Law both facilitates change and is an obstacle to change (Smart 1999, 154). These days Smart is not as critical of law, perceiving its positive capacity to adapt to social change and to offer recognition and affirmation alongside unwanted regulation and control (Smart 2012).

Considering the well-known and persistent disjuncture between formal and substantive equality between women and men in Portugal (Monteiro and Ferreira 2012; Amâncio and Santos 2021), fifty years later the consecration of equality brought about by the Carnation Revolution has yet to be fully fulfilled. A short overview of the legal reforms occurring with the democratic revolution, followed by a discussion of two recent legal reforms regarding domestic violence and abortion illuminates this. First, Law no 7/2000, enacted on 27 May, designating domestic violence as a public crime constituted a legal shift removing dependency on victim complaints. It allowed criminal proceedings based on reports or knowledge of the crime, even without the victim's formal complaint. Secondly, Law no 16/2007, established on 17 April, marked a significant milestone for sexual and reproductive rights. It decriminalised voluntary termination of pregnancy up to the tenth week, granting women the right to choose. Despite these legal reforms, a gap between the legislative framework and its practical implementation remains in both cases.

Women's Rights and Autonomy in Portugal: Abortion and Domestic Violence

Two crucial moments in Portuguese history are usually referred to as the milestones for women's rights and elimination of sexual discrimination in Portugal: the republican revolution of 1910 and the democratic revolution of 1974. Beyond these historical landmarks, the changes introduced regarding abortion and domestic violence in the twenty-first century represent two of the most significant for women's rights in Portugal.

The establishment of the Republic in 1910 led to some relevant legislative changes regarding sexual discrimination, namely Decree No 1 of 1910 on marriage, which adopted an innovative formulation at the time: "Conjugal society is based on freedom and equality". However, as Guilherme de Oliveira warns (2004, 42), "the wording of Article 39 was soon restricted by an unequal definition of marital roles", together with "an extensive unequal regulation of some personal effects and all property effects of marriage", showing clear supremacy of the husband over the wife. During the First Republic (1910–1926) women maintained a tense and contradictory relationship with the government. On the one hand, the new form of government actively promoted women's rights (education became mandatory for both sexes between the ages of seven and 11; the new laws of marriage ended the obligation of obedience to man; legalisation of divorce, with equal treatment for both sexes; new employment opportunities for women; two-month maternity leave for all workers (married or single)). On the other hand, attempts were made to exclude women from certain professions on the grounds of domestic duties.

With the establishment of the Estado Novo[5] on 28 May 1926, a period of regression commenced. The legal evolution previously advancing the elimination of sex-based discrimination began, with the reinstatement of discriminatory traits concerning married women. This included the husband's right to judicially compel his wife to return to him if she left the marital home without a "justifiable reason", or the husband's judicial request that his wife be handed over to him in court (as a mere object) when she had abandoned him without a justifiable reason, and the prohibition of divorce of people married by the church after the signature of the concordat. The 1933 Constitution excepted from the principle of equality between the sexes the limitations that derived, for women, from their biology or the good of the family (article 5). However, the Estado Novo also presented moments of hesitation, such as the 1971 constitutional revision of Article 5 which, in its wording, takes on the following formulation:

> Equality before the law involves (...) the denial of any privilege of birth, race, sex, [religion] or social condition, save, as regards sex, differences of treatment justified by nature (...).

For example, the need for a woman to gain her husband's permission to leave the country was revoked.

With the 1974 democratic revolution, the legal regime was purged of inequalities with the consecration and recognition of women's civil and political rights; the equality principle between spouses and the prohibiting of all discrimination; the end of the legal institution pater-familias; non-discrimination of children born in and out of wedlock; recognising catholic married couples' right to divorce; and even at the level of wording, the legislation was revised to scrupulously respect the principle of equality, always speaking indistinctly of "spouse", instead

[5] The official name of the Portuguese dictatorship, which was established by Carmona in 1926 and came to bear the imprint of Salazar (1928–68). Its central features were economic stringency and conservatism (which prevented industrial expansion), social conservatism and maintenance of good relations with the Roman Catholic Church, authoritarianism, and the maintenance of its colonies at all costs, tying them closer to metropolitan Portugal through administrative integration and the promotion of emigration to the colonies. After the replacement of Caetano in 1974, the Estado Novo collapsed concurrently with the colonial empire (Palmowski 2008).

of "husband" and "wife". Working rights and protection against gender discrimination were recognised and broadened as the country adopted and ratified the legal frameworks of international organisations such as the UN Commission on the Status of Women, the Council of Europe, and the European Economic Community (the European Union (EU) today), which Portugal joined in 1986 (Amâncio and Santos 2021).

Internationally, from the end of the nineteenth century to the beginning of the twentieth century, women were granted some civil and political rights. In Portugal the legislative evolution of law regarding women's condition was late, occurring mainly from 25 April 1974. Despite this lag, Portugal is now considered to be at the forefront in formal equality, namely legislation, action plans, general and specific rules, among others (Rolino et al. 2022). Furthermore, since 2010, Portugal's Score in the EU Gender Equality Index[6] has increased by 13.7 points, mainly due to improvements in the domains of time, that is, gender inequalities in allocation of time spent doing care and domestic work and social activities, and power, meaning gender inequalities in decision-making positions across the political, economic, and social spheres (EIGE 2023). Nevertheless, with 67.4 points out of 100, in 2023, Portugal score is 2.8 points below EU's score as a whole.

Focusing on two critical topics related to women's rights and autonomy in Portugal: abortion and domestic violence, provides an explicit insight into women's rights development. So, over the past five decades, significant legislative and policy changes have occurred, with particular emphasis on two pivotal laws from the 2000s.

Domestic Violence

Law no 7/2000 of 27 May attributed the categorisation of public crime to the crime of domestic violence, making the criminal procedure no longer dependent on the victim's complaint, changing article 152 of

[6] The Gender Equality Index gives the EU and the Member States a score from 1 to 100. A score of 100 would mean that a country had reached full equality between women and men: Gender Equality Index (nd); European Institute for Gender Equality (2025).

the Penal Code.[7] Furthermore, the illicit conduct (including physical, psychological and/or sexual violence) no longer implies reiteration, and a single and isolated act can form the practice of this crime. With Law no 59/2007 of 4 September, the concept of domestic violence was expanded to include ex-spouses, individuals who live or have lived in a de facto union, or who have maintained an intimate relationship without any cohabitation requirement.

Law No 104/2009 of 14 September approved the granting of compensation to victims/survivors, which may cover social and educational support components, as well as therapeutic measures adjusted to the physical, psychological, or professional areas, thus expanding protection for victims. In 2009 Law No 112/2009 of 16 September added other protection and prevention measures, creating the victim status, and introducing the use of technical means of remote control for the aggressor (electronic monitoring tag) and of teleassistance to the victim. In 2019, following a protocol signed between the Ministry of Justice and the Prosecutor General's Office to comply with article 27 of Law 112/2009, victim's assistance cabinets were created to support the Prosecutor's Office in establishing investigation departments equipped with a specialised section for processing investigations regarding domestic violence or gender-based violence crimes. Nevertheless, only ten cabinets have been installed so far. Thus, in March 2024 the political party PAN (People, Animals, Nature) presented to the Assembly of the Republic Draft Resolution No 6/XV/1.A to recommend that the Government takes the necessary steps to ensure the creation, in all judicial districts, of victim's assistance cabinets for victims of domestic violence until the end of 2028. Subsequently, the Assembly approved Resolution of the Assembly of the Republic no 35/2024 in May 2024 (Diário da Republica 2024).

Law no 44/18 of 9 August, introduced as "aggravated" domestic violence the so-called "net shaming" or illicit conduct of distribution, via Internet or other means, such as social networks like WhatsApp or

[7] For a complete version of the Portuguese Penal Code in English see *Penal Code—Portugal*, https://wfrtds.org/wp-content/uploads/2021/02/Portugal-Criminal-Code-2006-EN.pdf (accessed 1 November 2024).

Instagram, of personal data, namely image or sound, relating to the intimacy of the victim's private life without his/her consent, providing that a penalty of two to five years imprisonment can be applied.

Gaps Between the Law and Its Implementation

Domestic violence, unfortunately, continues to be the most common crime against people in Portugal, with 2/3 of victims being women who have had marital or similar relationships with the aggressor. According to Justice Statistics (DGPJ 2024), the crime of domestic violence against spouses or similar ranks first among the most frequent categories of crime, with 26,041 occurrences out of a total of 371,995 registered crimes for the year 2023. These numbers confirm that domestic violence continues to be a prevalent problem in Portuguese society. APAV (2023), the Portuguese NGO that assists victims/survivors, affirms that domestic violence affects victims of all conditions and different social and economic strata, and their aggressors are also from different backgrounds.

Between 2019 and 2021, 11,580 defendants were charged with this crime. Of these, 6588 were convicted (95.7 percent were male), corresponding to 57 percent of the total charges. However, in the same period, only 10 percent of those convicted were imprisoned. Of the remainder, 65 percent had their prison sentence suspended with probation. According to the recent opinion of the Economic and Social Council (*Conselho Económico e Social*/CES 2023), these numbers reveal a very high archiving rate of the processes by the Prosecutor; a conviction rate inferior to 50 per cent; and victim protection measures that are largely ineffective. Furthermore, as the opinion makes clear, the judicial system does not treat the crime of domestic violence as the violent crime it is. The frequent lack of timely and adequate response from the courts puts the safety of victims at risk.

Thus, the main difficulty lies in the need to establish an efficient communication and coordination routines system between the various public entities and bodies acting in the field of domestic violence, including courts (civil and criminal), police, prosecution services, the health system, and social security services, among others. Essential to this is interoperability of information systems and centralisation of relevant data (CES 2023).

Between Legal Frameworks and Societal Norms

With the 25 April 1974, and the consecration of the principle of equality in the Constitution of the Portuguese Republic of 1976, a process of intensive legislative modification began, motivated by political, economic, and social changes occurring at the time.

In Portugal, the fight against and prevention of domestic violence has been systematically addressed over the past two decades.[8] A robust political consensus facilitated the establishment of a legislative framework aligned with the Council of Europe Convention ("Istanbul Convention").[9] This legal context has played a pivotal role, effectively transforming domestic violence into a public crime. As asserted by Cerejo (2017), Law no 7/2000 marked a significant milestone, sending a clear societal signal regarding the seriousness of domestic violence. There is, therefore, a much more awakened collective and societal awareness regarding these issues.

The elimination of guilt in the context of divorce, with Law no 61/2008 of 30 November, occurred in the same period. The five years from 2005 to 2010 corresponds to a fruitful political cycle in terms of family law changes. Civil law is no longer responsible for verifying the violation or not of marital duties, only determining whether there is a definitive break in common life, and any idea of guilt becomes irrelevant, thus giving primacy to the individual will of the parties and their affective and sentimental choices. Thus, it is now for criminal law and justice to decide whether violence happened in the constancy of marriage or

[8] The National Support Network for Victims of Domestic Violence (RNAVVD), under the technical supervision of the Commission for Citizenship and Gender Equality (CIG), the national body for the promotion and advocacy of the principle of gender equality, is composed by 243 structures, 180 victim support centres, 28 emergency shelters and 35 shelters, with almost 800 professionals working in interdisciplinary teams (Neves et al. 2022).

[9] *Istanbul Convention*, https://www.coe.int/en/web/istanbul-convention (accessed 14 August 2024).

of a similar relationship, with or without cohabitation. The question of guilt was therefore transferred from civil law, focusing on affections, to criminal law, which turned domestic violence into a public crime, giving it the prominence civil law was concealing.

Nevertheless, the number of crimes and of victims remains high, as we could observe from the recent statistics detailed above. It is necessary to consider the sociocultural dynamics and civilisational values that have sustained gender imbalances and inequalities and are at the origin of their emergence and reproduction. The enduring social and historical legacy rooted in a patriarchal framework that perpetuates the notion of women's inferiority to men continues. Violence against women is a pervasive phenomenon that transcends social strata and age groups, its global prevalence underscoring its entrenched nature, intricately woven into diverse social frameworks (Cerejo 2017).

According to Neves and colleagues (2002), despite the inclusion of gender equality considerations in national public policies and the mandatory implementation of the National Strategy for Citizenship Education, there remains an imperative to consistently educate future generations toward greater equality.

Within the scope of the National Strategy for Equality and Non-Discrimination,[10] 2018–2030, "Portugal + Igual", the recent Action Plan to prevent and combat violence against women and domestic violence aims to promote awareness, accountability, and professional qualifications. At its core the plan seeks to eliminate social tolerance towards all forms of domestic violence and violence against women—this includes improving media reporting. The plan emphasises the importance of intervening with the aggressors, encouraging offenders to take responsibility for their actions and seek rehabilitation. Furthermore, the plan recognises the importance of qualified professionals (in the justice, health, social security and employment, and education services, and in the police forces) in addressing violence, and it aims to enhance their skills and knowledge to provide effective intervention and support.

---

[10] See Presidência do Conselho de Ministros. Resolução do Conselho de Ministros n.º 61/2018, www.cig.gov.pt/wp-content/uploads/2020/12/Resol_Cons_-Ministros_61_2018.pdf (accessed 24 August 2024).

In 2023, the Council of Ministers approved the first National Strategy for the Rights of Crime Victims, which is set to be effective from 2024 to 2028. The overarching goal of this strategy is to bolster crime prevention and victim support. It aims to facilitate access to justice, promote awareness, and foster a culture that prioritises victims' rights and empathy within institutions. To achieve these objectives, the strategy focuses on developing training programs for judicial professionals, law enforcement agencies, and multidisciplinary teams involved in addressing revictimisation, secondary victimisation, and victim interview techniques.

Abortion Rights

Portugal's abortion rights underwent significant transformation, influenced by the prolonged dictatorship (lasting 48 years—during that period, family planning and contraception were completely prohibited) and the powerful sway of the Roman Catholic Church (Barretto et al. 2022). In 1984, ten years after the Democratic Revolution of 1974, Law no 6/84 of 11 May was enacted, decriminalising abortions performed up to the twelfth week in cases of rape or when pregnancy posed a threat to a woman's physical or mental health. Additionally, abortions were permissible up to the sixteenth week in situations involving foetal malformation.

Nevertheless, implementation of the law was without practical application, since conscientious objection and absence of clinical services, either public or private, perpetuated clandestine abortion practices for years. As argued by Feio (2021, 133), the number of clandestine procedures, circa 17,000 in 2005, sometimes precipitated the women's death and criminalising women, as illustrated by the example of the mediatised trial of 17 women in Maia in 2002. This made abortion a political problem, leading to a referendum in 2007 with 59.2 per cent of voters replying positively to the question "do you agree with the decriminalization of voluntary interruption of pregnancy if carried out, at the woman's choice, in the first ten weeks, in a legally authorized health establishment?" The referendum culminated in the approval of Law no 16/2007, still in force today, changing article 142 of the Penal Code. The guarantee of professional secrecy and the right to conscientious objection were also incorporated.

According to this law, the circumstances that make the operation non-punishable must be certified by a doctor different from the one performing the termination. Ordinance No 741-A/2007 of 21 June, defined the administrative procedures and technical and logistical conditions for carrying out pregnancy termination, as well as the relevant information to be provided to pregnant women to form their free, conscious, and responsible choice. Moreover, the Ordinance establishes that the woman can freely choose the official health establishment where she wishes to terminate the pregnancy, within the limits of the applicable referral network.

Gaps Between the Law and Its Implementation

As mentioned, a significant discrepancy exists between the legal provisions and their practical application, particularly in the context of abortion rights. This divergence between the law and its practical implementation is notably pronounced in Portugal. Feio (2021) has soundly demonstrated that women, in reality, are confronted with several substantial barriers:

a. The stigmatizing attitudes exhibited by healthcare professionals, often expressed through conscientious objection.[11]

[11] As the Portuguese Health Regulatory Body concluded, it was clear there is no complete and updated register of all conscientious objector health professionals, both in hospitals and in primary care facilities, and thus the impossibility of establishing a relationship between the availability of non-conscientious objector doctors with an employment contract and pregnancy termination responsiveness (ERS 2023). According to calculations by journalist Fernanda Câncio in an article in the newspaper *Diário de Notícias*, published in 2023, seven hospitals stopped performing pregnancy termination procedures between 2009 and 2023. See Câncio (2023, "Acesso ao aborto no SNS. Entre 2009 e 2023, sete hospitais deixaram de fazer IVG", *Diário de Notícias*, March 3, 2023, https://www.dn.pt/sociedade/acesso-ao-aborto-no-sns-entre-2009-e-2023-sete-hospitais-deixaram-de-fazer-ivg-15934182.html/ (accessed 24 August 2024).

b. The consequential impact on the operation of health services across the various regions of the country, thereby revealing a geographical disparity in access to healthcare facilities.[12]
c. A pervasive lack of reliable information provided by the services, which consequently influences women's autonomous decision-making and the legally stipulated 10-week period.[13]

In any case, according to data from the General Directorate of Health (2023), the average waiting time between prior consultation and termination of pregnancy at the woman's option was of 6.4 days (above the 5-day period ascribed by the law), whereas the median gestational period of interruption was that of 7 weeks.

In 2023, the Portuguese Health Regulatory Body (*Entidade Reguladora de Saúde*) released a report indicating that between 2015 and 2022 it had initiated and concluded eight investigative processes directly linked to restrictions on access to pregnancy termination. These investigations culminated in the issuance of directives and recommendations to the implicated healthcare providers. The report also revealed the absence of a comprehensive and updated registry of all healthcare professionals who are conscientious objectors. Consequently, the Health Regulatory Body acknowledged the existence of challenges in securing timely access to pregnancy termination procedures, primarily due to the requirement for women to initiate their process with a consultation at the Primary Health Care services, which the body unequivocally identified as a hindrance (ERS 2023).

[12] The Portuguese Health Regulatory Body also concluded that, on February 28, 2023, only 31 health facilities out of 40 were carrying out pregnancy termination procedures, and two of which were private, mainly located in the Lisbon and Tagus Valley health region (ERS 2023).

[13] Between 2023 and 2024, journalist Fernanda Câncio wrote several articles on this matter, denunciating the obstacles women had to deal with, and confirming Feio's arguments (2021). See Câncio (2023); Câncio (2024).

Between Democratisation and Reactionary Forces

Even though left-wing political parties were predominantly responsible for initiating legislative measures on such issues, these parties demonstrated a considerable degree of subordination to the more conservative sectors of Portuguese society and institutions until the 2000s. In the year 2005, the Socialist Party (PS) incorporated the proposition of a referendum into its electoral program, pledging its commitment to the "yes" campaign. This commitment undeniably played a significant role in determining the outcome of the consultation in 2007, marking a milestone in the realisation of feminist demands that spanned over three decades (Monteiro 2012).

The year 2015, however, witnessed the single known attempt to modify the existing law. During that period, centre-right-wing parties were in government, thus the initiative to modify the law came as no surprise. Nevertheless, the laws that emerged from such initiative—Laws no 134/2015 and no 136/2015, both of 7 September—were subsequently repealed in 2016, thereby reinstating the original wording of the law.

At the time (2015), Isilda Pegado, president of the Federation for Life who led the legislative initiative signed by almost 50,000 citizens to change the law, generating Bill No 790/XII,[14] said that the subscribers of the legislative initiative only wanted to create "support mechanisms" for women who were considering abortion (Campos 2015). This Bill stemmed from the idea that Portugal was experiencing a serious and profound birth crisis with the State leaving human life completely unprotected until 10 weeks of gestation, actively collaborating with its elimination, even paying for the entire destruction process. The subscribers demanded an end to user fee exemptions, the imposition of mandatory psychosocial counselling, the requirement for women to sign an ultrasound, and the provision for health professionals to abstain from

[14] See *Parlamento,* https://app.parlamento.pt/webutils/docs/doc.pdf?path=6148523063484d364c793968636d356c6443397a6158526c6379395953556c4d5a5763765247396a6457316c626e527663306c7561574e7059585270646d45765a546c6c4e47526b4e7a45744d574e6d5a433030596d4d344c5467774d446374597a4e6a4d5755345a5755354e446b794c6d527659773d3d&fich=e9e4dd71-1cfd-4bc8-8007-c3c1e8ee9492.doc&Inline=true (accessed 13 June 2024).

declaring conscientious objection, thereby enabling their participation in prior consultations.

In the parliamentary debate[15] of July 2015, left-wing deputies heatedly contested the Bills drafted to modify the law. Deputy Helena Pinto (BE/Left Block) said that the proposals were presented as a "defence of the family" or a "promotion of birth rates", but in fact had a revanchist scent and aimed at penalising women who resorted to abortion. From the Socialist Party (PS), Deputy Isabel Alves Moreira emphasised the affront to women the fees represented, thus negating individual choice. For Deputy Paula Santos (PCP/Portuguese Communist Party), the Bills heralded a return to a not-too-distant past, endangering women's right to free choice, the right to access healthcare, and ultimately the right to dignity.

Soon after, in 2016, left-wing parties won the elections, and Parliament discussed the Repeal of Laws no 134/2015 and no 136/2015. The prior deputies (PS/BE/PCP) celebrated the revocation of a law deemed to be "insensitive, unethical, and detached from reality", and that promoted coercion and conditioned women's decisions.[16]

Currently, we witness, in Europe and elsewhere, the spread of a conservative movement based on the extreme right, which uses abortion as a battle horse. Portugal is not immune to such movement, and the existing conservative forces are regaining momentum. The 2024 legislative elections campaign demonstrated this. Paulo Núncio, a deputy candidate for the Democratic Alliance, a coalition of centre-right-wing parties, defended the need to "limit access to abortion as soon as possible" and proclaimed, in a boastful way, that the government in 2015 was "one of the first governments in the world to enact measures making access to abortion more difficult" (Expresso 2024). Soon after the elections, with the Democratic Alliance returning to government, a former conservative prime-minister, Pedro Passos Coelho, publicly presented the edited

[15] See *Parlamento,* https://debates.parlamento.pt/catalogo/r3/dar/01/12/04/107/2015-07-03/42?pgs=84-85&org=PLC&plcdf=true, pages 42 to 50 (accessed 13 June 2024).

[16] See *Parlamento,* https://debates.parlamento.pt/catalogo/r3/dar/01/13/01/036/2016-02-10 (accessed 13 June 2024).

collection entitled *Identidade e Família* (Identity and Family) (Bagão Félix et al. 2024). Most of the book's contributors belong to *MAE—Movimento Acção Ética* (Ethical Action Movement) and were subscribers of the 2015 legislative initiative. In a statement from January 2024, under the title "Macron and the right to abortion: a political urgency detached from reality", MAE, vehemently criticising the position taken by Macron, concludes by saying that "abortion contributes to the demographic decline the European Union is witnessing, with a real risk of implosion of communities in the not-so-distant future. These statements and intentions encourage and promote abortion at a time when the urgency is to reverse the process, promoting birth rates" (MAE 2022).

Just as in 2015, the arguments invoked are those of the demographic crisis narrative and the centrality of the traditional family, often used by right-wing parties to advance their demands regarding limiting access to abortion (Hall 2023). Another claim is that of "gender ideology" as a threat to the traditional family. As Garraio et al. (2023) argue, discourses against "gender ideology" in Portugal have occurred later than in neighbouring Spain and other European countries, but have become part of the repertoire used, espousing ideologies inherited from the dictatorship period.

Restrictions are hence justified by claiming that the family is the foundation of the nation, and thus the survival of both family, nation, and even of the EU, relies on female reproduction. The ideal woman is thus constructed on her ability to procreate, and the women who voluntarily choose to terminate pregnancy are negating this ideal and contributing to the implosion of the community. They are the witches Federici claims were hunted to consolidate the capitalist system, for women's bodies had to be made productive. This led to the redefinition of womanhood itself, while the heterosexual, patriarchal family became the engine of the new economy (Federici 2004). Furthermore, and as the Portuguese case shows, the legislative modifications of 2015 abolishing fee exemptions demonstrate, once again, that the capitalist system continues its witch hunt, forcing women to make monetary contributions as a way of punishing them by economically repaying for their refusal to contribute to the nation.

Conclusion

The 1974 democratic revolution played a pivotal role in promoting women's rights, ushering in the social and legal transformations that would ultimately lead to the legalisation of abortion and recognition of domestic violence as a public crime. The "daughters of the Carnation Revolution" have experienced great progress not only in terms of formal equality, but also in material equality. However, the gap between formal and material equality between men and women prevails. Despite the successful trajectory of women through the fields of education and work, the prevailing inequality of contributions of men and women to family life, the asymmetry of working hours and wages or the difference between the hours women and men spend caring for the family are undeniable.

This chapter reveals how, specifically in the areas of abortion and domestic violence, progress made in terms of written law does not always correspond to law practice. The judicial system's inefficiencies in the treatment of the crime of domestic violence and the substantial barriers women face in access to abortion seem to confirm the uneven development of law, which both facilitates change and is an obstacle to change (Smart 1999). While Portugal has made substantial advances in women's rights, the practical enforcement of these laws remains an ongoing challenge, shaped by historical legacies and contemporary political, economic, and social contexts. The impact of the democratic revolution on women's rights can only be understood holistically, considering both the continuity in change and the change in continuity. Challenges endure due to historical ideologies inherited from the dictatorship era (Amâncio and Santos 2021), which continue to influence current populist discourses. As we can witness and Monteiro (2012) highlights, the discourses surrounding abortion, for example, remain an open-ended debate within Portuguese society, with counter-movements persistently advocating for the retraction of legislative advancements. Further changes are needed. A transformation in men's attitudes towards their own masculinity and the way they have been socialised since birth (Rolino et al. 2022) is one. As the Portuguese rapper Capicua claimed when she released the song "Que força é essa, amiga?"[17] to celebrate International Women's Day and the fiftieth anniversary of the Carnation Revolution, what is at the root of inequality has a lot to do with what is happening at home. "There is a 25th of April that still needs to be done inside people's homes" (Capicua 2024) and minds.

These gaps reflect broader societal dynamics, including democratisation and reactionary forces. They highlight that the feminist and activist movements' struggles for equality remain relevant today. Fifty years later, the consecration of equality brought about by the Carnation Revolution has yet to be fully fulfilled.

Bibliography

Statutes and Conventions or Treaties

Decree No 1 of 1910 of 25 December, https://files.dre.pt/1s/1910/12/07000/09370938.pdf (accessed 28 June 2024).

Decree-Law no 485/77 of 17 November, <https://diariodarepublica.pt/dr/detalhe/decreto-lei/485-280540> (accessed 28 June 2024).

Decree-Law no 496/77 of 25 November, https://diariodarepublica.pt/dr/detalhe/decreto-lei/496-1977-300030 (accessed 28 June 2024).

Decree-Law no 392/79 of 20 September, https://diariodarepublica.pt/dr/detalhe/decreto-lei/392-1979-369814> (accessed 28 June 2024).

Istanbul Convention—Council of Europe Convention on Preventing and combating Violence Against Women and DomesticViolence, https://www.coe.int/en/web/istanbul-convention (accessed 14 August 2024).

Law no 6/84 of 11 May, https://diariodarepublica.pt/dr/detalhe/lei/6-1984-385266 (accessed 28 June 2024).

Law no 7/2000 of 27 May, https://diariodarepublica.pt/dr/detalhe/lei/7-2000-291937 (accessed 28 June 2024).

Law no 16/2007 of 17 April, https://diariodarepublica.pt/dr/detalhe/lei/16-2007-519464 (accessed 28 June 2024).

[17] It can be translated as 'What is that strength, my female friend?' (Capicua 2024).

Law no 59/2007 of 4 September, <https://diariodarepublica.pt/dr/detalhe/lei/59-2007-640142> (accessed 28 June 2024).

Law no 61/2008 of 30 November, <https://diariodarepublica.pt/dr/detalhe/lei/61-2008-439097> (accessed 28 June 2024).

Law No 104/2009 of 14 September, <https://diariodarepublica.pt/dr/detalhe/lei/104-2009-489757> (accessed 28 June 2024).

Law No 112/2009 of 16 September, <https://diariodarepublica.pt/dr/detalhe/lei/112-2009-490247> (accessed 28 June 2024).

Law no 134/2015 of 7 September, <https://diariodarepublica.pt/dr/detalhe/lei/134-2015-70196961> (accessed 28 June 2024).

Law no 136/2015 of 7 September, <https://diariodarepublica.pt/dr/detalhe/lei/136-2015-70196963> (accessed 28 June 2024).

Law no 44/2018 of 9 August, <https://diariodarepublica.pt/dr/detalhe/lei/44-2018-115946549> (accessed 28 June 2024).

Ordinance No 741-A/2007 of 21 June, https://diariodarepublica.pt/dr/detalhe/portaria/741-a-2007-442119 (accessed 28 June 2024).

Portugal 1976 (rev 2005) *Constitution—Constitute*, Portugal 1976 (rev. 2005) Constitution—Constitute, https://www.constituteproject.org/constitution/Portugal_2005 (accessed 2 April 2025).

Penal Code—Portugal, https://wfrtds.org/wp-content/uploads/2021/02/Portugal-Criminal-Code-2006-EN.pdf (accessed 1 November 2024).

Articles and Book Chapters

Amâncio L and Santos MH, "Gender Equality and Modernity in Portugal. An Analysis on the Obstacles to Gender Equality in Highly Qualified Professions" (2021) 10 *Social Sciences* 162 <https://doi.org/10.3390/socsci10050162> (accessed 13 June 2024).

Auchmuty R and Marle K, "Special issue: Carol Smart's *Feminism and the Power of Law*" (2012) 20(2) *Feminist Legal Studies* 65–69.

Barretto RS, Duarte M and Figueiredo AEB, "13 anos depois: diálogos sobre a Interrupção Voluntária da Gestação em Portugal" (2022) 27(4) *Ciência & Saúde Coletiva* 1525–1534.

Campos A, "Cavaco não deve promulgar nova alteração à lei do aborto, diz Isilda Pegado" *Público* (Público, 20 November 2015), <https://www.publico.pt/2015/11/20/politica/noticia/cavaco-silva-nao-deve-promulgar-nova-alteracao-a-lei-do-aborto-diz-isilda-pegado-1715046> (accessed 13 June 2024).

Câncio F, "Acesso ao aborto no SNS. Entre 2009 e 2023, sete hospitais deixaram de fazer IVG" *Diário de Notícias* (Diário de Notícias, 3 March 2023) <https://www.dn.pt/sociedade/acesso-ao-aborto-no-sns-entre-2009-e-2023-sete-hospitais-deixaram-de-fazer-ivg-15934182.html/> (accessed 19 June 2024).

Câncio F, "Abortar é legal, o acesso existe, mas é tudo menos fácil" *Diário de Notícias* (Diário de Notícias, 29 February 2024) <https://www.dn.pt/1515684282/abortar-e-legal-o-acesso-existe-mas-e-tudo-menos-facil/> (accessed 13 June 2024).

Casaleiro P, "O poder do direito e o poder do feminismo: revisão crítica da proposta teórica de Carol Smart" (2014) 29 *Ex aequo* 39–53 <https://doi.org/10.22355/exaequo.2014.29.03> (accessed 13 June 2024).

Cerejo D, "Emoções Sociais em Análise no Contexto da Violência Conjugal" (2017) Atas do IX *Congresso Português de Sociologia* <https://associacaoportuguesasociologia.pt/ix_congresso/docs/final/COM0760.pdf> (accessed 28 June 2024).

Expresso, "Mudar a lei do aborto? " February 28, 2024, https://expresso.pt/politica/eleicoes/legislativas-2024/promessas/2024-02-28-Mudar-a-lei-do-aborto--Nuncio-diz-logo-que-possivel-Montenegro-garante-que-nao-vai-mexer-na-lei-esquerda-fala-em-retrocesso-36bf4944 (accessed 24 June 2024).

Duarte M, "Entre o radicalismo e a contenção: O papel do direito na campanha Women on Waves em Portugal" (2007) *Oficina do CES*, n.º 279.

Duarte M, "O lugar do Direito nas políticas contra a violência doméstica" (2012) 25 *Ex aequo* 59–73.

Feio MA, "Lei do aborto em Portugal: barreiras atuais e desafios futuros" (2021) 97 *Sociologia, Problemas e Práticas* <http://journals.openedition.org/spp/9760> (accessed 28 June 2024).

Garraio J, Toldy T, Carvalho A de Sousa, Santos SJ and Amaral I, "'Gender Ideology' in Portugal: the Circulation and Political Performance of Anti-Gender Discourses in Society and Politics" in A Giorgi, J Garraio and T Toldy (eds), *Religion, Gender, and Populism in the Mediterranean* (Routledge 2023) 31–54.

Hall JE, "The Family and the Nation: The Centrality of Gender Politics in the Rise of European Illiberalism" (2023) Claremont-UC Undergraduate Research Conference on the European Union: vol 2023, Article 10 <https://doi.org/10.5642/urceu.EDBK1076> (accessed 28 June 2024).

Hunter R, "The power of feminist judgments?" (2012) 20(2) *Feminist Legal Studies* 135–148.

Kapur R, "Revisioning the role of the law in women's human rights struggles" in S Meckled-García and B Çali (eds), *The legalization of human rights: multidisciplinary perspectives on human rights and human* rights law (Routledge 2006).

Monteiro R, 'A descriminalização do aborto em Portugal: Estado, Movimentos de mulheres e partidos políticos' (2012) 204(xlvii) Análise Social 3 <https://estudogeral.uc.pt/bitstream/10316/40751/1/A%20descriminalização%20do%20aborto%20em%20Portugal_Estado%2c%20movimentos%20de%20mulheres%20e%20partidos%20políticos.pdf> (accessed 28 June 2024).

Monteiro R and Ferreira V, "Metamorfoses das relações entre o Estado e os movimentos de mulheres em Portugal: entre a institucionalização e a autonomia" (2012) 25 *Ex aequo* 13–27.

Neves S and others, 'Death Threats and Attempted Femicide in the Context of Domestic Violence in Portugal' (2022) 11 *Social Sciences* 347 https://doi.org/10.3390/socsci11080347 (accessed 28 June 2024).

Oliveira G, 'Dois numa só carne' (2004) 10 *Ex aequo* 41–49.

Rolino T, Pereira R, Mascarenhas M and Oliveira M, "Estudo de Diagnóstico sobre Estereótipos de Género nas Escolhas de Formação Profissional e das Profissões" (2022) <https://apf.pt/wp-content/uploads/2023/08/IGUALPRO_Estudo_digital_compressed.pdf> accessed 28 June 2024.

Sandland R, "Between 'truth' and 'difference': poststructuralism, law and the power of feminism" (1995) 3(1) *Feminist Legal Studies* 7–34.

Santos AC and Alves M, "Entre referendos: contributos e representações sobre a Campanha Fazer Ondas na luta pela despenalização do aborto em Portugal" (2009) 4 *E-cadernos CES* 47–78.

Valente L and others, "Mudar a lei do aborto? Núncio diz 'logo que possível', Montenegro garante que não vai mexer na lei, esquerda fala em 'retrocesso'" *Expresso* (Expresso 28 February 2024) <https://expresso.pt/politica/eleicoes/legislativas-2024/promessas/2024-02-28-Mudar-a-lei-do-aborto--Nuncio-diz-logo-que-possivel-Montenegro-garante-que-nao-vai-mexer-na-lei-esquerda-fala-em-retrocesso-36bf4944> (accessed 13 June 2024).

Books and Reports

Bagão Félix António, Victor Gil, Pedro Afonso and Paulo Otero eds., *Identidade e Família. Entre a consistência da tradição e as exigências da modernidade.* (Oficina do Livro 2024).

Elkins Z, Ginsburg T and Melton J, *Portugal 1976 (rev. 2005)* (Constitute) <https://www.constituteproject.org/constitution/Portugal_2005> (accessed 1 November 2024).

Federici S, *Caliban and The Witch: Women, The Body, and Primitive Accumulation* (Autonomedia, 2004).

Levit N and Verchick RRM, *Feminist legal theory. A primer* (New York University Press, New York, NY, USA 2006).

Palmowski J, *A dictionary of contemporary world history* (3rd edn, Oxford University Press, Oxford, UK 2008).

Smart C, *Feminism and the Power of Law* (Routledge, Oxford, UK 1989).

Smart, C, *Law, Crime and Sexuality. Essays in Feminism* (Sage, London, UK 1999).

Smart C, *Women, Crime and Criminology. A Feminist Critique* (Routledge Revivals, London, UK 2012)

Information Resources, Websites and Videos

APAV, "Estatísticas APAV Relatório Anual 2023" (2023) <https://apav.pt/apav_v3/images/pdf/APAV_Totais_Nacionais_2023.pdf> (accessed 13 June 2024).

APAV, "Estatísticas APAV: Violência Doméstica 2021–2023" (2024) <https://apav.pt/apav_v3/index.php/pt/3419-estatisticas-apav-vitimas-de-violencia-domestica-2021-2023> (accessed 28 June 2024).

Capicua, "Que força é essa, amiga?" (8 March 2024), Que Força É Essa Amiga, https://d:\AbortionAutonomy\Publisher\Publisher\Que, Força É Essa Amiga (accessed 2 April 2025). https://www.rimasebatidas.pt/capicua-sobre-que-forca-e-essa-amiga-sao-questoes-que-ainda-faltam-cumprir-na-luta-pelos-direitos-das-mulheres/

Conselho Económico e Social/CES, "Parecer sobre a Violência Doméstica" (2023) https://ces.pt/wp-content/uploads/2023/03/Parecer-VD-Aprovado-em-Plenario-3-marco.pdf (accessed 28 June 2024).

DGPJ, 'Estatísticas da Justiça. Destaque Estatístico Anual | N.º 92 | Março 2024' (2024) <https://estatisticas.justica.gov.pt/sites/siej/pt-pt/Destaques/20240328_D92_CrimesRegistados_2023.pdf> accessed 28 June 2024.

Diário da Republica 2024, https://files.diariodarepublica.pt/1s/2024/06/10900/0000500005.pdf (accessed 19 June 2024).

Direção-Geral da Saúde, 'Relatório de Análise dos Registos das Interrupções da Gravidez. 2022' (2023) https://www.spdc.pt/images/Relatorio_de_IG_2022_2.pdf (accessed 28 June 2024).

EIGE, *Gender Equality Index 2022 Portugal* (2023) <https://eige.europa.eu/modules/custom/eige_gei/app/content/downloads/factsheets/PT_2022_factsheet.pdf> (accessed 28 June 2024).

Entidade Reguladora de Saúde/ERS, *Acesso a interrupção voluntária da gravidez no Serviço Nacional de Saúde* (2023) https://www.ers.pt/media/besglp0x/acessointerrupcaovoluntariagravidezsns110923.pdf (accessed 28 June 2024).

European Institute for Gender Equality, *Gender Equality Index*, 2025, Gender Equality Index | European Institute for Gender Equality, https://eige.europa.eu/gender-equality-index/2024 (accessed 2 April 2025).

Gender Equality Index, *The EU Gender Equality Index*, nd, The EU Gender Equality Index by country 2023 | Statista, https://www.statista.com/statistics/1209683/the-eu-gender-equality-index-by-country/#:~:text=The%20Gender%20Equality%20Index%20benchmarks%20national%20gender%20gaps,100%20points%20indicate%20that%20gender%20equality%20is%20achieved. (accessed 2 April 2025).

MAE. *Macron e o direito ao aborto: uma urgência política desvinculada da realidade* January 22 2022, https://www.acaoetica.pt/comunicados/91-macron-e-o-direito-ao-aborto-uma-urgencia-politica-desvinculada-da-realidade (accessed 18 January 2025).

MAE—Movimento Acção Ética, 'Macron e o direito ao aborto: uma urgência política desvinculada da realidade' (*MAE—Movimento Acção Ética,* 22 January 2022) https://www.acaoetica.pt/comunicados/91-macron-e-o-direito-ao-aborto-uma-urgencia-politica-desvinculada-da-realidade (accessed 13 June 2024).

MAE. "«As Famílias Precisam De Ser Ajudadas» (Pedro Passos Coelho)," April 9, 2024, https://www.acaoetica.pt/noticias/115-as-familias-precisam-de-ser-ajudadas-pedro-passos-coelho (accessed 18 January 2025).

Parlamento, https://app.parlamento.pt/webutils/docs/doc.pdf?path=6148523063484d364c793968636d356c6443397a6158526c63793959535556c4d5a5763765247396a6457316c626e527663306c7561574e7059585270646d45765a546c6c4e47526b4e7a45744d574e6d5a433030596d4d344c5467774d446374597a4e6a4d5755345a5755354e446b794c6d527659773d3d&fich=e9e4dd71-1cfd-4bc8-8007-c3c1e8ee9492.doc&Inline=true (accessed 13 June 2024).

Parlamento, https://debates.parlamento.pt/catalogo/r3/dar/01/12/04/107/2015-07-03/42?pgs=84-85&org=PLC&plcdf=true, 42–50 (accessed 13 June 2024).

Parlamento, https://debates.parlamento.pt/catalogo/r3/dar/01/13/01/036/2016-02-10 (accessed 13 June 2024).

Presidência do Conselho de Ministros. Resolução do Conselho de Ministros n.º 61/2018, https://www.cig.gov.pt/wp-content/uploads/2020/12/Resol_Cons_-Ministros_61_2018.pdf (accessed 24 August 2024).
Que Força É Essa Amiga, https://www.youtube.com/watch?v=Xrx9sDyPr64 (accessed 2 April 2025).

4

Widows: Denial of Rights and Respect in Southern Nigeria

Wandoo Grace Aibangbee

Introduction

Women's rights and denial of them have been a significant source of advocacy and activism worldwide. The idea behind women's rights provokes the ideals of equality, acceptability, and the humane treatment of women. This idea has sparked and produced much international, continental, and national legislation.

Some of the laws worthy of note include:

(a) *Convention on the Elimination of All Forms of Discrimination against Women* (CEDAW) (1979), which Nigeria signed in 1984, ratified in 1985, signing the optional protocol in 2004;[1]

W. G. Aibangbee (✉)
Barrister & Solicitor, Member, Nigeria Bar Association, Abuja(Unity) Branch, Abuja, Nigeria
e-mail: waibangbee@yahoo.com

[1] UN Treaty Body Data Base, http://tbinternet.ohchr.org/_layouts/15/TreatyBodyExternal/Treaty.aspx?Treaty=CEDAW (accessed 1 November 2024).

J. A. Scutt (ed.), *Women, Power and Autonomy*,
https://doi.org/10.1007/978-3-031-97958-3_4

(b) *Universal Declaration of Human Rights* at the international level,[2] and the *African Charter on Human Rights* at the continental level.[3]

For Nigeria, some national legislation has attempted to address the denial of rights, discrimination, and dehumanization of women. Worthy of note are the 1999 Constitution of the Republic of Nigeria,[4] the *Violence Against Persons Prohibition (VAPP) Act* 2015,[5] and the Criminal Code of Nigeria.[6]

While these impressive legislative advances have done well in identifying the loopholes surrounding women's rights, very few sections of these laws have been dedicated at all levels to addressing the atrocious and despicable practices exercised against widows who are a marginalized group. Particularly in certain regional areas, women as widows have had to endure dehumanizing, oppressive, and repressive treatment from their community, ultimately stripping them of their rights, this being accepted generally as the norm, with no practical effects of the law.

In considering the treatment of widows and denial through customary practices and statutory perspectives of their rights and responsibilities in Southern Nigeria, this chapter is divided into four sections. For ease

[2] Universal Declaration of Human Rights | United Nations, https://www.un.org/en/about-us/universal-declaration-of-human-rights, https://www.african-court.org/wpafc/wp-content/uploads/2020/04/AFRICAN-BANJUL-CHARTER-ON-HUMAN-AND-PEOPLES-RIGHTS.pdf (accessed 1 November 2024).

[3] AFRICAN (BANJUL) CHARTER ON HUMAN AND PEOPLES' RIGHTS, https://www.african-court.org/wpafc/wp-content/uploads/2020/04/AFRICAN-BANJUL-CHARTER-ON-HUMAN-AND-PEOPLES-RIGHTS.pdf (accessed 1 November 2024).

[4] 1999 CONSTITUTION OF THE FRN.pdf, https://nhrc.gov.ng/files/publications/1999%20CONSTITUTION%20OF%20THE%20FRN.pdf (accessed 1 November 2024).

[5] *Nigeria: Violence Against Persons (Prohibition) Act*, 2015 (VAPP) | Refworld, https://www.refworld.org/legal/legislation/natlegbod/2015/en/105106 (accessed 1 November 2–24); The Violence Against Persons (Prohibition) Act, 2015—LawPavilion Blog, https://lawpavilion.com/blog/the-violence-against-persons-prohibition-act-2015/ (accessed 1 November 2024); FACT-SHEET ON THE VIOLENCE AGAINST PERSONS PROHIBITION ACT 2015—Partners West Africa Nigeria, https://www.partnersnigeria.org/factsheet-on-the-violence-against-persons-prohibition-act-2015/ (accessed 1 November 2024).

[6] *Criminal Code Act in Nigeria* 2024, https://jurist.ng/act/criminal_code_act (accessed 1 November 2024); Centre for Laws of Nigeria, CRIMINAL CODE ACT—Law Nigeria, https://lawnigeria.com/2025/01/28/criminal-code-act/ (accessed 1 November 2024).

of reference, the first part highlights Nigeria and the geopolitical divisions within Nigeria, and the background of marriage and widowhood practices. The second and third parts discuss marriage and widowhood in customary and statutory marriage and the denial of widows' rights across various categories. The chapter concludes with a summation of the issues that underpin the denial to women of Southern Nigeria the status and rights of women as widows, including the strength of patriarchal foundations that militate against changes to custom. It reflects upon the responsibility of government to fashion and foster changes based in human rights and human dignity to improve the status and rights of women as widows in Southern Nigeria, making recommendations to advance their rights and dignity.

It is essential to highlight that the chapter is intended to provide an opinion. Where women's rights are in issue, expert advice must be sought based on individual circumstances and the region in question.

Background

Nigeria is located in West Africa and is often described as Africa's most populous country due to its estimated population of 236.7 million people dwelling in an area of 923,768 km.[7] It comprises over 500 ethnic groups, and Statistica's 2023 report has life expectancy pegged at 60 years for men and 64 years for women, with the projection that there will be more widows than widowers. This follows because women marry far earlier than men and often to men older than them, as this is the norm.

Nigeria has 36 states and the Federal Capital Territory (FCT), and is referred to as the giant of Africa due to the country's size compared with other countries in the region. Nigeria has a democratic system of government, with Christianity and Islam as the two dominant religions. The country is divided into six (6) geopolitical zones: North-East, North-Central, North-West, South-East, South-West, and South-South. The government has faced significant security challenges in recent times, such

[7] *Nigeria—The World Factbook* (cia.gov), https://www.cia.gov/the-world-factbook/countries/nigeria/#people-and-society (accessed 28 August 2024).

as the Boko Haram insurgency[8] in the north, IPOB (Indigenous People of Biafra)[9] in the south, with farmer/herder clashes as well as kidnapping, which has accounted for a substantial number of deaths.

The southern part of Nigeria comprises the South-West (6), the South-East (4), and the South-South (5) regions. These regions account for 17 of the 36 states (47.2%) and are greatly influenced by their proximity, sharing similar customary, cultural, and religious practices.

Marriages across these regions are governed by the *Matrimonial Causes Act of Nigeria* 1970 and the *Marriage Act* 1900 (Nigerian legislation).[10] The Marriage Act recognizes two types of marriage: statutory marriage and customary marriage (including Islamic law marriage, which allows a man to marry a maximum of four wives, and traditional marriage). Religion is a critical factor that plays a vital role in the marriage process and, most often, statutory laws run concurrently with customary law.

Customary marriages have different rules regulating the rights and responsibilities of wives and widows. Though similar, these rights and responsibilities differ in many other ways from one region to another. The difference is significantly influenced by the customs and religious practices prevalent in that region. One must look at these rights from the Nigerian Constitution's fundamental human rights, customary rights, and statutory rights perspective to understand these differences.

It is a fact for humans that death, as we all know, is inevitable. However, in the region, reverencing death is often tilted to the side of the women, and widowhood is accompanied by specific expectations of the woman, not considering the increased psychological and emotional trauma. It is further gingered with significant degrees of discrimination and actions heralding dehumanization.

While modernization has improved some of these actions, among other factors culture, customs, and traditional beliefs still put the widow

---

[8] Officially known as ***Jamā'at Ahl as-Sunnah lid-Da'wah wa'l-Jihād***, an Islamic sectarian movement in Nigeria.

[9] The Indigenous People of Biafra (IPOB), founded by Nnamdi Kanu, is a separatist movement that seeks to establish an independent state for the Igbo people in south-eastern Nigeria.

[10] Matrimonial Causes Act 1970, http://www.commonlii.org/ng/legis/num_act/mca197/ (accessed 1 November 2024); Understanding Nigeria's Marriage Act: A Comprehensive Guide, https://marriageinnigeria.ng/nigeria-marriage-act/ (accessed 1 November 2024).

in a disadvantaged position. Under these circumstances, the widow's rights are not recognized. Customs and traditions are more concerned about the welfare of the widower, ensuring that he is not alone. Researchers agree that widows face more challenges than do widowers, and endure humiliating rituals not limited to mourning appearance, sexual activity, isolation, and physical and emotional trauma (Sassou 2002; Ewelukwa 2002), in addition to undue pressure.

Human rights can be defined and categorized in various ways. Amnesty International (Amnesty.org.uk 2022, 2024) defines human rights as:

> ... the fundamental rights and freedoms that belong to everyone, anywhere in the world. Human rights apply no matter where you are from, what you believe, or how you live your life.

The Federal Republic of Nigeria defines fundamental human rights in this chapter of the 1999 Constitution (sections 33–46). These are summarized as the right to life, the right to dignity of the human person, the right to personal liberty, determination of civil rights and obligations, the right to private and family life, freedom of thought, conscience, and religion, freedom of expression, freedom to move freely. As for property, the Constitution protects the freedom to acquire and own immovable property anywhere in Nigeria, and moveable property or any form of interest in such a property cannot be taken possession of forcibly, with no right over or interest in any such property to be acquired compulsorily in any part of Nigeria except in the manner and as prescribed by the law. Persons who claim that the provisions of this chapter relating to fundamental human rights have been, are being, or are likely to be contravened in any State may apply to a High Court in that State for dispute resolution.

For women as widows, denial of rights centered around the widow's dignity of the human person, inheritance, land, property, custody of children, and patriarchy is key. The importance of understanding the rights and responsibilities and the denial of them cannot be overstated. Some of these unfair practices come from deeply ingrained cultural beliefs, and traditional customs are carried out not only by men but by women who, despite education and awareness, hold on tight to the justification that it is a required cultural norm, failing to realize that all cultural norms can be changed. With no further support, the various dehumanizing practices are endured in silence, and widows are accorded inferior status in direct contradiction with their fundamental human rights that are protected as enshrined in the Constitution (*Constitution of the Federal Republic of Nigeria* 1999).

With fewer women in legislative positions at the current 10th Assembly of the country,[11] enacting women-related laws or simply localizing treaties and international laws touching on the subject is complex, considering Nigeria's patriarchal nature. This, in turn, lowers the chances of widowhood issues taking the frontline stage. Nonetheless, it remains a hope that lawmakers will consider these issues and implement laws to cover the gaps.

Widows and Marriage Laws

Widows in Customary Marriage

Marriage under customary law is considered a sacred union between a man and woman (or women where the custom allows for polygamy). There is no standard customary law across the country as these laws are community-based. Justice Karibi-Whyte[12] (as he then was) defined customary law as unwritten traditions and customs accepted by community members as mandatory for regulating the relations between its members.

Customary marriage in the South is an essential aspect of tradition. Most unions are acknowledged only after rites are performed and a bride price is paid and accepted. A significant condition for this to hold is the consent of both families, which, if not given, means a marriage cannot be validated (Nwabude 2022a).

[11] The Senate has three women out of 109 members (2.7%), while the House of Representatives has 17 women out of 360 members (4.7%).

[12] Late Justice of the Supreme Court of Nigeria and Professor of Law.

A bride price can be defined as the monetary sum given by the groom's family at the marriage rights "which signifies the acquisition of the rights by the groom of the bride's labor and reproductive ability" (Anderson 2007). The bride price is also the singular exchange that gives the wife a position, status, and a place of honor and dignity in the husband's family and community (Eniola and Aremo 2020). The marriage is often seen as a union of two different families, and it is generally accepted that the wife's family is married to the husband's family, with expectations of both families. In the Igbo region, as noted, women lose their fundamental rights and associated privileges by entering the customary union of marriage (Okpete 2001).

Following customary rites, should the couple wish, a church wedding celebrated by a documented minister in a registered church is conducted and duly recognized by the Marriage Act. However, it has become a familiar and unwritten practice that confirmation is requested before religious rites are performed to ensure that all customary rites are carried out in addition to the religious ones. This may differ slightly from one locality to another. Yet the rites are pre-eminent, and little is attended to about succession, property and inheritance rights, child custody rights, and the rarely discussed right to remarry.

While on paper most of these customary practices have been abolished, repealed, or completely upturned for their detrimental nature, this has not limited the practice of these repugnant customs in rural areas of the region. For instance, widows in most of these cultures have no right to the inheritance of (what is classed as) their husband's property and are left either with nothing or at the mercy of their husband's family, especially if there is no male son of age.

The environment and culture are significant factors in the social behavior of human beings (Nnachi 2007) and have aided customary practices over the years, even though these laws should change positively with evolving social conditions. In specific African communities, wives are outsiders among their husbands' families and, once widowed, families are willing to let the woman go, no matter how long the marriage to the deceased lasted.

The present-day Igbo community forms one of the major tribes in Nigeria. They are known for their business shrewdness and hardworking characteristics, which are indoctrinated at an early age. This makes the death of a male son and breadwinner an enormous event.

The woman must perform a variety of responsibilities, rites, and duties. Generally, the widow is expected to be in seclusion, wear black mourning clothing, and allow the married patrilineal daughters of the deceased's family (Umuada) of the community "to shave her head and pubic areas with razor blades" (Samuel 2011, 186). Once she has wholly mourned her deceased husband, she can mingle with others, but in a restricted manner. These practices are justified not as punishment of the widow but as age-long traditions that must be adhered to as a mark of respect for the late husband. In some extreme cases, the widow is expected to drink the water used to wash and clean the corpse of her late husband; this singular action is seen as proof that she had no hand in his death, even when there is a justifiable and proven cause of death.

However, with the advent of Christianity and modernization, these practices are not as often enforced. The Roman Catholic Church, which has a strong base in the region alongside other religious and social groups, campaigns vigorously against such practices and other cultural and burial rights, which are ancient and cause more pain and suffering for women.

The Yoruba community is also a prominent tribe in Nigeria and is reported as the second-largest ethnic group in the country. Yoruba are typically Muslims or Christians who firmly maintain traditional practices, culture, and beliefs, and regard marriage as a sacred institution where rites based on traditional and customary rites are performed to ensure a successful marriage.

The bride's price and consent are also significant factors in the consummation and acceptance of the union. Following a recognized marriage, the loss of a husband comes with its own set of rites and responsibilities. The widow must perform or uphold these rites as part of her role in the interment of her deceased husband. Like the Igbo people, the confinement period of a widow could be between three (3) to twelve (12) months. Some writers, having studied the community, state that widowhood practices and rights are performed in Yoruba land so that the woman is protected from being harmed by the spirit of her late husband, proving that she is not involved in his death and is innocent and free of any such allegation. It is believed that the spirits of the deceased can cause disturbances to the entire family, a belief which has further encouraged and enforced the continuing traditional rites applied to African widows (Oyeniyi and Ayodeji 2010).

However, customary laws for the Yoruba widow are not as stringent as those for other communities in the region and can be altered in consideration of certain circumstances. The social status of the bereaved in the community and the larger society is also a factor. The higher the status, the less forcefully imposed the rites. However, essential duties for the burial have not been altered.

The existence of the two dominant religions plays a significant role in what is expected. Islam has a straightforward and all-inclusive practice of widowhood, which is meant to guarantee the right to cleanliness, freedom, and decency during this period. For inheritance, even though the Quran has stipulated that she gets one-eighth of the husband's property, this may not be implemented in some instances due to the intrusion and enforcement of varying factors.

The Benin people, like the other cultures, require consent and the payment of bride price for the marriage to take place. They also insist that the widowed wife is subjected to swearing an oath that she has nothing to do with and is not involved in her husband's death. While this has gradually shifted, some rural communities and firm traditionalists still insist that the widow shave her hair, and drink and bathe with the water used to cleanse her husband's body. Undoubtedly this will be traumatizing!

Notably, these rights were and remain in place in most rural communities as a social obligation, a rite of passage, to be upheld by "right-standing members" of that community. However, most rural community members do not have access to modern-day information and realities, so they do not consider these practices derogatory. Also, because these practices usually have some religious-cultural flavor, adherence to them is predicated on fear of the repercussions as opposed to the willingness of its members to keep these practices. Thus, a widow would most likely not want to keep most of these practices due to their degrading nature, save the fear of their having "metaphysical repercussions."

Critics point out that the common factor for all customary marriage rites in the region is that the monetary bride price and all other associated requests can be extremely high, especially among the Igbos, who can portray women as commodities (Wendo 2004). However, it is strongly believed that a valid customary marriage is the only union that should bring forth and nurture children.

This position under customary law has been considered atrocious by women activists, researchers, academics, and (some) lawmakers as it reinforces the concept that traditionally, women are the property of their husbands and their families,[13] incapable of owning anything. It also blatantly forces the widow to become subject to the deceased family as the family will have "legal rights" over the children, with the ability to make life-changing decisions for the children on behalf of the deceased.

Widows in Court Marriage

Court marriages in Nigeria are governed by two principal laws, the Nigerian Marriage Act and the Matrimonial Causes Act, and a certificate constitutes evidence of this form of marriage. This is a state-backed union, usually between a man and a woman only, and it is expected to last throughout the spouses' lifetimes until either spouse dies or the union is dissolved through a divorce proceeding.

Upon the death of a man in a court marriage, the rights and responsibilities of the widow tend to be different from those of a widow under customary marriage. The widow of a court marriage is not obligated to follow most of the customary practices under the customs that apply to customary marriage. However, traditions are strong, and most people want to adhere to them to avoid being termed an outcast.

The idea of responsibilities for a widow in court marriage is to ensure that the widow does all she can to bury her deceased husband. There are usually no demeaning practices that she would have to keep up with

[13] *Iweloa Awero v Raimi Sadipe* (1983) 11 OYS HC (pt 11) 790, states that a widow without children is part of the property, and liable to be inherited with the other property of the husband; see also Akinnubi v Akinnubi (1997) 2 NWLR 144 (SC).

when burying her husband. The clear stipulation of a widow's responsibilities in a court marriage make this form of marriage desirable. The laws that govern her marriage during her husband's lifetime safeguard her roles, rights, and responsibilities then and upon his death.

Bearing in mind this background of some of widows' responsibilities and practices in customary and court marriages, it is timely to consider some of the rights afforded (and/or denied) to a widow.

Denial of Widows' Rights

Discrimination on the grounds of being a woman cannot or should not create a right in others. However, that it does emphasizes the fact that women are being denied human rights. This denial of rights in the southern region comes under four (4) main categories, namely:

Right to Dignity of the Human Person

This is such an essential right that it is enshrined in the grand norm of virtually every country of the world, including the *Constitution of Nigeria* 1999, particularly section 34(1). It is instructive to reproduce the content of that section:

> Every Nigerian individual is entitled to respect for the dignity of his person and accordingly (a) no person shall be subjected to torture or inhuman or degrading treatment ...

Cutting across all laws is the fundamental principle of the dignity of the human person. The underlying subject here is that *everyone* is treated humanely, not in any degrading, inhumane, or discriminatory manner. The keyword is everyone.

While this legal provision is a guaranteed right for everyone, under customary law marriages, widows are treated so inhumanely through the customary practices they are expected to endure an existence where section 34(1) appears to have little or no application.

The protocol to the African Charter on Human and People's Rights on the Rights of Women in Africa (Maputo Protocol) defines "Harmful Practices" as:

> ... all behavior, attitudes, and practices that negatively affect the fundamental rights of women and girls, such as their right to life, health, dignity, education, and physical integrity.[14]

While it is known that these customs are so degrading that no person would freely subject themselves to such practices, they continue to exist because of their origins and history. These practices prevailed for so long and have been passed down from generation to generation, that the members of these communities become indifferent to them. Protest becomes unthinkable, even when these abuses make women even more vulnerable as is so for the widow with no children or without a male child. This targeting of women because their reproductive capacity does not fulfill patriarchal requirements in and of itself amounts to torture and inhumane treatment, violating the rights and dignity of the human person.

Inheritance and Property Succession

The right of widows to succeed and inherit their deceased husbands' estate depends on the nature of the marriage, whether customary or court marriage (Falade 1999). While there is a practice of supporting and maintaining a widow after her husband's death, it differs depending upon the community. Maintenance and support of a widow are constituted by providing her basic needs through support from the husband's estate or family so that she may continue to survive. The concept of maintenance is that these widows are not left helpless or hopeless and are provided for. However, a woman who marries under customary law may not necessarily be maintained and may need other means of survival.

---

[14] MAPUTO PROTOCOL ON THE RIGHTS OF WOMEN IN AFRICA: COMMEMORATING 20 YEARS. | African Union, https://au.int/en/newsevents/20230705/maputo-protocol-20-years (accessed 1 November 2024).

Under court marriage, the laws regulating the marriage during the husband's lifetime in turn regulate the marriage after the husband's death (this applies to all widow rights). So, the law states that the estate must be shared according to intestacy rules where the man has written no will during the marriage. Thus, adequate support must be provided to the widow to cater for her needs and the needs of the children in the marriage (if any).

The law protects the right to inherit the properties of a deceased husband (Falade 1999). Under the Marriage Act, inheritance can apply whether testate or intestate. Inheritance by "testate" occurs when the husband leaves a will disposing of his assets amongst his wife and children. Here, the rules of testate succession apply, and the property is divided according to the wishes of the deceased husband as stated in the will. On the other hand, the rules of intestacy provide that if a man dies intestate (without a will), the wife will inherit a portion of the husband's estate. For instance, in the administration of estates law under the laws of Lagos state, in section 49(5):

> ... in the event of a spouse married under the Marriage Act dying intestate and being survived by his spouse and children, the surviving spouse shall be entitled to two-thirds of the real estate of the intestate.[15]

While this law relates primarily to inheritance and succession, its import ensures that the widow's and the children's needs are adequately provided for. This means that widows are relieved of the fear of not inheriting their spouse's property. With legal backing, widows under court marriage can now lay claim to their rights even though implementation is complex.

This law (among other forward-moving laws) is one of those few that seeks to preserve the rights of widows, thereby making it an essential right afforded to widows. Nevertheless, while this law may seem progressive, it is limited to marriages under the Marriage Act. Thus, this right may still be denied under customary marriage, as customs and traditions are highly respected, with severe consequences for non-adherence.

[15] LAGOS STATE ADMINISTRATION OF ESTATES LAW—Law Nigeria, https://lawnigeria.com/2019/10/15/administration-of-estates-of-lagos-state/ (accessed 1 November 2024).

In the Igbo community (South-East), the woman may be allowed to continue to reside in the house of her deceased husband (Chika and Nneka 2021), but she cannot inherit the property. This is one way she may be supported and maintained by extended family. However, the region has a very different approach to widows' inheritance. Upon the death of her husband, the woman cannot inherit property, but the property may go to the male children if they are of age or be kept in trust until they become of age. The idea is that inheritance should follow blood, and since the women—wives now widowed—are not related by blood to the deceased husband, they are not entitled to an inheritance.

This attitude toward inheritance is archaic and unfair. The proposition that she cannot inherit because she is not related by blood to the deceased husband should be approached with caution. Marriage is a union that makes the two a couple and is expected to create a lasting bond between spouses. Hence, women/wives not related by blood can argue that they are now united by marriage. All incidences and benefits are available in relationships by blood should also be available in relationships by marriage. Furthermore, the "related by blood" rule overlooks the contribution the woman makes to the marriage and the family, which preserves and maintains property and can add to its value.

Nonetheless, maltreatment and the denial of any associated rights or privileges may be resolved by the family or through authorities like the kindred (Umunna), which is generally revered and sometimes successful.

However, successes from community leaders and pressure groups are not recorded in all circumstances even though they are acknowledged as confirmed in the case of *Amaka Ezeaku v Delphine Zikere Okonkwo and Anor* (2011). Barrister John Okonkwo (SAN—Senior Advocate Nigeria) married his two wives according to Igbo Native law and customs. The first wife whom he married in 1976 had a daughter while the second bore two children (son and daughter). However, he was separated from his first wife in 1988, until he died in 2005. During this period, in 1992 he married his second wife and was with her until his death. There was no evidence that the marriage to the first wife was formally dissolved by the Native law and custom under which they married. At the same time, an affidavit was deposed by him at the registry of the Enugu High Court on the 15th day of June 1998 to the effect that his second wife was his only wife. The courts ruled that if there was no formal dissolution of the marriage in line with native law and custom, the first wife was also entitled to share his estate.

As recently as January 2024, the reported case of thirty-seven-year-old Chineneye Okonkwo saw her brother-in-law Boniface Okonkwo evict her and her five children from her husband Linus Okonkwo's house despite the community leader's plea and interventions of various groups. Boniface Okonkwo refused to give her access to her husband's land forcing her to seek refuge elsewhere (Obianeri 2024; Chukindi 2024).

The Yoruba people (South-West) who are married under statutory law are expected to share inheritance as enshrined by the law, whether the husband dies testate or intestate. Customarily, in the past, all the deceased's property was vested with the first son (Dawudo) upon the father's death. The first son held it in trust and for the benefit of all family members. He was restricted from selling or mortgaging the property in his care without the consent of the required family members (Elias 1971). If the property were to be divided, it would be divided via the Idi-igi inheritance. This is also known as per stripes, where the property is divided equally amongst the wives of the deceased husband if her children contribute to the deceased's burial expenses.

The number of children born to each wife is not considered under the per stripes. This was seen as unjust, prompting the introduction of the per capita (Ori-major) method. This method divides the property among all children irrespective of gender. It is more acceptable within monogamous homes. However, female children are not included in land inheritance as they are believed to be destined for marriage and thus expected to move away from home. In any dispute, the head of the household can decide what method will be used to ensure justice (Falade 1999, 110).

The community firmly believes that women/widows are themselves chattels to be inherited, so why would a chattel inherit property? This demeaning thinking has been passed down historically so that an average traditionalist has little or no regard for the female person.

Religion also plays a critical role in this region, as there is a mixture of Christianity and Islam. Inheritance under Islam has specific guidelines that should be followed, and daughters should be allowed to inherit.

With liberalism, these principles are not usually followed strictly by inheritance (Sodiq 2017). Christianity has no laid down rules for inheritance, but it is expected that division will be done in line with statutory law.

In the south-south regions, particularly the Edo community, there is a strong inheritance culture regarding property. The system is based on the primogeniture principle. Thus, when a man dies, the Igiogbe (the main house where he lived, died, and was perhaps buried) goes to his eldest living male son, excluding all other siblings. Native laws and customs do not permit women to inherit property. The widow is ultimately denied ownership over the property, putting her at the mercy of the first male child. In a polygamous family, the first son may not be her biological son, making the circumstances even more complicated. However, she may have access to other assets as these may be shared.

While some cultural practices in southern Nigeria (such as the South-West and South-South) relating to inheritance and property succession are somewhat progressive with enacted, some practices in other regions (like the South-East Region) outrightly deprive these widows of their rights. These practices in and of themselves are discriminatory and even outright inhumane. This is the sad reality, namely that not only are widows of customary marriage handicapped in the issue of inheritance (Emery 2013), but they are treated as less of a person and are considered chattels that can be inherited.

Custody of Children

The custody of children of a widow is a priority, for every widow desires to have custodial rights, that is, physical possession and rights over a child. Under Nigerian statutory laws, particularly the Matrimonial Causes Act, the focus is more on the custody rights relating to children of divorced couples, with little emphasis placed on widows. The Matrimonial Causes Act encompasses provisions relating to the institution of marriage, legal separation, and the equitable distribution of property. While the Act is not specific to the custodial rights of widows, it is a trite law that what the court looks out for is what is most beneficial to the child. One may also make specific references to sections of the Act relevant to widows' rights following the demise of their spouses and the allocation of marital assets.

The *Violence Against Persons (Prohibition) Act* 2015 encompasses prohibitions against a range of violent acts, including harmful practices associated with widowhood (Obi 2020). The denial of custody of children can be categorized as harmful due to the pain the loss of a child causes to the mother.

Under the Nigerian Constitution, enacted in 1999 and subsequently amended, section 42 ensures individuals' entitlements to freedom from discrimination based on various factors, encompassing gender. This section may be cited to emphasize the constitutional safeguard for widows based on gender and may be applied to child custody.

Under customary practices, the father has complete and total rights over his children during his lifetime. Upon his death, these rights are transferred to the eldest surviving brother of the deceased father. However, the mother of the children has an unfettered right to the day-to-day care of the child/children. The customary practice implies, however, that the mother has no legal rights over her children.

This position under customary law reinforces the concept that, traditionally, women are the property of their husbands and their families, incapable of owning anything (Nzewi 2019). It also blatantly forces the widow to become subject to the deceased family as the family would have "legal rights" over the children, with the ability to make life-changing decisions for the children on behalf of the deceased. Nonetheless, these practices are being challenged, as reported in the widely celebrated case in Anambra State (the Igbo region) (Ikeanvionwu 2024), where the Children, Sexual, and Gender-Based Violence Court (sitting at the Chief Magistrates Court, Awka) granted custodial rights of two children to a widow (Mrs Nkechi Maduakor), denying the husband's family the rights, adding that her late husband's relatives were not entitled to take away the children (ABS 2024). While this was a celebrated case, most widows are too overwhelmed by grief, helpless, and often weak, with no financial resources or long-term support to fight or advocate for justice, considering the economic hardship experienced in the country.

Right to Remarry

The right of a widow to remarry is an essential aspect. The loneliness and pain that comes with the loss of a spouse is traumatizing, not forgetting her physical needs. Under the Marriage Act, the union must last if possible or until a divorce is formalized. On religious grounds, it should last for a lifetime until the death of either spouse. So, when a man dies and leaves his wife, she is legally allowed to remarry.

The customary norms also allow remarriage after the death of a spouse. However, these norms encourages the widower to marry as soon as possible to heal his pain and to ensure care is available for his needs (Osagie and Oboite 2024). The widower also requires help in the care of their children, especially when he has one wife—now deceased. In polygamous circumstances, the expectation is that he will find comfort with the other wives (Bamgbose 2015). However, the reverse is the case for the widow. Even though she is allowed the option to remarry, she is seen as marrying too early and not mourning her husband enough after the mourning period, which is generally one year. Some communities believe that for a widow to marry early, she may have been having extramarital affairs before the death of her husband. So, to avoid such social judgement, she is expected to stay in single widowhood much longer. In addition, these women are encouraged to remain in the former husband's family home, which makes remarriage difficult as they are keenly watched. Some widows, however, opt to return to their father's house. This is not against tradition, especially where there are no children and in situations where she may not be at peace in her deceased husband's family.

Whatever decision she may choose, either to remain in her husband's home or to go back to her father's house, the marriage between her and the dead husband subsists. Thus, when the widow decides to remarry, her family must repay the bride price paid at the consummation of the union, which must be accepted before she can remarry. This repayment of the bride price is a condition precedent to her remarriage and is taken seriously as the action formally invalidates the marriage. If this is not done, any children born after a subsequent marriage are the children of the former husband and remain in the late husband's lineage.

This custom, therefore, does not afford widows unfettered rights to remarry, distinguishing their situation from that of the men of customary marriage who are widowed. So, realistically, the widow is partially denied her right to remarry. Yet if the death of a spouse brings an end to the marriage, then the woman should be allowed to remarry without recourse to the husband's family, just as the man would be allowed to remarry without recourse to the wife's family.

Conclusion

The combination of these cultural biases and legal inequality creates a powerful combination that sustains the marginalization and oppression of widows, leading to a cycle of disadvantage that can persist for multiple generations (Essien et al. 2020). Considering these situations and how widows in most southern states have been denied rights, it begs the question, aren't the numerous laws to help tackle this injustice against widows, especially under customary marriage, effective? Indeed, laws at all levels have attempted to provide remedies for these women.

The treatment and denial of rights of these women/widows persist because the communities do not want to change their norms. Very little is done by the government to curb these arbitrary practices. So, the perpetrators of acts that dehumanize widows, including taking custody of their children, continue in the perpetrators' belief that they would face no repercussions. Perhaps if stricter penal measures were in place, perpetrators would desist from their actions.

Patriarchy is a strong force in Nigeria, where men have dominated every aspect. Control is not limited to finances but includes other parts of women's lives. Resistance is rare as it is an acceptable norm. However, eliminating this culture and accepting gender equality can resolve these issues and stop the exploitation of widows socially, psychologically, emotionally, and mentally. Encouraging men to document their wills and update them regularly to avoid disputes at their death is a vital element.

Finally, illiteracy, poor education, and ignorance of the law play significant roles in the persistence of these actions against women which are vices against the Nigerian Constitution. Therefore, active intervention and implementation at all levels of government, including the local, state, national, and international levels, have become essential to aid the widowed women's stand.

Bibliography

Reported Cases

Akinnubi v Akinnubi (1997) 2 NWLR 144 (SC).

Amaka Ezeaku v Delphine Zikere Okonkwo and Anor (2011) LPELR-57009(CA)

Delphine Zikere Okonkwo v Amaka Ezeaku and Administrator-General/Public Trustee, Enugu State (2020) Legalpedia (SC) 11118

Iweloa Awero v Raimi Sadipe (1983) 11 OYS HC (pt 11) 790

Statutes, Treaties and Conventions

African (Banjul) Charter on Human and Peoples' Rights 1981, AFRICAN (BANJUL) CHARTER ON HUMAN AND PEOPLES' RIGHTS, https://www.african-court.org/wpafc/wp-content/uploads/2020/04/AFRICAN-BANJUL-CHARTER-ON-HUMAN-AND-PEOPLES-RIGHTS.pdf (accessed 1 November 2024).

Convention on the Elimination of All Forms of Discrimination Against Women (CEDAW), UN Treaty Body Data Base, https://tbinternet.ohchr.org/_layouts/15/TreatyBodyExternal/Treaty.aspx?Treaty=CEDAW (accessed 1 November 2024).

Criminal Code Act of Nigeria 2004, Centre for Laws of Nigeria, CRIMINAL CODE ACT—Law Nigeria, https://lawnigeria.com/2025/01/28/criminal-code-act/ (accessed 1 November 2024).

Constitution of the Federal Republic of Nigeria, 1999 CONSTITUTION OF THE FRN.pdf, https://nhrc.gov.ng/files/publications/1999%20CONSTITUTION%20OF%20THE%20FRN.pdf (accessed 1 November 2024).

Constitution of the Federal Republic of Nigeria 1999, Chapter 4 of the 1999 Constitution (Sections 34 (1), 33–46), The Nigerian Constitution_ https://nigerian-constitution.com/chapter-4-section-44-compulsory-acquisition-of-property (accessed 19 August 2024).

Criminal Code Act in Nigeria 2024, https://jurist.ng/act/criminal_code_act, https://lawnigeria.com/laws/2018/02/26/administration-of-estates-law/ (accessed 1 November 2024)

Jurist.ng, Section 33 of the Constitution of the Federal Republic of Nigeria. https://jurist.ng/constitution/sec-33-46 (accessed 29 July 2024).

Lagos Administration of Estates Law 2019, LAGOS STATE ADMINISTRATION OF ESTATES LAW—Law Nigeria, https://lawnigeria.com/laws/2018/02/26/administration-of-estates-law/ section 49(5)

Marriage Act 1900 (Nigerian Legislation), Chapter 218, Law of the Federation of Nigeria 1900, Marriage Act, http://www.commonlii.org/ng/legis/num_act/ma85/ (accessed 1 November 2024), M6.pdf, https://www.lawsofnigeria.placng.org/laws/M6.pdf (accessed 1 November 2024).

MAPUTO PROTOCOL ON THE RIGHTS OF WOMEN IN AFRICA: COMMEMORATING 20 YEARS. | African Union, https://au.int/en/newsevents/20230705/maputo-protocol-20-years (accessed 1 November 2024).

Matrimonial Causes Act 1970 (Nigeria), http://www.commonlii.org/ng/legis/num_act/mca197/ (accessed 1 November 2024)

Universal Declaration of Human Rights 1948, Universal Declaration of Human Rights | United Nations, https://www.un.org/en/about-us/universal-declaration-of-human-rights (accessed 1 November 2024).

Violence Against Persons (Prohibition) Act 2015, Nigeria: Violence Against Persons (Prohibition) Act, 2015 (VAPP) | Refworld, https://www.refworld.org/legal/legislation/natlegbod/2015/en/105106 (accessed 1 November 2024).

Articles and Book Chapters

ABS News (2024). "Court In Awka Grants Widow Custody Of Her Children", *Good Morning Anambra*, 7 July 2024, https://www.absradiotv.com/2024/07/07/court-in-awka-grants-widow-custody-of-her-children/ (accessed 1 November 2024).

AKANNI, Abdul Hakeem (2020). "Widowhood Practice among Contemporary Yoruba Muslims of South-West Nigeria", *NIU Journal of Humanities*,

[Sl], vol 5, no 1, 141–150, May 2020. ISSN 3007-1712, https://ijhumas.com/ojs/index.php/niuhums/article/view/787 (accessed 12 August 2024).
Anderson, S (2007). "The Economics of Dowry and Bride Price", *Journal of Economics Perspectives,* vol 21, 151–174. https://doi.org/10.1257/jep.21.4.151 (accessed 12 August 2024).
Aransiola, JO and Ayodeji, IGE (2010). "Widowhood practices among the Yorubas of south west Nigeria ...", *Gender and Behaviour*, vol 8, issue 2, 1 December 2010, Widowhood practices among the Yorubas of south west Nigeria: are there differences in what women experience due to their status? https://journals.co.za/doi/abs/https://doi.org/10.10520/EJC34645 (accessed 2 March 2025).
Bamgbose, O (2015). "Translating Traditional Concepts into Legislation and Practice: The Nigerian Woman in Focus", *International Journal of African and African-American Studies*, vol 62 (4) 71–92.
Chika, Sylvia and Nneka, Umejiaku (2021). "Discriminatory Cultural Practices and Women's Rights among the Igbos of South-East Nigeria: A Critique", *Journal of Law, Policy and Globalization*, vol 25, (PDF) Discriminatory Cultural Practices and Women's Rights among the Igbos of South-East Nigeria: A Critique, https://www.researchgate.net/publication/357368475_Discriminatory_Cultural_Practices_and_Women's_Rights_among_the_Igbos_of_South-East_Nigeria_A_Critique (accessed 1 November 2024).
Ikeanvionwu, Chidinma (2024). "Court grants widow ...", *Dateline Nigeria*, 6 July 2024, Court grants widow custody of her two children (dateline.ng) (accessed 18 August 2024).
Eghosa, Ekhator (2019). "Protection and Promotion of Women's Rights in Nigeria: Constraints and Prospects" in Michael Addaney (ed) *Women and Minority Rights Law: African Approaches and Perspectives to Inclusive Development*, Eleven International Publishing, Netherlands, https://ssrn.com/abstract=3799471 (accessed 7 July 2024).
Eniola, BO and Aremo, JI (2020). "Bride Price and Sexual and Reproductive Rights of Women: A Case Study of South Africa and Nigeria", *Journal of Law, Policy and Globalization*, vol 96, 26-33.
Essien, EEP, Gibson, MK, Essien, CKP and David E (2020). "Effects of widowhood practices on the physiological well-being and socio-economic stability of women in Nigeria", *Journal of the Social Sciences,* vol 48 (3), 568–576.

Ewelukwa, UU (2002). "Post-Colonialism, Gender, Customary Injustice: Widows: Widows in African Societies", *Human Rights Quarterly* 24, 424-486.

Falade, SA (1999), Marriage, Divorces and Inheritance in Nigeria, Igabalaye Printing, Lagos, Nigeria.

Law Pavilion, "The Violence Against Persons ...", *LawPavilion Blog*, 5 April 2016, The Violence Against Persons (Prohibition) Act, 2015—LawPavilion Blog, https://lawpavilion.com/blog/the-violence-against-persons-prohibition-act-2015/ (accessed 1 November 2024).

Mezieezieobi, Dan I, Mezieobi, Sam A and Iyamu, EOS (2011). "Widowhood Practices among Igbos of South Eastern Nigeria as a Betrayal of the Fundamental Human Rights of Women", *Journal of Contemporary Research,* vol 8 (no 2), 72–83.

Mamah, E, Ujumadu, V, Nkwopara, C, Okoli, A, Okonkwo, N and Ozoret, C (2016). "The cost of widowhood ...", *Vanguard News*, 8 June 2016, The cost of widowhood in Igboland—Vanguard News (vanguardngr.com) (accessed 30 July 2024).

Obi, Helen Obiageli (2020). "Violence against persons (prohibition) act 2015: Advancing legal protections of women against violence in Nigeria", *International Review of Law and Jurisprudence* (*IRLJ*), 2 (1) 116-122.

Osagie, E and Oboite, N (2024). "The impact of tradition on widowhood rites and property rights on women Inegor local government area of Edo state, Nigeria", *International Journal of Humanities and Social Development* vol 9 (1), (PDF) International Journal of Humanities and Social Development THE IMPACT OF TRADITION ON WIDOWHOOD RITES AND PROPERTY RIGHTS ON WOMEN INEGOR LOCAL GOVERNMENT AREA OF EDO STATE, NIGERIA, https://www.researchgate.net/publication/379542715_International_Journal_of_Humanities_and_Social_Development_THE_IMPACT_OF_TRADITION_ON_WIDOWHOOD_RITES_AND_PROPERTY_RIGHTS_ON_WOMEN_INEGOR_LOCAL_GOVERNMENT_AREA_OF_EDO_STATE_NIGERIA (accessed 2 March 2025).

Oyeniyim, Aransiola Joshua and Aydeji, IGE (2010). "Widowhood practices among the Yorubas of south-west Nigeria: Are there differences in what women experience due to their status?" *Gender and Behaviour*, vol 8 (2) Widowhood practices among the Yorubas of south west Nigeria: are there differences in what women experience due to their status? | Gender and Behaviour, https://journals.co.za/doi/10.10520/EJC34645 (accessed 1 November 2024).

Nwabude, AR (2022a). "Traditional African (the Igbo) Marriage Customs & the Influence of the Western Culture: Marxist Approach", *Open Journal of Social Sciences*, vol 10, 224–239. https://doi.org/10.4236/jss.2022.102016 (accessed 7 July 2024).

Nwabude, Aaron (2022b). "Traditional African (the Igbo) Marriage Customs & the Influence of the Western Culture: Marxist Approach", *Open Journal of Social Sciences*, vol 10 (2), January 2022, 224–239, https://www.researchgate.net/publication/358773938_Traditional_African_the_Igbo_Marriage_Customs_the_Influence_of_the_Western_Culture_Marxist_Approach (accessed 1 November 2024).

Obianeri, Ikenna (2024). "Anambra widow battling forced eviction by in-law seeks help", Punch (Nigeria), 28 January 2024, https://punchng.com/anambra-widow-battling-forced-eviction-by-inlaw-seeks-help/ (accessed 18 September 2025).

Oboite, VN and Egharevba, OJ (2024). "The impact of tradition on widowhood rites and property rights on women in Egor local government area of Edo state, Nigeria", *International Journal of Humanities and Social Development*, vol IX issue 1 March 2024, 38–48.

Odiaka, N (2013). "The concept of gender justice and women's rights in Nigeria: Addressing the missing link", *Afe Babalola University: Journal of Sustainable Development Law and Policy*, vol 2(I) ss 1, 190–205.

Okpete, RK (2001). "A Historical Analysis of Traditional Women Organisation As Agents of Progressive Change in Igboland", *Nigerian Journal of Research in Contemporary Issues*, vol 1 (no 2) 77.

Oyeniyi, A and Ayodeji, I (2010). "Widowhood practices among the Yorubas of southwest Nigeria: are there differences in what women experience due to their status?" *Gender and Behaviour*, vol 8 (1), 3152–3167.

Samuel, GCE (2011). "Emergent Issues on Widowhood Practices in Igbo Culture: Between the Video Screen and Reality", *Unizik Journal of Arts and Humanities* (UJAH), 184–193.

Sassou, MA (2002). "Widowhood Practices in West Africa: The Silent Victims", *International Journal of Social Welfare,* vol 11, 201-209.

Suraiya, S (2024), "Human Rights of Widows: A Study of Widowhood Practices in a Nigerian Society", *Global Online Journal of Academic Research* (*GOJAR*), vol 3 (1) file:///C:/Users/DoBUY/Downloads/2489–4907–1-SM.pdf, (accessed 7 July 2024).

Olowooke, Dipo (2016). "Inheritance: The First Son …", *Business Post Nigeria,* 1 November 2016. Inheritance: The First Son Takes All in Esan Culture | Business Post Nigeria (accessed 29 July 2024).

Wendo, C (2004). "African Women Denounce Bride Price". *The Lancet* vol 363, 716.

Books and Reports

Elias, TO (1971). Nigerian Land Law, 4th edn, Sweet & Maxwell, London, UK.

Emery, Vanessa (2013). *Women's Inheritance Rights in Nigeria: Transformative Practices,* https://nairametrics.com/wp-content/uploads/2013/02/WOMEN-INHERITANCE-RIGHTS-IN-NIGERIATRANSFORMATIVE-PRACTICES.pdf (accessed 7 July 2024).

Friday, AE and Akanni, IA (2017). *We Are Strangers in Our Homes: Older Widows and Property Inheritance among the Esan of South-South Nigeria* (https://www.inia.org.mt/wp-content/uploads/2017/01/1.2-4-Nigeria-90-to-112-Final.pdf) (accessed 7 July 2024).

Gbenga, EA (2015). *Widowhood Practices and the Rights of Women: The Case of South-Western Nigeria,* https://thesis.eur.nl/pub/10819/Research_Paper-Final-Gbenga_Afolayan-_Widowhood_Practices_and_the_Rights_of_Women_in_SW-Nigeria.pdf (accessed 18 September 2025).

Igbe, Chief Sam OU (2023). *From Birth to Death, A Benin Cultural Voyage,* From Birth to Death: A Benin Cultural Voyage by Sam Odighi Udiniyiwe Igbe | The StoryGraph (accessed 7 July 2024) p 125.

Mujibat, O (2023). *The inheritance rights of women in Nigeria,* (https://www.iawj.org/content.aspx?page_id=2507&club_id=882224&item_id=4986#:~:text=In%20Igbo%20customary%20law%2C%20widows,blood%20relatives%20of%20their%20husbands (accessed 30 July 2024).

Nnachi, RO (2007). *Advanced Psychology of Learning and Scientific Enquiries.* Enugu: John Jacob's Classic Publishers Ltd.

Nzewi, E (2019). *Widowhood practices: The Imo experience. Proceedings of the Better Life Programmes for Rural Women Workshop,* Owerri Government Publication, Nigeria.

Odimmegwa, Augustine Okwunna (2010). *Widowhood and the dignity of womanhood in Igboland: A pastoral challenge to the discipleship of the Roman Catholic Church in Igboland.* ETD Collection for Fordham University, NYC, NY, US, AAI3411005. https://research.library.fordham.edu/dissertations/AAI3411005 (accessed 7 July 2024).

Information Documents and Resources

Amnesty.org.uk (2022). "What are human rights?" *About Us*, 16 August 2022, What are human rights? https://www.amnesty.org.uk/what-are-human-rights (accessed 1 November 2024).

Amnesty.org.uk (2024). "What We Do", 2024, Campaigns and Issues (accessed 1 November 2024).

The annual population lecture series—APLS (pg.1 and 124) National Population Commission—NPC Nigeria. www.nationalpopulation.gov.ng. (accessed 22 November 2023)

BRIDE PRICE Definition & Meaning Dictionary.com (accessed 30 July 2024).

FACTSHEET ON THE VIOLENCE AGAINST PERSONS PROHIBITION ACT 2015—Partners West Africa Nigeria, https://www.partnersnigeria.org/factsheet-on-the-violence-against-persons-prohibition-act-2015/ (accessed 1 November 2024).

Isibor, PO (2020). Women's right and status under edo native law and custom: esanland.org, unpublished paper, Microsoft Word—WOMEN's RIGHTS.doc, https://nigerianlawguru.com/wp-content/uploads/2024/10/WOMEN-RIGHTS-AND-STATUS-UNDER-EDO-NATIVE-LAW-AND-CUSTOM-MYTHS-AND-REALITIES.pdf (accessed 29 July 2024).

Nigeria—The World Factbook (cia.gov), https://www.cia.gov/the-world-factbook/countries/nigeria/#people-and-society (accessed 24 August 2024).

Sodiq, Y (2017). A History of the Application of Islamic Law in Nigeria, Palgrave Macmillan, A History of the Application of Islamic Law in Nigeria. SpringerLink (accessed 2 October 2025).

Ukhuegbe, Solomon and Ewere, Anthony (2016). Gender-Based Violence/Social-Cultural Discrimination in Nigeria and the fate of the Gender and Equal Opportunities Bill 2015. Unpublished Paper presented at the International Conference on Strengthening Policy Implementation in a Contemporary World at the University of Benin, Nigeria.

Understanding Nigeria's Marriage Act: A Comprehensive Guide, https://marriageinnigeria.ng/nigeria-marriage-act/ (accessed 1 November 2024).

5

Forging the Right to Work with Metal: Women and the Struggle for Work in Wollongong

Janne Ellen Swift

Introduction

Most of history is written by observers after the fact. This chapter is written by someone who was there, someone who felt the handcuffs and the chains, someone who worked tirelessly, juggled the children and campaigning, someone who didn't get a job, was blacklisted and spied on by ASIO (the Australian Intelligence Organisation) hiding in sight.

Wollongong was a steel city. It lies below a high plateau on a strip of land, a coastline of a beautiful ocean. Our family, packed into two cars, began to descend the mountain to the land below. I thought this must be what hell is like. Black smoke belched from the industries and lay like thick fog, while barely a tree existed. The beautiful escarpment and mountain side were scattered with coal mines, an ugly scar among the

J. Ellen Swift (✉)
Wauchope, NSW, Australia
e-mail: jannell1224@gmail.com

J. A. Scutt (ed.), *Women, Power and Autonomy*,
https://doi.org/10.1007/978-3-031-97958-3_5

lush vegetation. Wollongong was owned by the company Broken Hill Propriety Ltd (BHP).[1]

We had lived the last six years settled in Bathurst, so why did our droving, itinerant worker Dad sell up all our beautiful animals and everything we owned to take us to this terrifying place? Many years later, reading *The Story of Bathurst*, "a book written by Bathurstians" and edited by Bernard Greaves, my sister and I discovered the reason (Greaves 1961; Etsy nd). From the end of WW2 Bathurst was one of the main towns to take in displaced people, the refugees forced to abandon home by bombs, guns, soldiers and threat. By 1952, 80,000 had come through the Migrant Centres and it was recommended that workers seeking employment could relocate to the steel town of Port Kembla (Greaves 1961, 229–230). What my lovely, dying Father didn't know was that his family of older girls who needed work faced life in a city where work was available only to men.

This was all about to change, due to the tireless work of women and the 1970s Women's Movement.

Jobs for Women

In 1973, a collective of working-class feminists as part of the Women's Liberation Movement (WLM) won the right for women to obtain work in the "male only" metal industry, BHP steel works in Port Kembla, Wollongong. By 1977 in an economic downturn the women were pushed out by the "last on, first off" rule. This union/employer rule ensures that if retrenchment of workers is required or programmed into the employer's management plans or economies of scale, then those employed the longest stay on, the most recently employed being first to go.[2]

[1] Schultz (1990) documents well BHPs control of the Illawarra district of New South Wales. The book is available in Wollongong Public Library.

[2] See Janne Ellen Swift, Chronicles of a Radical Feminist (unpublished), a record of history compiled from diaries and kindly typed for the author by Sandra Russell, Wendy Ogbourne and Raechel Ward (private collection). Additional material is available in the short movie DVD (2016) and Laurence (2016).

In 1980, four Sydney women, after being refused jobs in BHP, began the campaign again. Using the *Anti-Discrimination Act* (ADA) 1977[3] they won once more the right work. Again they were pushed out in an industry downturn. They challenged BHP with the law and after a protracted series of court cases in 1993 won again (Anderson 1994; Scutt 2003; Murphy 2020).[4]

Why were there no women in Australia in the metal industry, trades, building industry, waterfront, mines, or working as merchant seamen in Australia? Women workers at that time were employed in only six industries and all on lower wages, historically ranging from 50 per cent to 75 per cent of men's wages.

There Are Two Organisations That Work for Women: Trade Unions and Feminist Organisations

The Trade Unions

The Trade Union Movement (TUM) is the only defence working people have against capitalism, an economic system built on ownership, privilege and greed, at the expense of the working-class. Trade Unions (TU's) began early in Australia. In 1871, the UK Trade Union Act was implemented, securing the legal status of unions through voluntary registration.[5] Trade union structure was governed by democratic centralism, was patriarchal and male dominated, a product of history. The major policies and support in the TUs come from peak bodies. Local Trades

[3] ANTI-DISCRIMINATION ACT 1977 - As at 1 July 2024 - Act 48 of 1977 (accessed 1 November 2024); View - NSW legislation, https://legislation.nsw.gov.au/view/whole/html/inforce/current/act-1977-048 (accessed 1 November 2024).

[4] Australian Iron & Steel Pty Ltd v Banovic [1989] HCA 56; (1989) 168 CLR 165 (5 December 1989), https://www.austlii.edu.au/cgi-bin/viewdoc/au/cases/cth/HCA/1989/56.html (accessed 1 November 2024); *Nadjovska and Ors v Australian Iron and Steel Pty Limited* (1985) EOC #92-140; conversations between the author and filmmaker/activist Robyn Murphy.

[5] 1871 Trade Union Act, https://spartacus-educational.com/Ltrade.htm (accessed 1 November 2024); Section - the TUC's first victories | TUC, https://www.tuc.org.uk/research-analysis/reports/section-tucs-first-victories (accessed 1 November 2024); Trade-Union Act | United Kingdom [1871] | Britannica, https://www.britannica.com/topic/Trade-Union-Act-United-Kingdom-1871 (accessed 1 November 2024).

and Labour Councils (TLCs) are established in every Australian state, with unions electing delegates to the State Trades and Labour Councils (STLCs),[6] each a very powerful organisation within its respective state, electing delegates to the peak body, the Australian Council of Trade Unions (ACTU).

All the conditions most workers have today came from the militant actions of the workers in the TUs. The opposition to them has taken many forms from governments imposing penal clauses and using them to jail the officials and confiscate their finances (Ryan and Conlon 1975; D'Aprano 2001; Scutt 2024).[7]

Skills and Apprenticeships

In 1896, the number of apprentices male and female was about equal, yet by 1906 no women were apprenticed, all of them gone (Ryan 1983, 9, 15, 16; Ryan and Conlon 1975, 86). The states established Wages Boards (for example, Victoria) and Industrial Courts (for example, NSW), with the Commonwealth in 1902 establishing the Arbitration Court, cases at state and federal level focusing on the type of work undertaken in trades and professions. Despite some advances, male workers made slow progress, and women received very little (Bramble 2008, 39).

The Harvester Decision

In 1907, Henry Bournes Higgins, the judge heading the Arbitration Court, ruled in the "Harvester Decision" that men should have a decent wage to support a family. The Trade Unions hailed "the family wage" as a great victory. The decision established a male family wage that did not equate to women with families but did apply to single men (Wise

[6] For example VTHC (nd) and UnionsWA (nd).

[7] Victorian Tramways Union leader Clarrie O'Shea, in 1969 gaoled by Industrial Court judge John Kerr for non-payment of fines, became a trade union hero, ending gaoling of trade union leaders in these circumstances, see Merritt (2019), Scutt (2024).

1973; Scutt 2024).[8] The decision was used as the main argument against equal pay in every case until the Women's Liberation Movement (WLM), the National Council of Women (NCW) and the Union of Australian Women (UAW), defeated it in 1969 and 1972 (Ryan and Conlon 1975; D'Aprano 2001; Scutt 2024), gaining the right to equal pay for equal work, then equal pay for work of equal value, with the Women's Electoral Lobby (WEL) succeeding in having the minimum wage apply to women in 1974 (Ryan and Conlon 1975; D'Aprano 2001; Scutt 2024). Yet today women's earnings are still well below men's (D'Aprano 2001; Scutt 2024).

Feminist Organisations

Many feminist organisations in Australia fought hard and won conditions for women. Two of the issues were the women's right to own property—with wins in the 1880s and 1890s, and the vote in 1894 (South Australia) and 1899 (Western Australia) and federally in 1902 (Buczynski-Lee and Scutt 2002; National Museum of Australia nda; ndb).[9] An amalgamation of feminist organisations fighting for the vote formed the United Associations of Women (UA), working for equal pay and other rights for women at work and at home (Street 1966; Radi 1990; Sekuless 1978). The Union of Australian Women (UAW) began after WW2 from the Housewives Association and was part of the Communist Party of Australia (CPA), focusing on working-class women's rights (Stevens 1991; Reid 1987).

---

[8] *Ex parte HV Mckay* (1907) 2 CAR 1, *Ex parte H.V. McKay* (Harvester Case), (1907) 2 CAR 1, https://www.fwc.gov.au/documents/history/1907_2_car_1.pdf (accessed 1 November 2024); Wise (1973) includes a comprehensive account of the past attitudes of men in Trade Unions.

[9] Karen Buczynski-Lee, When Vida Met the President - Vida Goldstein takes on politics, and Mourning Becomes Electric: A drama/documentary film script, MA (Research), Melbourne University VCA 2010.

Women's Liberation Movement

A new feminist organisation under the banner of the Women's Liberation Movement (WLM) began in 1969 in Sydney. Although many of us involved were radical political activists, we had never heard the word "feminist". We didn't know that women for at least 200 years had been fighting for women to have many basic human rights, including some of the issues that existed for women in 1969/1970:

1. Women could not sign a lease, take a loan, begin a bank account, buy a property without a male guarantor.
2. Contraception was not freely available and abortion illegal.
3. Divorce laws favoured men, and children could be taken from women legally.
4. Childcare did not exist.
5. Domestic violence was not a concept. Men had the right to "chastise" wives.
6. Rape trials were held on the belief that men could not control their sexual urges. Women were seen as part of men's property. Rape in marriage was legal.
7. Child sexual abuse was not a concept. Despite laws against incest, the police put forward the notion that they did not have the power to charge a father for abuse. Young girls seen as sexually active could be sent to "Girls' Homes" charged with "being exposed to moral danger".
8. Women working in the public service in many categories were not classed as permanent, being "temporary" workers only, once they married.
9. Most women workers were employed in only about six industries, mainly related to the home or caring work. Women's wages ranged from 60 per cent to 75 per cent of the male rate.
10. Discrimination in employment was evident in most workplaces.
11. Married women were forced out of the workforce.
12. Low numbers of women were students in universities and many degree courses had few or no women in them.

These issues the WLM began to fight for, and as I have written in "Chronicles of a Radical Feminist":

It was a genius of a movement. It allowed the idea of women's freedom and equality to spread, unimpeded by structure. The small groups were called "Collectives". You didn't have to join anything, attend AGMS, elect officials, pay dues, and be a card-carrying member. All you had to do was form a collective around the fight for women. The (WLM) was the largest, most effective social and political movement of the twentieth century.

It began in consciousness raising (CR) where women talked about their personal lives and experiences, and discovered that as women, we too suffered political oppression. The personal is political.[10]

Working-Class Women and Domestic Responsibilities

Going back a long way in Australian history, for women's place in the workforce the same pattern emerges over and over:

1. The training of working-class women from childhood to view their lives as "homemakers, marriage and children" and not as workers.
2. The lengths that employers have gone to enforce that position so that women's pay remains below men's wages.
3. The TUs that have jealously guarded men's wages and conditions and have kept women out or underpaid.
4. Formal agreements between employers and TUs that kept women out of apprenticeships and training.
5. The non-recognition of women's skills in the work they do and the classifications of what is skilled and what is not.
6. Junior females as the lowest-paid workers in the country with the fewest career opportunities.

[10] Swift (n2).

World War 2

A most productive time for women and work was in WW2 1939–1945. From the early days, feminists in the UA fought for women as they entered and worked in all the male industries. During WW2 many women became TU leaders in their fight for equal wages and conditions as they entered male industries.

Organisations like the ACTU and the ALP (Australian Labor Party) moved to support equal pay for women entering male industries. Women worked in all those industries receiving between 60 to 98 per cent of the male rate. Most women workers (those in "women's industries") were still earning a little over half (54%) of the male rate. Strikes and stoppages became common as women fought the Manpower Directorate's regulations enforcing conscription of women into the workforce. The Arbitration Court lifted wages of women in women's industries to 75 per cent of males. At the end of the war women were sacked out of the male industry by government legislation (Ryan and Conlon 1975; D'Aprano 2001; Scutt 2024).

Back to the Kitchens

Post-war was an intense period of social conditioning aimed at women, and many TUs did not support them, choosing to protect men's jobs. The Arbitration Court in 1949 reversed WW2 pay rates into large pay cuts back to 54 per cent for women. In their book *Gentle Invaders*, Anne Conlon and Edna Ryan (1975, 140) remarked that no TU had ever allowed a cut like that, even in the Great Depression (Stevens 1976, 94).

The 1950s trained many women to again view their lives as devoted to men and households and bearing children. Many years of Liberal government saw the most draconian laws brought in against TUs. This conservative period slowly changed in the mid-60s (Stevens 1985; Mitchell 1979).

Women in the 1960s

The late 1960s brought a small breakthrough for women. The NSW Builders Labourers Federation (BLF) began to employ women on building sites in Sydney. Using strikes and "work ins" they forced employers to employ the women on equal pay (Burgmann and Burgmann 2017).

Probably in the 1960s some TUs had women officials, but they are difficult to locate as history is not generally a fair record of women's activity, particularly where it strays into fields seen as "for men only". At this time, I was the honouree (unpaid) secretary and organiser for the Amalgamated Postal Workers Union (APWU) in Wollongong and the only female member of the South Coast Trades and Labour Council. I was the only honouree in Trades Hall. The secretaries of TUs there had an office, personal secretary, wages, and car. None of these benefits were extended to me or my office.[11]

The Beginnings of the Women's Liberation Movement (WLM) "Wave" of 1970

Gill, a friend and political ally, told me to call in on my way home from work. Over a cuppa she produced a leaflet of meetings just beginning in 1969, location Glebe Point Road, Glebe, in Sydney, NSW. It was called "Women's Liberation" or "Women's Liberation Movement" (WLM) (Graham 1987, 182–183). At the meeting, I tasted with these women a touch of sisterhood, a consciousness raising. Although many of us were radical political activists, we had never heard the word "feminist". This is called, and is, "political erasure".[12]

I was also a member of the Union of Australian Women (UAW). A major split in the Communist Party caused most of the experienced left-wing women to oppose the WLM. I put word out for the women of Wollongong to start a new movement called Women's Liberation (Bevage et al. 1982; Beaton 1982, 81).

---

[11] Swift (n2).

[12] Swift (n2).

Jobs for Women Campaign

The new WLM group in Wollongong began with consciousness raising (CR) which led to all of us talking about the struggle we had to get work. Most of us had begun our working lives as young teenagers and always had trouble finding jobs. We formed and named the first Jobs for Women Campaign (JFWC) and decided to fight for the inclusion of women in the male only paid workforce. We were also working on many other issues affecting women.

The Jobs For Women Collective (JFWC) managed to get women into the rolling mills and tube makers jobs. But the main works refused to budge. After Sally Bowen, a Communist from the Miners Women's Auxiliary, joined the collective we decided that the JFWC would focus on the steel industry. AI&S (Australian Iron & Steel), a subsidiary of BHP, was the major steel works in Wollongong, employing approximately 22,000 men.

The First Barriers

Numbers of us had applied to work at AI&S and been refused. Sally Bowen had worked there during WW2. She said that many women did not want to leave after the war, as they liked the friendship and the money. So the WLM JFWC began the campaign with press interviews. The press also published interviews with Laurie Short, the national secretary of the very large and powerful Federated Iron Workers Association (FIA). He wouldn't meet with us and came out publicly not supporting the right for women to work ("City Women Fight ..." 1971).[13]

The Campaign

We started printing multilingual leaflets. We picketed and rallied, handing out leaflets to the men coming in and out on the three-shift work at AI&S. We set up at the bundy clocking-on entrance gate to

[13] Swift (n2).

distribute the leaflets. Most of the men were OK. Some said their wives had worked in industry in their own home country. However, we told them not to contact us. Anyone associated with our collective would not get work. But we kept in contact with a few men, giving them leaflets for their wives to pass around. We told them to tell their wives: "When jobs are advertised, go and apply", but warning "don't join us", and publicised as much as we could directly to the women, too. We were right in the "don't join us" action and decision.

The Lobbying and Action Continues

At the federal government level, the minister for immigration, Al Grassby, born in Brisbane, Queensland, to immigrant parents, delayed and delayed a meeting. It was 1972 and the Whitlam Labor government was in power. After many months of picketing, leafleting and speaking engagements, the momentum was picking up. BHP had requested a further migrant intake to fill the 800 vacant jobs. We were incensed and we all applied for jobs again. No response.

Trades Hall and left-wing women still were not supporting us, despite our requesting support and meetings with the relevant TUs. As the only woman delegate, I raised the issue constantly. Some men were great, Lenny Norris (Miscellaneous Workers Union [MWU]). Steve Quinn (Metal Trades Union [MTU]). Jim Reed, Jack Clare (Builders Workers Industrial Union [BWIU]), and Merv Nixon, secretary, South Coast Labour Council (SCTLC).

The Miners Women's Auxiliary requested we speak to them. These fierce political women had held the Miners Strikes together. Gill and I with shaking boots addressed them about the new WLM and the JFWC. We got great support.

The Chain Up

We began a vigil at 3.20 pm at the gates of BHP employment office. There were only about 20 of us, and three of us, Maureen Ballardie, myself, and Cathy Gordon, chained ourselves to the fence where the bundies were located. (For those who asked me, bundies are a mechanical device that records when you arrive at work and leave.) Police and security were called. The press was there. Sally Bowen, an articulate woman, spoke clearly to the police and press, saying:

> Women should be filling these positions and the money that they want to spend putting in housing for up to 800 migrant men could go towards housing, families, facilities and childcare for women and migrant families. The BHP has 800 workers, mostly migrant women; they just need to employ them.[14]

Our demand was: "Negotiations with the management, a tour of the steelworks, and (to follow) the employment of women on Equal Pay". Part of the campaign was getting young women into the trades apprenticeships. The Federated Ironworkers Association (FIA) insisted that no women could work in the steelworks, saying the work was too heavy. There were just a few jobs "possible" for women, out of 22,000 (approximate). The police kept watch but did not arrest us. We stayed until after the shift at 11.20 pm talking to the men on their way in and out. The manager of the works, Burgess, refused to meet with us.[15]

The Federated Ironworkers Association (FIA)

Over the time of the campaign, we continued to request interviews and meeting with the FIA. We met with the new Wollongong secretary, an Italian migrant named Nando Lelli. He said he supported women working there—reluctantly—but made the point strongly that women should not have special privileges. He was one of four officials at that meeting. The other three remained uncommitted and silent. They did agree we could address their committee of management. Meanwhile, the powerful National Secretary Mr Short refused all requests for a meeting. The local FIA committee reluctantly agreed that "if the women get in, they go in with equal pay". We were in the process of meeting

[14] Swift (n2). Newspaper reports included "Protesters" (1973).

[15] Swift (n2).

and addressing all the other TUs involved, a lengthy process given how reluctant they were.

The Opposition

Some of the opposition we faced politically included:

1 No showers and toilets for women.
2 Taking old men's and injured workers' easy jobs.
3 Prohibition by law from lifting more than 35 pounds (restricted to women).
4 Fear that women would use their sex to get seniority over men.
5 The work is too hot, heavy, arduous and dangerous for women.
6 Women would be cheap labour because women don't earn the same as men.
7 Taking men's jobs in general and shifting the men into the hard jobs and giving women the easy ones.

We needed more press coverage from the "big" papers to pressure Minister Al Grassby and BHP. BHP were doubling up security at the steelworks. We knew if we were to get women work there, we had to get publicity in the Sydney press. We just didn't have the support in Wollongong. The Trades and Labour Council (SCTLC) passed a resolution of support, but many delegates voted against it. Some of the men were great but the political split that occurred lost us some of the most experienced left-wing women and men. Within the left, in its beginnings, the WLM with its autonomy was a much-hated movement.[16]

The "Work In"

We planned a "work in". Why a "work in"? We were challenging one of the most important laws of capitalists, their right to hire and fire workers.

[16] See "Always Working at the Sink ..." (1971); *Illawarra Daily Mercury Reports* from 1972–1973; Swift (n2).

The steel industry had kept all radical action out by never hiring anyone they hadn't screened. The huge strikes in militant Wollongong had won working conditions for all Australian workers but not for the steel works. We worked out that the company's ability to hire and fire was paramount to them. We knew, too, that whoever went in to work in the steel mills would likely be arrested and it was unclear if Trades Hall would support us.

Our women were nervous. Women supporting kids couldn't do it. We didn't know how long we would be held when arrested or how serious they would make the charges. The steel industry was a protected industry. Unauthorised entry by us posing as workers could be classed as a security breach. We believed it would have to be ASIO vetting the workers for jobs there, deciding who did and who didn't.[17] We made a decision as a collective that I and Cathy Gordon would go in. We both had families and supportive partners, and both had applied to work there. I was friends with Ros Harrison, a feminist and Communist doctor who wanted to come. As we were often told how dangerous it was, and as we would be called reckless for going in, we took our doctor with us. Next, Ponch Hawkes, a journalist, came too. One of the first serious women reporters, she worked for a national newspaper, *Digger*.

We acquired overalls and black hardhats from some of the men we knew. We entered the steelworks via a bridge that spans across a road to Port Kembla. Workers went back and forth across the bridge, the works being on both sides of the road, and we had noticed this—although workers did not enter the works that way because they had to "bundy on". We thought we would try it. That was the only chink in AI&S armour that we knew, as we would not have enough time to cut wire fences.

When a group of men were walking across the bridge, we went up the steps and fell in behind them. Strangely enough, they did not challenge us nor notify anyone. We wandered around the works doing odd jobs, noting although the work was dirty there was little we couldn't do. We stayed a whole shift coming out late. A lot of the men knew we were

[17] South Coast District CPA Meeting of the Women Cadres, Report by ASIO No 1007/7, 10 November 1970, see Swift (n2).

there, but no one told on us. We thought we looked like blokes, but obviously we didn't altogether. Sometimes we got a wolf whistle, common in those days. At one point we had a foreman directing us to work. We did a few jobs, split up into twos a couple of times.

Our JFWC collective had notified the major press earlier as to why we were there and that a "work in" was in progress. We came out to a blaze of reporters. We had broken AI&S BHP's silence. The national press went over the top with it. Suddenly BHP AI&S were put on the spot asking for more migrant men when a huge pool of working women was already there. WLM was demanding action.[18]

Early April 4th, 1973

BHP announced that women were not in the steel works and hadn't worked, even though we were photographed when leaving and 20 members of the WLM were there to meet us coming out. Some men said: "Yes, they were working there." One man reported: "... the foreman hadn't realised they were women." 6th April press: *Illawarra Mercury*: "They Were Not There", reporting that AI&S insisted women could work there; they just had to apply at the employment office.

WE WON.

Most of us wanted to work there, so we went to the employment office at AI&S where we had been going all along with other women. We were accepted reluctantly and went to the Department of Labour where our formal arrangements for employment were made. We went public on the acceptance and encouraged women who wanted to work to follow. AI&S never confirmed they agreed, because they were saying they had never stopped women from employment in the first place.

As a result of the publicity, the past refusal to meet us at the local branch of the FIA was lifted and they invited us to address the branch. The hostility from many was obvious. As before, Nando was on side but

[18] Swift (n2). Reports included "Women Fool BHP Guards", "Girls Invade the Steel Works", "Four Women Claim A.I.&SA. Jobs Right", *Illawarra Daily Mercury* through to May 1973; "Meet the Women Who Were Never There", *Daily Telegraph*, May 1973; "Women Given Jobs", *Daily Telegraph* 28 April 1973.

was echoing the men's concern. Those of us from the campaign who applied for jobs never entered the steelworks as employees, and there was no acknowledgement of our campaign work. We had "put the word out", as the *Daily Mercury* called it, and women were now entering the steelworks. Famed photographer and journalist Ponch Hawkes wrote up a great article in *Digger*, heading the report "Women of Steel" (Hawkes 1973). Among us, the migrant women we knew all got jobs (Hawkes 1973).[19]

Our press releases reiterated again: WE WON.[20]

But tragedy hit early in the campaign when we gained 30 women employment at Tubemakers in Port Kembla. One of the women was killed. Her name was Francis Ryan ("Woman Dies ..." 1973; Reed 1973).[21] I received the news from the press early in the morning, as I was rushing to get the kids off for school. I was shocked all day at work. I kept asking myself "are we wrong? Are we sending young women to their death?" It was a sobering thought, and it is only now, decades later, that corporate manslaughter has gained legislative recognition. In June 2024, the NSW Parliament passed an amendment to the *Work, Health and Safety Act* 2011 (NSW), the Industrial Manslaughter Act, creating an offence of industrial manslaughter and specifically penalising industrial gross negligence.[22]

Meet the Press

The *National Times* magazine 19–24 May 1975 carried a double page spread by Glenys Bell, with photos of Gina Blanchtensky and Sophia Hayden, and Linda Pazzo working as an electrical fitter. Titled "Some women who have made it", it read positively for women. While acknowledging that "every girl" does not grow up "wanting to be a 'Crane

19 Swift (n2).

20 Swift (n2).

21 17 Apr 1973 - WHEN A WOMAN STEELE DIED - Trove, https://trove.nla.gov.au/newspaper/article/236857109 (accessed 2 November 2024).

22 Work Health and Safety Amendment (Industrial Manslaughter) Bill 2024 (nsw.gov.au), https://www.parliament.nsw.gov.au/bills/Pages/bill-details.aspx?pk=18597 (accessed 19 August 2024).

Chaser'", some did "want to be electricians or fitters and turners at AI&S BHP Port Kembla". (Crane chasers sling cranes and winches, and are responsible for ensuring that loads do not exceed lifting capacities.) The article went on with Glenys Bell citing the numbers (Bell 1975):

> There are now 800 women holding down jobs and earning the same pay as men in a period of high unemployment. No one in management or the union say that the women are taking the jobs away from men.

Noting that the women were scattered across the works in a wide variety of jobs, she commented on what they had to wear (Bell 1975):

> Their working clothes are utilitarian and ugly, mostly overalls and drab pants, sweaters and head gear.

No mention of the JFWC.

Mr Fancourt for the company commented "they work like Trojans". They took on all the jobs, the dirty jobs. If there was any discrimination against the women "it was for them by the foreman, but the women wouldn't have it". Next, the article had Margaret Pavelka, a Czech-Australian machine operator, speaking about her job, going on to point out that "60 per cent" of the women "are migrants, many with small children", all "doing their job, working as well as the men". The personnel department was quoted as stating that the women's "absentee rate was the same" as the men's. The question of promotion was met with the response that "seniority" is the criterion. The article was headed "Equality is head and feet high", beginning with a review of women in the steelworks (Ginnane 1975).[23] The first in a series in the *Illawarra Daily Mercury*, the front page is an interview with Carmel Harding, Illawarra's only crane chaser, being given a cuppa from her little son "when she gets home from work" at BHP AI&S.

---

[23] Swift (n2).

A Different World

By 1977 TUs, governments and the left wing of politics had been forced into acceptance of the issues and were on side with WLM. We changed the world for women at every level.

Collectives in the WLM in Sydney, Melbourne, Wollongong and elsewhere had formed and developed the Women's Charter Campaign challenging the restrictive position of women in the workforce, promoting our right work and many other issues (Stevens 1991; Scutt 2024). Our demands were being accepted by the ACTU. In Wollongong the terrible divisions between women had been resolved and the WLM became the accepted organisation for women. In 1977 feminists in Sydney from the WLM and the Women's Electoral Lobby (WEL) had the NSW *Anti-Discrimination Act* (ADA) passed in 1977, ensuring that the Anti-Discrimination Board (later the Equal Opportunity Tribunal then the Equal Opportunity Division of the NSW Civil and Administrative Tribunal) was set up.[24]

"Last on First Off"

I interviewed women about our experiences and wrote an article, "Women of Steel", published in the newly emerging feminist magazine *MABEL*. I reported on the "work in" and the women employed, then what happened when BHP AI&S "had a downturn" and closed some sections of the works. The women working there were sacked, using the "last on, first off" rule. Most men were transferred elsewhere, and any women transferred were sent to the worst jobs, the blast furnaces and coke ovens. There were no shower facilities, or not for women, so that the women had to double up in showers when they could get them, very difficult with buses to catch and the double job at home.

---

[24] *Anti-Discrimination Act* 1977 No 48 - NSW Legislation, https://legislation.nsw.gov.au/view/html/inforce/current/act-1977-048 (accessed 19 August 2024); Administrative and Equal Opportunity Division (nsw.gov.au), https://dcj.nsw.gov.au/content/dcj/ctsd/ncat/ncat/how-ncat-works/ncat-divisions-and-appeal-panel/administrative-and-equal-opportunity-division.html#:~:text=The%20Administrative%20and%20Equal%20Opportunity,Privacy%20of%20personal%20information (accessed 19 August 2024).

The women complained to their TU, the FIA. The FIA went along with management, saying that the women were not being discriminated against. Bella, a migrant friend, and two other women talked to me and said it was deliberate policy to get rid of women. Other women said foremen were picking on them and not on the men in other parts of the works. The picture slowly emerged that BHP were pushing them out. They were all TU women. AI&S BHP deliberately divided them by race/ethnicity to stop the communication between them (Swift 1975).

So, a mere two years after their showpiece on working women in 1977/1978, jobs again advertised by BHP AI&S said "AI&S BHP do not employ women". No comment from the FIA. Nevertheless, or because of this, the women were going into the TUs, joining up if they weren't already members, and working hard.

The 1980s

By the 1980s women had been working all over Australia in far reaching industrial jobs, including aircraft and engineering, and the strikes by women in industry must not be forgotten, an example being those working at Uniroyal in South Australia.[25] Yet BHP AI&S would still have female jobs lists but no jobs for women.

In the years to 1980, WLM had transformed women's position. The TU Movement had dramatically changed. Women were demanding that the TUs work for them; men had to change their attitude. Nando Lilli had become a much stronger voice for the FAI. Laurie Short was gone and no mention of him came up again.

Jobs for Women Begins Again

Four women from a socialist party went to live in Wollongong. Refused jobs, they decided to take on BHP AI&S. The 1980 Jobs for Women

[25] Originally SA Rubber, UniRoyal (together with Bridgestone) was built into a major industrial facility in South Australia, manufacturing amongst other items the Holden, Australia's own car. The women's strikes are ripe for the writing of a key part of the history of this complex: "Bob Footner ..." (2025).

Action Campaign (JFWAC) was formed and immediately registered a complaint with the Anti-Discrimination Board (ADB) in Sydney. The group began using the slogans of the previous campaign, as well as our byline "Women of Steel", all well recognised in Wollongong, and the fight began again.

The group campaigned in exactly the same place, using exactly the same tactics, leaflets, and publicity as the 1970 JFWC. This time the press were on side. The *Illawarra Daily Mercury* encouraged women to join them. Another big difference was technology, which had moved rapidly in the production of the necessary leaflets and letters: no more dirty Roneo machines or multiple carbon copies made with ink all over our fingers, our hands and our faces!

The Tent Embassy

Copying the Aboriginal Movement and the Tent Embassy in Canberra on the lawns of Parliament House,[26] the women set up a Tent Embassy to raise money and inform workers. A brilliant tactic, it meant that as well as building a fighting fund, they gathered hundreds of signatures on a petition. Some women from the first campaign joined them. They worked hard, raising money, writing leaflets, marching and, like the 1970s campaigners, used inventive tactics.[27]

The most enormous difference was the men in the TU Movement supporting them. The SCLC and several TUs now supported women's right to work. Included, too, were the many experienced left-wing women who had initially not supported the early campaign and the WLM. Wollongong TU women and the WLM set up a Women's House, Wollongong Women's Information and Referral Centre (Wollongong Women nd), where feminists were employed, working with domestic violence, too (Arrowsmith 2002).[28] The setting up of the Wollongong Migrant Resource Centre brought migrants of all nationalities together,

[26] Set up on 26 January "Australia Day" 1972, "Defining Moments – Aboriginal Tent Embassy ..." (2024).

[27] See for example Covell et al. nd, part of the Right to Defend Al Jobs campaign; Swift (n2).

[28] Swift (n2).

giving access to migrant women, translators and many who had been steelworkers in their home country. The Feminist collective of newly established Wollongong University gave full support.

These uniting changes meant that women in the campaign would be employed, not blacklisted as women in the first campaign were. The ADB's Carmel Niland, an Official of the FIA from Wollongong, and the JFWAC women met. After lengthy negotiations, 31 women complainants were employed. To follow, 300 were given work and then AI&S BHP closed their books again. Another "downturn". Retrenchments (sackings) began in 1982. The fight went on. Mass retrenchments saw 2300 workers lose their jobs. The FIA came out in support of married women, opposing their being sacked because they were married. Some women from the JFCAC who were sacked combined to challenge the sacking. Sacked because of lacking seniority—because they were not employed when they first applied (which would have saved their jobs), was unjust. Called "voluntary retirement" BHP paid a handout to sacked workers. The women received very little, again because they had not been employed for long. By now over 3,000 workers lost their jobs.

Backed by newly resurrected JFWAC, the women argued sex discrimination, direct and indirect, under the ADA. Thirty-four women lodged the complaint. BHP would not relent on their "recognition for seniority" rule. So the women lodged 55 complaints with the Equal Opportunity Tribunal (EOT). This required a costly legal team. The JFWAC began another fundraising campaign. A major difficulty was that it was not a class action, each case being separate, with each woman testifying and being cross-examined. An intimidating process at best, this action was very difficult for the migrant women involved.

Raising the Funds

The group could have challenged the FIA and TLCs to use their lawyers or pay for legal representation. Where was the well-off NSW TLC, and even the ACTU, large organisations with experienced legal teams? What about the FIA, a very large national TU with a large membership? The women eventually received $10,000 from the Women's Advisory

Council (WAC) set up by the Wran Labor government at feminist urging. Legal Aid, refused at first because some women had working husbands, was ultimately granted. The JFWAC remained as the organising group, meeting with the Public Interest Advocacy Centre (PIAC) which helped them sort out the process.

Another Victory

The EOT found in favour of the women, a landmark case stating that AI&S BHP had discriminated against them on grounds of sex. Justice Barbour awarded them $AUS 1.4 million. BHP appealed, and the case dragged on (Thornton 1993).[29]

1988 BHP Appeals Again

The NSW Court of Appeal dismissed the appeal and the women began to be paid the damages. An appeal to the High Court in May 1989 against eight of the 34 women retrenched on the "last on, first off" basis was lost, too.[30]

---

[29] *Australian Iron & Steel Pty Ltd v Najdovska and Ors* (1988) NSWLR 587, NSWLR | 12 NSWLR 587 | AUSTRALIAN IRON & STEEL PTY LTD V NAJDOVSKA AND OTHERS[EDITORIAL NOTE: An application for special leave to appeal to the High Court from part of the judgment herein has been lodged.], https://nswlr.com.au/view/12-NSWLR-587 (accessed 2 November 2024); Defeating sex discrimination at the Port Kembla steel works - Justice and Equity Centre, https://jec.org.au/impact/our-record/defeating-sex-discrimination-at-the-port-kembla-steel-works/ (accessed 2 November 2024); Law and the Quest for Gender Equality, https://press-files.anu.edu.au/downloads/press/n10614/html/ch09.xhtml?referer=&page=19 (accessed 2 November 2024).

[30] *Australian Iron and Steel Pty Ltd v Banovic* (1989) 168 CLR 165, Australian Iron & Steel Pty Ltd v Banovic [1989] HCA 56 - BarNet Jade - BarNet Jade, https://jade.io/article/67531 (accessed 2 November 2024); Australian Iron & Steel Pty Ltd v Banovic [1989] HCA 56; (1989) 168 CLR 165 (5 December 1989), https://www.austlii.edu.au/cgi-bin/viewdoc/au/cases/cth/HCA/1989/56.html (accessed 2 November 2024); Australian Iron & Steel Pty. Ltd. v. Banovic | Women and Justice | US Law | LII / Legal Information Institute, https://www.law.cornell.edu/women-and-justice/resource/australian_iron_steel_pty._ltd._v._banovic (accessed 2 November 2024); Discrimination law - Law School - University of Queensland, https://law.uq.edu.au/australian-feminist-judgments-project/mapping/discrimination-law (accessed 2 November 2024).

Class Action

The women decided to fight for class action provisions, enabling representation as a group to present the case, compensation being granted individually. They aimed at overcoming the "individual case" problem confronting the women in those earlier cases. The JFWAC decided to use one woman to take the stand as the claimant. In August 1989, Robynne Murphy took the stand in the EOT. Again the court stated that AI&S BHP had discriminated against all the women on the basis of sex between 1977 and 1981 at Port Kembla steel works. BHP did not appeal.

The Women Workers Step Up

The fight continued with now almost 300 women complainants and eye watering legal battles by BHP. Each woman had to apply through the ADB to make a claim of discrimination. BHP argued that under the ADA claimants had to apply for action within six months of the discrimination. This allowed BHP to offer a much smaller amount of compensation to the women. AI&S BHP dragged the case on and on until 1992, depriving the women of payment.

The Final Case

Altogether over 700 women registered claims with the ADB. In 1993, the case came to an end when AI&S signed an agreement with PIAC to pay. The original group received the large payout that they won initially. The second group received only a small amount. The final payout was never revealed.[31]

---

[31] Swift (n2).

Another Look at BHP

Why did BHP not settle the first claim quickly? The FIA was not organising the women. With the first group, the JFWAC were political organisers. Winning the campaign would have meant a payout equivalent of petty cash for a company the size of BHP, compared to court costs of nine years and the final payouts.

Around the same time, in 1984 women in the TU Movement had pressured RJ (Bob) Hawke in the ACTU about sex discrimination legislation. The Women's Movement was pressuring the Liberal-Coalition government and Labor opposition (particularly Susan Ryan as senator and MP Ros Kelly). The federal government set up a pilot program of 28 companies (including BHP) to test affirmative action. Whilst denying the Wollongong women justice, BHP set up affirmative action in their Whyalla and Queensland steel plants.[32]

I believe BHP was trying to break the new anti-discrimination laws because, like the 1973 "Work In" example, all capitalist companies firmly believe in the right to hire and fire. Anti-discrimination laws take away that right, imposing obligations to honour employment rights including anti-discrimination rights.

Both campaigns were politically amazing. The first campaign took the new WLM to Wollongong and challenged the gross discrimination of BHP. The second campaign held a group of women—including mostly migrant women with different languages—together to finally get justice for women in BHP. The BHP AI&S strategy was to instil fear. Campaign leaders were refused employment and forced to live in poverty and financial insecurity.

[32] Editor's Note: Australia under the Fraser Liberal Country Party (later National) government signed CEDAW (*Convention on the Elimination of All Forms of Discrimination Against Women*) in 1981 when the UN International Women's Conference (following up the 1975 Mexico Conference) was held in Copenhagen, Australia's delegation led by Beryl Beaurepaire as chair of the National Women's Advisory Council (NWAC) and RJ Ellicott as Minister for Home Affairs. When Labor won government in 1983 under Hawke, Australia ratified CEDAW and consistent with international obligations introduced the Sex Discrimination Act 1984 (Cth) with CEDAW attached as a Schedule to the Act. Senator Susan Ryan led the Second Reading Debate, and two years later introduced the Affirmative Action Act 1986 (Cth). Australia entered into the Optional Protocol later, in 2009 under the Rudd Labor government.

The anti-discrimination laws were established with good intentions. However, the legislation, both state and federal, is now used for vexatious and trivial reasons by men: to access Coogee women's pool (Spender 2021), to enter women's online support forums, to enter women's art spaces (Thomson and Stubbs 2024)[33] and more. Meanwhile, numbers of women in leadership roles in nursing and women's prisons staffing decline with no significant corresponding increase in other areas. The struggle continues.

Bibliography

Reported Cases

Australian Iron and Steel Pty Ltd v Banovic (1989) 168 CLR 165, Australian Iron & Steel Pty Ltd v Banovic [1989] HCA 56 - BarNet Jade - BarNet Jade, https://jade.io/article/67531 (accessed 2 November 2024).

Australian Iron & Steel Pty Ltd v Banovic [1989] HCA 56; (1989) 168 CLR 165 (5 December 1989), https://www.austlii.edu.au/cgi-bin/viewdoc/au/cases/cth/HCA/1989/56.html (accessed 2 November 2024).

Australian Iron & Steel Pty. Ltd. v. Banovic | Women and Justice | US Law | LII / Legal Information Institute (accessed 2 November 2024).

Australian Iron & Steel Pty Ltd v Banovic [1989] HCA 56; (1989) 168 CLR 165 (5 December 1989), https://www.austlii.edu.au/cgi-bin/viewdoc/au/cases/cth/HCA/1989/56.html (accessed 1 November 2024).

Australian Iron & Steel Pty Ltd v Najdovska and Ors (1988) NSWLR 587, NSWLR | 12 NSWLR 587 | AUSTRALIAN IRON & STEEL PTY LTD V NAJDOVSKA AND OTHERS[EDITORIAL NOTE: An application for special leave to appeal to the High Court from part of the judgment herein has been lodged.], https://nswlr.com.au/view/12-NSWLR-587 (accessed 2 November 2024).

[33] *Moorilla Estate Pty Ltd v Lau* [2024] TASSC 49 (27 September 2024), https://www.austlii.edu.au/cgi-bin/viewdoc/au/cases/tas/TASSC/2024/49.html (accessed 11 November 2024); *Lau v Moorilla Estate Pty Ltd* [2024] TASCAT 58, https://www.austlii.edu.au/cgi-bin/viewdoc/au/cases/tas/TASCAT/2024/58.html (accessed 11 November 2024).

Ex parte HV Mckay (1907) 2 CAR 1, Ex parte H.V. McKay (Harvester Case), (1907) 2 CAR 1, https://www.fwc.gov.au/documents/history/1907_2_car_1.pdf (accessed 1 November 2024).

Lau v Moorilla Estate Pty Ltd [2024] TASCAT 58, https://www.austlii.edu.au/cgi-bin/viewdoc/au/cases/tas/TASCAT/2024/58.html (accessed 11 November 2024).

Moorilla Estate Pty Ltd v Lau [2024] TASSC 49 (27 September 2024), https://www.austlii.edu.au/cgi-bin/viewdoc/au/cases/tas/TASSC/2024/49.html (accessed 11 November 2024).

Nadjovska and Ors v Australian Iron and Steel Pty Limited (1985) EOC #92-140.

Statutes, Conventions and Treaties

Anti-Discrimination Act 1977 No 48 - NSW Legislation, https://legislation.nsw.gov.au/view/html/inforce/current/act-1977-048 (accessed 19 August 2024).

ANTI-DISCRIMINATION ACT 1977 - As at 1 July 2024 - Act 48 of 1977, https://classic.austlii.edu.au/au/legis/nsw/consol_act/aa1977204/ (accessed 1 November 2024).

Convention on the Elimination of All Forms of Discrimination Against Women (CEDAW), Convention on the Elimination of All Forms of Discrimination against Women, https://www.un.org/womenwatch/daw/cedaw/ (accessed 1 November 2024).

Sex Discrimination Act 1984 (Cth), Federal Register of Legislation - Sex Discrimination Act 1984, https://www.legislation.gov.au/C2004A02868/latest/text (accessed 1 November 2024).

Trade Union Act 1871 (UK), 1871 Trade Union Act, https://spartacus-educational.com/Ltrade.htm (accessed 1 November 2024).

Trade-Union Act | United Kingdom [1871] | Britannica, https://www.britannica.com/topic/Trade-Union-Act-United-Kingdom-1871 (accessed 1 November 2024).

View - NSW legislation, https://legislation.nsw.gov.au/view/whole/html/inforce/current/act-1977-048 (accessed 1 November 2024).

Work, Health and Safety Act 2011 (NSW), Work Health and Safety Act 2011 No 10 - NSW Legislation (accessed 2 August 2025).

Work Health and Safety Amendment (Industrial Manslaughter) Bill 2024 (nsw.gov.au), https://www.parliament.nsw.gov.au/bills/Pages/bill-details.aspx?pk=18597 (accessed 19 August 2024).

Articles and Book Chapters

Aboriginal Tent Embassy established | Australia's Defining Moments Digital Classroom | National Museum of Australia, https://digital-classroom.nma.gov.au/defining-moments/aboriginal-tent-embassy-established (accessed 1 November 2024).

"Always Working at the Sink Never Allowed to Make Them" – Four Women Interview with the *Star*, 1971.

Anderson, Jill, "Iron Steel – An industrial landmark as Australian women take on the Big Australian", *Alternative Law Journal* 19 (no 3), June 1994, pp 107–110, Iron & steel: An industrial landmark as Australian women take on the big Australian | Alternative Law Journal, https://doi.org/10.3316/informit.T2024112500013691588004309 (accessed 1 November 2024).

Arrowsmith, Irene, "Wollongong Women's Centre - The Early Days", *Illawarra Unity* 2 (no 5) Illawarra Unity - Journal of the Illawarra Branch of the Australian Society for the Study of Labour History, https://paperity.org/journal/149559/illawarra-unity-journal-of-the-illawarra-branch-of-the-australian-society-for-the-study, Dec 2002.

Beaton, Lynn, "The Importance of Women's Paid Labour—Women at Work in WWII" in M Bevege, M James and C Shute (eds), *Worth Her Salt—Women at Work in Australia* (Hale & Iremonger, Sydney, 1982), 84–98.

Beaton, Lynn, "The importance of women's paid labour. Women at work in World War II" by Lynn Beaton, https://www.marxists.org/subject/women/authors/beaton/1982/world-war-two.htm (accessed 1 November 2024).

Bell, Glenys, "Some women who have made it", *National Times Magazine*, 19–24 May 1975.

"Bob Footner builds SA Rubber Mills complex in Edwardstown suburb of Adelaide ..." *Adelaide AZ*, 2025, Bob Footner builds SA Rubber Mills complex in Edwardstown suburb of Adelaide; then Uniroyal and Bridgestone ending | Adelaide AZ, https://adelaideaz.com/articles/bob-footner-builds-sa-rubber-mills-into-major-manufacturer-before-uniroyal-and-bridgestone-ending (accessed 19 August 2024).

"City Women Fight Discrimination, South Coast Women's Liberation Group", *Illawarra Daily Mercury*, 7 September 1971.

"Defeating sex discrimination at the Port Kembla steel works" - Justice and Equity Centre, https://jec.org.au/impact/our-record/defeating-sex-discrimination-at-the-port-kembla-steel-works/ (accessed 2 November 2024).
"Defining Moments – Aboriginal Tent Embassy …", 25 October 2024, Aboriginal Tent Embassy established | Australia's Defining Moments Digital Classroom | National Museum of Australia, https://digital-classroom.nma.gov.au/defining-moments/aboriginal-tent-embassy-established (accessed 1 November 2024).
Ginnane, Paddy, "Equality is head and feet high", *Illawarra Daily Mercury*, 10 April 1975.
Graham, Diana, "Through Life in Pursuit of Equality" in JA Scutt (ed), *Different Lives—Reflections on the Women's Movement and Visions of its Future* (Penguin Australia, Melbourne, Australia, 1987), 178–187.
Hawkes, Ponch, "Women of Steel" *Digger*, May 1973.
Laurence, Emily, "The Women Who were Never There …", *ABC*, 17 March 2016, The Women Who Were Never There: Wollongong steelworks history retold in dramatic short film - ABC News, https://www.abc.net.au/news/2016-03-17/wollongong-steelworks-history-retold-in-dramatic-short-film/7253948 (accessed 1 November 2024).
Merritt, John, "Clarrie O'Shea – The trade union leader who went to gaol …", *Australian Society for the Study of Labour History*, 2019, Clarrie O'Shea – The trade union leader who went to gaol | Australian Society for the Study of Labour History, https://labourhistorycanberra.org/2019/05/clarrie-oshea-the-trade-union-leader-who-went-to-gaol/ (accessed 1 November 2024).
Merritt, John, "The Trade Union Leader Who Went to Gaol", *Canberra Historical Journal*, September 2007, Merritt-Clarrie-OShea.pdf, https://labourhistorycanberra.org/wp-content/uploads/2019/05/Merritt-Clarrie-OShea.pdf (accessed 1 November 204).
"Meet the Women Who Were Never There", *Daily Telegraph*, May 1973.
"Protesters Chained to Fence", *Illawarra Daily Mercury*, 26 March 1973.
Reed, Janne, "When a Steely Woman Died", *Tribune*, April 1973; 17 Apr 1973 - WHEN A WOMAN STEELY DIED - Trove, https://trove.nla.gov.au/newspaper/article/236857109, https://trove.nla.gov.au/newspaper/article/236857109 (accessed 2 November 2024).
Reid, Elizabeth, "The Child of Our Movement – A Movement of Women" in JA Scutt (ed), *Different Lives – Reflections on the Women's Movement and Visions of its Future* (Penguin Australia, Melbourne, Australia, 1987), 8–20.
Ryan, Edna, "Introduction" in Ann Game and Rosemary Pringle, *Gender at Work* (Taylor & Francis, Sydney, Australia, 1983) 9–11.

Scutt, Jocelynne A, "Without Precedent ...", *Alternative Law Journal*, 2003, vol 28 (no 2), pp 74–79, Scutt, Jocelyn --- "Without precedent: Sexlgender discrimination in the High Court" [2003] AltLawJl 15; (2003) 28(2) Alternative Law Journal 74, https://www5.austlii.edu.au/au/journals/AltLawJl/2003/15.html (accessed 1 November 2024).

Swift, Janne Ellen, "Women of Steel", *MABEL*, No 1, 1975.

Thomson, Jane and Stubbs, Laura, "Tasmania's MONA's Ladies Lounge ...", October 2024, Tasmania's MONA's Ladies Lounge Wins Discrimination Appeal in Supreme Court | Moray & Agnew, https://www.moray.com.au/insights-media-events/publications/pro-bono-update/october-2024 (accessed 11 November 2024).

Thornton, Margaret, "The Indirection of Sex Discrimination"' UTasLaR 6, [1993] UTasLawRw 6; (1993) 12(1) *University of Tasmania Law Review* 88, imageREAL Capture, https://classic.austlii.edu.au/au/journals/UTasLawRw/1993/6.pdf (accessed 2 November 2024).

South Coast District CPA Meeting of the Women Cadres, Report by ASIO No 1007/7, 10 November 1970.

"Woman Dies on the Job", *Illawarra Mercury*, 19 April 1973.

"Women Given Jobs", *Daily Telegraph*, 28 April 1973.

"Working Women" series, "Women Fool BHP Guards", "Girls Invade the Steel Works", "Four Women Claim A.I.&SA. Jobs Right", *Illawarra Daily Mercury* from 1972 through to May 1973.

Books and Films

Bevege, Margaret, James, Margaret and Shute, Carmel (eds), *Worth Her Salt—Women at Work in Australia* (Hale & Iremonger, Sydney, Australia, 1982).

Bramble, Tom, *Trade Unionism in Australia—A History from Flood to Ebb Tide* (Cambridge University Press, Port Melbourne, Australia, 2008).

Buczynski-Lee, Karen and Scutt, Jocelynne A, *The Incredible Woman—Film* (shot in the Legislative Council Chamber, House of Parliament, Hobart, Tasmania, Australia, 2002).

Burgmann, Meredith and Burgmann, Verity, *Green Bans, Red Union—The Saving of a City*, 2nd edn (UNSW Press, Kensington, Australia, 2017).

D'Aprano, Zelda, *Kath Williams—The Unions and the Fight for Equal Pay* (Spinifex Press, Melbourne, Australia, 2001).

DVD 'The Women Who Were Never There', 2016, The Women Who Were Never There - Women's Voices Now, https://www.womensvoicesnow.org/films/the-women-who-were-never-there (accessed 1 November 2024).

Game, Ann and Pringle, Rosemary, *Gender at Work* (Taylor & Francis, Sydney, Australia, 1983).

Greaves, Bernard (ed), *The Story of Bathurst* (Angus & Robertson, Sydney, Australia, 1961).

Jessie Street, *Truth or Repose* (Australasian Book Society, Sydney, Australia, 1966).

Mitchell, Winifred Joyce, *Fifty Years of Feminist Achievement—A History of the United Associations of Women* (UA, Sydney, Australia, 1979).

Murphy, Robyn, Women of Steel (2020) | Australian film, https://www.womenofsteelfilm.com/ (Fan-Force.com, Dharawal nation, Wollongong, Australia, 2020) (accessed 11 November 2024).

Radi, Heather, *Jessie Street—Documents and Essays* (Women's Redress Press, Sydney, Australia, 1990).

Ryan, Edna and Conlon, Anne, *Gentle Invaders—Australian Women at Work 1788-1974* (Thomas Nelson, Sydney, Australia, 1975).

Schultz, Julianna, *Steel City Blues* (Penguin, Melbourne, Australia, 1990).

Scutt, Jocelynne A, *Wage Rage for Equal Pay—Australia's Long, Long Struggle*, (Palgrave Macmillan, London, UK, 2024).

Sekuless, Peter, *Jessie Street—A rewarding but unrewarded life* (Prentice Hall, Sydney, Australia, 1978).

Spender, Lynne, *The Women's Pool* (Spinifex Press, North Melbourne, Australia, 2021).

Stevens, Joyce, *A History of International Women's Day in Words and Images* (IWD Press, Sydney, Australia, 1985).

Stevens, Joyce, *Lightening the Load—Women and Work: A History of Women's Employment Action Centre (WEAC) 1982–1989* (WEAC, South Sydney, Australia, 1991).

Stevens, Joyce, *Taking the Revolution Home—Work Among Women in the Communist Party of Australia 1920-1945* (Sybylla Cooperative Press and Publications, Fitzroy, Australia, 1976).

Etsy, nd, The Story of Bathurst, Book Written by Bathurstians, Edited by Bernard Greaves, Plus Blue Mountains of NSW Photographic Booklet, History. - Etsy UK, https://www.etsy.com/uk/listing/1564011623/the-story-of-bathurst-book-written-by?gpla=1&gao=1&&utm_source=google&utm_medium=cpc&utm_campaign=shopping_uk_en_gb_b-books_movies_and_music-other&utm_custom1=_k_CjwKCAjw8fu1BhBsEiwAwDrsjPuEPYGdEZLeuLPJObhbhAhKuViJyuNZEXBOGcHmzKXsrIWZo71j-RoCXz0QAvD_BwE_k_&utm_content=go_12604173817_126677745264_508772828068_pla-314262775587_c__1564011623engb_102858184&utm_custom2=12604173817&gad_source=1&gclid=CjwKCAjw8fu1BhBsEiwAwDrsjPuEPYGdEZLeuLPJObhbhAhKuViJyuNZEXBOGcHmzKXsrIWZo71j-RoCXz0QAvD_BwE (accessed 16 August 2024).

Wise, Audrey, *Women and the Struggle for Workers Control* (Bertram Russell Peace Foundation, London, UK, 1973).

Information Documents and Resources

Administrative and Equal Opportunity Division (nsw.gov.au), https://dcj.nsw.gov.au/content/dcj/ctsd/ncat/ncat/how-ncat-works/ncat-divisions-and-appeal-panel/administrative-and-equal-opportunity-division.html#:~:text=The%20Administrative%20and%20Equal%20Opportunity,Privacy%20of%20personal%20information (accessed 19 August 2024).

Buczynski-Lee, Karen, When Vida Met the President—Vida Goldstein takes on politics, and Mourning Becomes Electric: A drama/documentary film script, MA (Research), Melbourne University VCA 2010.

Covell, D, Christine and Perez, D, *Jobs for Women*, Right to Defend Al Jobs campaign leaflet produced by Covell et al, nd.

Discrimination law - Law School - University of Queensland, https://law.uq.edu.au/australian-feminist-judgments-project/mapping/discrimination-law (accessed 2 November 2024).

Law and the Quest for Gender Equality, https://press-files.anu.edu.au/downloads/press/n10614/html/ch09.xhtml?referer=&page=19 (accessed 2 November 2024).

Section - the TUC's first victories | TUC, https://www.tuc.org.uk/research-analysis/reports/section-tucs-first-victories (accessed 1 November 2024).

Swift, Janne Ellen, Chronicles of a Radical Feminist (unpublished), a record of history compiled from diaries and kindly typed for the author by Sandra Russell, Wendy Ogbourne and Raechel Walsh (private collection).

UnionsWA, nd, About Us - UnionsWA, https://www.unionswa.com.au/about-us/ (accessed 17 August 2024).

VTHC, nd, VTHC - We Are Union VTHC, https://www.weareunion.org.au/vthc (accessed 17 August 2024).

Wollongong Women, nd, wollongong women info and referrals center 1980 photos - Search Images, https://www.bing.com/images/search?q=wollongong+women+info+and+referrals+center+1980+photos&qpvt=wollongong+women%27s+information+and+referral+centre+1980s+photos&form=IGRE&first=1 (accessed 1 November 2024).

National Museum of Australia, nda, Women granted the vote in federal elections | Australia's Defining Moments Digital Classroom | National Museum of Australia, https://digital-classroom.nma.gov.au/defining-moments/women-granted-vote-federal-elections (accessed 1 November 2024).

National Museum of Australia, ndb, Women's suffrage | National Museum of Australia, https://www.nma.gov.au/defining-moments/resources/womens-suffrage (accessed 1 November 2024).

6

Demanding the Right of Representation for Women in Corporate Structures and Policy in the United Kingdom

Natalie Turney

Introduction

The legacy of a society constructed by and for men is a persisting lack of representation of women across many industries, in both primary and secondary forms. In its primary form, we see sectors where women are not physically represented in-role, particularly in more senior roles: even in multilateral organisations (such as UNESCO): since 1945, only 12 per cent of leaders of key organisations have been women (GWL Voices 2024). A shift in recent history has seen greater levels of diversity across multilateral organisations and in corporations. However, the consequence of the historic lack of primary representation, and thus the secondary form, is a lack of representation of women and girls as considered parties and factors in decision and policymaking. Both primary

N. Turney (✉)
University of Reading, Reading, UK
e-mail: n.r.turney@reading.ac.uk

J. A. Scutt (ed.), *Women, Power and Autonomy*,
https://doi.org/10.1007/978-3-031-97958-3_6

and secondary forms of lack of representation—and in some cases exclusion altogether—pose significant risks to women and girls, in health and safety, access to basic resources, economic independence, and more.

Boardroom and Representation

Inclusion of women in the fabric of businesses is crucial to ensuring primary and secondary forms of representation, and recent years have seen a particular drive towards better representation of women on boards of directors and in key influential roles. However, the composition of corporate structures often leaves women vulnerable to exposure.

When it comes to corporate structure, shareholders represent the highest authority in a company. However, there is a separation between ownership and control. The directors of the company are not bound to follow shareholders' views,[1] and are statutorily bound to exercise independent judgement.[2] Therefore, there is a complex interplay between the two. The board of directors governs the company, applying the powers of management vested in it, having been (in most instances) appointed by the shareholders (Cadbury 1992).[3] Perhaps unsurprisingly, companies commonly adopt a shareholder-focussed approach to corporate governance, wherein the principal objective is to foster and nurture long-term relationships between a company's shareholders and its board of directors, often driven by profit. Whilst in some respects this can allow for a greater harmony in steering the company, it perpetuates an exposure whereby women are disadvantaged (Valsan 2016). One of the most evident examples is where the board of directors and/or shareholders are dominated by men, with women rendered under-represented (or indeed wholly unrepresented) in both the primary and secondary form.

---

[1] *John Shaw & Sons (Salford) Ltd v Shaw* [1935] 2 KB 113 (CA).

[2] *Companies Act* 2006 (UK), s 173.

[3] "Corporate governance is the system by which companies are directed and controlled with boards of directors responsible for the governance of the company while the role of the shareholders is to appoint the directors and the auditors and to satisfy themselves that an appropriate governance structure is in place", Cadbury (1992).

Directors must have regard to enlightened shareholder value as a core principle: the theory that directors are duty-bound to promote the success of the company for the benefit of its members as a whole.[4] This is expressed by statute, under section 172 of the *Companies Act* 2006 (UK), whereby directors are required to consider a range of factors in determining how best to promote the success of the company. Crucially, however, section 172 is not limited in scope to a contemplation of shareholders: as part of their fiduciary duties, directors are required to consider, too, the impact of company operations on stakeholders.[5] In dealing with the common law rule that became section 172,[6] the Company Law Review Steering Group (2001), charged with revolutionising company law, aimed to shift away from the traditional corporate focus on short-term shareholder wealth maximisation and instead sought to promote increased focus on directors' duties and corporate social responsibility. However, the issue remains that the duty is subjective[7]—based on the concept of good faith—and is thus difficult to enforce. Furthermore, it is for the company to enforce the duties and not for outsiders.[8] Accountability for lack of consideration of the impact of operations on women, intra and extra-corporately, is problematic, and the ultimate impact on female employees and consumers of a lack of representation can be significant and even life-threatening.

Enlightened shareholder value as a principle and foundation of the section 172 duty can be utilised in embracing the inclusion of women and fostering a more diverse and relational approach to the board. However, companies must be conscious of the bias it can perpetuate without proactivity regarding women, in some part due to an historic overrepresentation of men-in-role delivering on the principle (Wesley-Key 2007). Historic and inherent masculine dominance, and typification

---

4 *Companies Act* 2006 (UK), s 172.

5 *Companies Act* 2006 (UK), s 172.

6 The obligation to act *bona fide* in a manner in which the director considered to be in the company's interests and not for any collateral purpose. *See Re Smith & Fawcett Ltd* [1942] Ch 304 (CA) 306 (Lord Greene MR).

7 *Regentcrest Plc (In Liquidation) v Cohen* [2001] 2 BCLC 80 (Ch) [120] (Jonathan Parker J). Though there are circumstances where an element of objectivity may be considered. *See Charterbridge Corporation v Lloyd's Bank Ltd* [1970] Ch 62.

8 As the duties are owed to the company alone: *Companies Act* 2006 (UK), s 170.

of the role and skillsets attributed to it, means representation of women on the board remains too low. There is concern that, where driven by profit maximisation, "recruiters are guided by stereotyping and suspicion that women directors will follow a 'female agenda'" (Wesley Key 2007, 424; Kelly & Parkinson 1998, 176).[9] However, in 2019, McKinsey & Co reported that companies with gender-diverse boardrooms were 25 per cent more likely to experience above-average profitability and outperform on profitability companies with non-diverse boards (McKinsey & Co 2020). There are, particularly in more recent years, increased reviews and initiatives designed to combat historically shameful primary representation of women on boards.

In the UK, the Hampton-Alexander, Davies, and Women Leaders Reviews have all sought to assess periodically representation of women on the board, as the jurisdiction continues to take a voluntary approach to enhancing gender diversity on the board.[10] According to the government-appointed Hampton-Alexander Review of early 2021, the number of female executives on the boards of the UK's top listed companies increased by 50 per cent in the preceding five-year period. Following a "culture change" noted by Lord Davies in the foreword to his report in 2014 (Davies 2014), in 2022 (based on 2021 figures), it was reported in the Women Leaders Review that 39.1 per cent of UK FTSE 100 board members were women, compared with 12.5 per cent in 2011 (FTSE Women Leaders 2022).[11]

Substantive methods of ensuring board consciousness in regard to gender diversity typically take the form of reporting requirements: section 414(c)(8)(c) of the *Companies Act* 2006 (UK) requires quoted companies to specify in their annual Strategic Report the number of persons of each sex holding the positions of director, senior manager or employee of the company; similarly, the UK Corporate Governance

[9] Wesley-Key (2007, 424), citing Kelly and Parkinson (1998, 176).

[10] A quota approach had been threatened had the 25% target of women on boards of FTSE 100 companies by 2015 not been met: Company Lawyer 2013, citing Vince Cable (then-Business Secretary).

[11] UK figures in 2011 closely resembled those in the European Union in 2013: "85 per cent of non-executive board members and 91.1 per cent of executive board members are men, while women make up just 15 per cent and 8.9 per cent respectively", EU Focus (2013, 8).

Code (which operates on a comply or explain model) requires companies to disclose in their annual reports “the policy on diversity and inclusion, its objectives and linkage to company strategy, how it has been implemented and progress on achieving the objectives; and the gender balance of those in the senior management and their direct reports” (Financial Reporting Council 2018).[12] In 2022, amendments to the Listing Rules became active following a drive by the Financial Conduct Authority to require “at least 40% of women and those self-identifying as women” to be appointed to the board, and hold at least one senior board position (Financial Conduct Authority 2021), to be reported pursuant to a similar comply or explain model. Though progress is evidently underway, at each point of review it is evident that more must be done.

Questions arise as to whether an ‘artificial’ movement to see greater representation of women on the board is ultimately productive in the longer-term and in ensuring effective business. Though this movement may be perceived as artificial, such steps have become necessary for opening doors to women, allowing entry into spaces which would otherwise—as a default—be dominated by men. Caution as to ensuring talent and worthiness in role when it comes to inclusion is mitigated by implementing robust hiring procedures and competency-based frameworks for appointment—although this should surely apply to male appointments too and ought always to have done so. Thus, it becomes a point of applying equity in the hiring process. This is crucial because representation of women on the board, and at company policymaking level, is fundamental in promoting good corporate social responsibility and protection of women and girls through gender-aware policymaking. At policymaking level, women must be represented to enable adequate consideration of female impact of corporate activities, and this must be supported with the delivery of sufficient training company-wide to ensure those representing the company in society uphold this social responsibility. The representation of women in companies is a vital step in furthering the movement to encompass women and girls’ rights in everyday life. This is not solely a case of equal opportunities at work, a significant issue which demands address. Representation at higher levels

---

[12] NB: This language is retained in the 2024 UK Corporate Governance Code, effective 2025.

filters down to every aspect of the business, from profitability, to risk management on the board (Kaur 2023, 133; Credit Suisse 2012, 19), to work conditions of employees, and to rights of consumers.

Safety and Representation

Lack of representation in corporate policy has consequences experienced daily by women and girls. On occasion, these everyday effects—often costs—provoke a wider media reaction. In January 2022, a "lone woman whose car [had] broken down at night in the dark" was left stranded when she called The AA (Automobile Association) for breakdown assistance, to be told she was not a priority because "that's equality" (Mott 2022). She took to Twitter (now 'X') to contact The AA further, and therein they responded: "you've been advised correctly. We don't prioritise based on gender, we do consider the location so as an example we would prioritise someone on a motorway over someone in a supermarket carpark" (The AA 2022). This exchange prompted widespread attention, as the suggestion was made by The AA that the measure of priority is the risk to safety in the circumstances.[13]

What unfolded was a brief but stark interaction between the company and consumer, as Twitter bystanders intervened to offer their own thoughts on the purported company policy. A common reaction to The AA response was that there was a distinct lack of awareness. Most women and girls will have felt, at some point in their lives, a real sense of vulnerability in a supermarket carpark: the area passed off with ease as a comparative area of safety. I remember, at 16 years old, on a Saturday at midday, when I was followed from a busy shop into the carpark by three men as I made my way to catch my lift; when, at 17 years old, I had just passed my driving test and a man tried to gain access to my vehicle as I was about to drive out of my parking space at the restaurant where I worked. These are 'minor' interactions, and pale in significance in comparison to the experiences of too many others. In June 2017, 23-year-old Molly McClaren walked to her car which was parked in her gym

[13] Indeed, this was endorsed by The AA President Edmund King OBE in his own response to the original tweet: "Please rest assured we give priority to anyone at risk", King (2022).

carpark, and at 11.00 am—in broad daylight—was stabbed 75 times to death by her ex-boyfriend. The tragic event rightfully attracted media attention and the mass outrage of the public; however, often incidents in such environments are on a wider scale unknown. Yet, the issue is pervasive, and a search engine result will—at any time—reveal numerous recent instances of rapes and assaults upon women and girls in carparks, committed by persons known or unknown to the victim. The AA 'place of safety' is not safe.

The AA responder's example given in their measure of order of priority, influenced by a misconceived perception of equity (versus equality and equal rights to safety and service), fails to account for the risk to well-being that women face in everyday life. It is entirely routine for many women to lock their car doors as soon as they enter their vehicle, to enable safety lock features on their cars to protect themselves against risk, and to spread the word to female friends and family members. For men, the constant risk awareness, assessment, and risk management as a routine part of daily life simply does not exist, at least on the same level. Yet often it is men leading the narrative in developing policy that should, in its foundations, be influenced by the risk management and routine dominating a large proportion of its consumer-base—namely, women and girls.

The AA followed up with an apology, and assurance that lone women are indeed prioritised as part of a vulnerable group. However, this event demonstrates a complete lack of understanding by the respondent employees (both on the phone and via Twitter), which translated into actions and responses that placed a lone woman directly in harm's way. This singular event represents a clear manifestation of the need for women to be embedded in decision-making, policymaking, and training development. The life of a woman must be heard and reflected in business activity. The consequences of its absence are not irrelevant, and nor are they trivial. The representation of women is not merely a case for boardroom-related objectives, but must become part of the corporate fabric. Without this influence and insight from the female perspective, a vast number of stakeholders are forgotten or ignored, and the consequences can be extreme.

Wellbeing and Representation

Companies are increasingly under the spotlight for their impact on stakeholders external to the inner workings of the business, particularly with the growth of the 'ESG' movement (environment, social and governance). However, the responsibility for the health, safety and wellbeing of the workforce is paramount, particularly when considering the power imbalance systemic in the employer–employee relationship. Working conditions is a topic that often provokes media reaction, particularly in the fast-fashion industry, where workforces may be internationally based. Standard setting and accountability for poor working conditions must be at the forefront of the minds of those making and enforcing law and policy. Women must lead in, and be intimately connected to, these efforts, as women make up approximately 80 per cent of garment workers (Clean Clothes Campaign 2024). Upon seeking entry to the New York Stock Exchange, fast-fashion brand SHEIN faced resistance by lawmakers, due to concerns relating to supply chain issues, and use of trade law loopholes allowing importation of goods into the US without payment of duties or scrutiny by human rights reviews,[14] and ties to China (Fonrouge 2024; Cox 2023). Nonetheless, reports suggest that leading political parties in the UK continue to encourage SHEIN to float on the London Stock Exchange (LSE) (Briggs 2024). Though the UK has laws regarding human rights violations and high standards in relation to ESG,[15] this encouraged move is critical not only to the reputation of the LSE,[16] but—above all—to the workers. Flotation must carry significant expectations as to accountability, and the letter of the law and regulation must be enforced—irrespective of SHEIN's size and might—so to safeguard against and prevent the promotion of continued exploitation of women and girls.

---

[14] On SHEIN and TEMU, *see* Select Committee (2023).

[15] Particularly following the implications of the EU approval of the Corporate Sustainability Due Diligence Directive (CSD3).

[16] Particularly in light of a 2021 House of Commons Report which revealed evidence that the Uyghur population and other ethnic minorities in Xinjiang Uyghur Autonomous Region suffer systematic human rights violations, and—separately—continued suggestion that SHEIN engages business in the area concerned (Business, Energy and Industrial Strategy Committee 2019–2021, 1272; Oi 2023).

The health of the workforce is increasingly under the spotlight following a period of health-related tumult and focus on individuals' personal welfare. Consider, however, being faced with an epidemic whereby six million members of the workforce report suffering with one or more of the following symptoms: headaches, fatigue, low concentration levels, poor memory, low mood or depression, achy joints and muscles, low confidence. Some escape a number of those symptoms, but all experience physiological changes that affect their health. Research shows that 10 per cent of sufferers leave the workforce, with 25 per cent needing to take time off (Fawcett Society 2022). The impact on the country's economy alone is measured at approximately £10 billion.[17] Faced with this epidemic—as an employer, lawmaker or regulator, or enforcement officer—what would you do?

Fortunately, upon the rampant spread of COVID-19 in early 2020, swift action was taken by employers, and—at a point—by government, in implementing policies, procedures, and laws to ensure the health and wellbeing of the workforce. Flexible working arrangements became far more prevalent, and policies remain in place today in workforces across the world in respect of COVID-19, demonstrating that change and adaptation in the interests of employees' wellbeing is possible. However, say that the epidemic presented in the scenario facing you is *not* COVID-19: it affects the fastest growing demographic in the workforce, and it is the menopausal and peri-menopausal.

In July 2022, a House of Commons Committee report was published, with the government given two months to respond (Women and Equalities Committee 2022); the government responded six months later—in early 2023 (UK Government 2023). The response to the Committee report recommendations fell far short of effecting real and meaningful change. Whilst the government committed to reflect on the study of menopause in school education, promote a self-care factsheet, and create the position of 'Menopause Employment Champion' as a Department of Work & Pensions ministerial appointment, it *rejected* the recommendation to produce model menopause policies to assist employers. This

---

[17] "The team at balance used data from the Fawcett Society, the [Office for National Statistics], and drew from their own expert opinions to create the formula that reveals the true cost for organisations", Balance (2022).

arose during a period when the most common treatment available for menopause was impacted by severe supply shortages, meaning that those affected were experiencing, at times, unmanageable symptoms.

The government asserted the civil service already has the 2021 Menopause in the Workplace Policy and noted institutions that had launched guidance on menopause in the workplace (UK Government 2023, 13). However, this fails to accommodate the millions of women working in small to medium size enterprises lacking the resources of larger corporate counterparts to effect meaningful change beyond looking to guidance. In such instances, where a model policy would provide tangible and meaningful assistance, there was a refusal to do so. Thus, the onus falls on companies, but the difficulty with demanding change from and by companies alone is that not all businesses have equal access to resources to enable them to meet such demands. Government or regulator intervention is potentially amongst the most productive ways to ensure that objectives are met sector-wide.

Yet companies—irrespective of size and might in resourcing—have a legal responsibility to their employees to ensure a safe working environment,[18] and to provide protection against unfair treatment of employees going through menopause, pursuant to the protected characteristics of sex, age, and disability under the *Equality Act* 2010 (UK) (because menopause symptoms can indeed be disabling). Acknowledging this in theory is one thing, but in practice much remains to be done beyond the words on the page. Companies must do more to protect women, and to ensure the inclusion and representation of women at decision-making and policy level in order to do so; the government must be more proactive in its support of companies taking action, and there must be better enforcement of the laws and standards set. Where failures to act meaningfully arise, as in the government's response to the peri-menopause and menopause crisis, women are directly and significantly harmed.

The oversight of women's health and their welfare in the workplace is not reserved to 'women-related issues'. When it comes to burnout, for example, another epidemic of the current working environment, all sexes suffer. Burnout is not exclusive to women, and has been recognised

---

[18] *Wilsons and Clyde Coal v English* [1938] AC 57; *Cook v Square D* [1992] ICR 262.

by the World Health Organisation as an "occupational phenomenon" (2019). Indeed, the Burnout Report of 2024, commissioned by the charity Mental Health UK, revealed a brutal yet unsurprising account (Mental Health UK 2024). It shows 91 per cent of adults in the UK reporting having experienced high or extreme levels of pressure or stress in the year prior, with 20 per cent needing to take time off work due to poor mental health as a result. Yet women find themselves more greatly and disproportionately affected. Women were found to be five percentage points more likely than men to experience high or extreme levels of pressure or stress, yet a higher percentage of men stated that they had taken time off work due to poor mental health caused as a result.

Katie Jgln, in an article influenced by Penny Reid (a bestselling author), stated: "women should not set themselves on fire to keep others warm" (2024). Jgln was discussing a moment at the January 2024 Golden Globes ceremony when the male host made a 'joke' about Taylor Swift, and the singer was filmed as the joke was delivered: she didn't laugh, she just sipped her drink. Swift was criticised heavily online for her 'overreaction', and this prompted further discussion about how so often men are perceived to 'react' to situations whereas women in the same position are considered to '*over*react'. The article prompted the thought that "women should not set themselves on fire to keep others warm" is a mantra so close to home because it addresses all parts of women's lives—beyond regulation of emotions. According to UN Women in a report of late 2023, by 2050 women globally will spend 9.5 per cent more time on unpaid care and domestic work than men: that is 2.3 more hours per day per woman (UN Women 2023, 14).[19] The scale of unpaid work for others is so wide, that the monetary value of women's unpaid care work globally is three times the size of the world's tech industry (UN Women 2024, 24). Evidently, this takes the mantra from 'setting ourselves on fire' to burning *out* at an exponential rate.

Whilst the UN Women forecasted figures on unpaid care and domestic work are grave, the extent to which women are impacted

[19] Further: "On average globally, women spend around three times more time on unpaid care and domestic work than men", UN Women (2024, 8), citing ILO (2018).

by unpaidwork *within* their employment further compounds the issue. According to the Burnout Report, women are seven percentage points more likely than men to experience a high or increased workload of tasks unpaid, and six percentage points more likely to regularly work beyond their contracted hours (Mental Health UK 2024). The Working Time Regulations 1998 in theory set a restriction on this, yet the reality is that—especially post-COVID—many workers are stretched beyond their workload and companies relying on the good will of employees and the enforcement of stretched workloads are exhausting their staff, mentally and physically. The Health and Safety Executive (responsible for enforcing the Regulations) is under-resourced and struggling to keep pace with the "occupational phenomenon" (World Health Organisation 2019), and the Department of Work and Pensions has itself been under the spotlight as struggling civil servants within report "unbearable" workloads due to "improper" staffing levels (Markson 2023).

Stretch on resources is an issue for almost all workforces, as companies, government agencies, and employers continue to suffer post-pandemic, the cost-of-living crisis, Brexit, and so forth. However, there is an obligation—legal, ethical and moral—to safeguard the health of employees through robust internal policy and accountability on workload management and compliance with working hours. Mental health issues arising from pressure and stress is itself an epidemic. With women disproportionately affected, and as "[w]omen leaders are commonly people-orientated [and] empathetic" (Kaur 2023, 133; Credit Suisse 2012, 19), women must be accepted as forerunners in leading companies to change by raising the standards of the workplace and workers' welfare. As in relation to peri-menopause and menopause, the government must lead in investing resources to address the welfare crises prevalent in businesses, through support for development and implementation of internal policy, to legal and regulatory standards, and continued attention to board diversity. The work of not-for-profits and charitable organisations in demanding this rigour from government is critical, and must continue with utmost support of the wider public.

Gaps to Protection and Representation

The COVID-19 pandemic disproportionately impacted women in their own careers, in comparison to men (CEDAWinLaw 2021). In 2021, the European Institute for Gender Equality reported the unsurprising finding that women were overrepresented in roles deemed to be 'key-work', thus resulting in decreased flexible working arrangements and greater exposure to health threats (European Institute 2021, 35–36). Studies published by UN Women and by McKinsey confirm that female employment not only fell at a greater rate than in comparison to men, but the burden of unpaidwork increased (UN Women 2020; McKinsey & Co 2021). Women leaving employment to take up unpaid care roles, for example for children, increased (UN Women 2024, 9), and, consequently, financial dependency upon male wage-earners increased.[20] It is imperative that this disproportionate impact be recognised and companies work to ensure that this is not a continuing legacy of the recent pandemic. Similarly, it is crucial to recognise the health epidemics impacting women to avoid mass exodus or sidelining from the workplace. Access to meaningful and accommodating employment—"decent work" (UN Women 2024, 24)—for women is all-the-more crucial, particularly in upholding women's independence. UN Women considers that there are three critical elements of economic empowerment of women: power (agency, power, and autonomy), systems (policies, norms, and institutions), and resources (equal rights and access to, ownership of and control over assets) (UN Women 2024, 11). However, achieving this trinity for each woman cannot be accomplished by the individual alone.

Financial dependency does not stop at welfare inequities: some of the greatest exposures to women resulting from historically male-dominated workplaces is the persisting gender pay gap and pensions gap. According to figures released through the government's gender pay gap reporting system in early 2022, on average women are paid 90 pence to men's earned one pound (Duncan 2022; Government Equalities Office

[20] "Patriarchy is a root cause of gender inequalities and economic disempowerment, and historically unequal power relations between women and men have persisted within households and in society more broadly", UN Women (2024, 10).

2024).[21] Where the average pay gap increases for women, this is typically due to an overrepresentation of women in lower-paid industries, such as in health and social care. There are many contributing factors, including, for example, career breaks often taken by women who leave employment to raise children. This delay in progress and development is often accompanied by financial reliance. Consequently, with interruption to wage-earning comes disruption to pension payments, with comparatively smaller pension payments, leaving women in a more vulnerable position in later life and exposing women to old-age poverty, including hidden homelessness.

Some companies are already forced into some measure of accountability in respect of confronting the gender pay gap. As of 2017, employers with a headcount of over 250 employees must comply with regulations on gender pay gap reporting.[22] In making the report, there is the option to provide a supporting narrative and employer action plan (Government Equalities Office 2024). As many companies already publish their gender pay gap data alongside a measure of explanation, arguably this introspective measure should become compulsory. Resting the onus for change and good corporate responsibility solely on companies, without any measure of legal or regulatory guidance (at a minimum), is not the proactive and frequently not the productive solution in many instances: "[a]ddressing the barriers to economic empowerment requires work at multiple levels" (UN Women 2024, 12).

We have long lived in a society where women are financially dependent on men, but over time the number of female dependants has decreased. With the opening of more jobs and industries to women, female wage-earners have become normalised. However, when the COVID-19 pandemic imposed turbulent circumstances on so many, between April and June 2020 alone, there was a 65 per cent increase in calls to the National Domestic Abuse Helpline, when compared to the first three months of that year (Havard 2021). This number refers to calls in relation to domestic abuse generally, and includes financial abuse. Financial

[21] According to ILO (2022), globally women in the paid workforce earn 20% less than men on average: UN Women (2024, 8).

[22] The Equality Act 2010 (Gender Pay Gap Information) Regulations 2017.

abuse can occur, for example, when a woman feels unable to leave an abusive relationship because she has become financially reliant on her partner during the course of the relationship and does not have access to the necessary funds to leave. HSBC, an international bank (well known as a British bank), in recent years commissioned an advertisement campaign promoting the importance of financial independence. The advertisement depicts a woman staggering towards a dangling payment card, and the card is snatched from her grasp before she heads towards the door. However, she is pulled back, not by a person, but by chains restraining her ability to move free from control. "When an abuser controls your finances, they control you" (The Media Leader 2023), are the words that can be heard in narration to this harrowing but familiar scene. In the advertisement, the chains are visible, and the woman moves beneath them like a puppet on a string; in reality, the chains are invisible, but countless women remain shackled to those upon whom they rely to sustain their lives financially.

HSBC's advertisement, in collaboration with domestic abuse support charities Hestia and No More, is a great example of the good that companies can achieve, in taking corporate social responsibility and promoting stakeholder interests. As part of the UK Says No More campaign, safe spaces can be found not only in HSBC but also Metro Bank, NatWest, Santander, Nationwide, TSB Banks, Boots, Superdrug, Morrisons, Well pharmacies, and hundreds of independent pharmacies across the UK (and the list of companies providing safe spaces continues to grow). Providing safe spaces for vulnerable persons dependent on others for basic commodities is vital, and in a cost-of-living crisis can prove to be a lifeline. Companies must rise up to meet their social responsibilities and utilise their power to be a source of empowerment to those so desperately in need and must be empowered to do so by the attention and investment of law and regulatory bodies.

In circumstances whereby companies seek protection, perhaps due to lack of resources and/or struggle with a lack of guidance from lawmakers and regulators, the remedy is often insurance. Individuals often manage risk in the same way, obtaining insurance coverage to protect against risks faced in all aspects of life: for example, life, health, employment, liability, home, goods, and so forth. However, as with wages and pensions, the 'insurance gap' demonstrates a lacuna whereby women find themselves greater exposed as compared to male counterparts.

Beyond concerns as to career progression within the insurance industry (ABI 2018), the insurance gap represents the space between women and men whereby women face additional hurdles in accessing insurance provision (Hielkema 2024). The exposure faced by women due to the gender pay gap and pensions gap further exacerbates the consequences of the insurance gap, as the provision of insurance as a risk management tool is often obtained to remedy a lack of financial wherewithal upon the occurrence of (uncertain) events. It is crucial that women have access to insurance at the point of taking out a policy for protection, and also upon an event that triggers a claim for extension of cover: "Even when policies are available and affordable, they are often not tailored to meet women's needs" (Oyekan 2022). Insurance products are typically led and thus developed by the market, in pricing, drafting of policy wording, and associated matters. According to the European Insurance and Occupational Pensions Authority, 45 per cent of female consumers consider themselves unfairly targeted by exclusions in insurance contracts (Hielkema 2024). This is seen particularly in the case of rural women and migrant women (UN Women 2024, 14). Driven largely by the market, a responsibility lies on insurers as corporations to address the discriminatory effect of policy wording and to explore the impact of drafting and claims practices in their assessments of operational impact on consumers and stakeholders. This is largely self-regulatory, though there is arguably scope for oversight and/or supervision by regulatory bodies insofar as practices may be considered discriminatory.

Access to affordable insurance policies is a notoriously difficult task in low-income households. Women are particularly exposed to the risk of being priced out of the market: the gender pay gap and time out of employment to undertake unpaidwork (Teachers Financial Planning 2024) renders insurance less affordable and accessible. Thus, the microinsurance market—intended to be accessible and affordable—has proliferated. Microinsurance[23] offers coverage by way of social protection in absence of local or national support schemes, and by provision of support for low-income households by developing a business model that fosters a profitable (or sustainable) market segment for insurers (Churchill 2006, 15). Oyekan notes the outcome of two instances of illness in the African region: of Mary Anyango, who died of typhoid in Kenya, and of Betty Waswa, who survived complications during the delivery of her child. Waswa survived, though both she and Anyango earned a daily wage of $2 (USD), because she had microinsurance coverage (Oyekan 2022).

When out of employment and undertaking unpaid domestic and care work, many women will not take steps to obtain life insurance should something happen to them, though such provision is typically available (Todoroff 2023). Similarly, women are hugely under-represented in income protection cover.[24] This demonstrates the criticality of social protection schemes in safeguarding women's independence and consequently benefiting the communities built around women. In this regard, it is crucial to note that continued cuts to social security benefits disproportionately impact women, as women are twice as reliant on social security due to comparatively lower incomes, longer lives, violence against women, and time devoted to unpaidwork (Engender 2024). While women should not need to look to commercial options to see themselves protected, it is an increasing reality, and one requiring attention and—crucially—education (Churchill 2006, 20).

Protection in absence of social insurance and/or state-led support schemes is vital in order to combat the disproportionate impact of events (minor and catastrophic) on women: "Globally, only 26.6 per cent of women had comprehensive coverage compared to 34.3 per cent of men before the COVID-19 pandemic" (UN Women 2024, 14). Though

---

[23] "Microinsurance is the protection of low-income people against specific perils in exchange for regular premium payments proportionate to the likelihood and cost of the risk involved", Churchill (2006). 'Micro' is perhaps somewhat deceiving, as the scope of risk covered and indeed risk carrier need not be small.

[24] "A recent report by The Exeter discovered that only 11% of women either have, or are applying for income protection cover in 2023. Men are also under-insured in this area, with around 16% holding or applying for an income protection policy", Teachers Financial Planning (2024).

UN Women calls for greater investment to increase women's access to more comprehensive social insurance and assistance (UN Women 2024, 14), access to microinsurance at individual level, tailored to specific risks, provides a level of comfort and protection for women seeking to ensure their own independence. Indeed, it is estimated that women account for approximately 50 per cent of the lives covered by the microinsurance industry (Oyekan 2022). Frequently operating as risk managers of the home, allocating resources to meet the varying household demands (often from within: "setting themselves on fire"), this is a pertinent option in managing risk in a low-income setting. When women are protected, and households are protected, the collateral impact on the wider family network and community is overwhelmingly positive. Indeed, the benefits to the insurance industry of offering greater protection to women is huge: forecast at over $1 trillion (USD) by 2030.[25] Aside from ethical and moral motivations, the drive for profit and business development would also be supported by ensuring better representation of women.

Conclusion

A traditional male dominance of leadership positions in multilateral organisations and companies has perpetuated a continued caution towards the inclusion of women in key positions.[26] Recruiters can be wary of the inclusion of women in leadership positions within companies for the fear of a 'female agenda' being promoted, despite the fact that boards inclusive of women have proved profitable and better at risk management.[27] Where companies tend to focus narrowly on

[25] "According to IFC's 2015 SheforShield Report, the Insurance industry can play a major role in addressing this gap and earn up to $1.7 trillion by 2030 from women alone—half of it in emerging economies—if they target women", International Labour Organization (2024, 112).

[26] According to Clare Burton, the patriarchal foundations of many industries, roles and structures lead to "organisational politics", where businesses become "saturated with masculine values", Burton (1991, 3). This results from "embedding a gendered workplace culture, continuously replicating itself", which is not a practice exclusively exercised by men, but demonstrates the value seen in one's 'self' and its replicas: Scutt (2024, 16).

[27] Furthermore, male-dominated companies promote a 'male agenda' in any event.

enlightened shareholder value, which itself tends to strengthen male professional positions and relationships, inclusion of women on the board can ensure better contemplation of stakeholders in the execution of the business. The caution against women is at times accompanied by a general criticism of pro-gender diversity initiatives as being 'artificial' and providing opportunities without merit. However, in recent years there has been greater attention and review of the meritorious representation of women on boards, and 'comply or explain' models of transparency and accountability have increased. Moves to advance equitable access and opportunities prove positive as the number of women on boards increases, however the balance of power remains skewed, consequently impacting negatively on women as stakeholders and part of the wider community.

Where women are not represented in decision and policymaking roles, the impact on stakeholders exposed to such decisions and policies can be stark. Corporate policies that may on the face of it seem more minor—like vehicle recovery services prioritising vulnerable women, or hotels not reading aloud room numbers of female guests in an open reception—are critical as they impinge on women's safety. Representation of women's perspectives and lived experiences in the policymaking process, and consistent and robust training of staff throughout a business in ensuring the proper advocation of the policy's objectives, are key in ensuring that women are considered and safeguarded as stakeholders. Beyond consideration of consumers and members of the wider community, the interests of employees are of paramount importance due to the power imbalance between employers and their workforce. With this, working conditions and respect and regard for women's health, and the disproportionate impact of pandemics and epidemics on women, are crucial. When it comes to such issues, the responses of employers and the state are typically laboured with a distinct lack of urgency, which can force women into positions of vulnerability and reliance on male partners and relatives. Coupling the mass exodus of women from the workforce when struggling with issues otherwise ignored, with the immense burden of unpaid domestic and care work which typically persists, women are burning out at exponential rates and suffering a loss of independence.

Loss of economic independence is critical to women as it tends to force reliance on either a society typically developed by and for men, or on male counterparts directly. The role of women in society has over time been perceived as the homemaker and carer, and this continues to be balanced with employment as time progresses. The COVID-19 pandemic was a brutally stark demonstration of this dynamic, and many women left paid employment to take up more traditional (unpaid) domestic roles. Where women are employed, the gender pay gap and consequent pensions gap leaves them exposed to financial reliance on other individuals or on the state. This can be mitigated somewhat by social security and social insurance provisions, though these have been cut at a colossal rate in the UK in recent times, with a disproportionate impact on women (CEDAWinLaw 2022). Private insurance, in the form of microinsurance, is designed to assist with providing protection in cases of low-income households and offers some means of support, though the market must be conscious of continued biases in the development of the system and policy wording in remedying the insurance gap that follows the lacuna in pay and pensions.

Women must break through the glass ceiling. Their representation in primary and secondary forms across society is crucial, but must continue to be supported by employers, corporate policy, state-led initiatives, and by lawmakers and regulators. In all positions of support, women must be part of the conversation, as the life and perspective of womanhood cannot be replicated except to be lived.

Bibliography

Reported Cases

Charterbridge Corporation v Lloyd's Bank Ltd [1970] Ch 62.
Cook v Square D [1992] ICR 262.
John Shaw & Sons (Salford) Ltd v Shaw [1935] 2 KB 113 (CA).
Regentcrest Plc (In Liquidation) v Cohen [2001] 2 BCLC 80 (Ch) [120] (Jonathan Parker J).

Re Smith & Fawcett Ltd [1942] Ch 304 (CA) 306 (Lord Greene MR).
Wilsons and Clyde Coal v English [1938] AC 57.

Statutes, Regulations and Codes

Companies Act 2006 (UK), sections 170, 172, 173, https://www.legislation.gov.uk/ukpga/2006/46/contents accessed 2 October 2025.
Equality Act 2010 (UK), https://www.legislation.gov.uk/ukpga/2010/15/contents accessed 2 October 2025,
Financial Reporting Council, "UK Corporate Governance Code: July 2018" (*Financial Reporting Council*, July 2018) https://media.frc.org.uk/documents/UK_Corporate_Governance_Code_2018.pdf accessed 24 June 2024.
The Equality Act 2010 (Gender Pay Gap Information) Regulations 2017.

Articles and Book Chapters

Balance by Newson Health, "Menopause 'Cripples the UK Economy'" (*Balance*, 12 October 2022) https://www.balance-menopause.com/news/menopause-cripples-the-uk-economy/ accessed 24 June 2024.
Briggs, Fiona, "Shein: UK Party Leaders Mustn't Ignore Supply Chain 'Scandal', Expert Warns" (*Retail Times*, 17 June 2024) https://retailtimes.co.uk/shein-uk-party-leaders-mustnt-ignore-supply-chain-scandal-expert-warns/ accessed 25 June 2024.
Company Lawyer, "Davies Report Reviews Progress of Women in the Boardroom" (2013) 34(7) *Comp Law* 216–217.
Cox, Chelsey, "Retailers Shein and Temu Violate US Tariff Law and Evade Human Rights Reviews on Imports, House Report Says" (*CNBC*, 22 June 2023) https://www.cnbc.com/2023/06/22/shein-temu-evade-us-tariff-and-human-rights-law-on-imports-house-report.html accessed 25 June 2024.
Davies, Mervyn, "Women on Boards: Davies Review Annual Report 2014" (*GOV.UK*, 26 March 2014) https://assets.publishing.service.gov.uk/media/5a7effd340f0b62305b84802/bis-women-on-boards-2014.pdf accessed 24 June 2024.

Duncan, Pamela, "UK Gender Pay Gap: Women Paid 90p for £1 Earned by Men" (*The Guardian*, 6 April 2022) https://www.theguardian.com/world/2022/apr/06/uk-gender-pay-gap-women-paid-90p-for-1-earned-by-men accessed 24 June 2024.

EU Focus, "Women on Boards: Commission Proposes 40 Per Cent Objective" (2013) 303 *EU Focus* 8.

Fonrouge, Gabrielle, "NRF Rejects Shein Membership as Retailer Pursues US IPO" (*CNBC*, 13 May 2024) https://www.cnbc.com/2024/05/13/nrf-rejects-shein-membership-as-retailer-pursues-us-ipo.html accessed 25 June 2024.

FTSE Women Leaders, "FTSE Women Leaders Review: Achieving Gender Balance" (*FTSE Women Leaders*, 22 February 2022) https://ftsewomenleaders.com/wp-content/uploads/2022/02/2021-FTSE-Women-Leaders-Review-Final-Report.pdf accessed 24 June 2024.

Hielkema, Pietra, "Petra Hielkema: Bridging the Gender Gap in Insurance and Pensions" (*European Insurance and Occupational Pensions Authority*, 3 April 2024) https://www.eiopa.europa.eu/petra-hielkema-bridging-gender-gap-insurance-and-pensions-2024-03-26_en accessed 25 June 2024.

Jgln, Katie, "No, Women Should Not Set Themselves on Fire to Keep Others Warm" (*Medium*, 11 January 2024) https://medium.com/the-noösphere/women-should-not-set-themselves-on-fire-to-keep-others-warm-ff44bafd1220 accessed 24 June 2024.

Kaur (a/p Harbans Singh), Kashmirjit, "Women in Boardrooms: Accelerating the Agenda for a Post-Pandemic World" (2023) 44(4) *Comp Law* 132.

Kelly, Gavin and Parkinson, John, "The Conceptual Foundations of the Company: A Pluralist Approach" (1998) 2 *CFILR* 176.

Markson, Tevye, "EXCL: DWP Civil Servants Describe 'Unbearable' Workloads Amid 'All-Time Low Staffing' Levels" (*Civil Service World*, 4 December 2023) https://www.civilserviceworld.com/professions/article/excl-dwp-civil-servants-describe-unbearable-workloads-amid-alltime-low-staffing-levels accessed 25 June 2024.

Oi, Mariko, "Shein: China Fashion Giant Faces US Calls for Probe Over Uyghur Claims" (*BBC News*, 2 May 2023) https://www.bbc.com/news/business-65452976 accessed 25 June 2024.

Oyekan, Ola, "Closing the Gender Gap: The Role of Inclusive Insurance in Empowering Women Around the World" (*Reinsurance Group of America*, March 2022) https://www.rgare.com/knowledge-center/article/closing-the-gender-gap-the-role-of-inclusive-insurance-in-empowering-women-around-the-world accessed 25 June 2024.

Teachers Financial Planning, "The Gender Insurance Gap" (*Teachers Financial Planning*, 5 February 2024) https://www.teachersfp.co.uk/protection/the-gender-insurance-gap-2/ accessed 25 June 2024.

Todoroff, Natalie, "The Gender Gap in Life Insurance" (*Bankrate*, 28 December 2023) https://www.bankrate.com/insurance/life-insurance/gender-gap/ accessed 24 June 2024.

Valsan, Remus, "Board Gender Diversity and the Enlightened Shareholder Value Principle" (2016) 37(6) *Comp Law* 171–177.

Wesley-Key, Sophia, "Companies Act 2006: Are Cracks Showing in the Glass Ceiling?" (2007) 18(12) *ICCLR* 422–429.

Books and Reports

ABI, *Tackling the Gender Seniority Gap: What Works for the Insurance and Long-Term Savings Industry?* (Association of British Insurers, September 2018), https://www.abi.org.uk/globalassets/files/publications/public/diversity/tackling_the_gender_seniority_gap_what_works_for_the_insurance_and_long_term_savings_industry.pdf accessed 25 June 2024.

Burton, Clare, *The Promise and the Price: The Struggle for Equal Opportunity in Women's Employment* (Allen & Unwin, Sydney, Australia, 1991).

Business, Energy and Industrial Strategy Committee, *Uyghur Forced Labour in Xinjiang and UK Value Chains* (HC 2019-21, 1272).

Cadbury, Adrian, *Report of the Committee on the Financial Aspects of Corporate Governance* (The Committee on the Financial Aspects of Corporate Governance and Gee and Co Ltd, 1 December 1992) https://www.icaew.com/-/media/corporate/files/library/subjects/corporate-governance/financial-aspects-of-corporate-governance.ashx accessed 24 June 2024 ("The Cadbury Report").

CEDAWinLaw, *People's Tribunal: President's Report* (CEDAWinLAW, 2021) https://womensbillofrights.wixsite.com/website-1/copy-of-news accessed 25 August 2024.

CEDAWinLaw, *People's Tribunal on 1950s Women's Pensions: The Judge's Report* (CEDAWinLAW, 2022) https://womensbillofrights.wixsite.com/website-1/post/the-judge-s-report-2022 accessed 25 August 2024.

Churchill, Craig, *Protecting the Poor: A Microinsurance Compendium* (International Labour Organisation (ILO), Geneva, Switzerland, 2006).

European Institute for Gender Equality, "Gender Equality Index 2021: Health" (*European Institute for Gender Equality*, 2021) https://eige.europa.eu/publications-resources/publications/gender-equality-index-2021-health accessed 25 June 2024.

GWL Voices, "Women in Multilateralism 2024: Behind Closed Doors" (*GWL Voices*, 3 February 2024) https://gwlvoices.com/women-in-multilateralism-2024/ accessed 11 June 2024.

International Labour Organisation, *Care Work and Care Jobs: For the Future of Decent Work* (ILO, 2018) https://www.ilo.org/sites/default/files/wcmsp5/groups/public/@dgreports/@dcomm/@publ/documents/publication/wcms_633135.pdf accessed 25 August 2024.

International Labour Organisation, *Pay Transparency Legislation: Implications for Employers' and Workers' Organizations* (ILO, 2022) https://www.ilo.org/sites/default/files/wcmsp5/groups/public/%40ed_protect/%40protrav/%40travail/documents/publication/wcms_849209.pdf accessed 25 August 2024.

Mental Health UK, *The Burnout Report* (Mental Health UK, 1 January 2024) https://euc7zxtct58.exactdn.com/wp-content/uploads/2024/01/19145241/Mental-Health-UK_The-Burnout-Report-2024.pdf accessed 24 June 2024.

ILO, *Report – Care Work and Care Jobs*, 2018, Care work and care jobs for the future of decent work | International Labour Organization, https://www.ilo.org/publications/major-publications/care-work-and-care-jobs-future-decent-work#:~:text=This%20report%20takes%20a%20comprehensive%20look%20at%20unpaid,market%2C%20which%20are%20inextricably%20linked%20with%20care%20work. accessed 24 June 2024.

Scutt, Jocelynne, *Wage Rage for Equal Pay: Australia's Long, Long Struggle* (Palgrave Macmillan, London, UK, 2024).

The Fawcett Society, "Menopause and the Workplace" (*The Fawcett Society*, April 2022) https://www.fawcettsociety.org.uk/Handlers/Download.ashx?IDMF=9672cf45-5f13-4b69-8882-1e5e643ac8a6 accessed 24 June 2024.

The Company Law Review Steering Group, *Modern Company Law for a Competitive Economy: Final Report* (Department of Trade and Industry, 2001) https://webarchive.nationalarchives.gov.uk/ukgwa/20070603154510//www.dti.gov.uk/cld/final_report/prelims.pdf accessed 24 June 2024.

The Select Committee on the Chinese Communist Party, *Fast Fashion and the Uyghur Genocide: Interim Findings* (United States, 22 June 2023).

UN Women, "Progress on the Sustainable Development Goals: The Gender Snapshot 2023" (UN Women, September 2023) https://www.unwomen.org/sites/default/files/2023-09/progress-on-the-sustainable-development-goals-the-gender-snapshot-2023-en.pdf accessed 24 June 2024.

UN Women, "Women's Economic Empowerment Strategy" (*UN Women*, January 2024) https://www.unwomen.org/sites/default/files/2024-03/un-women-womens-economic-empowerment-strategy-en.pdf accessed 24 June 2024.

World Health Organisation, "Burn-Out an 'Occupational Phenomenon': International Classification of Diseases", WHO, Geneva, Switzerland (*World Health Organisation*, 28 May 2019) https://www.who.int/news/item/28-05-2019-burn-out-an-occupational-phenomenon-international-classification-of-diseases accessed 24 June 2024.

Information Documents and Resources

Clean Clothes Campaign, "Gender: Women Workers Mistreated" (*Clean Clothes Campaign*, 2024) https://cleanclothes.org/issues/gender accessed 25 June 2024.

Credit Suisse Research Institute, "Gender Diversity and Corporate Performance" (*Credit Suisse*, August 2012) https://www.publicappointmentsni.org/files/publicappointmentsni/media-files/Gender%20diversity%20and%20corporate%20performance%20-%20Credit%20Suisse%20Research%20Institute%20August%202012.pdf accessed 24 June 2024.

Engender Research and Policy, "Social Security" (*Engender*, 2024) https://www.engender.org.uk/research-social-security/ accessed 25 June 2024.

Financial Conduct Authority, "FCA Consults on Proposals to Boost Disclosure of Diversity on Listed Company Boards and Executive Committees" (*Financial Conduct Authority*, 28 July 2021) https://www.fca.org.uk/news/press-releases/fca-consults-proposals-boost-disclosure-diversity-listed-company-boards-executive-committees accessed 24 June 2024.

Government Equalities Office, "Statutory Guidance: Gender Pay Gap Reporting: Guidance for Employers" (GOV.UK, 9 January 2024) https://www.gov.uk/government/publications/gender-pay-gap-reporting-guidance-for-employers accessed 24 June 2024.

Government Equalities Office, "Statutory Guidance: Overview" (*GOV.UK*, 9 January 2024) https://www.gov.uk/government/publications/gender-pay-gap-reporting-guidance-for-employers/overview accessed 25 June 2024.

Havard, Tirion, "Domestic Abuse and Covid-19: A Year Into the Pandemic" (*House of Commons Library*, 11 May 2021) https://commonslibrary.parliament.uk/domestic-abuse-and-covid-19-a-year-into-the-pandemic/ accessed 24 June 2024.

International Labour Organization, "Targeting Women in Insurance" (*International Labour Organization*, 2024) https://www.ilo.org/projects-and-partnerships/projects/targeting-women-insurance accessed 25 June 2024.

King, Edmund, "Tweet" (*X*, 19 January 2022) https://x.com/AAPresident/status/1483896066902839296 accessed 12 June 2024.

McKinsey & Company, "Diversity Wins: How Inclusion Matters" (*McKinsey & Co*, May 2020), https://www.mckinsey.com/~/media/mckinsey/featured%20insights/diversity%20and%20inclusion/diversity%20wins%20how%20inclusion%20matters/diversity-wins-how-inclusion-matters-vf.pdf accessed 24 June 2024.

McKinsey & Company, "Seven Charts That Show COVID-19's Impact on Women's Employment" (*McKinsey & Co*, 8 March 2021) https://www.mckinsey.com/featured-insights/diversity-and-inclusion/seven-charts-that-show-covid-19s-impact-on-womens-employment accessed 25 June 2024.

Mott, Helen, "Tweet" (*X*, 19 January 2022) https://x.com/_HelenMott_/status/1483864107375808519 accessed 12 June 2024.

The AA, "Tweet" (*X*, 19 January 2022) https://x.com/TheAA_UK/status/1483867262373220356 accessed 12 June 2024.

The Media Leader, *HSBC Combines Mass Reach and Niche Targeting to Help Economic Abuse Victims* (YouTube, 2023). https://www.youtube.com/watch?v=LStknPNRmFI accessed 25 August 2024.

UK Government, *Menopause and the Workplace: Government Response to the Committee's First Report of Session 2022–2023* (HC 1060, 2022–2023).

UN Women, "Whose Time to Care? Unpaid Care and Domestic Work During Covid-19" (*UN Women*, 5 November 2020) https://data.unwomen.org/sites/default/files/inline-files/Whose-time-to-care-brief_0.pdf accessed 25 June 2024.

Women and Equalities Committee, *Menopause and the Workplace—First Report* (HC 91, 2022–2023).

7

Criminal Court Links to a Better Lifestyle and a Better Community in Queensland, Australia

Anne Thacker

Introduction

The criminal justice system was, historically, essentially devised and has been developed by men to manage male criminals with little amendment to acknowledge the lives of women defendants/offenders. In Queensland, Australia, this situation has been compounded by the smaller numbers of women facing criminal justice, a fact consistent with most countries and other Australian jurisdictions (gov.uk 2025; Pollak 1961; Hartz-Karp 1981).[1] Equal application of laws and criminal justice funding is a challenge in such circumstance. Consequently, women and girls tend to be ignored as a separate cohort of criminal defendants and offenders.

[1] See also Kilroy (2016); Jessica K Williams, "Lobbying for Change – One Woman's Experiences of Incarceration and Male Violence", Chapter 13 this volume.

A. Thacker (✉)
The University of Queensland, St Lucia, Qld, Australia
e-mail: Magistrate.thacker@courts.qld.gov.au

J. A. Scutt (ed.), *Women, Power and Autonomy*,
https://doi.org/10.1007/978-3-031-97958-3_7

The number of women recorded as committing criminal offences is increasing at more than three times the rate of men. Women are being charged with offences at a rapidly increasing rate with First Nations women significantly over-represented within this cohort (Women's Taskforce (WTF) 2022a, 2022b, 405, 418–427). Increased imprisonment of women and girls appears to be part of a broader imprisonment increase despite the crime rate having decreased over the past 20 years. Imprisonment has been the subject of much published discussion over the same period (Sarre 2021).

Worldwide evidence shows the use of prison is a function of government, police and judicial decision-making rather than a response to criminal activity directly (Cuneen 2010, 45). In America, Audre Lorde put it strongly, pointing at the patriarchy in a politically based world when she observed that the "master's tools" can "never dismantle the master's house" (Berkley 2007, 110). As she goes on to say, those tools may enable a temporary respite in beating the master "at his own game", but "genuine change" will never be brought about by using the master's own tools against him (Berkley 2007, 110).

Current sentencing of women and girls is reported by the Queensland Sentencing Advisory Council (QSAC) (nd)[2] in their 2022 "Engendering Justice Report" (QSAC 2022). The quantitative data analysis used came from Queensland courts during 2005–2006 to 2018–2019. The report is stark, showing the number of women receiving a prison sentence increased by 339 per cent from 2005–2006 to 2018–2019 (QSAC 2022, Figure 2, 2). Four in 10 women sentenced to imprisonment received a sentence under six months. Statistics on recidivism recorded 37.3 per cent of women and girls in this category (QSAC 2022, 38). The report remarks that the reasons behind this dramatic growth in imprisonment (especially for girls) are "complex and difficult to untangle" (QSAC 2022, 52).

The report examined differences between men and women sentenced, finding that offending patterns are highly gendered (QSAC 2022, 52):

---

[2] Other States in Australia have similar agencies for example Victoria has the Centre for Innovative Justice having the broader aim of "making the justice system act as a positive intervention in people's lives, and a strong record of delivering major reforms to criminal and civil justice systems at a state and national level" (RMIT, nd).

> Men were most commonly sentenced to imprisonment for committing the offences contravention of a domestic violence order, assaults occasioning bodily harm and unlicensed driving. For women, the most common offences for attracting a term of imprisonment were stealing, breach of bail – failure to appear, and possession of dangerous drugs.

My daughter read a draft of this essay and wrote to me saying:

> ... the topic of women and girls who go through the criminal justice system is something I noticed when I was a bailiff. Out of the whole year I was in that role I only had **two female defendants** and both were being charged with possession of dangerous drugs and both had severe mental health issues (schizophrenia and bipolar). They also acted in court as tho they knew what they had done was wrong and [they] were upset but the situations they were in were because of a partner in the drug business. And their mental health wasn't supported by their families – also both were white women.[3]

Factors Contributing to Rising Rates of Imprisonment

What is driving this increase in the rate of imprisonment for women and girls? Likely factors appear to include:

> **Lack of an appropriate gendered-responsive approach** to criminal justice, including moving beyond the "victim-offender binary", to ensure response to criminal offending is tailored to the particular needs and context of (especially) victimised women. (*Hear Her Voice* 2022a, 2022b, 427–429)
> **Increased visibility of certain types of offences**, including increased use of CCTV and Loss Prevention Officer positions for surveillance in shops, may well account for the larger number of cases involving theft offences which has nearly doubled for girls. Further, motor traffic offending caught by automated surveillance methods means that where once discretion to

[3] Email dated 10.16 am 15 May 2024 from Alice Thacker to the author.

charge was left to police officers who could listen to circumstance explanations, machine detection devices simply cause an infringement notice to be imposed.

Rising use of remand instead of bail, as one of the most common offences confronting women offenders is breach of bail by failing to appear. This suggests an application of the law equally across genders regardless of the additional duties women bear, caring for children and the elderly, as compared to men and which effectively prohibits women from complying with bail laws.

Legislated restrictions on judicial sentencing discretion remains a significant factor.[4]

Inappropriately taking the blame. Taking the blame for criminal behaviours of other members of their family. This is observed anecdotally, especially for motor traffic offending and drug related offending. It is a matter that often comes to light, if at all, solely by accident and suspicion based on other observable aspects of the family.

Consequences of a shorter term of imprisonment. The Australian Institute of Criminology (AIC) (2020) investigated recidivism among prisoners in 2016.[5] Their research showed women classified as "delayed" or "moderate risk" recidivists and who had received a shorter imprisonment sentence were associated with a higher risk of recidivism! (AIC 2020, 8). It was opined that this "might also reflect that offenders with shorter sentences receive less assistance both while imprisoned and upon release" (AOC 2020, 8). Specifically, women in the group of "moderate risk" recidivists may re-offend due to a gradual accumulation of social pressures when they re-enter the community (AIC 2020, 8). Previous research demonstrated that women can be especially likely to face social and economic marginalisation when they re-enter the community, a cumulative situation that may lead to eventual reoffending (AIC 2020, 8).

[4] For example, on 13 December 2024 the *Making Queensland Safer Act* 2024 (Qld), Making Queensland Safer Act 2024 - Queensland Legislation - Queensland Government, https://www.legislation.qld.gov.au/view/whole/html/asmade/act-2024-054 (accessed 2 February 2025) came into force with immediate effect removing from the Youth Justice Act 1992 (Qld), *Youth Justice Act* 1992, https://www.legislation.qld.gov.au/view/pdf/inforce/2024-11-03/act-1992-044 (accessed 2 February 2025) the principle of detention as a last resort and the principle that a non-custodial order is better than detention in promoting a child's ability to reintegrate into the community.

[5] It acknowledged some limitations to the research by the nature of available data.

Changed attitudes towards sentenced offenders. Australia differs in attitude from other countries that have a high standard of living. For example, Scandinavian social democracies (ranking highest on social expenditure within Europe) see offenders as needing re-socialisation and that this is the responsibility of the community as a whole (Naylor 2015). By contrast, the criminal justice system in Australia struggles against a relentless public news media focussing on a perception that there is a crime wave when analysis of data from the courts and insurance companies shows that no such phenomenon exists.

Changed funding support for the criminal justice system. In Queensland, the *Penalties and Sentences Act* 1992 (Qld) shifted the emphasis of sentencing from penalties to other sentencing considerations, especially rehabilitative community-based orders.[6] However, in the years since the mid-2000s these orders are not supported to the same extent as when initially introduced. For example, two significant changes have occurred over the past 20 years: community-based (unpaid) work-related programs no longer exist due to withdrawal of insurance protecting services that were once offered; and the Office of Corrections divided the probation officer role into two roles—compliance and social support. Since then, the compliance role has received direct funding while the Office of Corrections relies on outsourcing the social support role. This has largely relied on charities such as The Salvation Army and *ad hoc* funded programs. Most programs accommodate men as their focus of attention, for example, there are no drug rehabilitation facilities designed specifically for women or girls. Currently, in Queensland, the waiting list for access to almost all rehabilitation services is out by months or simply not available, exacerbated more recently by the COVID-19 pandemic closures that have not re-opened. Sentencing practices have skewed to accommodate this dearth of service by imposing imprisonment with a parole order (ordaining the social service is accessed), too often ending with the offender returning to prison for breach of parole when actual imprisonment was not an intention truly attached to the parole order.

---

[6] See also the *Legislative Standards Act* 1992 (Qld), https://www.legislation.qld.gov.au/view/html/inforce/current/act-1992-04 (accessed 2 February 2025) relating to standards of legislation, its drafting of legislation and "other purposes related to legislation", and under which the post of Queensland Parliamentary Counsel and Office of the Queensland Parliamentary Counsel are established.

Therapeutic Jurisprudence Introductions and Developments

Autonomy, in the sense of possessing self-directed freedom in an objectively right moral way, is a concept that the criminal justice jurisdiction reaches for when sentencing criminals. This has become the norm in many courts across the world where criminal justice systems are similar to that of Australia (publiclawlibrary.org 2024). This has developed alongside changes to the way criminal justice courts may regard the criminal defendant.

Once, courts were concerned with two significant factors only:

- Did the defendant commit the crime of which they are accused?
- What is the penalty for the criminal conduct?

Today, courts are more likely to ask:

- Is the defendant's criminal behaviour better understood as a consequence of underlying personal issues requiring management, rather than simply repugnant behaviour requiring punishment?

A more therapeutic jurisprudence focuses on behavioural contracting, prevention planning and reinforcing acceptable behaviour. In other words, looking to secure the future for society rather than merely punishing for past behaviour.

In 1987, the International Society for Therapeutic Jurisprudence (ISTJ) was co-founded in America by law professors David Wexler and Bruce Winick. The ISTJ advocates for therapeutic jurisprudence as an interdisciplinary philosophy and practice that examines the therapeutic and anti-therapeutic properties of laws, public policies and legal dispute resolution systems, including criminal justice systems.

In America, "problem-solving" courts (a term coined by Judge Peggy Horton Hora [2011]) began in 1989 with the first adult drug treatment court in Miami, Florida. Literature produced since then deals with the skills and behaviours stipulated as essential abilities of judges and magistrates. These include having emotional intelligence and motivational interviewing skills, as well as knowledge of the stages of behavioural change to manage participant defendant/offenders in a deeper way than merely calling them to account for the actions and/or omissions that brought them before the criminal court.

In Queensland, amendments to the *Penalties and Sentences Act* 1992 (Qld) as well as to the *Bail Act* 1980 (Qld) (Collins 2000), enable courts to impose more intrusive options to understand, manage and immediately commence some palpable improvement of the defendant's /offender's life circumstances.

These amendments clash with settled legal principles: the assumption that every person from the age of about seven years, knows right from wrong and makes decisions about their acts and omissions; and that a defendant is under no compulsion to do anything about their lifestyle unless and until they are found guilty of the criminal offence charged against them.

Of course, doing justice "differently" is fuelled by modern developments bringing about better knowledge of the human condition and our frailties in the face of mental health issues, substance dependence, gambling issues, ability to maintain housing, coping with domestic violence and other problems intractable for some people. Psychology and psychiatry have developed exponentially over the past one hundred years grounding this knowledge with evidence-based understanding.

Therapeutic jurisprudence has developed in Australia and gained traction over the past 25 years. Very briefly, significant events evidence how that occurred. In 2000, Queensland's first Drug and Alcohol Court was constituted under Part A of the *Penalties and Sentences Act* 1992 (Qld) (Queensland Courts nd). In 2006, a large legal focussed cohort attended at the International Therapeutic Jurisprudence Conference held in Perth, Western Australia. The conference encouraged think-tanks and policy-makers towards a more holistic approach to re-socialisation in preference to punishment of criminal offenders.

Reforming Management of Criminal Defendants

Increased rehabilitative response to crime has occurred across Australia, though largely in an *ad hoc* fashion, by the state, the police and the courts. Several examples illustrate this phenomenon.

In May 2006, the Queensland Justice Department supported a pilot "Brisbane Homeless Persons Court Diversion Program" commencing in the Special Circumstances Court presided over by Magistrate Christine Roney. This court offered help to homeless defendants charged with minor offences. Referral was available to appropriate support services and the opportunity to resolve issues related to their offending, often accommodation, health and/or substance misuse issues. Fines or imprisonment could be avoided for successful participation in the program. The Court was defunded, ceasing operation in 2012.

In 2021, *Lacey (a pseudonym) v NSW Attorney General*[7] a transforming criminal jurisdiction process was raised. Lacey was a 15-year-old girl who had been arrested and strip-searched by police. The prosecution case against her included video footage of the strip-search. Two First Nations women gave evidence about the impact of Aboriginal culture on gender considerations, arguing that showing a woman's sensitive parts is women's business and that "opening this up to men will likely result in cultural shame and lasting distress" for Lacey. The appeal was lost for technical reasons. However, the decision left open the possibility of re-arguing for a female magistrate to preside over the hearing of such a case in the original court.

The Magistrates Courts (in New South Wales called Local Courts) especially, are pushing further with more specialisation. Doing justice differently[8] shows a way forward integrating therapeutic jurisprudence as mainstream for the criminal justice system.

In Queensland, the *Women's Safety and Justice Taskforce* was established as an independent, consultative taskforce by the Queensland

---

[7] [2021] NSWCA 27.

[8] "Doing Justice Differently" is now the title of a video produced by the Queensland Sentencing Advisory Council describing and explaining Queensland's Court Link Program Court (QSAC, nda; ndb).

Government[9] to examine *inter alia* the experience of women across the criminal justice system. The Women's Taskforce (WTF 2021, 402, 442) examined:

> What should be done to address the alarming increase in the number of women and girls coming into contact with Queensland's criminal justice system. How do their offending patterns and needs differ from men and boys? How can they be diverted away from the criminal justice system before they become enmeshed in it? What can be done to heal these women and girls so that the community can gain from the realisation of their human potential?

The information gathered by the Taskforce included (WTF 2021, 408–409):

> Some women felt that they received inappropriate responses to their circumstances and offending, and were not being sufficiently diverted from the criminal justice system.
> Women reported feeling confused and unsupported in the legal system, and experienced difficulties in obtaining legal assistance.
> Many had not applied for bail, or did not have adequate support or suitable housing to successfully seek bail. Those who were granted bail spoke about the lack of support available to comply with bail conditions.
> On sentencing, women reported feeling that their victimisation history had not been adequately presented by lawyers or taken into account by judges. Some also felt that the fact they had dependent children was used against them at sentencing to characterise them as "bad mothers".

The Task Force's second report, titled *Hear Her Voice,* was published in 2022. It makes 188 recommendations for reform to improve women and girls' experiences of the criminal justice system. Recommendation 93 states (Women's Taskforce (WTF) 2022a, 2022b, 434):

---

[9] The Taskforce first report *Hear her voice - Report one* (November 2021) made 89 recommendations for domestic violence and justice system reform, all supported or supported in principle by the Queensland Government (Women's Task Force [WTF] 2021).

> The Queensland Government develop and implement a whole-of-government strategy for women and girls in the criminal justice system as accused persons and offenders. The strategy will incorporate a public health approach and aim to prevent women and girls offending, reduce the risk of reoffending and improve the experiences of women and girls who are involved in the criminal justice system as accused persons and offenders. The strategy will be co-designed with women and girls with lived experience, service system and legal stakeholders and First Nations peoples. It will incorporate the implementation of recommendations made by the Women's Safety and Justice Taskforce in Part 3 of this report. The strategy should have a particular focus on better meeting the needs of First Nations women and girls to complement the implementation of recommendation 1 from *Hear her voice: Report One*, addressing coercive control and domestic and family violence in Queensland, and to contribute to Queensland's achievement of the targets in the National Agreement on Closing the Gap.

Some of these recommendations are already the subject of legislative changes.[10]

> In May 2024 the Queensland police Drug Diversion Program was expanded and incorporates a 3-tiered health response graded from 'warning' to 'referral', to 'drug division assessment programs' before a criminal charge may be preferred.

Queensland's "Court Link Program" Court

The compromise achieved by some courts of leaning to rehabilitation-oriented sentencing, is being surpassed by "problem-solving" courts engaging a multi-disciplinary approach (Walsh 2011; Victorian Centre for Innovative Justice, nd). This has developed slowly but persistently over many years.

---

[10] For example, "coercive control" of a person will become a criminal offence in Queensland on May 26, 2025 pursuant to the *Criminal Law (Coercive Control and Affirmative Consent) and Other Legislation Amendment Act 2024* and will carry a maximum sentence of 14 years imprisonment.

In Queensland, around 2006, the Brisbane Special Circumstances Court was established and presided over principally by Magistrate Roney. This court started an important change in how justice was being done for defendants/ offenders who have difficult life circumstances. In 2010, the Queensland Supreme Court of Appeal commented on this court, in *R v AAM; ex parte Attorney General of Queensland,* observing[11]:

> It seems unsatisfactory that the laws of this State make no provision for the determination of the question of fitness to plead to summary offences. It is well documented that mental illness is a common and growing problem amongst those charged with criminal offences. The Magistrates Court has attempted to meet this problem through its Special Circumstances Court Diversion Program which apparently presently operates only in the Brisbane area.

The Court pointed out that the program "assists categories of vulnerable people including those with impaired decision-making capacity because of mental illness, intellectual disability, cognitive impairment, or brain and neurological disorders" and further[12]:

> This commendable initiative, which allows for suitable compassionate supervisory and supportive bail and sentencing orders to be made in appropriate cases, may well be effective in assisting these vulnerable people. But it does not and cannot provide a satisfactory legal solution where people charged with summary offences under the criminal justice system are unfit to plead to those charges. The legislature may wish to consider whether law reform is needed to correct this hiatus in the existing criminal justice system.

The Queensland Parliament responded by passing the *Mental Health Act* 2016 (Qld) giving magistrates the power to dismiss simple offences if the court is "reasonably satisfied, on the balance of probabilities, that

---

[11] [2010] QCA 305, at [9].

[12] At [9].

the defendant was, or appears to have been, of unsound mind when the offence was allegedly committed or is unfit for trial".[13]

In 2017, the Court Link Program Court (Court Link) was established and open to all adult criminal defendants at several Magistrates Court sites across Queensland (QSAC 2020; QSAC, nd). By 2024, Court Link has been available at eight Magistrates Court sites across Queensland.

Court Link is a bail-based program popular with defendants who wish to change their lifestyle away from activities or omissions bringing them into contact with the criminal justice system but at a loss how to achieve a change. This being quite separate from whether or not they are guilty of the criminal charge. Court Link incorporates an integrated court assessment, referral and support program. At the earliest opportunity willing defendants are linked to a social service able to assist them—inclusive of both case management by Court Link staff and supervision by the court. Ultimately, if the defendant is found guilty, or pleads guilty, the evidence of positive lifestyle change is presented as a factor to reduce the sentence that may otherwise have been imposed.

A wide variety of different, complex social and personal factors affect women differently from men. Social duties often avoided by men often include issues arising from domestic violence, unstable housing and trauma, as well as caring responsibilities and involvement with vulnerable members of their family including for some, the child protection system (Hidderley et al. 2022, 52). Thus, for women in particular, Court Link provides the opportunity to tailor a program and any sentence to the individual defendant's circumstances. Court Link also provides opportunity for women defendants to appear before court in a separate "women-only" list.

The *Engendering Justice Report* supports the therapeutic jurisprudence principal stating (Hidderley et al. 2022, 52):

> Nuanced, tailor-made crime prevention, diversion strategies and gender-specific criminal justice and rehabilitative responses are likely to yield the best outcomes to reduce female offending and recidivism rates.

---

[13] *Mental Health Act* 2016 (Qld) sections 172 and 173.

In March 2024, *The Court Link Evaluation Report* was published (Department of Justice 2023). It is an independent and very detailed review of Court Link. The sociodemographic characteristics of Court Link participants were self-reported by participants. The report examined the profiles and characteristics of people who engaged in Court Link with the aim of identifying specific groups who may or may not have benefited from Court Link. After applying various rules, a sample of 3,499 individuals referred to Court Link between 2017 and 2022 were studied. As no surprise, this showed that men account for the majority of referrals at 68 per cent of total referrals reviewed. However, a cluster analysis allowed for gendered extrapolation. Women were 1.6 times more likely than men to be admitted to Court Link case management despite their accounting for 32 per cent of referrals to Court Link (Department of Justice 2023, para 3.2.4).

The survey included questions about what participants learned through the program, what changes they made, what services they intended to continue using after the program, as well as their self-rated likelihood of future reoffending. Overall, respondents stated that they had learned "a lot" or "quite a bit" about a range of topics through their participation in Court Link. Of the different topics (for example, where to get help, how to cut down drinking and drugs, how to stay out of trouble) and of those who responded to this part of the survey, the following received the highest ratings from respondents:

- 78 per cent of respondents said they had learned a lot about "where I can get help";
- 75 per cent of respondents said they had learned a lot about "how to stay on track and make changes";
- 60 per cent of respondents said they had learned a lot about "how to keep healthy" and "how to get through Court".

Respondents were also asked to identify areas of their life that had improved since being admitted to Court Link. Reduced drug use emerged as the area with the most significant improvement—83 per cent described it as "a lot better". This was followed by mental health—78 per cent described it similarly as "a lot better". More than 70 per cent of respondents reported time management, physical health, drinking less alcohol and having identification documentation as being, again, "a lot better" as a result of Court Link.[14]

Unfortunately, *The Court Link Evaluation Report* does not analyse differences between men and women on Court Link. However, since 2019 as recommended in the *Hear Her Voice—Report two* (2022), Court Link staffing has included a dedicated Women's Case Manager position. The Women's Case Manager role was not sustained due to funding issues until around mid-2024, when this was corrected. In the meantime, Anglicare Southern Queensland—Women's Early Intervention Service outreach support has supplemented Court Link Program case management. Overall, therefore, a high degree of support aims specifically at the needs of women available through Court Link.

While future evaluations of Court Link may look at the breakdown and comparison between men and women, as the Court Link magistrate I observe better outcomes for women who engage in Court Link. There could be several reasons why this is being noticed:

- women are more ready and open to support based on societal norms and respond to the more holistic approach to meet their needs through Court Link; and/or
- the efficacy of management of women by woman-focussed agencies; and/or
- with woman-centred attention service offered is simply easier to accept and/or implement; and/or
- because there are fewer women there is an unconscious bias to noticing their outcomes.

Conclusion

My perspective on women and girls in the criminal justice system comes from a long career almost exclusively within criminal justice and as a

---

[14] As a result of the 2022 *Women's Safety & Justice Taskforce - Report 2* and its recommendations putting the spotlight on women's needs (Department of Justice 2023, para 3, 51).

magistrate presiding in criminal (including drug rehabilitation) courts for some 25 years. The recent reports by investigators independent of the courts, as well as my experience presiding at court hearings, show me (as a generalisation) that women very often acknowledge they have a problem or issue and accept appropriate support to change their lifestyle for the better. By contrast, men are more often procrastinators, and more willing to accept the simple age-old adage "if you do the crime, do the time."[15]

Court Link has demonstrated returning autonomy to a person with scaffolding for a better future is the better response to criminal behaviours. *The Court Link Evaluation Report* confirms that Court Link has a positive effect for defendants/offenders. Furthermore, its findings show this court process contains an ability to direct appropriate differences of response to individuals with the consequence that the whole community is advantaged by this restorative aspect of the criminal justice system.

Bibliography

Reported Cases

R v AAM; ex parte Attorney-General of Queensland [2010] QCA 305, R v. AAM; ex parte A-G (Qld) [2010] QCA 305 (5 November 2010), https://www.austlii.edu.au/cgi-bin/viewdoc/au/cases/qld/QCA/2010/305.html (accessed 2 February 2025).

Lacey (a pseudonym) v NSW Attorney General [2021] NSWCA 27, https://nswlr.com.au/view/104-NSWLR-333 (accessed 2 October 2025).

Statutes

[15] Anecdotally, generally the same type of problem as trying to get men to a medical appointment.

Bail Act 1980 (Qld), https://www.legislation.qld.gov.au/view/html/inforce/current/act-1980-035 (accessed 2 February 2025).

Criminal Law (Coercive Control ...) Act 2024 (Qld), *Criminal Law (Coercive Control and Affirmative Consent) and Other Legislation Amendment Act 2024* (accessed 2 February 2025).

Legislative Standards Act 1992 (Qld), https://www.legislation.qld.gov.au/view/html/inforce/current/act-1992-04 (accessed 2 February 2025).

Making Queensland Safe Act 2024 (Qld), Making Queensland Safer Act 2024 - Queensland Legislation - Queensland Government, https://www.legislation.qld.gov.au/view/whole/html/asmade/act-2024-054 (accessed 2 February 2025).

Mental Health Act 2016 (Qld) https://www.legislation.qld.gov.au/view/pdf/inforce/2021-03-08/act-2016-005 (accessed 2 February 2025).

Penalties and Sentences Act 1992 Qld) Penalties and Sentences Act 1992, https://www.legislation.qld.gov.au/view/pdf/inforce/current/act-1992-048 (accessed 2 February 2025).

Youth Justice Act 1992 (Qld), Youth Justice Act 1992, https://www.legislation.qld.gov.au/view/pdf/inforce/2024-11-03/act-1992-044 (accessed 2 February 2025).

Articles and Book Chapters

Collins, Kelly-Anne, "Queensland Bail Laws", *Legislation Bulletin* no 1/100, Queensland Parliamentary Library, Brisbane, 2000, rb0100kc.pdf (parliament.qld.gov.au), https://documents.parliament.qld.gov.au/explore/ResearchPublications/researchBulletins/rb0100kc.pdf (accessed 2 February 2025).

Cuneen, Chris, "Fear: Crime and Punishment" *Academy of the Social Sciences 2010*, Dialogue 29, 2/2010, 45

gov.uk 2025, Statistics on Women and the Criminal Justice System (publishing.service.gov.uk), https://assets.publishing.service.gov.uk/government/uploads/system/uploads/attachment_data/file/938360/statistics-on-women-and-the-criminal-justice-system-2019.pdf (accessed 2 February 2025).

Hartz-Karp, Janette, "Women in Constraints", chapter 8 in SK Mukherjee and Jocelynne A Scutt (eds), *Women and Crime*, AIC, Canberra, ACT, Australia, 1981; republished Taylor & Francis, London, UK, 2016.

Hora, Judge Peggy Fulton, "Courts New Solutions Using Problem-Solving Justice: Key Components, guiding Principles, Strategies, Responses, Models, Approaches, Blueprints and Tool Kits" *Chapman Journal of Criminal Justice* vol 2, no 1, 2011.

Kilroy, Debbie, Kilroy-Debbie-Women-in-Prison-in-Australia-paper.pdf (njca.com.au), 2016, https://www.njca.com.au/wp-content/uploads/2023/03/Kilroy-Debbie-Women-in-Prison-in-Australia-paper.pdf (accessed 2 February 2025).

Lord, Audre, "The Master's Tools Will Never Dismantle the Master's House" in CA Berkley (ed), *Sister Outsider: Essays and Speeches,* Crossing Press, NYC, NY, US, 2007) 110

Naylor, Bronwyn, "The evidence is in: you can't link imprisonment to crime rates", *The Conversation,* 23 April 2015, https://theconversation.com/the-evidence-is-in-you-cant-link-imprisonment-to-crime-rates-40074 (accessed 2 February 2025).

publiclawlibrary.org, "Judge Juan Merchan ..." *AP News,* 17 March 2024, Judge Juan Merchan runs a mental health court when he's not hearing a Trump case | AP News. 17 March 2024, https://apnews.com/article/trump-hush-money-criminal-trial-judge-merchan-c227f5eab200cccffb19ed931b4dac92 (accessed 2 February 2025).

Sarre, Rick, "Australia's prison rates are up but crime is down. What's going on?" *The Conversation,* 22 October 2021, https://theconversation.com/australias-prison-rates-are-up-but-crime-is-down-whats-going-on-170210 (accessed 2 February 2025).

Walsh, Tamara, "A special court ...", *University of Queensland Law Review,* 2011, Walsh, Tamara --- "A special court for special cases" [2011] UQLRS 8 (austlii.edu.au), https://classic.austlii.edu.au/au/journals/UQLRS/2011/8.html (accessed 2 February 2025).

Williams, Jessica K, "Lobbying for Change – One Woman's Experiences of Incarceration and Male Violence", chapter 13 this volume.

Books, Reports and Videos

Department of Justice and Attorney-General, *Final Outcomes and Impact Evaluation Report- Evaluation of Court Link – Department of Justice and Attorney-General*, Deloitte Access Economics June 2023, https://www.courts.qld.gov.au/__data/assets/pdf_file/0009/785808/court-link-evaluation.

pdf.courts.qld.gov.au/__data/assets/pdf_file/0009/785808/court-link-evaluation.pdf (accessed 2 February 2025).

Hidderley, Laura, Jeffs, Samuel, Thoms, Dimit and Klambauer, Dr Eva, *Engendering justice: The sentencing of women and girls in Queensland*, August 2022, QSAC, Sentencing-profile-on-womens-and-girls.pdf, https://www.sentencingcouncil.qld.gov.au/__data/assets/pdf_file/0008/735425/Sentencing-profile-on-womens-and-girls.pdf (accessed 2 February 2022).

Pollak, Otto, *The Criminality of Women*, AS Barnes, NYC, NY, US, 1961.

QSAC nda, "Doing Justice Differently", nda, https://www.sentencingcouncil.qld.gov.au/about-sentencing/ng-justice-differently/court-link (accessed 2 February 2025).

QSAC ndb, "Doing Justice Differently", ndb, https://www.facebook.com/qldsac/videos/ng-justice-differently-court-link/260931928573350/ (accessed 2 February 2025).

QSAC, "Engendering Justice Report", 2022, https://www.sentencingcouncil.qld.gov.au/__data/assets/pdf_file/0008/735425/Sentencing-profile-on-womens-andgirls.pdf (accessed 2 February 2025).

QSAC, "New video highlights … Queensland's Court Link", 29 January 2020, New video highlights the work of Queensland's Court Link | Sentencing Advisory Council Queensland, https://www.sentencingcouncil.qld.gov.au/about-us/news/archive-news/2020/new-video-highlights-the-work-of-queenslands-court-link (accessed 2 February 2025).

Women's Taskforce (WTF), *Hear Her Voice - Report one*, November 2021, https://www.womenstaskforce.qld.gov.au/ (accessed 2 February 2025).

Women's Taskforce (WTF), *Hear Her Voice – Report two,* 2022a, https://www.womenstaskforce.qld.gov.au/ (accessed 2 February 2025).

Women's Taskforce (WTF), *Hear Her Voice – Report two,* 2022b, https://www.womenstaskforce.qld.gov.au/__data/assets/pdf_file/0009/723843/Hear-her-voice-Report-2-Volume-2.pdf (accessed 2 February 2025).

Information Documents and Sources

Australian Institute of Criminology (AIC), *Trends & Issues*, 2020, https://www.aic.gov.au/sites/default/files/2020-05/tandi530.pdf (accessed 2 February 2025).

Queensland Drug and Alcohol Court | Queensland Courts, https://www.courts.qld.gov.au/courts/drug-court (accessed 2 February 2025).

Queensland Sentencing Advisory Council (QSAC), *All you need to know about sentencing in Queensland*, nd, https://www.sentencingcouncil.qld.gov.au/ (accessed 2 February 2025).

RMIT, Centre for Innovative Justice, nd, https://cij.org.au/about/what-we-do/ (accessed 2 February 2025).

Thacker, Alice, E-mail dated 10.16am 15 May 2024 to the author.

Victorian Centre for Innovative Justice, https://supportingjustice.net/ (accessed 2 February 2025).

Part II

Respect

You alone are enough. You have nothing to prove to anybody.
—Maya Angelou, Poet, Writer, Filmmaker, and Activist, nd

8

When a Woman's Body Is Not Her Own: Regulating Women Through Abortion Law

Jocelynne A. Scutt

Introduction

In November 2024, vice president and Democrat presidential candidate Kamala Harris, the first African-Indian American to stand for the US presidency, conceded defeat to her major opponent. On 14 November, writing for *The New Yorker* under the title "A New Rallying Cry for the Irony-Poisoned Right", Jia Tolentino (2024) observed:

> It took less than twenty-four hours after Trump's reëlection for young men to take up a slogan that could define the coming era of gendered regression: "Your body, my choice."

The catchphrase adopted by (some) young men was a riposte to the feminist slogan "My Body, My Choice" adopted at the end of the 1960s, accompanying women's demand for bodily autonomy, access to essential

J. A. Scutt (✉)
Department of Arts, Design and Architecture, School of Social Sciences, University of New South Wales (UNSW), Sydney, Australia
e-mail: jocelynne@fraserchambers.com

J. A. Scutt (ed.), *Women, Power and Autonomy*,
https://doi.org/10.1007/978-3-031-97958-3_8

health care, and a recognition of women's psychic integrity. This demand was replicated throughout the western world. In France, women marched in support of the 1971 Manifesto for Abortion Rights penned by Simone de Beauvoir and signed by 243 women who declared they had undergone abortion, a crime in the country at that time (Zarevich 2022). In the United Kingdom, the Abortion Law Reform Association (ALRA), established in 1935 (Abortion Law Reform Association [ALRC] 1930s–2000s), was a principal proponent of the *Abortion Act* 1967 (England, Scotland and Wales) putting into statute law the terms on which abortion could be conducted legally,[1] and in Australia the Abortion Law Reform Association (ALRA) was active in Victoria from the late 1960s (Evans 2012), as well as in New South Wales, the Australian Capital Territory (ACT), and other states,[2] with both South Australia (1969)[3] and the Northern Territory (1973)(Baird and Belton 2019) introducing legislation similar to the UK Act.[4]

Flaws in the common law approach, and continuing criminalisation of women's right to medical treatment despite what were seen as legislative advances, meant medical specialists in obstetrics and gynaecology, general practitioners, and medical associations agitated for legislative clarification to put an end to police intervention where doctors carried out abortions they considered conformed to the law, whether statutory or judge made. Women continued the campaign for their abortion rights, framed as "free contraception and abortion on demand". Ultimately, the aim was

---

[1] *Abortion Act* 1967 (England, Scotland and Wales), Abortion Act 1967, https://www.legislation.gov.uk/ukpga/1967/87/contents (accessed 2 November 2024).

[2] In Queensland known as Children By Choice, incorporated in 1972 (Children by Choice 2025).

[3] *Criminal Law Consolidation Act* 1935–1969, 1935.2252.pdf, https://www.legislation.sa.gov.au/__legislation/lz/c/a/criminal%20law%20consolidation%20act%201935/1992.01.15/1935.2252.pdf (accessed 2 November 2024); Abortion Law Reform Association | AWR, https://www.womenaustralia.info/entries/abortion-law-reform-association/ (accessed 2 November 2024); s82A, South Australia: Medical termination of pregnancy, https://www.consciencelaws.org/law/laws/australia003.aspx (accessed 2 November 2024); Abortion Regulations 1970, 1970.-.pdf, https://www.legislation.sa.gov.au/__legislation/lz/c/r/abortion%20regulations%201970/1996.08.31_(1991.07.18)/1970.-.pdf (accessed 2 November 2024).

[4] For Aotearoa/New Zealand see Royal Commission on Contraception, Sterilisation and Abortion June 1975–March 1977 (Cook 2011; Aotearoa/New Zealand, nd; 1976, 1977a, b; Goodyear-Smith 2023); for Canada see *Criminal Law Amendment Act, 1968–69* (Bill C-150) (Canada); (University of Toronto Libraries, nd).

to ensure that women's health and women's lives were given priority, and that rather than see the embryo or foetus as "the tiniest patient" with transcendent rights, abortion laws should prioritise women as patients.

Statutory Law—Progressive or Regressive Reform?

Legislative action allowing termination of pregnancy in specific circumstances was predated by *R v Bourne*,[5] decided in 1938. Campaigning by women to end women's deaths by backstreet abortion was well in hand. In 1934, the Conference of Cooperative Women passed a resolution advocating legal abortion. Then in 1935 Stella Browne, Janet Chance and Alice Jenkins led the 1935 establishment of the Abortion Law Reform Association (ALRA). ALRA advocated the right of free access to improved contraceptive services, legalisation of abortion by qualified practitioners "within such limitations as may be considered advisable" and, declaring that existing abortion laws would not "end the widespread practice of secret abortion, whereby unqualified persons endanger the lives of pregnant women", maintained "that this problem cannot be adequately solved until the reasons for the refusal of motherhood are given the attention they deserve" (Humanist Heritage 2023).

This led to gynaecologist Mr Bourne, having performed an abortion where the 14-year-old patient had been gang raped by five soldiers, presenting himself for prosecution under the *Offences Against the Person Act* (OAPA) 1861. Sections 58 and 59 of the OAPA criminalise attempts to procure abortion or supply the means for it. Section 58 makes criminal the "unlawful" administration of drugs ("poison or noxious thing") or use of instruments by a woman "with intent" to procure abortion on herself, or by anyone ("whosoever") on another woman, that offence being a felony. Section 59 extends to supply or procuring of "any poison

---

[5] *R v Bourne* [1938] 3 All ER 615, united_kingdom_1938_bourne.pdf, https://www.law.utoronto.ca/sites/default/files/documents/reprohealth/united_kingdom_1938_bourne.pdf (accessed 2 November 2024); see also Infant Life (Preservation) Act 1929, https://www.legislation.gov.uk/ukpga/Geo5/19-20/34/section/1 (accessed 2 November 2024.

or noxious thing, or any instrument or thing whatsoever" in the knowledge that it is "intended to be unlawfully used or employed with intent to procure the miscarriage of any woman" whether pregnant ("with child") or not, that offence being a misdemeanour. Earlier statutes of 1803, 1828, and 1837 had made termination of pregnancy illegal, with similar wording, however, although the phrase "wilfully, maliciously, and unlawfully" appeared, the 1837 Act did not include the words "with child", and the crime was classed a felony rather than misdemeanour.

Mr Bourne was charged under the OAPA with conducting an illegal abortion. The defence raised section 1(1) of the *Infant Life (Preservation) Act* 1929, providing that no person "shall be found guilty … unless it is proved that the act which caused the death of the child was not done in good faith for the purpose only of preserving the life of the mother". In addressing "child destruction"—the "destruction of the life of a child capable of being born alive" (defined in section 1 (2) as evidenced by a twenty-eight-week pregnancy), the Act was not directly relevant. However, the use of "unlawful" in the OAPA provisions enabled Justice McNaghten to embrace of the language of section 1(1), directing the jury that where a doctor "is of the opinion", based on "reasonable grounds" and "with adequate knowledge"[6]:

> … that the probable consequence of the continuance of the pregnancy will be to make the woman a physical or mental wreck, [they] are entitled to take the view that the doctor is operating for the purpose of preserving the life of the mother.

What must be proved beyond reasonable doubt was whether "the act which Mr. Bourne admittedly did was not done in good faith for the purpose only of preserving the life of the girl" or "not leaving her a mental or physical wreck". Failing that, Mr Bourne was entitled to an acquittal[7]:

---

[6] *R v Bourne* [1938] (n6) 617. This extract is from the Judge's directions to the jury, with the jury acquitting and hence ending the case.

[7] *R v Bourne* [1938] (n6), 616.

> On the other hand, if you are satisfied beyond all real doubt that Mr. Bourne did not do it in good faith for the purpose only of preserving the life of the girl, your verdict should be a verdict of guilty.

An argument arose between prosecution and defence as to the meaning of "preservation of life". Contending that Mr Bourne's aim was "preservation of health", the prosecution sought to make a distinction between it and the "preservation of life". Yet McNaghten considered there was little or no distinction to be made, for what could the expression mean other than "preserving health"? In this, he emphasised the importance of the woman's right to life[8]:

> The unborn child must not be destroyed except for the purpose of preserving the yet more precious life of the mother.

In the years following, common law jurisdictions and medical practitioners confronted with pregnancy termination relied on *R v Bourne*. Financially comfortable women who could seek a medical abortion did so. Others less well-placed either road out the pregnancy, whatever the circumstances of the conception, their economic circumstances or job and income prospects, or their desire for motherhood, attempted self-abortion, or sought out backyard abortionists with all the risks that entailed. A denial to women of essential health care, and explicit evidence of wilful ignorance of women's human rights, the situation was neither fair nor just. Nor was it healthy. Medical practitioners who wanted to provide proper medical care to women resented the uncertainty surrounding their legal position. In the 1960s and early 1970s and into the mid-1980s, this led to the introduction of abortion rights legislation or local common law decisions.

Seen at the time as an advance, in England, Scotland and Wales the *Abortion Act* 1967 provided security for medical practitioners. Whilst to some extent advantaging women, simultaneously it explicitly discriminated against them, simply because they were women. Discrimination was written into the very first section of the Act. Abortion was not

[8] *R v Bourne* [1938] (n6), 617.

decriminalised, for the OAPA provisions remained and added to them was section 5 of the Abortion Act itself, criminalising all pregnancy terminations not carried out strictly according to the Abortion Act provisions.

Reciting that no offence would lie where pregnancy "is terminated by a registered medical practitioner", the provision went on to qualify that by requiring that not only one, but two, registered medical practitioners be[9]:

> … of the opinion, formed in good faith –
>
> (a) that the continuance of the pregnancy would involve risk to the life of the pregnant woman, or of injury to the physical or mental health of the pregnant woman or any existing children of her family, greater than if the pregnancy were terminated; or
> (b) that there is a substantial risk that if the child were born it would suffer from such physical or mental abnormalities as to be seriously handicapped.

The only exception to the two-doctor requirement was contained in section 1(4), providing that a sole practitioner could carry out the operation where:

> … of the opinion, formed in good faith, that the termination is immediately necessary to save the life or to prevent grave, permanent injury to the physical or mental health of the pregnant woman.

No operation or health treatment for a man is required to be authorised by two practitioners, hence why for a woman the two-doctor rule and the need to make an exception for sole practitioner authority on the basis of her imminent death or grievously permanent mental or physical injury. Such a sex-discriminatory rule violates women's autonomy and right to make decisions about her health in independent consultation with her medical practitioner.

---

[9] *Abortion Act* (England, Scotland and Wales) 1967, Abortion Act 1967, https://www.legislation.gov.uk/ukpga/1967/87/contents (accessed 22 November 2024).

But this was not the only encroachment on women's equal rights. Section 2 required that the Minister of Health (England and Wales) and Secretary of State (Scotland) make regulations governing terminations and record keeping. Doctors conducting any abortion must certify compliance with section 1 and preserve and record any disposal of such certificates; must give such notice of the termination including information as the regulations require; are prohibited from disclosing information other than as prescribed; and must notify the abortion to the Chief Medical Officers of the Ministry of Health and the Scottish Home and Health Department, with identifiers. Hence, not only was a local record kept of every abortion carried out in England, Wales and Scotland, but a record is held by the Ministry of Health, and the Home and Health Department, that a woman has undergone this procedure—where, and possibly who she is. No similar recording governs health care operations in relation to male-related medical issues.

These discriminatory measures were incorporated into the South Australian (Symons 2014) and Northern Territory Acts (Baird and Belton 2019). Behind these limitations on women's access to medical care on equal terms with men was the hobbling of reformers' desire to advance women's interests and rights by a perception that the women were unreliable or that the electorate perceived them to be so, meaning that "safeguards" must be incorporated into the legislation to ensure that this necessary treatment was not sought and gained upon spurious grounds, or that anti-abortion rights lobbyists could not derail the reforms by such claims. But the registration requirement—in the British, Northern Territory and South Australian Acts—unknown to or not grasped by women now undergoing lawful surgery (if they were at all informed)—was a gross breach of privacy and medical confidentiality sanctioned by parliaments. In 2011 in *Department of Health, R (on the Application of) v Information Commissioner*[10] the UK Department of Health's concern that disclosure of late term abortion statistics would "create a

[10] *Department of Health (R on the Application of) v Information Commissioner* [2011] EWHC 1430(Admin), [2011] ACD 97, [2011] Med LR 363, Department of Health, R (on the application of) v Information Commissioner | [2011] EWHC 1430 (Admin) | England and Wales High Court (Administrative Court) | Judgment | Law | CaseMine, https://www.casemine.com/judgement/uk/5a8ff75360d03e7f57eab522 (accessed 21 November 2024).

real risk of patients being identified" was overruled by the High Court, the Department being ordered to release the information. From 1969 to 2022, the Office for National Statistics (ONA) had provided detailed records of abortions on all grounds, including foetal abnormality. This changed when responsibility for reporting statistics was transferred to the Department of Health which took a more restrictive view as to what ought be released publicly. It was this change in reporting, generated by privacy concerns, that led to an application under the *Freedom of Information Act* 2000 (UK) by the ProLife Alliance that in turn led to the determination that the information should be released. The Department's concern was that release of material with postcode signifiers could lead to personal identification of women who had undergone late term abortions. Notably, there is no comparable requirement of records being provided to the Chief Medical Officers of England, Wales or Scotland where patients undergo specifically male treatments or surgical interventions (Vasectomy-Information.com 1999–2025).[11] This followed vis-à-vis the SA and NT laws, too.

Common Law—Progressive or Flawed Reform?

Some thirty years after *R v Bourne*, medical practitioners' concerns about police interventions and "crackdowns" on doctors performing abortions in clinics and hospitals, together with women's campaigns for rights, led not only to legislative intervention but to common law rulings setting down local principles governing pregnancy termination. This superseded reliance on Bourne by courts in jurisdictions outside Britain. Jurisprudential developments occurred in the United States with

[11] Issues relating to vasectomies were based in eugenics and 'mental defectives', not subject to prohibitions and compulsory recording comparable to requested pregnancy termination by women.

Roe v Wade,[12] and in Australian states—Victoria: *R v Davidson*, "Menhennit Ruling" (1969)—"physical or mental wellbeing" (Naylor 2017a, b; Victorian Law Reform Commission (VLRC) 2007)[13]; NSW: *R v Wald*, "Levine Ruling" (1971)—"economic, medical or social ground" (Henry 1995; Douglas and De Costa 2016; Gotsis and Ismay 2017)[14]; US: *Roe v Wade*—individual privacy under the 14th Amendment (1973) (Center for Reproductive Rights, nd)[15]; then, later, Queensland: *R v Bayliss; R v Cullen*, "McGuire Ruling" (1986), confirmed *Vievers and Connolly* —"life, or mental or physical health" (1995)(Cica 1998; Bennet et al. 2015)[16]; and later again NSW *CES v Superclinics* (1995) (Graycar and Morgan 1986; Henry and Charlton 1994; Henry 1995; Bradstreet 2007).

Judicial decisions were important in the scope they provided in establishing legitimate grounds for women's right to abortion. Although there were some differences in ambit, decisions followed an identical pattern of setting down grounds for legality. In Victoria, *R v Davidson*[17] was, effectively, consistent with *R v Bourne* albeit relying on the defence of necessity. Here, Dr Davidson was charged with four counts under section 65 of the *Crimes Act* 1958 (Victoria). As with the OAPA, the use of the word "unlawful"—as in "unlawful use of an instrument or other means with the intention to procure the miscarriage of a woman

---

[12] *Roe v Wade* 410 US 113 (1973), Roe v. Wade | 410 U.S. 113 (1973) | Justia U.S. Supreme Court Center, https://supreme.justia.com/cases/federal/us/410/113/ (accessed 22 November 2024).

[13] R V. DAVIDSON Victorian Supreme Court [1969] Vicrp 85 Menhennitt, J - DocsLib, https://docslib.org/doc/850232/r-v-davidson-victorian-supreme-court-1969-vicrp-85-menhennitt-j (accessed 22 November 2024); *R v Davidson* [1969] Vic Rep 85, https://docslib.org/doc/850232/r-v-davidson-victorian-supreme-court-1969-vicrp-85-menhennitt-j, https://docslib.org/doc/850232/r-v-davidson-victorian-supreme-court-1969-vicrp-85-menhennitt-j (accessed 22 November 2024).

[14] *R v Wald* (1971) 3 DCR (NSW) 25, R v Wald | 28 October 1971 | Legal Helpdesk Lawyers, https://legalhelpdesklawyers.com.au/2014/10/28/r-v-wald-28-october-1971/ (accessed 22 November 2024).

[15] *Roe v Wade* 410 US 113 (1973), Roe v. Wade | 410 U.S. 113 (1973) | Justia U.S. Supreme Court Center, https://supreme.justia.com/cases/federal/us/410/113/ (accessed 22 November 2024).

[16] *R v Bayliss; R v Cullen* (1986) 9 Qld Lawyer Reps 8; *R v Bayliss and Cullen* (1986) 6 QLR 8; *Vievers and Connolly* [1995] 2 Qd R 326.

[17] *R v Davidson* (n13).

..."—arose, in that it implied that there could be "lawful use". Justice Menhennit relied on the common law principle of necessity, with some criticism of McNaghten's reference to "lawfulness" via the *Infant Life Preservation Act* 1929 (UK) and its use of "for the preservation of the life of the mother". Necessity as a defence required that an accused "honestly believed on reasonable grounds" that it was necessary to do what he did, and that a "reasonable man in his position would have considered that what he did was not out of proportion to the mischief to be prevented". Having canvassed several earlier cases that cited "good faith" and "preserving the life or health of the woman", Menhennit held that unlawfulness must be proven by the Crown through establishing lack of honest belief on reasonable grounds that the abortion was[18]:

> ... necessary to preserve the woman from serious danger to her life or her physical or mental health (not being merely the normal dangers of pregnancy and childbirth) which the continuance of the pregnancy would entail; or

> ... in the circumstances proportionate to the need to preserve the woman from a serious danger to her life or her physical or mental health (not being merely the normal dangers of pregnancy and childbirth) which the continuance of the pregnancy would entail.

Judge Levine of the NSW District Court went further, incorporating "any economic, social or medical ground or reason" a jury may find existed which "'in their view could constitute reasonable grounds upon which an accused could honestly and reasonably believe there would result a serious danger' to the woman's 'physical or mental health'".[19] The practitioner's "honest and reasonable belief" that the woman's mental health was seriously endangered "at the very time she was interviewed" by him, or that her mental health, "although not in serious danger" could be reasonably expected to be in serious danger "at some time during the currency of pregnancy, if uninterrupted" applied. In either circumstance,

[18] *R v Davidson* (n13), at 89–90.

[19] *R v Wald* (n14), at 29.

a "conscientious belief on reasonable grounds" required disproving before a breach of the *Crimes Act* 1900 (NSW) abortion provision (s 83) applied (Naylor 2017a, b).

Queensland medical practitioners were tried under the *Criminal Code* 1899 (Qld) section 224 (attempt to procure abortion whether the woman is or is not pregnant), section 225 (attempt whether the woman is pregnant), and section 226 (supplying drugs or instruments to procure abortion), with section 82 (later section 82(1)) providing a defence, but it was not until 1986 that District Court judge McGuire in *R v Bayliss and Cullen*[20] gave a ruling on the legality of abortion. McGuire adopted the "lawfulness" principle as where the termination "is carried out to prevent serious danger to the woman's physical and mental health" (Qld Health, Communities ... 2016). Then in 1995, almost ten years later, in *Vievers and Connolly*,[21] a single judge decision, the Supreme Court affirmed this interpretation. There, the claim was for damages from a doctor whom it was alleged had negligently failed to conduct blood testing to determine whether or not the first plaintiff was suffering from rubella. That diagnosis would have resulted in a recommendation for abortion due to the putative child's potentially suffering from severe physical and mental disabilities. As rubella was not diagnosed through the failure of testing, the pregnancy continued to birth. Rejecting the defence submission that "serious danger to mental health" as the foundation for lawful abortion related to the period of the pregnancy itself alone, de Jersey (the judge) held the "'serious risk" to the first plaintiff's mental health "crystallised with the birth of the terribly disabled child".

CES and Anor v Superclinics and Ors[22] was decided by the NSW Court of Appeal that year. Although the facts differed from those in *Vievers and Connolly* as there was no issue of ill-health of the mother or disability of

[20] *R v Bayliss and Cullen* (1986) (n16).

[21] *Vievers and Connolly* [1995] (n16).

[22] *Ces and Another v Superclinics (Australia) Pty Limited and Others* Nos. Ca 40266/94; Cl 14479/88 Criminal Law and Procedure - Damages - Negligence [1995] NSWSC 103 (27 October 1995), https://www.austlii.edu.au/cgi-bin/viewdoc/au/cases/nsw/NSWSC/1995/103.html (accessed 22 November 2024); *CES and Anor v Superclinics and Ors* [1995], Microsoft Word - SC 1995 - CES v. Superclinics.docx, https://www.globalhealthrights.org/wp-content/uploads/2013/02/SC-1995-CES-v.-Superclinics.pdf (accessed 22 November 2024).

the child, the question of "illegality" or lawfulness of pregnancy termination arose similarly. In *CES* the first plaintiff sought damages for failure by the respondents (a clinic and medical practitioners) to provide her with accurate pregnancy advice. Despite "repeated consultations", she having requested tests well within the period during which lawful pregnancy termination could be effected, she was advised too late that she was indeed pregnant. When the correct information was received, that period had passed. The pregnancy went ahead with a successful birth. The essence of the case was that the respondents owed the plaintiff a duty of care, the breach of which meant that she had suffered damage, including pain and suffering vis-à-vis pregnancy and birth, together with economic loss incurred and ongoing which comprised confinement and child-rearing expenses. The second plaintiff, her husband/partner, claimed damages in relation to confinement and child-rearing.

This being a civil rather than a criminal case, the trial judge (Newman) said that the onus rested on the respondents to establish the illegality of abortion in the first plaintiff's circumstances, just as in a criminal trial it lay with the prosecution. He then applied *R v Wald* and the Levine test, namely that lawfulness rested upon the doctor's honest belief on reasonable grounds of the necessity of termination to save the woman from "serious danger to her life, or physical or mental health" should the pregnancy continue, and "not merely the normal dangers of pregnancy and childbirth"; and that the danger of the operation was not, in the circumstances, "out of proportion to the danger intended to be averted". Newman then determined that the evidence of medical staff who saw the first plaintiff when she was pregnant established that her mental health was not at risk and her pregnancy "was no danger to either her life or her physical well-being". Termination would therefore have been unlawful under section 82 or 83 of the Crimes Act. The matter did not, however, rest there, with appeals to the Court of Appeal and the High Court. The Court of Appeal ordered a retrial, with the matter going to the High Court on points of law. A notice of discontinuance was filed in the High Court on 11 October 1996, so that the case did not proceed to a determination on the merits, the parties settling out of court (Kenny 2024; Henry 2018; Bradstreet 2007; Neville 1998; Wainer 1997; Kirkby 1996).

In the Court of Appeal, the trial judge was found to be wrong in his analysis and application of abortion law. Addressing *R v Wald* first, Justice Kirby observed that the test in *R v Wald* "had merit" apart from at what time the "danger posed to the woman's mental health" should arise or to which it should be limited. Levine's judgment seemed to assert that that danger "may not necessarily arise at the time of consultation with the medical practitioner", but a doctor's honest belief "may go to a reasonable expectation" that that danger may arise "at some time during the currency of the pregnancy, if uninterrupted". Kirby considered that there was no apparently logical basis for "limiting the honest and reasonable expectation of such a danger to the mother's psychological health to the period of the currency of the pregnancy alone". Once having acknowledged the relevance of other economic or social grounds potentially substantiating such a belief, he said it was[23]:

> ... illogical to exclude from consideration, as a relevant factor, the possibility that the patient's psychological state might be threatened after the birth of the child, for example, due to the very economic and social circumstances in which she will then probably find herself. Such considerations, when combined with an unexpected and unwanted pregnancy, would, in fact, be most likely to result in a threat to a mother's psychological health after the child was born when those circumstances might be expected to take their toll.

The respondents bore a heavy burden in asserting unlawfulness of the pregnancy termination, and that burden could not be discharged in regard to the foregoing, as trial judge Newman had not considered "the effect of continuation of the pregnancy on the psychological health of the first appellant after the birth of the child, when the economic and social circumstances in which she found herself would foreseeably have their greatest effect".

These common law developments were an advance. Yet they remained flawed for they were developed against the backdrop of criminal law provisions deeming abortion illegal. Why should essential medical treatment required by women only, be singled out? The law already governs

[23] *CES and Anor v Superclinics and Ors* [1995] (n22) [60].

crimes against the person, covering all surgical treatment which constitutes grievous bodily harm, unlawful wounding, or actual bodily harm unless consented to by the patient (or their guardian where the patient is not competent) and is for the patient's benefit. The abortion provisions constituted direct discrimination (unequal treatment) against women on the grounds of sex.

Decriminalising Women's Bodies

In 1998 Cheryl Davenport, MP, introduced a Private Members' Bill into the Western Australian Parliament's Legislative Council (Ferguson 2022) to repeal section 199 (attempt to procure abortion—14 years hard labour), section 200 (attempt by woman on herself—7 years hard labour),[24] section 201 (supplying drugs or instruments to procure abortion—3 years hard labour), and section 259 of the *Criminal Code Act* 1913 (WA).[25] The "defence" provision, section 259, was surprisingly liberal in its application to abortion:

> 259. A person is not criminally responsible for performing, in good faith and with reasonable care and skill, a surgical operation upon any person for his benefit, or upon an unborn child for the preservation of the mother's life, if the performance of the operation is reasonable, having regard to the patient's state at the time and to all the circumstances of the case.

Nonetheless, in a campaign seeking to elevate respect for women's bodily integrity and individual conscience, Western Australian women were determined to decriminalise pregnancy termination altogether. Abortion

---

[24] Curiously the marginal note is drafted wrongly as "The like by woman with child"—"The like" referring to attempt to procure abortion. All three provisions—ss 199, 200 and 201 are consistent in their wording: "a woman, whether she is or is not with child". It seems that the draftsperson must have had before him (sic) the OAPA 1861 which does make that distinction between sections 58 ("with child") and 59 ("be with or be not with child").

[25] *Criminal Code Act Compilation Act* 1913 - [00-00-00].pdf, https://www.legislation.wa.gov.au/legislation/prod/filestore.nsf/FileURL/mrdoc_13659.pdf/$FILE/Criminal%20Code%20Act%20Compilation%20Act%201913%20-%20%5B00-00-00%5D.pdf?OpenElement (accessed 22 November 2024).

rights were integral to Women's Movement activism, and the strength of the campaign was bolstered when in 1998 two Perth doctors were arrested for performing an abortion.[26] Along with the Davenport Bill, in the Legislative Assembly the Attorney General introduced an alternative retaining abortion in the Criminal Code but reducing abortion restrictions. This led to an amalgamation of the proposals. Section 199 of the Criminal Code remained, but the *Acts Amendment (Abortion) Act* 1998 (WA) made abortion performed by a medical practitioner legal, with the *Health (Miscellaneous Provisions) Act* 1911 (WA) section 334 setting out the "justification"[27]:

(a) the woman concerned has given informed consent; or
(b) the woman concerned will suffer serious personal, family or social consequences if the abortion is not performed; or
(c) serious danger to the physical or mental health of the woman concerned will result if the abortion is not performed; or
(d) the pregnancy of the woman concerned is causing serious danger to her physical or mental health.

"Informed consent" was defined as consent "freely given" by the woman, the doctor having[28]:

(a) properly, appropriately and adequately provided her with counselling about the medical risk of abortion and of carrying a pregnancy to term; and
(b) offered her the opportunity of referral to appropriate and adequate counselling about matters relating to abortion and carrying a pregnancy to term; and

[26] The author flew to Perth at the invitation of campaigners to speak at rallies and meetings, the organisers running a well-powered campaign with PR company Atticus. Hazel Hawke, former wife of Bob Hawke (Prime Minister 1983–1991) was involved also.

[27] *Health (Miscellaneous Provisions) Act* 1911 (WA), Abortion-Information-and-legal-obligations-for-medical-practitioners.pdf, https://wnhs.health.wa.gov.au/-/media/HSPs/NMHS/Hospitals/WNHS/Documents/Professionals/Abortion---Information-and-legal-obligations-for-medical-practitioners.pdf (accessed 22 November 2024); see also section 324 Public Health Act 2016, PUBLIC HEALTH ACT 2016 - SECT 324, https://classic.austlii.edu.au/au/legis/wa/consol_act/pha2016126/s324.html (accessed 22 November 2024).

[28] *Health (Miscellaneous Provisions) Act* 1911 (WA) (n27).

(c) informed her that appropriate and adequate counselling will be available to her should she wish it, following an abortion or after carrying the pregnancy to term.

The guidance for doctors emphasised that "counselling" means providing proper, appropriate and adequate information "on risks related to pregnancy and abortion", not "psychological counselling" relating to "decision-making about pregnancy choices". There is no legal requirement to provide "supportive counselling … in relation to informed consent". The aim was to ensure that women were accepted as competent decision-makers, entitled to exercise their autonomy when exercising their right to health care.

Following this, around Australia agitation for complete decriminalisation intensified. In 2016 the Health, Communities, Disability Services and Domestic and Family Violent Prevention Committee of the Queensland Parliament launched an Inquiry into Abortion Law Reform. In a comprehensive *Information Paper,* it set out the (then) state of the law in all Australian jurisdictions (Qld Health Communities … 2016).

Decriminalised—ACT (Australian Capital Territory, Canberra)—• Abortion is no longer a crime under the *Crimes Act* 1900 (ACT). • Under the *Medical Practitioners (Maternal Health) Amendment Act* 2002 (ACT), abortion is available on request.

Decriminalised—Victoria (*Abortion Law Reform Act* 2008) (Victoria) and repeal of provisions under the *Crimes Act* 1958 (Victoria) • Up to 24 weeks gestation: a registered medical practitioner may perform an abortion on a woman upon request; • After 24 weeks gestation: a registered medical practitioner may perform an abortion only where the practitioner and at least one other registered medical practitioner reasonably believes that the abortion is appropriate in all the circumstances.

Decriminalised—Tasmania • Abortion no longer a crime under the Tasmanian *Criminal Code Act* 1924. • Under the *Reproductive Health (Access to Terminations) Act* 2013 (Tas): • Up to 16 weeks: abortion is allowed, provided the woman consents; • After 16 weeks: two medical practitioners must agree that the woman's physical and/or mental health is at greater risk by continuing the pregnancy.

Criminal but exceptions—Queensland • Abortion is a crime for women and for doctors procuring it. • It is legal if the doctor believes a woman's physical and/or mental health is in serious danger.

Criminal but exceptions—New South Wales • Abortion is a crime for women and for doctors procuring it. • It is legal if the doctor believes that the woman's life or physical and/or mental health is in serious danger. Social, economic and medical factors may be considered.

Criminal but exceptions—South Australia • Under the *Criminal Law Consolidation Act* 1935 (SA): • Up to 28 weeks: abortion is lawful if two qualified medical practitioners agree the woman's physical and/or mental health is at greater risk by continuing the pregnancy than from termination, or that the child is at risk of being seriously handicapped. A two-month residency requirement applies; • After 28 weeks: the termination must be necessary to save the woman's life or prevent grave injury to her physical or mental health.

Criminal but exceptions—Western Australia • Abortion is illegal under the Western Australia Criminal Code unless performed by a medical practitioner in good faith, with reasonable care and skill and it is justified under the *Health Act* 1911 (WA): • Up to 20 weeks: justified with the informed consent of the woman. • After 20 weeks: not justified unless two appointed medical practitioners agree the woman or unborn child has a severe medical condition and the procedure is performed in an approved facility.

Criminal but exceptions—Northern Territory • Abortion is illegal under the *Criminal Code Act* 1983 (NT) but is lawful in certain circumstances provided under the Medical Services Act 1982 (NT): • Up to 14 weeks: if two medical practitioners agree the woman's physical and/or mental health is at greater risk by continuing the pregnancy, there is substantial risk of the child being seriously handicapped. Must be performed in a hospital. • After 14 weeks and up to 23 weeks: abortion is lawful if immediately necessary to prevent serious harm to the woman's physical or mental health.

Decriminalisation post 2016[29]:

[29] All states and territories generally make provision for termination by medication.

- ACT—committed to free (no cost) termination for Canberra residents and access to abortion from women from outside the ACT (ACT Government, nd; ACT Government 2024).
- NT—*Termination of Pregnancy Law Reform Act* 2017 (NT) came into effect 1 July 2017, retaining legal abortion up to 23 weeks gestation but failing to repeal the Criminal Code provisions so that "a woman who is 24 weeks pregnant and whose foetus has a fatal abnormality would have no choice but to continue with the pregnancy" and similarly "for women pregnant as a result of rape": here, women continue to be "forced to fly interstate". The new law does, however, provide for "access to health care from specialist health clinics" without the need to go to a hospital (Human Rights Law Centre 2018). However the *Termination of Pregnancy Law Reform Legislation Amendment Act* 2021 (NT) corrected this, legalising abortion under 24 weeks gestation, with abortion legal beyond this in certain special or emergency circumstances only, namely if one medical practitioner determines it is "necessary to preserve the patient's life".
- Queensland—*Termination of Pregnancy Act* 2018 (Qld) passed 50 to 41 (17 October), repealing the Criminal Code provisions and making abortion available "on request", up to 22 weeks gestation, with abortion after 22 weeks legal where the medical practitioner "performing the termination has consulted with a second medical practitioner and both agree that 'in all the circumstances' the abortion should be performed" (Horn 2018).
- NSW—*Abortion Law Reform Act* 2019 (NSW) repealing *Crimes Act* 1900 (NSW) provisions and abolishing common law prohibitions and making abortion legal up to 22 weeks gestation, with abortion after 22 weeks lawful if the "specialist medical practitioner" performing the termination and a second "specialist medical practitioner" determine that in all the circumstances there are sufficient grounds for the termination to be performed after considering all relevant medical circumstances, and the woman's current and future physical, psychological and social circumstances, and the professional standards and guidelines applicable, and (for the doctor performing the operation) any advice received to her/his request from a multi-disciplinary team

or hospital advisory committee. The Act further stipulates the requirement of informed consent from the woman or an authorised person (where the woman lacks capacity to consent), and termination must be performed at a registered hospital or approved health facility. An emergency termination save the woman's life or "save another foetus" is lawful after 22 weeks without compliance with the detailed provisions above.[30]

- South Australia—Termination of Pregnancy Act 2021 (SA) commencing 7 July 2022 provides for removal of criminal provisions from state law (*Criminal Law Consolidation Act* 1935 [SA]) and late term abortion legal after 22 weeks and six days if two doctors approve the termination and it is deemed medically appropriate. South Australia Health statistics indicate that in the first 18 months following implementation "fewer than five" woman had their pregnancies terminated after 27 weeks (South Australian Law Reform Institute [SALRI] 2019; SA Health 2023).
- Western Australia—*Abortion Legislation Reform Act* 2023 (WA) abortion legal for up to 23 weeks gestation and after 23 weeks accessible in certain special or emergency circumstances only (MSI 2024).

In the UK, the belief that pregnancy termination was solved by the *Abortion Act* 1967 was generated partly by the fact that Northern Ireland continued to enforce the OAPA provisions, the Abortion Act had never applied to it, and women were obliged to travel to England to secure proper health care. In 2018 the CEDAW Committee UK review, the government was told that action on Northern Ireland women's rights in this regard was imperative. This led to the Parliament's repeal in October 2019 of the OAPA abortion provisions, MPs voting 332 "for" to 99 "against"—but extraordinarily those provisions were not repealed for the entire country—hence, they remained for England and Wales (Bloomer and Campbell, nd; 2022; Bloomer et al. 2024). Until the *Abortion (Northern Ireland) Regulations* 2020 were agreed and passed into law setting out restrictions, abortion was, ironically, wholly decriminalised in

[30] *Abortion Law Reform Act* 2019 No 11 - NSW Legislation (accessed 22 November 2024); Public Health Amendment (Safe Access to Reproductive Health Clinics) Act 2018, https://legislation.nsw.gov.au/view/pdf/asmade/act-2018-26 (accessed 22 November 2024).

Northern Ireland while remaining criminal elsewhere in the UK unless conforming to the restrictive provisions of the Abortion Act. Even then, Northern Ireland remained ahead of the rest of the UK. There, a single doctor alone is required up to 10 weeks of pregnancy, with two medical opinions required up to 24 weeks. As to grounds where there is no gestational limit, abortion is legal[31]:

(1) "immediate necessity"—where a medical practitioner believes "in good faith" that termination "is immediately necessary to save the life, or prevent grave permanent injury [to the woman's] physical or mental health": reg 5
(2) opinion "in good faith" of two medical practitioners –

    (a) prevent grave permanent injury to the woman's physical or mental health, or
    (b) continuance of pregnancy would involve risk to the woman's life greater than if the pregnancy were terminated: reg 6

(3) opinion "in good faith" of two medical practitioners that the foetus' condition is such that –

    (a) death is likely before, during or shortly after birth, or
    (b) if the child were born, s/he would suffer from such physical or mental impairment as to be seriously disabled: reg 7

(4) the operation takes place in authorised premises—clinic, hospital, etc. except where the woman has visited same and, having been prescribed Mifepristone and Misoprostol for pregnancy termination ingests them at home: reg 8

Nonetheless, this does not mean that abortion is readily available to women in Northern Ireland. Following decriminalisation, women continue to travel to England to secure abortions under the *Abortion Act* 1967, as efforts to re-criminalise remain constant, and obstacles to access remain. Although Northern Ireland may be severe, both approaches

---

[31] The Abortion (Northern Ireland) Regulations 2020, https://www.legislation.gov.uk/uksi/2020/345/contents/made (accessed 22 November 2024).

arise in most—and likely all—jurisdictions where decriminalisation has occurred. This includes Australia, Canada and France.

As for the rest of the UK, in 2024 action was initiated in Westminster to decriminalise in England and Wales by extending the repeal of sections 58 and 59 of the OAPA, overlooked in 2019 when repeal was restricted to Northern Ireland. The vehicle was the Criminal Justice Bill 2024 (Hughes 2024).[32] Two amendments were introduced. Possibly their contradictory aims led to the lack of advancement, despite media reports anticipating success for abortion rights campaigners. The chair of the House of Commons Home Affairs Committee Dame Diana Johnson, Labour MP, who in 2018 had introduced a backbench Bill for decriminalisation, tabled an amendment seeking to "decriminalise abortion entirely for women" or abolish prosecution if women "ended their pregnancies beyond the 24-week legal time limit". This was reported as having "cross-party support from 20 MPs" and, saying she wished "to see how the debate develops", the Health Secretary, Victoria Atkins, Conservative MP, was reported by *The Telegraph* as "indicating that she would back decriminalisation of abortion". Having "previously supported decriminalisation, and backed buffer zones for abortion clinics ...", she added that her "voting record ... speaks for itself". Meanwhile, Caroline Ansell, Conservative MP, put forward the second amendment, proposing that the time limit on legal abortions be lowered from 28 to 24 weeks. This was said to be "supported by a cross-party group of 25 MPs" (Donnelly et al. 2024). Commitments on both sides followed the usual pattern, that abortion rights are not located in a particular party-political position. The paucity of numbers indicated that whatever the media's view, a successful outcome for either side was remote. As it stood at the end of 2024, the Bill contained no reference to either proposed amendment. However, in June 2025 Tonia Antoniazzi MP's amendment ensuring women terminating beyond the Abortion Act 24 week limit would not suffer criminal prosecution passed by a 242 majority.

---

[32] Criminal Justice Bill, https://publications.parliament.uk/pa/bills/cbill/58-04/0155/230155.pdf 2024 (UK) (accessed 2 November 2024); Criminal Justice Bill - Parliamentary Bills - UK Parliament, https://bills.parliament.uk/bills/3511 2024 (UK) (accessed 2 November 2024).

Anyone (including doctors) assisting in such an abortion could remain liable. Nevertheless, consistent with other jurisdictions, the UK had advanced the rights of women not to be harassed by the handing out of anti-abortion leaflets in "buffer zones" or obstructed when attending appointments or working at "abortion clinics". "Protection" or "buffer" zones were "strengthened" as from 31 October 2024 (Home Office et al. 2024).

Respect in Retreat—*Roe v Wade* versus *Dobbs v Jackson*

Just as in 2024 the UK parliamentary numbers revealed conflicting positions on abortion rights, so it has been throughout the western world (Marty and Pieklo 2019; Norris 2023). *Dobbs v Jackson,* in overturning *Roe v Wade,*[33] appears to have bolstered opposition campaigns. Decided in 1973, *Roe v Wade* was seen as a landmark for women, as was *Doe v Bolton,*[34] the Georgia case that was decided together with it. Covering both cases, the decision struck down a Georgia law heavily restricting abortion rights and invalidated a Texas law banning abortion unless the woman's life was in danger. In a 7:2 decision, the US Supreme Court ended state control of women's bodies through denying their right to health treatment constituting termination of pregnancy. Citing the right to privacy as implied in the First, Fourth, Fifth, Ninth and Fourteenth Amendments to the Constitution,[35] particularly the "due process clause" of the Fourteenth Amendment: "…nor shall any state deprive any person of life, liberty, or property, without due process of law", the decision established the trimester system, where abortion would be solely the woman's decision in the first trimester; could be subject to government regulation in the second trimester to protect the woman's

---

[33] *Roe v Wade* 410 US 113 (1973), Roe v. Wade | 410 U.S. 113 (1973) | Justia U.S. Supreme Court Center, https://supreme.justia.com/cases/federal/us/410/113/ (accessed 2 March 2025).

[34] *Doe v. Bolton* 410 US 179 (1973), Doe v. Bolton | 410 U.S. 179 (1973) | Justia U.S. Supreme Court Center, https://supreme.justia.com/cases/federal/us/410/179/ (accessed 2 March 2025).

[35] *Roe v Wade, Roe v Bolton* 410 U S (1973), 152–153.

health, without banning it; would be subject to prohibition in the third trimester, with a right to obtain an abortion if doctors certified it as necessary to save her life or health. Under the Fourteenth Amendment a foetus was determined as not having personhood, and the right to privacy was incorporated as embracing the right to abortion.

However, problems were readily predictable. The decision was located in the viability of the foetus. Even at that time, new reproductive technologies (NRTs) were in development. Miriam Menken had first fertilised a human ovum in a Petrie dish at the end of the 1950s (Gross 2020; Littleton et al. 2023a, b; Scutt 1988, 1990). The first "test tube baby" was born on 25 July 1978, merely five years after *Roe v Wade*, and some ten years after the Cambridge team had begun their research. Although few IVF procedures result in success—the "success" rate fixed at approximately 15 per cent—the fact that an embryo could be developed in a test tube and transferred into a woman's uterus inevitably raises the question whether an aborted embryo could be transferred in the same way. Further, the more technological developments led to potential survival of premature babies at a younger and younger stage of development, the more likely the proposal from those opposed to women's rights to establish a policy that a late term abortion should result in the premature baby being kept alive to be adopted by alternative parents. Both approaches would put women in the invidious position of being denied their rights, as many would decide on going ahead with the pregnancy rather than giving up their putative child to others by deciding on "termination".

Not long after the decision, Ruth Bader Ginsburg (later appointed to the Supreme Court by President Clinton) wrote critically of the decision principally on the basis that it ought to have been decided under the principle of women's right to equality under the equal protection clause of the Fourteenth Amendment rather than privacy (Ginsburg 1985; Ginsburg et al. 2018). Then in 1992 in a split decision (5:4) the Supreme Court in *Planned Parenthood of Southeastern Pennsylvania v Casey*[36] upheld *Roe v Wade* under the Fourteenth Amendment due

---

[36] *Planned Parenthood of Southeastern Pa. v. Casey* | 505 U.S. 833 (1992) | Justia U.S. Supreme Court Center, https://supreme.justia.com/cases/federal/us/505/833/ (accessed 22 November

process clause. The Court affirmed procedural and substantive rights to "liberty", holding that this incorporated the right and freedom to make "intimate and personal choices" that are "central to personal dignity and autonomy".[37] It reaffirmed viability (the stage at which a foetus can sustain life outside the uterus) as the crucially determining factor—although medical capacity to keep premature babies alive had developed twenty years on from the original decision, and NRTs had developed even further since that time. Furthermore, despite reiterating that states could not ban pregnancy termination where it helped to preserve the health or life of the woman, the Court held that states could pass valid laws protecting the life and health of the foetus or mother in far broader circumstances than in *Roe v Wade*. "Safeguarding of the woman's health" could render lawful a state law governing the first trimester though not to deny or limit a woman's access to abortion. In addition, the problematic nature of viability was recognised directly in its finding that "life-preserving medicines" could encroach on the division between second and third trimester, lessening the length of the former and expanding the length of the latter. The Court also introduced the "substantial obstacle" and "undue burden" test, saying that it was this test that should govern determination whether a state regulation violated a woman's constitutional abortion rights, and upholding all but one of the restrictions contained in the Pennsylvania statute (Oyez 1991; McBride 2006). By this time, Sandra Day O'Connor (the only woman then appointed to the Supreme Court) was one of the five, which included fellow justices Blackmun (who wrote the original decision), Kennedy, Stevens and Souter, with Rhenquist, White, Scalia and Thomas in dissent.

Changes in composition of the Supreme Court in the 2020s led to the overturning of *Roe v Wade* in a 6:3 decision: Justices Alito (writer of the decision), Barrett, Gorsuch, Kavanaugh (concurrence), and Thomas (concurrence), and (concurring) Roberts (writing his own judgment) (majority); Breyer, Kagan and Sotomayor (joint dissent). The

---

2024); *Planned Parenthood of Southeastern Pennsylvania v Casey* 550 U.S. 833, 997, 1001 (1992).

[37] *Planned Parenthood* (n36), 851.

principal judgment relied on a re-reading of history, resort to questionable authorities, and reverting to obsolete statute and common law. The majority judgment rejected the Fourteenth Amendment as underpinning women's right to autonomy in respect to her own health care constituting pregnancy termination, averring[38]:

> We hold that *Roe* and *Casey* must be overruled. The Constitution makes no reference to abortion, and no such right is implicitly protected by any constitutional provision, including the one on which the defenders of Roe and Casey now chiefly rely—the Due Process Clause of the Fourteenth Amendment.

The majority judgment ruled out any right to abortion on three bases[39]:

(1) There was no right conferred through the Constitution via the "freedom and liberty" clause of the Fourteenth Amendment, and the equality clause was ruled out because it had not been relied upon by either *Roe v Wade* or *Casey*;
(2) The contention that a right to obtain abortion was "rooted in the Nation's history and tradition" and a fundamental component of "ordered liberty" was unsustainable as abortion had ever been contrary to law, referencing English common law jurists Bracton, Blackstone, Coke and Hale;
(3) There was no basis for fixing the right as "part of a broader entrenched right" that is supported by other precedents; because appeals "to a broader right to autonomy and to define one's 'concept of existence'" could "license fundamental rights to illicit drug use, prostitution, and the like" and "the abortion right [is sharply distinguishable] from the rights recognized in the cases on which *Roe* and *Casey* rely is something that both those decisions acknowledged: Abortion is different because it destroys

---

[38] Perma | Dobbs v. Jackson Women's Health Organization:: 597 U.S. ___ (2022):: Justia US Supreme Court Center, https://perma.cc/3MC3-PD8F (accessed 22 November 2024).

[39] *Dobbs v Jackson* (n38), 30–32.

> what *Roe* termed "potential life" and what the law challenged in this case calls an "unborn human being".

Analysis and critique of *Dobbs v Jackson* deserves more than a cursory review. Save it to say, first, that termination of pregnancy does require a Fourteenth Amendment foundation in equal treatment and sex-based rights: as a condition that accrues to women only, on the basis of sex, and a health condition that women are entitled to have treated as such, discriminatory provisions harm women's entitlement to health treatment and breach women's equal rights to autonomy, dignity of the human person and personhood itself. As in other jurisdictions, no health issue specific to men as a sex is singled out for criminal sanctions. Secondly, a woman's right to life cannot be subjugated to the rights that an embryo or foetus might possess. Thirdly, reliance on historical treatises written by men alone is arguably ill-informed. This may be particularly so when at least one of them—Hale—revealed in his own writings an unremitting misogyny: he was the judge who sat on the last witch trial imposing death in England, declaring that witches were real because they had been found to be so in his court and in any event the bible said so; and the judge who determined so demonstrably erroneously that "rape is a charge easily made and hard to be defended against be the defendant never so innocent". A second—William Blackstone—was ignorant of women's rights to autonomy and independence, asserting that married women were advantage by being under a husband's power and control ("coverture"). Over two centuries before *Dobbs v Jackson,* the editor of the 1793 edition of *Blackstone's Commentaries* challenged this contention, noting (Christian 1753, 445fn):

> I fear there is little reason to pay a compliment to our laws for their respect and favour to the female sex.

Nevertheless, immediately following the decision, twenty-six conservative states were reported as "either certain or considered likely to introduce new abortion restrictions or bans" (BBC 2022). Some liberal states announced an intention to ensure that women from states with restrictive regimes denying women's autonomy would be able to access services across their borders, to be met with the threat from the states favouring restrictions that such provision would be subject to penalties, and by December 2024 Idaho and Tennessee courts were reported as ruling on "abortion trafficking" laws (Conley 2024). The need to travel interstate was emphatically illustrated when, six days after *Dobbs v Jackson*—on 30 June 2022 a ten-year-old girl, just over six weeks' pregnant and nine years at the time of conception, travelled from Ohio to Indiana because Ohio's abortion law made no exception for pregnancies consequent upon the rape of a minor. Concerned that this would not be the only instance of desperate need for accessible medical treatment untrammelled by restrictions based on ideological grounds rather than health, safety and psychological and bodily integrity, Dr Caitlin Barnard, the child's Indiana treating doctor, gave an interview to *The Indianapolis Star* which published the story. Almost a year later, the Indiana Republican attorney-general's complaint to the Indiana Medical Licensing Board resulted in a hearing lasting some fourteen hours, a fine of $3000 and a letter of reprimand, but no suspension of her licence. The outcome was based on the Board's acceptance of privacy breaches and rejection of failure to report child abuse and "being unfit to practice" (Bendix and Helsel 2023; PBS News 2023). Dr Barnard had reported child abuse consistent with Indiana law, and president of the Board, Dr John Strobel, said she was "a good doctor", and so long as consent was obtained, a medical practitioner was entitled to "talk about, and ... make some very good points and educate the public" (Magdaleno, nd; Nation 2023). Subsequent to Barnard's treating the child, Indiana's law was amended to make abortion illegal except to preserve the life and physical health of the woman, and in cases of fatal foetal abnormalities and rape or incest up to 10 weeks of pregnancy. The "near total ban" resulted in legal action and an injunction on the basis of the law violating the state Constitution, and a challenge that the ban violated religious freedom (Indiana Department of Health, nd; Molloy 2024). Contrarily, on 7 November 2023 a citizen initiated referendum "The Right to Reproductive Freedom with Protections for Health and Safety" passed by a majority of voters (56.8%), amending Ohio's state Constitution, codifying reproductive rights, including abortion in accordance with *Roe v Wade*, and extending to contraception, miscarriage care, and fertility treatment (Smyth 2023).

This reflects the US position post *Dobbs v Jackson.* Since the decision, many states have introduced harsh laws resulting not only in deaths of women seeking abortion, but of women suffering miscarriage whom hospitals are reluctant to treat whether due to replacing health care with religiously-based (non) treatment or for fear of prosecution. Medical practitioners are reported as fearing to assist women in dire need of treatment and prosecutions have eventuated. On the other hand, in the November 2024 presidential election, some ten states included abortion referenda on the ballot, proposing constitutional amendments to incorporate *Roe v Wade* at state level. These states were Florida—failed as not reaching 60 per cent majority required: abortions remain banned after six weeks pregnancy, "with rare exceptions" (Reuters 2024); Arizona—passed to "guarantee abortion rights" up to foetal viability (around 23–24 weeks) (Reuters 2024); Colorado—passed (meeting the requirement of "at least 55%"), to "guarantee abortion rights" by upholding current Colorado law, which makes abortion legal (Reuters 2024); Maryland—passed to amend the state constitution "to guarantee a 'right to reproductive freedom', including the ability to continue or end one's own pregnancy" with abortion remaining legal (Reuters 2024); Missouri—passed to "guarantee a 'right to reproductive freedom'" to replace a law banning abortion "with few exceptions" (Reuters 2024); Montana—passed "to guarantee abortion rights … upholding current law …, where abortion remains legal" (Reuters 2024); Nebraska—referendum guaranteeing abortion rights failed; competing referendum "prohibiting abortion beyond the first three months of pregnancy passed" (Reuters 2024; Zernike 2024); Nevada—passed to "guarantee abortion rights"' making it more difficult to "roll back" an existing right to abortion "up to 24 weeks"—though to be effective, "the measure [must be approved] twice" so requires approval in 2026 also (Reuters 2024); New York—passed, amending the NY Constitution equal protection clause "to enshrine access to abortion and guarantee individuals' autonomy over reproductive healthcare" with abortion remaining legal (Reuters 2024); South Dakota—failed and abortion "banned with few exceptions" (Reuters 2024; Pipia 2024).

The negative impact of *Dobbs v Jackson* is being experienced in Australia. Even before, around the country concerns about impediments to access were being raised. Then in 2021, a federal Liberal MP introduced a Bill, re-introduced in 2022 by two Liberal senators, requiring doctors to record "medical care, treatment and statistics on children born alive as a result of terminations". This was based on a contention that aborted foetuses were being born alive, but a parliamentary inquiry determined the Bill had no legal, ethical or medical basis (Shepherd 2024; Middleton 2024). A similar inquiry was initiated in Queensland. The "born alive" thesis continues to generate debate, as does the "lack of access" issue.

Tabled in the NSW Parliament on 29 November 2024, a review of the NSW law (under section 17 of the Act)[40] observed that "almost all submissions" confirmed a lack of "real and equitable" access to abortion, "particularly for women living in regional, rural or remote parts of NSW, Aboriginal women, culturally and linguistically diverse women and women who are not [sic] socially and/or financially disadvantaged". This accompanied reports that the service was not available at some hospitals although the minister for health subsequently apologised, with the health treatment apparently reinstated (Barbour 2024). In South Australia, consistent with concerns related to the trimester system and measures directed toward maintaining premature babies at lower and lower periods of gestation, a proposal to amend the law so that pregnant women would be induced at 27 weeks and six days with adoption if premature survival resulted was "narrowly lost" nine in favour, ten against (Holder and Leckie 2024). In Queensland, prior to the 2024 state election a minor party member foreshadowed moving a private members bill to "repeal abortion laws" apparently meaning to re-criminalise pregnancy termination. The then opposition leader—who shortly after became premier—lacked any real clarity as to his position (ABC North West 2024). In the UK in similar terms the leader of a minor party called for "stricter abortion limits" despite the regressive terms of the *Abortion Act* 1967 and the continuing impact of the OAPA (Mitchell 2024).

[40] *Abortion Law Reform Act* 2019 (NSW), View - NSW legislation, https://legislation.nsw.gov.au/view/whole/pdf/inforce/2024-12-02/act-2019-011 (accessed 22 November 2024).

A stark reminder of the need to repeal the OAPA abortion provisions for women in England and Wales, as well as section 5 of the *Abortion Act* 1967 making criminal any termination outside its terms, arose through the 2020 Covid 19 lockdowns. Criminal assault at home and other forms of domestic violence increased exponentially. Women finding themselves pregnant whether by consensual sex or rape (including within the family) and seeking abortion were limited in access to advice, with hospitals focused on pandemic patients and putting "regular" health care on the non-priority list. Two cases highlighted the failure to support all women's rights during the OAPA repeal for Northern Ireland alone, only the year before.

Carla Foster was prosecuted, tried, found guilty and on 18 July 2023 sentenced to 28 months imprisonment. Giving leave to appeal, the Court of Appeal quashed the sentence, substituting 14 months, suspended for 18 months, with a "rehabilitation activity requirement of up to 50 days". Due to time served, Foster gained immediate release (Scutt 2023a).[41] Originally charged with child destruction, Foster pleaded guilty to administering poison with intent to procure her miscarriage contrary to the OAPA section 58. Through the National Health Service (NHS) telephone service she gained and ingested mifepristone and misoprostol tablets despite the pregnancy being beyond the 24-week limit in the *Abortion Act* 1967. On the evidence, conception occurred during separation from her partner, she concealed it when they recommenced living together for the sake of their three children during the Covid lockdowns, and she told a friend of the pregnancy, saying: "I'm too old and I don't want to be a single mum." A postmortem examination determined that the abortion occurred at between 32- and 34-weeks' gestation. Despite concerns expressed as to the criminalisation of a woman trapped into an invidious choice, and police reports of upcoming prosecutions of women in a similar situation, as of 2024 the law remained in effect. In June 2025 the Crime and Policing Bill 2025 was amended (379 "for":137 "against")

---

[41] *Carla Foster v R* [2023] EWCA Crim 1196, 20231018-R-v-FOSTER-final-approved.pdf (accessed 22 October 2023); *Regina v Catt* [2013] EWCA Crim 1187, [REGINA v Catt | [2013] EWCA Crim 1187 | England and Wales Court of Appeal (Criminal Division) | Judgment | Law | CaseMine, https://www.casemine.com/judgement/uk/5a8ff70460d03e7f57ea5d5b (accessed 22 October 2023).

to counter this, providing that no woman terminating her pregnancy outside the 24 week limit would suffer police investigation. The amendment was scheduled to come into effect "within months" (so long as passing all stages of the legislative process)(Dyer 2025) although until that time women continued under threat.

The second Covid lockdown case saw Paris Mayo imprisoned for life, with a minimum of 12 years, for murder of the baby to whom at 15 years of age she gave, downstairs at night, all alone whilst her parents and brother slept unawares upstairs. Ironically, the conviction occurred in the same week the High Court refused Carla Foster's first appeal. Passing mention of infanticide (equivalent of manslaughter, on the basis that the death occurred during the mother's hormonal imbalance) made no impact on the jury. Eighteen years at the trial, Mayo said she was unaware initially of the pregnancy then hid it in denial, fear and dread of her parents, particularly her father (in relation to whom evidence was given of his "emotional cruelty" and other factors engendering a poor relationship), that the child fell onto the floor injuring his head, she put cotton balls into his mouth to clear the mucus, and concealed the body for disposal in a garbage bag. The prosecution said she intentionally bashed the child's head on the floor and smothered him with the cotton balls (Scutt 2023b).

The Baroness Casey Review (October 2022, March 2023) of the Metropolitan Police found misogyny embedded (Casey 2023; Analytical Report, nd). That the Criminal Prosecution Service (CPS) regularly drops rape, flashing, and criminal assault at home and other forms of domestic violence cases yet is pursuing with vigour women and girls—children—caught within a system that continues to criminalise abortion appears to confirm a potential bias there, also. This differential is emphasised, too, in the approach to killing where a man kills an intruder—the notion that "a man's home is his castle" continues to dictate the CPS approach to prosecution where factors such as age (elderly) and sex (male) of the killer, contrasted with age (child) and sex (female) in Mayo's case (Irish Times 2018; Morgan 2011; BBC News 2011; Scutt 2023b). Edward Christian's 1793 admonition that the law does not favour nor respect women remains intact.

Conclusion—On Respecting Women

A recurring feature of legal systems globally is a disrespect for women as human. In the common law system, this is confirmed in the series of cases in the UK, Australia, Canada and the US which labelled women "non-persons", so that it was not until 1929 that a British court acknowledged women's personhood (Scutt 1985, 2016).[42] That the law of abortion singles out women for punishment is indicative of a mindset and an ideology that sees as "right" the labelling of women as unable to make competent, moral or ethical decisions, incapable of appreciating the value of life (of others than themselves), and untrustworthy (Pringle 2007). At the heart of this misogyny is the reality that a pregnancy can result in the birth of a male child. It is the prospective ending of the potential for male life that operates in religion and law against women's own interests in preserving their own health and well-being and, ultimately, their own lives.

Until women are granted equal status as men, with a right to make determinations about their own selves, so that women's existence as human is fully affirmed, abortion will remain a crucial point of contention in law, politics and society. Surely it is ironic that it is the woman who is targeted when confronted with the question of ending a pregnancy. "Choice" is the mantra called upon to justify the decision not to carry a pregnancy to full term. Yet women in this situation make the "choice" to end the pregnancy because ultimately they have no choice. The lack of choice arises in two different ways. The first is where the fetus is diagnosed with anencephaly or spina bifida: the woman confronts ending the pregnancy where she desired to be a mother, but she puts the medically determined state of the child at birth above her own desire. The second arises where, if the circumstances ensured that she was emotionally, economically, financially and psychologically prepared and able to become a mother at that time, she would go ahead to bear the child. That she decides not to (a decision not easily made, and the

[42] *Jex-Blake and Others v. Senatus Academicus of the University of Edinburgh, and the Chancellor Thereof* | *[1873] SLR 10_549* | *Scottish Court of Session* | *Judgment* | *Law* | *CaseMine*, https://www.casemine.com/judgement/uk/5a8ff82760d03e7f57ebbed6 (accessed 22 November 2024).

proposition that women do "choose" abortion lightly confirms systemic socio-cultural misogyny embedded in the legal system) means she can make no other decision. Thus, there is no real choice.

That the law criminalises abortion is indicative of a society, culture and legal system that has directed its focus at the wrong target. Pregnancy should come within the criminal law only where it is forced upon a woman or girl as a consequence of rape—whether it be marital rape, rape by a father or other relative, a "friend" or "intimate partner", or a stranger. What requires attention is the crime and the man who perpetrates the crime. Not the woman who suffers the crime. That rape is so rarely pursued as an offence, yet abortion has been criminalised and prosecuted, penalised and punished globally for centuries, is the most unambiguous and glaringly blatant evidence of the denial of women's humanity. Until women are acknowledged as entitled to equal respect, every woman will ever run the risk of laws that demote her to a province she occupies as a being whose status is located alone in her reproductive facility. Yet a woman is more than a womb.

Bibliography

Reported Cases

R v Bourne [1938] 3 All ER 615, united_kingdom_1938_bourne.pdf, https://www.law.utoronto.ca/sites/default/files/documents/reprohealth/united_kingdom_1938_bourne.pdf (accessed 2 November 2024).

R v Bayliss; R v Cullen (1986) 9 Qld Lawyer Reps 8; *R v Bayliss and Cullen* (1986) 6 QLR 8.

Regina v Catt [2013] EWCA Crim 1187, [REGINA v Catt | [2013] EWCA Crim 1187 | England and Wales Court of Appeal (Criminal Division) | Judgment | Law | CaseMine, https://www.casemine.com/judgement/uk/5a8ff70460d03e7f57ea5d5b (accessed 22 October 2023).

R v Davidson [1969] Vic Rep 85, https://docslib.org/doc/850232/r-v-davidson-victorian-supreme-court-1969-vicrp-85-menhennitt-j, https://docslib.org/doc/850232/r-v-davidson-victorian-supreme-court-1969-vicrp-85-menhennitt-j (accessed 22 November 2024).

R V. DAVIDSON Victorian Supreme Court [1969] Vicrp 85 Menhennitt, J - DocsLib, https://docslib.org/doc/850232/r-v-davidson-victorian-supreme-court-1969-vicrp-85-menhennitt-j (accessed 22 November 2024).

R v Wald (1971) 3 DCR (NSW) 25; R v Wald | 28 October 1971 | Legal Helpdesk Lawyers, https://legalhelpdesklawyers.com.au/2014/10/28/r-v-wald-28-october-1971/ (accessed 22 November 2024).

R v Wald | 28 October 1971 | Peter O'Grady Lawyer, https://peterogrady.com.au/2014/10/28/r-v-wald-28-october-1971/ (accessed 22 November 2024).

Ces and Another v Superclinics (Australia) Pty Limited and Others Nos. Ca 40266/94; Cl 14479/88 Criminal Law and Procedure - Damages - Negligence [1995] NSWSC 103 (27 October 1995), https://www.austlii.edu.au/cgi-bin/viewdoc/au/cases/nsw/NSWSC/1995/103.html (accessed 22 November 2024).

CES and Anor v Superclinics and Ors [1995], Microsoft Word - SC 1995 - CES v. Superclinics.docx, https://www.globalhealthrights.org/wp-content/uploads/2013/02/SC-1995-CES-v.-Superclinics.pdf (accessed 22 November 2024).

Carla Foster v R [2023] EWCA Crim 1196, 20231018-R-v-FOSTER-final-approved.pdf, D:\busstuff.cttees\articles\my articles\EBylines\Abortion\20231018-R-v-FOSTER-final-approved.pdf (accessed 22 October 2023).

Department of Health (R on the Application of) v Information Commissioner [2011] EWHC 1430(Admin), [2011] ACD 97, [2011] Med LR 363, Department of Health, R (on the application of) v Information Commissioner | [2011] EWHC 1430 (Admin) | England and Wales High Court (Administrative Court) | Judgment | Law | CaseMine, https://www.casemine.com/judgement/uk/5a8ff75360d03e7f57eab522 (accessed 21 November 2024).

Perma | *Dobbs v. Jackson Women's Health Organization*:: 597 U.S. ___ (2022):: Justia US Supreme Court Center, https://perma.cc/3MC3-PD8F (accessed 22 November 2024).

Doe v Bolton 410 US 179 (1973), Doe v. Bolton | 410 U.S. 179 (1973) | Justia U.S. Supreme Court Center, https://supreme.justia.com/cases/federal/us/410/179/ (accessed 2 March 2025).

Jex-Blake and Others v. Senatus Academicus of the University of Edinburgh, and the Chancellor Thereof | [1873] SLR 10_549 | Scottish Court of Session | Judgment | Law | CaseMine, https://www.casemine.com/judgement/uk/5a8ff82760d03e7f57ebbed6 (accessed 22 November 2024).
Planned Parenthood of Southeastern Pennsylvania v. Casey | Oyez, 1991 https://www.oyez.org/cases/1991/91-744 (accessed 22 November 2024).
Planned Parenthood of Southeastern Pennsylvania v. Casey, 550 U.S. 833, 997, 1001 (1992), Planned Parenthood of Southeastern Pa. v. Casey | 505 U.S. 833 (1992) | Justia U.S. Supreme Court Center, https://supreme.justia.com/cases/federal/us/505/833/ (accessed 22 November 2024).
Roe v Wade, Roe v Bolton 410 US 113 (1973), Roe v. Wade | 410 U.S. 113 (1973) | Justia U.S. Supreme Court Center, https://supreme.justia.com/cases/federal/us/410/113/ (accessed 22 November 2024).
Vievers and Connolly [1995] 2 Qd R 326.

Statutes

Abortion Act 1967 (UK) Abortion Act 1967, https://www.legislation.gov.uk/ukpga/1967/87/contents (accessed 2 November 2024).
Abortion Law Reform Act 2019 (NSW), View - NSW legislation, https://legislation.nsw.gov.au/view/whole/pdf/inforce/2024-12-02/act-2019-011 (accessed 22 November 2024).
Abortion Law Reform Act 2019 No 11 - NSW Legislation, https://legislation.nsw.gov.au/view/html/inforce/current/act-2019-011 (accessed 22 November 2024).
Abortion Law Reform Act 2008 (Victoria), https://www.legislation.vic.gov.au/in-force/acts/abortion-law-reform-act-2008 (accessed 2 October 2025)
Abortion Legislation Reform Act 2023 (WA), https://www.legislation.wa.gov.au/legislation/statutes.nsf/law_a147399.html (accessed 2 October 2025).
Abortion Regulations 1970 (SA), 1970.-.pdf, https://www.legislation.sa.gov.au/__legislation/lz/c/r/abortion%20regulations%201970/1996.08.31_(1991.07.18)/1970.-.pdf (accessed 2 November 2024).
Abortion (Northern Ireland) Regulations 2020 (NI), The Abortion (Northern Ireland) Regulations 2020, https://www.legislation.gov.uk/uksi/2020/345/contents/made (accessed 22 November 2024).
Acts Amendment (Abortion) Act 1998 (WA), https://www.legislation.wa.gov.au/legislation/statutes.nsf/main_mrtitle_2880_homepage.html (accessed 2 October 2025).

Crimes Act 1958 (Victoria), https://www.legislation.vic.gov.au/in-force/acts/crimes-act-1958 (accessed 2 October 2025).

Crimes Act 1900 (ACT), https://www.legislation.act.gov.au/a/1900-40/default.asp (accessed 2 October 2025).

Crimes Act 1900 (NSW), https://legislation.nsw.gov.au/view/html/inforce/current/act-1900-040 (accessed 2 October 2025).

Criminal Code Act 1983 (NT), https://legislation.nt.gov.au/en/Legislation/CRIMINAL-CODE-ACT-1983 (accessed 2 October 2025).

Criminal Code 1899 (Qld), https://www.legislation.qld.gov.au/view/pdf/inforce/current/act-1899-009 (accessed 2 October 2025).

Criminal Code Act 1924 (Tasmania), https://www5.austlii.edu.au/au/legis/tas/consol_act/cca1924115/index.html (accessed 2 October 2025).

Criminal Code Compilation Act 1913 (WA), WALW - Criminal Code Act Compilation Act 1913 - Home PageCriminal Code Act Compilation Act 1913 - [00-00-00].pdf, https://www.legislation.wa.gov.au/legislation/prod/filestore.nsf/FileURL/mrdoc_13659.pdf/$FILE/Criminal%20Code%20Act%20Compilation%20Act%201913%20-%20%5B00-00-00%5D.pdf?OpenElement (accessed 22 November 2024).

Criminal Justice Bill, https://publications.parliament.uk/pa/bills/cbill/58-04/0155/230155.pdf 2024 (UK)(accessed 2 November 2024).

Criminal Justice Bill - Parliamentary Bills - UK Parliament, https://bills.parliament.uk/bills/3511 2024 (UK) (accessed 2 November 2024).

Criminal Law Amendment Act, 1968–69 (Canada), https://everything.explained.today/Criminal_Law_Amendment_Act%2c_1968%e2%80%9369/ (accessed 2 October 2025).

Criminal Law Consolidation Act 1935 (SA), https://www.legislation.sa.gov.au/lz?path=%2FC%2FA%2FCRIMINAL%20LAW%20CONSOLIDATION%20ACT%201935 (accessed 2 October 2025).

Criminal Law Consolidation Act 1935-1969 (South Australia), 1935.2252.pdf, https://www.legislation.sa.gov.au/__legislation/lz/c/a/criminal%20law%20consolidation%20act%201935/1992.01.15/1935.2252.pdf (accessed 2 November 2024).

Freedom of Information Act 2000 (UK), Freedom of Information Act 2000, https://www.legislation.gov.uk/ukpga/2000/36/contents (accessed 2 February 2025).

Health (Miscellaneous Provisions) Act 1911 (WA), Abortion---Information-and-legal-obligations-for-medical-practitioners.pdf, https://wnhs.health.wa.gov.au/~/media/HSPs/NMHS/Hospitals/WNHS/Documents/Professionals/Abortion---Information-and-legal-obligations-for-medical-practitioners.pdf (accessed 22 November 2024).
Health (Regulation of Termination of Pregnancy) Act 2018 (NI), Health (Regulation of Termination of Pregnancy) Act 2018, https://www.irishstatutebook.ie/eli/2018/act/31 (accessed 2 February 2025).
Infant Life (Preservation) Act 1929 (UK), Infant Life (Preservation) Act 1929, https://www.legislation.gov.uk/ukpga/Geo5/19-20/34/section/1 (accessed 2 November 2024).
Medical Practitioners (Maternal Health) Amendment Act 2002 (ACT), https://www.legislation.act.gov.au/a/2002-26/ (accessed 2 October 2025).
Medical Services Act 1982 (NT), Northern Territory Legislation, https://legislation.nt.gov.au/Legislation/MEDICAL-SERVICES-ACT-1982 (accessed 2 November 2024).
Public Health Act 2016, PUBLIC HEALTH ACT 2016 - SECT 324, https://classic.austlii.edu.au/au/legis/wa/consol_act/pha2016126/s324.html (accessed 22 November 2024).
Public Health Amendment (Safe Access to Reproductive Health Clinics) Act 2018, https://legislation.nsw.gov.au/view/pdf/asmade/act-2018-26 (accessed 22 November 2024).
Reproductive Health (Access to Terminations) Act 2013 (Tas), https://www.legislation.tas.gov.au/view/html/inforce/current/act-2013-072 (accessed 2 October 2025).
Termination of Pregnancy Act 2021 (SA), South Australia: Medical termination of pregnancy, https://www.consciencelaws.org/law/laws/australia003.aspx (accessed 2 November 2024).
Termination of Pregnancy Act 2018 (Qld), Termination of Pregnancy Act 2018, https://www.legislation.qld.gov.au/view/pdf/inforce/current/act-2018-023 (accessed 22 November 2024).
Termination of Pregnancy Law Reform Act 2017 (NT), https://legislation.nt.gov.au/en/Legislation/TERMINATION-OF-PREGNANCY-LAW-REFORM-ACT-2017 (accessed 2 October 2025).
Termination of Pregnancy Law Reform Legislation Amendment Act 2021 (NT), https://legislation.nt.gov.au/en/Bills/Termination-of-Pregnancy-Law-Reform-Legislation-Amendment-Bill-2021-S35?format=assented (accessed 2 October 2025).

Articles and Book Chapters

ABC North West Qld, "Could Robbie Katter's abortion views …", *ABC News*, 21 October 2024, Could Robbie Katter's abortion views cause backlash for his party in the Queensland election? - ABC News, https://www.abc.net.au/news/2024-10-21/katter-abortion-policy-influence-young-voters/104496092 (accessed 22 November 2024).

Abortion: A woman's right to choose | Green Left, https://www.greenleft.org.au/content/abortion-womans-right-choose (accessed 21 November 2024).

BBC News, "Salford burglar death …", *BBC News*, 22 July 2011, Salford burglar death: No prosecution over stabbing - BBC News, https://www.bbc.co.uk/news/uk-england-manchester-14248097 (accessed 22 November 2024).

BBC News, "Roe v Wade: What is US Supreme Court ruling …", *BBC News*, 24 June 2022, Roe v Wade: What is US Supreme Court ruling on abortion? - BBC News, https://www.bbc.co.uk/news/world-us-canada-54513499 (accessed 22 November 2024).

Baird, Barbara and Belton, Suzanne, "Feminism on the frontier …", *Women's History Review* vol 28, issue 1, 2019, 139–158 (24 April 2018 (online), 2 January 2019), Feminism on the frontier: the history of abortion law reform in 1973 in the Northern Territory, Australia: Women's History Review: Vol 28, No 1 - Get Access, https://doi.org/10.1080/09612025.2018.1464481 (accessed 21 November 2024).

Barbour, Lucy, "NSW Health apologises …" *ABC News*, 2 December 2024, NSW Health apologises to women affected by limited abortion services, following hospital bans in Queanbeyan and Orange - ABC News (accessed 2 December 2024).

Bendix, Aria and Helsel, Phil, "Indiana doctor Caitlin Bernard reprimanded …", *NBC News*, 25 May 2023, updated 26 May 2023, Indiana doctor Caitlin Bernard reprimanded over 10-year-old's abortion case, https://www.nbcnews.com/health/health-news/indiana-doctor-gave-10-year-old-girl-abortion-disciplinary-hearing-rcna86214 (accessed 22 November 2024)

Bloomer, Fiona, Roberts, Danielle and Campbell, Emma, "Competing framings of abortion in the Northern Ireland Assembly and Westminster: the long and winding road to abortion decriminalisation", *Irish Political Studies*, online, 28 July 2024, Full article: Competing framings of abortion in the Northern Ireland Assembly and Westminster: the long and winding road to abortion decriminalisation, https://www.tandfonline.com/doi/full/https://doi.org/10.1080/07907184.2024.2375095#:~:text=Abortion%20was%20decriminalised%20in%20Northern%20Ireland%20in%20October,international%20inquiries%2C%20and%20regional%20and%20national%20court%20cases. (accessed 22 November 2024).

Bradstreet, Katherine, "Abortion: A woman's right to choose", *Analysis*, Issue 709, 11 May 2007

Christian, Edward, *Blackstone's Commentaries on the Laws of England*, 1753, 1793 edn, vol 1, 445fn.

Conley, Julia, "Federal court rules ...", *Common Dreams*, 3 December 2024, Federal court rules Idaho can enforce so-called 'abortion trafficking' law, https://www.msn.com/en-gb/news/world/federal-court-rules-idaho-can-enforce-so-called-abortion-trafficking-law/ar-AA1vcFwv?ocid=msedgntp&pc=HCTS&cvid=522f7933a19a407bb29f46779914bed0&ei=15 (accessed 4 December 2024).

Cook, Megan, "Abortion - Controversy: 1974 to 1980s", *Te Ara - the Encyclopedia of New Zealand*, 5 May 2011, reviewed and revised 8 November 2018, http://www.TeAra.govt.nz/en/abortion/page-4 (accessed 28 February 2025).

Donnelly, Laura, Hymas, Charles, Turner, Camilla, "Health Secretary could back decriminalisation ...", *Telegraph*, 23 February 2024, Health Secretary could back decriminalisation of abortion, https://www.telegraph.co.uk/politics/2024/02/23/parliament-historic-vote-decriminalising-abortion/?msockid=12ff2003749a674e082b352875056688 (accessed 22 November 2024).

Douglas, Heather and De Costa, Caroline, "Time to repeal outdated abortion laws ...", *Medical Journal of Australia*, 205 (8), 353–354, Time to repeal outdated abortion laws in New South Wales and Queensland - Douglas - 2016 - Medical Journal of Australia - Wiley Online Library, https://doi.org/10.5694/mja16.00807?msockid=12ff2003749a674e082b352875056688 (accessed 22 November 2024).

Dyer, Clare, "MPs vote to end prosecution of women who terminate pregnancy at any stage", BMJ, 18 June 2025, 389;r1261, MPs vote to end prosecution of women who terminate pregnancy at any stage | The BMJ (accessed 2 October 2025).

Evans, Richard, "Bertram Barney Wainer (1928–1987), *Australian Dictionary of Biography*, vol 18, 2012, Biography - Bertram Barney Wainer - Australian

Dictionary of Biography, https://adb.anu.edu.au/biography/wainer-bertram-barney-15900 (accessed 2 November 2024).
Ferguson, Samantha, "Former Labor MP Cheryl Davenport says it's time to refine her monumental 1998 bill", *Mandurah Mail*, 8 July 2022, updated 13 July 2022, Former Labor MP Cheryl Davenport says it's time to refine her monumental 1998 bill | Mandurah Mail | Mandurah, WA, https://www.mandurahmail.com.au/story/7812142/trailblazer-who-legalised-abortion-in-wa-says-its-time-to-further-refine-the-bill/ (accessed 2 February 2025).
Ginsburg, Ruth Bader, "Some Thoughts on Autonomy and Equality in Relation to *Roe v. Wade*," *North Carolina Law Review* 63 (1985) 384.
Goodyear-Smith, Felicity, "Abortion Law in Aotearoa New Zealand", *NZ Medical Journal*, 136 (150), 72077 (4 August 2023).
Graycar, Reg and Morgan, Jenny, "*Before the High Court* 'Unnatural rejection of womanhood and motherhood': Pregnancy, Damages and the Law – A note on *CES v Superclinics (Aust) Pty Ltd*", *Sydney Law Review* vol 18, 1986, 323–341, imageREAL Capture, https://www.austlii.edu.au/au/journals/SydLawRw/1996/16.pdf (accessed 2 February 2025)
Gross, Rachel E, "The female scientist …", *BBC Future*, 6 January 2020, The female scientist who changed human fertility forever - BBC Future, https://www.bbc.com/future/article/20200103-the-female-scientist-who-changed-human-fertility-forever (accessed 22 November 2024).
Henry, Catherine, "Abortion Retried – the legal status of abortion: under question again", *Alternative Law Journal* vol 20, no 5 (October 1995), pp 239–241, 103.pdf, https://www5.austlii.edu.au/au/journals/AltLawJl/1995/103.pdf (accessed 22 November 2024).
Henry, Catherine, "The case that changed me", *Law Society Journal*, Issue 47 (August 2018), 66.
Henry, Catherine and Charlton, McCourt, "CES & Anor v Superclinics Australia Pty Limited & Ors - Unreported NSW Supreme Court Newman, 18 April 1994", *APLA Update*, August Issue 1994, ScanGate document, https://classic.austlii.edu.au/au/journals/AUPLAUpdate/1994/25.pdf (accessed 21 November 2024).
Holder, Sophie and Leckie, Evelyn, "South Australian upper house narrowly votes down …", 16 October 2024, *ABC News*, South Australian upper house narrowly votes down late-term abortion law amendments, with controversy between MP's - ABC News, https://www.abc.net.au/news/2024-10-17/abortion-legislation-vote-south-australia/104477762 (accessed 22 November 2024).

Horn, Allyson, "Abortion legalised in Queensland ...", *ABC News*, 17 October 2018, Abortion legalised in Queensland after historic vote in Parliament - ABC News, https://www.abc.net.au/news/2018-10-17/abortion-legal-in-queensland-after-historic-vote/10382538 (accessed 22 November 2024).
Hughes, Laura, "MPs in push to decriminalise abortion ...", *Financial Times*, 9 May 2024, MPs in push to decriminalise abortion in England and Wales, https://www.ft.com/content/4135e2ae-330c-471a-bb08-a80d69524773 (accessed 22 November 2024).
Irish Times, "Pensioner who fatally stabbed burglar ...", *Irish Times*, 6 April 2018, Pensioner who fatally stabbed burglar will not be prosecuted – The Irish Times, https://www.irishtimes.com/news/world/uk/pensioner-who-fatally-stabbed-burglar-will-not-be-prosecuted-1.3453280 (accessed 22 November 2024).
Kenny, Susan, "Interveners and Amici Curiae in the High Court", image-REAL Capture, https://www.austlii.edu.au/au/journals/AdelLawRw/1998/14.pdf (accessed 22 November 2024).
Kirkby, Margaret, "Abortion ...", *Green Left Weekly*, issue 248, 25 September 1996, Abortion: A woman's right to choose | Green Left, https://www.greenleft.org.au/content/abortion-womans-right-choose#:~:text=The%20case%2C%20CES%20%26%20otrs%20v%20Superclinics%20%26,several%20doctors%20who%20failed%20to%20diagnose%20her%20pregnancy. (accessed 22 November 2024).
Littleton, Fiona, Kisby, Bewley and Drife, James, "Introduction – Presenting the First Test-Tube Baby", *The Edwards and Steptoe Lecture of 1979*, 9781009211031_excerpt.pdf, https://assets.cambridge.org/97810092/11031/excerpt/9781009211031_excerpt.pdf (accessed 22 November 2024).
McBride, Alex, "The Supreme Court. Expanding Civil Rights ...", *PBS*, December 2006, The Supreme Court. Expanding Civil Rights. Landmark Cases. Casey v. Planned Parenthood (1992) | PBS, https://www.thirteen.org/wnet/supremecourt/rights/landmark_casey.html (accessed 22 November 2024).
Magdaleno, Johnny, "Indiana doctor Caitlin Bernard reprimanded ...", *Indianapolis Star*, nd, Indiana doctor Caitlin Bernard reprimanded over 10-year-old's abortion case, https://www.nbcnews.com/health/health-news/indiana-doctor-gave-10-year-old-girl-abortion-disciplinary-hearing-rcna86214 (accessed 22 November 2024).
Middleton, Karen, "Greens to ask Senate ...", *Guardian*, 19 November 2024, Greens to ask Senate to vote to jettison anti-abortion bill in bid to split

Coalition on issue | Abortion | The Guardian, https://www.theguardian.com/world/2024/nov/19/greens-to-ask-senate-to-vote-on-anti-abortion-bill-in-bid-to-split-coalition-on-issue?utm_term=673d0a63de16d337c18f0994f2b4ed9d&utm_campaign=AustralianPolitics&utm_source=esp&utm_medium=Email&CMP=aupolitics_email (accessed 20 November 2024).

Mitchell, Archie, "Nigel Farage calls for parliament …", *Independent*, 28 November 2024, Nigel Farage calls for parliament to debate stricter abortion limits | The Independent, https://www.independent.co.uk/news/uk/politics/farage-abortion-limit-reform-b2655446.html (accessed 29 November 2024).

Molloy, Mary Claire, "Explaining what's legal and illegal …", *Indianapolis News*, 1 May 2024, Explaining what's legal and illegal under Indiana's abortion law - Indianapolis News | Indiana Weather | Indiana Traffic | WISH-TV |, https://www.wishtv.com/news/health-spotlight/explaining-whats-legal-and-illegal-under-indianas-abortion-law/ (accessed 22 November 2024).

Morgan, Lee, "Is it right …", *BBC News*, 22 July 2011, Is it right to stab an intruder? - BBC News, https://www.bbc.co.uk/news/uk-england-manchester-14253259 (accessed 22 November 2024).

Naylor, Bronwyn, "Judge-Made Law: The 'Menhennit Ruling' and Abortion Law Reform in Victoria", *Victorian Historical Journal,* vol 88, no 1, June 2017a, Judge-Made Law: The 'Menhennit Ruling' and Abortion Law Reform in Victoria by Bronwyn Naylor:: SSRN, https://papers.ssrn.com/sol3/papers.cfm?abstract_id=3011276 (accessed 22 November 2024).

Neville, Warwick, "Abortion before the High Court – What Next? Caveat Interventus: A Note on *Superclinics Australia Pty Ltd v CES*", *Adelaide LR*, vol 20, 1998, 183–192, Abortion before the High Court: what next? Caveat Interventus: a note on Superclinics Australia Pty Ltd v CES. | The Adelaide Law Review, https://doi.org/10.3316/agis_archive.19990366 (accessed 22 November 2024).

Oyez, "Planned Parenthood of Southeastern Pennsylvania v. Casey." *Oyez,* www.oyez.org/cases/1991/91-744 (accessed 2 February 2025).

PBS News, "Indiana doctor reprimanded …", *PBS News – Nation,* 26 May 2023, Indiana doctor reprimanded, fined $3,000 for talking publicly about Ohio 10-year-old's abortion | PBS News, https://www.pbs.org/newshour/nation/indiana-doctor-reprimanded-fined-3000-for-talking-publicly-about-ohio-10-year-olds-abortion#:~:text=An%20Indiana%20board%20decided%20Thursday%20night%20to%20reprimand,to%20a%2010-year-old%20rape%20victim%20from%20neighboring%20Ohio. Nation 26 May 2023 (accessed 2 February 2025).

Pipia, Lindsey, "South Dakota voters defeat effort ...", 6 November 2024, South Dakota voters defeat effort to put abortion rights in the state constitution, https://www.nbcnews.com/politics/2024-election/south-dakota-voters-defeat-abortion-rights-ballot-measure-rcna177402 (accessed 22 November 2024).

Pringle, H, "Urban Mythology: The Question of Abortion in Parliament", *Australasian Parliamentary Review* 22(2), 2007, 5-22.

Reuters, "Results of state-level abortion ballot measures ...", Results of state-level abortion ballot measures in the US election | Reuters, https://www.reuters.com/world/us/results-state-level-abortion-ballot-measures-us-election-2024-11-06/ (accessed 22 November 2024).

Scutt, Jocelynne A, "Sexism in Legal Language", *Australian Law Journal* vol 59, no 10, 1985, 163–174.

Scutt, Jocelynne A, "Abortion rights – and wrongs", *East Anglia ByLines*, 22 June 2023a, my-body-my-choice-scaled-e1687371067253.jpg (1200×900), https://eastangliabylines.co.uk/wp-content/uploads/2023/06/my-body-my-choice-scaled-e1687371067253.jpg (accessed 22 November 2024).

Scutt, Jocelynne A, "Abortion, infanticide, murder ...", *East Anglia ByLines*, 18 July 2023b, Abortion, infanticide, murder – does the legal system differentiate? https://eastangliabylines.co.uk/politics/justice/abortion-infanticide-murder-does-the-legal-system-differentiate/ (accessed 22 November 2024).

Shepherd, Tory, "Australian conservatives claim ...", *Guardian*, 27 August 2024, Australian conservatives claim babies are sometimes 'born alive' after an abortion. What's the truth? | Australia news | The Guardian, https://www.theguardian.com/australia-news/article/2024/aug/28/australian-conservatives-claim-babies-are-sometimes-born-alive-after-an-abortion-whats-the-truth (accessed 22 November 2024).

Smyth, Julie, "Ohio voters pass amendment ...", *AP News*, 8 November 2023, Ohio voters pass amendment protecting access to abortion | AP News, https://apnews.com/article/ohio-abortion-amendment-election-2023-fe3e06747b616507d8ca21ea26485270 (accessed 22 November 2024).

Symons, Ainsley, "Anti-Abortion Campaigning and the Political Process" *Recorder* (Melbourne Branch, Australian Society for the Study of Labour History), no 279, March 2014, 2, (99+) Anti-Abortion Campaigning and the Political Process (2014) | Ainsley Symons - Academia.edu, https://www.academia.edu/6714935/Anti_Abortion_Campaigning_and_the_Political_Process_2014_ (accessed 21 November 2024).

Tolentino, Jia, "A New Rallying Cry …", *The New Yorker*, 14 November 2024, "Your Body, My Choice": A New Rallying Cry for the Irony-Poisoned Right | The New Yorker, https://www.newyorker.com/news/the-lede/your-body-my-choice-a-new-rallying-cry-for-the-irony-poisoned-right (accessed 15 November 2024).

Wainer, Jo, "Abortion before the High Court", *Australian Feminist LJ*, vol 8, 1997, 133-138.

Zarevich, Emily, "The Manifesto of the 343", *JSTORE Daily*, 14 November 2022, The Manifesto of the 343 - JSTOR Daily, https://daily.jstor.org/the-manifesto-of-the-343/ (accessed 2 November 2024).

Zernike, Kate, "Nebraska Voters Pass Measure …", *New York Times*, 6 November 2024, Nebraska Voters Pass Measure Limiting Abortions - The New York Times, https://www.nytimes.com/2024/11/06/us/nebraska-abortion-ballot-measure.html (accessed 22 November 2024).

Books and Reports

Analytical Report, nd, Analytical Report - evidence to support Baroness Casey of Blackstock's conclusions about the current misconduct system in the Metropolitan Police Service, London, UK, https://www.met.police.uk/SysSiteAssets/media/downloads/met/about-us/baroness-casey-review/baroness-casey-review-interim-report-on-misconduct.pdf (accessed 22 November 2024).

Aotearoa/New Zealand, *Report of the Royal Commission*, Wellington, Aotearoa/NZ,1976, Royal Commission on Contraception, Sterilisation and Abortion, 1976, https://teara.govt.nz/en/photograph/29028/royal-commission-on-contraception-sterilisation-and-abortion-1976 (accessed 28 February 2025).

Bennett, C and Landers, B, in consultation with Children by Choice, Professors Heather Douglas and Caroline de Costa, *Reform of Queensland's Abortion Laws* (accessed 22 November 2024), UQ Pro Bono Centre, 2015.

Bloomer, Fiona and Campbell, Emma, *Decriminalizing Abortion in Northern Ireland – Allies and Abortion Provision*, Perlego e-book, nd; Bloomsbury, London, UK, 2022.

Casey, Baroness, *An Independent Review into the standards of behaviour and internal culture of the Metropolitan Police Service by Baroness Casey of Blackstock DBE CB*, March 2023, BARONESS CASEY REVIEW Final Report, https://www.met.police.uk/SysSiteAssets/media/downloads/met/about-us/baroness-casey-review/update-march-2023/baroness-casey-review-march-2023a.pdf (accessed 22 November 2024).

Casey Review of Met Police—discrimination 'baked' into the system | News | LexisNexis, https://www.lexisnexis.co.uk/legal/news/casey-review-of-met-police-discrimination-baked-into-the-system?msclkid=73032e85117e14dff82a49ca1180e3d5&utm_source=bing&utm_medium=cpc&utm_campaign=BL%20%7C%20MS%20%7C%20LN%20%7C%20Prospecting%20Search%20%7C%20DSA%20%7C%20DA&utm_term=%2Flegal%2Fnews%2F&utm_content=DSA%20-%20News%20-%20Generic (accessed 22 November 2024).

Ginsburg, Ruth Bader with Hartnett, Mary and Williams, Wendy W, *My Own Words – Ruth Bader Ginsburg*, Simon & Schuster, NYC, NY, US, 2018.

Gotsis, Tom and Ismay, Laura, *Abortion Law – A National Perspective, Briefing Paper No 02/2017,* Abortion Law.pdf, Canberra, ACT, Australia, https://www.parliament.nsw.gov.au/researchpapers/Documents/Abortion%20Law.pdf#page=30 (accessed 22 November 2024); Download the full paper as PDF, https://www.parliament.nsw.gov.au/researchpapers/Documents/Abortion%20Law.pdf Parliament of NSW, *Advice on legislation or legal policy issues contained in this paper is provided for use in parliamentary debate and for related parliamentary purposes. This paper is not professional legal opinion.*

Littleton, Fiona Kisby, Bewley, Susan and Drife, James Owen, *Presenting the First Test-Tube Baby – The Edwards and Steptoe Lecture of 1979*, Cambridge University Press, Cambridge, UK, 2023.

Marty, Robin and Pieklo, Jessica Mason, *The End of Roe v. Wade – Inside the Right's Plan to Destroy Legal Abortion*, Ig Publishing, NYC, NY, US, 2013, 2019.

Norris, Sian, *Bodies Under Siege – How the Far-Right Attack on Reproductive Rights Went Global*, Verso, London, UK, 2023.

Queensland Health, Communities, Disability Services and Domestic and Family Violence Prevention Committee, *Inquiry into Abortion Law Reform Paper*, Parliament of Queensland, 2016, 14-infop-16June2016.pdf (accessed 22 November 2024).

Scutt, Jocelynne A (ed), *The Baby Machine – Reproductive Technology and the Commercialisation of Motherhood*, McCulloch Publishing, Australia, 1988; republished Green Press, UK/France, 1990.

Scutt, Jocelynne A, *Women and Magna Carta – A Treaty for Rights or Wrongs*, Palgrave Macmillan, London, UK, 2016.

Victorian Law Reform Commission, *The Law of Abortion – Information Paper*, Melbourne, Australia, September 2007, Microsoft Word - Final web version info paper 27 Sep.doc, https://www.lawreform.vic.gov.au/wp-content/uploads/2021/07/law-of-abortion-final_web_version_info_paper.pdf (accessed 22 November 2024).

Information Documents

ACT Government, Abortion - ACT Government, https://www.act.gov.au/health/topics/sexual-health/abortion#:~:text=It%20is%20legal%20to%20get%20an%20abortion%20in,live%20in%20the%20ACT%20to%20access%20free%20services, nd (accessed 22 November 2024).

ACT Government, "No-cost abortions now accessible …", 8 April 2024 No-cost abortions now accessible at more Canberra locations - Our Canberra, https://www.act.gov.au/our-canberra/latest-news/2024/april/no-cost-abortions-now-accessible-at-more-canberra-locations (accessed 22 November 2024).

Abortion Law Reform Association | AWR, https://www.womenaustralia.info/entries/abortion-law-reform-association/ (accessed 2 November 2024).

Abortion Law Reform Association SA/ALR. *Abortion Law Reform Association 1930s-2000s*, Abortion Law Reform Association | Wellcome Collection, https://wellcomecollection.org/works/h278gyy2 (accessed 2 November 2024).

Aotearoa/New Zealand, "Abortion Controversy: 1974 to 1980s", nd, *Te Ara Encyclopaedia of New Zealand*, Controversy: 1974 to 1980s – Te Ara Encyclopedia of New Zealand, https://teara.govt.nz/en/abortion/page-4 (accessed 2 November 2024).

Aotearoa/New Zealand, *Contraception, Sterilisation …*, 1977a, Contraception, Sterilisation, and Abortion Act passed, https://nzhistory.govt.nz/page/contraception-sterilisation-and-abortion-act-passed (accessed 2 November 2024).

Aotearoa/New Zealand, "NZ History, Contraception, Sterilisation, and Abortion Act passed 16 December 1977", 1977b, *New Zealand History: Nga korero a ipurangi o Aotearoa*, 4 August 2023, https://www.bing.com/search?q=abortion+rights+new+zealand+1970s&form=ANNTH1&refig=5bd67cda5c2648dfb7dfe32bdfb79da6&pc=HCTS (accessed 2 November 2024).

Children By Choice, Inc. 1972, Children By Choice Association Incorporated | AWR, https://www.womenaustralia.info/entries/children-by-choice-association-incorporated/ (accessed 2 November 2024).

Cica, Natasha, *Abortion Law in Australia – Research Papers 1998-99*, Australian Parliamentary Library, 31 August 1998, Research – Parliament of Australia, https://www.aph.gov.au/About_Parliament/Parliamentary_departments/Parliamentary_Library/Research (accessed 22 November 2024).

Home Office, Department of Health and Social Care (UK), "Protection zones around abortion clinics ...", 18 September 2024, Protection zones around abortion clinics in place by October - GOV.UK, https://www.gov.uk/government/news/protection-zones-around-abortion-clinics-in-place-by-october (accessed 22 November 2024).

HR Law Centre, 30 June 2018, One year on, it's time for NT Government to finish the job on outdated abortion laws | Human Rights Law Centre, https://www.hrlc.org.au/news/2018/6/29/a-year-on-its-time-for-nt-government-to-fully-update-outdated-abortion-laws (accessed 22 November 2024).

Humanist Heritage, *Abortion Law Reform Association*, 2023, Abortion Law Reform Association | Humanist Heritage - Exploring the rich history and influence of humanism in the UK, https://heritage.humanists.uk/abortion-law-reform-association/ (accessed 22 November 2024).

Indiana Department of Health, Health: Consumer Services & Health Care Regulation: Abortion Information Center, https://www.in.gov/health/cshcr/acute-and-continuing-care/abortion-information-center/, nd (accessed 22 November 2024).

MSI Australia, *Abortion Law in Australia*, updated September 2024 (MSI Australia 2024), Abortion Law in Australia | MSI Australia, https://www.msiaustralia.org.au/abortion-law-in-australia/ (accessed 22 November 2024).

NT Laws, Northern Territory Legislation, https://legislation.nt.gov.au/en/Bills/Termination-of-Pregnancy-Law-Reform-Legislation-Amendment-Bill-2021-S35?format=assented (accessed 22 November 2024).

Naylor, Bronwyn, *Research Paper No 3011276*, 2 August 2017b, Monash University – Faculty of Law; RMIT University – Graduate School of Business and Law, 2017b, *Monash University Faculty of Law Legal Studies Research Paper No. 3011276*, https://papers.ssrn.com/sol3/papers.cfm?abstract_id=3011276 (accessed 22 November 2024).

Roe v. Wade - Center for Reproductive Rights, https://reproductiverights.org/roe-v-wade/ (accessed 22 November 2024).

SALRI, South Australian Law Reform Institute | Adelaide Law School | University of Adelaide, https://law.adelaide.edu.au/south-australian-law-reform-institute (accessed 22 November 2024).

SA Health, Abortion legislation reform and the new Termination of Pregnancy Act 2021 | SA Health, https://www.sahealth.sa.gov.au/wps/wcm/connect/public+content/sa+health+internet/conditions/abortions/abortion+legislation+reform+and+the+new+termination+of+pregnancy+act+2021#:~:text=As%20recommended%20by%20SALRI, (accessed 22 November 2024).

SA Health, *Abortion legislation reform …*, 2023, Abortion legislation reform and the new Termination of Pregnancy Act 2021 | SA Health, https://www.sahealth.sa.gov.au/wps/wcm/connect/public+content/sa+health+internet/conditions/abortions/abortion+legislation+reform+and+the+new+termination+of+pregnancy+act+2021#:~:text=As%20recommended%20by%20SALRI, (accessed 22 November 2024).

South Australian Law Reform Institute (SALRI 2019, *South Australian law practice review reform Report* 13 October 2019, Abortion Report 281119.pdf, https://law.adelaide.edu.au/ua/media/996/Abortion%20Report%20281119.pdf (accessed 22 November 2024).

State Library of Western Australia, *W.A. Abortion Law Reform Papers*, COLLECTION NAME, https://slwa.wa.gov.au/pdf/mn/mn3001_3500/mn3184.pdf (accessed 22 November 2024).

University of Toronto Libraries, *Post-1969*, nd, Post-1969: The Omnibus Bill and Abortion · The State in the Bedroom - The Evolution of Reproductive Rights in Canada · Exhibits, https://exhibits.library.utoronto.ca/exhibits/show/stateinthebedroom/omnibusbill (accessed 2 November 2024).

Vasectomy-Information.com, *History of Vasectomy 1999–2025*, History of Vasectomy: Brief history of the procedure, https://www.vasectomy-information.com/what-to-know/history/ (accessed 21 November 2022).

9

Surrogacy: A Question of Women's Right to Self-Determination or Exploitation of Women's Bodies?

Maja von Bolton

Introduction

Surrogacy exists in two forms: altruistic and commercial. Neither altruistic nor commercial surrogacy is permitted in Sweden; however, it is not prohibited for Swedes to travel abroad to engage in surrogacy arrangements. Altruistic surrogacy is thus possible for Swedish couples in countries where it is allowed. The difference between the two forms is that commercial arrangements involve payment, while altruistic agreements occur without payment, for instance, to help a friend, sister, or daughter who cannot become pregnant for various reasons. It also occurs to help unknown persons, although this is less common (SOU 2016:11, 373).

Whether surrogacy is altruistic or commercial, it involves a woman (the surrogate mother) giving birth with the intention of handing the child over to the commissioning couple, the intended parents (Saldeen

M. von Bolton (✉)
Uppsala University, Uppsala, Sweden
e-mail: majavonbolton@gmail.com

J. A. Scutt (ed.), *Women, Power and Autonomy*,
https://doi.org/10.1007/978-3-031-97958-3_9

2023, 131). Because surrogacy is not allowed in Sweden, it is common for individuals to travel abroad to have a child via a commercial surrogate (Norstedts Juridik 2022). Today, more children come to Sweden through commercial surrogacy arrangements than through adoptions (Bergström 2023). In 2014, the majority of those who had children via commercial surrogacy arrangements were heterosexual couples, despite surrogacy often being portrayed as an LGBTQI issue, specifically for male same-sex couples (Gondouin 2014, 109).

In a 2013 report by the Swedish National Council on Medical Ethics (Smer), all council members deemed commercial surrogacy ethically indefensible (Smer 2013, 171). The arguments against commercial surrogacy are numerous, including that it often occurs under exploitative and coercive conditions. When surrogacy is commercialised, children are turned into products to be bought and sold. Commercial surrogacy is also said to harm surrogate mothers because they are often in an economically and socially disadvantaged position (Baker 1995, 35). Therefore, Sweden would never allow commercial surrogacy. However, the majority of the council considered that altruistic surrogacy could be justifiable under certain conditions, while a minority believed that both commercial and altruistic surrogacy should remain prohibited (Smer 2013, 171). The debate on altruistic surrogacy has grown and evolved in recent years in Sweden, shifting from being seen as an unusual reproductive method to becoming an important "family policy" issue (Gondouin 2014, 109). The discussion about allowing altruistic surrogacy in Sweden has resurfaced several times recently, both in investigations and parliamentary motions. Following the 2013 report, most recently in a 2016 official government inquiry, the approval of altruistic surrogacy was discussed (SOU 2016).

The Swedish Debate on Altruistic Surrogacy

Whether altruistic surrogacy should be allowed or not is highly debated in Sweden. The divided nature of the debate and the fragmented political stance on its allowance generates interest in examining the elements of the ongoing societal contest (Wilhelmson 2022). It is especially valuable to study the arguments from an ethical perspective grounded in human rights. Attention is usually focused on human rights violations within the commercial surrogacy trade, but relatively little information exists on human rights violations within altruistic surrogacy arrangements. This chapter focuses on the debate surrounding altruistic surrogacy, currently the only form of surrogacy that might be approved in Sweden.

This requires examination of the arguments for and against the prospect of altruistic surrogacy in Sweden by analysing arguments in the public realm. Arguments then require assessment by reference to three ethical principles: respect for human dignity (non-discrimination and exploitation), self-determination, and self-ownership, to determine whether altruistic surrogacy should be permitted in Sweden. Articles examined and analysed for this purpose were published between 2016 and 2023, this timeframe selected to comprehensively understand the current societal debate on altruistic surrogacy. The decision to run from 2016 is due to publication in that year of the government inquiry "Olika vägar till föräldraskap" (Different Paths to Parenthood), which prompted a surge in publications "for" or "against", "why" and "why not".

Ethical Principles

Altruistic surrogacy raises three fundamental ethical principles: respect for human dignity (non-discrimination and exploitation), self-determination, and self-ownership (Smer 2013, 165). Discussion on the meaning of these ethical principles and how they can be linked to human rights is essential to highlight and categorise the different types of argument for and against altruistic surrogacy. Ethical principles form the basis for how analysis of the topic is conducted. In compiling the arguments, I assess whether, for example, those presented are cognisant with the right to self-determination or human dignity, and so on. The ethical principles are intended to enable identification of the arguments for and against. They are chosen because they are grounded in human rights and are, in many respects, interconnected and share the same foundations.

Human dignity is the more fundamental principle, with the others being interpretations of it. The ethical principle of greatest significance for the analysis is therefore respect for human dignity, as it underpins the concept of human rights and signals that there is something inherently worthy of respect. Human dignity thus forms the basis for the other ethical principles and, therefore, arguments related to human dignity carry the most weight. Without human dignity, human beings do not have the right to self-determination or the right to self-ownership; having human dignity means there is something that must be respected. Without human dignity, people could treat each other as mere resources, disregard others' self-determination, and make decisions about each other's bodies. Since human dignity is the foundation of what deserves respect, contentions related to respect for human dignity carry the most weight in the evaluation of arguments. Following this, an analysis of the arguments requires their categorisation into pro-surrogacy and anti-surrogacy perspectives for each ethical principle. Firstly, each ethical principle requires a brief explanation before the arguments are presented.

What Is Respect for Human Dignity?

Human dignity and human rights are closely interconnected, with dignity featuring prominently in many human rights. Oscar Schachter argues that human dignity is a universally accepted ideal, reflecting the notion that each of us possesses an inherent value that deserves respect (Schachter 1983, 849). Since human rights stem from the idea of inherent value, a violation of human rights constitutes a violation of our dignity (Beyleveld and Brownsword 1998, 665). The humanistic view of humanity suggests that people are more than just their biological or economic value. Human dignity is tied to our existence rather than our actions; it is not our attributes that determine our dignity, but something independent of our status or societal roles. This means that everyone has an equal right to life, fair and just treatment, freedom, and to have their rights respected (Smer 2018, 36).

Human dignity, therefore, does not pertain to some people more than others. A person using a wheelchair for mobility has the same dignity as an elite athlete, just as an illiterate individual has the same dignity as a Nobel prize winner (Smer 2018, 36). Individuals should not be subjected to discrimination based on specific traits such as skin colour, gender, age, sexual orientation, or political or religious affiliation. This principle of non-discrimination encompasses, according to Jack Donnelly, the right not to be excluded from the legitimate enjoyment of human rights (Donnelly 2013, 275). Another significant aspect of human dignity comes from Immanuel Kant, who drew a distinction between what can and cannot be bought, proposing that there are things that can be priced, bought, and sold, such as milk and laundry detergent, yet human life can never be bought or sold (McManus 2022). This follows because human life possesses an intrinsic value that cannot be exhausted or violated. Kantian ethics also asserts that individuals should be treated as ends in themselves, not merely as means to an end. According to this logic, practices like slavery are unacceptable, as they constitute a violation of human dignity (Smer 2013, 111). Respect for each individual's inherent value implies that people should not be used to satisfy others' needs or desires. I interpret this as the right to not be exploited.

Human Dignity (Non-discrimination)

Pro-surrogacy Arguments

Non-discrimination refers to the right not to be excluded from the legitimate enjoyment of human rights (Donnelly 2013, 272). How discrimination is considered to occur in the context of altruistic surrogacy arrangements can be perceived in different ways. One argument identified in the debate is that a ban on altruistic surrogacy is discriminatory against childless individuals seeking to have children. The groups affected include single individuals, women with non-functioning wombs, and homosexual men, who would be deprived of the opportunity to become parents if such a ban on surrogacy were imposed in Sweden (Ekelund Nachman 2016). The group most commonly cited as being adversely affected by a ban constitutes homosexual male couples who cannot conceive children in other ways (Nilsson 2023). Homosexual men face significant challenges in adopting, partly due to the limited number of children available for adoption and restrictions from countries driven by homophobia. Therefore, a ban is argued to be discriminatory against this group, who would essentially have no other means of becoming parents except through surrogacy. Due to the limited options available to homosexual men, pro-surrogacy advocates argue that altruistic surrogacy should be permitted (Westerholm 2016).

A ban on altruistic surrogacy is also argued to be an attempt to undermine LGBTQI families, as it would particularly impact childless homosexual men. Such a ban would generally make it more difficult for involuntarily childless individuals to receive assistance either abroad or in Sweden in the future, which is seen as a regressive way to restrict freedoms. In this context, having children is understood as a freedom (Svensson 2019). Consequently, a ban on altruistic surrogacy could be perceived as discriminatory. Arguments in favour of allowing altruistic surrogacy suggest that it would help those struggling with involuntary childlessness and provide equal opportunities for LGBTQI individuals to have children (Nilsson 2023). It would enable more people to "experience the joy of parenthood" (Svensson 2019). Thus, permitting altruistic surrogacy would ensure that childless individuals have the same opportunities as others to have children, hence promoting equal treatment. What can be inferred from these arguments is that allowing altruistic surrogacy would contribute to equal treatment and respect for human dignity regardless of sexual orientation (Westerholm 2016).

Anti-surrogacy Arguments

The anti-surrogacy side of the debate argues against the pro-surrogacy perspective, contending that a ban on surrogacy is not homophobic because the majority of those currently having children through surrogacy are heterosexual couples. This suggests that a ban would not disproportionately affect homosexual men (Samuelsson 2023). Claiming that a ban on surrogacy is homophobic, according to anti-surrogacy writers, undermines an extremely complex issue (Andersson 2023). They argue that a ban on altruistic surrogacy is necessary to ensure that women are not discriminated against and are not deprived of their rights. Sweden has an obligation to ensure that women are not excluded from the legitimate enjoyment of human rights, which is necessary to prevent discrimination. A ban on altruistic surrogacy is argued as necessary to protect fundamental humanitarian values and moral norms (Rollén and Olin Wikman 2019). Thus, a ban on altruistic surrogacy is not aimed at specific groups unable to have children but is about protecting women and affirming women's humanity. An additional argument is that permitting altruistic surrogacy reflects a negative view of women's rights (Ohlsson 2021). Furthermore, there are arguments that Sweden should implement a complete ban on foreign surrogacy arrangements to uphold the international commitments made to protect women from human trafficking (Winberg 2016). Prohibiting altruistic surrogacy is viewed as a measure to protect women and acknowledge women as human.

Human Dignity (Non-exploitation)

Anti-surrogacy Arguments

Respect for each individual's inherent value means that people should not be used to satisfy the needs or desires of others; in other words, individuals should be treated as ends in themselves, not merely as means (Smer 2013, 111). Arguments from the anti-surrogacy side of the debate suggest that allowing altruistic surrogacy exploits women, as women's bodies are used solely as a means to an end.

Ekis Ekman describes this perspective on altruistic surrogacy:

> The moment one sees another person as a "possibility"—an extension of one's own desires, thus requiring them to forego their own feelings—a power relationship begins (Ekis Ekman 2019).

This argument suggests that perceiving individuals as instruments to fulfil our desires initiates and condones exploitation. Moreover, the argument can be understood as suggesting that when individuals are exploited for others' desires, they are reduced to mere instruments. The power dynamic described involves the actor who views the other as a possibility and thus exerts power over them. The argument can be seen as a warning that surrogacy leads to people being used to satisfy others' needs or desires, violating human dignity. Ekman's stance also implies that there is something wrong with wanting to use another person's body solely to achieve one's own goals (Eris Ekman 2019). Altruistic surrogacy is perceived as promoting a view of women's reproduction as something that can be exploited by a third party (Kakabaveh 2018). That the practice allows one to rent or take control of parts of someone else's body is another argument against altruistic surrogacy (Winberg 2016).

A further proposition is that all forms of surrogacy, even altruistic ones, are commercial transactions because they always involve a contract between the childless couple and the woman, whose body is treated as a "vessel" (Inci 2016). The notion that the female body becomes a vessel in altruistic surrogacy refers to the idea that it contributes to a demeaning view of the female body as merely a carrier of a child. According to this view, the surrogate mother is reduced to the function of "baby creator".

Lindquist highlights this:

> Apparently, there is at least some opinion that does not see the "woman as vessel" concept as a problem—as long as she chooses to be reduced to such (Lindquist 2019).

This propounds that a segment of society, in viewing as acceptable the use of women's bodies to fulfil their desires, does not consider problematic the vision of women as vessels. Yet when women are used as vessels for reproduction, their bodies are reduced to existing solely to satisfy others' needs, contradicting the principle of human dignity. Linquist conveys the notion that even if individuals voluntarily choose to be surrogate mothers, it becomes problematic when others are willing to use another person as a resource for their desires. In this view, surrogacy, whether altruistic or commercial, and whether it is voluntary or coerced, is always exploitative because the female body is used solely as a means. No one should exploit another person's humanity for their own purposes, no matter how strong the desire is for children (Lindquist 2019).

Due to our inherent value, individuals should be treated as ends in themselves and not merely as means, but using someone else's body—even voluntarily—reflects a view of the female body as a means. Therefore, anti-surrogacy advocates call for a ban on altruistic surrogacy because using the female body as a vessel or means for reproduction violates human dignity (Rollén and Olin Wikman 2019). Furthermore, altruistic surrogacy is criticised as perpetuating an outdated patriarchal notion of women as helpful, even self-sacrificing, and the female body as a tool to satisfy others' needs (Inci 2016). The anti-surrogacy debate generally agrees that using others' bodies for one's own ends is wrong according to the principle of human dignity, and thus altruistic surrogacy should be banned.

Pro-surrogacy Arguments

Altruistic surrogacy should be permitted because, in the long term, it will lead to Swedes ceasing to use commercial surrogates, is one type of argument advanced in the discourse. The argument posits that if Sweden does not allow altruistic surrogacy, people will continue to use commercial surrogates because those longing for children will act on their desires (Karlsson 2019). Allowing altruistic surrogacy would reduce the need for Swedes to seek commercial surrogates abroad, as other options would be available in Sweden (Wojciechowski 2023). From this perspective, permitting altruistic surrogacy is desirable because otherwise, we would be condoning the exploitation and use of women, which undermines individual human dignity. An additional argument is that Sweden currently relies on poorer countries to fulfil the desires of childless individuals, which contributes to women risking their health and lives for financial gain (Ekelund Nachman 2016). Consequently, current Swedish legislation contributes to the ongoing exploitation and use of commercial surrogates. To reduce the exploitation of commercial surrogates, pro-surrogacy advocates argue that we should establish international norms for surrogacy arrangements, similar to those for international adoptions. This would ensure that surrogates, prospective children, and intended parents are not harmed within these arrangements (Engberg 2023).

A ban on altruistic surrogacy will not resolve the issues associated with surrogacy. Instead, it will continue to contribute to the uncontrolled foreign market, according to pro-surrogacy writers. Problems with surrogacy could instead be addressed by providing access to safe and reliable options in Sweden where the free choice of surrogates is prioritised, but this can occur only through the legalisation of altruistic surrogacy (Dousa 2019). Thus, pro-surrogacy writers argue that allowing altruistic surrogacy would reduce the demand for commercial surrogates abroad.

Anti-surrogacy Arguments

The anti-surrogacy side of the debate, however, remains sceptical of the contention that altruistic surrogacy would reduce the use of commercial surrogates. They argue that allowing altruistic surrogacy would increase a demand that could not be met within Sweden, resulting in more people travelling abroad for surrogacy arrangements. This trend is observable in other countries where altruistic surrogacy is permitted (Sjöberg 2023). The UK, for example, where altruistic surrogacy is legal, has not been able to ensure a reduction in British citizens using commercial surrogates. The UK has had too few domestic women willing to act as altruistic surrogates, leading to an overrepresentation of UK citizens among Europeans travelling abroad for commercial surrogacy arrangements (Kakabaveh 2018).

Similarly, in Australia, where altruistic surrogacy is allowed (Kirkman and Kirkman 1989) (with varying differences in technical rules between the six states and two territories), the use of commercial surrogates abroad has not decreased. The reasons appear to be a lack of suitable surrogates, a lengthy and complicated domestic process, and concerns that the surrogate might want to keep the child. The increase in the use of overseas commercial surrogates is attributed to altruistic surrogacy normalising the use of surrogates. If there are not enough women willing to be altruistic surrogates, individuals will instead opt for commercial surrogates abroad (Lindquist 2019). In the US, where altruistic surrogacy is permitted in certain states, it has become more accepted to travel to countries where commercial surrogacy is legal. This acceptance has arisen as a consequence of permitting altruistic surrogacy, as it implies that using others' bodies for personal needs is sometimes acceptable (Ohlsson 2016). In contrast to the pro-surrogacy side of the debate, the anti-surrogacy perspective argues that permitting altruistic surrogacy in Sweden would not decrease the use of commercial surrogates abroad; rather, this would increase it. These arguments show that altruistic surrogacy normalises the use of others' bodies solely as a means. If there are no willing altruistic surrogates in the vicinity, individuals will seek commercial surrogacy arrangements outside Sweden, perpetuating the exploitation of women.

A further argument is that allowing altruistic surrogacy is merely "an interim halt on the road to commercialisation" (Birgersson 2019). Birgersson argues that decision-makers will eventually realise it is unreasonable for surrogates not to be compensated for the significant risks of pregnancy. Additionally, they will recognise that it is unfair to restrict "having children" to childless couples with friends or family members willing to act as surrogates. Therefore, decision-makers will ultimately allow commercial surrogacy (Birgersson 2019).

A related viewpoint is that altruistic surrogacy should not be permitted because it risks "altruism" sliding pragmatically into surrogacy's commercial forms. Firstly, it is difficult to guarantee that no pressures or receipt of payments or gifts occur within the arrangements. Secondly, a certain form of financial compensation is often involved in altruistic surrogacy, such as reimbursement for lost wages or potential sickness leave due to pregnancy (Heiman and Rose 2016). According to the anti-surrogacy debate, there are tangible risks that altruistic surrogacy arrangements could transition to commercial forms, which in itself violates human dignity as women in commercial surrogacy arrangements are exploited. As a result, altruistic surrogacy risks infringing on human dignity (Kakabaveh 2018). For this reason, the anti-surrogacy side argues that altruistic surrogacy should not be permitted.

What Is Self-Determination?

Altruistic surrogacy brings to light ethical aspects of self-determination. The right to self-determination means that everyone has the right to make decisions about their life based on their own understanding of what constitutes a good life. This means that each individual has the right to live their life in accordance with their own values and desires. For example, each person has the right to decide if and when they want to have children. This is an example of how one exercises their self-determination (Smer 2013, 114). Human dignity is respected by allowing individuals to exercise their right to self-determination. Ronald Dworkin argues that individuals should be treated with respect and regarded as beings capable of forming their own views on how they wish to live their lives, making decisions based on those views (Nickel 1982). The right to self-determination means that individuals should have the ability to make independent decisions about their own lives without interference from others (Smer 2013, 114). This, together with Dworkin's view of self-determination, is used in this chapter to explore arguments on how altruistic surrogacy can either violate or strengthen the right to self-determination. The right to self-determination applies as long as it does not harm or violate someone else; however, it is only in exceptional cases that no other individual is affected by the decisions of others (Smer 2018, 39).

Furthermore, it is important to understand that our capacity for self-determination depends on our situation. There is a difference between the decision-making capacity of an adult and that of an elderly person with dementia. This means that our life situation determines our ability to express our values, opinions, or desires (Smer 2018, 38). To be able to exercise one's right to self-determination, informed consent is required. It is important that one is well-informed and understands the outcomes that follow certain decisions. Additionally, consent is meaningful or real only in the absence of coercion, and a person must not be in a dependent position where free and informed choice is an illusion. Informed consent is necessary for a person to make decisions independently and to morally defend their decision (Smer 2013, 116). Informed consent is therefore essential when discussing surrogacy. This is a crucial aspect when it comes to respecting a person's self-determination. Without informed consent, it is not possible to be self-determining, because if one has incorrect information, consent is not genuine.

Pro-surrogacy Arguments

The right to self-determination involves respecting individual choices and acknowledging personal responsibility. Recognising that people are responsible for their decisions is a way to affirm our distinct identities and decision-making abilities (Schachter 1983, 850). From the standpoint of self-determination, surrogacy-positive advocates argue that it is self-evident that women should have the option to decide if they want to be surrogate mothers to help others become parents (Wojciechowski 2023). Altruistic surrogacy is argued to be an important feminist issue because it concerns women's right to decide for themselves whether they want to be surrogates (Westerholm, Heimbrand och Nordquist 2021). The argument states that Swedish women wishing to be surrogate mothers are prevented from doing so by current Swedish legislation (Skanne 2018). Once again, the focus shifts to the problems with existing Swedish laws, this time positing that they limit the right to self-determination.

Dousa discusses allowing altruistic surrogacy and women's self-determination as follows:

> Sweden faces a crossroads: to protect women's right to decide over their own bodies or to take a path where someone other than the woman decides over her body (Dousa 2019).

This argument constructs the issue as if it is one of Sweden letting women decide over their own lives or letting others decide for them. It is seen as inconceivable that anyone other than ourselves should have the power to make decisions over our lives (Dousa 2019). The argument states that allowing altruistic surrogacy would strengthen women's right to self-determination because individuals have the right to make decisions about their lives based on their own understanding of what constitutes a good life (Smer 2013, 114). If an individual wants to be a surrogate mother, that person should have the right to choose that possibility. Allowing altruistic surrogacy thus defends women's right to choose for themselves, which is a fundamental right that should never be compromised (Dousa 2019).

An important part of the right to self-determination is that decisions must be made with informed consent and voluntarily. Arguments for allowing altruistic surrogacy include that as long as all parties involved in altruistic surrogacy arrangements act of their own free will, it harms no one and should be permitted. Allowing altruistic surrogacy is also understood to strengthen the belief in an individual's ability to make decisions about their own life (Fölster 2016). The surrogacy-positive side of the debate argues that allowing altruistic surrogacy strengthens individual self-determination based on the principle that each individual has the right to live their life in accordance with their own values and desires (Smer 2013, 114). They specifically argue that allowing altruistic surrogacy defends women's right to self-determination.

Anti-surrogacy Arguments

In contrast to surrogacy-positive writers, surrogacy-negative advocates argue that altruistic surrogacy may instead limit individual self-determination. It can be difficult for people to say no to childless friends or family members who ask them to be surrogate mothers, thus there is a high risk that a woman will be coerced into becoming a surrogate. The risk that women will be forced to be surrogates cannot, therefore, be ruled out (Inci 2016). If individuals are coerced into being surrogate mothers, it is not of their own free will, and thus the right to self-determination is not relevant, or indeed is contradicted. A complementary argument is that it cannot be proven whether bribes or gifts equivalent to financial compensation have taken place, which would mean that altruistic surrogacy shifts to being commercial (Sjöberg 2023). If individuals have been coerced or bribed into being surrogate mothers, there has been no informed consent, which is required to make independent decisions and morally defend them. The surrogacy-negative side of the debate argues that surrogacy limits women's right to self-determination if they are coerced or bribed into participating. Due to the risk that women could be forced into being surrogates, surrogacy-negative writers argue that it should not be allowed.

Pro-surrogacy Arguments

The surrogacy-positive side of the debate, however, argues that the view of surrogate mothers as coerced reflects a skewed perception of women as incapable of making their own decisions. Arguments against this view suggest that women, just as they can decide to donate organs or undergo transplants, can also decide if they want to be surrogate mothers. If the Swedish healthcare system believes that organ donors make their decisions without coercion, they should similarly believe that altruistic surrogate mothers make their decisions without coercion. Regarding the belief that women are coerced into being surrogate mothers, surrogacy-positive advocates argue that this reflects a view of women as incapable of assessing what is best for themselves (Schottenius 2019). Our right to self-determination means that each individual has the right to live their life in accordance with their own values and desires, which should mean that those who want to be surrogate mothers should be allowed to do so as long as no one is harmed (Smer 2013, 114).

A ban on altruistic surrogacy reflects a negative view of women, seeing them as incapable of making decisions they deem best for themselves. Allowing altruistic surrogacy thus strengthens the belief in women's self-determination.

What is Self-Ownership?

The concept of self-ownership is similar to the right to self-determination in many ways. Self-ownership primarily comes from Robert Nozick's book *Anarchy, State, and Utopia* (2001) and is fundamentally a libertarian idea asserting that individuals have an inherent right to decide over their own bodies. The right to self-ownership posits that a person's skin, teeth, hair, and so on constitute a moral boundary that cannot be crossed without consent, akin to bodily integrity, implying that we, as individuals, have an invisible sphere that others have no right to interfere with or approach. Nozick explains that individuals have a complete and unique right to control and have power over themselves. The right to self-ownership dictates that others should never interfere with what another person chooses to do with their body, the exception being the protection of self-ownership—that is, one may exercise their right to self-ownership as long as ownership encompasses both the right to self-determination and bodily integrity (Marceta 2022, 19). According to Martha Nussbaum, respect for bodily boundaries, freedom of movement, and reproductive choices are integral to bodily integrity. Nussbaum's idea is based on the simple notion that the individual who controls their own body should be the only one making decisions regarding it—essentially, that one possesses self-ownership (Patosalmi 2009, 125–126).

Anti-surrogacy Arguments

Individuals have an inherent right to decide over their own bodies, meaning that others should never interfere with what someone else chooses to do with their body (Marceta 2022, 19). Arguments surround the issue of how self-ownership can either be violated or strengthened through altruistic surrogacy. Those opposed to surrogacy propose that allowing altruistic surrogacy promotes a misleading notion that it is acceptable for others to control someone else's body (Inci 2016). In one argument from the anti-surrogacy side, surrogacy is compared to prostitution in that both provide access to women's bodies (Winberg 2016). This perspective maintains that women's bodies are not meant to satisfy others' needs and that it is unacceptable to use other women's body to fulfil one's own desire for children (Inci 2016). Altruistic surrogacy should not be permitted because it risks establishing a norm that women's bodies and reproductive organs are available for others to use. Allowing altruistic surrogacy runs directly contrary to ensuring women retain their self-ownership (Kakabaveh 2018). From the debate, it can be interpreted that permitting altruistic surrogacy restricts women's self-ownership by normalising the use of women's bodies and reproductive organs for others' needs.

Pro-surrogacy Arguments

The pro-surrogacy side argues that a ban on altruistic surrogacy is a prohibition on women exercising their full autonomy. They argue that women in Sweden do not have the opportunity to decide to carry someone else's child even if they want to, but every woman should have the right and the opportunity to decide what she wants to do with her body (Dousa 2019). Further arguments suggest that Sweden should not prevent women from exercising their full bodily rights but should instead lead in promoting women's choices and strengthening women's self-ownership over their bodies (Dousa 2019). The government should never hinder individuals from having control and decision-making power over themselves (Fölster 2016). A ban on altruistic surrogacy is seen as a way of depriving women of their self-ownership, given that every individual has a right to their own body and to make decisions about it. Arguments advanced in this vein contend that since individuals have an inherent right to decide over their own bodies, women who want to be surrogate mothers should have the opportunity to do so.

Additional arguments draw parallels between surrogacy and abortion. An example of such an argument is that the contemporary struggle for surrogacy rights is reminiscent of the struggle to strengthen abortion rights during the 1970s (Westerholm et al. 2021). Another argument highlights that the opposition to altruistic surrogacy mirrors the opposition to abortion and contraceptives (Douhane 2023). The debate about allowing altruistic surrogacy shares many similarities with the abortion issue, considering that when abortion was illegal in Sweden, Swedish women had to travel abroad to have abortions and, similarly, those wanting to have children through surrogacy must travel abroad to achieve their goal (Skanne 2018). The argument that abortions will continue to occur even if they are banned is also relevant to the surrogacy debate, indicating that people will continue to enter surrogacy arrangements even if they are prohibited. Pro-surrogacy advocates argue that those who support abortion rights based on women's self-ownership should, logically, also support surrogacy (Karlsson 2019). Based on our self-ownership, individuals who want to be surrogate mothers should be allowed to be so, just as individuals who want to have an abortion are allowed to do so.

Anti-surrogacy Arguments

The anti-surrogacy side of the debate also addresses the abortion issue but argues that altruistic surrogacy is incompatible with women's self-ownership and reproductive rights. An example of such an argument is that the right to abortion vanishes when surrogate mothers carry someone else's child (Westerstrand 2018). What happens if the intended parents no longer want the child and ask the surrogate mother to have an abortion, despite her not wanting to? Is the surrogate mother bound to comply with the intended parents' request, or does she have the free will to decide over her body and not undergo the abortion (Birgersson 2019)? What if she decides she cannot go ahead with the birth, deciding on a legal abortion: is she precluded from exercising that right because the intended parents say "no"? Since it always involves an agreement between the intended parents and the surrogate mother, the surrogate mother contracts away her rights to her own body, as well as the care of the child after birth (Inci 2016).

Discussion of the Arguments

A positive perception of altruistic surrogacy is that it would enable more childless people to have children. This is particularly relevant for homosexual men, who currently can have biological children only through surrogacy, as the number of adoptions has decreased and homosexual men are banned from adopting from certain countries due to homophobia. Allowing altruistic surrogacy thus promotes equal treatment, which is part of the respect for human dignity, stating that individuals should be treated with equal consideration and respect. Permitting altruistic surrogacy would ensure that LGBTQI individuals, a marginalised group, are not discriminated against. This argument is well-formulated considering Sweden's commitment to preventing discrimination based on specific characteristics such as sexual orientation. Achieving non-discrimination means that individuals should not be deprived of their rights due to their sexuality. However, there is no right to have children, and heterosexual individuals who cannot have children naturally would also be prevented from using surrogates if a ban on surrogacy were imposed. Moreover, it appears that the majority of those currently acquiring children through surrogacy are heterosexual couples. Consequently, a ban would not target a specific group such as homosexual men. Thus, this argument for allowing altruistic surrogacy is not particularly strong.

Today, Swedish childless couples travel abroad to engage in commercial surrogacy arrangements because they have no other options in Sweden. Hence, current Swedish legislation perpetuates the commercial surrogacy trade, contributing to an exploitative industry where poor women are both vulnerable and targeted. Therefore, allowing altruistic surrogacy would enable people to enter surrogacy arrangements within Sweden. By permitting altruistic surrogacy, people would no longer need to use commercial surrogates abroad as there would be safer and better options available in Sweden. The argument advanced is that there are good reasons to believe that allowing altruistic surrogacy would lead to a reduction in the exploitation of women in commercial surrogacy arrangements. If altruistic surrogacy were allowed in Sweden, the Swedish companies that facilitate connections between commercial surrogates and commissioning couples would diminish or be outcompeted. The result of allowing altruistic surrogacy would thus be a decrease in the use of commercial surrogates, leading to fewer women being exploited abroad. Therefore, altruistic surrogacy can be seen as positive from a human dignity perspective as it contributes to fewer people using commercial surrogates.

While this may appear compelling, the opposing arguments demonstrate that it lacks validity. There are several negative perceptions of what allowing altruistic surrogacy would entail. Contrary to what pro-surrogacy writers have argued, allowing altruistic surrogacy risks increased use of commercial surrogates. Examples from the UK, Australia, and the US show that people continue to travel abroad to use commercial surrogates despite altruistic surrogacy being allowed in their home country. Principally the reasons are that people do not have sufficient individuals in their vicinity willing to be surrogates. For altruistic surrogacy to be effective, a balance of supply and demand is required, with demand often exceeding supply, which drives individuals to seek surrogates abroad. This makes altruistic surrogacy comparable to a market. It shows that allowing altruistic surrogacy does not decrease the use of commercial surrogates. Allowing altruistic surrogacy seems to normalise rather than reduce it.

This reasoning is well-founded because it is reasonable to say that not everyone has people in their vicinity who want to be altruistic surrogates. It is likely more probable that fewer people in one's vicinity are interested in being surrogates than those who are not. Pregnancy is not as simple as pro-surrogacy writers sometimes make it seem. Even though maternal mortality in Sweden is not high, pregnancy always carries risks, and women in Sweden do die during childbirth (RFSU 2022). Currently, it is also possible for Swedes to enter into altruistic surrogacy arrangements by travelling to countries where it is allowed and getting support from fertility clinics. Therefore, the possibility for Swedes to use altruistic surrogates already exists and its legalisation is not essential. Likely, people would prefer to use an altruistic surrogate they know and who lives in Sweden. Nevertheless, Swedish couples choose to use commercial surrogates despite altruistic surrogacy arguably being possible for Swedes by their going overseas. Therefore, the pro-surrogacy argument that allowing altruistic surrogacy would reduce the use of commercial surrogates falls apart.

Commercial surrogacy has been established as a form of human trafficking and involves the exploitation of women. If altruistic surrogacy leads to more people using commercial surrogates, implementing it would be reprehensible as it would mean that Sweden contributes to the exploitation of poor women abroad. It seems reasonable to assume that allowing altruistic surrogacy normalises the use of other people's bodies for one's needs, thereby increasing the use of commercial surrogates. This results in a violation of human dignity, as it means using others merely as a means to achieve one's goals.

The right to self-determination and the right to self-ownership are similar in many respects. Each concerns an individual's right to make decisions about themselves. Allowing altruistic surrogacy is projected as promoting and benefiting both women's right to self-determination and to self-ownership. The contention is that women should have the right to decide if they want to be surrogates as long as it is done willingly and without harm to others. Due to our self-ownership, individuals have a clear right to do what they want with their own bodies, which should reasonably include allowing women who want to use their bodies to help others become parents to do so. This perspective sees altruistic surrogacy as a factor strengthening our self-ownership through enabling women to make decisions about their bodies as they wish.

Similarities between the abortion issue and surrogacy are identified in that a ban on both restricts women's bodily self-ownership. The contention is that just as Swedish women previously had to travel abroad to undergo abortions, people today need to travel abroad to enter surrogacy arrangements. The similarity between the struggle for abortion rights and the struggle for surrogacy rights is advanced by Kutte Jönsson in *Det förbjudna mödraskapet* (*The forbidden motherhood* 2003), where he explains that the fight for abortion led by feminists and the women's movement has largely been about the right to make decisions about one's own body. Here, Jönsson argues that the right to self-ownership can equally mean the right to reproduction, that is, the right to freely choose if one wants to be a surrogate (Jönsson 2003, 180).

Arguments that allowing altruistic surrogacy increases women's right to self-determination and self-ownership are strong. However, as pointed out, the opportunity for Swedish women to be altruistic surrogates already exists. It is forbidden to arrange surrogacy within Sweden, but the law says nothing about arranging surrogacy abroad. Thus, those who want to be altruistic surrogates for a friend or family member can get help from foreign fertility clinics with embryo transfer or insemination (Canoilas 2020). Therefore, allowing altruistic surrogacy in Sweden is not crucial for women's self-determination or self-ownership since the opportunity to be an altruistic surrogate as a Swede exists.

This has not been raised by either the pro-surrogacy or anti-surrogacy sides in the articles considered in writing this chapter, but my assessment is that the argument that altruistic surrogacy strengthens women's self-determination and self-ownership is not strong enough to justify allowing it.

The desire to use women's bodies as a resource for one's own goals is also problematic. Altruistic surrogacy promotes a view of women's bodies as something to rent or control. Allowing altruistic surrogacy fosters a perception of the female body as merely a vessel for carrying children. With this view, the surrogate is reduced to the role of the child's carrier and creator only. This is confirmed in Johanna Gondouin's study of the Swedish documentary series "Barn till varje pris?" ("Children at all costs"), where she describes how the surrogate's emotions are disregarded in the series, making it more difficult for viewers to identify with her and to see her with understanding and compassion. This creates and compounds an image of the surrogate as merely a vessel (Gondouin 2014, 126).

Allowing altruistic surrogacy risks establishing a norm that says women's bodies and reproductive organs are for others to use. Allowing altruistic surrogacy also conveys an outdated patriarchal idea of women as eternally benevolent, placing others' desires, wants and needs above their own. This is reflected by Sharyn Roach Anleu in her study "Reinforcing Gender Norms: Commercial and Altruistic Surrogacy". Anleu posits that altruistic surrogacy contributes to maintaining female gender norms. Gender norms create a distinction between altruistic and commercial surrogacy, with the former being more accepted. Typically, altruistic surrogates are honoured, while commercial surrogates are demeaned (Anleu 1990, 64). Anleu argues that a ban on commercial surrogacy reflects gender norms that view pregnancy and motherhood as inherently (unpaid and self-negating) female roles, and that decrees it as unnatural if a woman relinquishes a child she has carried. Furthermore, becoming a surrogate for financial reasons is perceived as selfishly money-orientated and contrary to traditional female gender norms, whereas being a surrogate for altruistic reasons aligns with gender norms of female selflessness and sacrifice (Anleu 1990, 71–72).

As noted, there are perceptions that altruistic surrogacy risks sliding into commercial forms if the intended parents choose to give financial compensation in the form of payments or gifts to the altruistic surrogate. Commercial surrogacy is unlikely to be permitted in Sweden. If the allowance of altruistic surrogacy poses a risk of transitioning into commercial practices, this provides compelling reasons to refrain from permitting it. Regarding altruistic surrogacy arrangements, an overwhelming risk exists of individuals being coerced into becoming surrogates. Where altruistic surrogacy arrangements occur between friends or family members, it can be difficult to say no to a close relative. This is corroborated by the findings in Anleu's empirical study, where she claims that there is a risk that women enter into altruistic surrogacy arrangements due to pressure or guilt imposed by family members, consistent with what the anti-surrogacy side of the debate argues. Anleu has found that because of this, altruistic surrogacy arrangements can be more exploitative than commercial agreements (Anleu 1990, 72). If a person is coerced or bribed into being a surrogate, there is no informed consent, a crucial requirement for self-determination. The arguments raise a question about whose right to self-determination holds the greatest weight. Should the risk that some are coerced into being surrogates prevent those who genuinely want to be surrogates?

When surrogates are pregnant, their self-ownership is restricted: for example, their right to abortion may be compromised. Uncertainties arise regarding the rights and limitations faced by a surrogate, which could potentially undermine her self-ownership. If she is not permitted to have an abortion or is forced to undergo one because the intended parents no longer wish to keep the child, her self-ownership is emasculated. It seems reasonable to assume that when a woman is a surrogate for a friend or family member, it may be even more difficult for her to consider abortion due to the close relationship with the intended parents and their expectation that she will carry their child to term. It is almost as if the intended parents exert a form of control over the surrogate's body, thereby limiting her autonomy. In surrogacy arrangements, especially commercial ones but also those deemed altruistic, the surrogate is bound by a contract. Signing this contract may tie her to certain conditions, such as if she were to seek an abortion, it is not her own child she is aborting. Jönsson's dissertation indicates that this awareness might cause a surrogate to complete the pregnancy against her will if she had originally wished to have an abortion (Jönsson 2003, 179). Thus, altruistic surrogacy may be perceived as limiting individuals' self-ownership to the extent that surrogates are either reluctant to seek an abortion or are forced to do so against their will.

Conclusion

What emerges from the analysis and discussion is that both sides of the debate find the current Swedish legislation, which neither permits nor prohibits surrogacy, problematic. However, the emerging conclusion is that it would not be advantageous for Sweden to permit altruistic surrogacy. This conclusion is drawn primarily because altruistic surrogacy risks causing more harm than good. Several arguments suggest that altruistic surrogacy would lead to positive changes, such as increasing women's self-determination and self-ownership, but Swedish women already have the opportunity to be altruistic surrogate mothers if they travel abroad. This means that allowing altruistic surrogacy in Sweden would not significantly enhance women's self-determination and self-ownership.

Although it is undoubtedly a more complicated process to travel abroad to fertility clinics for embryo implantation or insemination, after that, one can return to Sweden, where Swedish maternity care takes over, and the child can be born in Sweden. Altruistic surrogacy can be carried out by Swedes, yet people still choose to use commercial surrogate mothers, making it uncertain that permitting altruistic surrogacy would reduce the use of commercial surrogate mothers. Examples from other countries have also shown that allowing altruistic surrogacy has increased the use of commercial surrogate mothers. The practice, therefore, seems to normalise a view of the female body merely as a means to achieve others' goals. It is more important to ensure that women's bodies are not seen as a resource or a tool than for people to have children through surrogacy. The risk that women could be coerced or bribed into being surrogate mothers makes it hazardous to allow altruistic surrogacy, a practice that risks becoming commercialised. If childless individuals, regardless of sexual orientation, whether couples or single, should have their desire for children fulfilled, then whether this should be through the allowance of altruistic surrogacy in Sweden remains questionable.

Bibliography

Articles (Print Media)

Andersson, A Daniel (2023) "Det är en ideologisk fråga—inte homofobi", *Expressen*. 13 February, https://www.expressen.se/debatt/det-ar-en-ideologisk--fraga-inte-homofobi/ (accessed 22 March 2024).

Bergström, K (2023). "Lika självklart som att få hjälp vid fysisk smärta", *Svenska Dagbladet*. 11 May, https://www.svd.se/a/P4axm5/surrogatmamma-i-ukraina-gav-svenska-paret-en-son-fantastiskt (accessed 22 March 2024).

Birgersson, Sussana (2019). "Ska staten tvinga unga kvinnor att göra abort?" *Expressen*. 28 July, https://www.expressen.se/ledare/susanna-birgersson/ska-staten-tvinga-unga-kvinnor-att-gora-abort/ (accessed 21 March 2024).

Canoilas, V (2020). "Linnea födde sin brors och svägerskas barn", *Dagens Nyheter*. 19 February, https://www.dn.se/nyheter/sverige/linnea-fodde-sin-brors-och-svagerskas-barn/ (accessed 21 March 2024).

Douhane, P (2023). "Gör surrogatvärdskap lagligt i Sverige i stället", *Aftonbladet*. 26 April, https://www.aftonbladet.se/debatt/a/q17bag/m-c-och-l-politiker-gor-surrogatvardskap-lagligt (accessed 22 March 2024).

Dousa, B (2019). "Muf: Inskränk inte kvinnans rätt till sin kropp", *Svenska Dagbladet*. 13 October, https://www.svd.se/a/kJ1enX/muf-inskrank-inte-kvinnans-ratt-till-sin-kropp (accessed 21 March 2024).

Ekelund Nachman, A (2016). "Cyniskt av feminister säga nej till surrogatmammor", *Dagens Samhälle*. 9 March, https://www.dagenssamhalle.se/opinion/gastkronika/cyniskt-av-feminister-saga-nej-till-surrogatmammor/ (accessed 21 March 2024).

Ekis Ekman, K (2019). "Surrogatmamman säljer hela sitt liv", *Aftonbladet*. 29 May, https://www.aftonbladet.se/kultur/a/70BeBo/surrogatmamman-saljer-hela-sitt-liv (accessed 21 March 2024).

Engberg, CO (2023). "Värdgraviditeter bör tillåtas i Sverige", *Svenska Dagbladet*. 24 March, https://www.svd.se/a/9zx689/vardgraviditeter-bor-tillatas-i-sverige-skriver-hbt-liberaler (accessed 21 21 March 2024).
Fölster, S (2016). "Vänd inte de ofrivilligt barnlösa ryggen till", *Dagens Samhälle*. 24 March, https://www.dagenssamhalle.se/styrning-och-beslut/demokrati/vand-inte-de-ofrivilligt-barnlosa-ryggen-till/ (accessed 20 March 2024).
Heiman, I and Rose, N (2016). "Surrogatmödraskap måste förbjudas även utomlands", *Göteborgs-Posten*. 2 July, https://www.gp.se/debatt/surrogatmodraskap-maste-forbjudas-aven-utomlands.7083aab9-e5ce-4006-91f9-928e36fcf2ea (accessed 2 March 2024).
Inci, Z (2016). "Kvinnors kroppar är inte till för att tillfredsställa andras behov", *Sydsvenskan*. 12 January, https://www.roks.se/nyheter/debatt-kvinnors-kroppar-ar-inte-till-att-tillfredsstalla-andras-behov (accessed 19 March 2024).
Kakabaveh, A (2018). "Surrogatmödraskap öppnar för utnyttjande", *Svenska Dagbladet*. 28 November, https://www.svd.se/a/J1e5rm/surrogatmodraskap-oppnar-for-utnyttjande (accessed 22 March 2024).
Karlsson, N (2019). "Släpp makten över kvinnors livmödrar, regeringen", *Dagens Samhälle*. 1 March, https://www.dagenssamhalle.se/opinion/gastkronika/slapp-makten-over-kvinnors-livmodrar-regeringen/ (accessed 20 March 2025).
Lindquist, K (2019). "Surrogatfrågan handlar om att underkasta människan en marknadslogik", *Dagens Nyheter*. 30 June, https://www.dn.se/kultur-noje/kulturdebatt/kristina-lindquist-surrogatfragan-handlar-om-att-underkasta-manniskan-en-marknadslogik/ (accessed 21 March 2024).
Nilsson, K (2023). "S inleder offensive—mot regnbågsfamiljer", *Expressen*. 6 February, https://www.expressen.se/debatt/s-inleder-offensiv-mot-regnbagsfamiljer/ (accessed 19 March 2024).
Ohlsson, C (2016). "Därför säger vi kraftfullt nej till surrogatmödraskap", *SVT Nyheter*. 15 February, https://www.svt.se/opinion/vi-sager-kraftfullt-nej-till-surrogatmodraskap (accessed 20 March 2024).
Ohlsson, C (2021). "Gör inte kvinnor och barn till varor", *Svenska Dagbladet*. 22 June, https://www.svd.se/a/qAGole/gor-inte-kvinnor-och-barn-till-varor (accessed 20 March 2024).
Rollén, B and Wikman, Olin Wikman (2019). "Schottenius förenklar en fråga med djupa etiska dimensioner", *Dagens Nyheter*. 27 May, https://www.dn.se/kultur-noje/schottenius-forenklar-en-fraga-med-djupa-etiska-dimensioner-skriver-berit-rollen-och-monika-olin/ (accessed 22 March 2024).

Samuelsson, S (2023). "Surrogatmödraskap är ingen hbtqi-fråga", *Göteborgs-Posten*. 11 February, https://www.gp.se/kultur/kulturdebatt/surrogatmodraskap-ar-ingen-hbtqi-fraga.1a8a7214-32c3-4c8e-80ad-ca4c6f93d72b (accessed 20 March 2024).
Schottenius, M (2019). "Jag provoceras av beskäftigheter som det är ingen mänsklig rättighet att få barn", *Dagens Nyheter*. 20 May, https://www.dn.se/kultur-noje/maria-schottenius-jag-provoceras-av-beskaftigheter-som-det-ar-ingen-mansklig-rattighet-att-fa-barn/ (accessed 20 March 2024).
Sjöberg, S (2023). "En legalisering löser inte surrogathandeln", *Aftonbladet*. 3 May, https://www.aftonbladet.se/debatt/a/Xbevpb/en-legalisering-loser-intesurrogathandeln (accessed 20 March 2024).
Svensson, M (2019). "Säg ja till surrogatmödraskap", *Dagens Nyheter*. 29 July, https://www.dn.se/ledare/mattias-svensson-sag-ja-till-surrogatmodraskap/ (accessed 20 March 2024).
Skanne, H (2018). "Kakabavehs motion baserad på fördomar", *Svenska Dagbladet*. 21 November, https://www.svd.se/a/oROBKR/kakabavehs-motion-baserad-pa-fordomar (accessed 22 March 2024).
Westerholm, B (2016). "Oacceptabelt att säga surrogatbarn", *Dagens Samhälle*. 25 February, https://www.dagenssamhalle.se/styrning-och-beslut/demokrati/oacceptabelt-att-saga-surrogatbarn/ (accessed 19 March 2024).
Westerholm, B, Heimbrand, C and Nordquist, L (2021). "Det handlar om kvinnans rätt att välja", *Svenska Dagbladet*. 23 June, https://www.svd.se/a/2dLWQr/det-handlar-om-kvinnans-ratt-att-valja (accessed 19 March 2024).
Wilhelmson, A (2021). "Politikerna splittrade i frågan om surrogatmödraskap", *Dagens Nyheter*. 12 June, https://www.dn.se/insidan/politikerna-splittrade-i-fragan-om-surrogatmodraskap/ (accessed 26 March 2024).
Wilhelmson, A (2021). "Politikerna splittrade i frågan om surrogatmödraskap", *Dagens Nyheter*. 12 June, https://www.dn.se/insidan/politikerna-splittrade-i-fragan-om-surrogatmodraskap/ (accessed 26 March 2024).
Winberg, M. (2016). "Krav: Förbjud alla former av surrogatarrangemang", *Dagens Samhälle*. 12 July, https://www.dagenssamhalle.se/styrning-och-beslut/demokrati/krav-forbjud-alla-former-av-surrogatarrangemang/ (accessed 21 March 2024).
Wojciechowski, A (2023). "Vi är hänvisade till andra länders lagar", *Svenska Dagbladet*. 27 March, https://www.svd.se/a/4oxGo6/vi-ar-hanvisade-till-andra-landers-lagar-skriver-debattorer (accessed 20 March 2024).

Articles (Journals) and Book Chapters

Anleu, SLR (1990) "Reinforcing gender norms: Commercial and altruistic surrogacy", *Acta Sociologica*, 33(1), 63–74.

Baker, B (1996). "A Case for Permitting Altruistic Surrogacy", *Hypatia* 11 (2): 34–48.

Beyleveld, D and Brownsword, R (1998). "Human Dignity, Human Rights, and Human Genetics", *Modern Law Review.* vol. 61, no 5. https://doi.org/10.1111/1468-2230.00172.

Gondouin, J (2015). "Gay Fathers, Surrogate Mothers and the Question of the Human: A Postcolonial Feminist Analysis of Emotions", *Barn till varje pris?. Föreningen Lambda Nordica.* vol. 19, nr 3–4, 109–139.

McManus, Matt, "Immanuel Kant—Kant's Theory of Human Dignity", *Philosophy Now*, 2022, Kant's Theory of Human Dignity | Issue 150 | Philosophy Now, https://philosophynow.org/issues/150/Kants_Theory_of_Human_Dignity (accessed 8 November 2024).

Marceta, Ahlin, J (2022). "Does Libertarian Self-Ownership Protect Freedom?" *De Ethica* 7.1:19–30. https://doi.org/10.3384/de-ethica.2001-8819.227119.

Nickel, WJ (1982). "Equal Respect and Human Rights", *Human Rights Quarterly* 4(1):76 https://doi.org/10.2307/761991.

Norstedts Juridik (2022). *Surrogatmoderskap—ett rättsligt dilemma och "haltande föräldrarskap"*, https://www.nj.se/nyheter/surrogatmoderskap-ett-rattsligt-dilemma-och-haltande-foraldraskap (accessed 25 February 2024).

Patosalmi, M (2009). "Bodily Integrity and Conceptions of Subjectivity", *Hypatia* vol 24, no 2 (Spring, 2009), 125–141.

"Riksförbundet för sexuell upplysning (RFSU) (2022). *Mödradödlighet i världen*, https://www.rfsu.se/vad-vi-gor/nara-dig/barnvagnsmarschen/modradodlighet-i-varlden/ (29 April 2024).

Schachter, O (1983). "Human Dignity as a Normative Concept", *American Journal of International Law.* vol 77, no 4 (October 1983), 848–854.

Books and Reports

Donnelly, J, *Universal Human Rights in Theory and Practice*, 3rd edn, Cornell University Press, Ithaca, NYC, NY, US, 2013.

Kirkman, Maggie and Kirkman, Linda, *My Sister's Child—A Story of Full Surrogate Motherhood Between Two Sisters Using in Vitro Fertilisation,* Penguin, Melbourne, Australia, 1989.

Nozick, Robert, *Anarchy State and Utopia,* John Wiley & Sons, NYC, NY, US, 2001.

Saldeen, Å, *Barn- och föräldrarätt,* 7. uppl., Iustus Forlag, Uppsala, Sweden, 2013.

Statens offentliga utredningar (SOU)(Swedish Government Official Report) (2016) 2016:11, 373, Olika vägar till föräldraskap—Regeringen.se, https://www.regeringen.se/rattsliga-dokument/statens-offentliga-utredningar/2016/02/sou-201611/ (accessed 8 November 2024).

Statens medicinsk-etiska råd (Smer) (Swedish National Council on Medical Ethics) (2018). *Etik - en introduktion.* 4 uppl. Elanders Sverige ab.

Statens medicinsk-etiska råd (Smer) (Swedish National Council on Medical Ethics) (2013). *Assisterad befruktning—etiska aspekter,* Assisterad befruktning—etiska aspekter, https://smer.se/wp-content/uploads/2013/02/Smer_rapport_2013_1_webb.pdf (accessed 2 March 2025).

Information Resources and Documents

Jönsson, K (2003). *Det förbjudna mödraskapet: en moralfilosofisk undersökning av surrogatmödraskap.* Diss. Lund: Univ., Sweden, 2003.

10

The Prostitution System as the Wreckage of Women's Autonomy: Revising Sexual Assault Law to Undermine Structural Coercion

Simone Watson and Helen Pringle

Introduction

This chapter first took shape in 2023 as a submission to an Australian commonwealth government inquiry into consent in sexual assault laws.[1] The committee terms of reference were animated by sympathy for models of "affirmative consent", driven by concern about the ubiquity of sexual violation of women alongside low rates of reporting, arrest, prosecution and conviction. However, the committee contemplated a

[1] Parts of this chapter have been presented previously in submissions to the Senate Inquiry into Current and Proposed Sexual Consent Laws in Australia 2023; Queensland Parliament Inquiry on the Criminal Code (Decriminalising Sex Work) and Other Legislation Amendment Bill 2024; New South Wales (NSW) Legislative Council Inquiry into the Equality Legislation Amendment (LGBTIQA+) Bill 2024); in papers to the 2023 Australian Political Science Association (APSA) Annual Conference, the 2023 FiLiA (formerly, Feminism in London) conference and is referenced Alsalem (2025, fn 92). In all our work together, we acknowledge that we live and work on unceded land and, in particular, we acknowledge the wrongs and sorrows of a long history of sexual violence and exploitation of Indigenous women that scars this land but is yet to be fully and truthfully understood as part of genocide in Australia.

S. Watson (✉)
Perth, WA, Australia
e-mail: simonewatson3@gmail.com

J. A. Scutt (ed.), *Women, Power and Autonomy*,
https://doi.org/10.1007/978-3-031-97958-3_10

narrowly confined examination of consent in terms of general provisions of criminal law and policy. From our perspective, such a focus leaves behind those women who are most at risk of systemic sexual assault, and who are most in danger of their wrong being ignored, together with their injuries (and, in many cases, even mocked). A comprehensive and systematic rethinking of sexual assault legislation in terms of human rights principles—autonomy, dignity and anti-discrimination—must explicitly address the question of consent and coercion in the prostitution system. This area was not raised as a specific concern in the terms of reference of the 2023 Australian inquiry (Senate Inquiry 2023), and the majority of submissions to the committee did not even make note of the prostitution system at all. A similar lack of consideration of the connection between prostitution and sexual assault laws marks academic literature.[2] Academic and popular literature do regularly take up at a very general level the question of whether consent is present in prostitution, but there is little that insists on the importance of sustained and rigorous attention to prostitution in laws that address sexual assault as a criminal matter.

A striking example of such absence of reference to prostitution in terms of rape law is the 2021 report to the Human Rights Council by Dubravka Šimonović,[3] who was at that time UN Special Rapporteur on Violence against Women, its Causes and Consequences. The report was entitled *Rape as a Grave, Systematic and Widespread Human Rights Violation, a Crime and a Manifestation of Gender-based Violence against Women and Girls, and its Prevention* (Šimonović 2021a). The Special Rapporteur

H. Pringle
School of Social Sciences, University of New South Wales, Sydney, NSW, Australia
e-mail: h.pringle@unsw.edu.au

[2] For exceptions, see for example, Bacik 2020; Bacik 2021; Farley 2018; also Chatterjee 2021; Buggs and Hoppe 2023. An earlier project addressing prostitution in relation to rape more broadly is Cotton et al. 2002.

[3] For further information on the office of "Special Rapporteurs" see United Nations, Special Procedures of the Human Rights Council, https://www.ohchr.org/en/special-procedures-human-rights-council (accessed 13 January 2025), and for a more expansive examination, Nolan et al. (2017).

provided an addendum to her report, entitled *A Framework for Legislation on Rape (Model Rape Law)* (Šimonović 2021b), the purpose of which was set out in these terms:

> The Model Rape Law provides States and other stakeholders with a tool for implementing international standards on rape, as established under international human rights law, international humanitarian law and international criminal law, including as interpreted in the jurisprudence of relevant tribunals and soft law produced by expert mechanisms. These standards are presented in the report of the Special Rapporteur on violence against women on rape as a human rights violation and a manifestation of gender-based violence against women (A/HRC/47/26), and are applicable both in times of peace and during conflict (Šimonović 2021b, 3).

At no point in this projection of a model law on sexual assault did the sSpecial rapporteur make mention of the specific problems of the prostitution industry in regard to sexual assault law—or of the specific problems of sexual assault law in addressing prostitution. Our argument attempts to fill those gaps. At the centre of our argument is a proposal for revision of sexual assault law/s based on an understanding of the prostitution industry *as* systemic coercion, in which we draw out what needs to follow in how law responds to claims of sexual violation. Our perspective also envisages such legal changes as steps towards the *abolition* of the prostitution system, not solely as ameliorative measures for women and girls already damaged by living in that system.

In this chapter, we focus on principles that should underlie legal provisions on sexual assault. Our central recommendation is that we take seriously the necessity of *explicitly* including prostitution in any consideration of the framework of sexual assault laws. This would involve understanding the prostitution system within a human rights framework, as a form of gender inequality, of violence and coercion against women in particular, and of sexual exploitation.[4] On this basis, our specific recommendations in this chapter are twofold:

1. An explicit clarification in all legal statements on sexual assault that a person accused of sexual assault or rape[5] cannot rely on a consent achieved by payment of a monetary sum, or in the course of a commercial transaction, as a defence; and
2. An explicit legal formulation of a civil action for sexual assault committed in the context of the prostitution system and associated forms of exploitation, whether involving direct commission or complicity in the act. This second proposal for civil action takes as its model the Illinois Predator Accountability Act 2005 (Ill), now entitled the Trafficking Victims Protection Act, passed in 2018, coming into effect 1 January 2019.[6]

We also urge any considerations of such legal changes to invite and hear testimony and evidence from survivors of the prostitution system as preparatory to reform, indeed as a matter of signal importance to all deliberations on consent and sexual assault.

---

[4] Our approach is similar to that of the current (as of 2025) Special Rapporteur on Violence against Women, its Causes and Consequences, Reem Alsalem, as set out in her report (Alsalem 2024). This approach is also known as the Nordic or Equality Model, and is perhaps best exemplified in the French Loi n° 2016–444 du 13 avril 2016, *visant à renforcer la lutte contre le système prostitutionnel et à accompagner les personnes prostituées*, https://www.legifrance.gouv.fr/jorf/id/JORFTEXT000032396046 (accessed 13 January 2025) (Pringle 2016).

[5] We prefer to use the term "sexual assault" here because it catches a wider range of sexual violation than penile penetration, an over-narrow stipulation that figures in many conventional and some legal understandings of the term "rape", as in English common and statute law for example.

[6] Illinois General Assembly, 740 ILCS 128/ Trafficking Victims Protection Act [formerly, Predator Accountability Act], http://www.ilga.gov/legislation/ilcs/ilcs3.asp?ActID=2812&ChapterID=57 (accessed 13 January 2025). Please see other references to this Act noted below.

Background to Problems of Consent and Autonomy in Sexual Assault Law

The argument here is made with primary reference to Australia, although it is advanced in the hope that what we say might be useful as a model in considering sexual assault laws elsewhere. In particular, we refer to recent (2022) changes made to sexual assault provisions in the *Crimes Act* 1900 of the Australian state of New South Wales (NSW).[7] The impetus to the enactment of these changes came from the process and aftermath of the 2017 acquittal of a young man accused of the anal rape of a young woman in Sydney in 2013.[8] The 2022 reform emerged after a familiar procedure of reports and consultations together with invited public submissions, with the final draft of the law designed to put in place some form of "affirmative consent" as a governing principle.

We refer to the NSW reforms because we find much that is worthy of wider implementation in these changes as they stand. However, we argue for a further shift in the legislative *framing* of these and similar provisions, so as to bring their interpretation into line with an overarching definition of sexual assault as **a violation of a sexual nature under circumstances of threat or use of force, fraud, coercion, abduction, or of the abuse of power, trust, or a position of dependency or vulnerability**. This definition is adapted from a proposal by Catharine MacKinnon (2016, 469–470), who draws on the language and reasoning of international law on sexual assault developed in the International Criminal Tribunal for the Former Yugoslavia, the International Criminal Tribunal for Rwanda, and the International Criminal Court (ICC), as well as on the language of the Protocol to Prevent, Suppress and Punish Trafficking in Persons, Especially Women and Children [Palermo Protocol] (UN General Assembly 2000).

---

[7] *Crimes* Act 1900 (NSW), https://legislation.nsw.gov.au/view/html/inforce/current/act-1900-040 (accessed 13 January 2025).

[8] In the Luke Lazarus case, the process involved two trials (first before a jury and a retrial before a judge sitting alone), and two appeals, the main features of which are outlined in Mason and Monaghan (2019). The path to enactment of the 2022 NSW reforms is usefully set out in brief in Quilter (2020).

Although we are in broad agreement with principles of mutual affirmative consent in acting upon sexual assault and ensuring sexual justice, we consider that understanding and recognition of *free (autonomous) consent* should be not solely a matter of actions and words (speech acts) between individual persons in specific sexual encounters and relationships. The "background conditions" within which individual and collective sexual power and preferences are formed must be acknowledged, particularly how women as a class are culturally and socially marked as vulnerable and at risk, through which *some* women are culturally and socially designated with the status of *legitimately accessible* to male sexual entitlement. The "*some* women" here are women in the prostitution system. The way the law operates is to ostensibly punish instances of sexual assault, but simultaneously and contiguous with this, it provides sexual *permissions* to *all* men that there is a class of women sexually available on a different understanding of "consent" from other women. Not all men act on these permissions, but the prostitution system is built out of them.

Over the last ten years or so, the problem of sexual assault has gained in its national and international prominence.[9] Along with women in such movements as #MeToo (Chandra and Erlingsdóttir 2021; Cheema 2023; McGowan 2018), sex trade survivors have campaigned with other women's rights campaigners for our voices to be given a central place in legislative contexts and considerations of consent in relation to sexual assault. Survivors of prostitution draw attention to the fictive character of the "consent" that is often invoked as underlying prostitution (Lloyd 2012; Moran 2015; Norma and Reist 2016; Döring 2022; Bender 2020). The point is that agreement on payment for sex cannot be considered as *consent reflecting and performing autonomy*: even a consent "given" without an outward show of force does not displace the coercive context

[9] The 1970s and 1980s were a time of dedicated attention to rape law reform, generated and driven by the persistence of women and broadly sympathetic governments. In Australia, see for example the South Australia (SA) and NSW experience.

of the prostitution system in which individual sexual transactions take place. With prostitution, money (or other forms of payment) provides the initial and framing coercive element. What is purchased in prostitution transactions is not sex or consent itself, but the temporary suspension of a woman's desire not to consent—and that is coercion (Watson 2014; Eagers and Kennedy 2015). The acceptance of this coercion as "free agreement" weaves the web of systemic violation. The prostitution system lies at the epicentre of violence against women and girls, while masquerading as a benevolent institution that provides "sex work" for women in poverty or desperate circumstances.

We view the problem of sexual consent achieved by payment, and in particular, payment within the (global) prostitution system, as a "blind spot" in popular and academic discussions of sexual consent. A system of payment for sex constructs a framework of coercion and constraint, which vitiates not only particular individual expressions of "consent", but the very conditions of free consent. This form of systemic coercion is exacerbated by the highly gendered structure of the prostitution system, as a network of asymmetrical relationships between prostituted women, and buyers and pimps: on the one hand is the extreme vulnerability of women, with on the other hand a heightened form of male entitlement to access women's bodies.

A discussion of sexual consent in sexual assault laws that does not comprehensively include the prostitution system in its deliberations remains seriously incomplete, and amplifies the vulnerability of women in that system. There is a widespread cultural illusion as to the distinctness of sex in prostitution from "normal" sex, which both reflects and reinforces the illusion of the distinctness of women in prostitution from "other" women. We refuse to embed such a distinction into consideration of the legal or cultural status of sexual assault. This distinction would mean leaving behind those women most vulnerable to sexual assault, that is, those vulnerable to continual and approved systemic rape in prostitution. Our law, no matter how it valorises affirmative consent in individual transactions, still shrugs and looks away from systemic sexual assault, and leaves our citizens "free" to do the same.

What is the cost of this shrug and who pays that cost can be illustrated by cases where women report sexual violence against them in the course of prostitution. The cultural "blind spot" in not understanding the prostitution system as coercive can be deadly for women in prostitution. An illustrative case is that of Henry Jiang.[10] Mr Jiang was a real estate agent in Melbourne who broke into a vacant house and paid an escort agency for a woman to come there. At the end of the hour, during which Mr Jiang experienced sexual incapacity, the woman made to leave, but was blocked by Jiang, who put a sponge in her mouth and bound her across the face and by the hands with electrical cable. The woman alleged that Jiang then vaginally, anally and digitally anally raped her, performed unprotected oral sex on her, and indecently assaulted her, before she escaped from the house without her clothes. The police called to the scene had to use bolt cutters to release her bound hands. The magistrate at first instance refused bail to Jiang on the basis of what he characterised as a case of "sustained torture" and "brutal rape". Jiang's defence at trial was that there was consent to the whole encounter, for which he had paid. A jury acquitted him on seven charges of false imprisonment and sexual assault. Jiang pleaded guilty to a separate charge of theft, involving a dispute over drugs, a small amount of money and the woman's mobile. In this latter case, the judge suggested (with apparent disbelief) that the jury members in the previous case had seemingly made their decision on the basis that Jiang had paid for the woman, and that he was within his rights in seeking the completion of their mutually consented-to agreement.[11]

It is often alleged that the reason for women's infrequent reporting of sexual violation in prostitution, and for the low rate of convictions

---

[10] *DPP v Jiang* [2016] VCC 494 (26 April 2016), https://jade.io/article/463191?at.hl=DPP+v+Jiang+%255B2016%255D+VCC+494+(26+April+2016 (accessed 13 January 2025).

[11] *DPP v Jiang* [2016] VCC 494 (26 April 2016), Sentencing Remarks.

when they do, is a matter of "stigma" (Stardust et al. 2021; Treloar et al. 2021)[12]—hence the frequent advocacy of a strategy that works to change long-standing social attitudes to women in prostitution as being sinful, dirty, disreputable and so on. The question of stigma and stigmatisation in and towards the prostitution system is complex, but the *Jiang case*, and others, leads us away from seeing stigma towards women in prostitution as a discriminatory factor in criminal law: the jury found itself able to convict Mr Jiang for theft of the property of a woman in prostitution, but not for the violation of her person and personal autonomy. He had after all paid, he had thereby kept his side of the "bargain", and he asserted his right to fulfilment of what he believed he had paid for. The "contract" of prostitution was the stumbling block to conviction, not the character of the woman or the credibility of her voice. To emphasise: the problem of prostitution as coercion inheres in its very purpose and structure, not only in public attitudes towards it or to those in the prostitution system.

We understand of course that a change in law cannot singlehandedly or immediately transform entrenched social, cultural and economic practices and institutions. However, law is not only punitive, but is permissive, particularly in the sense of permitting and approving certain categories of entitlement. Law is moreover a form of (sex) education: the words of legislation, the conduct of trials and the remarks of judges convey ideas about sex, love and justice that powerfully shape our perspectives and values of what is acceptable and reasonable in our intimate lives (Pringle 1993). Human rights perspectives and treaties, with a central focus on the autonomy and dignity of the person and on her claims to equal enjoyment of the world and its benefits, are key in guiding our argument. Those claims are systematically violated in the prostitution system, although not for buyers or pimps, whose experience of "stigma" takes dramatically different forms.

[12] We refer readers to our current work in progress on understanding the concept of stigma, on file with authors.

Sexual Assault: A Crime of Sex Inequality and Discrimination

As we noted above, changes to the NSW Crimes Act sections on sexual assault[13] provide a working model around which to build our proposals. The 2022 changes are clarified in the Act by a statement of their aim in the following terms:[14]

An objective of this Subdivision is to recognise the following—

(a) every person has a right to choose whether or not to participate in a sexual activity,
(b) consent to a sexual activity is not to be presumed,
(c) consensual sexual activity involves ongoing and mutual communication, decision-making and free and voluntary agreement between the persons participating in the sexual activity.

Making explicit the objective of the law on sexual assault in this way as written into the law itself is important in setting out its values and boundaries, and the character of its permissions. We note briefly in passing that "ongoing and mutual communication" cannot *by definition* be accomplished (or even be a possibility) where a partner to the act is unconscious, even if made so by a preceding act or acts of mutual agreement. However, we caution that sustaining the conditions of "ongoing and mutual communication" does not require "enthusiasm". We do not agree that it is the role of law to investigate and monitor levels of enthusiasm in sexual acts, and believe it is a fundamental mistake to require enthusiasm of sexual partners, or to use the term as another way of speaking about affirmative consent (ABC 2018; University of Sydney 2022).

---

[13] *Crimes Legislation Amendment (Sexual Consent Reforms) Act* 2021 (NSW), 3.10.1A, https://legislation.nsw.gov.au/view/html/inforce/current/act-1900-040#pt.3-div.10-sdiv.1A (accessed 13 January 2025), now incorporated in *Crimes Act,* Subdivision 1A Consent and knowledge of consent, 61HF.

[14] *Crimes* Act 1900 (NSW), https://legislation.nsw.gov.au/view/html/inforce/current/act-1900-040#pt.3-div.10-sdiv.1A (accessed 13 January 2025).

However, the stated objective in the NSW Crimes Act significantly displaces recognition that sexual assault is most appropriately defined in terms of acts and/or a context of *coercion*, covering not only brute force but other factors that make impossible a full equality and mutuality in sexual or intimate relationships. The basic objective in law should include an understanding of sexual assault as, in the terms noted above, "**a violation of a sexual nature under circumstances of threat or use of force, fraud, coercion, abduction, or of the abuse of power, trust, or a position of dependency or vulnerability**". This formulation of what constitutes sexual assault draws on the reasoning of international legal forums in deliberations on prosecutions in this area.[15] The pivotal Rwanda case of Akayesu (1998a, b) defines rape in international law as "a physical invasion of a sexual nature, committed on a person under circumstances which are coercive", coercion being explained in this way: "Threats, intimidation, extortion and other forms of duress which prey on fear or desperation may constitute coercion, and coercion may be inherent in certain circumstances".[16] In turn, Catharine MacKinnon's formulation of sexual assault is as "a physical invasion of a sexual nature under circumstances of threat or use of force, fraud, coercion, abduction, or of the abuse of power, trust, or a position of dependency or vulnerability" (MacKinnon 2016, 432). We have slightly modified MacKinnon's formulation by substituting "a violation" for "a physical invasion". We do this because in our view, sexual assault need not involve "invasion", or even physical contact, as for example in the incidents addressed in the cases of *Akayesu* and *Muhimana* at the International Criminal Tribunal for Rwanda (ICTR).[17] Although the reasoning in the *Akayesu* decision

[15] Possible additions here could include "false imprisonment" and "detention".

[16] *The Prosecutor v Jean-Paul Akayesu (Trial Judgement)*, ICTR-96-4-T, International Criminal Tribunal for Rwanda (ICTR), 2 September 1998, paras 598 and 688, https://www.refworld.org/cases,ICTR,40278fbb4.html (accessed 13 January 2025), and discussed in MacKinnon (2016) The discussion in Cole (2008) provides a useful summary of some unresolved problems in regard to questions of the salience of consent in sexual assault cases in international law.

[17] See respectively *The Prosecutor v Jean-Paul Akayesu (Trial Judgement)*, ICTR-96-4-T, International Criminal Tribunal for Rwanda (ICTR), 2 September 1998, para. 429, https://www.refworld.org/cases,ICTR,40278fbb4.html (accessed 13 January 2025); and *The Prosecutor v Mikaeli Muhimana (Judgement and Sentence)*, ICTR-95-1B-T, International Criminal Tribunal for Rwanda (ICTR), 28 April 2005, paras. 32, 65, https://www.refworld.org/cases,ICTR,429c29694.html (accessed 13 January 2025).

does not confine the term "invasion" to penetration, the use of "invasion" could potentially be confusing or misleading in popular discussions of sexual assault, perhaps entailing a non-cognisance of various acts of sexual violation as serious criminal matters.

At this point we do not, of course, refer to these cases in international law, the law of armed conflict, as binding precedents in domestic law, whether in Australia or elsewhere. Rather, as leading thinking on questions of sexual assault, these cases provide valuable and insightful guidance as to how to understand the respective salience of coercion and of consent in legal (and popular) consideration of sexual interactions. The concept of "norm transfer" is useful in this context, that is, in exploring how principles, deliberations and procedures in international criminal law forums and courts are brought to bear on our thinking about sexual assault in domestic contexts (Pringle 2005; Dowds 2020). The violations of women that occur in every culture are sometimes spoken of or described as "a war against women" (Dworkin 1974, 1993; Smith 1991).

Moreover, the point we draw from the guidance provided by sexual assault cases in international law is not a denial of the importance of consent. Rather, we wish to draw attention to the way in which a *context* of inequality of standing in sexual encounters can be mobilised such as to make those encounters themselves into occasions for the further unfolding of inequality in the absence of mutuality. That is, a form of systemic *sex discrimination* is constructed, in the sense given to that term by the Convention on the Elimination of All Forms of Discrimination against Women (CEDAW):[18]

> For the purposes of the present Convention, the term "discrimination against women" shall mean any distinction, exclusion or restriction made on the basis of sex which has the effect or purpose of impairing or

[18] UN General Assembly, *Convention on the Elimination of All Forms of Discrimination Against Women*, 18 December 1979, U.N.T.S., vol. 1249, p. 13, Art 1, https://treaties.un.org/pages/viewdetails.aspx?src=treaty&mtdsg_no=iv-8&chapter=4&clang=_en (accessed 13 January 2025).

> nullifying the recognition, enjoyment or exercise by women, irrespective of their marital status, on a basis of equality of men and women, of human rights and fundamental freedoms in the political, economic, social, cultural, civil *or any other field* [emphasis added]

The understanding of "discrimination" set out in CEDAW is perhaps not how discrimination is always or even usually understood in popular and media forums, but it does provide a good fit for understanding sexual assault as an action "which has the effect or purpose of impairing or nullifying the recognition, enjoyment or exercise by women,... on a basis of equality of men and women, of human rights and fundamental freedoms in the political, economic, social, cultural, civil or any other field". General Recommendation No 19 (GR19) of the Committee on the Elimination of Discrimination against Women further succinctly explains: "The definition of discrimination includes gender-based violence, that is, violence that is directed against a woman *because she is a woman or that affects women disproportionately* [emphasis added]" (UN Committee 1992).

The 1993 Declaration on the Elimination of Violence against Women (DEVAW) sets out a suitable formulation of what counts as violence in such contexts of discrimination against individuals as members of the class of women:

> For the purposes of this Declaration, the term "violence against women" means any act of gender-based violence that results in, or is likely to result in, physical, sexual or psychological harm or suffering to women, including threats of such acts, coercion or arbitrary deprivation of liberty, whether occurring in public or in private life (UN General Assembly 1993).

That is, the Declaration understands "violence" in terms of what it *does* to women and to women's lives, rather than using the word to name specific (physical) actions against individuals such as punching, choking, hitting etc.

In summary, we believe that the approach in international law of emphasising a context of coercion, rather than an examination for the presence or absence of consent, as defining and addressing sexual assault offences is best practice.[19] The presence of consent as indicated by mutual affirmation may serve as *evidence* of whether a coercive context exists in regard to particular incidents, and hence of whether a specific act was an expression of inequality and/or exemplar of discrimination. The presence of consent may also serve in some limited circumstances as a defence to a charge of sexual assault. In other words, it is the existence of coercion (which may or may not include brute force) rather than the non-communication of mutual consent that is best understood as definitional of the offence. Our attention in these matters should focus directly on elements of coercion as the overall framework for understanding sexual assault. We now turn to what this approach to sexual assault broadly would mean for considering claims of sexual assault in the prostitution system.

Prostitution and Sexual Assault: Disqualifying Reliance on "Consent" as a Defence

The new NSW sexual assault provisions include, in section 61HJ, a list of "circumstances in which there is no consent", circumstances indicating coercion, deception, and inequality in trust, dependence, authority etc. Section 61HJ (2) adds, "This section does not limit the grounds on which it may be established that a person does not consent to a sexual activity". If the prostitution system is understood as a framework of coercion, it is conceivable that reliance on consent achieved by payment might be already disqualified under this provision. However, an *explicit* undertaking should be made in the law of sexual assault that a further ground on which it may be established that a person does not consent to a sexual activity is where payment is made in consideration of acts within the prostitution system.

Payment for sex is itself a form of coercion that is the heart of the prostitution transaction. In these circumstances, the payment is not for

[19] There is a lively discussion about the question of the relation of coercion to consent in terms of definitions and understanding of sexual assault in law. McLoughlin and Ringin (2024) provide an excellent introduction to this discussion, although their emphasis on consent differs from that taken in this chapter. See also Couvret (2024).

a specific good or a service, but rather a payment for *suspension of the women's desire not to consent*, as noted above. Contempt for women's autonomy is in this way definitive of the act of payment to prostitute women, even if its brutality is attenuated (for any number of reasons) by particular buyers in individual transactions. In its submission to the 2018 NSW Law Reform Commission Review of Consent in relation to Sexual Offences, the Sex Workers Outreach Project (SWOP) estimated that there was a minority population of buyers given free leash to act out "consent violations" in the prostitution system:

> While most clients of the NSW sex industry are respectful, and stick to the agreed sexual services, at SWOP we often hear about clients who are serial offenders at consent violations. They get away with this repeated behaviour because of under-reporting and under-prosecution, *and are thus free* to continue assaulting other sex workers. They use this success to develop their skills at pushing the boundaries of consent [emphasis added] (Sex Workers Outreach Project (SWOP 2018)[20]

The SWOP submission traces the existence of serial offenders to patterns of under-reporting and under-prosecution, patterns attributed in turn to the criminalisation of "sex work" even though NSW is regarded as a decriminalised jurisdiction. The submission met this objection to its analysis by noting that migrant and other women in the system are often not aware that "sex work" has been decriminalised in NSW, and hence a similar dynamic is at work in relation to reporting assault to police.

Contrary to the SWOP submission, however, there is ample evidence that the prostitution system is not "mostly populated" by buyers who are "respectful clients" when they "see" or "visit" a "sex worker".[21] Further, the minimisation by SWOP of the occurrence and intensity of sexual assault and physical violence committed by buyers in the prostitution system is accompanied by a blindness to another primary source of

---

[20] Other submissions to the review and documents related to the Commission review can be found at NSW Law Reform Commission 2021 (dated November 2021 yet said to have been tabled in the NSW Parliament 2020).

[21] Perhaps the fullest account of violence in prostitution in Australia was provided by Quadara 2008: clearly, updated research is needed. A useful research project is reported in Dalla et al. (2003).

violence, that is, pimps as third parties in prostitution transactions.[22] In a largely American-focused study, Lisa Thompson drew on US Army Field Manual classifications and prohibitions, together with Biderman's Chart of Coercion, in using the category of "torture" in order to classify and analyse accounts by women of their treatment in prostitution. Including references to other sources (Royal 2018)[23] Thompson (2011, 297) found:

> The comparison exposes the multiple ways in which some pimps replicate methods of physical abuse and psychological coercion used in political interrogation, thereby revealing pimp-controlled prostitution's proclivity for oppression and dehumanization. Forced nudity; rape; humiliation; food, water, and sleep depr[i]vation; beatings; confinement; isolation; and mock executions are among the tactics of torture demonstrated to be in the repertoire of some pimps. This being the case, the practice of torture may be much more commonplace than is recognized by important groups such as human rights activists, trauma experts, politicians, and the general public.

Accurate data on sexual and other violence against women in prostitution can be difficult together and analyse, the reasons varying to some extent across different spaces of prostitution (for example, brothel vs street) and different jurisdictions. But in terms of DEVAW's understanding of violence against women as noted above, a common thread of different forms of violence is what they *do* in the prostitution system. Judith Herman (2003, 4) sums up the collective impact:

> The ultimate goal in this, as in all systems of domination, is to destroy the autonomy of the victim and induce as far as possible a state of willing submission.... Under conditions of prostitution, autonomous self-regulation of any sort is a form of insubordination; it is expressly forbidden and actively suppressed.

---

[22] For an overview of the role of the pimp in prostitution, within the English context, see Tiggey May et al. (2000).

[23] See also Spidel et al. (2006, 193).

The wreckage enacted on women by prostitution does not necessarily rest on or require continuous application of acts of violence. It is enough that a state of threat of violence exist in order for autonomy to be destroyed, as indicated by Lisa Thompson's archive of women's experience, which reflect the infliction of a deep harm on women in prostitution and a generalised threat to women of the cost of subordination. The violence of prostitution is systemic in its coercive denial of women's autonomy.

This form of systemic coercion is exacerbated by the gendered nature of the prostitution system and the fundamental inequality and asymmetry both of prostitution relationships and of the system itself, placing an inequitable burden of vulnerability on women. The Preamble to the 1949 *Convention for the Suppression of the Traffic in Persons and of the Exploitation of the Prostitution of Others* (which Australia has not—yet—signed or ratified) notes that "Prostitution and the accompanying evil of the traffic in persons for the purpose of prostitution are incompatible with the dignity and worth of the human person" (UN General Assembly 1949, vol 96, 271). This portrait of the prostitution system outlined by the 1949 Convention is echoed in later global trafficking instruments such as the 2000 Palermo Protocol, which notes (UN General Assembly 2000, Art 3):

> For the purposes of this Protocol:
> (a) "Trafficking in persons" shall mean the recruitment, transportation, transfer, harbouring or receipt of persons, *by means of the threat or use of force or other forms of coercion, of abduction, of fraud, of deception, of the abuse of power or of a position of vulnerability or of the giving or receiving of payments or benefits to achieve the consent of a person having control over another person, for the purpose of exploitation* [emphasis added]. Exploitation shall include, at a minimum, the exploitation of the prostitution of others or other forms of sexual exploitation, forced labour or services, slavery or practices similar to slavery, servitude or the removal of organs;
> (b) The consent of a victim of trafficking in persons to the intended exploitation set forth in subparagraph (a) of this article shall be irrelevant where any of the means set forth in subparagraph (a) have been used; ...

The provision explicitly disallows reliance on the consent of a person achieved by payment as a defence to a charge of trafficking. Domestic criminal law should echo this disallowance in its application to sexual assault.

Many discussions of prostitution proceed on the basis that there is bright line between trafficking and prostitution, with trafficking defined in terms of physical force (for example, women handcuffed to beds) and/or fraud (for example, women induced into trafficking for purposes of sexual exploitation by false or misleading promises). Such a distinction between trafficking and prostitution cannot be maintained as a notation of reality. Trafficking across borders of women into brothels, for example, acts as a feeder system into prostitution in national states. Moreover, the element of crossing national borders is not maintained in the Australian legal understanding of trafficking: the federal *Criminal Code* 1995 (Cth) includes "domestic trafficking" in its provisions on Trafficking in Persons, covering movement across state borders within Australia.[24] In this case, consent cannot be relied upon as a defence, providing:

> 271.11B (Offences against Division 271—no defence of victim consent or acquiescence)
> To avoid doubt, it is not a defence in a proceeding for an offence against this Division that a person against whom the offence is alleged to have been committed consented to, or acquiesced in, conduct constituting any element of the offence.

Moreover, throughout this section of the Code, "coercion" is required to be given the same meaning as in Division 270 (Slavery and slavery-like offences), where the term includes coercion by any of the following: force; duress; detention; psychological oppression; abuse of power; taking advantage of a person's vulnerability.

Our claim is that prostitution as a system of violence and exploitation is not only connected to trafficking empirically on the ground, in the streets. The global prostitution system exhibits features of coercion that should lead us to address it in largely similar terms as trafficking, in

---

[24] *Criminal Code Act* 1995 (Cth), Division 271, https://www.legislation.gov.au/C2004A04868/latest/text/2, Volume_2. Section 271.11, (accessed 15 September 2025), Jurisdictional requirements—offences of domestic trafficking in persons or organs, clarifies the reach of the term "domestic trafficking".

particular, that consent should not be permissible as a defence where coercion is accomplished by such factors. This position is supported by a wide variety of women's organizations around the world which draw attention to the wrong of prostitution as a human rights violation similar to and empirically related to trafficking. The distinctiveness of this approach is the framework of human rights in which it is centred, as marked by close adherence to the principles and text of particular human rights instruments, and by upholding the central principle or value of the *dignity* of the person that is the chief animator of human rights talk and action, and of (sexual) autonomy.[25]

Autonomy, Dignity and the Prostitution System

These principles and commitments are the basis of the "Nordic model" endorsed in 2014 by resolutions of the peak European parliamentary bodies, the European Parliament (Resolution 2014, based on European Parliament Report 2014; also European Parliament Resolution 2023), and the Parliamentary Assembly of the Council of Europe (PACE) (Resolution 1983 of 8 April 2014 based on PACE Report of 26 April 2012). The common concern here is with the human rights of women, in protecting the autonomy and dignity of *all* women equally, and in bringing an end to all forms of the subordination and degradation of women.

Defenders and beneficiaries of the prostitution industry do frequently portray prostitution as a relationship between individuals, in which one person provides sexual services (or performs "sex work") to another person in exchange for money. Portraying prostitution as a series of such individual, and un-gendered, transactions is a fundamental misunderstanding and, indeed, a misrepresentation, of the historical and current

[25] Although it is important to do so, it is beyond the scope of this chapter to explore the meaning/s of dignity and autonomy in greater detail, and also to explore the difference in emphasis between these two general principles as a site of disagreement in discussions of sexual assault. For a comprehensive coverage of "dignity" generally as a principle in the Constitutions of South Africa and Ireland, see Hughes (2014).

organization of prostitution. Prostitution is a *system* that includes not only sellers ("sex workers") but crucially, buyers, as well as pimps and other beneficiaries of the industry (particularly through its close links with the pornography industry). The prostitution system is also deeply and fundamentally gendered, with the majority of buyers being men, and the majority of those from whom sex is bought being women and girls. An attempt to consider consent to prostitution outside a full understanding of prostitution as a *system* fails to comprehend the inequality and subordination, violence and exploitation lying at its foundation.

Closely linked to a defence of prostitution as a series of individual transactions is the emphasis placed by its defenders on women's "choices" in the industry. Women's choices (that is, the "choices" of "sex workers"), important as they are, do not form the driver of the prostitution industry, just as they do not form the foundation of trafficking. Prostitution as a social institution is driven by (male) *demand*, that is, the choices that *men* make in choosing to buy sex and the bodies of women. We now know a great deal about the character of those choices through what are sometimes called "punter sites", on which sex buyers review brothels and the women with whom they have had a paid relation. Even in the course of "ordinary" transactions, those choices are brutal. The Invisible Men Project, for example, collates reports from these sites, providing a chilling picture of the reality for most prostituted women: a reality of violence, desperation, subordination and despair. The main danger to women in prostitution comes from those who prostitute them, and/or who financially and in other ways benefit from their prostitution and the trauma it perpetuates throughout the lives of women.

PACE Resolution 1983 (PACE 2014) noted above states at ¶6:[26]

> Forced prostitution and sexual exploitation should be considered as violations of human dignity and, as women are disproportionately represented among victims, as an obstacle to gender equality.

Both the European Parliament and PACE resolutions draw attention to the violence of exploitation in prostitution and trafficking. It is for

[26] See also European Parliament Resolution of 26 February 2014.

this reason that the PACE resolution in particular notes that sex worker organizations are not the sole stakeholders in considering measures that address prostitution in one way or another. The PACE resolution notes in ¶10:

> In designing and enforcing prostitution legislation and policies, public authorities should strengthen co-operation with civil society, particularly non-governmental organisations (NGOs), assisting victims of forced prostitution and trafficking, as these are not represented by sex workers' organisations.

Consultation with *survivors* of the prostitution system is crucial to any project for its reform and to any specific reform options advanced, as well as to the implementation and monitoring of such measures.

There has been little attempt in Australia at a state or federal level to address prostitution within a framework of human rights and its guiding principles of human dignity and autonomy. We believe that our recommendation to disqualify reliance on consent as a defence to a charge of sexual assault in prostitution would go some way towards doing this via legislative reform. Our proposal also has the potential to remove disincentives to reporting by individual women of sexual assault in the ordinary course of prostitution, which is endemic, as noted in a classic study by pro- "sex work" researchers (Roxburgh et al. 2006) of street prostitution in the Greater Sydney area:

> Given that current PTSD among these women is related to adult sexual assault (which was reported as the most prevalent and most stressful trauma), establishing a safe environment and minimising their ongoing exposure to trauma would entail leaving the sex industry, where occupationally they are at risk of sexual assault on a daily basis.

In contrast, the "Nordic Model" works, in the sense of working to narrow the range of sex inequality and of exploitation in our society. It benefits *all* women, whether they are currently in the prostitution system, survivors of the system, or women affected by it. *All* of us are affected by prostitution in various ways, but it is those most affected and most damaged by it who are owed our urgent efforts in working towards its abolition. Our argument here is that *any* legal provision that places the burden of criminal sanctions on those who are bought and sold in the prostitution system should be slated for removal, but this should not be accompanied by the removal of criminal sanctions against those who buy and sell women in prostitution and trafficking (sex buyers, pimps and brothel owners, auxiliaries etc.). The present global and domestic situation calls for a comprehensive and systematic rethinking of sexual assault in terms of human rights principles, particularly autonomy and dignity. The complete decriminalisation of the prostitution system as a whole, an aim with which the current law in certain Australian states is aligned, fails to make much distinction in terms of unlawfulness between prostituted persons (mainly but not entirely women and girls) and those who prostitute them and profit from their subordination. We conclude with a set of practical reform options requiring legislative changes, some of which could be immediately put in place.

Steps in Another Approach to Prostitution

The approach advocated by propagandists of the prostitution industry has failed prostituted women. Legalization does not tackle the systemic violence of prostitution. Decriminalisation does not attenuate trauma—because the infliction of trauma on persons in prostitution is chiefly by buyers and pimps in the course of prostitution transactions. The main danger to women in prostitution comes from those who prostitute them, or who financially and in other ways benefit from their prostitution. **Prostitution can be made safe only through abolishing it.**

Abolition is not a utopian model. It is the aim of the "Nordic model", first implemented in Sweden through the Sex Purchase Law of 1998, and since adopted in various forms in Norway and Iceland, Northern Ireland, Ireland, France, Canada and Israel. It is the approach recommended by the European Parliament and the Parliamentary Assembly of the Council of Europe as forming a basis for a pan-European approach to prostitution and trafficking. The French legal measures directed towards the abolition of the prostitution system were found by the European Court of Human

Rights in 2024 to be not incompatible with the human rights framework of the European Convention on Human Rights.[27]

Most countries up to now have adopted an approach assuming that the prostitution of women is in some way "a fact of life", that it is "inevitable", that it is (as in the cliché) "the oldest profession" that will always be with us. The 2014 EP resolution however adopted the perspective of the Declaration on the Elimination of Violence against Women which understands that forms of violence, like prostitution and sexual exploitation, are a "manifestation of historically unequal power relations between men and women", and are in no sense natural or biological phenomena. The EP press release (20140221IPR36644_en) summed up succinctly the meaning and significance of its 2014 resolution:

> It stresses that prostitution violates human dignity and human rights, whether it is forced or voluntary, and calls on member states to find exit strategies and alternative sources of income for women who want to leave prostitution.

The 2014 PACE resolution noted in similar tones:

> Forced prostitution and sexual exploitation should be considered as violations of human dignity and, as women are disproportionately represented among victims, as an obstacle to gender equality (¶6).

This chapter recommends the following proposals for reform as parts of an extended action plan. These options are adapted from the 2014 PACE resolution (¶12) as a guide to best practice in addressing the prostitution system, in legislative terms and beyond. These revisions would also have a significant impact on public attitudes and practices towards violence and discrimination against women.

1. Putting in place of "exit programs" for those who wish to leave prostitution. Exit programs must be based on a holistic approach,

[27] *M.A. and Others v France* (App. Nos. 63664/19 and others) European Court of Human Rights (Fifth Section): Judgment of 25 July 2024, https://hudoc.echr.coe.int/fre?i=001-235143 (accessed 31 December 2024). As of March 2025 the decision is under appeal.

with mental health and other health-care services, housing support, education and training, and employment services, focused on career paths and good job prospects. Adequate financing and resourcing is required to make exit a realistic option for women to aspire to and to achieve. Information on the human rights of those in prostitution, as well as contact details of exit programs and anti-trafficking services, need to be clearly displayed in any spaces concerned with prostitution.

2. Criminalization of sex purchase as an effective way of preventing and combating prostitution and trafficking. These measures should include making unlawful the related activities of pimping and keeping a brothel or similar premises, and making unlawful the advertising of sexual services, including disguised advertising for prostitution.
3. Raising public awareness of the need to change attitudes to sex purchase and to prostitution. These efforts should be designed to increase awareness through the media and school education, particularly among young people, of the importance of mutually respectful, gender-equal and violence-free sexuality and sexual practices.
4. The promotion of systematic quantitative and qualitative research on prostitution and trafficking within a human rights framework, with a government mandate for independent and regular assessments of the impact of the regulation of prostitution on those persons who remain in the system.

Beyond these steps, an immediate practical measure recommended by this chapter is that sustained consideration be given to the meaning and significance of consent in the law of sexual assault, so as to further protect women in prostitution from sexual assault, particularly by sex buyers and pimps. This proposal would remove reliance on "consent" as a defence to assault charges for actions against prostituted women. Our specific legislative proposals would also serve to raise public awareness of the need to change actions and attitudes to the purchase of sexual services and to prostitution. We do not have to wait for attitudes to change before actions change. Crucially, such public educative efforts via the law have the potential to raise general awareness with regard to the importance of mutually respectful sexuality and sexual practices. At the heart of these proposals is a call for radical change to the basis of disrespect for prostituted women, namely the lack of respect for women as equal participants in society which is evident in the toleration of the form of exploitation of women that is prostitution.

It can sometimes be difficult to understand prostitution *as* coercion, even despite the high incidence of acts of violence in the "normal" course of prostitution transactions being widely known. There is a general cultural consensus in Australia (and elsewhere) that payment for sex presents no general barrier to recognising the presence of consent, or indeed the presence of mutual affirmative consent. This understanding is held across the board. It is not a left–right issue. The costs to women of this cultural failure in understanding the prostitution system as coercive can be deadly for women in prostitution, exemplified in the case of Henry Jiang where a jury was able to find him not guilty despite the gross levels of violence and abuse to which he subjected his victim. In such cases, and particularly where there is a history of repeated violation of women in prostitution (a notorious Australian example is that of Adrian Bayley, convicted of having murdered Jill Meagher an ABC journalist)[28] the coercive context of prostitution should disqualify prima facie any reliance on consent in answer to a charge.

Recommendations for Ending Denial and Disrespect

Our first recommendation as was noted above is:

> **An explicit clarification in all legal statements on sexual assault that a person accused of sexual assault or rape cannot rely on a consent achieved by payment of a monetary sum, or in the course of a commercial transaction, as a defence**

To give "teeth" to this provision, we recommend a civil action for sexual assault and abuse in the context of prostitution:

---

[28] See *The Queen v Bayley* [2013] VSC 313 (19 June 2013), (accessed 15 September 2025).

An explicit legal formulation of a civil action for sexual assault committed in the context of the prostitution system and associated forms of exploitation, whether involving direct commission or complicity in the act.

This provision might seem in some way superfluous if there is an effective and enforced law on sexual assault on the ground of coercion. However, this recommendation represents a response to *aggravated* sexual assault, relating to the systemic and organised character of sexual assault both in the structural set-up of prostitution, and incidental to it. The enabling of such a cause of civil action was pioneered by the Illinois *Predator Accountability Act* 2006 (Ill).[29] The Act allowed "persons who have been or who are subjected to the sex trade to seek civil damages", with the "sex trade" being defined widely so as to include soliciting a woman in prostitution, pandering, keeping a place of prostitution, pimping, obscenity, trafficking over the areas of street prostitution, pornography, escort services, and massage parlours and brothels.

Prostitution is not a victimless crime, and it would be unjust and at odds with human rights principles to punish those who are its victims and who suffer its wrong and injuries often throughout the whole of their lives, once having entered the territory. Moreover, our proposals in tandem would serve as a reminder to popular culture and the media that sexual assault of women in coercive circumstances is not to be mitigated by reference to her ostensible consent. An expression of consent born of vulnerability, powerlessness, of poverty does not indicate the free consent of citizens in a democracy. If we as a society and culture continue to fail to comprehend this, we ensure that some women are left behind in the wreckage of prostitution. And we thereby ensure that it is no great matter that they are left behind, and that not all women have a human right to the enjoyment of the world on equal terms with other women, and with men.

---

[29] Illinois General Assembly, 740 ILCS 128/ Predator Accountability Act, http://www.ilga.gov/legislation/ilcs/ilcs3.asp?ActID=2812&ChapterID=57 (accessed 13 January 2025). For further discussion of the Act, and the obstacles to its wider use, see Goswami (2011), Singh (2007), and the shorter useful account of Keleher (2010).

Bibliography

Reported Cases

DPP v Jiang [2016] VCC 494 (26 April 2016), Sentencing Remarks, https://jade.io/article/463191?at.hl=DPP+v+Jiang+%255B2016%255D+VCC+494+(26+April+2016) (accessed 13 January 2025).

M.A. and Others v France (App. Nos. 63664/19 and others) European Court of Human Rights (Fifth Section): Judgment of 25 July 2024, https://hudoc.echr.coe.int/fre?i=001-235143 (accessed 31 December 2024).

The Prosecutor v Jean-Paul Akayesu (Trial Judgement), ICTR-96-4-T, International Criminal Tribunal for Rwanda (ICTR), 2 September 1998, paras. 598 and 688, https://www.refworld.org/cases,ICTR,40278fbb4.html (accessed 13 January 2025).

The Prosecutor v Jean-Paul Akayesu (Trial Judgement), ICTR-96-4-T, International Criminal Tribunal for Rwanda (ICTR), 2 September 1998, para. 429, https://www.refworld.org/cases,ICTR,40278fbb4.html (accessed 13 January 2025).

The Prosecutor v Mikaeli Muhimana (*Judgement and Sentence*), ICTR-95-1B-T, International Criminal Tribunal for Rwanda (ICTR), 28 April 2005, paras. 32, 65, https://www.refworld.org/cases,ICTR,429c29694.html (accessed 13 January 2025).

The Queen v Bayley [2013] VSC 313 (19 June 2013), https://jade.io/article/296990?at.hl=Bayley (accessed 13 January 2025).

Statutes and Treaties or Conventions

Crimes Act 1900 (NSW), https://legislation.nsw.gov.au/view/html/inforce/current/act-1900-040 (accessed 13 January 2025).

Crimes Legislation Amendment (Sexual Consent Reforms) Act 2021 (NSW), 3.10.1A, https://legislation.nsw.gov.au/view/html/inforce/current/act-1900-040#pt.3-div.10-sdiv.1A (accessed 13 January 2025).

Criminal Code Act 1995 (Cth), Division 271, https://www.legislation.gov.au/Details/C2021C00183/Html/Volume_2.Section 271.11 (accessed 13 January 2025).

European Parliament Resolution of 26 February 2014, Sexual Exploitation and Prostitution and its Impact on Gender Equality, https://www.europarl.europa.eu/doceo/document/TA-7-2014-0162_EN.html?redirect (accessed 13 January 2025).

European Parliament Resolution of 14 September 2023, Regulation of Prostitution in the EU: Its Cross-border Implications and Impact on Gender Equality and Women's Rights, https://www.europarl.europa.eu/doceo/document/TA-9-2023-0328_EN.html (accessed 13 January 2025).

France Loi n° 2016–444 du 13 avril 2016, *visant à renforcer la lutte contre le système prostitutionnel et à accompagner les personnes prostituées*, https://www.legifrance.gouv.fr/jorf/id/JORFTEXT000032396046 (accessed 13 January 2025).

Illinois General Assembly, 740 ILCS 128/ Trafficking Victims Protection Act [formerly Predator Accountability Act], http://www.ilga.gov/legislation/ilcs/ilcs3.asp?ActID=2812&ChapterID=57 (accessed 13 January 2025).

Parliamentary Assembly of the Council of Europe (PACE) Resolution 1983 of 8 April 2014, Prostitution, Trafficking and Modern Slavery in Europe 2012, https://assembly.coe.int/nw/xml/XRef/Xref-XML2HTML-en.asp?fileid=20716 (accessed 13 January 2025).

UN General Assembly, *Convention on the Elimination of All Forms of Discrimination Against Women*, 18 December 1979, UNTS, vol. 1249, p. 13, Art 1, https://treaties.un.org/pages/viewdetails.aspx?src=treaty&mtdsg_no=iv-8&chapter=4&clang=_en (accessed 13 January 2025).

UN General Assembly, *Convention for the Suppression of the Traffic in Persons and of the Exploitation of the Prostitution of Others*, 2 December 1949, U.N.T.S., vol. 96, p. 271, https://treaties.un.org/pages/viewdetails.aspx?src=ind&mtdsg_no=vii-11-a&chapter=7&clang=_en (accessed 13 January 2025).

UN General Assembly, *Declaration on the Elimination of Violence against Women*, 20 December 1993, A/RES/48/104, https://digitallibrary.un.org/record/179739?ln=en (accessed 13 January 2025).

UN General Assembly, *Protocol to Prevent, Suppress and Punish Trafficking in Persons, Especially Women and Children, Supplementing the United Nations Convention against Transnational Organized Crime* (Palermo Protocol), 15 November 2000, Article 3, https://treaties.un.org/Pages/ViewDetails.aspx?src=ind&mtdsg_no=XVIII-12-a&chapter=18&clang=_en (accessed 13 January 2025).

Articles and Book Chapters

ABC, "Enthusiastic Consent': What Is It, How Do You Prove It, and Will It Work in Court?" 8 May 2018, https://www.abc.net.au/triplej/programs/hack/how-do-you-prove-enthusiastic-consent-in-court/9740214 (accessed 13 January 2025).

Bacik, Ivana, "'If Consent is Bought, It Is Not Freely Chosen': Compromised Consent in Prostituted Sex in Ireland," *Dignity* 5, Article 6 (2020).

Bacik, Ivana, "#MeToo, Consent and Prostitution—The Irish Law Reform Experience," *Women's Studies International Forum* 86 (2021) 102457.

Chatterjee, Sudeshna, "#MeToo from the Margins: Rethinking Consent-Coercion Binaries with Commercial Sex Work in India," *Feminist Formations* 33 (2021) 289.

Cole, Alison, "*Prosecutor* v. *Gacumbitsi:* The New Definition for Prosecuting Rape under International Law," *International Criminal Law Review* 8 (2008) 55.

Cotton, Ann, Farley, Melissa and Baron, Robert, "Attitudes Toward Prostitution and Acceptance of Rape Myths," *Journal of Applied Social Psychology* 32 (2002) 1790.

Couvret, Genevieve, "Affirmative Consent is Not Enough: A Feminist Critique of the NSW Reforms and the Limits of Consent under Patriarchy," *Australian Feminist Law Journal* 50 (2024) 131.

Dalla, Rochelle L, "'You Just Give Them What They Want and Pray They Don't Kill You': Street-Level Sex Workers' Reports of Victimization, Personal Resources, and Coping Strategies," *Violence against Women* 9 (2003): 1367.

Farley, Melissa, "#MeToo Must Include Prostitution," *Dignity* 3, Article 9 (2018).

Goswami, Samir, "From Street Corner to Statehouse: Survivors' Struggle for Civil Rights" in *Global Perspectives on Prostitution and Sex Trafficking: Europe, Latin America, North America, and Global*, Rochelle L Dalla et al. (eds) (NYC, NY, US: Lexington Books 2011).

Herman, Judith Lewis, "Introduction: Hidden in Plain Sight: Clinical Observations on Prostitution" in *Prostitution, Trafficking, and Traumatic Stress*, Melissa Farley (ed), (NYC, NY, US: Haworth Maltreatment & Trauma Press, 2003) 4.

Keleher, Christopher P, "The Illinois Predator Accountability Act: A Sleeping Giant," *Illinois Bar Journal* 98 (2010), https://web.archive.org/web/20240330182825/ (accessed 13 January 2025).

McLoughlin, Kasey and Ringin, Adrienne, "Giving Meaning to Consent at the International Criminal Court and Beyond: A (Qualified) Defence of Consent," *Australian Feminist Studies* 38 (2023) 503.

MacKinnon, Catharine A, "Rape Redefined," *Harvard Law & Policy Review* 10 (2016) 432.

Mason, Gail and Monaghan, James, "Autonomy and Responsibility in Sexual Assault Law in NSW: The *Lazarus* Cases," *Current Issues in Criminal Justice* 31 (2019) 24.

Pringle, Helen, "Acting Like a Man: Seduction and Rape in the Law," *Griffith Law Review* 2 (1993) 64.

Pringle, Helen, "France's Abolition Day: The Dream of a Society without Prostitution," *ABC Religion & Ethics* 12 April 2016, https://www.abc.net.au/religion/frances-abolition-day-the-dream-of-a-society-without-prostitutio/10097120 (accessed 13 January 2025).

Pringle, Helen, "Lessons from Abroad," *UNSW Law Journal* 28 (2005) 20.

Quilter, Julia, "Getting Consent 'Right': Sexual Assault Law Reform in New South Wales," *Australian Feminist Law Journal* 46 (2020) 225.

Roxburgh, Amanda, Degenhardt, Louisa and Copeland, Jan, "Posttraumatic Stress Disorder among Female Street-Based Sex Workers in the Greater Sydney Area, Australia," *BMC Psychiatry* 6 (2006), https://bmcpsychiatry.biomedcentral.com/articles/ (accessed 13 January 2025).

Singh, Shay-Ann M Heiser, "The Predator Accountability Act: Empowering Women in Prostitution to Pursue Their Own Justice," *DePaul Law Review* 56 (2007) 1035.

Spidal, Alicia, Greaves, Caroline, Hervé, Hugues, Cooper, Barry, Hare, Robert and Yuille, John, "The Psychopath as Pimp," *Canadian Journal of Police and Security Services*, 4 (2006) 193.

Stardust, Zahra, Treloar, Carla, Cama, Elena and Kim, Jules, "'I Wouldn't Call the Cops if I was Being Bashed to Death': Sex Work, Whore Stigma and the Criminal Legal System," *International Journal for Crime, Justice and Social Democracy* 10 (2021) 142.

Thompson, Lisa L, "On a Street Near You: Pimps as Practitioners of Torture Rights," in *Global Perspectives on Prostitution and Sex Trafficking: Europe, Latin America, North America, and Global*, Rochelle L Dalla (ed) (NYC, NY, US: Lexington Books 2011) 297.

Treloar, Carla, Stardust, Zahra, Cama, Elena and Kim, Jules, "Rethinking the Relationship between Sex Work, Mental Health and Stigma: A Qualitative Study of Sex Workers in Australia," *Social Science & Medicine* 268 (2021) 1.

University of Sydney, "What Enthusiastic Consent Actually Looks Like: If It's Not an Enthusiastic Yes, It's a No," 21 September 2022, https://www.sydney.edu.au/study/why-choose-sydney/student-life/student-news/2022/09/21/what-enthusiastic-consent-actually-looks-like-html (accessed 13 January 2025).

Books, Videos and Reports

Alsalem, Reem, UN Special Rapporteur on Violence Against Women and Girls, *Prostitution and Violence against Women and Girls*, A/HRC/56/48, 7 May 2024, https://documents.un.org/doc/undoc/gen/g24/078/81/pdf/g2407881.pdf (accessed 13 January 2025).

Alsalem, Reem, UN Special Rapporteur on Violence Against Women and Girls, *Guidance Document - The Concept of Consent in Relation to Violence Against Women and Girls*, Special Procedures, UN Human Rights Council, 20 September 2025, https://www.ohchr.org/sites/default/files/documents/issues/women/sr/activities/consent-guidance-document.pdf (accessed 20 September 2025).

Bender, Rebecca, *In Pursuit of Love: One Woman's Journey from Trafficked to Triumphant* (Grand Rapids: Zondervan, 2020).

Buggs, Shantel Gabrieal and Hoppe, Trevor (eds), *Unsafe Words: Queering Consent in the #MeToo Era* (New Brunswick NJ, US: Rutgers University Press, 2023)

Chandra, Giti and Erlingsdóttir, Irma (eds), *The Routledge Handbook of the Politics of the #MeToo Movement* (Oxford: Routledge, 2021).

Cheema, Iqra Shagufta (ed), *The Other #MeToos* (Oxford: Oxford University Press 2023).

Döring, Mia, *Any Girl: A Memoir of Sexual Exploitation and Recovery* (Dublin: Hachette Books Ireland, 2022).

Dowds, Eithne, *Feminist Engagement with International Criminal Law: Norm Transfer, Complementarity, Rape and Consent* (Oxford: Hart, 2020).

Dworkin, Andrea, *Woman Hating* (New York: Dutton, 1974).

Dworkin, Andrea, *Letters from a War Zone* (Chicago: Lawrence Hill, 1993).

Eagers, Damien and Kennedy, Jason, "'Prostitution: We Don't Buy It', Campaign Launch by Jill Meagher's Husband Tom," Wed 22 Apr 2015 at 13:27, https://www.independent.ie/videos/irish-news/video-archive-prostitution-we-dont-buy-it-campaign-launch-by-jill-meaghers-husband-tom-31163021.html (accessed 13 January 2025).

European Parliament, Report of 4 February 2014, on Sexual Exploitation and Prostitution and its Impact on Gender Equality, https://www.europarl.europa.eu/doceo/document/A-7-2014-0071_EN.html?redirect (accessed 13 January 2025).

Hughes, Anne, *Human Dignity and Fundamental Rights in South Africa and Ireland* (Hatfield, South Africa: Pretoria University Law Press, 2014).

Lloyd, Rachel, *Girls Like Us: Fighting for a World Where Girls are Not for Sale: A Memoir* (NYC, NY, US: HarperCollins, 2012).

McGowan, Rose, *Brave* (NYC, NY, US: Barnes & Noble, 2018).

May, Tiggery, Harocopus, Alex, Hough, JM, *For Love or Money: Pimps and the Management of Sex Work*, Police Research Series Paper 134 (2000).

Moran, Rachel, *Paid For: My Journey through Prostitution* (NYC, NY, US: Norton, 2015).

NSW Law Reform Commission, *Consent in Relation to Sexual Offences Report*, https://lawreform.nsw.gov.au/completed-projects/recent/consent.html (accessed 13 January 2025).

NSW Law Reform Commission, Review of Consent Publication, https://lawreform.nsw.gov.au/documents/Completed-projects/2010-onwards/consent/NSWLRC_Statement-Report-138-6-Dec-2021.pdf (accessed 2 February 2025).

Nolan, Aoife, Freedman, Rosa and Murphy, Thérèse (eds), *The United Nations Special Procedures System* (Leiden, The Netherlands: Brill Nijhoff, 2017).

Norma, Caroline and Reist, Melinda Tankard (eds), *Prostitution Narratives: Stories of Survival in the Sex Trade* (North Melbourne, Australia: Spinifex Press, 2016).

PACE, *Report of 26 April 2012, on Prostitution, Trafficking and Modern Slavery in Europe*, https://pace.coe.int/en/files/20559 (accessed 13 January 2025).

Parliament of Australia, *Final Report*, Senate Inqury into Current and Proposed Sexual Consent Laws in Australia, https://parlinfo.aph.gov.au/parlInfo/download/committees/reportsen/RB000074/toc_pdf/CurrentandproposedsexualconsentlawsinAustralia.pdf (accessed 25 January 2025).

Quadara, Antonia, *Sex Workers and Sexual Assault in Australia: Prevalence, Risk and Safety*, Australian Institute of Family Studies (AIFS) Issues no. 8 (2008).

Queensland Parliament, *Report No 4, 57th Parliament—Criminal Code (Decriminalising Sex Work) and Other Legislation Amendment Bill*, https://www.parliament.qld.gov.au/Work-of-Committees/Committees/Committee-Details?cid=240&id=4366 (accessed 2 March 2025).

Mickey Royal, *The Pimp Game: Instructional Guide* (New Edition) (NYC, NY, US: Sharif Publishing, 2018).

Šimonović, Dubravka, *Report of the Special Rapporteur on Violence against Women, Its Causes and Consequences: Rape as a Grave, Systematic and Widespread Human Rights Violation, a Crime and a Manifestation of Gender-based Violence against Women and Girls, and its Prevention,* https://www.ohchr.org/en/documents/thematic-reports/ahrc4726-rape-grave-systematic-and-widespread-human-rights-violation (accessed 2 February 2025).
Šimonović, Dubravka, *Report of the UN Special Rapporteur on Violence Against Women and Girls, A Framework for Legislation on Rape—Addendum,* https://digitallibrary.un.org/record/3929055?ln=en&v=pdf, 2021b.
Smith, Joan, *Misogynies: Reflections on Myths and Malice* (London, UK: Fawcett, 1991).
UN General Assembly, *Protocol to Prevent, Suppress and Punish Trafficking in Persons, Especially Women and Children, Supplementing the UN Convention against Transnational Organized Crime,* U.N.T.S., vol. 2237, U.N.T.S., p. 319, 15 November 2000, https://treaties.un.org/Pages/ViewDetails.aspx?src=ind&mtdsg_no=XVIII-12-a&chapter=18&clang=_en (accessed 13 January 2025).

Information Documents and Resources

A/HRC/47/26/Add.1, 15 June 2021, https://digitallibrary.un.org/record/3929055?ln=en&v=pdf (accessed 13 January 2025).
New South Wales Legislative Council Inquiry into the Equality Legislation Amendment (LGBTIQA+) Bill, 2024, Equality Legislation Amendment (LGBTIQA+) Bill 2023 https://www.parliament.nsw.gov.au/bills/Pages/bill-details.aspx?pk=18460 (accessed 2 March 2025).
Parliament of Australia, *Senate Inquiry into Current and Proposed Sexual Consent Laws in Australia,* 2023, Current and proposed sexual consent laws in Australia—Parliament of Australia, https://www.aph.gov.au/Parliamentary_Business/Committees/Senate/Legal_and_Constitutional_Affairs/sexualcontentlaws/ (accessed 2 March 2025).
Queensland Parliament, *Explanatory Notes,* Queensland Parliament Inquiry on the Criminal Code (Decriminalising Sex Work) and Other Legislation Amendment Bill, 2024, https://www.parliament.qld.gov.au/Work-of-the-Assembly/Tabled-Papers/docs/5724t206/5724t206-b09c.pdf (accessed 2 March 2025).
Sex Workers Outreach Project (SWOP), Preliminary Submission to NSW Law Reform Commission Review of Consent in Relation to Sexual

Offences, 6, https://lawreform.nsw.gov.au/documents/Current-projects/Consent/Preliminary-submissions/PCO103.pdf (accessed 13 January 2025).
UN Committee on the Elimination of Discrimination Against Women, CEDAW General Recommendation No 19: Violence against Women, ¶6, U.N. Doc. CEDAW/C 1992/L.1/Add.15 (1992), https://www.un.org/womenwatch/daw/cedaw/recommendations/recomm.htm#recom19 (accessed 13 January 2025).
United Nations, Special Procedures of the Human Rights Council, https://www.ohchr.org/en/special-procedures-human-rights-council (accessed 13 January 2025).
Watson, Simone, Open Letter to Amnesty International (2014).

11

Informed Consent and Preventing Loss of Innocence: Child and Forced Marriage in the United States

Shabina Begum

Introduction

According to the United Nations (UN Population Fund 2025):

> Child marriage is a human rights violation. Despite laws against it, the practice remains widespread: Globally, one in every five girls is formally married or in an informal union, before reaching age 18.

The US does not currently have a working definition of child and forced marriage. Thus the starting premise in itself is limited. Turning to the Convention of the Rights of the Child which the US has signed but not ratified (Hill 2021), this refers to child marriage as unions of minors below the age of 18, yet does not discuss a child being forced into a marriage.

S. Begum (✉)
Goodman Ray Solicitors, London, UK
e-mail: shabinabegum@goodmanray.com

J. A. Scutt (ed.), *Women, Power and Autonomy*,
https://doi.org/10.1007/978-3-031-97958-3_11

The recent legislative change in the US on a state-by-state level to raise the age of marriage suggests that child marriage is being viewed as a problem, and a majority of the discussions have focused around outlawing child marriage by raising the age of marriage to 18 years. Some discussions on criminalizing the act are occurring, but no active steps have been taken to create specific legislation to tackle the issue at a state or federal level.

Statistics

In one of the largest studies conducted by Tahirih Justice Center (2017), it was found that between the years 2000–2015, 200,000 children under the age of 18 were married in America. Breaking down the statistics and looking across the states, an even more harrowing picture emerges (Tahirih Justice Center 2017):

> For example, records from the Virginia Department of Health show that from 2004 to 2013, nearly 4,500 children were married. Nearly 90% of them were girls, nearly 90% married adults, and some of those adults were decades older. Similar records from Maryland show that 3,100 children were married from 2000 to 2014.

The Pew Research Center analyzed the data from the Census Bureau's American Community Survey in 2014, finding: "About 57,800 minors in the U.S. ages 15 to 17 were married as of 2014" (McClendon and Sandstrom 2016). This provides a snapshot of the number of child marriages in one year. The research also highlighted that child marriage is more common in the Southern States. It is, however, silent on the ethnicity, religious group, or socio-economic class of the children involved in the cases.

Although the US government recognizes child marriage as a domestic issue, the responsibility of providing any form of support is shouldered by a limited number of NGOs which undertake the work of providing direct services and protecting and supporting survivors of child marriage on a domestic level. The main NGOs identified are Unchained at Last (nda, b), Tahirih Justice Center (2017), Sauti Yetu (NYC Service 2023), Manavi (1985–2025), and AHA Foundation (2025). Notably no coordinated government service deals with child and forced marriage, meaning that these NGOs are undertaking either advocacy work or providing support services to protect potential victims or actual survivors of child and forced marriage. This lack of US government action, whether federal or state, and reliance on NGOs, is concerning given the statistics and how widespread child marriage is across the US.

There are many reasons for child marriage occurring as a global practice, and there are, equally if not more, factors which place a girl at risk of being subjected to child marriage. According to UNICEF some of the reasons include "poverty, the perception that marriage will provide 'protection', family honour [sic], social norms, customary or religious laws that condone the practice, an inadequate legislative framework and the state of a country's civil registration system" (AHA Foundation 2025). It is due to these wide-ranging reasons that eliminating child marriage is complex. From the outset it is apparent that the changes must be made on a social, cultural, religious, economic, and legislative level. An added complexity is that the same practice "will vary from one community to the next and the practice may look different across regions ... even within the same country" (Girls Not Brides 2025a, b). Therefore to eliminate the problem the subtle differences and cultural contexts need to be addressed carefully.

Federal vs State

On 16 February 1995 the US signed the *Convention on the Rights of the Child*. The failure to ratify it leaves the US as the only member state of the UN not to have done so (Humanium 2015; Human Rights Watch 2023; Human Rights Watch 2025). According to this treaty,[1] nation states are prohibited from permitting or giving validity to marriages of minors below the age of 18 (Unite for Children 2008, 2).

[1] Article 1, *Convention on the Rights of the Child* (1989).

It is shocking to realize that in the US each state varies in the legal age of marriage and, in effect, in the way a minor is defined at the point of marriage, this meaning that an individual does not have to be aged 18 or below to be regarded a minor at the point of marriage. This is a surprising position for the US to adopt, considering that it has expressed globally how harmful underage marriage is and recognizes the significance of raising to 18 the age of marriage. Bearing this in mind, it is an unmissable oversight that the US government is allowing for child marriage to subsist within its own borders.

As of 2017, child marriage, or marriage before age 18, was legal in all 50 US states (Unchained at Last nda, b). In August 2017, Tahirih Justice Center noted the different minimum legal ages of marriage across each state in the US, summarizing their initial findings as the following (Tahirih Justice Center 2017):

- 25 states do not set any age floor by statute;
- Three states (Virginia, Texas, and New York, in order of enactment) limit marriage to legal adults[2];
- In eight states and Washington DC, clerks alone—without judges—can approve marriages of all minors;
- Only 17 states require judges to consider the minors' best interests;
- Nine states expressly permit pregnancy as a basis on which to lower the minimum marriage age.

The expression "no floor age" (noted above) is used in the context of "if the statutory exceptions are met, a child of any age could be married" (Tahirih Justice Center 2016). According to Humaniam, before 2017, 24 states[3] did not have a floor age, when a statutory exception applied. Since 2017 this number has been reduced to 21, as Massachusetts, New Jersey and Rhode Island have raised the minimum

[2] The age limit of an adult is not 18 for all three states, this is further discussed below.

[3] Arizona, Arkansas, California, Colorado, Connecticut, Delaware, Idaho, Kentucky, Louisiana, Maine, Massachusetts, Michigan, Mississippi, Missouri, Nevada, New Jersey, New Mexico, Ohio, Oklahoma, Pennsylvania, Rhode Island, Tennessee, West Virginia and Wyoming (Tahirih Justice Center 2016). Note: The number of states has been amended according to the relevant statutory changes taking place since November 2016.

age of marriage on a state level to 18. A close look at the legislative mechanisms across states demonstrates that the most common exceptions appearing in the state statutes enabling a minor to be married are parental consent or judicial approval, and nine states (Arkansas, Florida, Illinois, Iowa, Kentucky, Montana, Nevada, Ohio and South Carolina)[4] expressly mention pregnancy as an exception. According to Tahirih Justice Center (2016):

> Lax statutory exceptions based on parental consent (which can hide parental coercion) or pregnancy (which can be evidence of rape) can actually *facilitate* forced marriages and often leave older minors especially unprotected.

These exceptions emphasize how certain states in the US are united with other jurisdictions around the world where child and forced marriages are motivated by the desire to control the sexuality or reproductive rights of girls (Girls Not Brides 2022).

Many states in the US have attempted to raise the legal age of marriage to 18 in order to outlaw child marriage. One such example is Virginia, which is the pioneer state to increase the age of marriage to 18 with no exceptions (Virginia Decoded nd).[5] The Bill came into effect on July 1, 2016,[6] and prior to this date, girls as young as 13 or those who fell pregnant could legally be married in Virginia (Portnoy 2016). In 2016, according to the National Conference of State Legislatures, similar Bills were introduced in California, Maryland, New Jersey and New York (Portnoy 2016). The State of New York passed Senate Bill 4407B which raised the age of marriage from 14 to 17 years of age.[7]

---

[4] Understanding State Statutes on Minimum Marriage Age and Exceptions (Tahirih Justice Center 2016). (This data was extracted from the report after the author of this chapter conducted a search of which states included the pregnancy exception.).

[5] Va. Code Ann, § 20–48, http://law.lis.virginia.gov/vacode/20-48. (The minimum age at which persons may marry shall be 18, unless a minor has been emancipated by court order. Upon application for a marriage license, an emancipated minor shall provide a certified copy of the order of emancipation.).

[6] Va, SB415 (2016).

[7] New York Senate Bill 4407B, 2016 (2017 in force), NY State Senate Bill 2017-S4407B, https://www.nysenate.gov/legislation/bills/2017/S4407 (accessed 2 March 2025).

This came into force in July 2017, and then in 2021 New York passed "Naila's Law," raising the age of marriage to 18 years (Tahirih Center 2023; Grey 2021; Ramos 2021). Texas Senate Bill 1705 came into effect on 1 September 2017,[8] stating that parties can be married only if they are 18 or emancipated minors (Samuels 2017). Florida approved Senate Bill 140 on 5 March 2018,[9] incorporated a committee amendment permitting the marriage of a pregnant 16- or 17-year-old (Human Rights Watch 2018) or if there is parental consent and the partner is no more than two years older (Ceballos 2018).

Since 2017 as a result of the strong advocacy campaign led tirelessly by Unchained at Last (nda, b), various states have raised the age of marriage. This includes Delaware and New Jersey in 2018, followed by American Samoa in 2018, the US Virgin Islands, Pennsylvania and Minnesota in 2020, Rhode Island and New York (as mentioned above) in 2021, Massachusetts in 2022, Vermont, Connecticut and Michigan in 2023, and Washington, Virginia and New Hampshire in 2024 (Unchained at Last nda). Raising the age of marriage to 18 is a good starting point for a better future for all minors. But is this sufficient in the absence of protective and preventive legislative mechanisms to minimize the risks of child and forced marriage?

Legislative Framework

Currently no federal law exists to combat child and forced marriage in the US (Landau 2016). The current examples of child and forced marriage legislation which do exist, do so on a state level across 10 states (Tahirih Justice Center 2016)[10]: California, Maryland, Minnesota, Mississippi, Nevada, Oklahoma, US Virgin Islands, West Virginia, Virginia District of Columbia, and Florida. These states either have

[8] Texas Senate Bill No (1705), 85(R) SB 1705—Enrolled version, https://capitol.texas.gov/tlodocs/85R/billtext/pdf/SB01705F.pdf (accessed 2 March 2025).

[9] Florida Senate Bill 140 (2018), Senate Bill 140 (2018)—The Florida Senate, https://www.flsenate.gov/Session/Bill/2018/140 (accessed 2 March 2025).

[10] Compiled from Tahirih Justice Center 2016, the number of states has been amended according to the relevant statutory changes taking place since November 2016.

restrictive legislation which do not protect minors and male victims, or categorize child and forced marriage under ancillary crimes such as human trafficking or prostitution.

These state statutes do not deal with child and forced marriage as a free-standing issue. Instead, they rely on other crimes which may be ancillary risks and harms to which a minor may be subjected to as a result or as part of the child and forced marriage transaction. These statutes can therefore be criticized for being "antiquated [as they]... fail to address the complicated dynamics [and] characteristic[s] of forced marriage" (Landau 2016, 2). Wrongful categorization of child and forced marriage can have various consequences, for instance the District of Columbia deals with child marriage as prostitution, arguably harmful as "[l]abeling forced marriage victims as prostitutes can lead to blaming the victim for what has been done to her and cause feelings of shame that could make her less likely to seek help" (Landau 2016, 4). It must also be noted that "[c]onflating human trafficking with forced marriage ignores the complex family law dynamics that are unique to forced marriage" (Landau 2016, 4). Furthermore these statutes "fail to hold accountable the variety of perpetrators involved, such as extended family or influential community members" (Alanen 2012, 4). Further, as Sri and Raja (2013, 7) observe:

> ... most of the statutes fail to empower authorities to intervene *before* a forced marriage occurs, when there is still an opportunity to prevent a host of harms that often flow from forced marriage.

The American Bar Association (2014, 2) summed up the legislative gap in the following manner:

> State level legal responses to forced marriage are limited, and while existing laws can be tools to prevent forced marriages or protect victims in some cases, they are not widely used or may offer inadequate protections... At a federal level, little effort has been made to address forced marriages involving US citizens or residents.

The fact that the US lacks a working definition of child and/or forced marriage means that not only, as noted above, is the starting premise limited, but it draws open a wider gap in overlooking a large category of children and vulnerable adults at risk of forced marriage. Turning to the *Convention on the Rights of the Child*, there is reference to child marriage as unions of minors below the age of 18, however it does not discuss a child being forced into a marriage. The definition of forced marriage set out in the US State Department travel page (2024) refers to minors being forced into marriage, but does not fully explain the key components of a forced marriage.

Forced marriage is often mistaken with arranged marriage despite the two being distinct practices, the distinguishing aspect being located in the principle or notion of consent.[11] The US Department of State recognizes the difference between the two practices and states in this regard (2005):

> … arranged marriages have been a long-standing tradition in many cultures and countries. The Department respects this tradition and makes very clear distinction between a forced marriage and an arranged marriage.

Yet effective legislation for child and forced marriage is possible only if the key components of a forced marriage are identified.

In the absence of a definition of child and forced marriage in the US, it useful to turn to a jurisdiction in the global north which is further ahead in the journey to eradicate child and forced marriage, namely the UK. The UK Government's characterization of forced marriage incorporates its definition in the following terms[12]:

---

[11] For an exploration of the law of consent in the context of forced and arranged marriage, see Scutt (2014).

[12] *Marriage and Civil Partnership (Minimum Age) Act* 2022 (legislation.gov.uk) (accessed 27 August 2024); Marriage and Civil Partnership (Minimum Age) Bill—House of Lords Library (parliament.uk) (accessed 27 August 2024); and see also College of Policing 2023. Forced marriage—GOV.UK (https://www.gov.uk/guidance/forced-marriage (accessed 13 September 2025); England and Wales, Section 121 of the Anti-social Behaviour, Crime and Policing Act 2014.

> ... forced marriage is [a marriage] where one or both people do not (or in cases of people with learning disabilities, cannot) consent to the marriage and pressure or abuse is used.

Forced and child marriage are indefensible practices recognized in the UK as a form of violence against women and men, domestic/child abuse, and a serious abuse of human rights. The pressure exerted on people to marry against their will can be physical (including threats, actual physical violence, and sexual violence) or emotional and psychological (for example, when someone is made to feel they are bringing shame on their family). Financial abuse (taking the individual's wages or not giving them any money) can also be a factor (Foreign and Commonwealth Office 2013/2023). The definition recognizes the issue of an individual's ability to consent to a marriage; it recognizes forced marriage is a human rights abuse, and expressly recognizes that women and men, girls and boys can be victims. In providing specificity to the range of conduct which comes within its purview, the legislation in the UK sets out the various types of pressure which can be placed to coerce an individual into marrying against their will. It should further be noted that whilst forced marriage is considered a criminal offence throughout the UK, in England and Wales there are also civil remedies available to forced marriage victims. The civil remedies are set out under the *Forced Marriage (Civil Protection) Act* 2007 (FMA 2007) which came into effect in 2008 and was incorporated into the *Family Law Act* 1996. Section 63A(1) of the *Family Law Act* 1996 (FLA) awards protection in the form of a forced marriage protection order to victims who are about to be subjected to a forced marriage and it also protects those who have already been forced into a marriage. This enhances protection for potential victims and serves as a preventative mechanism.

Informed Consent

A defining feature of child and forced marriage is the concept of informed consent. This is perhaps where the most confusion arises in the context of arranged and forced marriages. The pivotal point in an arranged marriage scenario is often when an adult individual in this arrangement may be unable to retract their consent from their initial "yes." As stated by Marai Larasi: "Your yes is only as good as your ability to say no" (Otoo-Oyortey and Pobi 2003). Therefore if an individual is placed in a situation where they cannot withdraw their initial consent it is very likely that they have been placed under some kind of external pressure, whether cultural, societal or religious, and as a consequence they say "yes," but this consent is in effect tainted (Scutt 2014).

Arranged marriages have been upheld by UK courts as a legitimate cultural practice[13] and perhaps it is no more than being introduced to a would-be spouse by a friend or a matchmaking website. But caution is essential. Once there is no consent the marriage can no longer be regarded as an arranged marriage, and it becomes a forced marriage (Scutt 2014).

Often it is imagined that an individual's ability to consent is effected through domestic violence inflicted upon them. The US Department of Justice (2025) defines domestic violence in the US as:

> A pattern of abusive behavior in any relationship that is used by one partner to gain or maintain power and control over another intimate partner. Domestic violence can be physical, sexual, emotional, economic, or psychological actions or threats of actions that influence another person. This includes any behaviors that intimidate, manipulate, humiliate, isolate, frighten, terrorize, coerce, threaten, blame, hurt, injure, or wound someone.

Although in the US this definition is limited to intimate partners, in the UK the definition is extended to include family members. However, it is a mistake to categorize the level of pressure and coercion exerted in forced marriage situations among family members as a simple extension of what

[13] "A forced marriage is entirely different from an arranged marriage in which, in conformity with their cultural expectations, two persons consent to marry each other pursuant to an arrangement negotiated between their respective families": Lord Wilson SJC (para 9). *R (on the application of Aguilar Quila) v Secretary of State for the Home Department (Aguilar, interested party); R (on the application of Bibi and another) v Secretary of State for the Home Department* [2011] UKSC 45, R (on the application of Quila and another) (FC) (Respondents) v Secretary of State for the Home Department (Appellant)—UK Supreme Court, https://supremecourt.uk/cases/uksc-2011-0022 (accessed 2 March 2025).

is routinely understood as domestic violence. Forced marriage cases are more nuanced, complex, and specific, usually involving an element of so-called honour-based violence (Gill et al. 2014).

Many researchers, activists, and practitioners make the distinction between "honour"-based violence and typical domestic violence due to the nature of the crimes and the way they manifest. As Nazir Afzal (2014; cited Helba et al. 2016) has said:

> Honor violence is a form of family violence in that it is committed by family members against other family members. However, unlike "traditional" family or domestic violence in extreme cases of honor violence there is a conspiratorial and less impulsive quality, evidenced by the systematic surveillance of the victim, involvement of one or more family members, and, in some instances, the family engagement of bounty hunters or assassins to find and kill victims.

Perpetrators of "honor" based violence have a sense of "honor" rather than one of wrongdoing and believe that coercing, harming, or killing the victim is the only way to either prevent behavior that would bring dishonor to the family or to restore the family's damaged honour (Helba et al. 2016, 3). The concept of "honor" is especially intrinsic to the entire family's conduct, as even girls are raised from a young age to believe that their ability to choose a boyfriend or life partner and ultimately their sexuality is linked to the "honor" of the family. Thus, what may appear to be free and full consent is in fact skewed, as the option to say "no" would be at the cost of the honor of the family. The scale of consent is already weighted heavily on one side.

Preventing Loss of Innocence

When minors end up being forced into a marriage, they face a panoply of difficulties in leaving the situation as in the US they have no access to shelters and are unable to petition for a divorce or annulment, as they are under 18 (Gunaratna 2017):

> One dominant reason that advocates are concerned with married minors having access to divorce is because data shows [HAQ nd] that child marriage leads to higher risk of domestic violence.

These barriers confirm how child marriage makes girls further vulnerable and open to abuse.

To mobilize the movement of ending child and forced marriage at a faster pace, the US should consider broadening the remit of the federal law to include "child marriage" as a form of child abuse, thereby also urging states to broaden their definition of "child abuse" and consider it a child protection issue. Then young girls may have a better chance of being protected from a harmful and dangerous practice. The additional protection that this would provide is that it would enable girls to approach teachers or child protection services at schools for advice or support (HM Government 2014). This could in turn enable authorities to intervene legitimately to prevent the practice or assist a child at potential risk of marriage to escape the situation safely—and to safety.

To ensure effective protective mechanisms exist and are operative, the US must consider implementing legislation to prevent child and forced marriage from taking place, US legislators need to think about the different points at which a child may require preventative or protective measures, and at what point prosecution would be a necessary and proportionate response.

Current measures in the US arguably fall short of a proper solution to child and forced marriage, and the danger is a short-sighted solution that could fuel the problem. Arguably an apt response would be combined civil measures and criminal sanctions, as adopted by England and Wales.[14] This would mean passing civil legislation specific to child and forced marriage, so that it captures various stages and is preventative as well as protective; which would mean preventing the risk of a child being subject to a child and forced marriage; and also protecting the child or vulnerable adult if the actual marriage does take place.

[14] The recommendations will be gender neutral, applying the principle that legislation should not be restricted by gender.

Bibliography

Reported Cases

R (on the application of Aguilar Quila) v Secretary of State for the Home Department (Aguilar, interested party); R (on the application of Bibi and another) v Secretary of State for the Home Department [2011] UKSC 45, R (on the application of Quila and another) (FC) (Respondents) v Secretary of State for the Home Department (Appellant)—UK Supreme Court, https://supremecourt.uk/cases/uksc-2011-0022 (accessed 2 March 2025).

Statutes and International Conventions or Treaties

Convention on the Rights of the Child, Article 1, 1989, Convention on the Rights of the Child text | UNICEF, https://www.unicef.org/child-rights-convention/convention-text (accessed 2 February 2025).

Article 24(3) of the *Convention on the Rights of the Child*, Article 24(3), 1989, Convention on the Rights of the Child text | UNICEF, https://www.unicef.org/child-rights-convention/convention-text (accessed 2 February 2025).

Florida Senate Bill 140 (2018), Senate Bill 140 (2018)—The Florida Senate, https://www.flsenate.gov/Session/Bill/2018/140 (accessed 2 March 2025).

Marriage and Civil Partnership (Minimum Age) Bill—House of Lords Library (parliament.uk), https://lordslibrary.parliament.uk/marriage-and-civil-partnership-minimum-age-bill/#:~:text=The%20main%20legislation%20covering%20marriages%20and%20civil%20partnerships,is%20under%20the%20age%20of%2016%20is%20void. (accessed 27 August 2024).

Marriage and Civil Partnership (Minimum Age) Act 2022 (legislation.gov.uk), https://www.legislation.gov.uk/ukpga/2022/28 (accessed 27 August 2024).

New York Senate Bill 4407B, 2016 (2017 in force), NY State Senate Bill 2017-S4407B, https://www.nysenate.gov/legislation/bills/2017/S4407 (accessed 2 March 2025).

Texas Senate Bill No 1705, 85(R) SB 1705—Enrolled version, https://capitol.texas.gov/tlodocs/85R/billtext/pdf/SB01705F.pdf (accessed 2 March 2025).

Va. Code Ann, § 20–48, § 20–48. Minimum age of marriage, https://law.lis.virginia.gov/vacode/title20/chapter5/section20-48/ (accessed 2 March 2025).

Va, SB415 (2016), Bill Text: VA SB415 | 2012 | Regular Session | Engrossed | LegiScan, https://legiscan.com/VA/text/SB415/id/565630 (accessed 2 March 2025).

Articles and Book Chapters

Afzal, Nazir, "Project Interview", 2014, cited Cynthia Helba, Matthew Bernstein, Mariel Leonard and Erin Bauer, Report on Exploratory Study, U.S Department of Justice, May 2015, Report on Exploratory Study into Honor Violence Measurement Methods | Office of Justice Programs, https://www.ojp.gov/library/publications/report-exploratory-study-honor-violence-measurement-methods (accessed 20 November 2024)

Alanen, Julia, "Shattering the Silence Surrounding Forced and Early Marriage in the United States", *Child. Legal Rights Journal* vol 32, no 2, 8 May 2012, http://preventforcedmarriage.org/wp-content/uploads/2016/05/Elizabeth-Landau_Custom-or-Crime-II.pdf (accessed 3 May 2024).

Ceballos, Ana, "Senate, House Reach Compromise on Controversial Child Marriage Bill", FLORIDA POLITICS, 5 March 2018, https://floridapolitics.com/archives/258162-senate-house-reach-compromise-controversial-child-marriage-bill (accessed 2 March 2025).

Girls Not Brides, "About child marriage", 2025a, https://www.girlsnotbrides.org/about-child-marriage/ (accessed 2 March 2025).

Girls not Brides, "Girls' education and child marriage", 15 September 2022 https://theirworld.org/news/getting-girls-into-school-is-best-way-to-stop-child-marriage/ (accessed 20 November 2024).

Girls Not Brides, "Why Does Child Marriage Happen?" 2025b, https://www.girlsnotbrides.org/about-child-marriage/why-child-marriage-happens/ (accessed 2 March 2025).

Gray, Lucy Ann, "New York only just ended child marriage—but what about the rest of America?", The Independent, 10 August 2021 https://www.independent.co.uk/news/world/americas/child-marriage-us-age-ny-b1897500.html (accessed 2 March 2025).

Gunaratna, Shanika, "The 'ugly' reality of child marriage in the U.S.", CBS NEWS, 5 May 2017 https://www.cbsnews.com/news/child-marriage-in-the-u-s-surprisingly-widespread/ (accessed 2 March 2025)

Hill, Nicholas, Explanation of Position for the Rights of the Child Resolution—United States Mission to the United Nations, 2021 (usmission.gov) (accessed 2 March 2025).

Humaniam, "Convention on the Rights of the Child: the United States lags behind", 8 December 2015, https://www.humanium.org/en/usa-and-crc/, https://usun.usmission.gov/explanation-of-position-for-the-rights-of-the-child-resolution/ (accessed 3 May 2018).

Human Rights Watch, “Florida: Child Marriage Ban Hits a Bump Legislators Should Support Bill Setting Minimum Age at 18”, 4 February 2018, https://www.hrw.org/news/2018/02/05/florida-child-marriage-ban-hits-bump, https://www.hrw.org/news/2018/02/05/florida-child-marriage-ban-hits-bump (accessed 24 August 2024).

Human Rights Watch, “How Do US States Measure Up on Child Rights?” 2023, https://www.hrw.org/feature/2022/09/13/how-do-states-measure-up-child-rights (accessed 27 August 2024).

Landau, Elizabeth M, “Custom or Crime?: Part II of IV: Legal Remedies for Forced Marriage Victims and Survivors”, *American Journal of Family Law,* Spring 2016, Volume 30, Number 1, at 46–57, reprinted online, available at: http://preventforcedmarriage.org/wp-content/uploads/2016/05/Elizabeth-Landau_Custom-or-Crime-II.pdf (accessed 3 May 2024).

McClendon, David and Sandstrom, Aleksandra, “Child Marriage is Rare in the U.S., Though This Varies by State”, *Pew Research Center*, 1 November 2016, http://www.pewresearch.org/fact-tank/2016/11/01/child-marriage-is-rare-in-the-u-s-though-this-varies-by-state/ (accessed 3 May 2018).

Otoo-Oyortey, Naana and Pobi, Sonita, “Early Marriage and Poverty ...”, Forum on Marriage and the Rights of Women and Girls, *Gender and Development*, vol 11 no 2, 2003, 42–51, Early Marriage and Poverty: Exploring Links and Key Policy Issues on JSTOR, https://www.jstor.org/stable/4030639 (accessed 2 March 2025).

Portnoy, Jenna, “Why 13-year-olds ...”, *The Washington Post*, 3 July 2016, Why 13-year-olds can no longer marry in Virginia—The Washington Post, https://www.washingtonpost.com/local/virginia-politics/why-13-year-olds-can-no-longer-marry-in-virginia/2016/07/03/03849e46-3ef9-11e6-a66f-aa6c1883b6b1_story.html (accessed 2 March 2025).

Samuels, Alex, “New law seeks to reduce number of child brides in Texas”, *The Texas Tribune*, 26 September 2017 https://www.texastribune.org/2017/09/26/new-law-seeks-reduce-number-child-brides-texas/ (accessed 2 March 2025).

Scutt, Jocelynne A, “Arranged’ Marriages And Nullity Law: Should Culture Override Or Inform Fraud And Duress?” *Denning Law Journal,* vol 26, 62–97, 2014, human Rights, (ubplj.org), https://www.ubplj.org/index.php/dlj/article/view/935 (accessed 27 August 2024).

Sri, Vidya and Raja, Darakshan, Voices from the Frontline: Addressing Forced Marriage Within the United States, Gangashakti: 2013, at 7, available at http://www.hks.harvard.edu/cchrp/research/working_papers/VidyaSri_VoicesFromTheFrontline.pdf(last visited 3 May 2024).

Tahirih Justice Center, "Ending Child Marriage in the United States: Progress, Lessons Learned, and Where We Go from Here" 6 November 2023 https://www.tahirih.org/news/ending-child-marriage-in-the-united-states-progress-lessons-learned-and-where-we-go-from-here/ (accessed 2 March 2025).

Tahirih Justice Center, "Falling Through The Cracks, How Laws Allow Child Marriage to Happen in Today's America", August 2017, http://www.tahirih.org/wp-content/uploads/2017/08/TahirihChildMarriageReport-1.pdf (accessed 2 March 2025).

Tahirih Justice Center, "Understanding State Statutes on Minimum Marriage Age and Exceptions", November 2016 https://www.tahirih.org/pubs/understanding-state-statutes-on-minimum-marriage-age-and-exceptions/ (accessed 2 March 2025).

Books and Reports

American Bar Association, *Resolution and Report 112B*, American Bar Association Commission on Domestic and Sexual Violence, 12 August 2014, http://www.americanbar.org/ content/dam/aba/administrative/house_of_delegates/resolutions/2014_hod_annual_meeting_112b.authcheckdam.pdf (accessed 15 April 2018).

Gill, Aisha K, Strange, Carolyn and Roberts, Karl (eds), *'Honour' Killing and Violence—Theory, Policy and Practice*, Palgrave Macmillan, Basingstoke, UK, 2014.

HM Government, *Multi-Agency Practice Guidelines: Handling Cases of Forced Marriage*, June 2014, https://assets.publishing.service.gov.uk/government/uploads/system/uploads/attachment_data/file/322307/HMG_MULTI_AGENCY_PRACTICE_GUIDELINES_v1_180614_FINAL.pdf HM Government Multi-agency practice guidelines: Handling cases of Forced Marriage, (accessed 2 March 2025).

Human Rights Watch, *World Report*, 2025, World Report 2025 | Human Rights Watch, https://www.hrw.org/world-report/2025 (accessed 2 February 2025).

Information Documents and Sources

About Us—Girls Not Brides, "Girls not Brides", 2022–2025, https://www.girlsnotbrides.org/about-girls-not-brides/ (accessed 2 February 2025).

Aha*foundation* (Aryan Hirsi Ali Foundation), 2025, https://www.theahafoundation.org (last visited 3 May 2018).

Child Marriage and the Law, *Legislative Reform Initiative Paper Series,* Background paper for UNICEF Report on State of the World's Children 2007, https://www.wcwonline.org/pdf/asia2007conf/Child%20Marriage%20and%20the%20Law.pdf (accessed 2 February 2025).

College of Policing, Legislation prohibits child marriage | College of Policing, https://www.college.police.uk/article/legislation-prohibits-child-marriage, 21 April 2023 (accessed 27 August 2024).

HAQ, Centre for Child Rights, Child Marriage in India: Achievements, Gaps and Challenges, Response to Questions for OHCHR Report on Preventing Child, Early and Forced Marriages for Twenty-sixth Session of the Human Rights Council, nd, http://www.ohchr.org/Documents/Issues/Women/WRGS/ForcedMarriage/NGO/HAQCentreForChildRights1.pdf (accessed 3 May 2024).

Manavi, *Our Mission*, 1985–2025, http://www.manavi.org (last visited 3 May 2018).

NYC Service, *Sauti Yetu*, 2023, https://www.nycservice.org/organizations/index.php?org_id=2551, https://www.nycservice.org/organizations/index.php?org_id=2551 (last visited 3 May 2018).

Ramos, Phil, *Assembly Man Ramos Passes Bill Raising Age of Consent for Marriage to 18, Protecting Minors from Predators*, Phil Ramos—Assembly District 6 |Assembly Member Directory | New York State Assembly, https://nyassembly.gov/mem/Phil-Ramos/story/97385 (accessed 2 March 2025).

UK Gov, Forced marriage Information and practice guidelines for professionals protecting, advising and supporting victims, Foreign & Commonwealth Office and Home Office, Forced marriage—GOV.UK, https://www.gov.uk/guidance/forced-marriage (accessed 2 March 2025).

UN Population Fund, *Child marriage*, 2025, https://www.unfpa.org/child-marriage (accessed 9 July 2024).

U.S. Department of Foreign Affairs Manual, 7 FAM 1743 (2005) http://www.state.gov/documents/organization/86822.pdf (accessed 27 August 2024)

U.S. Department of State—Bureau of Consular Affairs, Forced Marriage (international travel, Emergencies), 2024, https://travel.state.gov/content/travel/en/international-travel/emergencies/forced-marriage.html (accessed 3 May 2018).

Unchained at Last, *Child Marriage in the US*, nda, http://www.unchainedatlast.org (accessed 2 March 2025).

Unchained at last, *50 for 50*, ndb, https://www.unchainedatlast.org/child-marriage-in-the-u-s/ (accessed 19 June 2024).

Unite for Children, *Child Marriage and the Law Legislative Reform Initiative Paper Series*, UNICEF, January 2008, https://www.unicef.org/policyanalysis/files/Child_Marriage_and_the_Law(1).pdf (accessed 27 August 2024).

United States Department of Justice, *Domestic Violence*, 2025 https://www.justice.gov/ovw/domestic-violence (accessed 2 March 2025).

Virginia Decoded, *Minimum age of marriage; History*, Minimum age of marriage (§ 20–48)—Virginia Decoded - Virginia Decoded, nd, https://vacode.org/2016/20/3/20-48/#:~:text=The%20minimum%20age%20at%20which%20persons%20may%20marry,a%20certified%20copy%20of%20the%20order%20of%20emancipation. (accessed 2 March 2025).

12

Between Legal and Non-legal Terrains: Religious Nationalisms and Racialized Women Immigrants in the United States

Rianka Roy, Bandana Purkayastha, and Anjana Narayan

Introduction

Religious nationalism—or nationalist practices and discourses shaped by religious dogmatism—strikes at the heart of laws that are designed to provide human rights for all in secular societies. Within secular and democratic nation-states like the US, scholars studying religious nationalism have typically focused on groups that share a primary marker of identity with the dominant group, for example, whiteness, but they build their cause against both the mainstream as well as minoritized groups.

R. Roy (✉)
Wake Forest University, Winston-Salem, NC, USA
e-mail: royr@wfu.edu

B. Purkayastha
University of Connecticut, Mansfield, CT, USA
e-mail: bandana.purkayastha@uconn.edu

A. Narayan
California State Polytechnic University, Pomona, CA, USA
e-mail: anarayan@cpp.edu

J. A. Scutt (ed.), *Women, Power and Autonomy*,
https://doi.org/10.1007/978-3-031-97958-3_12

Within the larger agenda of grasping power—and gaining more adherents to their cause—religious-nationalist groups build narratives of their victimization in ways that label marginalized groups as perpetrators of violence and threats to national security. Along with explicit or implicit messages, religious nationalists castigate those who practice different religions (Blee 2004; Banerjee 2010; Sarkar 1995)—such as immigrants of diverse faiths, nationalities, and cultures. In the US, this is evident in the growing xenophobic rhetoric among religious nationalists criminalizing immigrants. As gendered minorities, women, however, are central to religious nationalist projects—both as patriarchal cultural symbols and as foot soldiers to the cause (Blee 2002; Peters 2024a, b). Evidence of this is seen in the recent resurgence of religious nationalist attempts to control women's reproductive choices in the US. Women have been enthusiastically involved in both "pro-choice" (that is, pro-abortion) and "pro-life" (that is, anti-abortion) movements.

In focusing on an immigrant group in the US—Hindu Indian American women—we have two aims—(1) to examine the larger structures that foster religious nationalisms and shape their relations with racialized and gendered minorities; and (2) to determine the location and agency of immigrant women within these structures. We choose this group because it is positioned at the intersection of two strands of religious nationalism—white Christian nationalism in the US, and Hindu nationalism or Hindutva in India (and in the Indian diaspora in the US). We discuss how as gendered and racialized minorities in the US, Hindu Indian immigrant women navigate the otherness imposed on them by Christian nationalism; and how they simultaneously navigate their gendered position within Hindutva, or the nationalist manifestation of their native religion (Narayan and Purkayastha 2009).

We situate our observations within the current rise of religious nationalism in both countries where the governments and judicial institutions are officially secular, and apparently distinct from the direct control of dominant religions. However, we stress a well-established postcolonial critique of nation-states in colonial modernity. The critique suggests that this emergence of religious nationalism in secular states is *not* a paradox. Rather, the instruments of laws and governance in both countries are steeped in religious models of statecraft and citizenship.

In the US, Christian symbols and practices are normalized in legal and political rights, institutions and practices (Joshi 2020, 2006). Similarly, in postcolonial India, secularism was adopted as a framework in its Constitution to ensure that all members of the diverse population could exercise their freedom to practice their faith. This meaning does not necessarily align with the Western idea of secularism as a hard separation of religion and the state (Chatterjee 1994). But Nandy (1997) adds that the legal frameworks of secular governance, too, was an outcome of colonial modernity—that normalizes the marginality of colonized, racialized and gendered populations. Therefore, while Hindu nationalists castigate secularism (Jaffrelot 2018), they also coopt it and turn the inclusive religiosity of the Hindu faith into a machinery to govern the secular state (Nandy 1997). As a result, the so-called "neutral" laws (Korteweg 2017; Purkayastha and Roy 2023) in modern secular and liberal democracies marginalize some communities—such as racialized and religious minorities, women, and immigrants.

We draw upon previously published research that we have conducted over nearly two decades, much of this research specifically about women, and present two observations about the relationship among women immigrants, religious nationalism, and laws in the US. First, we discuss the legal constraints within the US that affect people who are neither Christian nor white. We mark persistent legal and political discourses inflected with colonial and racial imageries. We demonstrate how the legitimate models of citizenship and governance in the US accommodates Christian nationalist abhorrence toward racialized immigrants. We also argue that the same Christian nationalism makes room for other religious-nationalist discourses—such as Hindutva—in the US. Facing marginality in and exclusion from legal rights, many racialized and gendered minorities seek an alternative that enables them to assert their own religious affiliations and nationalist pride (Kurien 2001, 2004).

Second, we show that these so-called secular laws create a vacuum—or a non-legal terrain—where practices and discourses of religious nationalism leading to discrimination and violence against minoritized groups go uncontested. Here, we spotlight the transnational spread and connections of religious nationalism, and its ability to cross borders via institutional and interpersonal means. We underscore the importance of considering lives on virtual spaces—often uncharted legal territories—where the ecosystems of religious-nationalist discourses thrive (Banaji and Bhatt 2019; Zavos 2010; 2015a, b).

The chapter is divided into the following sections. First, we discuss the existing literature on secular laws, religious nationalism, migration and women in the US context. Then, following the methods section, we first describe the legal terrain that shapes and constrains lives of Indian Americans—especially women—that leads to many of them toward Hindutva. Following this, we discuss the larger, non-legal context in which Hindu women in the US interact with Hindutva. We conclude with some insights into the interaction of religious nationalisms and secular laws for women immigrants in the US and beyond.

Literature: Secular Laws, Religious Nationalism, Migrants, and Women

Secular Laws as a Premise of Religious Nationalism

The recent rise of religious nationalism worldwide evokes some intriguing questions about its legal and political contexts: does religious nationalism mark the decline of liberal democracies? How does religious nationalism emerge even in countries with secular governments? Does it suggest a paradox?

The questions are pertinent to the US, where in recent years, white Christian nationalism (namely, Christianity espoused by practitioners who believe that the US is a Christian nation, and Christian culture and practices should be strengthened in all aspects of public life) has taken center stage in democratic politics. Lawmakers have relentlessly criminalized those deemed "outsiders" to the country. Seemingly secular political and legal institutions have curtailed women's reproductive rights in the name of Christian nationalism, and "foreigners" are often targets.[1]

[1] An instance was seen in Purvi Patel's case in Indiana, US. In 2015, Patel was sentenced to prison for an exemplary duration of 20 years for "illegally" inducing her abortion. Outdated

A recent outcome is the overturning of *Roe v Wade* in 2022—which had protected women's right to abortion in the US for fifty years.

Many scholars, however, do not see the presence of religious nationalism in a secular state as an aberration (Joshi 2020; Nandy 1997; Yountae 2024). Rather, they remind us of the fraught colonial and racial history of secularism, and the privileges it grants to the dominant groups to practice their beliefs and faith. As a discourse/ideology, secularism had historically normalized the imposition of Eurocentric and Christian ideals around the world,[2] and justified violence on non-white colonized subjects, including enslaved and Indigenous populations in the US (Carr 2022; Perry 2018).

The separation of religion and politics in modern nation-states (more specifically, of the Church and the State)—a product of European Enlightenment—was an alien concept to non-European populations (Carr 2022; Miró 2019; Yountae 2024); we have argued elsewhere that in the formulation of secular, Western nation-states have operated on the basis of separating structures typical within Christianity as the foundation for this separation. But the persistence of colonial modernity has led even postcolonial non-Western countries to adopt secular legal and political structures. In these countries, secularism sits awkwardly with religion-driven local values, customs and practices (for example, the ambiguous nature of secularism in India's legal institutions, see Chatterjee 1994), especially if these do not fit the congregation-type, faith-based, religious organization and practices.

---

medical tests were used to prove that the fetus was alive after the abortion, and that she was guilty of feticide (see Bazelon 2015).

[2] There are various non-Western and precolonial instances of secular governance, for example, in India, Emperor Ashoka's Edicts, which separated institutional religion from the state, and Mughal Emperor Akbar's Din-i-Ilahi religion in India which was syncretic in form and combined practices from multiple religions. The Indian Constitution primarily upholds this diversity in its understanding of secularism (Chatterjee 1994). Similarly, Indigenous secularism in North America recognized the importance of embracing diversity in faith, and resisted forced religious conversion because it turned religion into a tool of secular statecraft (Carr 2022). But Western secularism was exclusionary, and originally assigned legal subjecthood to white, property-holding, able-bodied, heterosexual men alone (Perry 2018). Western notions of secularism became the dominant form of governance in most modern nation-states, as the ideology was globally disseminated through colonization.

In both Western and non-Western societies, secularism normalizes the marginality of religious, ethnic, caste, and gender minorities (the most prominent contemporary example is the hijab ban in France in the name of secular modernity and religious equality (see Anand 2023; Korteweg 2017; also Kannabiran 2014)). At times—as Nandy (1997) astutely observes in the case of Hindutva in India—secularism forms the core of the dominant group's religious nationalism and its aspirations for governing the state by the dual logic of religion and the free market (see also Harvey 2005).

In the US, purportedly secular judicial and legal institutions carry imprints of Christianity, and privilege Christianity-based practices over other religious activities even in a supposedly multicultural context (see Harding 2000). Joshi (2020) identifies it as Christian privilege, and highlights its entanglements with white supremacy. Weed (2017) even conceptualizes white supremacy as a religion, based on Christian traditions, that reinscribes the racial order in the US. White Christian supremacy, thus, remains lodged within the so-called secular legal and political institutions, and limits the scope of religious freedom for non-white and non-Christian subjects.

Overall, secular laws and politics constitute the premise (as well as target, see Jaffrelot 2018; Nandy 1997) of religious nationalism that minoritizes non-adherent racial, ethnic, and religious groups. In the next section, with a focus on the US, we will discuss how religious nationalism treats two such minoritized groups—migrants and women.

Women and Migrants in Religious Nationalism

Women and migrants feature among the minoritized groups which religious nationalism attempts to govern and exclude from established rights granted by the state.

Women hold an ambivalent position in terms of their agency and autonomy within the framework of religious nationalism. On the one hand, religious nationalism identifies women as the carriers and protectors of traditions and cultures, their role being central to training future citizens. On the other hand, religious nationalism imposes narrowly defined heterosexual gendered reproductive roles on women fully or partially excluding them from citizenship (Chatterjee 1989; Peterson 1999; Narayan and Purkayastha 2011; Sarkar 1992; Yuval-Davis 1997). This is evident in the US, where religious-nationalist groups have foregrounded women's role in nation-building, while simultaneously attempting to curb their social, political and economic choices.

Migrants—particularly non-white and non-Christians—represent another group that religious nationalists label as misfits. Historically, the creation of legal subjects in secular Western laws involved the gendered and racialized attribution of "personhood" to able-bodied, heterosexual, property-holding white men (Glenn 2002; Perry 2018). Migrants—including enslaved and indentured labor populations—were always constructed as the "figure of the unnatural" (Samaddar 2020). Current immigration laws in the US perpetuate the same gendered and racialized logic to control the flow of migrant labor into US territory (Espiritu 2003), while instituting laws curtailing their access to political rights.

As the "figure of the unnatural," racialized immigrants in the US have historically been characterized as a threat to national security and harmony. Nationalist governments[3] in the US have relentlessly deployed judicial apparatus to criminalize immigrants, separate their families, and dehumanize them to distance them from human rights (Menjívar et al. 2018). Some notable instances of legally enforced discrimination against migrants are the bans on Asian immigrants in the late nineteenth to early twentieth centuries (Espiritu 2003), and the surge of racist bans imposed on Muslims and South and Central American immigrants in recent years (Al-Khersan and Shashahani 2022).

But how do legal and political institutions in the US—with overt and covert structures of white Christian nationalism—treat women immigrants? In other words, we attempt to understand how subjects positioned within the intersecting marginality as women *and* migrants experience religious nationalism in the host country. Studies and

[3] There is a broad zone within with explicitly Christian nationalist groups and implicitly Christian nationalist groups overlap in their political orientation. The latter's politics certainly shore up the power of the former.

media reports demonstrate that religious-nationalist groups quite explicitly exclude racialized immigrant women from socioeconomic rights, including the human rights to employment and families (Espiritu 2003; Purkayastha and Abraham 2019). These discriminatory practices are often legally enforced. For example, the Page Law of 1875[4] prohibited the entry of Asian women to US on account of their suspected moral depravity. This ban preceded the Chinese Exclusion Act of 1882[5] and the Immigration Act of 1917[6] which also restricted the entry of Asian men.

These restrictions were shaped by xenophobic sentiments that were rooted in religious nationalism, and its racist ideals of gender and morality (Nagel 2001). In these immigration laws, Christianity was often a code or a "proxy" for whiteness (Al-khersan and Shahshahani 2022: 143). In recent years, South and Central American immigrant women have also faced similar discrimination, family separation, and exploitation. Dominant nationalist narratives about immigrants continue to emphasize their moral depravity. Racialized women immigrants in particular are accused of giving birth to "anchor babies"—born citizens of the US, who would afterwards sponsor the immigrant parents' citizenship (Chavez 2017).

Following the Civil Rights Movements, immigration laws in the US have apparently been less discriminatory and more inclusive by allowing immigrants' claims-making (Bloemraad 2022). The Immigration and Nationality Act of 1965 ended the ban on Asian immigrants, and introduced skill-based labor migration free from all forms of discrimination.[7] In reality, however, the under-representation of women in skill-based employment visas, restrictions on employment and mobility on the

---

[4] The Page Act of 1875 (Immigration Act), https://loveman.sdsu.edu/docs/1875Immigration%20Act.pdf (accessed 10 November 2024).

[5] Chinese Exclusion Act (1882) | National Archives, https://www.archives.gov/milestone-documents/chinese-exclusion-act (accessed 10 November 2024).

[6] Immigration Act of 1917 (Barred Zone Act)—Immigration History, https://immigrationhistory.org/item/1917-barred-zone-act/ (accessed 10 November 2024).

[7] *Immigration and Nationality Act* 1965 (US), Text of H.R. 2580 (89th): An Act to amend the Immigration and Nationality Act, and for other purposes (Passed Congress version)—GovTrack.us COMPS-1376.pdf, https://www.govtrack.us/congress/bills/89/hr2580/text (accessed 2 March 2025).

dependent visas which are mostly assigned to women, and women immigrants' underemployment in the US expose the systemic persistence of racial and gendered marginality even in seemingly "neutral" immigration laws (Purkayastha 2004; Purkayastha and Roy 2023).

Scholars have argued that such systems of "immigrant integration" and inclusion also perpetuate the colonial mission of "rescuing" and "civilizing" non-white and non-European subjects—especially women—from their "backward" cultures and religions (Korteweg 2017; Schnikel 2018). Farris (2017) identifies this "rescue"-driven approach toward immigrant women as "femonationalism." Femonationalists accuse male immigrants of stealing citizens' jobs, but try to "rescue" non-white immigrant women. This approach is driven by the neoliberal agenda of retaining immigrant women's carework in the host society. This means, beside legal terrains, religious nationalism creates some extra-legal spaces that perpetuate gendered and racialized immigrant women's marginality.

Racialized and gendered immigrants—especially women—respond to this marginality in host societies by turning to their own cultures, including religion. Many non-Christian religions grant women a central space in their rituals (see Narayan and Purkayastha 2009). Besides, religion also connects immigrants to social networks in the host society, while the emphasis on religious affiliation allows them to mask their racial marginality (Kurien 2004, Narayana and Purkayastha 2009).

But what happens when women immigrants' native religion too takes nationalist turns, so they end up in a marginalized position even within the institutions of their own religion? The short answer is that they seek a relatively more supportive space within their communities, but, despite their efforts, they do not regain full autonomy. We present findings from several of our research projects on Hindu women in the US, and see how they navigate both Christian nationalism in the host society and Hindu nationalism in the diaspora.

Methods and Methodological Decisions

We have conducted a meta-analysis of a body of work on highly educated (with at least one college degree) first and second-generation Indian origin women over the last 15 years. The original studies ranged from a variety of interviews with highly educated Indian Americans, to ethnographies and quantitative analyses of networks of websites. We have not directly interviewed members of religious-nationalist groups though we have analyzed the pattern of their discourse on social media (see Narayan, Purkayastha and Banerjee 2010; Narayan and Purkayastha 2011). Our work on accounts of living Hinduism provides a profile of investment in and reaction against Hindutva—the word used to describe the political mobilization of *selected aspects* of Hinduism by the religious-nationalist group (who claim that their activities are to defend Hinduism).

A key issue for understanding the legal terrain of religious nationalism is to highlight the terrain of legal opportunities and constraints. Since religious nationalism exists and grows within the nexus of political and cultural rights, we focus on an immigrant group to unravel the nature of the structural intersection between the dominant groups' religious nationalism and religious nationalism among an immigrant group. We draw upon the experiences of Hindu Indian American women—citizens and migrants on different types of visas—to highlight the terrain of formal laws as well as the factors that exist beyond formal laws but profoundly shape the context of religious nationalisms.

The pattern of Indian migration to the US reflects the selection criteria of US immigration laws, which, following a global ban on migration of Asian origin people, opened the doors, in 1965, for highly skilled migrants from Asian countries and, later, their nuclear families (Purkayastha and Roy 2023); because of the way in which "high skills" were defined, the men arrived first, followed by their highly educated spouses as dependants (Purkayastha 2004). By the 1990s, the job-related visa categories changed to temporary permits to reside in the US, contingent upon the economic needs of employers. Hence, focusing on Indian Americans not only allows us to look at religious nationalism within the community, but to analyze the trends with a clear understanding that various sections of Indian Americans—and women in this group—have variable rights within the country (full citizenship rights, and very limited political and social rights as temporary guest workers). Outlining these general constraints provides some insights into questions of religious nationalisms.

The second methodological decision we made is to focus on cadences of lives beyond laws. The human rights-oriented work has focused on the legal edifices within states including multicultural citizenships (see also Iwata and Purkayastha 2011). There is a growing body of work on countries where more conservative groups have lobbied for separate laws and courts for people practicing different faiths. To address this, we present the constraints in which Hindu immigrants exist in spite of the US's much heralded secularism.

The third decision is to periodically refer to strident Christian religious nationalism, which thrives on racist stereotyping against (and sometimes, aligning with) which the Hindu religious-nationalist groups organize. That discussion is not restricted to the Christian religious-nationalist groups alone, but also to seemingly secular or neutral discourse which continues to belittle Indian Americans by using racist tropes.

Analysis

Legal Constraints

At a time when scholars have been writing about religious-nationalist groups, in societies like the US, laws against violence (and hate crimes), which religious-nationalist groups direct against others, have been growing more robust. It is important to note, however, that the US does not allow parallel courts or adjudication systems similar to those existing in the UK or Canada. So which aspects of the legal terrain are relevant? We document that the laws governing how religion is to be practiced, based on what is the norm for the majority group, is relevant. Relatedly, the laws governing the rights of migrant groups—including the graduated restrictions imposed upon non-white citizens and guest workers—shape the larger landscape of rights and protections these groups can access.

Most of our work, and that of others, shows that immigration laws reflect a racialized, gendered order that constrains or restricts access to rights (depending on citizenship or visa status). For Indians, access to the US was opened after several decades of migration bans against Asian origin people. When the door to migration was opened, it was restricted to highly skilled people and their nuclear families. The definition of high-skills was gendered (Purkayastha and Roy 2023; Kibria et al. 2014) and women, highly educated themselves, were mostly seen as dependants (that is, at least initially, they have little access to rights on their own). Most of the post-1965 migrants were able to access citizenship though the path to citizenship was delayed by multi-year delays built into the US quota system. Without citizenship no migrant has full access to the protection of laws.

By the 1990s, immigration laws shifted so that highly skilled migrants were redefined as guest workers. Guest workers are legally in the country, they contribute to the economy, but they are denied political rights. While there is a path to citizenship, it takes nearly twenty years for Indians to move from guest worker status to citizenship (for details read Purkayastha and Roy 2023; see also Banerjee 2021; Roy 2024). In addition, the laws of deportation have been strengthened over the 2014–2024 decade. Paradoxically, this is partly in response to women's lobbying to address violence against women in homes, which carries penalties of deportation. The deportation requirement has had the effect of dampening reporting of domestic violence (DV) and other gendered crimes within homes and communities (Das Gupta 2007, 2014). This variable terrain of visas and rights codifies the vulnerability of women.

A second level of laws intersects with this problematic terrain of rights. These are laws and policies guiding the practice of religion. In India, Hinduism includes a significant variety of beliefs, norms and practices (and states set their own holidays to reflect locally relevant practices). Many versions are constituted by practices outside temples and congregations (Narayan and Purkayastha 2008); a significant section of those adhering to the religion *do not* need to go to temples to "be Hindus." In the US, religious practice is defined in terms of Christianity and its church focused congregations. The US requires places of worship to conform to its 501(c) laws.[8] According to the requirements, formally recognized places of worship are defined institutions such as temples; these laws *require* temples to have congregations (members), priests, and to be built in places approved by local planning and zoning boards. As a result, Hindu temples in the US have adapted their practices to fit local circumstances, creating a unique pattern of participation not typically found in India. Religious holidays is also an issue. Since Christian holidays are paid holidays, Hindus are automatically disadvantaged. Currently, most institutions will allow other religious practitioners to take time off; but the work or education enterprise does halt its operation, so taking time off by practicing Hindus means making up the work some other time.

Consequently, religious events are primarily held on Sundays, the only neutral holiday available, as Hindu holy days vary across different regions in India, not falling on the same days each week. Consequently, major temple events are scheduled on weekends. The temple's structure is centered around a faith-based *guru-sisya* (teacher-disciple) relationship, where a male guru is revered by his followers, similar to evangelical Christian faith-based missions. These temples also initiate cultural activities to instill pride and teach religious practices, aiming to educate the next generation about Hinduism. This includes creating new ceremonies like a gift-giving tree in December, establishing Hindu Sunday schools, and offering lessons on performing pujas—all practices modeled on practices of Christianity. However, these practices tend to homogenize Hindu rituals, reducing the diversity inherent in the religion. Temples in America are adopting church-like organizational practices, simplifying Hinduism to fit better within American society, which diminishes the variety of opinions and beliefs that define the religion.

As Roy and Williamson (2014) have written, over time, these restrictions led to the establishment of temples which also became de facto

---

[8] 501(c) Organization: What They Are, Types, and Examples, https://www.investopedia.com/terms/1/501c.asp#:~:text=501(c)(1)%3A,%2C%20scientific%2C%20literary%2C%20or%20educational (accessed 10 November 2024): governing tax exempt status.

community spaces. The vast majority of the temples follow a conservative, Brahmanical version of Hinduism with a male priest, and a mostly male board, as authoritative arbitrators of Hindu practices. In the absence of other opportunities to practice Hinduism, many priests begin to enhance the most patriarchal rules and norms during rituals. In our interviews and podcasts several women have pointed out how single women, or married women without children, become uncomfortable in these spaces; others simply delink from Hindu "communities."

In sum, despite avowals of non-alignment and non-discrimination in terms of religion, these combinations of laws position women and men in ambiguous positions. However, the intersection of the patriarchal (racist) immigration laws and specific policies and practices surrounding religion that uphold patriarchy, position women in disadvantaged positions.

Laws and Practices

Scholars have noted that the Indian American case challenges the long-held belief that relatively affluent, English-speaking migrants become assimilated into the US. Yet in reality, as brown skinned people existing in white dominant America, they encounter multiple challenges. Joshi (2006) has written about the second generation growing up in different parts of the country where the prelude to sports events are Christian prayers. Even as the country progresses and multifaith leaders are invited to public ceremonies, the vast majority of "priests" continue to be men. Consequently, when representatives of Hinduism are called to say prayers at multifaith events, the public face of Hinduism is a male priest.

More salient is the discourse of the religious-nationalist Christian right. With their claims that the US is a Christian nation, much of their discourse against other religions (including Islam) is about the supposedly non-modern character of these religions. Women become symbols of the discourse, identified as subservient and non-modern. While religious nationalists such as ultra-right Christians use racist/gendered discourse, there is a wider normalized set of stereotypes constantly circulated among the secular mainstream. This other group often draws on transnational assemblage of a knowledge bank developed by colonial powers to rationalize their presence in the colonies. Both Christian missionaries who wished to convert the heathen, and colonial powers wishing to "modernize" colonies, developed discourses characterizing colonial subjects in terms of subservience, immorality, and/or unfettered violence. As Patil and Purkayastha demonstrated more recently (2018) these traces of knowledge continue to circulate, including in media depictions of Indian women and Indian American women and men.[9]

The rejection of religions other than Christianity is sometimes taken to extremes through hate crimes. Harvard University's Pluralism Project[10] lists some of the violence committed against places of non-Christian worship in the US. Whether the attacks are on gurudwaras, mosques, synagogues or temples, non-Christian groups remain wary of their vulnerability. So too with attacks on women identified racially as foreigners. Joshi and Purkayastha (2018) have written about some of these crimes by "Dot Busters"[11] and attacks against turban wearing people. This is another arena where the lack of rights to demand justice or the uncertainty about support from law enforcement, both for cultural reasons and related to the individual's temporary visa status makes reporting a fraught process.

Situated within these legal constraints and persistent discourses, Indian Americans seek community in temples and related spaces. A veritable series of new institutions, such as Hindu Sunday schools, evangelizing efforts and institutions have developed in the US.

As we have documented elsewhere (including chapters written for the co-written autoethnographies on Living Our Religion, or through the Walking a Fine Line podcasts),[12] women, including highly educated women, who do not subscribe to these conservative, and Christian-normed versions of religions, find themselves battling with other head-winds (Roy et al. 2025).

---

9 While well-known public figures of Indian-descent in the US—such as Nikki Hailey or Kamala Harris, who have at least one parent who is not Christian—might appear to refute this conclusion, in reality none of them claims any religion other than Christianity.

10 The Pluralism Project (accessed 10 November 2024).

11 The term coined to "stand for" the bindi, a dot painted or pasted on, the term "dot busters" denoting violence directed against persons of the Hindu faith wearing a bindi or "dot" on the forehead:

12 Walking a Fine Line: Voices of Hindu Women in the US (accessed 16 November 2024).

The Non-legal Terrain: Racism Head Winds of Transnational Religious Nationalism

The legal terrain has intersected with the spaces beyond the laws of a single nation-states. A brief outline of the transnational influences on the Indian diaspora in the US, and how these influences can shape Hindutva, illustrates this point.

Since the 1980s, the Indian government has actively engaged with its diaspora, a shift influenced by globalization and a move from state-driven to neoliberal economic policies in India. Initiatives aimed at strengthening ties with the diaspora included flexible citizenship options like Persons of Indian Origin (PIO) and Overseas Citizens of India (OCI), voting rights for Indian passport holders abroad, the establishment of a Ministry of Overseas Indian Affairs, and the celebration of Pravasi Bharatiya Divas (or Non-Resident Indian Day) to honor the contributions of overseas Indians. The rise of the Hindu nationalist Bharatiya Janata Party (BJP) in the 1990s further spurred policies to attract the diaspora, using their achievements to promote India's global presence (Kapur 2010; Mishra 2016; Varadarajan 2010).

The affluent Indian diaspora has also become notable for its philanthropic activities. As the world's largest recipient of remittances, India received $87 billion in 2021, with the US contributing over 20 percent of these funds. Beyond remittances, various organizations, including professional and ethnic groups, have been active in philanthropy, focusing on areas such as education, health, and disaster relief both in India and the US.

Amid these developments, there has been growing scholarly attention to the role of religious organizations within the US Indian diaspora and their involvement in nationalist movements in South Asia. While Sikh and Tamil diasporas have pursued separate state agendas, Hindu nationalist groups have used Hindu traditions like *seva* (selfless service) to enhance their influence and promote their values. Unlike other diasporic nationalisms, Hindu nationalism does not seek a separate homeland but aims to assert the dominance of Hindu values, particularly against Islam and Christianity. Bhattacharjee (2021) describes *seva* as a foundational pillar of the Hindu nationalist movement, enhancing its appeal in both

India and the US diaspora. Research shows that Hindu nationalist organizations engage in a broad range of philanthropic and humanitarian activities in India, including support for women's self-help groups, micro enterprises, milk cooperatives, and various conservation and educational projects (Sarkar 1994; Jaffrelot 2006; Katju 2003; Bhattacharjee 2021; Zavos 2015a, b). In the US, these groups contribute to food banks, tutoring, disaster relief, medical support, and COVID relief efforts, among other activities. These initiatives help Hindu nationalist organizations project a compassionate image, strengthen their networks, and expand their influence into new areas (Bhattacharjee 2021).

Despite their positive public image, Hindu nationalist organizations have faced scrutiny for redirecting philanthropic funds toward anti-minority activities in India. Historical examples include funding for the construction of a Hindu temple on the site of a mosque in Ayodhya and donations to the Indian Development Relief Fund (IDRF), which supported anti-minority campaigns (Kurien 2007; SACW 2002). More recently, organizations like Sewa International have come under criticism for using COVID relief funds to support Hindu nationalist causes (Pahwa 2001). Nonetheless, these groups have successfully used their philanthropic and service initiatives to strengthen their presence and influence within both the Indian American community and India.

Unregulated Digital Spaces and Religious Nationalism

A key aspect of religious nationalism's growth is the political economy of manufacturing and disseminating misinformation and hate content, often through "WhatsApp universities," a term coined by noted journalist Ravish Kumar.[13] These networks produce and circulate content

[13] Ravish Kumar is an Indian journalist, author and media personality. Until recently, he was the Senior Executive Editor of NDTV India, hosting a number of programs including the channel's flagship weekday show Prime Time, Hum Log, Ravish Ki Report, and Des Ki Baat. He has been twice conferred with Ramnath Goenka Excellence in Journalism Award for the Best Journalist of the Year and became the fifth Indian journalist to receive the Ramon Magsaysay Award in 2019: Ravish Kumar | Center for Contemporary South Asia, https://watson.brown.edu/southasia/people/ravish-kumar (accessed 10 November 2024).

profitably using technology. Like mainstream media, where sensationalism drives market share, "IT cells" running these social media networks for nationalist political parties boost the influence of religious-nationalist groups (say, white nationalists, Hindu nationalists) through rapid misinformation spread on WhatsApp. Kumar highlighted that these "universities" operate outside traditional educational or journalistic standards, leveraging the platform's widespread reach and lack of oversight to influence and manipulate public perception. Banaji and Bhatt (2019) have, among others, documented the reach and impact of WhatsApp misinformation on hate crimes.

In our earlier research (Narayan and Purkayastha 2011; Narayan, Purkayastha and Banerjee 2011), we examined how gendered imagery—often seemingly positive about women—is circulated online through a wide network of diaspora groups supporting Hindu nationalism. These groups utilize numerous websites and a robust social media presence to present themselves in the US as the unified voice of Hindus. Their goal is to construct a positive identity for Hindus to counter ideologies that stigmatize their culture as inferior and backward. To address the racialization and denigration typically symbolized by perceptions of women's inferior status, these groups emphasize the unique and distinctive identities of Hindu women. They do so through depictions of powerful goddesses like Durga and Kali, as well as obedient epic figures like Sita. This portrayal suggests that Hinduism offers women significant public roles if they remain compliant in private. They argue that Hinduism uniquely empowers women compared to other South Asian religions, particularly Islam, and dismiss Western influences such as feminism as irrelevant to Hindu women. Additionally, these groups aim to appeal to Western audiences by highlighting prominent Western women who have embraced Hinduism. Furthermore, they have actively campaigned to correct perceived misrepresentations of Hinduism, especially in educational contexts such as textbooks, to protect Hindu cultural identity and address the alienation of Hindu American students in public schools. However, this discourse often reinforces patriarchal ideologies under the guise of empowerment.

These images provide powerful counterpoints to women's personal reflections on their lives (Narayan and Purkayastha 2009). Conversations with educated Hindu and Muslim women revealed (Kibria et al. 2021) that many feel the impact of friends and family who, despite their limited historical knowledge or critical perspective, share information from "WhatsApp universities" within their networks globally. At the same time, women who criticize Hindutva often encounter severe online harassment, including threats of violence against their families residing in other countries. Women journalists and academics who challenge Hindu nationalism face significant online trolling, which includes harassment, threats, and abusive language aimed at intimidating and silencing them. This trolling is frequently organized and coordinated, utilizing social media platforms to amplify the abuse (Sen and Jha 2024). These attacks not only target their professional work but also invade their personal lives, highlighting the broader issue of gendered online violence in spaces that are often beyond legal regulation.

More recently, as we talked with women who are not part of the religious-nationalist groups, we found that some were beginning to resist by creating alternative material. Our analysis (Narayan and Smith 2019) reveals that Hindu women, particularly from post-immigrant generations, are creating their own alternative online spaces where they engage with their own constructs of feminism and challenge prevailing notions of Hindutva. They are creating an online space to address gender inequities within their communities and challenge stereotypical, discriminatory nationalist views of Hindu women. Through blogs and online discussions, these women share personal experiences and critique orientalist perceptions. These voices also critique conservative Hindu organizations for promoting victimhood narratives that erase the experiences of Dalits[14] and women. Organizations like Hindus for Human Rights are mobilizing both online and offline to challenge right-wing Hindu rhetoric while advocating for inclusivity and social justice. This emerging online discourse represents a collective effort by Hindu

[14] Formerly known in derogatory and discriminatory terms as 'Untouchables' or 'Outcasts': India's "Untouchables" Face Violence, Discrimination, https://www.nationalgeographic.com/pages/article/indias-untouchables-face-violence-discrimination (accessed 10 November 2024).

women to redefine their roles and create a more inclusive and progressive narrative of Hinduism.

Despite this growing presence, Hindu nationalist rhetoric continues to dominate virtual spaces. Most online content about Hinduism and gender is still produced, controlled, and disseminated by well-financed and technologically adept right-wing Hindu groups in the diaspora. These groups use sophisticated, networked websites and forums to attract Hindus worldwide, including in Europe, Canada, and Australia (Smith and Narayan 2019). While feminist groups are increasingly visible online, their presence is primarily focused on the Hindu diaspora in the US and remains fragmented with limited global reach. Overall, women who are hungry for alternative discourses are caught between the counter currents of entrenched racism of the mainstream, particularly the strident white religious nationalists, and the power of Hindutva to define and control them.

Conclusion

This brief overview demonstrates the interplay of legal terrains and the spaces shaped by practices beyond laws and policies shape the positions and practices surrounding women within religious-nationalistic efforts and movements. As an extension to the discussions above, we emphasize three insights that are important to discussions about women and religious nationalisms.

First, religious nationalism is often studied as binaries. We tend to focus on religious-nationalist groups and assume there is a clear line between them and others in secular, democratic nation-states. The case of Indian Americans—a relatively affluent and seemingly integrated group—shows that the process is more complex. "Secularism" itself has multiple meanings across national contexts, and often it is coopted in by religious nationalists. Besides, a series of seemingly disparate and seemingly secular laws come together, such as the immigration laws and the laws governing religious practice intersect to enhance and entrench racialized minority positions within which the right to religious practice is made vulnerable. But these laws, in turn, intersect with the discourses of strident religious nationalists among the dominant white population as well as the "soft" racism of wider secular groups. In fact, we argued that the "soft" religious-nationalist practices that normalize Christianity enhance the reach of some of the claims strident nationalists claim in their quest for a Christian (non-secular) nation.

These conditions of vulnerability lead minoritized gendered people to seek communities for support and identity. Yet, at this point, these spaces for communities are being shaped powerfully by religious nationalists so many women and gender non-conforming individuals do not find a space for building autonomous lives. The very structures of religious freedom, which entrench the norms of the dominant religion both enhance the power of Christian religious nationalists, and religious nationalists of other religions.[15] Culture provides the toolkit used for inventing and crafting the discourse and the practices, which can now be circulated widely through new platforms.

Second, most of the religious nationalism studies focus on single countries, with a focus on laws in these countries. By introducing the transnational dimension, we show how the fodder for religious nationalism can be developed and disseminated transnationally. There are no borders for targeting "consumers" of religious nationalism via social media. In fact, consumable information and misinformation is widely circulated to enhance the authority and power of religious-nationalist groups (challenging the secular discourse and understandings. The consequences play out in specific locales, including through violence (including violence on social media), trolling and hate crimes. There is a growing literature on weaponization of language and growth of political authoritarianism. On the basis of this chapter, we would argue that a critical question, yet understudied, is the link between explicit, strident religious nationalism and political authoritarianism, and how these circulate transnationally.

---

[15] As we have written earlier (Purkayastha and Narayan 2009), even more open religious communities try to downplay symbols and representations that might draw negative attention to them by dominant groups. These representations include transgendered forms and representations of unclad female goddesses in fierce modes. The benign imagery that is normalized in places of worship reinscribes gender hierarchies to fit the "good," "non threatening" immigrant imageries within the US.

Third, much has been written about women as the targets of control of religious nationalisms. We show that the reality is more complicated. On the one hand seemingly neutral and secular laws can empower patriarchal structures within groups; on the other women seeking respite from racism can search out those patriarchal institutions as the groups that stand up for their religious identities. Women can be depicted as powerful within the religious communities (and social media discourses) but these tools, which appear to be challenging racist tools of dominant religious nationalists, also enhance patriarchal power within the minoritized groups. Our brief discussion about the need to examine political economies of messaging also challenges us to rethink the notion of "traditional cultures." Instead, the culture in such transnational messaging as a very modern tool of contemporary political economies is what should be considered.

Finally, from the 1980s ongoing feminist debates about the role of groups' rights on women's positions in society have dominated the discourse. Most Western scholars have argued that nation-states needed a single set of laws for women, and because non-Western cultures were bad for women, there should be no discussion of groups' rights. Some of that approach continues to shape the human rights field when people consider the position of women amidst patriarchal cultures. Here we show that binary ways in which Western rights vs non-Western traditional practices are being conceptualized is not enough. In fact, the interaction of immigration laws, racist discourse, laws and structures normed on Christianity, create contexts in which to survive with dignity requires creating zones of resistance to explicit or implicit Christian nationalism (and racism). These resistance contexts create sweet spots where religious nationalism flourishes among minority groups. At the same time the growing political economy of hate-message consumers are adding new dimensions to a variety of religious-nationalist groups among the dominant and minoritized communities. For both, women remain the symbols and foot soldiers. In the context of intersecting politics and economics of religious nationalism, women are likely to remain enablers and victims.

Bibliography

Reported Cases

Roe v Wade 410 US 113 (1973), Roe v Wade | 410 U.S. 113 (1973) | Justia U.S. Supreme Court Center (accessed 2 March 2025).

Statutes

Chinese Exclusion Act 1882 (US), Chinese Exclusion Act (1882) | National Archives, https://www.archives.gov/milestone-documents/chinese-exclusion-act (accessed 10 November 2024).

Immigration Act 1917 (Barred Zone Act) (US), Immigration Act of 1917 (Barred Zone Act)—Immigration History, https://immigrationhistory.org/item/1917-barred-zone-act/ (accessed 10 November 2024).

Immigration and Nationality Act 1965 (US), Text of H.R. 2580 (89th): An Act to amend the Immigration and Nationality Act, and for other purposes (Passed Congress version)—GovTrack.us COMPS-1376.pdf, https://www.govtrack.us/congress/bills/89/hr2580/text (accessed 2 March 2025).

Page Act 1875 (US), The Page Act of 1875 (Immigration Act), https://loveman.sdsu.edu/docs/1875Immigration%20Act.pdf (accessed 10 November 2024).

Articles and Book Chapters

Al-khersan, Tina, and Shashahani, Azadeh, 2022. "From the Chinese Exclusion Act to the Muslim Ban: An Immigration System Built on Systemic Racism". *Harvard Law and Policy Review* 17:132-156.

Anand, Aleena, 2023. "Hijab is Our Right: An Analysis of Muslim Girls' Veil Ban Protests in India". *Embodied: The Stanford Undergraduate Journal of Feminist, Gender, and Sexuality Studies* 2(1).

Banerjee, Sikita, 2010. "Women, Muscular Nationalism and Hinduism in India: Roop Kanwar and the Fire Protests". *Totalitarian Movements and Political Religions* 11(2-3):271-287. https://doi.org/10.1080/14690764.2010.546085.

Bazelon, Emily, 2015. "Purvi Patel Could Be Just the Beginning" *The New York Times Magazine*, 1 April. https://www.nytimes.com/2015/04/01/magazine/purvi-patel-could-be-just-the-beginning.html (accessed 11 November 2024).

Bhattacharjee, M, 2021. "Building a 'Hindu Rashtra' through 'seva'". *Economic and Political Weekly* 56(3), https://www.epw.in/engage/article/building-hindu-rashtra-through-seva (accessed 11 November 2024).

Bloemraad, Irene, 2022. "Claiming Membership: Boundaries, Positionality, US Citizenship, and What It Means to Be American". *Ethnic and Racial Studies* 45 (6): 1011–33.

Carr, Ryan, 2022. "Indigenous Secularism and the Secular-Colonial." *Critical Research on Religion* 10(1): 24-40.

Chatterjee, Partha, 1994. "Secularism and Toleration". *Economic and Political Weekly* 29(28):1768-1777.

Chinkel, W, 2018. "Against 'Immigrant Integration': For an End to Neocolonial Knowledge Production". *CMS* 6:31, https://doi.org/10.1186/s40878-018-0095-1 (accessed 11 November 2024).

Das Gupta, Monisha. 2014. "'Don't Deport Our Daddies': Gendering State Deportation Practices and Immigrant Organizing". *Gender and Society* 28(1):83-109.

Iwata, Miho, and Purkayastha, Bandana, 2011. "Cultural human rights" in *Human Rights in Our Own Backyard: Social Justice and Resistance in the*

U.S., William Armaline, Davita Glasberg, and Bandana Purkayastha (eds). Philadelphia, PA, US: University of Pennsylvania Press.

Jaffrelot, C, 2018. "Indian Secularism and Its Challenges" in *Forms of Pluralism and Democratic Constitutionalism*, J. Cohen, A. Arato, and A. von Busekist (eds), 184–196. Columbia University Press.

Jaffrelot, C and Therwath, I, 2007. "The Sangh Parivar and the Hindu Diaspora in the West: What Kind of Long Distance Nationalism?" *International Political Sociology* 1(30): 278-295.

Kapur, D, 2003. "Indian Diaspora as a Strategic Asset". *Economic and Political Weekly* 38(5): 445-448.

Kibria, Nazli, Purkayastha, Bandana, Narayan, Anishka, Khan, Kaneez and Yousaf, Farah N, 2021. "Living Religions Across Transnational Spaces: Experiences of South Asian American Hindu and Muslim Women". *Contemporary South Asia* 29(2): 243–256, https://doi.org/10.1080/09584935.2021.1915243 (accessed 11 November 2024).

Korteweg, Anna C, 2017. "The Failures of 'Immigrant Integration': The Gendered Racialized Production of Non-Belonging". *Migration Studies* 5(3): 428–444, https://doi.org/10.1093/migration/mnx025 (accessed 11 November 2024).

Kurien, Prema, 2004. "Multiculturalism and Ethnic Nationalism: The Development of an American Hinduism". *Social Problems* 51(3): 362-385.

Kurien, Prema, 2001. "Religion, Ethnicity and Politics: Hindu and Muslim Indian Immigrants in the United States". *Ethnic and Racial Studies* 24(2): 263-293.

Kurien, Prema, 2012. "What is American About American Hinduism? Hindu Umbrella Organizations in the U.S. in Comparative Perspective" in *Public Hinduisms*, J Zavos, P Kanungo, D Reddy, M Warrier, and RB Williams (eds), 90–111. New Delhi: Sage Publications.

Menjívar, Cecilia, Cervantes, Andrea Gómez and Alvord, Daniel, 2018. "The Expansion of 'Crimmigration,' Mass Detention, and Deportation". *Sociology Compass* 12(4): e12573.

Miró, Gisela Carrasco, 2019. "Encountering the Colonial: Religion in Feminism and the Coloniality of Secularism". *Feminist Theory* 21(1):91-109.

Mishra, AK, 2016. "Diaspora, Development and the Indian State". *The Round Table* 105(6): 701-721.

Nagel, Joane, 2001. "Racial, Ethnic, and National Boundaries: Sexual Intersections and Symbolic Interactions". *Symbolic Interaction* 24(2): 123-139.

Nandy, Ashis, 1997. "The Twilight of Certitudes: Secularism, Hindu Nationalism, and Other Masks of Deculturation". *Alternatives: Global, Local, Political* 22(2): 157–176.

Narayan, Anjana and Purkayastha, Bandana, 2020. "Modernity in the Service of Tradition: Women and Gender within Hinduism in the United States" in *Religion, Race, and Asian Americans*, D Yoo and Khyati Joshi (eds), 184–196. Hawaii: University of Hawaii Press.

Narayan, Anjana and Purkayastha, Bandana, 2011. "Talking Gender Superiority in Virtual Spaces". *Journal of South Asian Diaspora* 3(1): 53-69.

Narayan, Anjana and Smith, Lise-Helene, 2019. "Gender, Religion and Virtual Diasporas", *Economic and Political Weekly* 54: 77-85.

Narayan, Anjana, Purkayastha, Bandana and Banerjee, Shubhra, 2011. "Constructing Transnational and Virtual Identities: A Study of the Discourse and Networks of Ethnic Student Organizations in the U.S. and U.K". *Journal of Intercultural Studies* 32: 495-517.

Pahwa, N, 2021. "Covid relief donations are supporting a project to 'hinduize' India: why are Twitter, Microsoft and Google promoting a charity with ties to right-wing nationalism?" *Slate Magazine*. 8 June 2021, https://slate.com/news-and-politics/2021/06/covid-india-charity-sewa-hindu-nationalism.html (accessed 3 June 2022).

Patil, Vrushali and Purkayastha, Bandana, 2015. "Sexual Violence, Race and Media (In)Visibility: Intersectional Complexities in a Transnational Frame". *Societies* 5: 598-617. https://doi.org/10.3390/soc5030598.

Peters, Katie, 2024. "Not My Fault: Far Right Women and the Emancipatory Narratives of Misogyny and Infantilization". *Feminist Philosophical Quarterly* 10(1–2).

Peters, Ted, 2024. "Gender and Race in Christian Nationalism". *Public Theology*, 18 May 18, https://www.patheos.com/blogs/publictheology/2024/05/gender-and-race-in-christian-nationalism-parts-78/ (accessed 11 November 2024).

Peterson, VS, 1999. Political Identities/Nationalism as Heterosexism. *International Feminist Journal of Politics*, 1(1), 34–65.

Purkayastha, Bandana, 2004. "Skilled Migration and Cumulative Disadvantage: The Case of Highly Qualified Asian Indian Immigrant Women in the U.S." *Geoforum* 36: 181–196. https://doi.org/10.1016/j.geoforum.2003.11.006.

Purkayastha, Bandana and Narayan, Anjana, 2009. "Bridges and Chasms. Orientalism and the Making of Indian Americans in New England" in *Asian*

Americans in New England, Monica Chiu and Durham, NH (eds). Lebanon, NH, US: New England University Press.
Purkayastha, Bandana and Roy, Rianka, 2023. "Hidden in Plain Sight: 'Neutral' Enclosures for High-Skilled Immigrants During COVID-19". *Sociological Forum* 38. https://doi.org/10.1111/socf.12965.
Ranjeet, Bidya and Purkayastha, Bandana, 2007. "Minority within a Minority: Reflecting on Marital Violence in the Nepali American Community" in *Body Evidence: Intimate Violence Against South Asian Women in America*, Shamita Das Gupta (ed), 38–52. Rutgers University Press, http://www.jstor.org/stable/j.ctt5hj900.7 (accessed 11 November 2024).
Roy, Devparna, and Williamson, Lola, 2012. "The Changing Face of Hindu Identity in Jackson, Mississippi" in *Ethnic Heritage in Mississippi: The Twentieth Century*, S. Walton and B. Carpenter (eds), 153–171. Mississippi Scholarship Online. doi:10.
Roy, Rianka. 2024. "Covert Carcerality for 'High-Income Cheap Labor': Indian Tech Workers in the US". *Sociological Forum* 40(1): 50–64. https://doi.org/10.1111/socf.13028
Roy, Rianka, Bandana Purkayastha, and Anjana Narayan. 2025. "Gendered Patterns of Counter-dissemination: Hindu Women Navigating Religious Nationalism in the United States". *Sociological Bulletin.* https://doi.org/10.1177/00380229251349577
Sarkar, Tanika, 1994. "Educating the Children of the Hindu Rashtra: Notes on RSS Schools". *Comparative Studies of South Asia, Africa, and the Middle East* 14(1): 10-15.
Sen, R and Jha, S, 2024. "Women Under Hindutva: Misogynist Memes, Mock-Auction and Doxing, Deepfake-Pornification and Rape Threats in Digital Space". *Journal of Asian and African Studies* 0(0). https://doi.org/10.1177/00219096241257686 (accessed 11 November 2024).
Sreepada, Nihar and Coman, Ioana, 2024. "The Aftermath of the 2019 Pulwama Terror Attack—Religion, Nationalism and Exclusion in Online News Comment Sections". *The Journal of International Communication.* https://doi.org/10.1080/13216597.2024.2339883.
Yuval-Davis, Nira, 1997. "Women, Citizenship and Difference". *Feminist Review* 57(1):4–27. https://doi.org/10.1080/014177897339632 (accessed 11 November 2024).
Zavos, John, 2015. "Digital Media and Networks of Hindu Activism in the UK". *Culture and Religion* 16(1): 17-34.
Zavos, John, 2015. "Small Acts, Big Society: Sewa and Hindu (Nationalist) Identity in Britain". *Ethnic and Racial Studies* 38(2): 243-258.

Zavos, John, 2010. "Situating Hindu Nationalism in the UK: Vishwa Hindu Parishad and the Development of British Hindu Identity", *Journal of Commonwealth and Comparative Politics* 48(1): 2-22.

Books and Reports

Banaji, Shakuntala and Bhatt, Ram, 2019. *WhatsApp Vigilantes: An Exploration of Citizen Reception and Circulation of Misinformation Related to the Mob*, https://www.lse.ac.uk/media-and-communications/assets/documents/research/projects/WhatsApp-Misinformation-Report.pdf (accessed 11 November 2024).

Blee, Kathleen, 2002. *Inside Organized Racism: Women in the Hate Movement*. Berkeley, CA, US: University of California Press.

Chavez, Leo, 2017. *Anchor Babies and the Challenge of Birthright Citizenship*. Stanford, CA, US: Stanford University Press.

Das Gupta, Shamita (ed), 2007. *Body Evidence: Intimate Violence Against South Asian Women in America*. New Brunswick, NJ, US: Rutgers University Press.

Espiritu, Yen Le, 2003. *Homebound: Filipino American Lives Across Cultures, Communities, and Countries*. Berkeley, CA, US: University of California Press.

Farris, Sara R, 2017. *In the Name of Women's Rights: The Rise of Femonationalism*. Durham, NC, US: Duke University Press. Retrieved August 2, 2024 (http://www.jstor.org/stable/j.ctv11sn2fp) (accessed 11 November 2024).

Glenn, Evelyn Nakano, 2002. *Unequal Freedom: How Race and Gender Shaped American Citizenship and Labor*. Cambridge, MA, US: Harvard University Press.

Harding, Susan. 2000, *The Book of Jerry Falwell: Fundamentalist Language and Politics*. Princeton, NJ, US: Princeton University Press.

Joshi, K, 2006. *New Roots in America's Sacred Ground: Religion, Race, and Ethnicity in Indian America*. New Brunswick, NJ, US: Rutgers University Press.

Joshi, Khyati, 2020. *White Christian Privilege: The Illusion of Religious Equality in America*. NYC, NY, US: NYU Press.

Joshi, Khyati and Purkayastha, Bandana, 2018. *Faith and Religion: South Asian Americans in the US*. South Asian Digital Archives.

Kannabiran, Kalpana (ed), 2014. *Women and Law: Critical Feminist Perspectives*. New Delhi, India: SAGE Publications.

Katju, M, 2003. *Vishva Hindu Parishad and Indian Politics*. New Delhi, India: Orient Longman.
Kibria, Nazli, Bowman, Cathy and O'Leary, Michael, 2014. *Race and Immigration*. Cambridge, UK: Polity Press.
Kumar, Ravish, 2018. *The Free Voice: On Democracy, Culture and the Nation*. Translated from Hindi by Chitra Padmanabhan, Anurag Basnet, and Ravi Singh. New Delhi, India: Speaking Tiger Publishing Private Limited.
Kurien, P, 2007. "*A Place at the multicultural table: the development of an American Hinduism.*" New Brunswick, NC, US: Rutgers University Press.
Narayan, Anjana and Purkayastha, Bandana, eds. 2009. *Living Our Religions: Hindu and Muslim South Asian American Women Narrate Their Experiences*. West Hartford, CT, US: Kumarian Press.
Perry, Imani, 2018. *Vexy Thing*. Durham, NC, US: Duke University Press.
Samaddar, Ranabir, 2020. *The Postcolonial Age of Migration*. 1st ed. Routledge India, New Delhi, India. https://doi.org/10.4324/9780429324697 (accessed 11 November 2024).
Sarkar, Tanika, 1995. *Women and the Hindu Right*. New Delhi, India: Kali for Women.
Varadarajan, L, 2010. *The Domestic Abroad: Diaspora in International Relations*. Delhi, India: Oxford University Press.
Weed, Eric, 2017. *The Religion of White Supremacy in the United States*. Lanham, MD, US: Lexington Books.
Yountae, An, 2024. *The Coloniality of the Secular: Race, Religion, and Poetics of World-Making*. Durham, NC, US: Duke University Press.

Information Documents and Resources, inc Podcasts

Blee, Kathleen, 2004. "Positioning Hate." Paper presented at the Conference to Establish Hate Studies, Spoke Washington, March 20, 2004.
India's "Untouchables" Face Violence, Discrimination, https://www.nationalgeographic.com/pages/article/indias-untouchables-face-violence-discrimination (accessed 10 November 2024).
Pascale, Celine Marie, 2024. *Weaponization of Language*. Manuscript in preparation.
Ravish Kumar | Center for Contemporary South Asia, https://watson.brown.edu/southasia/people/ravish-kumar (accessed 10 November 2024).

South Asian Communalism Watch (SACW), 2002. *The Foreign exchange of hate: IDRF and the American funding of Hindutva,* http://www.sacw.net/2002/FEHi/FEH/ (accessed 13 June 2022).
Walking a Fine Line: Voices of Hindu Women in the US. https://open.spotify.com/show/1XHBKFobcTHrS146hpMHf1 (accessed 16 November 2024).

13

Lobbying for Change: One Woman's Experiences of Incarceration and Male Violence

Jessica K. Williams

Introduction

When I was 16 years old, I met a man eight years my senior who would soon become my boyfriend. It was one of those romances they make movies about; wild, passionate, dangerous, and intense. The power dynamic between us was one-sided in his favor. Roughly one year into our relationship, my boyfriend confronted me with a "choice". Along with another grown man nearly eight years my senior, I was asked to partake in committing crimes so that the two men could break into homes to steal household items and resell them for profit. I resisted. Yet it turned out that these two men were very serious about committing these crimes and needing my assistance: I was the only one with a car. The second man came armed with a loaded handgun, bringing it into my car to apply pressure on me to say "yes" in response to their demand

J. K. Williams (✉)
Independent Scholar and Women's Rights Advocate, Victoria, Australia
e-mail: contactjwilliams@yahoo.com

J. A. Scutt (ed.), *Women, Power and Autonomy*,
https://doi.org/10.1007/978-3-031-97958-3_13

that I be the driver for their crime spree. Begrudgingly, I said yes, not knowing what might happen to me if I continued to refuse.

I wish this was the end to this chapter in the story of my life …

After several stints of dropping the men off and picking them up after they had broken into a home, and upon seeing the rush of adrenaline the two men displayed upon returning to my car, at the impressionable age of 16 I was enticed to join them. Entering several homes with the two men, I participated in stealing personal belongings from the victims of our crimes. It was a "choice" that I still deeply regret, a permanent tarnish on the record of my life. Once we were caught and I was arrested, I was first taken to Cleveland County to be interviewed by the detectives who arrested me. They gave me the opportunity to word my witness statement to admit to being coerced into committing these crimes by older men and by threat of harm. This was a life-changing moment for me, and I can confidently say that today, as a 42-year-old woman, I realize that I made the wrong choice. At the time, I could not fathom betraying my boyfriend, so I said that I was as guilty as he. I was charged and convicted of numerous felonies in three separate counties across North Carolina. As a result, I was sentenced to a mix of probation and active time.

In total, over the course of the years 1999 and 2000, I was incarcerated in five separate penal facilities. Of these facilities, three are jails (McDowell County jail, Cleveland County Detention Center, Burke County jail) and two are prisons (North Carolina Correctional Institution for Women and Fountain Correctional Center for Women, which has since closed). Of the prisons, one was maximum-medium custody/security and the other was minimum security, and both were "closed" prisons. My age (as well as my naivety) was a crucial factor in my incarceration: I was 16 and later 17 years old, with no prior criminal history. I did not know what I was in for. My still-developing brain could not comprehend what was happening to me when I was ripped away from my mother's home, my friends, my church, my community, and my pets, and thrown into a hellish nightmare from which I could not awaken.

I felt hopeless, afraid, and overwhelmed with sorrow and despair. I was an adolescent who had never committed any crimes before this. I was a good student, a good daughter, and a good friend to many peers, but none of that could save me. While I was in prison, I was frequently threatened or intimidated by a handful of women who had far more serious convictions, and longer sentences, than I did. Thankfully, my mother was either there on Sunday—visitation day—or she would organize someone from the church I grew up attending (Mount Calvary Baptist Church), or a childhood friend, to be there to visit me. She did not falter in her support and love for me. I will never be able to repay my mother for everything she did for me during that time of my life (and beyond that).

Advocating for Women's Rights as Prisoners and Ex-prisoners

Before this relationship and my incarceration, I was exceptionally smart and capable. I was raised in a Christian home, and we regularly attended church on Sunday mornings and evenings, as well as Wednesday evenings. I was raised by a loving, hard-working, single mother. Nevertheless, I suffered with depression, suicidal thoughts, harmful behaviors, and eating disorders throughout my adolescent and teenage years. I was molested as a child, and I suffered sexual, physical, and psychological bullying and harassment throughout my years of schooling.

I am a survivor of extreme forms of male physical, psychological, and sexual violence, to the degree of non-state torture (Sarson and MacDonald 2016, 2020, 2022; Human Rights, Human Dignity 2025). I have likely suffered numerous Acquired Brain Injuries (ABI) from numerous occurrences of involuntary restriction of oxygen and/or restriction of blood supply to my brain, and have numerous Traumatic Brain Injuries (TBI) from multiple repeated, severe blunt force traumas to my skull. These ABI's and TBI's occurred after I was incarcerated and to my knowledge, I suffered nil brain injuries before incarceration. I entered into an abusive, heterosexual relationship post-brain injuries and post-incarceration. This may have implications regarding how patterns of abuse relate to patterns of criminality for women. As highlighted, I have suffered from ongoing depression and poor mental health from a young age. I left school before completing my high school education and obtained a General Educational Development (GED) certificate (high school diploma equivalency) while incarcerated at Fountain Correctional Center for Women. I am now a disabled woman with diagnosed Complex Post-Traumatic Stress Disorder (CPTSD) and fibromyalgia.

Due to my personal experiences of arrest, incarceration, strip searches, and male physical, sexual, and psychological violence, I have been compelled to advocate for women's rights, in particular, for incarcerated and ex-incarcerated women and girls and other women who have survived male violence. Having immigrated from the US to Australia in November 2010, my interest and participation in research and advocacy spans across the US and Australia, also including the United Kingdom.

Since moving to Australia, I have consistently undertaken political lobbying, advocacy, writing, and related research. I have studied corrections legislation, policies, and practices from different states and countries for my research, writing, and advocacy purposes. I have reviewed numerous international human rights instruments including the *International Covenant on Civil and Political Rights* (ICCPR), *International Covenant on Economic, Social and Cultural Rights* (ICESCR), *Convention on the Elimination of All Forms of Discrimination against Women* (CEDAW), *Convention against Torture and Other Cruel, Inhuman or Degrading Treatment or Punishment* (CAT), *Universal Declaration on Human Rights* (UDHR), United Nations Standard Minimum Rules for the Treatment of Prisoners (the Nelson Mandela Rules) (NMR), United Nations Rules for the Treatment of Women Prisoners and Non-custodial Measures for Women Offenders (the Bangkok Rules) (BGR), and the third and fourth Geneva Conventions in relation to women deprived of their liberty. This work has informed my understanding of the importance of laws, yet has exposed their failure to ensure women's safety in the outside world, much less in the world of imprisonment.

In addition to my own experience of incarceration, I have accumulated over three years of research and advocacy experience in this field, and have accumulated more than seven years of lobbying experience in related fields. I have reviewed research and literature relating to particular physical, psychological, and social vulnerabilities of women in general terms and of women specifically as a cohort of incarcerated people, including, but not limited to, Woolhouse et al. (2018) and Timonen et al. (2002). I have reviewed scholarly literature on this topic and related issues including, but not limited to, the work of Pratt (Pratt and Erikson 2011), of George (1993), of Mjåland et al. (2023), and of Crewe (2011, 2015) and Crewe et al. (2017, 2023). I provided expert witness testimony (Williams, CEDAW witness statement, 2023) for a hearing, hosted by Dr Jocelynne Scutt (University of Buckingham) through the University of New South Wales (UNSW), regarding Australia's obligations pursuant to CEDAW in relation to incarcerated women, and this chapter incorporates elements from that testimony. I wrote and submitted a stakeholder submission (SSPA 2023) to the Human Rights Framework inquiry by the Parliamentary Joint Committee on Human Rights (PJCHR), and research conducted for that submission helped shape perspectives for this chapter.

I have learned a great deal about the experiences of women and girls as a sex class, and of incarcerated and ex-incarcerated women as a sub-group of that sex class, through research, advocacy, lobbying, and through my experiences over four decades. This has taught me that when it comes to the treatment of incarcerated women, there is still so much work to be done.

Historical and Present Reality of Prison as an Institution

Closed and Open Systems?

Historically, prison systems have featured inhumane conditions, built designs and practices stemming from outdated beliefs. The Pennsylvania system, established in 1682 (McWilliams 2002; Brittanica 1998; Coyle 2025), aimed at rehabilitation, but its solitary cell design proved mentally and physically harmful to prisoners and was economically unsustainable. The Auburn system, which emerged in the early 1820's (Rubin 2017; Handley-Cousins 2018), improved conditions slightly, but still fell short of modern human rights standards; some commentators called it the "silent system" because prisoners were forbidden from speaking to one another during the work day (Rubin 2017). Many current facilities reflect remnants of these outdated systems, with individual cells and limited contact between the incarcerated population. The Scandinavian open prison model, originating in the 1930s (Reiter et al. 2018; Baker and Quince 2022), prioritizes rehabilitation for community reintegration.

Numerous academics have theorized which prison system ("open" or "closed") is more or less humane and to what degree of failure or success the system has in relation to rehabilitation and recidivism (Crewe et al. 2023; Crewe et al. 2017; Mjåland et al. 2023; Pratt and Eriksson 2011; Swavola et al. 2016). Research suggests that open prison systems positively impact policies, practices, and built design, surpassing closed systems in achieving humaneness and reducing recidivism. Norway has one of the lowest recidivism rates in the world at 20 per cent (Deady 2014, 3). As Tieman-Koster (2023) states, "only 20 per cent of inmates released commit another crime within two years of being released". The low recidivism rate has been attributed to prison policies which "directed prisons toward imitating community living" (Tieman-Koster, 2023) which Deady refers to as the "normalization approach".

Positive outcomes in open prison systems are accompanied by critiques that require further evaluation to determine their validity and applicability. Crewe (2011) spoke of the "tightness" of penal power, exemplified by invasive forms of psychological power and demands that prisoners regulate their conduct and construct their identities in alignment with institutional objectives. Smith and Ugelvik (as cited by Crewe 2023) noted that "there is a fine line between rehabilitation and authoritarian intervention." Authoritarian intervention, which involves regulating conduct and identities to align with institutional objectives, is a common aspect of daily life for humans, regardless of their liberty status. This intervention can appear in various forms, such as political governance, education, employment, religion, parenting, and societal norms. It is natural to expect some level of authoritarian intervention within correctional facilities, but this should not diminish the evident benefits of open prison systems. Crewe et al. (2023) observed: "Even in an unusually humane prison system, prisoners report considerable pain and frustration." This aligns with my own experiences of incarceration and that of my associates, one of whom was incarcerated in an open prison in Canada. I agree with observations from Sykes (1958) as cited by Mjåland et al. (2023), that one of the "fundamental processes" prisons share is the "capacity for prisons to produce pain, of which none is more immediately obvious than the loss of liberty". This experience of incarceration is evident in both open and closed prison systems. As observed and stated by Mjåland et al. (2023, 1651); citing Sykes (1958):

> Contrary to the qualitative literature that documents the *specific pains* experienced by prisoners in open prisons these results suggest that the most pressing pains of imprisonment are similar in both closed and open establishments.
>
> The deprivation of liberty, and the loss of contact with family and friends, is what hurts most in both types of prisons and in both countries. This finding is slightly at odds with the qualitative research on open prisons, highlighting that open prisons produce a distinct set of pains, related to ambiguity, ambivalence and self-regulation.

Notably, Neumann's assessment that psychological burdens "inherent in the loss of freedom" are "especially salient when prisoners are in open establishments" (2011, 5) does not align with my own experience of incarceration when reflecting on the weight or heaviness, breadth, tightness, and depth of incarceration between maximum-security and minimum-security closed prisons. Neither does her connection between an obligation to "build inner bars" as a means of self-discipline contributing significantly to these "inherent" psychological burdens. Mjåland et al. (2023, 1642) found "there is little in our survey data that supports the idea that open prisons produce a distinct set of pains" and "open prisons are still very much experienced as prisons". However, they concluded that "the main difference is that these pains are experienced as less acute" (Mjåland et al. 2023, 1642).

Open prison systems offer clear benefits, in comparison to closed prisons, to incarcerated women and their dependants and other family members, corrections staff, and society. There is ample punitive value within open prison systems despite the positive benefits extended to the incarcerated population and, in my opinion, these benefits should not serve to minimize the perpetual negative impact of being deprived of one's liberty.

Previous researchers may have unintentionally underestimated the severe and devastating impact of the loss of freedom, especially for incarcerated women and particularly those with children. This could stem from a superficial understanding of the incarceration experience. Deprivation of liberty feels as if a part of oneself has been cut away, leaving a hollow shell. Time seems to halt, isolating the incarcerated individual while the world continues moving forward, oblivious to their plight. From my own experience, the loss of freedom resembles glimpsing a life after death while still alive—a dark, heavy emptiness consumes a person. Regret, worry, and isolation intensify, compounded by separation from loved ones and the uncertainty of when normalcy will return. Even the most humdrum interactions "on the outside" become moments desperately longed for. Incarcerated women also face fears of losing employment, housing, or custody of their children. For me, being torn away from my mother's home, my pets, my friends, my family, my community—my entire world, was utterly devastating and debilitating.

Despite efforts to create humane prison systems, significant suffering persists; it is prison after all.

Women and Prison as "Humane" System?

Built Design and Construction

Many prisons housing females, along with their policies and practices, were originally intended for males, designed and built by males or based on male prison designs (Blakinger 2019; Fair 2009; Maiello and Carter 2015). Deady (2014) concluded that the "principle of normality" should guide the built design of prisons and jails.

Through my experiences in five different correctional facilities of varying sizes, types, locations, and security levels, I gained unique insights into how the built design affects the overall incarceration experience. While two of the prisons provided relatively humane conditions with more interaction and freedom, the practices within them were often inhumane, fostering tense and hostile environments and interactions between the women prisoners. The predominant use of steel, metal, and concrete in building materials created poor comfort and exacerbated feelings of depression and isolation. Fixtures bolted to the ground or walls making areas static or fixed in design creating an unnatural and discomforting atmosphere, seemingly based on assumptions of extreme violent behavior not supported by research on incarcerated women's behavior. Lack of privacy, such as uncovered showers and toilets, is degrading treatment which violates international human rights standards (viz NMR, ICCPR) and adds to feelings of shame and distress, particularly for women who have experienced assault which studies show is a high proportion of the incarcerated female population (Bagaric and Bagaric 2016; McDaniels-Wilson and Belknap 2008; McMillan et al. 2021; O'Rourke et al. 2018; Woolhouse et al. 2018). These design aspects do not reflect normal life and are often unjustified for security in women's prisons. Extreme security measures like armed guards and barbed wire are unnecessary in these facilities. This is in line with Maiello's and Carter's view (2015):

> When large, foreboding facilities are replaced with a more appropriate scale and normative design (like the San Diego facility), the buildings fit well within their physical environment. Because women are not prone to escape, there is less of a need for high security fencing topped with ominous razor wire. In some instances, the building itself can provide the secure perimeter, making the prison a "good neighbor" within its community, often mistaken for a school, or a college campus.

Searches and Body Cavity Searches

One of the vilest practices used by the criminal justice system against incarcerated women and girls is that of strip searches and body cavity searches as a form of security. While the exact steps required of incarcerated women during a strip search vary from prison to prison, common requirements include removing all clothing—including underwear, raising arms, raising feet, lifting breasts (and possibly having corrections staff run their hands underneath), bending over and spreading the buttocks; in some prisons the practice of "squatting and coughing" is still used. Each step of an invasive search comes with its own degree of humiliation and shame to add to the overall demeaning experience. Unsurprisingly, strip searching is often experienced as sexual assault by incarcerated women, and revictimizes women (WIPAN 2017). Amanda George (1993, 33) states:

> What we must acknowledge is that in giving officers the power to strip search and to use force, we are giving them the right to sexually assault. At the same time, we are removing any right of the victim to resist, to complain, and to have their experience of the assault legitimated.

In addition to regular strip searches, incarcerated women undergo routine strip searches before and after visitation. From my experience, this practice reinforces feelings of unworthiness for positive treatment and experiences. Strip searches strain relationships between corrections staff and the incarcerated population, particularly when women are compelled to obey orders of staff who have, by definition, sexually assaulted them. During visits to incarcerated women, strip searching may extend to family and friends, potentially burdening incarcerated women with guilt, and extending inhumaneness and sexual assault to additional parties. The degrading, humiliating, and demeaning act referred to as the "squat and cough" strip search technique is widely viewed as unacceptable, and in some jurisdictions is perceived as an unlawful body cavity search (Grewcock and Sentas 2019; Woods 2023; Daoud Legal 2025) for which police may need to seek a court order.[1] In some jurisdictions, there

[1] See generally *Law Enforcement Powers and Responsibilities Act* 2002 (NSW), http://www5.austlii.edu.au/au/legis/nsw/consol_act/leara2002451/ (accessed 22 March 2025); http://www5.austlii.edu.au/au/legis/nsw/consol_act/leara2002451/s31.html (accessed 22 March 2025). For searches without warrant, see Part 4 "Search and Seizure Powers without Warrant", Division 4 Provisions Relating to Personal Searches: s 31 governs strip searches, s 32 relates to "preservation of privacy and dignity during search", s 33 covers "rules for conduct of strip searches", s 34 provides that no strip searches can be conducted on children under 10 years, and s 4A governs searches "carried out with consent". Unless these provisions are complied with, noting

are calls to end routine strip-searching of women altogether (Victoria Ombudsman 2017).

In my research (Williams 2024), I have learned just how nefarious the Australian criminal justice system can be when it comes to strip-searching and keeping—or failing to keep—records. In 2022, a landmark class action lawsuit was filed with the Supreme Court in New South Wales alleging police unlawfully strip-searched people, including children, some as young as 10 years old (NSW Government 2024; Cueto 2024; LECC 2023; Woods 2023; Daniel 2022).[2] NSW Police committed a series of "unlawful acts" such as assault and battery during those searches over a six-year period from 2018 at the "Splendour in the Grass" festival. The plaintiffs alleged some people—again, including children without the support of a parent or guardian—were told to lift or move their genitals, strip naked, and squat and cough during searches, and women "were ordered to remove sanitary products so they too could be inspected". This lawsuit only came after a mountain of evidence about the misuse of strip searches by police stemming from police watchdog investigations, coroner's reports, and internal police documents had failed to convince lawmakers to push for legislative change.

In 2019, NSW police officers allegedly strip-searched at least 25 children illegally at the Sydney-based "Lost City Music Festival" which was for teens aged 13–17 years (Grewcock and Sentas 2019; Thompson 2019; Kontominas 2020). In one case, a child known as GEN15C told the NSW LECC (Law Enforcement Conduct Commission) that he was strip-searched by an officer who was not wearing gloves. He said the officer touched his testicles and rubbed his buttocks during the search. It is further alleged that after doing so, the officer moved around behind the boy, placed both hands inside his shorts and ran his hands around his buttocks, in a circular motion, in an effort to find drugs. No drugs were found (Mayers 2019).

---

s 31, a court order is required. Formerly the Crimes Act 1900 (NSW) governed conduct of a strip search, these provisions continuing to be incorporated in the Crimes Act 1900 (ACT), s 228, https://classic.austlii.edu.au/au/legis/act/consol_act/ca190082/s228.html (accessed 22 March 2025).

2 *Raya Meredith v State NSW* File No 2022/214157, https://supremecourt.nsw.gov.au/documents/Class-Actions/Music-Festival-Searches---Meredith/17_Orders_with_Schedules_A_B_C_3.5.24.pdf (accessed 22 March 2025).

In Tasmania, the Human Rights Law Centre (HRLC) obtained documents under *Right to Information Act* 2009 (Tasmania) requests which revealed that 841 strip searches of women in Tasmanian prisons took place in a seven-month period (between October 2020 and April 2021), with concealed items turning up in only three cases. The concealed items were pain medication; tobacco and a lighter; and tobacco and matchsticks. The HRLC says: "Tasmanian prisons searches [are] conducted too frequently, [and] not in line with international standards" (O'Brien 2021).

Freedom of Information responses (under the *Information (Public Access) Act* 2009 NSW) reveal that NSW Corrections does not record strip searches of women prisoners (Ryan 2021):

> The Human Rights Law Centre submitted a freedom of information request to Corrective Services NSW for the records of strip-searches on women in prison between October 2020 and April 2021. In response, the agency said there are no registers or log books where the searches are recorded.

This is in opposition to Rule 51 of the Nelson Mandela Rules regarding keeping records of strip searches. In Victoria, Australia, 1992, George (1993) reported that when asked to provide information on the number of strip searchers done by police, Victoria police replied that "no requirement" directed such searches to be "centrally documented," adding that consequently "no statistical data exists."

A NSW Inspector of Custodial Services Report (2020) into the Mary Wade Correctional Centre for women found strip searches are rife at the center, with the practice occurring when leaving the center, after contact and non-contact visits, as well as at times when women have gone nowhere or have not been visited. Strip searches are recorded only if something is found. This means there is no record of when, where, how or why searches are conducted: despite this being a routine practice, over 12 months ending in October 2019 no contraband had been found, so no record exists of how many women were subjected to a search for no reason, other than possibly degrading them.

To shed more light onto just how many strip searches occur within prisons across Australia, a WA Office of the Inspector of Custodial Services Report (2022) into strip-searching practices in Western Australian facilities revealed that almost 900,000 strip searches were conducted on prisoners over five years, with only 571 contraband items found, none of which were drug or weapons related. One could extrapolate that due to the contraband not being drug or weapons related, the assumption that this is a total of strip searches inflicted upon women is plausible. At least there, it appears that searches are recorded contrary to the position in New South Wales.

In 2017, then Ombudsman Deborah Glass conducted an independent inspection of the Dame Phyllis Frost Centre in Victoria over seven days (Victorian Ombudsman 2017a). Ms Glass said the inspection had uncovered some serious issues, including particular concerns related to the routine practice of strip searching the women before and after contact visits. Ms Glass said she was disappointed the Victorian Department of Justice and Regulation had not accepted her recommendation to stop the practice and instead undertake targeted strip searching when justified by intelligence or risk (which would be very rare). She said her office was also concerned about the high incidence of force and restraint being used at the prison, including reports of pregnant women being handcuffed when attending external medical appointments (Victorian Ombudsman 2017b).

If it even needs to be said, I will say it—the use of the "squat and cough" method within women's jails and prisons should cease immediately. Body-scanning technology (BST) should replace strip searches for incarcerated women at all points of detainment, arrest, or incarceration, including before and after visitation. BST should also replace strip-searching and watching women before, during, and after urine testing. *If* a strip search is deemed necessary, it must be conducted by (natal) female staff only.

Solitary Confinement and Prison Segregation

Australia's horrifying reputation extends to the use of solitary confinement. In a 2023 submission to the United Nations Committee Against Torture from the Australian Human Rights Commission (AHRC), numerous violations of human rights standards in regard to solitary confinement are listed, including that "1,876 separation and segregation notifications (exceeding 24 hours) in youth detention for the 2021–2022 period …" had been received by the New South Wales Ombudsman (AHRC 2023; Walsh and Blaber 2023). A 2022 review of the use of confinement and management regimes in Western Australia revealed that prisoners "are often held in their cells for 20–23 hours a day with little sensory or mental stimulation" (WA Office of the Inspector of Custodial Services 2022). Solitary confinement of women and children is prohibited by Rule 45 of the NMR yet is clearly still used in the sector. In Queensland *Owen D'Arcy v Chief Executive, Queensland Corrective Services and Ors* found procedural breaches in decision-making where a prisoner was precluded from contact with other prisoners, so that decision to so confine him was ruled unlawful and vacated.[3] In South Australia, despite its absence for some 19 years, solitary confinement was reinstated in 1990 under Section 32 of the *Correctional Services Act* 1982 (SA) (Legal Services Commission, SA 2025).[4]

A growing concern for me, and a growing challenge in the sector, is the embrace of political ideology by state and national governments, particularly regarding the recognition, or its lack, of the immutable nature of natal sex and the necessity of sex-segregation, and sex-focused provisions, in prisons. This lack of recognition of natal sex conflicts with international human rights standards, especially concerning the treatment of incarcerated women, creating a disconnect between state legislation/policy and international standards. As of 2023, all states and territories in Australia (SSPA 2023) have legislative or policy provisions allowing the

---

[3] Owen-D'Arcy v Chief Executive, Queensland Corrective Services [2021] QSC 273 (22 October 2021), https://www.austlii.edu.au/cgi-bin/viewdoc/au/cases/qld/QSC/2021/273.html (accessed 22 March 2025).

[4] Correctional Services Act 1982 (SA), https://www.legislation.sa.gov.au/lz?path=%2FC%2FA%2FCORRECTIONAL%20SERVICES%20ACT%201982 (accessed 22 March 2025).

transfer of a male prisoner to a female estate to be housed with female prisoners. These provisions fail to meet certain standards set in the NMR, BGR, CEDAW, ICCPR, and CAT, despite Australia being a member of the United Nations. Foregoing a crucial safeguarding method for female prisoners is inexplicable.[5]

Segregation of prisoners based on natal sex is a basic tenet of humane corrections for women and girls. *If* women and girls are to be incarcerated, international standards stipulate they must be afforded the basic dignity and safeguard of sex-segregation (NMR, Rule 11; Geneva Convention III: Art's 25, 29, 97, 108 and Geneva Convention IV: Art's 27, 76, 85, 124). As NMR Rule 11 states, in part:

> The different categories of prisoners shall be kept in separate institutions or parts of institutions, taking account of their sex, age, criminal record, the legal reason for their detention and the necessities of their treatment; thus: (a) Men and women shall so far as possible be detained in separate institutions; in an institution which receives both men and women, the whole of the premises allocated to women shall be entirely separate.

This basic requirement must extend to the staff and management of penal facilities. Same-sex supervision is another basic tenant of humane corrections (Geneva Convention III: Art's 97 and 108 and Geneva Convention IV: Art's 76 and 124). Female-only staff for women's prisons must be a sector-wide minimum-standard. As Rule 52 of the NMR states, in part:

> Intrusive searches, including strip and body cavity searches, should be undertaken only if absolutely necessary. Prison administrations shall be encouraged to develop and use appropriate alternatives to intrusive

[5] Editor's Note: Whether Australin courts will apply the jurisprudence of the UK Supreme Court in *For Women Scotland Ltd (Appellant) v The Scottish Ministers (Respondent)* UKS/2024/0042, https://www.supremecourt.uk/cases/uksc-2024-0042 (accessed 17 April 2025) that a person born male (sex = XY), holding a full gender recognition certificate ("GRC") which recognises that their gender is female, is not a "woman" (sex = XX) for the purposes of the *Equality Act* 2010 (UK) remains to be seen. Legislative changes to Australian sex discrimination/equal opportunity/anti-discrimination laws may mean that the UK decision does not apply or is interpreted not to do so.

> searches. Intrusive searches shall be conducted in private and by trained staff of the same sex as the prisoner.

This suggested minimum-standard is justified further by Maiello and Carter (2015):

> Trauma histories that accompany women to prison affect their perceptions of (typically male) authority, and inhibit their ability to navigate a seemingly threatening and authoritarian environment. For women with trauma histories, the controlling prison atmosphere can trigger a traumatic memory, and elicit a reaction that can be perceived by staff as uncooperative or disruptive.

As reported by Cat Woods (2023):

> Silke Meyer, former Deputy Director of the Gender and Family Violence Prevention Centre and Associate Professor of Criminology at Monash University reported that approximately 98 per cent of incarcerated women have histories of victimisation [*sic*] and trauma, and close to 85 per cent have been the victims of violence. Disturbing, also, is the research that estimates between 40 and 73 per cent of female prisoners have acquired brain injuries.

The sexual and physical violence that women suffer is overwhelmingly committed by males. Men account globally for around 90 percent of the suspects of intentional homicide (UNODC 2023), and in Australia, 97 per cent of sexual assault offenders are male (Australian Bureau of Statistics 2022). Accordingly, women and girls need safeguards to protect them from male violence while incarcerated.

Conclusion—Incarceration as Discrimination Against Women

In my expert witness testimony for the hearing at UNSW Sydney regarding Australia's obligations pursuant to the CEDAW in relation to imprisoned women, I go into detail regarding how incarcerating women is, in and of itself, an act of discrimination against women, and should be formally classified as such by the United Nations and all other relevant bodies (Williams 2023). There is a prevalence of (incarcerated) women suffering from Acquired Brain Injury (ABI) and Traumatic Brain Injury (TBI) (O'Rourke et al. 2018; Woolhouse et al. 2018), Post-Traumatic Stress Disorder (PTSD) (Baranyi et al. 2018), poor mental health and depression (Stathopoulos et al. 2012), histories of sexual assault and histories of physical and psychological abuse (ANROWS 2020).

Considering this, and given the correlation between Acquired Brain Injury (ABI) and Traumatic Brain Injury (TBI) with criminal behavior (Timonen et al. 2002), along with the increased suffering, stigma, and discrimination experienced by incarcerated women compared to men, and the detrimental effects of incarcerating women on families and communities, we must question the humanity of incarcerating such a vulnerable and mistreated population. The fact that 80 percent of incarcerated women are mothers, and many of them are single mothers, presents alarming implications for those women, their dependents, and society at large. As noted in *Overlooked: Women and Jails in an Era of Reform* (Swavola et al. 2016):

> As U.S. Attorney General Loretta Lynch said in her remarks at the White House Women and the Criminal Justice System Convening on March 30, 2016, "Put simply, we know that when we incarcerate a woman, we often are truly incarcerating a family, in terms of the far-reaching effect on her children, her community, and her entire family network."

There are more troubling stats on head injury that should be considered, too. McMillan et al. (2021) found:

> Significant head injury (SHI) was found in 85 (78%) of 109 women, of whom 34 (40%) had associated disability. Repeat head injury was reported in 71 (84%) of the 85 women with SHI and, in most cases, this resulted from domestic abuse that had occurred over many years. Women with a history of SHI were significantly more likely to have a history of violent offences than those without a history of SHI (66 [79%] of 85 women in the SHI group *vs* 13 [54%] of 24 women in the no-SHI group had committed a violent offence; odds ratio [OR] 3·1, 95% CI 1·2–8·1).

Based on these findings, it can be inferred that female-pattern criminal behavior often indicates victimization, typically by male violence. In addition to the previously mentioned reasons for considering female incarceration a form of discrimination, there are further justifications for this classification as a human rights standard. As Maiello and Carter (2015) state:

> For one, women's offenses are generally less serious than men's – primarily drug and property crimes, as opposed to violent offenses against the person. Female offenders are also less likely to have a prior offense history and they generally recidivate less often than their male counterparts. These factors alone suggest that community-based sanctions are an appropriate first choice for many female offenders.

Research and my personal experiences of incarceration (including stigma post-incarceration) support the notion that criminalizing and incarcerating women and girls offers minimal benefits to both the individual and the community. Incarceration "should be reserved for criminals who commit the most serious of deprived (sic) acts" (Mirko Bagaric 2016). The conclusion from Bagaric and Bagaric (2016) that "the default position is that no woman should be imprisoned" stands.

Sex-based criminal, violence, and security-risk patterns, as well as general differences between males and females, necessitate a distinct and sex-based approach toward the treatment and rehabilitation of criminally-at-risk women and girls. A radical approach of assisting criminally-at-risk women in overcoming existing psychosocial and trauma-based barriers, substance abuse issues, and other obstacles to successful rehabilitation, rather than resorting to incarceration, should be adopted across the sector and across society. The incarceration of girls and women constitutes discrimination against them and violates international human rights standards. It is cruel and is of little to no benefit in many circumstances; it perpetuates violence against women as well as within our families and communities. We should all want more from the society of which we are a part.

Bibliography

Reported Cases

For Women Scotland Ltd (Appellant) v The Scottish Ministers (Respondent) UKS/2024/0042, UK Supreme Court, https://www.supremecourt.uk/cases/uksc-2024-0042 (accessed 17 April 2025)

Owen-D'Arcy v Chief Executive, Queensland Corrective Services [2021] QSC 273 (22 October 2021), https://www.austlii.edu.au/cgi-bin/viewdoc/au/cases/qld/QSC/2021/273.html (accessed 22 March 2025).

Raya Meredith v State NSW File No 2022/214157, https://supremecourt.nsw.gov.au/documents/Class-Actions/Music-Festival-Searches---Meredith/17_Orders_with_Schedules_A_B_C_3.5.24.pdf (accessed 22 March 2025).

Statutes and Conventions or Treaties

Government Information (Public Access) Act 2009 (NSW), https://legislation.nsw.gov.au/view/whole/html/inforce/current/act-2009-052 (accessed 2 October 2025).

Convention on the Elimination of All Forms of Discrimination Against Women (CEDAW), New York, 18 December 1979 | OHCHR, https://www.ohchr.org/en/instruments-mechanisms/instruments/convention-elimination-all-forms-discrimination-against-women (accessed 2 March 2025).

Correctional Services Act 1982 (SA), South Australian Legislation, https://www.legislation.sa.gov.au/lz?path=%2FC%2FA%2FCORRECTIONAL%20SERVICES%20ACT%201982 (accessed 22 March 2025).

Crimes Act 1900 (ACT), https://www.legislation.act.gov.au/a/1900-40/ (accessed 2 March 2025).

Crimes Act 1900 (NSW), NSW Legislation, https://legislation.nsw.gov.au/view/html/inforce/current/act-1900-040 (accessed 2 March 2025).

Geneva Conventions – Third Geneva Convention, IHL Treaties - Geneva Convention (III) on Prisoners of War, 1949, https://ihl-databases.icrc.org/en/ihl-treaties/gciii-1949 (accessed 2 March 2025).

Geneva Conventions – Fourth Geneva Convention, IHL Treaties - Geneva Convention (IV) on Civilians, 1949, https://ihl-databases.icrc.org/en/ihl-treaties/gciv-1949 (accessed 2 March 2025).

International Covenant on Civil and Political Rights (ICCPR), OHCHR, https://www.ohchr.org/en/treaty-bodies/ccpr/background-international-covenant-civil-and-political-rights-and-optional-protocols (accessed 2 March 2025).

International Covenant on Economic, Social and Cultural Rights (ICESCR), OHCHR, https://www.ohchr.org/en/instruments-mechanisms/instruments/international-covenant-economic-social-and-cultural-rights (accessed 2 March 2025).

Law Enforcement (Powers and Responsibilities) Act 2002 (NSW), https://classic.austlii.edu.au/au/legis/nsw/consol_act/leara2002451/ (accessed 22 March 2025).

Right to Information Act 2009 (Tas), https://www.findandconnect.gov.au/entity/right-to-information-act-2009-2/ (accessed 2 October 2025).

United Nations Office on Drugs and Crime, Global Study on Homicide 2023—Report—Special Points of Interest. https://www.unodc.org/unodc/en/data-and-analysis/global-study-on-homicide.html https://www.unodc.org/documents/data-and-analysis/gsh/2023/GSH23_Special_Points.pdf

United Nations Standard Minimum Rules for the Treatment of Prisoners (the Nelson Mandela Rules) (NMR), Nelson Mandela Rules (NMR, Rule 11), https://www.unodc.org/documents/justice-and-prison-reform/Nelson_Mandela_Rules-E-ebook.pdf (accessed 2 March 2023).

United Nations Rules for the Treatment of Women Prisoners and Non-custodial Measures for Women Offenders (the Bangkok Rules) (BGR), OHCHR, https://www.ohchr.org/en/instruments-mechanisms/instruments/united-nations-rules-treatment-women-prisoners-and-non-custodial (accessed 2 March 2025).

Universal Declaration on Human Rights (UDHR), United Nations, https://www.un.org/en/about-us/universal-declaration-of-human-rights (accessed 2 March 2025).

Articles and Book Chapters

Bagaric, M and Bagaric, B, "Mitigating the Crime that is the Over-Imprisonment of Women: Why Orange Should Not be the New Black", *Vermont Law Review*, 2016, vol 41, https://papers.ssrn.com/sol3/papers.cfm?abstract_id=2773341 https://books.google.com.au/books/about/Mitigating_the_Crime_That_Is_the_Over_Im.html?id=aQUBzwEACAAJ&redir_esc=y (2 February 2024).

Baker, Nick and Quince, Annabelle, "Does it work?" Topic: Prisons - Rear Vision, 4 October 2022, *ABC Radio National*, Nordic criminal justice: How does it differ from Australia and does it work? - ABC News, https://www.abc.net.au/news/2022-10-05/what-are-nordic-prisons-like-criminal-justice/101481590 (accessed 8 September 2024).

Baranyi, G, Cassidy, M, Fazel, S, Priebe, S, Mundt, AP. "Prevalence of Posttraumatic Stress Disorder in Prisoners". *Epidemiol Rev*. 2018 Jun 1;40(1):134–145. https://doi.org/10.1093/epirev/mxx015. Erratum in: Epidemiol Rev. 2018 Jun 1;40(1):166. https://doi.org/10.1093/epirev/mxy007. PMID: 29596582; PMCID: PMC5982805.

Blakinger, K, "Can We Build a Better Women's Prison" *The Washington Post* 28 October 2019, https://www.washingtonpost.com/magazine/2019/10/28/prisons-jails-are-designed-men-can-we-build-better-womens-prison/ (accessed 3 March 2024).

Brittanica, The Editors of Encyclopaedia Britannica (1998, July 20). *Pennsylvania system. Encyclopedia Britannica.* https://www.britannica.com/topic/Pennsylvania-system (accessed 8 September 2024).

Canales, Sarah Basford, "Australia's freedom of information system 'dysfunctional and broken', inquiry finds", Australia news | The Guardian, https://www.theguardian.com/australia-news/2023/dec/09/australias-freedom-of-information-system-dysfunctional-and-broken-inquiry-finds (accessed 2 March 2025).

Coyle, Andrew G, "Pennsylvania system—Prison Reform ...", *Encyclopaedia Britannica*, 3 March 2025, Pennsylvania system | Prison Reform, Quaker Influence & Solitary Confinement Britannica, https://www.britannica.com/topic/Pennsylvania-system (accessed 8 September 2024).

Crewe, B, "Depth, weight, tightness: Revisiting the pains of imprisonment", *Punishment & Society*, 2011, 13(5), 509–529, https://journals.sagepub.com/doi/abs/10.1177/1462474511422172 (accessed 8 September 2024).

Crewe, B, "Inside the belly of the penal beast: Understanding the experience of imprisonment", *International Journal for Crime, Justice and Social Democracy*, 2015, vol 4(1) 50–65, https://doi.org/10.5204/ijcjsd.v3i2.201 (accessed 8 September 2024).

Crewe, B, Hulley, S and Wright, S, "The Gendered Pains of Life Imprisonment", *The British Journal of Criminology*, November 2017, vol 57(6) 1359–1378, https://doi.org/10.1093/bjc/azw088 (accessed 8 September 2024).

Crewe, B, Ievins, A, Larmour, S, Laursen, J, Mjåland, K and Schliehe, A, "Nordic Penal Exceptionalism: A Comparative, Empirical Analysis", *The British Journal of Criminology*, 2023, vol 63 424–443, https://doi.org/10.1093/bjc/azac013 (accessed 8 September 2024).

Cueto, Jonalyn, "NSW Supreme Court sets trial date …", *Australasian Lawyer*, 20 May 2024, NSW Supreme Court sets trial date for landmark strip search class action | Australasian Lawyer, https://www.thelawyermag.com/au/news/general/nsw-supreme-court-sets-trial-date-for-landmark-strip-search-class-action/489828 (accessed 22 March 2025).

Daniel, Sue, "Hundreds join class action …", 23 July 2022, Hundreds join class action against NSW Police strip searches at music festivals - ABC News, https://www.abc.net.au/news/2022-07-23/legal-action-launched-in-nsw-over-police-strip-searches/101263616 (accessed 22 March 2025).

Fair, H, "International Review of Women's Prisons", *Prison Service Journal* 2009, vol 184, https://www.prisonstudies.org/resources/international-review-womens-prisons-prison-service-journal-article (accessed 3 March 2024).

George, Amanda, "Strip searches: Sexual assault by the state" [1993] *Alt LawJ* 8; (1993) 18(1) Alternative Law Journal 31. Retrieved from http://www.austlii.edu.au/au/journals/AltLawJl/1993/8.html (accessed February 24, 2024).

Handley-Cousins, Sarah, "The Auburn System …", 11 March 2018, The Auburn System: Prisons and Punishment in the 19th Century United States – DIG, https://digpodcast.org/2018/03/11/auburn/ (accessed 8 September 2024).

Kontominas, Bellinda, "NSW Police watchdog finds strip searches of four teenagers …", *ABC News*, 8 May 2020, NSW Police watchdog finds strip searches of four teenagers at music festivals were 'unlawful' - ABC News, https://www.abc.net.au/news/2020-05-08/nsw-police-watchdog-finds-teen-festival-strip-searches-unlawful/12229188 (accessed 2 March 2025).

McDaniels-Wilson, C and Belknap, J, "The extensive sexual violation and sexual abuse histories of incarcerated women", *Violence Against Women*,

October 2008, vol 14 (1)) 1090–112, https://doi.org/10.1177/107780120 8323160 (accessed 3 March 2024).

McMillan, TM, Aslam, H, Crowe, E, Seddon, E, and Barry, SJ (2021, May 13). "Associations between significant head injury and persisting disability and violent crime in women in prison in Scotland, UK: a cross-sectional study". https://doi.org/10.1016/S2215-0366(21)00082-1 (accessed March 3, 2024);

Maiello, Laura and Carter, Stephen, "Minus the urinals and painted pink? What should a women's prison look like?" 9 December 2015, *Penal Reform Blog*, https://www.penalreform.org/blog/10020/ (accessed 3 March 2024).

Mayers, Lily, "NSW Police asked 15 year-old to expose himself ...", *ABC News*, 2 December 2019, *NSW Police asked 15yo to expose himself as part of festival strip search, inquiry hears,* https://www.abc.net.au/news/2019-12-02/nsw-pol ice-strip-searched-25-children-at-festival-inquiry-hears/11756902 (accessed 3 March 2024).

Mjåland, K, Laursen, J, Schliehe, A, and Larmour, S (2023). Contrasts in freedom: Comparing the experiences of imprisonment in open and closed prisons in England and Wales and Norway. *European Journal of Criminology, 20(5)*, 1641–1662, https://doi.org/10.1177/14773708211065905 (accessed 8 September 2024).

Neumann, Cecilie Basberg (2011). Chapter 7 "Imprisoning the soul". In Routledge, *Penal Exceptionalism?* (1st ed) 1–17.

O'Rourke, C, Linden, MA and Lohan, M (2018). "Traumatic brain injury and abuse among female offenders compared to non-incarcerated controls". *Brain Injury*. https://doi.org/10.1080/02699052.2018.1539872 (accessed February 24, 2024).

Pratt, J, and Eriksson, A (2011). "'Mr. Larsson is walking out again'. The origins and development of Scandinavian prison systems". *Australian & New Zealand Journal of Criminology, 44(1)*, 7-23, https://doi.org/10.1177/000 4865810393105 (accessed 8 September 2024);

Reiter, Keramet, Sexton, Lori and Sumner, Jennifer, Theoretical and empirical limits of Scandinavian Exceptionalism: Isolation and normalization in Danish prisons. *Punishment & Society, 20*(1), 92–112.https://doi.org/10. 1177/1462474517737273 (Original work published 2018).

Rubin, Ashley, "New York (Auburn) Prison System", *Wiley Online Library*, 1 August 2017, Rubin - Major Reference Works, https://onlinelibrary.wiley. com/doi/abs/ https://doi.org/10.1002/9781118845387.wbeoc259 (accessed 8 September 2024).

Ryan, H, "NSW fails to log strip searches of women", *Blue Mountains Gazette*, 9 December 2021, https://www.bluemountainsgazette.com.au/story/7544753/nsw-fails-to-log-strip-searches-of-women/ (accessed 27 August 2024).

Sarson, Jeanne and MacDonald, Linda, "Non-State Torture of Women: Reclaiming Their Human Right", *Witness: The Canadian Jurnal of Critical Nursing Discourse*, 2022, https://witness.journals.yorku.ca/index.php/default/article/view/121 (accessed 12 March 2025).

Sarson, Jeanne and Macdonald, Linda, "Seeking Equality – Justice and Women's and Girls' Right Not to be Subjected to Non-State Torture" in J Scutt (ed), *Women, Law and Culture – Conformity, Contradiction and Conflict*, Palgrave Macmillan, London, UK, 2016, 263–281.

Stathopoulos, M., with Quadara, A., Fileborn, B., & Clark, H. (2012). Addressing women's victimisation histories in custodial settings (ACSSA Issues No. 13). Melbourne: Australian Centre for the Study of Sexual Assault, Australian Institute of Family Studies.

Thompson, Angus, "NSW Police admits breaching strip-search laws", *Sydney Morning Herald*, 23 June 2019, *SW Police admits breaching strip-search laws,* https://www.smh.com.au/national/nsw/nsw-police-admits-breaching-strip-search-laws-20190620-p51zny.html (accessed 2 March 2025).

Tieman-Koster, C (2023). "Comparison of Open and Closed Prison Systems: Can These Systems Be Implemented in Australia?" *University of South Australia Law Review* 5. https://doi.org/10.21913/USLRunisalr.v5.1663 (accessed 8 September 2024).

Timonen, M, Miettunen, J, Hakko, H, Zitting, P, Veijola, J, Wendt, L von and Räsänen, P, "The association of preceding traumatic brain injury with mental disorders, alcoholism and criminality: the Northern Finland 1966 Birth Cohort Study", *Psychiatry Research* 2022, vol 113 (3) 217–226, https://doi.org/10.1016/S0165-1781(02)00269-X https://psycnet.apa.org/record/2003-01501-003 (accessed 8 September 2024).

Walsh, Tamra and Blaber, Helen, "Solitary Confinement and Prisoners Human Rights", *Monash University Law Review* vol 49, no 1, 2023 232–260, SOLITARY CONFINEMENT AND PRISONERS' HUMAN RIGHTS TAMARA WALSH* AND HELEN BLABER** https://www.austlii.edu.au/au/journals/MonashULawRw/2023/7.pdf (accessed 22 March 2025).

Woods, Cat, "Women in Prison", Jan 17, 2023, *Law Society of NSW Journal*, https://lsj.com.au/articles/women-in-prison/ (accessed 22 March 2025).

Woods, Cat, "NSW Police powers to search ...", 18 October 2023, *Law Society Journal online*, NSW Police powers to search, detain and arrest require overhaul - Law Society Journal, https://lsj.com.au/articles/nsw-police-powers-to-search-detain-and-arrest-require-overhaul/ (accessed 22 March 2025).

Woolhouse, R, McKinlay, A and Grace, RC, "Women in Prison With Traumatic Brain Injury: Prevalence, Mechanism, and Impact on Mental Health" *Int J Offender Ther Comp Criminol,* August 2018, vol 62 (10) 3135–3150, https://doi.org/10.1177/0306624X17726519 (accessed 8 September 2024).

Books and Reports

Australian Bureau of Statistics (ABC), *97 per cent of sexual assault offenders are male*, 2 February 2022, https://www.abs.gov.au/media-centre/media-releases/97-cent-sexual-assault-offenders-are-male (accessed 27 August 2024).

Deady, CW, *Incarceration and Recidivism: Lessons from Abroad*, Pell Center for International Relations and Public Policy, 2014, https://salve.edu/sites/default/files/filesfield/documents/Incarceration_and_Recidivism.pdf (accessed 3 March 2024).

Grewcock, Michael and Sentas, Vicki, *Rethinking Strip Searches by NSW Police*, UNSW Works, 2019, https://unsworks.unsw.edu.au/handle/1959.4/unsworks_64696 https://doi.org/10.26190/unsworks/27582 (accessed 22 March 2025).

Legal Services Commission SA, *Report – Solitary Confinement*, 2025, https://lawhandbook.sa.gov.au/ch33s03s04.php (accessed 22 March 2025).

McWilliams, John C, *Two Centuries of Corrections in Pennsylvania: A Commemorative History*, 2002, Office of Justice Programs (ojp.gov), https://www.ojp.gov/ncjrs/virtual-library/abstracts/two-centuries-corrections-pennsylvania-commemorative-history (accessed 8 September 2024).

NSW Inspector of Custodial Services, *Inspection of Mary Wade Correctional Centre Report*, October 2020, https://inspectorcustodial.nsw.gov.au/documents/inspection-reports/inspection-of-mary-wade-correctional-centre.pdf (accessed 2 March 2025).

Sarson, Jeanne and Macdonald, Linda, *Women Unsilenced*, Friesen Press, Canada, 2020.

Swavola, E, Riley K and Subramanian, R, *Overlooked: Women and Jails in an Era of Reform*, August 2016, Vera Institute, https://www.vera.org/publications/overlooked-women-and-jails-report (accessed 2 March 2025).

Sykes, GM, *The society of captives: A study of a maximum security prisoni,* 1958, Princeton University Press, https://psycnet.apa.org/record/2007-05794-000 (accessed March 3, 2024);

WA Office of the Inspector of Custodial Services, *Reports and Publications – Conclusion (Solitary Confinement),* 19 April 2022, Conclusion - Office of the Inspector of Custodial Services, https://www.oics.wa.gov.au/reports/141-inspection-of-the-intensive-support-unit-at-banksia-hill-detention-centre/conclusion/ (accessed 22 March 2025).

Information Resources and Documents

AHRC (Australian Human Rights Commission), Follow Up Procedures to Australia's Sixth Periodic Review – Submission by the Australian Human Rights Commission, 2023, https://humanrights.gov.au/sites/default/files/ahrc_-_follow-up_to_un_cat_concluding_observations_15.09.23_1.pdf (accessed 22 March 2025).

ANROWS, *Australia's National Research Agenda to Reduce Violence against Women and their Children,* 2020, ANROWS - Australia's National Research Organisation for Women's Safety, https://www.anrows.org.au/about/national-research-agenda-to-reduce-violence-against-women-and-their-children/ (accessed 22 March 2025).

Daoud Legal, *Strip Search Laws NSW,* 2025, Strip Search Laws in NSW: Know Your Legal Rights, https://sydneycriminaldefenceandtrafficlawyers.com.au/blog/strip-search-laws-and-rights-in-nsw/ (accessed 22 March 2025).

Human Rights, Human Dignity, 2025, *Persons Against NST – Non-State Torture,* https://nonstatetorture.org/ (accessed 8 September 2024); What is NST?: Persons Against NST, https://nonstatetorture.org/what-is-nst, 2025

Law Enforcement Conduct Commission (LECC), *Inquiry into NSW Police Force strip search practices,* 2023, Law Enforcement Conduct Commission, https://www.lecc.nsw.gov.au/pdf-files/inquiry-into-nsw-police-force-strip-search-practices (accessed 22 November 2024).

NSW Government, "Important Notice About The Festival Strip Searches Class Action", 5 September 2024, Opt Out Orders, https://supremecourt.nsw.gov.au/documents/Class-Actions/Music-Festival-Searches---Meredith/18_OPT_OUT_ORDERS_5.9.24.pdf (accessed 22 March 2025).

O'Brien Criminal & Civil Solicitors, *Tasmanian female inmates subjected to 841 strip-searches in 7 months,* September 2021, https://obriensolicitors.com.au/tasmanian-prisons-female-inmates-subjected-841-strip-searches-7-months/ (accessed 1 March 2024).

SSPA, Single Sex Prisons Australia – Submission, 2023, *Single Sex Prisons Australia stakeholder submission to the Parliamentary Joint Committee on Human Rights for the Australian Human Rights Framework Inquiry,* https://www.aph.gov.au/Parliamentary_Business/Committees/Joint/Human_Rights/HumanRightsFramework/Submissions (accessed 8 September 2024).

Victorian Ombudsman, Report and inspection of dame Phyllis frost centre, Victorian Ombudsman, Melbourne, 2017a, Victoria, https://preview.ombudsman.vic.gov.au/our-impact/investigation-reports/implementing-opact-in-victoria-report-and-inspection-of-dame-phyllis-frost-centre (accessed 2 September 2025).

Victorian Ombudsman, *Concern about routine strip searching and high incidence of force and restraint in women's prison,* 30 November 2017b, https://www.ombudsman.vic.gov.au/our-impact/news/concern-about-routine-strip-searching-and-high-incidence-of-force-and-restraint-in-womens-prison/ (accessed 27 August 2024).

Williams, Jessica, *Case of Wayne Gregory Astill, NSW Correctional Officer who sexually assaulted 14 women prisoners – an overview of Australian police and correctional officer failures re: strip-search,* June 2024, https://jkwilliamsofficial.wordpress.com/2024/06/17/nsw-correctional-officer-sexually-assaulted-14-women-prisoners-with-overview-of-failures-re-strip-search/ (accessed 3 March 2024).

Williams, Jessica, *CEDAW witness statement*, CEDAW Hearings UNSW, June 2023, https://jkwilliamsofficial.wordpress.com/2024/01/26/university-of-nsw-cedaw-hearing-witness-statement/ (accessed 2 March 2025).

Part III

Representation

We are here, not because we are lawbreakers; we are here in our efforts to be law-makers.

—Emmeline Pankhurst, *My Own Story,* Eveleigh Nash, London, 1914.

14

Representation: Making the Absent Present

Ameena Zia

> It is because the signifier exists, because it represents (through symbolic action), that the group being represented and symbolized exists and that, in return, it causes its representative to exist as representative of a group.
> —Pierre Bourdieu, La délégation et le fétichisme politique, 2001

Introduction

Women's equality is fundamental to democracy and women's equal representation in democratic institutions is vital. Without these non-negotiable requirements, democracy is lacking. As the UN General Assembly (2011) argues, "women in every part of the world continue to be largely marginalized from the political space, often as a result of discriminatory practices and laws, attitudes and gender stereotypes,

A. Zia (✉)
Division of Humanities, Brevard College, Asheville, NC, US
e-mail: AmeenaMZia@gmail.com

J. A. Scutt (ed.), *Women, Power and Autonomy*,
https://doi.org/10.1007/978-3-031-97958-3_14

low levels of education, lack of access to healthcare, and a disproportionate effect of poverty on women". This effectively acknowledges that cultural, socioeconomic, and political variables impacting on women and women's participation are essential to democracy and to the concept of representation and the notion of working *on behalf of*.

As gender emerges as a significant force, the pervasive disparity in the distribution of power and decision-making across the political system serves as a barrier to women's leadership opportunities. Through this constructivist understanding of representation, examination relies on elements of power and decision-making in the political environment as barriers to women's political participation. For this investigation, Pitkin's (1967) standardized conceptualizations of representation in the field of gender politics serve as a method by which to observe women's political power and influence in the political space as it intersects with sociocultural and socio-historical perspectives.

By including those marginalized by and deemed vulnerable to the pervasive global model of economics, namely women and minorities, within the international development framework, sets the tone for international policy to promise the achievement of the abstract notion of women's equality in society. This chapter begins first with a basic reflection of women's representation as a performative agent in society by examining representation as a mobilizer of women's participation. Secondly, the inclusion of women's political representation is defined as a means to ease inequalities of the neo-liberal economic order around the world. Next, the focus shifts to the role of the electoral system of proportional representation within parliaments as conduits to achieving justice in women's political representation through gender quotas. These reflections of broader understanding of representation as a facilitator of women's political participation provide insight and the potential for ensuring that women can and do take their rightful role as equals in the polity.

Conceptualizing Representation

Drawing from Weberian methodology, the concept of representation is constructed through historical and sociological abstractions of the term towards an empirical presentation of its value to help capture present realities. As science depends on concepts that grow from ideas, it is through inquiry into these constructions[1] of representation that researchers are led to ask questions and seek explanations. In this, concepts are essential in drawing lessons across national boundaries because they provide a common vocabulary that allows for comparative analysis.

The constructivist perspective examines social groups and political communities as socially constructed entities and, therefore, the examined political representation as being performative, contributes to the shaping of the social *doxa*, normalized public opinion. Representation is defined as a production of images and dialogues exchanged in the public sphere through various actors, including artists, media, the academy, social movement organizations, and ordinary citizens. Together, these actors construct a reality and provide a space to act and to engage even for the most marginalized segments of the population.

Representation has been designated and legitimated through labels of ambassadors, elected officials, and leaders dating back to the Middle Ages and is outlined in writings of Bartolus de Saxoferrato (1313–1356) as "to represent someone else by establishing fictitious juridical unity between the representative and the represented was a development in various domains but did not necessarily project consent by the represented". Fast forward to the modern era, Hobbes constructed a more developed understanding of representation as the relationship between the sovereign and the citizens and has been utilized by scholars as a foundation for all examinations of the concept.

Representative democracy is defined as *responsiveness of the government to the preferences of its citizens.* As this traditional model of representation places responsiveness at the core of representation, it draws heavily on the fundamental assertion of the role of democratic representation. With roots in revolutions of the West (United States and France), it identifies sources of power through legitimate delegation. As scholarship confirms, representation is not easy to operationalize and is mostly captured empirically through data or data-driven understanding of constituent preferences and legislator responsiveness. However, mere numbers do not capture the entire scope of the concept and therefore elements of participatory representation must be examined. Participatory democracy is representative and here understood as all active engagement through non-elected or government channels, and is defined as "democratic rediscovery of representation". Further analysis must include channels of women's participation that are examined through informal measures of mobilization and organization towards seeking alternatives to the existing patriarchal *doxa.*

Similarly, French political historian Marcel Gauchet (1997) conceptualizes the symbolic dimensions of political representation, arguing that "democracy, being essentially representative and far from reducing itself to the people's exercise of sovereignty, inseparably requires the institutional production of this sovereignty in its true nature. It seeks a collective disposition of its own, but a disposition that exists only if self-signified and for which it is not less indispensable to be imagined than to be executed". In this chapter, democratic representation is defined as mobilization that actively works to recruit constituencies and systems because it closely mirrors historical conceptualization of representation traced back to the eighteenth-century democratic revolutions. These constituencies go beyond the traditional legislator and voter relation, and include civil society forces with similar agendas, and draw on political identity as a response to oppression and a call to mobilize (Illustration 14.1).

Impactful Representation

Without representation, "we are without a conception of what political reality—the represented—is like" ...and without representation there is no representation—and without political representation there is no nation as a truly political entity (Ankersmit 2002).

To understand the change in power relations in the political realm, representation is understood as "acting in the interest of the represented,

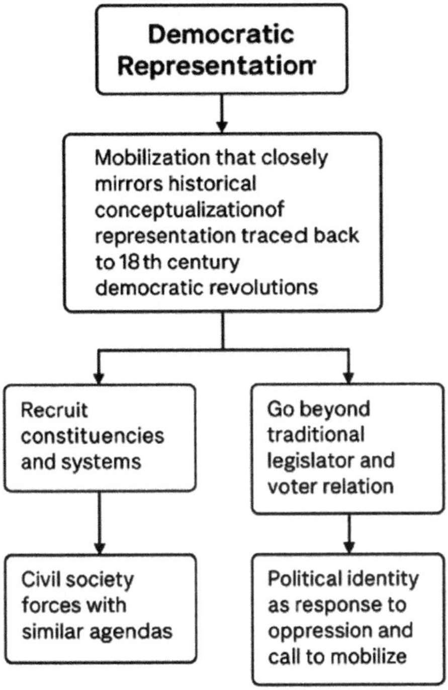

Illustration 14.1 Democratic representation

in a manner responsive to them" and this responsiveness is emphasized as the central focus of a representative government. Looking at the etymological origins of the word, "re-presentation" means "…making present again" which serves as the distinction between democratic leadership and authoritarian manipulation. Representation is regarded as a hallmark of democratic political representation because it provides space outside the confines of the legislator and constituency relation with an expansive role of influence.

As democracy is viewed to represent the interests of the voters and/or constituency, the model of representation is utilized to review the oppression and/or marginalization of women's participation in politics. The constructed framework assigns four different values to political representation. These include symbolic representation which embodies an idea or an entity; formal representation refers to institutional rules and procedures that designate representation; descriptive representation refers to the identity or attributes that are used to describe the representative (including gender, race, and age); and substantive representation refers to policies supported and advancements made as a representative.

The formalistic representation refers to institutional arrangements mandating representation through authority of power and accountability by constituency, outlined by "the rules that empower representatives to act and by which constituents hold representatives accountable" (Jalalzai 2016). Descriptive representation caters to the mirroring effect of the representative in attributes, characteristics, and experiences of the represented. Substantive representation, on the other hand, refers to the responsiveness to the political interests of women capturing the process (interventions made on behalf of constituents) and the outcomes (legislation and policies). Symbolic representation "engages emotional responses and relates to the extent to which constituencies believe their representatives support their interests" (Pitkin 1967).

Descriptive representation focuses on the increase in women's presence in parliaments as the identity of female legislators and institutional characteristics that constrain or enable participation (Mansbridge 2009). Advocates of gender quotas claim that a certain "critical mass" (Childs and Krook 2008). Women will change the agenda and outcomes in favor of women because numerical strength will allow them to coordinate with each other and exert feminizing influence (Bratton and Ray 2002). Along with their presence in numbers, women can lead the path towards inclusive women's agenda through their structural positions, life experiences, and behavior resulting in a unique perspective on identity (Phillips 1995). However, it is necessary to be cautious in assigning a unified agenda and collective legislative identity across the board to all women because there are differences in class, age, race, priorities, and so on between them.

Symbolic representation of women can have a positive impact on engagement and participation (Lawless 2004) as they break stereotypes of the dominance of "the male" or masculine in the political space. Although women may ascend the political ladder within the male-dominated political realm, this ascendency does not necessarily translate into transformation of power relations within the larger political sphere. Examples often (always?) work as outliers, especially in the case of Benazir Bhutto as the first female head of state of the Muslim world and the first female Prime Minister of Pakistan. Margaret Thatcher as first woman leader of a major political party (the Conservative Party) in the United Kingdom and first United Kingdom Prime Minister would be classified in this way by political (and feminist) analysts. Julia Gillard, first female prime minister of Australia but not the first major party leader (of the Australian Labor Party (ALP), Australian Liberal Party or Australian Greens is most likely not to be seen as an "outlier" (Williams 2017).

In assessing the performative nature of representation as a transformative agent of broader power relations in the political world, it is important to focus on representation as a mobilizer of the comparatively young democracies in the world with a special relationship to the ideals of securing minority presence in political arenas. As most debate on representation centers on demands for political inclusion from marginalized segments of population, exclusion of minorities from decision-making signifies a lack of representation. Fair representation must include similar experiences, and the representation must mirror the representative and, therefore, the historical significance of the electoral system under review.

Representation as a Mobilizer

The majority of work in political science limits the understanding of political representation to the legitimacy of elective representation in parliaments. It is important to contextualize specific variables that affect the political system and impact representation in setting forth a collective effort towards women's participation and, in turn, empowerment. This chapter focuses on representation as transcending descriptive understanding between a defined constituency, the represented, and its elected representative representor.

Political representation is contextualized within the confines of mobilization of women's agency, and majority of political discourse is a product of “crafted talk” (Jacobs and Shapiro 2000) developed by elites as messaging for support in a bid for power. Within the power and influence dialogue, civil society (women’s organizations, academia, and so on) serves to provide representation outside the traditional bounds of citizenship and elections, as “citizens…form themselves into constituencies … debate and struggle over the wisdom and implications of policy decisions” (Young 1999). This mobilization of the citizenry is a function of information networks of discussions within the public space, directed towards the formation of specific political identity around an issues agenda. It is within this space that an inclusive civil society, consisting of political parties, political challengers, the media, interest groups, hearings, opinion surveys, and other processes of communications, promotes the process of interest formation within the system, leading to recognition and mobilizing the need to seek alternatives to the dominant culture.

Political representation is a “public, institutionalized arrangement” not because of any single action by any one participant, but from the overall structure and functioning of the system (Disch 2015). It places importance on existing systems that work within the political sphere as collective relations and influences of mobilization. It serves as a platform for engagement that leads to the actualization of the marginalized power relations along gender lines. In addition, participatory representation is a process of forming demands and social cleavages (Childs and Krook 2008) as it not only allows the social to be translated into the political, but … facilitates the formation of political groups and identities (Phillips 1995). This performative element of representation allows space for agendas to form and paves the way for identity politics to emerge along dimensions of women’s political inequalities (Young 2000).

Understanding women’s mobilization is necessary IF the performative nature of representation is to be captured. Theories emphasize that political identities and demands emerge from social differences. As these conceptualizations follow the poststructuralist or pro-Marxist pluralist frameworks, a movement—or the potential of a movement—emerges within a democratic constituency. The mobilization effects of political movements frame events and conditions in ways that are intended to mobilize potential adherents and constituents, to garner bystander support, and to demobilize antagonists.

Case Study: Women's Representation in Pakistan

For the analysis of the changing power relations for women parliamentarians in Pakistan, it is important to understand the socially constructed Islamization of society. Historical analysis observes its implications, the result being the narrowing of women's agency by creating an imbalance in the social fabric of Pakistani society through the mobilization of identity politics along religious and gender lines. Active participation of societal elites in Pakistan such as party leaders, military junta, and religious leaders facilitated the art of persuasion in the adoption of societal values and beliefs in further inserting masculine domination in political power relations. As the collective mobilization of Pakistani society along religious and gender lines furthered the oppression of women, in the same manner, women's collective mobilization efforts surfaced in response to resistance to the power elites and decision-makers. Further, by deconstructing the popular *doxa*, representation facilitates constituency to action by enabling a viable space for the recognition of an issue and paving the path towards its narration defined as issue framing. Women's informal mobilization around issues has led to more formal movements which have successfully shifted institutional paradigms to mandate representation. To examine this transition in the context of the inclusion of women's issues into larger global discourse on the conditions and status of women it is important to trace the emergence of the rhetoric around the mobilization of women's political participation (in response to the need to alleviate inequalities).

Mandating and Mobilizing Women's Political Participation in the Development Framework

> *Human rights are women's rights…*
> —Hillary Rodham Clinton, Beijing Conference, 1995

Feminization of Inequality as a Consequence of Globalization

To understand the global mobilization and facilitation of the need to mandate women's political participation, efforts to advance women's agenda did not occur in a vacuum in the absence of women's mobilization, but as "part of the success of the emerging second wave of feminism that put women's lives and feminist questions onto the formal agenda of the foreign policy establishments of dozens of nation-states and international agencies (Enloe 2000). In 1975, women's political participation in Colonias Populares en Guadalajara, Mexico (United Nations 1976) highlighted the need to include women's movements in understanding the larger participation of women in politics. Held during the UN Year of the Woman or International Women's Year, this International Conference predated the international conference held in China, the Beijing Conference where Hillary Clinton made her "women's rights are human rights, human rights are women's rights" declaration. Women's movements cultivate a trail of motivated, skilled, and politically active women that result in the mobilization and facilitation of citizenship and political subjectivity among the women involved. The women may have initially joined the movement or organization as a response to curtailed rights as mothers or to protect their children or women, but in the process, may result in discovering a new political identity (Tripp 2000) and the actualization of their marginalized power relations in the political sphere. Participation of women in movements may alter the way in which women view themselves and result in more advanced participation such as running for higher political positions when opportunities arise. This mobilization serves as a participatory act for the marginalized segments of society to fight for change. The transformative nature of political identity is present in the 2015 efforts of collective political participation in the United States witnessed through the passing of the LGBTQ advocacy and Ferguson activism.

Transformative Power of Political Identity

The political landscape of the United States has experienced transformative shifts in recent years, particularly in the context of marginalized groups seeking greater political representation and justice. Key movements, including LGBTQ advocacy, the Ferguson activism, and Hillary Clinton's candidacy as the first woman presidential candidate for a major political party, have reshaped how political identity is understood and exercised. These movements demonstrate how collective political participation can alter individual and societal perceptions, inspiring new generations of marginalized individuals to engage in political life and pursue leadership roles that were once out of reach.

LGBTQ Advocacy

The LGBTQ rights movement has profoundly influenced the political landscape in the US, both in terms of policy change and the way marginalized groups view their political power. LGBTQ activists have long fought for equal rights, particularly in areas like marriage equality and anti-discrimination protections. The passage of same-sex marriage legislation in 2015 marked a pivotal moment in this struggle, reflecting the success of decades of grassroots political participation (Dugan and Reece 2014). The victory not only demonstrated the power of collective action but also encouraged more individuals within the LGBTQ community to participate in political processes, from voting to running for office.

LGBTQ advocacy has also played a critical role in redefining political participation. By emphasizing the importance of inclusion and rights for all people, the movement has empowered marginalized communities to assert their political voice. As Faderman (2015) explains in *The Gay Revolution: The Story of the Struggle*, the movement's success in achieving legal recognition for same-sex marriages is just one example of how political activism can lead to societal shifts in understanding and acceptance (Faderman 2015). This activism has prompted increased visibility and engagement from LGBTQ individuals in political spaces, paving the way for future advances in political representation.

Ferguson Activism: Mobilizing for Racial Justice

The Ferguson protests, sparked by the police shooting of Michael Brown in 2014, were another defining moment in American political activism. The movement, largely led by the Black Lives Matter (BLM) organization, catalyzed a nationwide conversation on systemic racism, police brutality, and the need for social justice reform. The protests underscored the power of collective political participation in confronting structural inequalities and demanded greater accountability for law enforcement.

Ferguson activism represented a transformative shift in political identity, as it mobilized marginalized groups—particularly African Americans—to not only demand policy changes but also assert their agency in challenging political structures. *From #BlackLivesMatter to Black Liberation*, Ferguson became a focal point for larger debates on race, policing, and justice, fundamentally altering the political conversation in the United States (Taylor 2016). The activism surrounding Ferguson also fostered a new sense of political identity among African Americans, signaling that political participation is a critical tool in fighting against racial oppression. This newfound mobilization directly influenced future generations of activists and politicians, further reinforcing the importance of political engagement in shaping societal change.

Hillary Clinton's Candidacy: Breaking Barriers for Women in Politics

Hillary Clinton's candidacy in the 2016 US presidential election marked a significant milestone in American politics. As the first woman to be nominated for president by a major political party, Clinton's campaign represented not just a personal achievement but also a broader transformation in the way women viewed their political potential. Her candidacy demonstrated how political identity could be shaped by collective action, as it was part of a larger wave of increasing female participation in political movements and leadership roles.

Clinton's campaign was not only a reflection of her individual political aspirations but also a result of decades of political activism by women who fought for gender equality in politics (Freeman 2017). Clinton's candidacy was a visible manifestation of how political mobilization and participation can break down traditional gender barriers. Her run for president, while unsuccessful, shattered long-standing expectations and encouraged other women to envision themselves in high political offices. Clinton's candidacy altered the political narrative for women, fostering an environment in which female political leaders could be more readily accepted (Murray 2017).

The mobilization of women in political movements over the years paved the way for Clinton's candidacy, reinforcing the idea that women's involvement in political life could redefine the trajectory of US politics. Clinton's campaign not only transformed her political identity but also encouraged future generations of women to participate more actively in political life, pushing for greater representation and leadership in all areas of government.

The political identities of marginalized groups in the United States have been significantly shaped by movements like LGBTQ advocacy, Ferguson activism, and Hillary Clinton's groundbreaking candidacy. These movements demonstrate how collective action can lead to political transformation, both in terms of policy change and the way individuals view themselves in the political arena. LGBTQ advocacy has empowered the LGBTQ community to demand equality and pursue political representation. Ferguson activism has redefined political engagement for African Americans, creating a broader conversation on racial justice and accountability. Finally, Hillary Clinton's candidacy served as a catalyst for women's political empowerment, breaking down gender barriers, and encouraging more women to pursue leadership roles. Together, these movements illustrate the transformative nature of political identity, showing how marginalized groups can alter the political landscape by actively participating in the fight for change.

Contextualizing the Inequality of Women's Political Participation

The role of women's mobilization within the context of a transformative impact on society has been highlighted to illustrate that, as stated previously, mobilization is a response to the actualization of oppression or injustice. To understand the broader dimensions of women's inequality of women's political participation, it is necessary to examine global structures of development. Research indicates that inequality is present and visible across the world as women continue to lack the authority of political power and decision-making. These disparities are a product of the lack of a middle class and of the concentration of wealth in a small segment of the population. International development actors at the United Nations, the World Bank, the International Monetary Fund (IMF), and other transnational networks have tried to resolve these inequalities on the ground, as prompting change is different from delivering on the promise. Although international agencies have the power to lobby nations, they do not have the power to coerce. However, through structural policies wrapped in economic aid packages, the West has been successful in rolling out descriptive change in developing countries from the top down through mandates.

Extreme poverty remains a constant in much of the world population and serves as a key factor inhibiting women's advancement and participation. In the developing world, poverty issues are concentrated around access to the allocation and inequality of resources between men and women (Kabeer 2015). Despite a focus on economic information levels, these are not the sole indicators of poverty because additional dimensions of empowerment include lack of access and a paucity of or no physical security. As the face of poverty around the world has constantly been that of women, clearly women's participation in the public sphere cannot make substantive strides unless poverty balances and inequalities are eradicated.

Most of the post-colonial developing world suffers from inadequate access to resources, representation, and social justice. Existing research notes that "globalization is the inexorable integration of markets, nation-states, and technologies to a degree never witnessed before" (Friedman

2005, 7) and therefore its profound effects on both international and domestic systems are real. The effects of globalization for women require examination because traditionally the condition of women has been salient and absent from mainstream theoretical and empirical research. The negligence of accounting for women as players in society has resulted in a distortion to ubiquitous social and political phenomena because gender does, in fact, have social, cultural, political, and economic implications across societies. The United Nations Development Programme (UNDP)'s Human Development Index attempts to capture and quantify levels of quality of life of citizens from over 187 countries and, in so doing, reflects increased degrees of inequality in achievements between men and women in all facets of society. Similarly, the World Economic Forum (WEF)'s Global Gender Gap Index ranks countries according to gender gaps in inequalities including economic participation and opportunity; educational attainment; political empowerment; and health and survival.

Globalization united women by highlighting the commonalities of economic restructuring and increasing the divide between winners and losers. In addressing the process, scholars theorize that this growth in nationalism facilitated the increase in mobilization of women's movements. International development agendas and treaties have assisted in slowly shifting global gender paradigms as pressures are placed on governments to honor commitments made on the international stage to establish national-level commissions as an access point for domestic women's movement and advocacy and to provide opportunities to team up with international networks to place pressure on governments to respond to the constituency.

Mobilization of women's movements on the international scene and global pressures in favor of women's access to political representation are important variables in explaining the growing feminization of legislative arenas around the world.

According to Henderson and Jeydel (2014), "challenge for the future is to continue to forge stronger links between women across cultures without obliterating their differences". Further, if power continues to rest in national institutions, "global women's movements will have to respond with new strategies, new tactics … to keep pace with the ever-changing international structures".

Globalization integrated economies and societies and aimed to improve lives around the world by providing economic opportunities that lead to the reduction of poverty. Opponents of globalization note that these neo-liberal economic policies increased disparities rather than eradicating them, further marginalizing citizens of the world. Due to the constant evolution of global realities, narrow approaches do not address discrepancies between men and women as new challenges of the international political economy are met with the increase in trans-border migration and war. Further, by viewing the women's empowerment process strictly out of the poverty lens, development policies gloss over the number of women and girl migrants crossing borders as they impact demographic shifts within the country's formal government policies, institutional structures, and resource allocation.

Trajectory of Women's Development Agenda

The foregoing established the pervasiveness of gender inequality. The trajectory of women's development agenda as a response to this increased inequality is essential to unpacking the need and demand for women's representation in the policy. The role of international policy was sanctioned to guide, encourage, or mandate countries (based on their circumstances) to develop national agendas and policy frameworks that would facilitate the alleviation of poverty and inequality. History notes that in the first two decades of international development work (1940s–1960s), organizations did not consider gender as a salient analytical tool. The inclusion of women's advancement within the development framework is a comparatively recent addition within the confines of the United Nations and other transnational networks.

As international organizations began to include economic and social designs to improve quality of life in the 1950s, '1960s, and '1970s and to stimulate economic growth for men, there was an assumption that eventually, overall growth would reach women (Boserup 1970). Women's development practitioners mobilized in the international development community and lobbied for increased funding for women's programs by arguing that the development process was not gender-neutral and women did not benefit from development in the same way as did men. It wasn't until 1963 that the idea of using development aid monies (proposed by feminist Ingra Thorsson in the Swedish Parliament) led to the (government) funding of two distinct positions to the United Nations to ensure a voice for women at the policy level. Thorsson proposed using development aid funds to create two key positions within the United Nations to ensure that women had a voice at the policy level. This led to the establishment of the position of a Women's Adviser to the United Nations, tasked with integrating gender issues into UN development programs and ensuring that women's concerns were considered in international development discussions (True 2012). Additionally, a Special Adviser on Women's Affairs was appointed within the UN Secretariat, a role designed to provide strategic advice on advancing gender equality and supporting the inclusion of women's rights in broader UN policies (United Nations 1975). These positions were a significant step towards institutionalizing women's voices in global policymaking.

Similarly, in the United States, Mildred Marcy of the US Information Agency made similar arguments for the integration of women into US-funded development programs, ultimately securing a position for women through the Percy Amendment in the Senate (Momsen 2004). Historical analysis confirms that these Women in Development (WID) approaches were closely linked to the second wave of feminism, grounded in liberal egalitarianism. This movement, which gained traction across the industrialized North, continued to highlight the development agenda's failure to address women's needs, advocating for their inclusion in global development policies (Moser 1993). Following these efforts, the UN Commission on the Status of Women (CSW), under feminist Helvi Sipila of Finland, successfully mobilized the passage of a UN General Assembly resolution calling for the broader integration of women into the development agenda (True 2012). These advancements culminated in the 1970s being recognized as the "Decade for Women" or International Women's Year (IWY).

The "Decade for Women" represented a pivotal era in the global recognition of women's rights as a central pillar of international development and policy reform. This designation emerged in response to growing awareness of gender inequalities and the pressing need for systemic changes to enhance women's political, social, and economic participation. During this time, the UN intensified its commitment to integrating women's issues into mainstream development policies, leading to the establishment of institutional frameworks and initiatives that sought to promote gender equality on a global scale.

The 1970s acted as a catalyst for both institutional and grassroots activism, prompting governments to establish national women's bureaus and specialized policy mechanisms dedicated to advancing gender equality. Many nations created ministries for women's affairs and enacted laws addressing gender disparities in key areas such as education, employment, and political representation. Additionally, this period saw the rise of transnational feminist movements, which facilitated cross-border collaboration and the exchange of strategies among women's organizations worldwide.

The achievements of the decade laid a strong foundation for continued global advocacy, influencing subsequent conferences expanded on the progress, refining approaches to integrating gender equality within national, and international development policies.

The First World Conference on Women held in Mexico (Mexico City 1975), followed by the Second World Conference on Women held in Denmark (Copenhagen 1980) and the Third World Conference on Women held in Kenya (Nairobi 1985) galvanized public interest, raised awareness on women's issues, and adopted international plans of action relating to women. These conferences were integral in jump-starting the mobilization which led to the recognition of the women's development agenda, reviewing progress, bringing awareness, and encouraging senior government officials from around the world to include women in their national development frameworks. As the Mexico City Conference Plan of Action called for government-prepared reports on the status of women, countries established women's ministries with hopes of creating access points for domestic women's movements to lobby, advocate, and work for explicit policies affecting women's status. These conferences led to the facilitation of transnational feminist networks in the 1970s and the emergence of the NGO Forum (Non-Government Organizations

Forum n.d.) which brought together women activists to exchange experiences and build on translational alliances. During these conferences, women formed networks and identities while acknowledging their differences. This led to "a new era and the sisterhood" that became active in advocating women's issues at the international level. The impact of these networks as policy machines is crucial.

The historical 1995 Fourth Conference on Women and the Beijing Platform upheld women's rights to participate in public life and called for the removal of barriers to equal participation. This acknowledgment of women's political representation was critical in ensuring equality and recognizing structural barriers for women through discriminatory laws and institutions which limited women's access to the political sphere. The UN Millennium Development Goals (MDGs) built on these outcomes and set measurement guidelines which included the proportion of women in parliamentary seats. As UN Women provided training and capacity building, it also advocated the inclusion of women in political parties and governments.

An increased attention to issues of motherhood surfaced in the 1970s on the international development platform and CSW (Commission on the Status of Women) emerged to promote, report, and monitor the progress of various treaties. In addition, the United Nations adopted the *Convention on the Elimination of All Forms of Discrimination Against Women* (CEDAW) in 1979 and defined what constitutes discrimination against women. A total of 173 countries around the world served as signatories, with ratification legally binding national agendas to put provisions into practice domestically. Development agencies, utilizing these frameworks, actively lobbied for time, research, and resources to advance gender equality and continue to serve as critical players in developing and filling spaces in women's policy machinery impacting developing policy.

As development agencies navigate the twenty-first century, shifting political economies must navigate the intersection of gender with poverty, political instability, and social changes in economic, social, and political infrastructures. As a result, development agencies recognized that the increase in wars in the developing countries in the last few decades resulted in an increase in war crimes and other violence against women within the context of poverty and deprivation. Just before and following the year 2000, in the last few decades the UN has focused on women, peace, and security by recognizing the importance of women as integral in resolving issues of peace and security, negotiating peace agreements, and reconstructing war-torn countries (CEDAW n.d.).

In the decade of the 2000s, leaders and development agencies renewed efforts for women's advancement by integrating gender within the larger development agenda as a result of the failed ambitious Millennium Development Goals (MDGs) adopted by the UN with the promise to eradicate world poverty by the year 2015. Although MDG 3 focused on empowering women by achieving education parity, equalizing representation in Parliament, and increasing the share of women in wage employment in non-agricultural sectors, critics argue that it did not encompass broader dimensions of tackling challenges of women and girls' disenfranchisement. Women's advancement agenda includes equality dimensions around access to education, stable employment, adequate political representation, and physical and mental well-being, with the assumption that to ensure strong families and communities, development efforts must cater to raising quantity and quality of life for world citizens. Although overly ambitious, the MDGs, for the first time, included gender equality as central to the larger societal development.

Institutional Policy Machines

As an economic indicator of development goals, women's political empowerment is regarded as a political public good. In unpacking the term empowerment, it is defined here as the existing systematic marginalization of women and the process of transformation from no or little agency to that of self-actualization and decision-making.

Women's movements, as a response to international women's participation awareness, led to the creation of women's policy machines (True 2012) and included the emergence of ministries and bureaus that specifically addressed women's issues (nominated as "institutional mechanisms" in the Beijing Platform and Declaration of Action arising out of the

1995 Beijing Conference (United Nations 1995). Although these agencies mushroomed in industrialized countries in the 1970s and 1980s, it wasn't until 1990s and into the 2000s that developing countries, such as Pakistan, recognized and created these policy machines. As these shifts were regarded as consequences of feminist movements to pursue alliances with political parties to push for policy reform along with pressure from "femocrats" they played an influential role in outlining gender equality policies (Moser 1993). These institutionalized women's policy machines ranged from equal opportunity commissions and councils to departments and ministries of women with the aim of integrating gender concerns and international policy agendas. Researchers note these avenues provided further access to institutional politics (Keck and Sikkink 1998).

In addition, peace movements adopt feminist ideology frames and organizational structures to build on feminist processes and adapt tactical innovations of women's movements. Similarly, women's mobilization has resulted in an increase in the study of women in leadership positions at research institutions. The rise of interest in examining women's organizations and facilitation of change in public space reflects the broad transformational effects of women's mobilization. Although the change is more visible in postindustrial societies, industrial and agrarian societies have depended on larger processes of socioeconomic modernization with the women's movements central to transformation.

As gender disparities continue to exist, even in the advantaged and interconnected societies institutions, like women's machines, are linked to the pervasive basis for such differentiations as institutions involve the exercise of power to the advantage of some and the disadvantage of others.

The UN through its own policy machinery devoted efforts to women's agenda through the platform of political machines like CSW and its administrative arm known as the Division for the Advancement of Women (now UN Women). These avenues lobbied national governments to establish similar structures and to assess the progress of women's advancements. The UN estimates nearly three-quarters of national governments have established national machinery (or 'institutional mechanisms') for the advancement of women especially since the Fourth World Conference of Women (1995) in Beijing. With the historic passage and adoption of the UN Sustainable Development Goals (SDGs) in 2000 (United Nations n.d.a), following on from or replacing the Millennial Goals, 180 nations around the globe committed to the intersecting 17 development goals, including Global Goal 5 aimed to achieve gender equality and empower all women and girls (United Nations n.d.b). Subsequently, conferences, high-level conferences and high-level meetings and commissions have incorporated gender into development dialogues with the recognition that gender intersects all other development in achieving sustainability. On the national level, politicians were forced to pay more attention to women's issues, organizations, and voters. As women's ministries and bureaus emerged in national institutional structures as women's political machines, so did the introduction and passage of moral laws with positive impact on women, political parties around the world also made an increased effort to organize women's sections within party structures.

Case Study: Women's Representation in Pakistan

Pakistan adopted the model of women's political machines with the emergence of the National Commission of the Status of Women (NCSW) a statutory body created by the government in 2002, with the objective to ensure that all women parliamentarians focus on ensuring gendered legislation and policy. Similarly, the Women's Parliamentary Caucus (WPC) was established in 2008 to facilitate coordination among all women parliamentarians across party lines. I expand further on the role of women's political machines and the behavior of women parliamentarians within the case study of the National Assembly of Pakistan from 2008 to 2013.

Gender Quotas to "Fast-Track" Development

Just as women's political machines are adopted as tools to alleviate inequalities, gender quotas, in the form of reserved seats, are also mandated in efforts to secure descriptive representation of women to allow for broader participation. Gender quotas serve as gatekeepers to representation. It is the very role of gender quotas in political space to operationalize the inclusion of minority representation. Intersectional scholars claim women as being oppressed on the basis of gender, class, race, and other social constructions. As women, historically, have been marginalized (due to a multitude of factors ranging from patriarchal social structures, economic dimensions, social capital, and political capacities) gender quotas are viewed as a productive strategy for advancing women's representation in hopes of increasing women's empowerment through political representation.

On average, gender quota laws translate into a 10 percent increase in the number of women in office when there is cultural support and less party leadership constraints. And newly elected women under the quota system can provide substantive representation by pursuing policies related to women's status (through policies related to reproduction, childcare, gender violence, and work-life balance) in the public space.

Although research supporting and positively linking descriptive representation to women- friendly policies exists, scholars nonetheless claim that results are inconclusive as to whether quotas result in a shift in women's status and in influencing political institutions for sustainable change. Perhaps quotas are necessary, but certainly not sufficient, in securing gendered representation in public offices. Therefore, it is important to expand the scope of inquiry and include other variables in assessing why quotas are not enough (Zia 2019).

Injecting Gender Quotas in Electoral Systems

Do electoral systems play a role in the adoption of gender quotas? If the mechanics of a particular electoral system exclude a large number of members of a particular ascriptive group (women or otherwise) then more often than not that is damning evidence that the system is excluding the interests of that particular group from the structures of decision-making power. The importance of electoral systems in the introduction of affirmative action mandates should be obvious but may require contextualization.

Electoral systems do not act in isolation within the political space and there is constant interaction with a host of cultural, socioeconomic and political variables to create a political dynamic that influences the curation of legislative assemblies. Although globalization can be a counterweight to the resistance of certain voting systems of the election of women, scholars note that women's political mobilization can overcome the anti-women friendly electoral systems. Therefore, an electoral system is an important variable to women's representation in legislatures because it determines the type of affirmative action that can be utilized and scholars in the field argue that the electoral system is neither an unnecessary nor sufficient condition to guarantee women's representation.

Research in the field identifies electoral systems as a determinant in ensuring women's political representation indicates that the proportional representation system, although having achieved only a modest proportion of female legislators, allows for an increase in women in parliaments when compared to majoritarian systems.[1] Scholars note that the proportional representation government model is more conducive to effective gender quotas through its inclusive nature, because both the majority and minority proportionally translate party votes into party seats in parliaments. In contrast to the majoritarian system, based on principal-agent representation that reserves power to the winner (winner-take-all), proportional representation secures space for minorities. However, scholars have also indicated that perhaps there has been an exaggeration in assessing whether voting systems promote or hinder achievement of women's presence in parliaments.

[1] Editor's Note: Preferential voting as applied in federal government elections in Australia: Preferential voting - Australian Electoral Commission (accessed 21 November 2024), and termed "ranked choice" in New York: Ranked choice voting | NYC Board of Elections (accessed 21 November 2024) has—together with affirmative action established by the Australian Labor Party (ALP)— resulted in vastly increased numbers of women (including minority ethnic and First Nations) in federal, state and territory parliaments. Preferential voting can achieve government by the political party of one's first (or second etc.) choice, rather than proportional representation which achieves multi-party governments as for example in Italy (and earlier under a mixed-member majoritarian system).

The representative government is democratic because it realizes not the (dominant) majority rules but (disadvantaged) minorities rule, and therefore, scholars argue that parliamentary systems of government provide a healthy platform for the success of gender quotas. As a mechanism for achieving gender equality, gender quotas are mandatory for targeted percentages of women candidates for public elections in forms of constitutional, legislative or political party quotas. Quotas, an institutional tool, help women gain descriptive representation in parliaments and legislatures and potentially enable women's representation.

Gender Quotas as Descriptive Representation

Political representation of women has been a topic of interest over the course of the last few decades as work around the gendering of political space has infiltrated national development agendas. Gender quotas are viewed as an institutional tool in achieving gains for women in political offices as mandatory or percentages of women candidates for public elections. Quotas are administered in forms of constitutional, legislative and/or political party quotas and apply to minority or oppressed populations along religious, regional, ethnic and linguistic lines to fulfill the mandate of increasing the presence of women in the political space, defined as descriptive representation. Reserved seat quotas, as a policy measure, aim to fulfill international and domestic objectives of securing women's political participation. On the international level, nation-states secure these commitments through the ratification of treaties such as the Universal Declaration of Human Rights and CEDAW. On the state level, mandates are introduced as a dialogue on the under-representation of women from the political space which serves as messages to the citizenry at large that reforms are on the way. This provides opportunity for male-dominated elites to agree to the separate process of allocation of additional seats to women because it does not interfere; nor does it take away seats from male candidates.

Scholarship in the field asserts that an increase in women in legislatures is witnessed as quotas are implemented into the national policy which leads to an increase in women's representation as a "fast-track" approach or a "jumpstart-mechanism" (Krook and O'Brien 2012). The assumption is that a mere increase in numbers is sufficient as a temporary fix until women's participation in politics normalizes. Comparatists in gender politics and similar academic disciplines have examined the impact of quotas by measuring the outcome of women's representation. According to The Quota Project (n.d.), countries have adopted reserved seat quotas for women with the explicit intention to ameliorate and end the under-representation of women in national legislatures. More than 84 countries around the globe have mandated some form of quotas to enhance women's representation in legislatures. Although the rules and implementations vary, legislative quotas require parties to field a certain number of women candidates. Pakistan adopted the development path crafted by the international community as mandated specifically by economic packages.

As international policy makers shifted their focus on increasing inequalities and poverty linked to neo-liberal economic policies, social policy began to surface as a tool to assist the poor and to masque its failed promises. These evolved social policies included elements of targeting, privatization and pluralization of service provides, along with a great reliance on the market for poverty relief, mostly evident in micro-credit programs and were viewed as (pro-market and anti- poverty) market fundamentalism as they were packaged in strict controls imposed by International Financial Institutions (IFIs). Due to pressure and resistance, especially from Latin America, IFIs started pushing their role as more of facilitators in state-building.

Case Study: Women's Representation in Pakistan

As a response, in the 1990s Pakistan women activists loosely protested these social policies, however, not under the formal umbrella of neo-liberal impacts but as critics of market led priorities instead of rights based. As the 4th World Conference on Women (WCW, Beijing, 1995) emphasized participation and empowerment of women, donor led projects surfaced in Pakistan as a result of World Bank's New Poverty Agenda (which later translated into the Millennium Development Goals, MDGs) stressing gender equality and good governance as measurable goals of development.

In Pakistan, the mandate of reserved seats is a top-down policy which parallels the country's checkered past of frequent leadership changes (due to military takeovers and shifts in governments). Military General Zia ul-Haq expanded reserved seats in the national assembly from 2–3 percent (reserved in 1954, 1956, 1962, 1967, 1970 and 1973) to 9 percent in mid 1980s and General Musharraf increased them further to 17 percent in national assembly and senate in post 9–11 Pakistan (in 2002). The impact on these mandates is void of organic grassroots efforts of women's organizations.

The support for gender quotas draws on the potential link between descriptive representation and women friendly policies. The creation and strength of quota adoption is linked to the mobilization of activists who support the introduction as a positive mechanism. Quotas do disproportionately result in a labeling effect that further stereotypes the quota legislator as unqualified and appointment as lacking meritocracy. Further, studies reflect on the top-down approach of quotas indicating that the increase in numerical representation is likely to benefit elite women who are disenfranchised from the women voters or women's organizations (and movements). At times regimes have used reserved seats to meet political agendas through patronage and power and ensuring party loyalty or as bargaining tools to secure coalition partners.

Summary

From local to global dimensions, women's leadership, and political participation are restricted as women are underrepresented in the public sphere as voters, leadership positions, elected offices, civil service, private sector and academia. In the post MDG world, women continue to be underrepresented despite proven abilities as leaders and agents of change, and despite rights to participate equally in democratic governance.

As women's empowerment increases in society, distributions of power relations should shift as entrenched patterns of gender inequality across economic and social (in private and public) space are also re-configured. Through inquiry, this study analyzes historical and feminist dimensions of representation. In doing so, this chapter examined the conceptualization of representation and the contextualization of formal and informal mobilization of women's political participation. If representing means "acting in the interests of the represented, in a manner responsive to them" then, that quality of representation depends on the mechanisms to hold representatives accountable. This chapter facilitates the argument of this study serving as a foundational link between the linear relationship of politics of idea and politics of presence.

Bibliography

Conventions and Treaties

Convention on the Elimination of all Forms of Discrimination Against Women (CEDAW), Convention on the Elimination of All Forms of Discrimination against Women New York, 18 December 1979 | OHCHR (accessed 2 March 2025).

Articles and Book Chapters

Bratton, Kathleen A and Ray, Leonard P (2002). "Descriptive Representation, Policy Outcomes, and Municipal Day-Care Coverage in Norway", *American Journal of Political Science* 46(2): 428- 437.

Childs, Sarah and Krook, Mona Lena (2008). "Critical Mass Theory and Women's Political Representation", *Political Studies* 56: 725-736.

Disch, Lisa (2015). "The Constructivist Turn in Democratic Representation: A Normative Dead-End?" *Constellations*, 22(4): 487–499.

Dugan, AG and Reece, RR (2014). "The political impact of LGBTQ activism in the U.S." in *LGBTQ Politics: A Critical Reader* 119–136.

Freeman, L (2017). "Hillary Clinton's Campaign and the Politics of Gender in the 2016 Election", *Politics & Gender* 13(4), 686-694.

Jalalzai, F (2016). "Shattered Not Cracked: The Effect of Women's Executive Leadership", *Journal of Women, Politics & Policy 37*(4), 439–463.

Kabeer, N (2015). "Gender, poverty and inequality: a brief history of feminist contributions in the field of international development", *Gender and Development*, vol 23, no 2, 189-205.
Krook, ML and O'Brien, DZ (2012). "All about structures? Political parties and women's representation", *Politics & Gender* 8(1), 1-34.
Lawless, Jennifer L (2004). "Women, war, and winning elections: Gender stereotyping in the post September 11th Era", *Political Research Quarterly* 53(3): 479-490.
Mansbridge, Jane (2009). "A 'Selection Model' of Political Representation", *The Journal of Political Philosophy* 17(4): 369-398.
Murray, R (2017). "Women and Political Leadership: The Gendered Impact of the 2016 Presidential Election", *Journal of Women, Politics & Policy 38*(2), 123-141.
True, J (2012). "The Political Economy of the United Nations and the Women's Movement: The Decade for Women", *Global Governance* 18(4), 473-490.
Young, Iris Marion (1999). "Justice, Inclusion, and Deliberative Democracy" in Macedo, Stephen (ed). *Deliberative Politics*. Oxford, UK, Oxford University Press.
Williams, B (2017). "A gendered media analysis of the prime ministerial ascension of Gillard and Turnbull: He's 'taken back the reins' and she's 'a backstabbing' murderer", *Australian Journal of Political Science 52*(4), 550–564.
Zia, Ameena (2019). "Descriptive to Substantive Representation: A Study of Gender Quotas in the National Assembly of Pakistan, 2002–2018", *Dissertations* 811.

Books and Reports

Ankersmit, FR (2002). *Political Representation*. Stanford University Press, Stanford, CA, US.
Boserup, E (1970). *Women's Role in Economic Development*. St Martin's Press, NYC, NY, US.
Enloe, Cynthia H (2000). *Manuevers: The International Politics of Militarizing Women's Lives*, University of California Press, Oakland, CA, US.
Faderman, L (2015). *The Gay Revolution: The Story of the Struggle*. Simon & Schuster, NYC, NY, US.

Friedman, TL (2005). *The World is Flat: A Brief History of the Twenty-First Century*. Farrar, Straus and Giroux, NYC, NY, US.
Gauchet, M (1997). *The Disenchantment of the World: A Political History of Religion* (Burge, O, Trans.). Princeton, NJ, US: Princeton University Press.
Henderson, SL and Jeydel, A (2014). *Women and Politics in a Global World*. Oxford University Press, Oxford, UK.
Jacobs, Lawrence R and Shapiro, Robert Y (2000). *Politicians Don't Pander: Political Manipulation and the Loss of Democratic Responsiveness*. University of Chicago Press, Chicago, Ill, US.
Keck, ME and Sikkink, K (1998). *Activists Beyond Borders: Advocacy Networks in International Politics*. Cornell University Press, Ithaca, NY, US.
Moser, C (1993). *Gender Planning and Development: Theory, Practice, and Training*. Routledge, Oxford, UK.
Momsen, JH (2004). *Gender and Development*. Routledge, Oxford, UK.
Phillips, Anne (1995). *The Politics of Presence*. Oxford University Press, Oxford, UK.
Pitkin, H F (1967). *The concept of representation*. University of California Press, Oakland, CA, US.
Taylor, K-Y (2016). *From #BlackLivesMatter to Black Liberation*. Haymarket Books, Chicago, Ill, US.
Tripp, AM (2000). *Women and politics in Africa: The power of participation*. Cambridge University Press, Cambridge, UK.
Young, Iris Marion (2000). *Inclusion and democracy*. Oxford University Press, Oxford, UK.

Information Documents and Resources

CEDAW (nd). *CEDAW and Security Council Resolution 1325: A Quick Guide*, UN Women, https://www.unwomen.org/en/digital-library/publications/2006/1/cedaw-and-security-council-resolution-1325-a-quick-guide (accessed 2 March 2025).
Non-Government Organisations Forum (nd). *About the NGO CSW Forum | NGO CSW/NY*, https://ngocsw.org/ngocswforum/ (accessed 2 March 2025.
The Quota Project (nd). *Global database of quotas for women*, Gender Quotas Database | International IDEA, https://www.idea.int/data-tools/data/gender-quotas-database#:~:text=The%20Global%20Database%20of%20Gender%20Quotas%20in%20parliaments,reserved%20seats%20might%20also%20have%20political%20party%20quotas (accessed 2 March 2025).

United Nations (nda). *The 17 goals | Sustainable development*, Sustainable Development Goals (SDGs) | UN Office for Sustainable Development, https://unosd.un.org/content/sustainable-development-goals-sdgs (accessed 2 March 2025).

United Nations (ndb). *Goal 5: Gender equality - The global goals*, https://www.globalgoals.org/goals/5-gender-equality/ (accessed 2 March 2025).

United Nations. (1995). *Beijing Platform for Action.* United Nations, https://www.un.org/womenwatch/daw/beijing/pdf/BDPfA%20E.pdf (accessed 2 March 2025.

United Nations (1976). *Report of the World Conference of the International Women's Year, Mexico City, 19 June-2 July 1975.* United Nations, https://digitallibrary.un.org/record/586225 (accessed 2 March 2025).

United Nations (1975). *World Conference on Women: The United Nations and the Women's Decade.* United Nations, https://www.un.org/en/conferences/women/mexico-city1975 (accessed 2 March 2025).

15

"Thieving Rorters!" A Linguistic Analysis of Construction of Australian Female Politicians in Public Comments in the Post-Gillard Period

Karen Dacy

… not how she behaves but how she is treated ….
—Eliza Doolittle, *Pygmalion*, George Bernard Shaw, 1912

Introduction

On 24 June 2010, Julia Gillard became Australia's first female prime minister, replacing then prime minister Kevin Rudd. This change came through an internal Labor Parliamentary Party process, with Rudd standing down when Gillard called for an internal ALP (Australian Labor Party) leadership ballot and the numbers were discerned as unlikely to go Rudd's way. On 23 August 2010, the governor-general having called an election at her request, Gillard won as Australia's forty-seventh prime minister and as leader of a minority government. Her term of office and

K. Dacy (✉)
Independent Scholar, Melbourne, Australia
e-mail: kdacy@unimelb.edu.au

J. A. Scutt (ed.), *Women, Power and Autonomy*,
https://doi.org/10.1007/978-3-031-97958-3_15

her accession to power were the subject of distinctive media commentary—with radio commentators being seen by many as misogynistic in their approach, and the opposition Liberal National Party demonstrating anti-woman bias both within the Parliament and outside it. As a linguistic analyst, I saw it as important to research the public critique of women politicians within this new setting—where a woman was in the principal political role in Australia for the first time.

Using appraisal theory and critical discourse analysis, my research found that commenters constructed genders differently, finding greater negativity toward female politicians, stronger emotional reactions as demonstrated in vocabulary; more extended arguments, which were more highly defended; and more frequent omission of females from debate. Conversely, issues around male politicians contained greater concentration on positive achievements and mitigatory language in comments around their alleged misdemeanours. Such linguistic strategies have much in common with discrimination against other social cohorts grouped by features including ethnicity or class. These findings indicate that pejoration in comments about female politicians may be a reaction by social elites to what they perceive as a legitimate threat to power.

The prime ministership of Julia Gillard was a tumultuous time, punctuated by frequent leadership challenges and disrespectful verbal attacks on both Gillard and her female colleagues. Blatant sexism ricocheted around parliament: senator David Bushby meowed at finance minister Penny Wong; the then leader of the opposition proffered a clunky double entendre in parliament that PM Gillard should "Make an honest woman of herself" weeks before leading a demonstration of fellow parliamentarians against her, in which placards were held reading "ditch the witch". Members of the media were equally brazen. Sydney radio shock jock Alan Jones rebuked prime minister Gillard on air for lateness and exhorted that she be *"put…* in a chaff bag and throw[n] out to sea" (Murphy and Coorey 2012). His Perth counterpart Howard Sattler asked if her male partner was gay. The cavalier remarks met with public outcry, one or two dismissals and some legal sanctions, showing that they clearly breached community standards: 62 percent of members of the public surveyed agreed that Gillard had been treated more harshly than her male colleagues (Stevenson 2013, 54).

Research further demonstrates a deeper level of gendered mediation in the way the press represents women in politics. Several studies have examined the construction of female politicians by mainstream media, both internationally and in Australia, revealing that female politicians are subjected to greater gender stereotyping and personalisation: that is, attention to details of their private lives and appearance (Ahmad 2020; Collier and Raney 2018; Conway 2016; Dolan and Lynch 2016; Donaghue 2013; Evershed and Liu 2016; Gooch 2015; Harmer 2021; Holland and Wright 2017; Honig 2016; Hunt and McKay 2016; Southern and Harmer 2021; Trimble et al. 2021; Williams 2019). While the majority of these studies demonstrate that such personalisation worked against the female politicians, they perhaps do not explain why. After all, the campaigns of many male politicians have been dominated by images of male candidates engaging in hobbies or domestic chores, or enjoying the company of their families, which suggests that they actively seek personalisation in their public image. Evidently personalisation, by emphasising the candidates' gender, produces different outcomes for males than females and is unlikely to explain everything in their different reception by the media and public, particularly the negativity and harshness met by female politicians in this period.

To describe the extent of sexism aimed at female politicians it is necessary to look beyond stereotyping and blatant gender-based discrimination. Such research is complicated by the adversarial nature of politics, often reflected in disorderly and vituperative dialogue within parliament. To test this perception, it is necessary to sample extensive amounts of text from a variety of individuals to indicate that women are represented differently and more negatively in terms of quantity, and to describe the nature of that negativity.

Another limitation of studying how mass media portrays female politicians is that the media is frequently made up of powerful institutions with their own values and fiscal motives, which may not always align with public opinion. Methods of measuring public opinion such as surveys and polls are likewise limited because people may not be prepared to reveal, or yet even be aware of, certain attitudes they hold. Unsolicited and relatively anonymous attitudes have been sampled by Stantic (2019) in a study of comments about the 2019 election in social media.

He found that they predicted the election outcome more accurately than traditional polls and surveys, indicating that citizen commentary potentially offers a more diverse and nuanced view than polling or the mainstream press.

Therefore, this study sought unsolicited opinions from the public and aimed to look beyond overt judgement to what is revealed about attitudes to female and male politicians A linguistic analysis was undertaken of a large corpus of public comments to newspapers, since discourse analysis has the capacity to reveal strength and direction of emotion and implicit attitude. This analysis divided comments on a wide variety of politicians into male and female corpora. It revealed wide differences in prominent themes found in reader comments about women and men and also, stronger negative emotional response to female politicians, tendencies to amplify perceived wrongdoings of females and soften or mitigate those of males, regardless of their party affiliation. A number of arguments, here called topoi (Wodak and Meyer 2014), were repeatedly raised in relation to female politicians which were consistent with perceived lower status of female politicians relative to the commenters. Using the model of social stratification proposed by Fiske (2010), such strategies represent defence of status by a high-status group which believes its position to be threatened.

This chapter analyses one particularly prominent theme arising in the sample of comments on females: that of their handing of or relationship to money. This theme is especially relevant to an examination of power relations within different social cohorts, having been described as a major conduit of "transferable power" (Hartsock 1983), historically firmly in the male domain (Burgoyne 2004) with women still often dependent on men for financial security, because the traditional economic model of society is the family with a male breadwinner. In the recent past, similar topoi were prominent in society: women seeking financial security were stereotyped as "gold-diggers" in popular culture (Ibroscheva 2006; Sandlin et al. 2011), an accusation even more prominently aimed at female politicians from particular ethnic groups in Brazil (Trinidade 2020). Similarly, Van Dijk (2017) demonstrated that the media attacks which facilitated impeachment of Brazilian President Dilma Roussef centred around embezzlement and fiscal dishonesty, as did those against

Ukrainian past president Tymoshenko (A'Beckett 2012). It was therefore of central interest to determine how female politicians were represented in relation to money and fiscal responsibilities.

Extracted from a sample of 20,000 comments, 2200 were analysed because they included the central theme of money. These were then analysed using the principles of Corpus Assisted Discourse Studies (CADS) (Partington and Marchi, 2015) which enables interrogation of text at multiple levels (Mautner 2005). Features of interest are noted at both corpus and comment level in a "flexible and recursive" manner (Gillings et al. 2023, 43) and observations are checked at each level for quantitative information and/or distinctive structures (Partington 2008). CADS also focuses on how a topic/subject is evaluated, making it particularly suited to this study. I therefore examined the "money subcorpus" for prominent features, whether linguistic or in terms of "ideological motifs and metaphors" (Partington 2008, 7), or "metapoesis" (Van Leeuwen 2008) which are contentions, or narrative themes presented in a text, such as "she steals public money for her own benefit".

Language and Appraisal

Before proceeding with the analysis, I will outline the reasons why a linguistic analysis, particularly one examining naturally occurring language, has potential beyond mere thematic or quantitative investigations. The language we hear and speak has been identified as central to how we construct our view of individuals and institutions (Fairclough 2001; Reisigl and Wodak 2017; Van Dijk 2015a, 2017) and hence our cognitive and social biases (Van Dijk 1999, 146). Everyday text and talk also creates and perpetuates attitude in a reciprocal fashion: the individual informing the social group and also taking attitudes from it (Gill 2007; van Dijk 1999; van Leeuwen 2008; Woolard and Schieffelin 1994, 55). One major function of transmission of attitude and cognitive bias in text and talk is the perpetuation of power relations within society, the powerful being afforded more attention from, and having access to, wider distribution platforms (Baker 2014; Fairclough 2001; Reisigl and Wodak 2017; Van Dijk 1999, 2017). The other result of this feature of discourse, however, is that it is also the site of shifts in power relations and hence documents unfolding social change (Lacan 1977).

How we as society members write or speak about public figures reveals much about our approval or disapproval of them and the esteem in which they are held. This in turn can influence community beliefs and, potentially, the success or failure of a public figure in their role (Harmer 2021, 2). When discourse is viewed as a conduit of social power, it can be seen to map closely onto the social psychology model of social stratification (Fiske 2010). In this model, society is composed of hierarchical strata, and people in that society attribute greater moral virtue, greater visibility, and greater credibility to the actions and values of high-status cohorts, this effect reversing down the hierarchy so that lower strata are judged negatively, omitted, or dismissed by the majority of all strata (Fiske 2010). By looking at the language with which people construct others around them, appraising or judging them, much can be deduced about what is important to society as a whole and, correspondingly, society's attitude toward the various groups within it. Different strata of society are determined by a range of factors: gender, religion, age, ethnicity, class, financial standing, and even ability. Each of us occupies multiple positions in the hierarchy, depending on which factor is relevant to the event or situation we are in, or the combination of factors which apply to us. Thus, a woman of wealth and influence may be perceived in the main as high status, but simultaneously of lower status to males in the same cohort, and lower again depending on the prestige or otherwise of her race, religion and ethnicity.

Martin and White's (2007) study of appraisal in language has demonstrated that people appraise others in ways that correspond closely to the model of social stratification: moral grounds, credibility, and visibility. Moral behaviour is determined by the values of the most prestigious class and is by no means universal. For example, in a society which values patriarchal dominance, treating women as equals can be perceived as immoral, in stark contrast to a society which favours gender equality. Martin and White's (2007) study has subsumed moral appraisal into two main categories: "social esteem" describes those qualities or abilities and their inverse which are valued in society, such as "bravery/cowardice, beauty/ugliness". The second, "social sanction" appraises how an individual adheres to standards of "veracity" and "propriety": whether they are authentic or truthful or adhere to socially valued actions: "good", "caring", and "unfair". In terms of social stratification, moral judgements reflect values of high-status cohorts, while those of low status are likely to be omitted or represented as violating.

In discourse, appraisal of morality and credibility are expressed through judgement, implicit in the word, or constructed in phrases "*She's evil; she is not up to scratch; she's talking rubbish*". Visibility is determined by omission or inclusion of people and actions that should or should not be present. For example, one may say "*the police dispersed the demonstrators*", indicating who acted upon whom, or alternatively "*the police restored order*", omitting the demonstrators from the discourse. Another feature of appraisal is "Engagement" or the extent to which a comment invites or precludes dialogue from the listener/reader. Phrases such as "*in my opinion*", "*I think*" attribute a view to the commenter only, thus permitting dis/agreement, while declarative statements: ("*he is corrupt*") preclude argument from the receiver. A final and important aspect of appraisal is graduation, or how the commenter amplifies or softens the strength of their discourse, so that a comedian can be described as "*amusing*" or "*hilarious*", or a similar statement may be amplified using intensifiers such as "*very, highly, extremely*" or even maximisers "*never*", "*always*", "*complete*", "*total*". More extreme efforts to convince of our judgement can result in high redundancy, or "saturation" of judgement or supporting arguments as in "*rotten, stinking, no good scoundrel*" or "*she stole something which was not hers*". Conversely, statements are mitigated using linguistic devices such as softeners: "*somewhat*", "*possibly*"or litotes: "*he's not very bright*".

Van Leeuwen's (2008) sociolinguistic model also informs about mechanisms of interpersonal stratification because it examines social and semantic roles in discourse. Such roles include the agent, or who is performing the action in a sentence; the patient, or who is acted upon, as in the sentence "*they sacked her*", defining respectively the agent and patient. The model also examines how the action or verb is realised in specificity, judgement or even in the formality of language. Compare for example "*She took it*" versus "*she pinched it*", or "*she stole it*". The first example is generalised and not incriminating; the second uses informality to present the act as less grave, while the last clearly incriminates. Such realisations of the roles in discourse are called "transformations". A role can be transformed with differing levels of specificity to reveal the focus of the communicator's interest: a woman in parliament can be described by name, as "*a woman*", "*female minister*" or "*former lawyer*" thus directing the reader's or listener's focus to different aspects of her identity. In describing events surrounding a particular person, a sentence can be constructed to include or omit the roles of various actors in the sentence. For example, one may say "*her party sacked her*" or "*she was sacked*". Van Leeuwen (2008) also describes the prominent role of legitimation within representation, where a writer/speaker gives credibility to their statements through appeals to common sense ("*everyone knows*", "*it's obvious*"), authority *("experts agree")* and rationalisation, which uses such devices as maxims and traditions "*a good mother wouldn't leave her sick child*". Semantic roles can also determine if politicians and other actors are cast as stimulus of an emotional reaction *("we love **her**")* and naturally all such roles can be softened or amplified to indicate strength of feeling.

Thus, this study examined comments by the public appended to newspaper articles which mentioned one of the politicians under investigation to answer the questions:

(1) What are the major ideological topoi arising within comments about money associated with male and female politicians?
(2) What attitudes are conveyed within these topoi?
(3) How are these attitudes constructed in linguistic choices?

Methods

Online reader comments to news outlets provided the largest, most relevant samples of comments on politicians. Reader comments were collected from the two publications which are the widest circulating national newspapers, *The Australian:* centrist to right (Beattie 2019) and

The Guardian (Australian Edition): centrist to left (Mediabias/fact check, 2022). Articles were chosen if they included a politician's name in the headline as this quite reliably indicated that the politician would be discussed in the comments.

Comments were collected on each of 27 politicians, with near even numbers across the political spectrum: 13 male and 14 female, because fewer comments were available on each female. The date range of sampling was extended both back and forward in time from 2015 until we reached 500 comments for each politician, the final range being 2013–2018. To compare comments by gender and publication, we created a male and female corpus from each publication, totalling four corpora: comments on female politicians in *The Australian* (FA), on males (*The Australian*) (MA), female politicians in *The Guardian* (Australian Edition) (*FG*) and males in *The Guardian* (*MG*). By comparing comments within publications, we achieved maximum uniformity in the data in terms of time period, likely readership, and wholly Australian content. The names, gender and political affiliation of leaders included in this study are presented in Table 15.1.

It included all prime ministers in the data collection period and a range of prominent figures, either as cabinet or shadow cabinet ministers and cross benchers. Three senior public figures were included as their work was closely aligned to the government, including the president of the Australian Human Rights Commission (AHRC), secretary of the Australian Council of Trade Unions (ACTU) and the Australian solicitor general. The two major parties are the Australian Labor Party (ALP) (left to centre) and the Liberal-National Coalition (LN) (centre to right) (Robert Manwaring 2017, 122).

The four corpora each contained approximately 120,000 words, or between 4500 and 5000 comments. As Table 15.2 shows, there was high agreement in comment length, types (different lexical items), tokens (number of each type) and the ratio of types to tokens (TTR) for the two *Australian* corpora which indicated the richness of the lexicon, or how frequently individual words were reused. Such uniformity is a good indication that the samples were sufficiently large to be representative of this type of text. For *The Guardian*, average numbers of types and tokens were significantly higher for the female corpus, but overall TTR was slightly

Table 15.1 Politicians and governmental leaders included in this study

Female leaders	Political affiliation and position(s) 2013–2018	Male leaders	Political affiliation and position(s) 2013–2018
Berejiklian, Gladys	Premier of the state of New South Wales, 2017–end of sampling period	Albanese, Anthony	Labor Minister and Leader of the Opposition
Bishop, Bronwyn	Coalition Senator Speaker of the House of Representatives 2013–2015	Abbott, Tony	Coalition Prime Minister 2013–2015
Bishop, Julie	Deputy Leader of Liberal Party, Minister for Foreign Affairs 2013–2019	Bandt, Adam	Deputy leader of The Greens 2012–end of sample
Bligh, Anna	Former Premier of the state of Queensland 2007–2012	Bernardi, Cory	Coalition Senator 2006–2017, defected to Independent Senator
Cash, Michaelia	Coalition Frontbencher, Minister for Women; Minister for Employment; Minister for Jobs and Innovation 2017–present	Brandis, George	Coalition Attorney General 2013–2017
Gillard, Julia	Labor Prime Minister 2010–2013	Cameron, Doug	Labor Senator 2007–2019
Hanson-Young, Sarah	Green Party Senator 2007–present	Cormann, Matthias	Leader of Government in the Senate, Minister for Finance 2013–2020
Lambie, Jacqui	Independent Senator for Tasmania 2013–2017	Dreyfus, Mark	Attorney General 2010–2013 Shadow Minister 2013–2022

(continued)

Table 15.1 (continued)

Female leaders	Political affiliation and position(s) 2013–2018	Male leaders	Political affiliation and position(s) 2013–2018
Ley, Sussan	Coalition Front Bencher, Assistant Minister for Education, Minister for Health, Minister for Sport; Minister for Aged Care 2013–end of sample	Joyce, Barnaby	MoHR and Deputy Prime Minister (2016–2022)
McManus, Sally*	Sec. Australian Council of Trade Unions (ACTU) 2015–	Gleeson, Justin*	Solicitor General 2012–2016
O'Dwyer, Kelly	Coalition Minister for Small Business; Assistant Treasurer Minister for Revenue and Financial Services; Minister for Jobs and Industrial Relations 2013–2019	Shorten, Bill	Leader, Federal Australian Labor Party, Leader of the Opposition; Shadow Minister Indigenous Affairs. 2013–2019
Peris, Nova	Labor Senator for the Northern Territory 2012–2016	Turnbull, Malcolm	Coalition Frontbencher; Prime Minister 2015–2018
Plibersek, Tanya	Labor Minister for Health and Medical Research, Deputy Leader of the Opposition; Shadow Minister for Foreign Affairs; Shadow Minister for Education and Training. 2007–	Xenophon, Nick	Independent Senator for South Australia 2008–2017
Triggs, Gillian*	President, Human Rights Commission 2012–2016		
Wong, Penny	Labor Senator, Leader in the Senate 2007–present		

* Indicates the referent is not a member of parliament, but in a public leadership position of notable political influence

Table 15.2 Total number of comments, lexical types, tokens (total words) and mean comment length included in this study by publication and gender

Publication	Gender in corpus	Total comments	Mean comment length (in words)	Types	Tokens	TTR
The Australian (FA)	F	4958	24.08	13,757	119,381	11.52
The Australian (MA)	M	4736	25	13,661	118,429	11.53
The Guardian (FG)	F	4979	58.98	25,242	293,691	8.6
The Guardian (MG)	M	4790	35.57	18,379	170,382	10.7

lower indicating that overall, comments were significantly longer with a broader lexicon in the female corpus.

Comments were downloaded or "scraped" from the net using Outwit Hub Pro and identifiers were removed. Comments were not analysed in any sequence but through examination of extracted features. To analyse the corpus, I employed WMatrix (Rayson 2002), software which groups synonymous words into semantic, or "key concepts". Key concepts may be topical (politics, housing) or more abstract, (emotions, time concepts) including appraisal-rich parts of speech such as adjectives, adverbs, and modal verbs. Key concepts are also divided into subthemes, such as "Money: debt", "Money: affluence" thus indicating the variety of topoi within each concept. All analyses were examined at a line-by-line level to ensure accurate classifications by Wmatrix and recategorized where necessary. Once semantic tagging was complete, I also identified further subthemes within the major key concept concordances which were not identified automatically. I used a verbatim or "In Vivo" approach (Saldana 2012, 16): in which recurrent key words/phrases in the comments, such as "entitled" were identified, followed by a search for synonymous phrases from other commenters.

Statistical measures undertaken were log likelihood, a statistic which takes into account the patterned nature of language in calculation of difference (Rayson 2002), log ratio (Hardie 2014a, 2014b) as a measure of effect size and logistic regression to determine whether gender determined the presence of money-themed comments more or less than other variables such as political party of the politician. Log likelihood is considered significant at $p < 0.01$ if it has a value over 7 (Rayson 2002) and log ratio enables meaningful comparison of numbers of greatly differing size. Corpus analysis included type/token ratio, which indicates the text's lexical richness. Other measures include number of comments and mean length of comment, which can indicate the degree of commenter engagement and ratio of key concepts, words, or parts of speech for the whole corpus.

Results

Money as a Prominent Theme

The theme of money was immediately evident, with money-themed comments in each corpus varied from three per cent (*Male Australian*) to 22 per cent (*Female Guardian*). Both female corpora had significantly more money-related lexical items than both male corpora at $p < 0.01$(*The Australian*: LL = 123.6, Log Ratio = 1.44; *The Guardian*: LL = 206.8, LR = 1.08) with a greater range of lexical types. Money related comments had more words for females than males within each publication. Negative evaluations as a percentage of total comments on money were considerably higher for the female corpora, and positive evaluations slightly lower (Table 15.3).

Logistic Regression

Logistic regression was performed to compare the relative influence of factors such as gender or political party on the prominence of key concepts arising. For *The Australian*, femaleness significantly determined the presence of key concepts of money and spending, being present in four sub-categories ("money and pay", "money general", "debts", "cost and price"). A further association was found between money/spending of politicians, (un)employment: frequently consisting of calls for sacking or retirement of the female politician, and use of travel allowances.

Table 15.3 Numbers and percentages of money-themed comments in the four corpora, including percentage of positive and negative evaluations

Corpus	Total money-themed comments	% of total corpus	x̄ words/ comment	word types	word tokens	TTR	neg. eval	(%)	pos. eval	(%)
FA	420	8.47%	46	267	2008	7.5	279	77	1	1
MA	148	3.10%	27	183	835	4.6	156	55	12	7
FG	1097	22%	101	238	2581	11	234	21	23	2
MG	500	10%	62	146	816	5.6	93	18	21	4.2

Similarly, comments in the key concepts of "future"', "investigate" and "using" largely dealt with themes of female politicians' destiny beyond politics, legal investigation of alleged misuse of employment allowances, and thus extended the theme of use of money by female politicians.

For *The Guardian*, the effect of gender on frequency of money-related key concept was significant at $p < 0.001$ for only two money concepts and "(un)employment" indicating far lower consideration of gender in commenter concerns about money (see Table 15.4).

For *The Australian*, key concepts in the money theme dominated the female corpus, occupying five of the top most frequent key concepts, with log likelihood from 8.27 to 293.68 ($p < 0.05$) (moderately to highly significant) and odds ratio from < 2.07–3.41, while in the male corpora, no key concepts related to "money" reached statistical significance. The female corpus contained almost 2.5 times more money-related comments than the male, and comments for females under this concept were substantially longer ($\bar{x}$ F = 45.5, M = 26.5 words) despite

Table 15.4 Significant results of logistic regression analysis for the two publications, measuring the strength of association of gender (femaleness) in determining key concepts within each political party

Key concept	Party	OR	(95%CI)	P-value
The Australian				
Cost and Price	Liberal	3.73	(1.54, 9)	**< 0.001**
Cost and Price	NA	6.67	(1.26, 35.2)	0.003
Cost and Price	ALP	1.92	(1.07,3.43)	0.025
Debts	ALP	2.13	(1.4, 3.25)	0.028
Debts	Greens	5.85	(2.28,14.99)	**< 0.001**
Debts	Liberal	2.39	(1.26, 4.54)	**< 0.001**
Debts	NA	3.6	(1.26, 10.3)	0.008
Money and pay	ALP	2.61	(1.9, 3.6)	0.017
Money and pay	Greens	5.07	(2.33, 11.02)	**< 0.001**
Money and pay	Liberal	3.63	(2.22, 5.93)	**< 0.001**
Money and pay	NA	3.96	(1.88, 8.37)	**< 0.001**
Money General	ALP	1.97	(1.49, 2.61)	**< 0.001**
Money General	Liberal	1.74	(1.12, 2.7)	**< 0.001**
The Guardian				
Money and pay		1.62	(1.42, 1.85)	**< 0.001**
Money General		1.59	(1.41, 1.79)	**< 0.001**

$p < 0.05$ or lower

that fact that in the entire corpora, the average length of comments for females was shorter than for males (F = 26.3, M = 26.7). It is interesting that while in general, commenters had more words to say about males, in this topic, they were far more voluble about females. Further, TTR within this key concept indicates a richer lexicon for females or a wider range of topic matter within this key concept, in contrast to the wider corpus, a feature which generally indicates a search for precision in order to convince the reader. Negative evaluation within each money-themed comment was substantially higher for females (F = 77%, M = 55%) and positive was lower (Table 15.3).

In *The Guardian* corpora differences between the two genders were less pronounced. However, the overall number of statistically differing key concepts concerning money was seven for ***FG*** and three for ***MG***, the former with log likelihoods ranging from seven to 470.45 while the latter ranged from 14.5–20.38, indicating a far higher preponderance of money topics in the female corpus.

Linguistic Features Within the Money Theme

For both *The Guardian* and *The Australian*, "Money" themed comments about female politicians included more semantic roles than did comments on males demonstrating that there were more stakeholders in the commenters' argument and again, greater attention by the commenter to presenting a watertight argument. Commenters named the supplier of money for both job-related spending and salary in such semantic roles as "*taxpayer*", "*I*", "*we*", "*myself*", "*the government*". Hence, stakeholders were foregrounded as possible victims of the politicians' wrongdoing, as was the accountability of politician receiving or spending money. In fact, where mentioned, the source of the politician's income is stressed in the female corpora through naming of "*taxpayer*" at a ratio of 3:1 compared to males, for whom the source of their income is not mentioned. Inclusion of any "payer" was more frequent for women in both newspapers (FA: 56%, ***FG***: 24%) than for males (***MG***: 6% MA: 1.5%), further reinforcing such inclusions as a strategy to foreground possible negative impact on stakeholders. For example:

Table 15.5 Use of terms "taxpayer" and pronouns "I" and "we" in association with comments about spending of government money: raw numbers and percentages of comments on money

	FA No. comments	%	FG No. comments	%	MA No. comments	%	MG No. comments	%
taxpayer	33	35.87	23	47.9	8	13.73	4	4.35
I-WE	19	20.65	4	8.33	5	8.62	1	1.09

(1) *You used tax payers money for something that you are not morally meant to spend it on. You and you families indulgence. Taxpayers are sick of it (FA)*

(2) *Triggs is a public servant paid for by taxpayers, by myself (**FG**)*

Inclusion of personal pronouns "*you*"/ "*I*"/ "*we*" in money-themed comments (we will have to pay you a pension; I pay to fund your lifestyle) was four times more frequent for female than male politicians in both publications (see Table 15.5), thus further emphasising personal consequences of politicians' actions around money. Direct address (you) of female politicians may also reflect a device to reduce social distance between themselves and those commented on, or even assume higher agency and authority over the commentee, as noted by Van Leeuwen (2008). Conversely, mention of salary and spending with no reference to the provider of funds was found in *The Australian* and only for males (14 percent of MA money comments).

Subthemes Within the Money Theme

Misuse of public funds was a topos in 45 percent of money-themed comments about female politicians in *The Australian*. Similar topoi predominated for females in *The Guardian*, but at the lower level, of 13 percent of comments. Another topos was commentary that female politicians should reimburse from their own savings, while such personal penalties were absent for males. Meanwhile mention of spending in relation to public policy was more frequent for females. As shown in Fig. 15.1, inclusion of stakeholders and topoi of misuse are more common in female than male corpora for both publications.

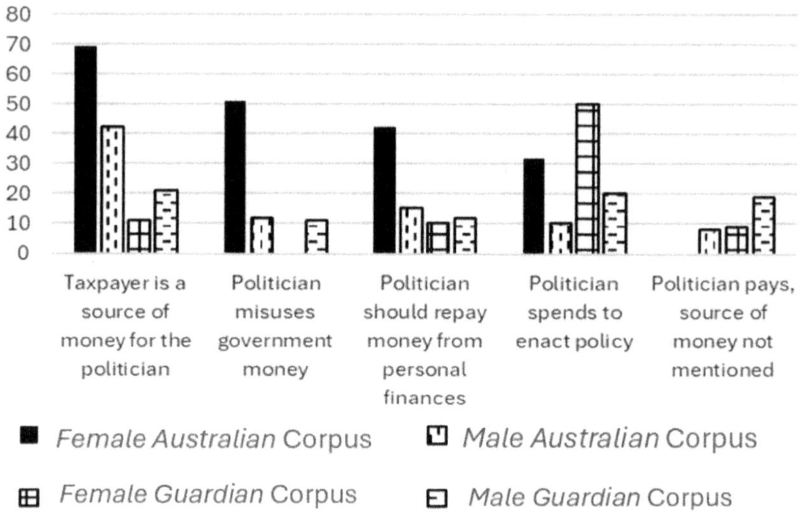

Fig. 15.1 Number of topoi in comments per thousand emerging within the key judgement of "Dissatisfaction with Money Handling" for comments to *The Australian* and *The Guardian*

The other large monetary subtheme in the corpora was that of monetary policy which entailed comments about decisions re government spending. In this theme, percentages of comments were higher for male politicians of both publication than females (*MA* 50%, *FA* 34%; ***MG*** 23%, ***FG*** 8%).

One frequently mentioned stakeholder, the taxpayer, was further analysed due to its very high occurrence for female politicians. While considerable ire was raised for both male and female politicians spending of taxpayer funds, the number of mentions of *taxpayer*, the number of comments containing intensifications and the total number of intensifications was considerably higher in the female corpora, while the number of softened/neutral comments was lower. Below are all examples in the topos of politicians' spending/income in *The Guardian* (Intensified concordances ***FG*** = 20, ***MG*** = 10; softened/neutral ***FG*** = 2; ***MG***: = 12). Compare the intensified negative lexicon for females: "*Good grief!*" "*Apologise*", "*rack up*", "*vile piece of work*", "*gall*", "*shonks*", "*spivs*", "*rip off*", "*disastrous*" (female) where judgement is clearly inscribed, in contrast to "*world of grandeur*", "*extravagant*" (male) in which judgement depends on reader interpretation, with only one negative inscribed judgement: "*obscene abuse*". For example, comments 7 and 8 on male politicians rely on narrative ("*So the justification…is…*") and sarcasm ("*taxpayer pay[s]..added bonus*") rather than judgement to present a case against the politicians, while the phrases "*personal fetish*", "*taxpayer welfare*"," *added bonus*" represent euphemistic, indirect or softened references to the disfavoured spending.

Guardian Male sample			
(3)	*world of grandeur at the expense of the*	***taxpayer***	*and Abbott must have been aware of this*
(4)	*or backing extravagant spending instead of the*	***taxpayer***	*He is sworn to SERVE AUSTRALIAN PEOPLE,*
(5)	*By the people of Queensland .... his obscene abuse of*	***taxpayer***	*funds to indulge his own personal fetish*
(6)	*a cosy chat with Fran Kelly, she can ask him how much*	***taxpayer***	*Welfare he's collected over the years*
(7)	*So the justification for Cormann spending $37,000*	***taxpayer***	*'s money is to argue for tax cuts for the wealthy*
(8)	*when your consort lives a long distance. Having*	***taxpayers***	*pay for your jaunts is an added bonus*
Guardian Female sample			
(9)	*Good grief; She should be apologising to the*	***taxpayer***	*for racking up a lawyers bill approaching 200 k*
(10)	*The vile piece of work even has the gall to bill*	***taxpayer***	*for her legal bills I would have a great deal*
(11)	*while she avoids answering!; As an Australian*	***taxpayer***	*I demand an apology from Cash for her wasting*
(12)	*March 2015 she was happy to hand over $500,000*	***taxpayers'***	*money to a so-called Melbourne Islamic Museum*
(13)	*her only contribution seemed to be appearing at*	***taxpayers'***	*expense at gala social functions*
(14)	*Minister, must immediately explain whether the*	***taxpayer***	*funded residence was used in any way to help*
(15)	*She will leave with a couple of hundred thousand*	***taxpayer***	*dollars per year as a pension from her defined*

Intensification Within Theme of Politician Misuses Government Money

Where female politicians were accused of misusing public funds, intensification was inscribed in lexicon of strong negative judgement including moral evaluation (“*demand*”, “*abuse*”, “*serial offender*”, “*despicable*”, “*caught out*”, “*blames*”, “*rant*”, “*extremism*”, “*fucking*”, “*rorter*”). There is more frequent use of maximisers (“*always*”, “*clearly*”, “*more than once*”, “*serial*”, “*anybody else for that matter*”). Further, lexicon such as “*demand*”, “*justification*”, “*pulled into line*”, indicates intention to invert the power relationship of commenter and politician. This is reinforced by the question in (16) demand[ing] documentary evidence for the trip expenditures, a redundant stipulation since this is a legal requirement for all spending of public monies by Australian politicians. (Australian National Audit Office 2022). Such requirements further represent a delegitimation of the politician through what Theo classifies as “appeal to authority” (2008, 110) (*“documentary evidence”* (16) *“since when”* (25). Supposition is presented as fact without evidential support (17, 18, 19, 22, 23) or cast while possible future monetary claims are presupposed (18). Doubt is also expressed toward spending within the politician’s role: “*disability care*” (21), *“so called, lectures to China”* (23) Only one example from ***FG*** (21) demonstrates mild mitigation by avoiding negatively infused words (“*she spent plenty*”, *“she was good at seeming to care”*).

FA

(16)	*Demand that she produces the documentary evidence for the trip*	*expenditures*	*and justification. Jonathan Was she alone in a hotel room?*
(17)	*this issue would not go away easily so, imho, she should have*	*paid*	*it back as it was always going to reflect badly on her*
(18)	*had the child ’s condition worsened she also expect for taxpayers to*	*pay*	*for her abuse of the tax payer How lucky can you get.?*
(19)	*She is a serial offender, having had to*	*pay back*	*more than once*
(20)	*Perhaps even further recognise that the money she is*	*spending*	*is not HERS. How despicable, she is caught out*

FG

(21)	*Disability Care, and others.; She spent plenty of*	*taxpayers*	*money.; She was good at seeming to care*
(22)	*I guess building costs have gone up a tad since Gillard spent $450 k*	*taxpayers*	*money on renovations to her Adelaide home*
(23)	*in March 2015 she was happy to hand over $500,000 of*	*taxpayer's*	*money to a so-called Melbourne "Islamic Museum"*
(24)	*Question: Why should the*	*taxpayer*	*pays for her fucking 'whiteboard' fees?*
(25)	*Since when do we pay this travel*	*rorter*	*for giving lectures to China or anybody for that matter*

In contrast, concordances with male politicians' spending in *The Guardian* contained fewer intensifications and were characterised by a non-judgemental presentation of "facts" and narrative explanation, whether to support (examples 26–29) or oppose (30–33) the use of government funds. Both supporting and opposing comments contain numerical and factual detail ("*193*", "*39*", "*CL 604 Challenger*") and rationalisation with legitimating evidence (26–29) which, as Van Leeuwen notes (2008, 106) confer legitimacy to the commenters' stance.

MG

(26) Of the 193 requests for special purpose aircraft in the first half of 2018, only Senator Cormann's booking for June 22 involved a single plane

(27) because 1) scheduled flights to Perth are plentiful and much cheaper on all four airlines, 2) his family was waiting for him in Perth,

(28) in fact because the fleet is based in Canberra his jet flew the route 39 times without him or any other passengers aboard.

(29) its a sign of respect to fly out to meet someone one on one.

(30) He booked flights on a CL604 Challenger defence jet, attracting a cost 20 times the price of the ticket if he wanted to wrap up negotiations shortly thereafter ...

(31) ridiculous. Corman did nt get this amount as cash. It was the notional cost of him flying on the charter. For parliamentary business. Because he has a job and a purpose.

(32) *number of hours flying each year and it might as well take Mathias where he wants rather than flying around empty. Dan Tehan has defended the finance minister Mathias Cormanns decision.*

(33) *So he just wasted his time flying to see them. For what possible personal benefit? Your comment does nt pass the sniff test*

Only one comment from ***MG*** also expressed strong negative judgement:

(34) *SOLE PASSENGER on a $37,000 taxpayer funded flight. Truly vile and disgusting*

"Entitled" was a strong key concept for women, comments describing unfair access to money, especially government allowances, desire for an extravagant lifestyle, and an attitude of disregard for taxpayers (M = 21, F = 60). By contrast, mentions of personal wealth for males attracted minimal negative commentary. In ***FA*** qualitative analysis revealed high levels of lexical intensification in appraisal, presented below in **bold.**

Female

(35) ***All*** *day serving the people to earn her* ***massive taxpayer*** *salary.*

(36) *She's still collecting her* ***massive pay*** *with a* ***slight*** *pay cut, and will* ***still*** *be getting a pension*

(37) *She* ***certainly*** *appears to have the* ***taxpayer-funded spending credentials*** *to fit* ***right*** *in*

(38) ***complaining*** *here,* ***understand this****. She will not be required to pay it back, and* ***her party will not sanction her***

(39) ***Grumpy*** *with the attitude of this career* ***leech****. Probably* ***never*** *paid tax* ***in her life****. (I don't count tax paid when you're already on the government* ***teat***

(40) *she is* ***close*** *friends with Sarina Russo.* ***No wonder*** *she wanted to spend new years eve on the Gold Coast in her company.* ***That wasnt working***

(41) ***indulgent junket*** *why would she? She clearly feels* ***entitled*** *to spend as much as she likes of* ***other people's*** *money under the* ***pretence***

(42) *like all politicians goes there regularly. She seems to spend an inordinate amount of time in Qld, more so than in her own electorate*

Male

(43) ***picture*** *of an* ***"entitled"*** *member of the* ***soft-popular left****. No* ***loss*** *when he quits.*

(44) ***We the taxpayers*** *are paying* ***handsomely*** *for his time, so he has* ***plenty*** *available to answer questions*

(45) *Abbott could pick up probably* ***in excess of*** *ten million dollars for a speaking tour he wanted to, also he could retire and his pension*

In ***FA***, lexicon used to appraise the politician and her relationship to money is frequently intensified and judgemental: (35, 36) *"massive"*, (37) *"taxpayer-funded spending credentials"*, (39) *"career leech"*, *"on the government teat"* (41) *"indulgent junket"*, *"under the pretence"* (42) *"inordinate amount of time"*. Behaviours and duration are maximised: (35) *"all day"*;; (37) *"fit right in"* (41) *"as much as she likes"* while potentially positive information is minimised *("slight")*. Repetition is employed to intensify messages (38) *"complaining here, understand this"* (36) *"still collecting...still getting a pension"*. Commenters employ devices to encourage readers to concur: (37) *"certainly appears"* (40*) "no wonder"* (41*) "she clearly feels"*.

For ***MA*** (44) *"paying handsomely"* and (45) *"in excess of"* lack clear negative judgement, compared to descriptions of female income. Although male is described as (43) *"entitled"*, this is expressed indirectly as *"a picture of"* and therefore mitigated, and the description of his political affiliation is softened as *"soft popular left"*, again presenting mild judgement, while a potential income is described as (45) *"pick up in excess of 10 million dollars"*.

Overall, the topic of money arose significantly more frequently for females in the lexicon of both publications; logistic regression results support the notion that gender was a determining factor and collocations with "man" and "woman" further adding weight to this finding. Subthemes within this topic focused on unfair access to funds (entitlement), illegitimate use of government funding by female politicians and overspending, while for males the most common mention of money was in relation to policy and performance (goals, responsibility, management) with government money. Males were commonly judged as incompetent with government money; however, this judgement was not associated with illegitimate use of funds and was accompanied by less intensified judgement. For females, in contrast, comment on spending of government money as part of their portfolio was rarely commented on. While intensification was common for both genders, it was more extreme and denser for females including considerable repetition of words and argument, indicating saturation of judgement in the text. Softened judgement was noted for males and absent for females. Negative evaluation of female relationships to money was higher for both female corpora and source of money spent as well as money to be repaid more commonly raised for females, with higher use of pronouns I, we, emphasising the personal impact of the female politicians' decisions on commenters.

Discussion

This chapter incorporates results and analysis of a study that was part of a larger CADS investigation about how female politicians were represented relative to male in two national Australian newspapers. The study focused on the prominent theme that emerged of how commenters represented the politicians' use of and relationship to money, finding more comments, negative judgements, and extreme reactions to female than male politicians in relation to financial responsibilities.

Overall, appraisal of both males and females was largely negative in the theme of money, and substantially in the form of "judgement". This tendency is consistent with earlier findings of high overall negativity in reader comments (Cavasso and Taboada 2021) and possibly further exacerbated by a broader negative attitude toward politicians. However, analysis of subthemes revealed that male politicians were largely criticised for spending decisions made as part of their professional role, while for females, negative judgement was largely related to claims of illegitimate use of government allowances.

The clear dominance in the female corpus of "money" related key concepts, consisting of judgements of entitlement and possible misuse/abuse of government funds suggests a delegitimization of women from their elected/appointed roles, as does the high level of association with illicit spending, which may serve to question the legitimacy of motives for entering politics. By contrast, comments on money for men focused predominantly on policy and performance in financial management, denoting goals, responsibility, and management, reinforcing that roles are perceived differently by gender, although this effect was undoubtedly exacerbated by the overall paucity of female politicians with ministerial portfolios at the time of data collection. Intensification as an indicator of strength of feeling was high for both corpora, but higher for females with more saturation and stronger lexical intensification, a finding consistent with more frequent negative judgements of females. Several examples in the female corpus showed especially high levels of intensification and maximisation, and a paucity of softeners to mitigate strength of negative judgement; however, such softeners were more common in comments on males.

Personalisation of female politicians was relatively low compared to previous findings, with minimal mention of appearance[1] or traditional female duties. Instead, comments appeared to focus on non-gender-related evaluations. As Van Dijk (2015b) noted in the field of racism, blatantly discriminating discourse tends to decrease due to caution around public sanction but instead tends to attribute universally stigmatised actions to the disfavoured group. For example, in the case of race and ethnicity, crime and lack of hygiene were often attributed to migrants as reasons for disapproval by the traditional population. Meanwhile, similarly targeted criticisms were found in evaluation of female journalists, who were labelled "poor writers" (Mitchelstein 2011).

[1] Editor's Note This contrasts vividly with the premiership of Joan Kirner (1990-1992) the first female leader of a major political party in the state of Victoria, and first female premier, whose dress in particular was targeted when a cartoonist represented her consistently as dressed in polka dots (albeit she had never worn such a frock), leading to a feminist fightback in the holding of the Spot on Joan Concert where the premier performed on stage playing the guitar as "Joan Jet" with a "Labor Women" back-up band. So well-embedded in the media imagination at least, it was referenced in news coverage upon her death: Lucy Thackray, "Joan Kirner dead ...", *Daily Mail Online*, 1 June 2015, 2 June 2015, https://www.dailymail.co.uk/news/article-3105910/Tributes-pour-political-pioneer-Joan-Kirner.html (accessed 21 November 2024); AAP, "Joan Kirner ...", *SBS News*, 1 June 2015, https://www.sbs.com.au/news/article/joan-kirner-the-polka-dot-premier/g0665q75a (accessed 21 November 2024); 9News, "Joan Kirner ...", 1 June 2015, https://www.9news.com.au/national/joan-kirner-the-polka-dot-premier/8fc6439d-47fa-466f-a991-7744a29d5889 (accessed 21 November 2024).

The preoccupation with females and money whether earning or spending their own or public funds is not without precedent. The findings support Hartsock's (1985) and Burgoyne's (2004) contentions that money is "the male domain". McElhinny (2003) extends this contention, arguing that the professions themselves are "gendered", politics, like policing and the trades being traditionally masculine, therefore raising doubt about the motivations or competence of women who enter them. Another explanation for the focus on money is a possible tendency for critics to find fault in individuals in skills or qualities which are fundamental to the profession (Johnson and Ensslin 2007; Bruns 2018; Axelson et al. 2010). Distribution of funding and claiming of expenses are central to the politician's role as well as evident to the public, and ostensibly more easily judged than complex policy decisions or negotiations.

A future area of investigation is to compare the relative focus of frequency of key concepts in headlines and articles with those in reader comments to ascertain the degree of influence of journalistic appraisal on members of the public. Preliminary investigations suggest that when journalists raise sensitive themes such as politicians' spending, a disproportionally strong reaction is provoked in readers. It is possible that the gender bias revealed by this study arises from attitudes which are unconscious in journalists, commenters, or both. Identifying the probable sources of such attitudes could provide powerful evidence about forces working against female politicians.

To further determine the contribution of gender to commenters' attitudes, it would be useful to examine data with equal numbers of male and female politicians holding portfolios, as was not possible when the data for this study was collected.

Finally, devices such as understatement, sarcasm and register were frequent in the corpora and flagged but minimally analysed in this study. This presents a rich area source of commenter attitude for future research.

Limitations

This chapter draws on a modest quantity of data. However, the study on which it is based was drawn from four large corpora and includes all the money-themed comments. That the corpora were adequately large is indicated by consistent percentages of many parts of speech across corpora. Collection of a considerably larger corpus could enable sampling of an extensive number of money-themed concepts to check for the replicability of the findings reported above.

Conclusions

The study of the impact of gender on appraisal of politicians as analysed in this chapter identified a strong tendency to delegitimise female politicians in their professional roles by under-representing them both in number of comments and by appraisal which undermines their moral (or ethical) and professional standing. The contrastingly close scrutiny by commenters on female use of funds marginalises women as legitimate participants in political decision making, indicating that their interest in politics was strategic and self-serving rather than for public good. Such representation is conceivably a form of implicit discrimination, overt sexism being evidently suppressed by wider community or legal standards. It is likely that the arguments and the money focus contained within these comments was triggered by a focus in the media on misuse by politicians of government funds. However, these results indicate that either such a media strategy is more closely aimed at female politicians, or the reputational effect is in fact stronger for women in politics than men. These findings build on the work by Van Dijk (2017) and Caldas-Coulthard and Moon (2010, 2016) which demonstrated that judgement has an important role in creating and perpetuating perception of public roles and public figures, in this case, women in politics. The findings together indicate that female participation is not yet regarded as normative and indicate that research on appraisal of females in public office should include themes beyond traditionally gendered stereotypes, to examine more implicit forms of discrimination, such as found here in the theme of money.

Note: The author reports there are no competing interests to declare.

Bibliography

Reported Cases

FORMER FIFTH SECTION CASE OF TYMOSHENKO v UKRAINE (Application no. 49872/11) JUDGMENT This version was rectified on 26 June 2013 under Rule 81 of the Rules of Court. STRASBOURG 30 April 2013 FINAL 30/07/2013 This judgment has become final under Article 44 § 2 of the Convention. It may be subject to editorial revision. C:\Users\scutt\Downloads\001–119382.pdf (accessed 2 March 2025).

Articles and Book Chapters

Ahmad, A, Rashid, M and Shahbaz, M (2020). "'Sell - outs, Fatsos or Whores?' Representation of Politically Active Pakistani Women on Social Media". *Pakistan Social Sciences Review (PSSR)* 4 (1), 40-50.

Axelson, RD, Solow, CM, Ferguson, KJ and Cohen, MB (2010). "Assessing Implicit Gender Bias in Medical Student Performance Evaluations". *Evaluation and the Health Professions*, 33(3), 365–385, https://pubmed.ncbi.nlm.nih.gov/20801977/ (accessed 2 March 2025).

Baker, EH (2014). "Socioeconomic Status. Definition". *The Wiley Blackwell Encyclopedia of Health, Illness, Behavior, and Society*, Socioeconomic Status, Definition - Baker - Major Reference Works - Wiley Online Library (accessed 2 October 2025).

Beattie, Peter (2019. "The Supply Side: What Affects the Supply of Information Provided by the Media" in Peter Beattie, *Social Evolution, Political Psychology, and the Media in Democracy: The Invisible Hand in the US Marketplace of Ideas*. Palgrave Macmillan, London, UK, 219-271.

Burgoyne, Carole (2004). "Heart-strings and purse-strings: Money in heterosexual marriage". *Feminism and Psychology* 14 (1) 165-172.

Caldas-Coulthard, CR and Moon, R (2010). "'Curvy, hunky, kinky': Using corpora as tools for critical analysis". *Discourse and Society* 21(2) 99–133, https://www.jstor.org/stable/42889310 (accessed 2 March 2025).

Caldas-Coulthard, CR and Moon, R (2016). "Grandmother, gran, gangsta granny semiotic representations of grandmotherhood". *Gender and Language*, 10(3).

Cavasso, L and Taboada, M (2021). "A corpus analysis of online news comments using the Appraisal framework". *Journal of Corpora and Discourse Studies* 4 1-38.

Collier, CN and Raney, T (2018). Understanding Sexism and Sexual Harassment in Westminster Parliaments in Australia, the United Kingdom, and Canada. *Social Politics: International Studies in Gender. State and Society*, 25 (3), 432–455, Understanding Sexism and Sexual Harassment in Politics: A Comparison of Westminster Parliaments in Australia, the United Kingdom, and Canada (accessed 2 October 2025).

Conway, D (2016). "Margaret Thatcher, Dress and the Politics of Fashion" in A Behnke (ed), *The international politics of fashion: being fab in a dangerous world*. Routledge, Oxford, UK.

Donaghue, N (2013., April 13). Gender bias: Why appearance focus fuels sexism in media. "Gender ... media". *The Conversation*, 13(2013). https://theconversation.com/gender-bias-why-appearance-focus-fuels-sexism-in-media-13325 (accessed 2 March 2025).

Evershed, Nick (2013, June 28). "Was Julia Gillard the most productive prime minister in Australia's history?" *The Guardian*. https://www.theguardian.com/news/datablog/2013/jun/28/australia- productive-prime-minister (accessed 2 March 2025).

Evershed, N and Liu, R (2016, June 26) "From Julia Gillard to Hillary Clinton: online abuse of politicians around the world". *The Guardian*. https://www.theguardian.com/technology/datablog/ng-interactive/2016/jun/27/from-julia-gillard-to-hillary-clinton-online-abuse-of-politicians-around-the-world (accessed 24 January 2024).

Fiske, ST (2010). "Interpersonal Stratification: Status, Power, and Subordination" in Fiske, ST, Gilbert, DT and Lindzey, G (eds). *Handbook of Social Psychology*, vol 1. John Wiley & Sons, London, UK.

Holland, J and Wright, KAM (2017). "The Double Delegitimatisation of Julia Gillard: Gender, the Media, and Australian Political Culture". *Australian Journal of Politic and History*, 63(4), 588–602.

Honig, M (2016, September 6). "Why Criticism of Hillary Clinton's $12,000 Jacket Is Sexist and Hypocritical". *Observer*, https://observer.com/2016/06/why-criticism-of-hillary-clintons-12000-jacket-is-sexist-and-hypocritical/ (accessed 2 March 2025).

Hunt, E, Evershed, N and Liu, R (2016, June 26) "From Julia Gillard to Hillary Clinton: online abuse of politicians around the world". *The Guardian*, https://scholar.google.com/scholar?cluster=316520198254 1157375&hl=en&oi=scholarr (accessed 2 March 2025).

Ibroscheva, E (2006). "The New Eastern European Woman: A Gold Digger or an Independent Spirit?" *Global Media Journal*, 5(9).

Johnson, S and Ensslin, A (2007). "'But her language skills shifted the family dynamics dramatically': Language, gender and the construction of publics in two British newspapers". *Gender amd Language*, 1(2), 229–254. https://doi.org/10.1558/genl.v1i2.229 (accessed 24 January 2025).

Manwaring, R (2017). "New developments: Recalibrating civil society—the case of Australia". *Public Money and Management*, 37(2), 121-125.

Mautner, G (2005). "Time to get wired: Using web-based corpora in critical discourse analysis". *Discourse and Society*, 16(6), 809–828.

McElhinny, B (2003). "Theorizing Gender in Sociolinguistics and Linguistic Anthropology" in J Holmes and M Meyerhoff (eds), *The Handbook of Language and Gender*, Blackwell, Oxford, UK, 21–40.

Mitchelstein, E (2011). "Catharsis and community: Divergent motivations for audience participation in online newspapers and blogs". *International Journal of Communications,* 5(21).

Murphy, P and Coorey, D (2012, October 2). "Insults and Chaff Bags Leave Jones in Bad Odour". *Sydney Morning Herald*, https://www.smh.com.au/politics/federal/insults-and-chaff-bags-leave-jones-in-bad-odour-20121001-26vla.html (accessed 2 March).

Partington, A (2008). "The Armchair and the Machine: Corpus-Assisted Discourse Research". *Corpora for University Language Teachers*, 74, 95–118.

Partington, A and Marchi, A (2015). "Using corpora in discourse analysis" in D Biber and R Reppen (eds.) *The Cambridge Handbook of English Corpus Linguistics*, vol 1, 216–234. Cambridge University Press, Cambridge, UK.

Reisigl, M and Wodak, R (2017). "The Discourse-Historical Approach (DHA)" in *The Routledge Handbook of Critical Discourse Studies.* (Issue January, 63–94).

Saldana, Johnny (2012). "An Introduction to Codes and Coding" in *The Coding Manual for Qualitative Researchers*, no 2006: 1–8. https://doi.org/10.1519/JSC.0b013e3181ddfd0a (accessed 24 January 2025).

Sandlin, JA, Stearns, J, Maudlin, JG and Burdick, J (2011). "'Now I Ain't Sayin'She a Gold Digger' Wal-Mart Shoppers, Welfare Queens, and Other Gendered Stereotypes of Poor Women in the Big Curriculum of Consumption". *Cultural Studies – Critical Methodologies* 11(5), 464–482.

Southern, R and Harmer, E (2021). "Twitter, incivility and 'everyday' gendered othering: an analysis of tweets sent to UK members of Parliament". *Social Science Computer Review*, 39(2), 259-275.

Stevenson, A (2013). "Making gender divisive: 'Post-Feminism', sexism and media representations of Julia Gillard". *Burgmann Journal*, 1(2), 53-63.

Trimble, L, Curtin, J, Wagner, A, Auer, M, Woodman, VKG and Owens, B (2021). "Gender novelty and personalized news coverage in Australia and Canada". *International Political Science Review*, 42(2), 164-178.

Trindade, LVP (2020). "Disparagement humour and gendered racism on social media in Brazil". *Ethnic and Racial Studies*, 43(15), 2766–2784.

Van Dijk, T (2015a) "Critical Discourse Studies: a sociocognitive approach" in Ruth Wodak and Michael Meyer, *Methods of Critical Discourse Analysis*. 2nd ed, 62–86. London: Sage, 2009. 3rd ed, London: Sage, 2015.

Van Dijk, TA (2015b). "Racism in the press" in N Bonvillain (ed), *The Routledge Handbook of Linguistic Anthropology*, Routledge, Oxford, UK 384–392 https://doi.org/10.4324/9780203492741 (accessed 24 January 2025).

Van Dijk, TA (2017). "How globo media manipulated the impeachment of Brazilian president Dilma Rousseff". *Discourse and Communication*, 11(2), 199–229.

Wodak, R and Meyer, M (2014). "Critical Discourse Analysis: History, Agenda, Theory, and Methodology". *Methods of Critical Discourse Analysis*, 1–33. https://doi.org/10.1016/S0376-7361(09)70018-4 (accessed 24 January 2025).

Woolard, Kathryn A and Bambi B Schieffelin (1994). "Language ideology". *Annual Review of Anthropology*, 23, 55–82, https://www.annualreviews.org/doi/abs/10.1146/ annurev.an.23.100194.000415 (accessed 24 January 2025).

Books and Reports

Australian National Audit Office (2022). *Administration of Travel Entitlements Provided to Parliamentarians.* https://www.anao.gov.au/work/performance-audit/administration-travel-entitlements-provided-parliamentarians (accessed 2 March 2025).

Bruns, A (2018). *Gatewatching and news curation: Journalism, social media, and the public sphere. Digital Journalism*, Series Digital Formations vol 113, Peter Lang, Frankfurt am Main, Germany.

Dolan, K and Lynch, T (2016). *The Impact of Gender Stereotypes on Voting for Women Candidates by Level and Type of Office*. Cambridge University Press, Cambridge, UK. https://doi.org/10.1017/S1743923X16000246 (accessed 24 January 2025).

Fairclough, N (2001). *Language and power* (2nd ed). Routledge, Oxford UK.

Gillings, M, Mautner, G and Baker, P (2023). *Corpus-assisted discourse studies*. Cambridge University Press, Cambridge, UK.

Gill, R (2007). *Gender and the media*. Polity Press, Cambridge, UK.

Gooch, K (2015). *Because She's a Woman: Gender Stereotypes and Women's Participation in Australian Politics*. University of Western Sydney, Sydney, Australia.

Hardie, A, Lancs. Ac. Uk, Hardie, A (2014). *Log Ratio--An Informal Introduction*. http://cass.lancs.ac.uk/log-ratio-an-informal-introduction/ (accessed 24 January 2025).

Harmer, E (2021). *Women, Media, and Elections: Representation and Marginalization in British Politics*. Policy Press, Bristol, UK.

Hartsock, N (1983). *Money, sex, and power: toward a feminist historical materialism*. Longman, New York, NY, US.

Hartsock, N (1985). *Money, sex, and power: toward a feminist historical materialism*. Northeastern University Press, Chicago Ill, USA.

Lacan, J (1977). *The four fundamental concepts of psycho-analysis*. Hogarth Press, London, UK.

Martin, JR and White, PRR (2005). *The Language of Evaluation: Appraisal in English*. Palgrave Macmillan, London, UK.

Martin, JR and White, Peter RR (2007). *The Language of Evaluation. Appraisal in English*, Palgrave Macmillan, Basingstoke, UK, The Language of Evaluation: Appraisal in English | Springer Link (accessed 2 October 2025).

McArthur, T (1981). *Longman Lexicon of Contemporary English*. Longman, London, UK.

Rayson, PE (2002). *Matrix: A statistical method and software tool for linguistic analysis through corpus comparison*. Lancaster University, Lancashire, UK.

Van Dijk, TA (1999). *Discourse and Racism*. Sage Publications, https://www.academia.edu/19984991/Discourse_and_Racism (accessed 2 March 2025).

Van Leeuwen, T (2008). Discourse and practice: New tools for critical discourse analysis. Oxford University Press, Oxford UK.

Williams, BE (2019). *From tightrope to gendered trope: a comparative study of the print mediation of women prime ministers*. Australian National University, Canberra ACT.

Information Resources and Documents

A'Beckett, L (2012). Resolution on the situation of Yulia Tymoshenko AP. Euronest Parliamentary Assembly, May 3–5, https://eur-lex.europa.eu/legal-content/EN/TXT/PDF/?uri=CELEX:52012XP0530(05 (accessed 2 March 2025).

Australian National Audit Office. (2022). *Administration of Travel Entitlements Provided to Parliamentarians.* https://www.anao.gov.au/work/performance-audit/administration-travel-entitlements-provided-parliamentarians (accessed 2 March 2025).

Hardie, A, Lancs. Ac. Uk, Hardie, A (2014). *Log Ratio--An Informal Introduction.* http://cass.lancs.ac.uk/log-ratio-an-informal-introduction/ (accessed 24 January 2025).

Stantic, Bela (2019). "It Was Not a Miracle; It Was Just Mathematical Certainty". Interview. Breakfast. Australian Broadcasting Commission (ABC). *Breakfast News.* Australian Broadcasting Commission. June18, 2019. https://www.facebook.com/watch/?v=293013414977783 (accessed 24 January 2024).

Williams, BE (2019). *From Tightrope to Gendered Trope: A Comparative Study of the Print Mediation of Women Prime Ministers.* PhD Thesis, Australian National University (ANU), Canberra, ACT, Australia.

16

Structural Inequality, Women's Safety and the Funding Cliff Edge: The Impact of the New Funding Policy in Meeting the Needs of Black and Minoritised Women

Baljit Banga

This chapter is part of the doctoral thesis by the author. The reference for the doctoral thesis is Banga, B, 2025. The Impact of the New Funding Policy (Commissioning and Procurement) on Women's Refuges in the United Kingdom. PhD Thesis. Bath. School of Social and Policy Sciences. Institute of Policy Research. University of Bath.

Note: 'By and for' women's refuges support Black and minoritised women who are represented at staff and board levels by the women they serve. They differ from generic women's services providing specialist support to all women without addressing such defined specific needs, and from non-specialist VAWG providers like housing associations which complete for refuge contracts as non-specialists.

B. Banga (✉)
Institute of Policy Research, University of Bath, Bath, UK

J. A. Scutt (ed.), *Women, Power and Autonomy*,
https://doi.org/10.1007/978-3-031-97958-3_16

The New Funding Policy—Shift from By and For Women's Refuges to Generic Non-Specialist Provision

The so-called new funding policy for the provision of services was introduced following a series of austerity measures by the Conservative government in 2010 that strategically aligned funding for social services under neoliberalism. It included local authority commissioning policy that replaced local authority grants operating prior to austerity (Rees 2014; MHCLG 2019)[1]. Under the new funding policy, women's organisations running emergency refuges experienced opportunities for both growth and development as well as reduction in services and consolidation due to under-resourcing. Women's organisations made difficult decisions to either meet high demand with fewer resources or create efficiency savings reducing both frontline support and infrastructure costs alongside reductions to staff support systems—training and wellbeing programmes designed specifically to address workplace trauma associated with delivering violence against women and girls (VAWG) services. Efficiency savings helped some women's organisations in competitive tendering however, they also led to changes in the service delivery model in favour of more cost-effective options. For others, it led to mergers with bigger and non-specialist providers that altered the nature of feminist rights-based trauma-informed support.

While adaptation under efficiency was one aspect of austerity that served some organisations well, it represented a threat to sustainability and subjected organisations to long periods of insecure and short-term funding creating financial pressures. This is also called the cliff edge where organisations operated on deficit budgets relying on reserves to

[1] These austerity policies introduced by the Conservative government in 2010 were designed to reduce public expenditure through funding cuts to women's organisations as part of the package of measures that required more services for less funding and reduction of overheads. Local authorities previously providing grants to local services replaced grant funding with service contracts containing, among other measures, target-hardening and a reliance on data monitoring. Women's services were pressured to evidence move-on and resettlement from women's refuges in shorter periods of time rather than focus on trauma-informed support.

sustain frontline services and ultimately, risk closure.[2] The new funding policy had both positive and negative impacts changing delivery models towards quick outputs, shifting the strategic direction of organisations to align them to the demands of statutory funders, and raising critical questions about the response to VAWG and the role of the state vis-a-vis policy to address a serious social problem disproportionately impacting women and their rights to safety, to rebuild their lives and to thrive in the fields of their choosing.

Impact on By and For Women's Refuges

Women's refuges were directly impacted by the new funding policy. In 2003 the Support People Programme (SP) made up one part of the funding to women's refuges while housing benefit (HB) covered the other part (Magnusson and Davidge 2020). The revenue stream that generated income through HB covered the following costs: housing management charges to housing associations for renting the property[3] (Magnusson and Davidge 2020) minor refurbishments and repairs to refuges that were not covered by housing associations; and overhead costs associated with management, finance and administration. The grant income stream or SP covered salary costs of refuge support workers. Overall, refuges provided some women's organisations with close to 40 per cent of their

[2] The cliff edge represents a period of significant crisis for organisations where the following happens: organisations utilise reserve income to offset funding shortfalls to support back office and frontline delivery costs; the more the reserves are used, the closer the organisation is to operating on a deficit budget; and finally, an assessment of funding prospects is carried out and where the prospects are low (unable to offset the shortfalls) then the organisation is at the cliff edge and at risk of closure. A few sources analysed the financial crisis facing organisations following the COVID pandemic when funding to the charities sector slowed down. Further insight is provided by King et al. (2022) and Charities Commission (2021).

[3] Most women's organisations rent property from housing associations to run refuge services. They are not outright owners of property. The arrangement is managed through a service level agreement with housing associations. The woman's organisation is effectively the tenant of the housing association.

funding and covered their running costs.[4] Additional income for other support services such as counselling and therapeutic work, and advocacy and advice came from grant income however grant income was restricted and rarely covered core costs. In other words, core funding served as a lifeline for women's organisations managing refuges supporting their financial sustainability and enabling these organisations to absorb shocks from the funding system itself (short-term funding, lack of core funding and limitations due to restricted funding).

SP was ring fenced requiring local authorities to allocate an agreed amount to support women's refuges. This arrangement changed in the later stages of SP with the removal of the ring fence (LGA 2008) and the introduction of commissioning and procurement policies (discussed below). During austerity there were changes to the funding formula (ring-fenced SP income) for women's refuges: first, the amount of time women could spend in refuges was reduced to about nine months (and later to three months under public procurement) and second, the SP grant was reduced when the ring fence was lifted. These measures are called throughput and introduced by local authorities believing that more women (and children) could be supported if throughput was increased by reducing the amount of time women spent in refuges (Sisters for Change 2017; LGA 2022). However, by and for organisations argued that trauma-informed support over a longer duration was needed to prevent repeat (and secondary) victimisation and to ensure women had the resources to enable their independence and freedom from violence. Equally important to note is the crisis in affordable housing that meant fewer affordable housing options were available to women especially under the increased throughput model.

In 2009, the ring fence on SP was removed and the central government response to VAWG began to change.[5] First, the response focused on domestic abuse rather than VAWG. By and for organisations delivering holistic support were marginalised in a response that

[4] This figure is estimated as an average from seven organisations that were part of Participant Group 1 in my fieldwork interviews. It is used as an illustrative figure to indicate the level of dependency women's refuge providers had on HB and SP income to sustain their organisations and meet overhead and infrastructure costs.

[5] See also Adisa (2020) and Steel et al. (2011).

heavily focused on delivery by statutory agencies and government-led programmes. Second, funding was aligned with these responses and many local authorities began retaining funding for in-house services. Third, by using the term "domestic abuse", the response was gender neutral and failed to recognise the disproportionate impact of violence against women and girls, on women and girls and hence, the service delivery models were changed from tailored specialist and holistic support towards cost efficient responses and schemes like the one stop shop that delivered co-located services to both women and men (Vachelli et al. 2015). Women's organisations, under some commissioning plans, were thereby required to deliver services to men. Finally, the approach to risk assessment replaced the needs-led trauma-informed approach used by women's organisations (Steel et al. 2011; Adisa et al. 2020). The shifting landscape focused on the systemisation and standardisation of the response to VAWG defined as efficiency measures under new funding policy. In 2014, refuges were directly targeted by central government funding cuts that recommended a three per cent cut to SP however, without the ring fence and due to the pressure on budgets, some local authorities introduced 40 per cent cuts over five years (Jarrett 2012).

The above provides an overview of the funding and resourcing approach related to women's refuges but more broadly, it speaks to the vital importance of sustaining an economy of provision that is gendered, that is, providing services to women in women only safe space and employing women in diverse occupational fields across organisations. The gendered economy also had wider impact. For example, women's labour was appropriately recognised, valued and remunerated by organisations. Women-centred policies such as extended maternity leave and flexible working to care for dependents formed part of human resource management policies. The feminist rights-based social justice approach was embedded in concepts such as equality and representation, fair play, advancement of opportunity, and flexibility among other measures that enabled women to participate in employment and create work-life balance.

Move from Gendered, Specialist Support

Local authority commissioning and procurement frameworks began to view women's refuges as non-specialist providers under a generic model (Vachelli et al. 2015). The consequence of reframing a vital service to women subjected to violence was that it invited all types of providers to bid for refuge contracts under the rules of open competition. The introduction of procurement and commissioning led to market expansion by diversifying suppliers especially for housing associations as direct service providers (Hilditch 2018). There was also market reduction leaving many smaller grassroots women's organisations unable to compete in the open market. Further, due to the reframing of services around cost effectiveness, grassroots women's organisations were unable to demonstrate social value. By 2017, many by and for women's refuges were unable to fully participate in commissioning and procurement due to the rigid assessment criteria favouring cost of delivery over quality of provision.

The new funding policy was not linked to demand but rather to efficiency inviting economies of scale in order to achieve faster throughput. The overview above provides an important context for understanding the need for women's refuges as part of a vital and diverse economy of provision addressing VAWG. Not all women have equal access to a criminal justice system-led response or statutory pathways to support (Lilley-Walker et al. 2019). For some groups of women, there is a need for specialist tailor-made pathways to report violence and access support. For Black and minoritised women confronting socio-economic barriers, this is called the intersectional approach that links social, economic and political factors confronting women's lives and the dynamics of power they must manage within structures of society, institutions and their interactions with them (True 2012). Such pathways view inequality as structural addressing patriarchy as institutionalised sexism and misogyny alongside compound trauma experienced from systemic racism.

Sustainability and Financial Security for By and For Women's Organisations: Preserving Women's Rights, Access to Safety and the Feminist Ethos

As stated above, the primary data and the analysis in this section was collected as part of a doctoral thesis by the author. Two groups of participants were interviewed referenced as Participant Group 1 (PG1) and Participants Group 2 (PG2).[6] Participants in PG1 who managed women's refuges said that 49 per cent of the provision they provided was independent and came about under the following circumstances: they were decommissioned by local authorities however organisations continued to manage refuges through independent means; they lost tenders to a WSS (women's specialist service) or a generic non-specialist provider resulting in the loss of by and for provision prompting organisations to replace the provision to ensure services to Black and minoritised women; or, by and for refuges were excluded from local authority commissioning plans that prioritised non-specialist generic provision.

However, independent provision carried significant risk for organisations as they relied totally on HB to generate income to run refuges to replace SP funding that was lost through decommissioning. Where

[6] The primary data was collected using a qualitative questionnaire with in-depth open-ended questions. Two groups of respondents were interviewed. The first group is called Participant Group 1 (PG1) and comprised interviews with 10 senior staff, mostly directors and chief executives, in by and for organisations and Women's Specialist Services (WSS) and 6 of these organisations directly managed refuges. The remaining interviews were held with organisations providing other specialist services including strategic advocacy however they did not manage refuges. Thematic analysis was used to code the data. The data collected included details of the operating and strategic context of organisations and experiences relating to development, strategic planning and the new funding policy. The second group is called Participant Group 2 (PG2) and comprised interviews with policy and decision makers in local and national government who had a role in the commissioning of services under the new funding policy where the commissioning of VAWG and/or domestic abuse services were part of their commissioning portfolios. The data was anonymised and to ensure confidentiality references to specific localities, job titles, names of organisations, and the names of funders (where there is a risk that an organisation could be identified) were deleted and/or replaced with generic names that prevent identification. The following references are used against direct quotes: for PG1 the participant is call PG1.1 or PG1.2 and so forth replacing names or initials with numbers. A similar system of used for PG2.

the revenue was used to cover all refuge costs, the accounts were squeezed with no surplus to meet repair costs, furniture replacement, and overheads associated with running a refuge. This placed pressure on management accounts coupled with additional funding shortfalls which meant that organisations were running close to the cliff edge and were unable to achieve a healthy period of sustainability. The fact that at least half the refuges managed by PG1 were independently funded suggests a failure in the new funding policy to support local by and for refuges. The evidence further suggests that local authorities were unable to meet the diverse needs of local communities and risked losing the value-added aspect of provision which included diverse language support to women, and specialist trauma-informed provision preventing repeat victimisation and reducing the burden on statutory services which also operated on limited budgets.

Impact of Austerity Cuts and the COVID Pandemic

Participants in PG1 suggested that funding after the COVID pandemic was steadily decreasing despite the emergency influx of funding during the pandemic. While this was viewed as exceptional to meet emergency needs there were no long-term plans to fund organisations through sustainable ring-fenced funding. This was occurring at a time of increased demand for services however participants were also managing the long-term consequences of political realities in the country. Austerity cuts from 15 years prior had targeted by and for organisations and neoliberal policies such as one size fits all created a preference in funding policy for generic non-specialist services. The policy was rationalised as a cost saving measure producing efficiency in public spend however it lacked an understanding around the pathways to support that women accessed and relied on streamlined accessibility measures centred on a revolving door delivery mechanism that reduced the duration of support to meet increasing demand with fewer resources. For service providers, models of provision that did not meet the new service specification under the efficiency policy were defined as less competitive.

Complexity in meeting need, or the intersectional lens advocated by the by and for sector was replaced by the economies of scale producing savings. This paved the way for the expansion of public procurement policy to include women's refuges. Participants in PG1 managed a precarious funding situation with historical underfunding (defined as services delivering more for less funding), defunding (defined as decommissioning through public procurement specifically through competitive tendering), lack of commitment to full cost recovery (FCR) which prevented core cost recovery, and commissioning tendencies that continued to weigh price (lowest cost) over the quality of provision hence pressuring services to change the nature of provision to compete.

The COVID emergency funding was the first sign of a cliff edge or financial crisis for these organisations. Participants noted that while funding had increased to keep services afloat, emergency funding only addressed immediate need arising from the COVID crisis. The new funding did not address the situation of chronic underfunding. The early signs of a "cliff edge" for organisations is noticed in the response to the COVID pandemic. The cliff edge describes the financial situation of organisations running deficit budgets where funding forecasts fall short. The difference from pervious cycles of deficit budgets is that the recovery for organisations is slower. For at least 6 organisations in PG1 that had secured less than one-third of their income, time was running out and they had real insecurities about the continuation of services, reduction of support staff and depletion of reserves. One participant described this as the false economy produced by emergency funding during the pandemic this way:

> We are small even though we have £1 million. I find the £1 million threshold a bit difficult…I feel that for the amount of work we do and the fact that we are a by and for and community-led organisation, we don't have these amazing salaries, we are still a small organisation, we have a lot of demand and trying our best to cope with it. Even if it was through emergency funding to reach the £1 million mark…we can't apply for sources of funding because our income now puts us as a medium sized organisation …. (PG1.4)

Another participant suggested confusion about thresholds which were artificial targets applied to the annual income of organisations that determine their size in relation to the bidding process:

> PG1.2: "We are medium because this year it was brilliant that there were small pots of money coming in because of COVID…But in the sector how do you say it is small, medium, is it based on income…how do you categorise it…".
> Interviewer: "We are using income as the threshold because in commissioning they use income to distinguish the size of organisation for example, if the income is £1 million and sometimes it is not clear because the organisation is holding income as lead partner but commissioning frameworks might expect organisations to be in a generic lot and not in the specialist lot if the income exceeds a certain threshold".
> PG1.2: "How would you characterise small, medium or large, is it over a million?"
> Interviewer: "In some tenders if it is over a million then they define you as a big organisation".
> PG1.2: "But I think we have to wait until next year because of the sudden [up]lift because of the small pots that came from everywhere".
> Interviewer: "You are absolutely right about that because during the COVID period with the emergency money there was an uplift, but it was only temporary".
> PG1.2: "Temporary for six months, something like this".

In describing the experiences of participants in PG1, it was evident that they were serving in senior posts within their organisations through times of national crisis that came in quick succession. In the recent period, it was marked by BREXIT, the COVID pandemic and then followed by the prolonged economic crisis. These crises produced new austerity measures at a time when organisations had not recovered from previous cutbacks in public spending. The false economy that created a boost in funding temporarily was followed by longer-term depression described as follows:

> …We did have an increment during the COVID period of emergency funding that came through and inflated the figures but that was very short-term. (PG1.3)

"I am worried that we can't apply for pots of funding, and we have to compete in a robust market with charities with a better infrastructure...We are trying to retain current salaries for staff, so we have not been able to increase salaries to offset the cost of living for staff. It is a complex picture. Funders and commissioners approach charities, and the size of charity is based on arbitrary numbers, and it is a trend that keeps coming up with commissioners and funders...When you go with funders that have established connections with other charities it is difficult to open that door. (PG1.4)

Managing Priorities Addressing VAWG and Domestic Abuse Services and Balancing Limited Budgets

Participants in PG2 managed diverse priorities within their commissioning portfolios that included the commissioning of VAWG and domestic abuse services alongside other priorities. The diverse portfolios with limited budgets were stretched very thinly funding frontline services without back office or infrastructure investment; reducing budgets even where there was evidence of high demand; and shifting priorities to address an emergent picture of need. They worked at strategic level focusing on addressing funding policy gaps caused by funding constraints that reduced priority on funding VAWG services. However, there was a lack of long-term planning in commissioning priorities addressing multiple crises. For example, needs assessment were completed inconsistently across diverse commissioning areas and focused on immediate needs addressed through short-term commissioning decisions where victim-survivor engagement was a priority for some commissioners but not for all; consultation with by and for services (and WSS) was not always done; and commissioners focused on immediacy, with no long-term plans to address the persistent nature of crisis in the post pandemic period with a prolonged economic crisis. Two participants from PG2 discussed the balancing act managing diverse priorities and addressing immediate needs as follows:

Our services are predominantly grant funded as we are a big team we have better capacity to pull in grant funding...In terms of the market

> engagement, we are not making savings...we have bigger budgets but things will be more expensive. For clients, we have asked for funding for offending services but not for VAWG services...The council has a cost of living team, they were the COVID team but it has meant that there is wider provision there and generally, things like refuges have had uplift through safe accommodation funding. We have internal funding for specialist posts in children's services and housing, and we have coordinated between all our services about how we maximise that funding...We are trying to offer increased specialist provision in housing, I remember as a frontline worker how much of my time was spent doing work that was not my work because services had been more than decimated, absolutely stripped back...A key thing will be the strategy and partnership action plan...We want systems change and proper community-based response. (PG2.7)
>
> Domestic abuse is challenging because it sits across many sectors and areas. We have invested in needs assessment to support the commissioning strategy and there have been a lot of gaps that we have identified through this work. There are many expectations from central government that we have to manage. We have realised that there are some gaps in the systems, and we have to meet these. We are in between stages for example we are improving information and partnership work and at the same time we are delivering on the new strategy, so things are happening together. (PG2.8)

Commissioning practices can be understood as providing both opportunity and disadvantage for organisations. Where there was opportunity, commissioners relied on two factors: influx of funding to support local priorities and embed funding for VAWG and domestic abuse services within their overall strategy. It is evident from the interviews with PG2 that due to the size of budgets they manage, commissioning pots and other funding was directed to meeting immediate needs. However, organisations managed prolonged periods of multiple crises and required different strategies as short-term approaches failed to address the scale of demand they faced. The cliff edge from the perspective of PG2 resulted from the lack of financial recovery over prolonged periods of time that weakened organisational infrastructure, and lack of long-term planning considering the breadth and depth of work delivered by organisations. The notion of the false economy permeated through funding policy for example, it relied on exclusions from participation by setting arbitrary thresholds based on previous year income or by "revamping" the previous policy of "one size fits all" which worked well within limited budgets.

There was concern that the system of commissioning perpetuated crisis by responding to immediate pressure points at the expense of long-term sustainable solutions. The preoccupation with the former created dependency for organisations existing at the cliff edge. Funding policy governing commissioning decisions and public procurement was therefore non-responsive to specific needs addressed by the by and for organisations. The exclusion of these organisations could be systemic in nature. Under public procurement, during times of crisis and with introduction of Part 4 Statutory Duty of the *Domestic Abuse Act* 2021 (UK),[7] recovery mechanisms provided temporary solutions that could include participation of by and for (and WSS) organisations. For example, the introduction of the specialist lot under national and regional procurement activity to enable smaller organisations, mostly by and for, to participate in public procurement after the COVID pandemic supported by and for organisations to win tenders. The policy recognised the value of by and for organisations in meeting local needs. The availability of funding to support women's refuges in local areas during the introduction of the duty is another example of supporting the management and delivery of services. One participant from PG2 discussed the opportunity for recovery as follows:

> From what providers are telling us, I am talking about women's refuges and especially by and for services is that they are being excluded from procurement and losing out on funding and we know that some have closed doors. The number of providers from the women's sector has changed because there are some who do not or cannot participate in procurement. Part 4 is supposed to address some of these barriers for

[7] *Domestic Abuse Act* 2021, https://www.legislation.gov.uk/ukpga/2021/17/contents (accessed 2 March 2025).

organisations and hold local authorities to account for their commissioning practices. (PG2.4)

Public Procurement and the Impact of Competitive Tendering on Rights-Based Services

Competitive tenders are designed around defined criteria that include some organisations into the bidding process. Likewise, the criteria are also used to exclude organisations from bidding. The culture surrounding public procurement is often described as open competition where all potential bidders participate in a level playing field for example, any qualifying organisation can submit a bid and be assessed using the same criteria. However, participants in PGI considered that exclusion from participation was part of the culture even before they were engaged in competitive processes. Exclusion criteria served as gatekeeping imposing arbitrary criteria on organisations based on size, financial turnover and the make-up of communities supported (with a preference for the generic model of service provision). There were less obvious criteria that could support organisations to participate in the open market if they significantly changed the service model moving from trauma-informed delivery (which was developed from the ethos of organisations) towards one producing efficiency savings.

Participants in PG1 had strong local connections to grassroots communities identifying their ethos around intersectionality and social justice aims and objectives (equality, economic justice, racial justice and gender justice). They understood their ethos as one that stood in sharp contrast to market-driven forces describing their service delivery model as holistic, wrap-around and trauma-informed designed to prevent violence and reduce secondary and repeat victimisation. They understood this model as costly due to the intensive nature of support however, with the potential to yield cost savings on public expenditure by preventing violence escalation. The ethos was embedded in service design, staff training and development and infrastructure. Such an organisation could not easily transition from a social justice organisation directly responding to community needs to a competition model responding to the marketplace. In this sense, the funding culture influenced by public procurement excluded organisations on the bases of their ethos. One participant said:

> How funding structures were designed so we all fit into boxes, became technical and how grassroots work was taken away, there was no innovation, we couldn't provide this or tackle it because we had to fit into the boxes, we carried on doing this and finding a way to fit into the box, all grassroots was taken away... We can't fit into a box, managing all of that has been a success but it also takes its toll.... (PG1.5)

For participants in PG1, the funding culture had three features: adaptability, the temporary fix and tick-box inclusion making it non-responsive to diverse needs witnessed during the COVID pandemic when some commissioners created specialist lots to ensure the participation of by and for organisations. Other adaptations included fast-track applications processes. However, these were temporary fixes that encouraged participation in the system, legitimising the system as the best way to secure public services and expanding it to include more services under public procurement including women's refuges. The tick-box (or critical self-check) ensured legitimacy through the increasing inclusion of services under the framework. One participant discussed the funding journey as follows:

> As it [VAWG] is going up on the political agenda the income is going up and it has slightly increased, but this is quite a recent thing since 2017 when one funder prioritised harmful practices and then [others] followed suit...We have been doing this work for years... and this includes work around supporting women with NRPF [no recourse to public funds] and we always have to dig into core costs around that, but even funders that do fund us, it barely covers all of the work, it literally covers a post but there are no ongoing resources to develop. Recently what we are finding is that overheads are completely cut out and because we have been keen to offer services, we have to keep the same level of services but that impacts on core.... (PG1.8)

Grant funders were perceived to participate in the culture through a mirroring effect described by participants in PG1 as the regular shifting of priorities, demanding higher outputs for fewer resources and short-term funding. In times of crisis, and multiple crises as witnessed recently with the COVID pandemic, the grant funding culture became more competitive reducing selection criteria and making onerous demands on organisations around data. One participant said:

> There is less funding…available from grants and foundations and trusts for the kind of work we want to do, and donations are going down, and the kinds of funds that were available in pandemic and pre-pandemic are not available anymore…so it will have an impact on us and our operations…[Back then] our income expanded rapidly, we expanded rapidly during that period as lots of funding was diverted to domestic abuse…we spent a lot of money on services, we expanded services…. (PG1.1)

Participants in PG2 were balanced in their assessment of commissioning and tendering under public procurement. For them the funding culture could be defined as procedural, reactive, or dismissive. The procedural elements of the culture relied on the policy itself and the requirements under law. While this made it a highly bureaucratic and costly system especially where short-term contracts were awarded, for participants in this group, it contained certain safeguards in making decisions about resource allocations. The culture was also reactive, responding quickly to high profile cases of VAWG and racial injustice where the system was able to shift resources, where these were available, to respond to immediate community needs. Where resources were not available, the culture promoted community engagement to build evidence of need. But equally, it could also be described as dismissive where there was a lack of inclusion relying instead on the least complex contracts, emphasising cost and efficiency, and ease of administration by establishing lead partnership arrangements usually held by big non-specialist providers who sub-contracted to small specialist organisations to deliver support. In short, the culture from the perspective of PG2 could respond quickly to emerging need however these responses were not sustainable in the long-term mainly due to the lack of resources. The views below expressed elements of the procedural, reactive and the dismissive cultures as well as corrupt engagement and contract processes during times of crises, expressed by participants in PG2 as risks:

> There have not been changes that I know of through DLUHC. It is challenging to bring in the new duty although the commissioning ask is not different. There are specific requirements on what we need to look for as commissioners and we were doing commissioning in a different way involving communities and services, and [now] we have to evidence the framework we are using. (PG2.8)
>
> In the past two years, when the pandemic hit, we were like is this going to cause austerity? The conversations that we were having, I cannot imagine we would have had 3 or 4 years ago. There was the George Floyd murder and the pandemic, there was more focus on domestic abuse, there were different conversations, and that created unprecedented interest. Things in the news that you never saw, that created interest by elected members and senior managers and in our borough...we had Sarah Everard kidnapped and murdered...all of that in a short space of time, in a year... so for us the strategy was adopted by council, there were motions being passed and a huge focus on VAWG and safety of women in public and private spaces so our strategy got a bigger commitment and buy-in. The political prioritisation and VAWG as a strategic programme means it is chosen, it is a strategic priority for the council...We got additional funding...This puts us in a different position moving into the commissioning cycle and we will not need to make a political case. We will see what happens as we move into another round the austerity... I can call on the specialisms of organisations, I didn't have to embed an intersectional and anti-racism approach in the strategy or ask how we were meaningfully doing this. It has all been straight forward. (PG2.7)
>
> The biggest change is the movement to have competitive tendering with very long contracts, like 5+2+2. To me I couldn't understand when tendering for quality, and not just price...you want flexibility to meet needs of emerging policy areas that you would tender and the contract... It gives little flexibility to change those services. The way contracts are awarded is interesting, it is like you can predict who is awarded.

> There were conversations with networks, cliques and favours prior to the contract being awarded like we have seen with the roll out during the pandemic. I know contracts went to friends and family, there was cronyism, and it did not go to the organisations that should have been awarded.... (PG2.3)

Funding Priorities—Professionalisation, Emergent Needs and Responding to High-Profile Cases of VAWG

While commissioners aimed to fund local priorities with the resources they had, they were also able to respond to emerging need especially highlighted in high profile cases garnering media attention. For commissioners, while the culture enabled quick reaction, the normal practice was influenced by procedure, policy and commissioning practices that required evidence of need, and arduous and bureaucratic processes to ensure a commitment of resources. For by and for organisations, even in the best of times when they were successful in their funding endeavours, the culture lacked flexibility and rather than open competition, they faced a closed process where they struggle to participate and gain the level playing field. Finally, points of crisis were viewed by both groups of participants as posing risks as decisions were made on a more arbitrary bases favouring some groups (through the golden handshake or designated as preferred suppliers) over others.

While participants in PG1 saw some benefits in adapting to more professional cultures such as introducing new standards for operating women's refuges and casework standards supporting women to move-on to independent housing, there were also concerns about how organisations would benefit in the long-term. Participants in PG2 also agreed that there would be changes to organisations as they became more competition-ready and remodelled services as corporate and business-like entities to fit better with public procurement culture. The idea of competition for participants in PG1, and to some extent, participants in PG2, embeded the ideas of disconnection to achieve efficiency (as described under rules of competition). One participant from PG1 said:

> Looking at it as a business, there are some concerns if this happens because we are not a business. I know there is funding for this type of approach. Are you looking at the service as a business, I don't know, as long as it is good to have a business model so you can have a plan, but it shouldn't take us away from what we are doing now, we are there for the women, we are grassroots. (PG1.2)

However, efficiency changes to provision were not enough to level the playing field. Efficiency increased opportunity to participate in competitive processes however, organisations also experienced disconnection from their ethos. Fundamentally, the landscape of service provision was changed by squeezing out by and for (and WSS organisations) and the specialisms (trauma-informed, rights-based and holistic support modelled from feminist values) they offered from the perspectives they brought. A participant described it as follows:

> I don't think in terms of an organisation like ours and the size we are, that we cannot operate business like, I don't agree with it. We have to have systems and structures and infrastructure, but it is not business like...How we do that [become business-like]...Because it is a requirement but the way we work with women we change all of that...women do the talking rather than us saying or asking questions that fits the business like model. (PG1.5)

The evidence suggested that the competition systems focusing on commercialisation and professionalisation forming the corporate and business-like entity were imposed systems, not emerging from within the values of organisations and the ethos they upheld. As imposed systems they challenged the justice goals in organisations. One respondent said:

> ...You know being a BME organisation it shouldn't be like that but out there when you say BME organisation people have assumptions that you somehow don't work under professionalism and you have no rules and I always want to fight against that thing that people talk about and I think that's what we recognise as achievement, people recognise we do things right. (PG1.2)

The level playing field is an allusive end goal. The evidence suggested that as organisations engaged in the level playing field, through the imposed competition systems and rules such as sub-contracting in loosely defined partnerships, they ended up creating distance and disconnect from the communities they served in three ways: through changes in the service model which required faster throughput; by implementing performance-driven indicators which were far-removed from the victim-survivor experience; and through social and behavioural change by staff delivering support. With regards to the latter, the language of organisations was transformed from social justice values to operating as the corporate and business-like entity as suggested here:

> When we got into the subcontracting, you lose your voice, and the commissioner body is there but the main organisation that is sub-contracting you is in the middle and you are at the bottom. How information gets to you, how you send information has to be through the main organisation that sub-contracts you. Monitoring meetings are happening with the contracting agent not with you. If we have issues, we have to go through the contracting agent, and they have contact with commissioners. We have to contact the contracting agency to see if contracts are being extended… Not being part of the process, you lose your voice totally and at the same time the contracting agency is using your outcomes as [their] results. We have to go on to their case management system and the other challenge is…even though you are sub-contracted, they [commissioners] expect certain things from you. (PG1.5)

Competition and Commercialisation vs Equality of Representation and the Rights-Based Ethos

The competition system also co-opted the ethos of organisations, watering it down to support the new system. For instance, survivor-victim centred work was changed from intensive support addressing complex need to the "revolving door" approach that focused on the basic needs of women fleeing violence for housing without trauma-informed support. For participants in PG2, the price over quality equation used to assess bids was about the commercialisation and professionalisation of the service model and there was acknowledgement that this will fundamentally change the ethos of organisations. While some commissioners identified the need for local provision vested in by and for (and WSS services), practice around this was inconsistent and could reinforce the postcode lottery of provision.

In the analysis of the data, the theme of exclusions was referenced throughout with various experiences specifically expressed by participants in PG1. The term exclusion was experienced as follows by the by and for organisations: discrimination and exclusion from processes based on the established criteria; racism experienced from hostile local authorities against groups of women supported by the by and for organisations; and sexism and misogyny where the structures, institutions and policy mechanisms failed to understand women's unequal status and systemic discrimination against them. The examples of exclusion included lack of representation where strategic decisions were made; lack of participation in competitive tenders and other funding where rigid criteria served as a gatekeeper to limit organisations from participation; lack of understanding of by and for organisations by defining them only as delivery organisations without strategic and influencing work where they represented diverse needs; and absence from processes such as needs assessments that did not fully represent local needs. Exclusions were also historical in that, there had been a long history of exclusion by local authorities directed at organisations that offered a critical voice in areas of policy and strategic planning. This was mostly evident when providing feedback to local authorities highlighting how strategies failed to consider VAWG and the role of by and for services.

Participants in PG2 were not unaware of some of these concerns however, they phrased them differently. For example, discussion on national versus local need for women's refuges indicated exclusions and often short-sightedness in local planning frameworks which ignored women's access to safe refuges. Participants understood that when women fled violent relationships, they travelled outside the borough to access support in another borough. They also suggested that this had a negative effect creating a postcode lottery (as some areas could be favoured in funding over others) and inconsistency in funding services for women.

It is clear exclusions operated in funding policy and that the new statutory duty could fall short in addressing these structural gaps. The lack of data and inconsistent monitoring were some of the reasons for the gaps however, there were also deep-rooted structural inequalities apparent on partnership boards and in funding structures that often failed to address the needs of women affected by violence and more specifically, the needs of Black and minoritised women.

The issues around funding were critical and there were two perspectives that shaped such decisions. First, resourcing while balancing multiple crises was limited therefore the idea of more for less was a convenient one however, it was based on the gatekeeper role promoting economies of scale and defining them as efficient providers. The problem was that such providers could be generic non-specialist that operated service models that were not consistent with feminist values that addressed inequalities, and that created the conditions where women were subjected to violence. The multiple crises rationale can easily be used to reduce the marketplace (as defined under public procurement policy), reduce competition, and redefine services using efficiency calculations. The risk was that such inequalities, if not addressed, could lead to further victimisation, the risk of homicide (due to inappropriate services) and death by suicide.

Second, specialist funding for by and for services did not feature consistently as priorities especially during times of crisis. Domestic abuse and VAWG priorities were often dispersed to other services such as housing, health and safeguarding under a coordinated approach or they were recognised as social problems without a commitment in funding. The experience of funding also suggested a piecemeal approach for example, funding IDVAs (Independent Domestic Violence Advocates) but not the services that could house the model and support its development. It has been argued that the experience of exclusion was embedded in the systems and policies where funding decisions were made creating disadvantage either by limiting participation and hence the visibility of by and for services in strategic spaces or through austerity policies where cost savings became the bottom line. One participant from PG2 said:

> For survivors the question is what are we doing that is preventing them from coming forward and how do we need to address this. I am hoping that the [Domestic Abuse] Act will support staff [at local authorities] to believe the survivors, I am hoping the Act will address that. The hope of local authorities is to see this duty, that should encourage them to take a partnership approach to meet the needs of survivors and that they are part of puzzle, piece of the puzzle and how they work with by and for services. (PG2.9)

Legal and Policy Measures to Stop the Reversal on Women's Rights

The doctoral research analysed the impact of the new funding policy (commissioning and procurement) as part of neoliberal measures designed to reshape social services as commercially viable provision. The research focused specifically on sustaining by and for women's refuges in the United Kingdom. The primary data covered the degree to which the new funding policy met the needs of women's refuges ensuring their financial stability and sustainability enabling organisations to respond to emerging needs (women's safe access to refuges after leaving violence) and addressing VAWG in a changing policy landscape driven by open market competition and a rigid contract compliance regime. The feminist rights-based social justice approach embedded in women's services and the intersectional lens applied in by and for organisations is met by the commercialisation of essential services. This tension challenges the feminist ethos of safe space forged around intersecting identities combining race and gender (and other inequalities) where struggle, resistance and a sense of collective solidarity challenge wider structural and systemic inequalities. In this interaction these services are remodelled as commercially viable and cost-effective provision that significantly alters the delivery model from a trauma-informed approach incorporating concepts like empowerment and independence of women through intensive support to one based on throughput to meet quick targets with fewer resources.

Under the new funding policy, a two-tier system of refuge funding emerged as described by PG1 who created independent non-State funded refuges which posed significant financial risk to these organisations however, the decision to operate independently was made to address the risk of decommissioning and to continue to deliver services to groups of women they served. This was a direct consequence of State funding allocated in open competition to generic non-specialist services. This raised questions about perceptions of fairness and equality within the funding system where women's experiences of violence were not centred in the design of tender specifications or included in strategic priorities governing the allocation of resources. The system also failed to address issues of systemic discrimination advocating instead, for statutory pathways (or those more closely aligned to them) for support. The independently funded model created insecurities for organisations while responding to immediate needs. Beyond the financial insecurities, organisations grappled with long-term sustainability including the need for holistic service continuity, ongoing infrastructure development, and meeting salary expectations and flexible HR systems development especially during economic crisis, of a predominantly female workforce.

PG2 in their commissioning role, worked to create the level playing embedding concepts fairness and equality within their thinking and by addressing some of the negative consequences for by and for organisations however PG2 also recognised the limitations of the new funding policy especially in weighing the needs for efficiency and effectiveness while addressing the problem of VAWG against the service delivery ethos advocated by PG1. There was evidence from PG2 on their understanding of the local economy of provision and the role of grassroots organisations such as by and for. Some participants in PG2 responded to this by creating separate lots of funding to enable participation by PG1 without competition from non-specialist providers. The "separate specialist lot solution" was a process similar to ring-fenced funding within a competitive environment however, it was based on the idea of like-for-like organisations "competing" against each other to level the playing field. The research found that while some organisations benefitted from these adjustments, the practice itself was inconsistent with little distinction between specialist and non-specialist services. The deliberate mandate within tender specifications was ill-defined and the focus on VAWG, as a core service requirement, could be easily used by non-specialist services in bidding for contracts.

Two-Tier Provision—Sustaining a Feminist Intersectional and Social Justice Service

In the context of the new funding policy, and the emergence of a two-tier system of refuge provision, the feminist, intersectional and social justice ethos of by and for organisations is safeguarded through the independent model however there is little evidence that this approach is sustainable as suggested by participants in PG1 who were concerned about the financial health of their organisations while acknowledging the temporary boost on the balance sheet during the period of national and global crisis. This raised questions about the degree to which new funding policy is able to meet diverse needs, or does it simply absorb these needs within generically funded provision that addresses the least complex need.

With regards to the latter, the data found that the complexity of need and intersectional concerns of organisations was replaced by economies of scale under the new funding policy. This significantly impacted by and for refuge provision who then created independent approaches to continue their refuge services. However, the new funding policy was built upon a false economy relying on price over quality and through open competition, by and for organisations were undercut in the bidding process through the price they offered (too expensive and therefore unable to produce efficiency). Exploring the false economy further, the data found that by and for organisations operated without full cost recovery thus creating budgetary pressure points and this increased the cost of provision as organisations were being squeezed—receiving consistently less funding to meet higher demand and sustain cost-effective targets. The lack of both FCR and proportionality (the price versus quality equation) were key factors in the new funding policy affecting by and for organisations.

PG2 highlighted the lack of long-term planning to identify commissioning priorities as most commissioning frames were short-term (one year with extension to two or three years) addressing immediate needs. During the period of the fieldwork, emergency funds was released during the COVID pandemic resulting from the short-term nature of the framework. For PG1, this meant that they could be embedded temporarily into the wider funding ecosystem producing immediate financial benefits. The data suggested the need for a more meaningful understanding of the problem of VAWG within a long-term funding solution to ensure stability and sustainability for organisations and to safeguard their ability to meet complex needs and the goals of intersectionality. The short-term nature of funding cycles perpetuated crisis rather than alleviating it thus impacting the ability of organisations to develop a strategic approach.

The market was open for some providers namely the bigger non-specialist providers operating economies of scale and closed for grassroots by and for participation. This also meant that the ideas on social justice, fairness, equality and representation were not dominant in the new funding policy. The exclusion of by and for organisations through the market process is understood as a price versus quality equation based on driving out, the high cost of service delivery and shifting the provision model through neoliberalism away from rights-based work. PG2 discussed safeguards within the funding culture suggesting that it is reactive to crisis prompted by the political situation—responding with COVID emergency funding, reacting to high profile cases of violence against women, and encouraging the State's response to VAWG—hence drawing a critical link between the nature of the political environment, the influence on public opinion and priority-setting in commissioning.

The emergency response and the ability of the system to react to crisis, models an alternative approach to the new funding policy and creates evidence of the positive impact based on the inclusion of organisations responding to diverse needs. These points of crisis were based around concepts such as reasonable consideration of by and for organisations participating in new funding policy as bidders, and fairness and equality albeit these are short lived approaches that are not embedded in policy but rather determined its adaptability to special and emerging circumstances. Finally, the data found evidence of the changing roles managed by PG2 during points of multiples crisis navigating between the gatekeeping commissioner operating systems of expediency (prompted by a partnership approach as solutions to competition-driven funding policy for smaller organisations) ensuring cost effectiveness to a strategic stakeholder and collaborator working to end VAWG alongside the sector.

The new funding policy required organisations to be competition-ready and to remodel their services. This required some degree of shift to ensure involvement in the system, rather than outright change to delivery models, as well as financial compromises (reductions on salaries, overheads and infrastructure). While some change was welcome such as the introduction of quality and professional standards it was more difficult for organisations to change, adapt or alter their service delivery ethos as this formed their identity around women's rights and equality. This created an uneasy tension for organisations who required resources to deliver their services and at the same time, understand that outcomes for women were driven by the ethos they held such as prevention of repeat victimisation, addressing the risk of death by homicide and suicide, responding to suicidal ideation by women subjected to VAWG and the risk of violence escalation. These outcomes were integrally linked to the ethos held by organisations and achieved through intensive women-centred trauma-informed that was challenged under the new funding policy.

Addressing Gaps and Omissions under the Neoliberal Approach to Funding Policy

The data found that the new funding policy and the neoliberal approach to commissioning and contracting services is likely to remain. Both groups of participants grappled with ways to address the gaps and omissions in policy and the consequences such as exclusion that the policy embedded. However, this was also a question of proportionality and reasonability (discussed above). The data found that for both groups, long-term sustainable funding solutions addressing VAWG and funding by and for (as well as WSS services) was needed. These solutions could consider investment in core support to sustainability efforts by organisations; a return to local authority grant funding replacing the contracts model introduced under commissioning; the outright removal of VAWG services from public procurement recognising these services as delivering rights-based support addressing women's equality; a financial settlement taking a comprehensive and holistic approach to resourcing considerations and meeting diverse needs (centring Black and minoritised and other groups of women); and for PG2, where new funding policy operated, an inclusive commissioning approach involving these services based on a deliberate mandate and recognition of VAWG as both a historical and core function of these services.

There was more synergy in the ways of thinking about the new funding policy between the two groups of participants as they argued for adjustments enabling organisations to participate as feminist and women's rights organisations. The emergency response to the COVID pandemic is a useful example here demonstrating how a reformed system of funding could operate where feminist social justice services could be recognised as operating a rights-based provision however, success is dependent upon the suspension of new funding policy for women's rights-based services. To achieve this, PG1 suggested that funding should model future need with the specific objective to end VAWG; that commissioners should take a longer-term view around resourcing decisions; and that the role of commissioners was to work to end VAWG by focusing on the dedicated commitment of resources. PG2 agreed however, suggested that within commissioning, outcomes should ensure the sustainability of refuges through longer-term solutions which would mean less frequent commissioning activity and ring-fenced commissioning ensuring the participation of by and for (and WSS) services. PG2 also suggested a wider review of commissioning principles with the aim to centre social justice values within new funding policy, and by developing less contentious and more collaborative systems.

This research was done to consider the impact of the new funding policy on vital women's services, specifically addressing the need for safe refuges. The research focused on by and for organisations as these were most targeted under neoliberal policy funding cuts. The threat to the by and for sector and Black and minoritised women who use services is not just a financial threat for survival, but it is compounded by a hostile environment that presents barriers to support for many groups of women. The new funding policy is also implemented during a time of backlash against women's rights and in women's spaces where women receive the support they need, to address the harms of violence and move-on to achieve economic and social independence. The backlash, as evidenced in the new funding policy, favours a neutral approach to funding that is, it fails to recognise the role of vital women's services in offering life-saving support to women subjected to VAWG, the service ethos that embeds women's equality and the need for by and for services that incorporate the intersectional lens. Providers of frontline by and for services and commissioners agree that a better solution is possible by centring women's representations within policy. The research concludes that the new funding policy fails in meeting the needs of diverse groups of women and an alternative funding model is needed.

Bibliography

Statutes

Domestic Abuse Act 2021, https://www.legislation.gov.uk/ukpga/2021/17/contents (accessed 2 March 2025).

Articles and Book Chapters

Lilley-Walker, SJ, Hester, M and P Rumney, 2019. "Rape, Inequality and the Criminal Justice Response in England. The Importance of Age and Gender", *Criminology and Criminal Justice*. 21:3, 297–315, https://doi.org/10.1177/1748895819863095 (accessed 2 March 2025).

Rees, J, 2014. "Public Sector Commissioning and the Third Sector: Old Wine, New Bottle?" *Public Policy and Administration*. 29:1, 45–63.

Vachelli, E, Kathrecha, P and N Gyte, 2015. "Open Space is it Really Just Cuts? Neo-liberal Tales from the Women's Voluntary and Community Sector in London", *Feminist Review*. 109:1, 180–189.

Books and Reports

Adisa, O, 2020. *Professionals' Perception of MARACs and Barriers to Attendance: Headline Findings from the "Are MARACs Still Fit for Purpose" Survey*. University of Suffolk, https://www.researchgate.net/publication/343745206_Professionals%27_perceptions_of_MARACs_and_barriers_to_attendance_Headline_findings_from_the_%27Are_MARACs_still_fit_for_purpose%27_survey_Briefing_paper (accessed 2 August 2025).

Adisa, O, Allen, K, Kumari, M, Weir, R and E Bond, 2020. *Mapping the Funding Ecosystem in England and Wales*. Suffolk. University of Suffolk.

Barter, C, Bracewell, K, Stanley, N and K Chantler, 2018. *Scoping Study: Violence Against Women and Girls*. Lancashire. University of Central Lancashire.

Hilditch, M, 2018. *Shelter Chief Warns Associations are Damaging Local Women's refuges*. Inside Housing. 2 May.

King, D, Chan, O, Coule, T, Dahill, D, Mainard-Sardon, J, Martin, A, Rossiter, W, Smith, S, Stuart, J, Vahidi, G and N Ibokessien, 2022. *Respond. Reset, Recover: Two Years On*. Nottingham. Nottingham Business School, https://cpwop.org.uk/what-we-do/projects-and-publications/covid-19-vcse-organisation-responses/ (accessed 2 August 2025).

Local Government Association (LGA). 2008. *Ring Fence Removed from Supporting People*, LocalGov, https://www.localgov.co.uk/Ring-fencing-removed-from-supporting-people/31127 (accessed 2 March 2025).

Local Government Association (LGA), 2022. *The Councillor's Workbook on Commissioning Services*. London. LGA.

Magnusson, L and S Davidge, 2020. *The Domestic Abuse Report 2020: The Hidden Housing Crisis*. Bristol. WAFE.

Ministry of Housing, Communities and Local Government (MHCLG), 2019. *Future Delivery of Support to Victims and Their Children in Accommodation-based Domestic Abuse Services: Consultation Responses*. London. OGL.

Sainsbury, R and Oldman, C, 2001. *The Transitional Housing Benefit Scheme: A Three-Way Process*. York. University of York. Social Policy Research Unit and Centre for Housing Policy, https://eprints.whiterose.ac.uk/id/eprint/73457/1/Document.pdf (accessed 2 August 2025).

Sisters for Change, 2017. *Unequal Regard, Unequal Protection. Public Authority Responses to Violence Against BME Women in England*. London. Sisters for Change.

Steel, N, Blakeborough, L and S Nicholas, 2011. Supporting High Risk Victims of Domestic Violence: A Review of Multi-agency Risk Assessment Conference (MARACs), https://www.researchgate.net/publication/332320398_Supporting_high-risk_victims_of_domestic_violence_a_review_of_

Multi-Agency_Risk_Assessment_Conferences_MARACs (accessed 2 March 2025).
True, J, 2012. *The Political Economy of Violence*. Oxford, UK, Oxford University Press.
WAFE, 2020. *Domestic Abuse Annual Report*. Bristol, UK, WAFE.

Information Documents and Resources

Banga, B, 2025. The Impact of the New Funding Policy (Commissioning and Procurement) on Women's Refuges in the United Kingdom. PhD Thesis. Bath. School of Social and Policy Sciences. Institute of Policy Research. University of Bath.
Charities Commission. 2021. COVID 19 Survey. London. Charities Commission.
Jarrett, T, 2012. *The Supporting People Programme*. Research Paper 12/40. Westminster, London, UK, House of Commons Library.

17

Women and Property: An Early Literary Response

Robin R. Joyce

Introduction

For Richer, for Poorer: Money, Marriage and Property Rights by Jocelynne A Scutt and Di Graham was published in 1984. The cover shows a newly married couple performing the traditional cake cutting ceremony. On top of the cake is a house, through which the knife slices cleanly, decisively in the hands of the couple. In another slice or two they will equally distribute the car on the second layer, and the $ at the bottom. The reality is somewhat different: a smiling couple does not distribute the property of the marriage cleanly and equally; a woman's ownership is not always recognised—victims of domestic violence are advised that they should leave the home. Scutt and Graham's book argues that legal and social recognition of women's property rights is essential. That the book was published in Australia some 40 years ago does not render this

R. R. Joyce (✉)
Independent Scholar, Canberra, Australia
e-mail: robrjo6@gmail.com

J. A. Scutt (ed.), *Women, Power and Autonomy*,
https://doi.org/10.1007/978-3-031-97958-3_17

"old news." Today women's contribution to marital assets remains a field of contention.

At times young women's literature has embodied the idea that women and girls can own property and can make decisions about property. Some of this literature was read from as early as the 1940s.[1] Some authors validate girls' and women's ownership of property; many recognise the importance of women's impact on property; some refer to the influence of economic independence or marriage. Property and its relevance to women is given significance through detailed descriptions of the properties and the characters' connection to it. Authors who were available in Australian school libraries during the 1950s and 60s, and to young women in Canada, America and Britain[2] who acknowledged women's right to property were the Australian, Mary Grant Bruce; Canadian, LM Montgomery; and the British writers, Elsie J Oxenham and Roberta Moss.

Land, Property Ownership and Connection

Mary Grant Bruce's Billabong books acknowledge the reality that Billabong is family property that the male heir will inherit. "Billabong" appears in many of the titles. While no ownership is implied, they make a strong association of character and property by linking characters with titles in the following instances: *Norah of Billabong*, *Bill of Billabong*, *Mates of Billabong*, *Billabong's Daughter*, *Billabong Riders* and *Son of Billabong*. In contrast with the reality, Norah is associated with the property in the titles more than any other character.

Billabong is described throughout the novels, demonstrating Grant Bruce's concern with the magnitude of the property surrounds as well as the rambling house, and later her emphasis on Norah's right to a Billabong homestead, if not the original.

The first book in the series is *A Little Bush Maid*, acknowledging the importance of Norah whose story dominates much of the series.

[1] Appendix.

[2] Appendix.

Although Norah cannot inherit, Grant Bruce bestows upon her putative ownership of Billabong, giving the main female character a strong connection with property. This connection becomes more domestic as the series progresses and Norah attains young adulthood. Upon their marriage, she and her husband become the owners of Little Billabong, maintaining some links with the main property through name and propinquity.

The English writers' property introduces the romanticism of a castle, abbey and manor, reflecting the class-based society with its greater distinctions than Canada and Australia. The British Abbey Girl series by Elsie J Oxenham gives primacy to property and women's agency in the main characters' lives. Cousins, Joan and Joy live at the Abbey where Joan's mother is the caretaker. Nearby is Abinger Hall, where Joy's previously estranged grandfather, Sir Anthony, resides. Upon his death, fifteen-year-old Joy inherits the Hall where she, Joan and her mother then live. Joy's inheritance relies on the death of the male heir. Joan inherits the Abbey and its grounds because of her love and knowledge of the property and enthusiasm for imparting this to visitors.

Both girls' inheritances are described throughout the novels and reiteration of their ownership is an essential part of the cousins' depiction when meeting new friends. For example, in *Strangers at the Abbey*, the massive dimensions of the land and building are highlighted. Initially the building cannot be seen because of the expansive lawns, there is an orchard of blossoming apple trees, and a winding road, gated before reaching a beech lined carriageway where leaves have fallen for years on the ground, and all this leads to a home park and a garden. When it comes into view the mansion is described as having a terrace, mullioned windows and a "great door" opening into the "great hall" with dark furniture, long stained glass, coats of arms and a "wide staircase leading to a gallery" (Oxenham, *Strangers at the Abbey*, 57). Joy's marriage does not affect her relationship with the Hall as it remains her home. The Abbey is partially a ruin but has historical status as well as housing jewels found by the schoolgirls. Joan leaves the Abbey upon marriage, but her connection with it remains intact.

Land, Property Ownership and Inheritance

Roberta Moss wrote three novels, featuring Jenny Fairfax as the main protagonist, closely followed by Lorna Adair, the heir to a castle. Although Lorna's ownership is overturned, the new owner is another young woman, the previously lost heiress, Isabel Courtenay. The resolution fits the schoolgirl-reader nature of this trilogy, the three girls living at the castle with the newly married couple, Jenny's aunt and Lorna's father. However, the owner of Courtenay Castle is indubitably Isabel Courtenay.

Although her relationship with property is changed, Lorna's diminished financial situation is short lived. Her independently wealthy aunt, a newspaper owner, makes Lorna her heir. The Moss books not only give the castle a woman owner, but another is media mogul with a female heir.

There are some descriptive passages, but these novels concentrate on schoolgirl adventures as well as the ownership tangle. The castle description features in the first novel where the most important point made is the gallery of portraits, about to become the source of Lorna's loss and Isabelle's gain. (Moss, *Jenny of the Fourth*, 19–23)

LM Montgomery novels are the strongest in imparting a strong sense of women's connection to property, their right to be owners, a beneficiary of a will or inherited property, love for property resulting in their independent care for it, and contributors to the purchase of property. The Canadian works also deal well with the sexual division of property ownership. In the Anne of Green Gables series Anne Shirley's changing status demonstrates the impact of marriage; in contrast, *Jane of Lantern Hill* places Jane, the daughter of separated parents, in an equal relationship with her father in choosing a property and taking charge of what happens there. *Magic for Marigold* uses a great grandmother's talk with her great granddaughter, Marigold, to explain the role of inheritance. *Pat of Silver Bush* explores Pat's dedication to the family farm and its house which takes over her life. The *Emily of New Moon* trilogy shows Emily's dependence on marrying a male inheritor to remain in a beloved home, and her determination to be independent. *The Blue Castle* features an imaginary dwelling, which becomes a reality in a marriage chosen by Valancy, the central character.

Anne leaves an orphanage to live at Green Gables with Marilla and Mathew Cuthbert. Green Gables is described as:

> … a big, rambling, orchard-embowered house …The kitchen at Green Gables was a cheerful apartment — or would have been cheerful if it had not been so painfully clean as to give it something of the appearance of an unused parlor. Its windows looked east and west; through the west one, looking out on the back yard, came a flood of mellow June sunlight; but the east one, whence you got a glimpse of the bloom white cherry-trees in the left orchard and nodding, slender birches down in the hollow by the brook, was greened over by a tangle of vines. (Montgomery, *Anne of Green Gables*, 3)

Inside the house:

> The hall was fearsomely clean; the little gable chamber in which she presently found herself seemed still cleaner… The whitewashed walls were so painfully bare and staring that she thought they must ache over their own bareness. The floor was bare, too, except for a round braided mat in the middle such as Anne had never seen before. In one corner was the bed, a high, old-fashioned one, with four dark, low-turned posts. In the other corner was the aforesaid three-corner table adorned with a fat, red velvet pin-cushion hard enough to turn the point of the most adventurous pin. Above it hung a little six-by-eight mirror. Midway between table and bed was the window, with an icy white muslin frill over it, and opposite it was the wash-stand. The whole apartment was of a rigidity not to be described in words … (28–29)

Anne's agency is asserted initially though her adorning her room with branches, and eventually she makes it her own.

Anne's education is a continuing theme. She recognises that to follow her aspirations she must leave her beloved friend, Diana, behind, choosing teaching as her career and a future that is based developing beyond life at Green Gables. Anne's first role in determining the fate of property reorders her priorities. She uses her teaching certificate to work rather than study for her Bachelor of Arts to ensure that Marilla keeps Green Gables after Mathew's death. This is Anne's last independent connection with property.

Marriage to Gilbert Blythe makes a difference. Gilbert chooses where he will work; joining his uncle in his medical practice makes sense. However, Gilbert also chooses the first house in which he and Anne will live. One proviso that needs to be acknowledged, is distance and the time it takes to travel what would be considered short distances today. Anne does not travel with Gilbert until they are married, and she arrives at her house of dreams, described by Gilbert as:

> … a little white house on the harbor shore, half way between Glen St. Mary and Four Winds Point…The situation is beautiful. It looks to the sunset and has the great blue harbor before it. [It is] Not very large, but large enough for us. There's a splendid living room with a fireplace in it downstairs, and a dining room that looks out on the harbor, and a little room that will do for my office. It is about sixty years old--the oldest house in Four Winds. But it has been kept in pretty good repair, and was all done over about fifteen years ago--shingled, plastered and re-floored. (Montgomery, *Anne's House of Dreams*, 14–15)

Anne's response sets her priorities, and these are met:

> The first glimpse of her new home was a delight to eye and spirit--it looked so like a big, creamy seashell stranded on the harbor shore. The rows of tall Lombardy poplars down its lane stood out in stately, purple silhouette against the sky. Behind it, sheltering its garden from the too keen breath of sea winds, was a cloudy fir wood, in which the winds might make all kinds of weird and haunting music… The door of the little house opened, and a warm glow of firelight flickered out into the dusk. (38)

However, it is also apparent that over time Anne's independent relationship with property is further diminished. When "the house of dreams" becomes too small, Gilbert decides that the family should move. The discussion is a meeting of equals, but those equals having a very different relationship to work and economic independence. Anne's opinion is sought, but she has lost her agency in choosing property, defending it on her own or someone else's behalf. Gilbert decides to buy Ingleside, then discusses the decision with Anne. She is not pleased but the move is determined by the family size and Gibert's job. However, eventually:

> ... I found little rootlets of affection for Ingleside beginning to sprout out...It isn't too old a house . . . too old houses are sad. And it isn't too young . . . too young houses are crude. It's just mellow. I love every room in it. Every one has some fault but also some virtue . . . something that distinguishes it from all the others . . . gives it a personality. I love all those magnificent trees on the lawn...every time I go upstairs I stop on the landing ... you know that quaint window on the landing with the broad deep seat ... and sit there looking out for a moment and ...bless the man who planted those trees whoever he was. (Montgomery, *Anne of Ingleside*, 11–12)

Ingleside is a house to which she wants to return after a holiday at Green Gables:

> Her heart sang all the way because she was going home to a joyous house... rooms that would welcome her... where the chairs waited patiently and the dresses in her closet were expecting her . ... Ingleside was all lighted up, with gay Japanese lanterns hanging on the veranda. Anne ran gaily along the walk bordered by daffodils. (15)

Land, Property Ownership and Economic Power

Economic power over property in these books is alleviated by their titles: *Anne's House of Dreams* and *Anne of Ingleside*. Whether LM Montgomery's writing had a particular feminist intent is not clear.[3] However, girls and women were central figures and had some agency over property,

---

[3] Since 1961 no fewer than 114 theses or dissertations are reported to have been written about LM Montgomery and her work (Lefebvre 2007/2025) and analyses that consider her and her work as feminist, or that critique her life and work through a feminist lens, are included in the many published works relating to her as an important Canadian writer and identity. See for example Pike and Robins (2021); Pacheco (2021).

giving readers every opportunity to interpret the titles as defining Anne's central role in decision-making about the properties in which she lives.

The *Pat of Silver Bush* series introduces a daughter to whom the farmhouse, Silver Bush, is an enduring love and occupation. The house becomes a point of contention when her brother, heir to the farm and house, marries Pat's school hood adversary. This series again underlines the reality that men are more likely to inherit property.

Pat's home, Silver Bush, is in the title of both books in association with Pat. The house is lovingly described as seen through Pat's eyes:

> … How beautiful it was, nestled against its wooden hill, as if it had grown out of it . . . a house all white and green, just like its own silver birches, and now patterned over charmingly with tree shadows cast by a moon that was floating over the Hill of the Mist. She always loved to stand outside of Silver Bush after dark and look at its lighted windows. There was a light in the kitchen… a light in the parlor… a light up in mother's room. A light for a moment flashed in the hall, as somebody went upstairs, bringing out the fan window over the front door. "Oh, I've got such a lovely home," breathed Pat, clasping her hands. "It's such a nice friendly house. Nobody . . . nobody . . . has such a lovely home…" (Montgomery, *Pat of Silver Bush*, 22)

Pat's dream that she and her brother remain unmarried at Silver Bush is unrealistic, but her having to accept reality is short lived when Silver Bush burns down. The siblings lose the property and must accept alternatives—the male heir a new house built on Silver Bush foundations and Pat a new house designed for her by her long-term architect friend and eventual husband, Hilary.

Hilary's intervention introduces another type of property ownership. Rather than Pat being depicted as the independent owner of property, this instance mirrors the way in which property ownership by a female protagonist is dealt with in *The Blue Castle*. For Pat, a dream and obsession are replaced with a reality of equal partners in a house with her as its inspiration. Like the example in *Pat of Silver Bush*, Valancy's blue castle dream is also changed through her marriage.

Valancy's blue castle is described in several ways. It is first an imaginary escape from her real home, contrasting with an ugly, small bedroom over which she has no control, in a house dominated by her widowed mother and aunt. Then it becomes a manifestation of that dream, much reduced in grandeur, described by Barney as:

> The jolliest place in the world…a little shack [on an island that he owns]…the lean-to…[with the] door locked…one big living room and one small bedroom…Well built…The beams…are cedar and the rafters fir…the living room windows face west and east…you can see both sunrise and sunset… (Montgomery, *The Blue Castle*, 192–193)

When the blue castle is seen through Valancy's eyes it is given a reality that is hers alone:

> Valancy looked - and looked again. There was a diaphanous lilac mist on the lake, shrouding the island. Through it two enormous pine-trees that clasped hands over Barney's shack loomed out like dark turrets. Behind them was a sky still rose-hued in the afterlight. Valancy shivered…"My blue castle!…Oh, my blue castle". (193–195)

In acquiring her "blue castle" Valancy is drawn as a woman with agency. Not only has she proposed to Barney but in doing so achieves the dream with which she has erased her past lack of control over property. Shared the blue castle may be, but her independent ownership is suggested through the realisation of her ideal in circumstances that she influenced.

Magic for Marigold and *Jane of Lantern Hill* also demonstrate women's control over property. Marigold is only 6 years of age—very young to be acknowledged as a property owner, or in this case, heir. Jane is 12 years of age, significantly the age around which readers might gather.

Marigold inherits because there are no male descendants in the Lesley clan. The property is:

> Cloud of Spruce, the original Lesley homestead…on the harbour shore, far enough out of Harmony village to be in the real country; a cream brick house — a nice chubby old house — so covered with vines that it looked more like a heap of ivy than a house; a house that had folded its hands and said, "I will rest." Before it was the beautiful Harmony Harbour; with its purring waves, so close that in autumnal storms the spray dashed over

> the very doorsteps and encrusted the windows. Behind it was an orchard that climbed the slope. (Montgomery, *Magic for Marigold*, 2)

Great Grandmother tells her:

> Cloud of Spruce will be yours some day, Marigold… And you must always love it. Places know when they're loved — just the same as people. I've seen houses whose hearts were actually broken. This house and I have always been good friends. I've always loved it from the day I came here as a bride. I planted most of those trees. You must marry some day, Marigold, and fill those old rooms again. But not too young — not too young. I married at seventeen and I was a grandmother at thirty-six. It was awful. Sometimes it seems to me that I've always been a grandmother. (75)

The title, *Jane of Lantern Hill*, acknowledges Jane's connection to the property while not necessarily being the owner. She is a significant decision-maker—deciding upon the purchase of the property, the allocation of the rooms, and the domestic tasks that are undertaken within the property. Her initial choice is dependent on her father's economic capacity rather than hers, but while he moots finding a house for the summer she decides on the house:

> Jane saw the house first, at least she saw the upstairs window in its gable end winking at her over the top of a hill… And then, right before them, was the house . . . their house! …It squatted right against a little steep hill whose toes were lost in bracken. It was small…It had a garden, with a stone dike at the lower end of it to keep it from sliding down the hill, a paling and a gate, with two tall white birches leaning over it, and a flat-stone walk up to the only door, which had eight small panes of glass in its upper half. The door was locked but they could see in at the windows. There was a good-sized room on one side of the door, stairs going up right in front of it, and two small rooms on the other side whose windows looked right into the side of the hill where ferns grew as high as your waist, and there were stones lying about covered with velvet green moss. (Montgomery, *Jane of Lantern Hill*, 96)

The detailed description of house and environs confirms the importance of Jane's discovery:

> On one side of the house was a clover field and on the other a maple grove, sprinkled with firs and spruces, and separated from the house lot by an old, lichen-covered board fence. There was an apple-tree in the corner of the yard, with pink petals falling softly, and a clump of old spruces outside the garden gate. "I like the pattern of this place," said Jane. …Jane had been so taken up with her house that she had not looked at the view at all. Now she turned her eyes on it and lost her breath over it. Never, never had she seen . . . had she dreamed anything so wonderful. Lantern Hill was at the apex of a triangle of land which had the gulf for its base and Queen's Harbour for one of its sides...And over it all the indefinable charm of a Prince Edward Island landscape. Just below Lantern Hill, skirted by spruce barrens on the harbour side and a pasture field on the other, was a little pond . . . absolutely the bluest thing that Jane had ever seen…She had never been there before, but it seemed as if she had known it all her life. The song the sea-wind was singing was music native to her ears. She had always wanted to "belong" somewhere, and she belonged here. At last she had a feeling of home. "Well, what about it?" said dad … (96–98)

Jane's agency is confirmed when she not only combats her father's concerns but is handed the key:

> "Jane, I have a suspicion that the roof leaks." "You can put some shingles on it." "There's a lot of burdocks in the yard." "We can root them out." "The house may have once been white . . ." "It can be white again." "The paint on the front door is blistered." "Paint doesn't cost very much, does it?" "The shutters are broken." "Let's fix them." "The plaster is cracked." "We can paper over it." "Who knows if there's a pantry, Jane?" "There are shelves in one of the little rooms on the right. I can use that for a pantry…"(98)
>
> Jane clutched [the key] tightly all the way back to Brookview… Think what it would open for her…There were three rooms upstairs . . . a quite large one to the north, which Jane decided at once must be father's. … I want this dear little one at the back. I want a little room, dad… Everything she looked at belonged to dad and her. She was mistress of

> this house — her right there was none to dispute. She could do just as she wanted to without making excuses for anything. (100–105)

Jane also decides upon the house she and her reunited parents will own:

> Jane thought of the little stone house in Lakeside Gardens. It had not been sold yet. They would buy it. "Oh, dad," cried this happiest of all Janes, "I know the very house." "You would," said dad". (271)

Land, Property Ownership and Woman-as-Property

Emily of New Moon, *Emily Climbs* and *Emily's Quest* is a trilogy that raises a host of issues related to property, including the complex one of women as property. Like *Anne of Green Gables*, the trilogy begins with a young girl arriving at a house with land comprising orchards, a dairy farm, and potato crops. The property to which Emily can never be an heir is described in detail, as is the one that she will eventually own, the "disappointed house".

Marriage is an important factor in whether Emily can live at New Moon after the death of her spinster aunt's ownership of the farm. Montogomery deals with Emily's dilemma elegantly. The disappointed house becomes hers after she rejects the man with whom she furnished it in preparation for their marriage. This relationship is one that Montgomery writes as a feminist demand for a woman's right to independence, to be seen as herself rather than the property of a man. The depiction of Emily brings two images of property that impact on a woman's life: her as a man's property, and her eventual ownership of the house in which the couple were to live. Emily eventually does marry, but this relationship is one of equals. Emily retains ownership of the former disappointed house, in the story as far as it goes. Emily's first choice that she should own property independently is highlighted when, although she refuses to leave beloved New Moon to follow a career in New York, she refuses the heir's marriage proposal. She recognises that he would ignore her opinions about New Moon. (Montgomery, *Emily's Quest*, 150)

Emily loves things as much as she loves people, and the fields around New Moon, the woods with names she has crafted to denote the ageing of the paths through which she and her friends wander, and Cousin Jimmy's garden are part of her world.

Emily's first sight of New Moon is:

> … through a veil of tall old trees - no mushroom growth of yesterday's birches but trees that had loved and been loved by three generations - a glimpse of silver water glistening through the dark spruces - that was the Blair Water itself, she knew - and a tall, golden-white church spire shooting up above the maple woods in the valley below. But it was none of these that brought her the flash--that came with the sudden glimpse of the dear, friendly, little dormer window peeping through vines on the roof… (Montgomery, *Emily of New Moon*, 63)
>
> She sat on a long wooden bench that was satin-smooth with age and scrubbing, and watched Aunt Elizabeth lighting candles here and there, in great, shining, brass candlesticks--on the shelf between the windows, on the high dresser where the row of blue and white plates began to wink her a friendly welcome, on the long table in the corner. And as she lighted them, elvish "rabbits' candles" flashed up amid the trees outside the windows. Emily had never seen a kitchen like this before. It had dark wooden walls…
>
> The sanded floor was spotlessly white, but the boards had been scrubbed away through the years until the knots in them stuck up all over in funny little bosses, and in front of the stove they had sagged, making a queer, shallow little hollow. In one corner of the ceiling was a large square hole which looked black and spookish in the candlelight [one of the Murray traditions] and made her feel creepy.
>
> … the sitting-room was much more cheerful than the kitchen. The floor was covered with gay-striped homespun, the table had a bright crimson cloth, the walls were hung with pretty, diamond-patterned paper, the curtains were of wonderful pale-red damask with a design of white ferns scattered all over them. They looked very rich and imposing and Murray-like. Emily had never seen such curtains before. But best of all were the friendly gleams and flickers from the jolly hardwood fire in the open stove

> that mellowed the ghostly candlelight with something warm and rosy-golden… What lovely little leaded glass doors closed the china closets on either side of the high, black, polished mantel! (63–65)

Emily becomes acquainted with more of the physical aspects of her new home, and its history:

> Everything was fascinating from the moment she came down the long, polished staircase into the square hall that was filled with a soft, rosy light coming through the red glass panes of the front door. Emily gazed through the panes delightedly…There was a certain charm about the old house which Emily felt keenly and responded to, although she was too young to understand it. It was a house which aforetime had had vivid brides and mothers and wives, and the atmosphere of their loves and lives still hung around it, not yet banished by the old-maidishness of the regime of Elizabeth and Laura. "Why--I'm going to love New Moon" …(73)
> Delicious smells were coming from the cook-house--a little, slant-roofed building at the corner where the big cooking-stove was placed in summer. It was thickly overgrown with hop vines, as most of the New Moon buildings were. To the right was the "new" orchard, very wonderful now in The blossom, but a rather commonplace spot after all, since Cousin Jimmy cultivated it in most up-to-date fashion and had grain growing in the wide spaces between the straight rows of trees that looked all alike. But on the other side of the barn lane, just behind the well, was the "old orchard," where Cousin Jimmy said the columbines grew and which seemed to be a delightful place where trees had come up at their own sweet will, and grown into individual shapes and sizes, where blue-eyed ivy twined about their roots and wild-briar roses rioted over the grey paling fence. Straight ahead, closing the vista between the orchards, was a little slope covered with huge white birches, among which were the big New Moon barns, and beyond the new orchard a little, lovable red road looped lightly up and up, over a hill, until it seemed to touch the vivid blue of the sky. (75)
>
> Emily looked about her with delight. The garden was lovely and the house quite splendid to her childish eyes. It had a big front porch with Grecian

> columns. These were thought very elegant in Blair Water, and went far to justify the Murray pride. A schoolmaster had said they gave the house a classical air. To be sure, the classical effect was just now rather smothered in hop-vines that rioted over the whole porch and hung in pale-green festoons above the rows of potted scarlet geraniums that flanked the step-s…It's a noble house, she said. "And what about my garden?" demanded Cousin Jimmy jealously. "It's fit for a queen," said Emily, gravely and sincerely. (81–82)

Emily's room is her writing haven—by candlelight, in keeping with Murray tradition. Because of her love for New Moon and its surrounds, she refuses the opportunity to follow a writing career opportunity in New York:

> What charm and dignity and fineness the old rooms had, with their candles and their ladder backed chairs and their braided rugs! How dear and entreating was her own little room with its diamond paper and its guardian angel, its fat black rose-jar and its funny kinky window pane!...How beautiful was this old garden…How beautiful was old New Moon farm!...How could she leave this old house that had sheltered her and loved her…the graves of her kin…the wide fields and haunted woods … (*Emily Climbs*, 300–301)

She believes that she can succeed while living at New Moon and, in this novel dedicated to seeing young women as capable of success as well as property ownership, of course she does.

Emily dreams of buying the disappointed house when as children, she and her future husband, Teddy, kindle a fire in the fireplace in an unfinished room. Emily's early determination to be independent is foreshadowed when she rejects the idea that they would need to be married to buy the house together.

The disappointed house's importance is demonstrated by the detailed description early in *Emily of New Moon*, it is:

> Off to the right, on the crest of a steep little hill, covered with young birches and firs, was a house that puzzled and intrigued Emily. It was grey and weather-worn…Why had it never been finished? And it was meant to

> be such a pretty little house--a house you could love--a house where there would be nice chairs and cosy fires and bookcases and lovely, fat, purry cats and unexpected corners; then and there she named it the Disappointed House, and many an hour thereafter did she spend finishing that house, furnishing it as it should be furnished… (Montgomery, *Emily of New Moon*, 77–78)

Later, as a young adult she walks alone to the house and wishes that she owned it. After her engagement to Dean Priest, he tells her that he has bought it:

> … their house. A house with the mystery of woods behind it and around it, except on the south side where the land fell away in a long hill looking down on the Blair Water, that was like a bowl of dull gold now, and across it to meadows of starry rest beyond and the Derry Pond Hills that were as blue and romantic as the famous Alsatian Mountains. Between the house and the view, but not hiding it, was a row of wonderful Lombardy poplars. They climbed the hill to the gate of a little enclosed garden — a garden far older than the house which had been built on the site of a little log cabin of pioneer days…She looked at the Disappointed House adoringly. Such a dear thoughtful little house. Not an old house — she liked it for that — an old house knew too much — was haunted by too many feet that had walked over its threshold — too many anguished or impassioned eyes that had looked out of its windows. This house was ignorant and innocent like herself. Longing for happiness. It should have it…(Montgomery, *Emily Climbs*, 72–73)

The couple furnish it together:

> … doing everything possible themselves and fixing it up exactly as they wanted it… They replaced the old, unused, temporary board steps, left by the carpenters thirty years before, with broad, red sandstones from the shore. Dean had casement windows put in with diamond shaped panes… And he added a dear little window over the front door with a little roof over it like a shaggy eyebrow and in the living-room they had a French window from which you could step right out into the fir wood. And Dean had jewels of closets and cupboards put in everywhere... Emily

> insisted on papering [the room] with a shadowy grey paper with snowy pine branches over it. (74–76)

The description of Emily's belongings provides another aspect of inheritance and property ownership when her mother's belongings are given to her:

> … long undisturbed boxes and chests, china and silver …some lovely things among them — especially a priceless pink lustre jug and a delightful old dinner-set of real willow-ware… the Chippendale sideboard and the claw-footed mahogany table [from] New Moon were Emily's... Emily brought her [favourite pictures] up, including the Lady Giovanna and Mona Lisa…Emily put the chessy-cat on the front porch door of the Disappointed House and hung the great silvery gazing-ball from the Venetian lantern… They locked the door of the Disappointed House one November evening and Dean gave the key to Emily. "Keep it till spring," he said …(76–84)

The handing over of the key replicates Jane's ownership of the key to the house at Lantern Hill and foreshadows Emily's eventual ownership of the disappointed house. When she breaks her engagement she is released from bondage:

> "… Emily, I give your life back to you. It has been mine, remember, since I saved you that day on Malvern rocks. It's your own again …"
> "Dean — here is the key." Dean shook his head. "Keep it till I ask for it". (96)

Dean eventually gives her the deeds, but at the moment she and her readers believe she has lost the house, Emily buys her own property with her earnings from writing—Lofty John's wood which has protected the New Moon and its garden. The wood is the source of an old feud which one of Emily's adventures stirs up into a threat to demolish it. Emily's successful bid to save the wood then is the success of a child, but nevertheless her action retains the beauty and comfort of the property she loves. As an adult with an income from her writing she is able to pay for it:

> I bought it to-day, with the proceeds of my latest serial. And it is mine — mine — mine… No one can ever cut it down or desecrate it in any way. (157)

Conclusion

Each of the writers gave the girls who read their books the opportunity to see themselves as the owners of property or at least the decision makers about property. In many cases economic independence is a factor in the characters' ability to have an impact on the purchase of property or decision-making about property, and this is the essential factor in today's reality. This applies to inheritance or having an independent income. However, this is not to say that the possibly romanticised version of control over property illustrated in *Jane of Lantern Hill* would not have been instrumental in influencing young women's beliefs about their right to property. Women and girls in the books were represented as concerned and knowledgeable about land and property, ownership and inheritance.

Whether the young women readers were influenced is not able to be answered, although one might surmise that women's activism in the 1970s, as well as being based in family influences, schooling, and engagement with a socio-political world, had some foundation in their reading of these perceptive writers. Women of the 1970s confronted head-on the requirement by banks and finance companies that a man's signature must accompany theirs on a mortgage or borrowings, as a woman's signature was considered insufficient (Warren 2009): today the ignominy of their second class citizenship continues to insult, popular media being replete with reflections such as this, the lead-in statement being "remember 50 years ago …," remarking on the struggle to end this imposition (Brownson 2021; also Bulbeck 1997, 1988). Upon marriage and purchase of the family home, they considered whether joint ownership or tenancy in common of the matrimonial home was better (Scutt and Graham 1984; Gov.UK nd). They laughed wryly at real estate agents' assumptions that they could not possibly earn sufficient to buy property unaided by a superior male income.[4] 1970s women's resistance to their demotion into a minority-like status, their demands for personhood and recognition of their independent identity, could have arisen out of their juvenile reading and the representation of women and girls' understanding of the importance of land and property, the risk they ran of being deprive of it or never being considered as entitled to it, yet their determination not to be demoted from their right to connection with land and property and potential economic power. Whatever the truth in that regard, it is certainly the case that writers such as Mary Grant Bruce, LM Montogomery, Roberta Moss and Elsie J Oxenham gave property ownership and control a significance in their novels which should be recognised.

Appendix

I posted this notice on the Facebook Historical Fiction Group:

> I'm researching young people's fiction from the 1950s. My junior high school library included LM Montgomery books such as *Anne of Green Gables*; the Abbey Girls series by Elsie J Oxenham; the Billabong books by Mary Grant Bruce and books by Roberta Moss, such as *Jenny's Exciting Term*. I am wondering if any other people from around 12 years of age to 15 years of age had these books in their school libraries?
> I'm particularly interested in the Australian readers but would like to know what was happening the rest of the world too, of course. I'm also interested in people who read any of these books independently of their school libraries/school.

The anecdotal responses have been drawn together, providing some insight into young women's experiences in reading, and at times continuing interest in, LM Montgomery's, Elsie J Oxenham's, Mary Grant Bruce's, and Roberta Moss' literature.

[4] Personal communication. See also Kearns 2025; Trapasso 2021; [HomeStreet]Bank 2024).

The most widely read books were those by LM Montgomery, and included the Anne, Pat, Story Girl, and Emily books, as well as *The Blue Castle*. They were read by girls in Canada, America, Australia, and Britain. So many of the readers enjoyed Montgomery books while young and returned to them as adults. One did so when suffering from depression. Another woman said that she had kept the Anne books—the only set of books she had retained from her childhood reading: they were her "go-to books" when growing up. Some women had seen the *Anne of Green Gables* television series and then read the books. One referred to loving both. Another woman mentioned her age, 73, writing that she continues to enjoy reading the Anne books, originally read when she was young. As well as revealing that they returned to the books in maturity, respondents specifically refer to reading them in the 1940s, 1950s, 1960s, 1970s and 1980s.

Prince Edward Island (PEI), the setting for the Anne of Green Gables, Pat of Silver Bush and Story Girl books read by respondents featured in several comments. One woman's grandmother was born there in 1881. She, like another reader, had grown up on PEI and as well as saying she loved the Anne books, thought about her grandmother's life on the Island. One woman read *Rilla of Ingleside* as social history as well as beloved literature, commenting on the way in which Montgomery's depiction of Canadian attitudes toward World War One reflected reality. Another visited the homestead that inspired Montgomery's writing. Grandmothers and mothers also provided the books for their granddaughters and daughters having read them themselves (one respondent has copies from 1919 and 1920). One mother is regretful that her love for Anne has not been replicated by her daughter. But others were more fortunate. One noted that her 11- and 12-year-old daughters are reading them at the same age at which she did. Another wrote about the family reading aloud the Anne books. A school age daughter followed her mother's newfound adult interest in LM Montgomery, and both are reading her books.

Only some respondents found the books in their school libraries, but at times they were available through public libraries. Sometimes they were accessible in both. One woman wrote that as Canadians LM Montgomery was always on their reading list. A mobile library brought the books to another respondent.

Several women referred to *The Blue Castle* as their favourite LM Montgomery work. Others preferred the Emily series to the Anne series. None mentioned *Jane of Lantern Hill* or *Magic for Marigold* (both of which I refer to in this chapter).

Where women mentioned other authors, they often referred to LM Montgomery as well. One growing up in England in the 1960s also the read Elsie J Oxenham books, and refers to loving them both, then and now. Another who read Montgomery when she was young, read Roberta Moss' books when she was in college where she was given them by South African relatives. The reading matter of another covered both the Anne books and television series and Mary Grant Bruce's Billabong books, which she refers to as being a large part of her childhood. She comes from Aotearoa/New Zealand, has an Australian mother brought up in the outback, and has a continuing interest in the Billabong books, as does her younger sister. The latter received them as presents; the respondent borrowed them from the school library. An Australian respondent read and enjoyed both the Anne books and Billabong books.

An Australian visiting her grandfather's farm in Victoria read all the Mary Grant Bruce books there. She lives in Queensland and read the Elsie J Oxenham books from the school library. She bought *Anne of Green Gables* as an adult and refers to it as her all-time favourite. The Facebook question has encouraged her to seek others in the series. She also read some of the Elsie J Oxenham books.

Some had not read LM Montgomery but referred to two of the other authors. One retains her collection of Elsie J Oxenham books and read the Billabong books when she visited her aunt. Another read all the Billabong books, loving them when she was 11 to 15 years of age in the 1950s.

I appreciate the women's responses to my Facebook query. Their comments have not only upheld my idea that the books were read, but the women were advocates for the impression they made. The issues that I raise in the chapter were not part of this endeavour. Rather, I wanted to know that my understanding from my own experience, namely that the authors were widely read, could be supported. This has been the case, and the way in which women now view property ownership and economic independence may have some foundation in some of the literature of the writers' attitudes to these issues analysed in this chapter.

Bibliography

Cited Authors Books

Grant Bruce, Mary [Mary Grant Bruce (24 May 1878 – 2 July 1958)].

Billabong Riders, Lock & Co, Limited, London and Melbourne, UK/Australia, 1942.

Bill of Billabong, Ward, Lock & Co, Limited, London and Melbourne, UK/Australia, 1931.

A Little Bush Maid, Lock & Co, Limited, London, Melbourne and Capetown, UK/Australia/Sth Africa, 1910.

Mates at Billabong, Lock & Co, Limited, London and Melbourne, UK/Australia, 1912.

Montgomery, LM [Lucy Maud Montgomery OBE (November 30, 1874 – April 24, 1942)].

Anne of Green Gables, Angus & Robertson, Sydney, Australia, 1935.

Anne's House of Dreams, George G Harrap & Co Ltd London, UK, 1926.

Anne of Ingleside, Angus & Robertson Limited, Sydney and London, Australia/UK, 1949.

Emily of New Moon, Virago, London, UK (1923), 2014.

Emily Climbs, Hodder and Stoughton, London, UK, 1925.

Emily's Quest, Dell-Laurel Leaf, NYC, NY, US (1927), 2003.

Jane of Lantern Hill, George G Harrap & Co Ltd London, Toronto, Bombay, Sydney, UK/Canada/India/Australia (1927), 1949.

Magic for Marigold, Angus & Robertson Limited, Sydney, Australia (1929), 1936.

Pat of Silver Bush, Angus & Robertson Limited, Sydney and Melbourne, Australia (1932), 1941.

Mistress Pat, Angus & Robertson Limited, Sydney and London, Australia/UK (1935), 1940.

The Blue Castle, Angus & Robertson, London, Sydney, Melbourne, Singapore, Manila, UK/Australia/Singapore/Philippines (1926), 1980.
Moss, Roberta [Robert Moss (1903–1994) pseudonym].
Jenny of the Fourth, Andrew Dakers Limited, London, UK, 1957.
Jenny's Exciting Term, Andrew Dakers Limited, London, UK, 1954.
Oxenham, Elsie J [Elsie Jeanette Dunkerley (25 November 1880 – 9 January 1960) pseudonym].
Jandy Mac Comes Back, Collins, London and Glasgow, UK, 1941.
Strangers at the Abbey, Collins, London and Glasgow, UK, 1958.

Articles and Book Chapters

[HomeStreet]Bank, "From Struggle to Triumph …", *FDIC, Education Center*, 3 July 2024, From Struggle to Triumph: The History of Women and Real Estate, https://www.vibrantlivingnewsletter.com/single-post/from-struggle-to-triumph-the-history-of-women-and-real-estate (accessed 22 November 2024).
Deborah Kearns, "The history of women in real estate, *Bankrate* (Troy Segal, ed), 19 March 2025, The History Of Women In Real Estate | Bankrate, https://www.bankrate.com/real-estate/history-of-women-in-real-estate/ (accessed 22 November 2024).
Adriana Pacheco, "L.M. Montgomery: A Woman History Can't Forget", *Anne of Green Gables*, L.M. Montgomery: A Woman History Can't Forget, https://www.anneofgreengables.com/blog/l-m-montgomery-a-woman-history-cant-forget#:~:text=L.M.%20Montgomery%20was%20a%20prolific%20writer%2C%20and%20through,the%20expectations%20of%20women%20during%20the%20time%20period (accessed 21 November 2024).
Clare Trapasso, "A Forgotten Chapter in U.S. History: When Women Had To Choose Between Mortgages and Motherhood", *News & Insights – Trends*, 31 March 2021, When Women Had To Choose Between Mortgages and Motherhood, https://www.realtor.com/news/trends/untold-history-discrimination-against-women-seeking-mortgages/?msockid=12ff2003749a674e082b352875056688 (accessed 22 November 2024).

Books and Reports

Lucy Brownson, Feminist Housing Activism in the 1970s–1980s …, *Glasgow Women's Library*, 17 August 2021, Feminist housing activism in the 1970s-1980s, #1: Making space for feminist infrastructures | Glasgow Women's Library, https://womenslibrary.org.uk/2021/08/17/feminist-housing-activism-in-the-1970s-1980s-1-making-space-for-feminist-infrastructures/ (accessed 22 November 2024).

Chilla Bulbeck, *Living Feminism—The Impact of the Women's Movement on Three Generations of Australian Women*, Cambridge University Press, Cambridge, UK, 1997.

Chilla Bulbeck, *One World Women's Movement*, Pluto Press, London UK, 1988.

E Holly Pike and Laura M Robins, *L.M. Montgomery and Gender*, McGill-Queen's University Press, Montreal, Canada, 2021.

Jocelynne A Scutt and Di Graham. *For Richer, For Poorer: Money, Marriage, and Property Rights*, Penguin, Victoria, Australia; NYC, NY, US, 1984.

Joyce W Warren, *Women, Money, and the Law—Nineteenth-Century Fiction, Gender, and the Courts*, University of Iowa Press, Iowa City, IA, US, 2009.

Information Documents and Resources

Gov.UK, *Joint property ownership*, nd, Joint property ownership: Overview - GOV.UK, https://www.gov.uk/joint-property-ownership (accessed 22 November 2024).

Benjamin Lefebvre, Bibliography – Dissertations/Theses, *L.M. Montgomery Online*, 11August 2007/31 January 2025, Dissertations/Theses » L.M. Montgomery Online, https://lmmonline.org/bibliography/dissertations-and-theses/ (accessed 21 November 2024).

Spark21, *Women, their Money, and the Law - 100 First Hundred Years*, 22 June 2016, Women, their Money, and the Law - First 100 Years, https://first100years.org.uk/women-their-money-and-the-law/ (accessed 22 November 2024).

18

Lolita: The Mocked Female Reader

Judy Anne Forshaw

Bonding and Estranging

At the time *Lolita* was first published in 1955 there were readers who fell into Humbert's artful trap. Dorothy Parker (1958, 102–103), in a review of *Lolita* for *The New Yorker*, writes:

> It is the engrossing, anguished story of a man, a man of taste and culture, who can love only little girls. They must be between the ages of nine and fourteen, and he calls them nymphets.

Parker goes on to describe Dolores (I shall use her real name, not the one Humbert Humbert bestowed on her), as "a dreadful little creature, selfish, hard, vulgar, and foul-tempered. He knows that he knows all of what she is".

J. A. Forshaw (✉)
Cambridge, UK
e-mail: forshawjudy@gmail.com

J. A. Scutt (ed.), *Women, Power and Autonomy*,
https://doi.org/10.1007/978-3-031-97958-3_18

Now, nearly seventy years later, despite Humbert's apparent contrition for the harm he has done Dolores, readers cannot forgive him. In this chapter, my focus is on what Phelan (2008) calls bonding unreliability, in which the narrator, in this case Humbert, seduces the reader into sympathising with him, whilst remaining uneasily aware that they abhor his way of thinking. This seduction is encouraged by "an element of the novel's aesthetics, Nabokov's stylistic virtuosity" (2008, 22). Nevertheless, as early as Chapter 5 in the novel (2008, 18–21), Humbert's reasoning is "exposed as an elaborate rationalization of pederasty" (2008, 25) when he introduces his theory of "nymphets". From here on, the reader becomes increasingly estranged, so that Humbert's argument throughout Part I of the novel, which claims a grown man can be sexually manipulated by a child, is demolished by the start of Part II, as the full horror of his crime becomes apparent.

The Story

Humbert's story is as bizarre as it is unsettling. He marries Charlotte Haze in order to gain access to her twelve-year-old daughter Dolores; Lolita is his pet name for her. When the mother is fortuitously (for him) run down in a random accident, he becomes Dolores' "parent". The second half of the book focuses on his flight from his "daughter's" hometown on a road trip across America. After months of staying in seedy motels, he settles in a small town called Beardsley, named after Aubrey the paedophile artist, where he rents a house and sends Dolores to school. She eventually escapes, aided by another paedophile, the mysterious Clare Quilty. The novel is told in recollection; Humbert is awaiting trial for the murder of Quilty and has written his confession from his prison cell. Although he is being tried for murder, the focus of his confession is his obsessive "love" for Dolores, whilst the murder of Quilty is an annoying adjunct as far as he is concerned.

The final pages of Humbert's confession are chilling. Five years after having escaped his clutches, Dolores writes to him asking for money. He drives out to a remote shack in a dusty wasteland, and finds her married, heavily pregnant and desperately poor. He gives her the $400 in cash she asked for, and "a check for three thousand six hundred more" (Nabokov 2015, 278). She is overwhelmed by his "gift" but what he doesn't tell her is that he has pocketed the money from the sale of her dead mother's house, money that he knows full well Charlotte Haze would have wanted to go to her daughter rather than a husband she hated. This apparently insignificant detail is telling; despite Humbert's protestations of remorse, he just can't help himself. The final blow is contained in Dolores' letter to her "Dad" in which she signs herself "Dolly (Mrs Richard F. Schiller)" (2015, 266). We remember the name from the Foreword written by the prosecution's psychiatrist, John Ray Jr. His account lists the names of those involved in his patient's confession, their whereabouts and occupations, years after the events described, and we recall that a Mrs Richard Schiller died in childbirth.

Critical Reception

Christine Clegg (2000), in her overview of the critical history of *Lolita,* points out that despite an unofficial ban of his novel in America and Britain, Nabokov was never officially brought to trial on charges of pornography and obscenity. In 1956, a year after the novel was published in France, Nabokov felt compelled to write an afterword, "On a Book Entitled Lolita" (2015, 311–317), to accompany the American debut, in which he is at pains to make a clear separation between artistic and moral concerns:

> For me a work of fiction exists only insofar as it affords me what I shall bluntly call aesthetic bliss, that is a sense of being somehow, somewhere connected with other states of being where art (curiosity, tenderness, ecstasy) is the norm. (2015, 314–315)

Clegg maintains that since *Lolita* has generated so much debate about "the relationship between aesthetic form and sexual content [...] the question of morality and art is central to the unfolding critical history of *Lolita*" (2000,. 12). When, as Nabokov insists, the artistic form is paramount, then the issue of the problematic content becomes less important. Whilst formalist criticism of the 1950s and 1960s tends to focus on the formal features of the narrative, thereby overlooking what happens to Dolores, from the 1980s onwards there is a shift in emphasis. Greater attention is given to "the ethics of human relations, [and] the old opposition between morality and art starts to undergo a transformation" (2000, 13). Clegg contends that this shift is made easier now that *Lolita* has entered the literary canon, making it less contentious to discuss its disturbing content, a key concern in feminist criticism of the novel.

Although the novel was published in America in 1958 to great popularity and critical success, Clegg (2000, 18) points out that critics from the late 1950s through into the 1970s, unnerved by the book's rocky reception, were at pains to keep a distance from "the spectral question of pornography", claiming that the subject had "no bearing on the discussion of literature". The influential American critic Lionel Trilling's (1958) broadly humanist critique of the novel, "The Last Lover", focuses on romantic parody and evocations of courtly love:

> Lolita is about love. Perhaps I shall be better understood if I put the statement in this form: Lolita is not about sex, but about love. Almost every page sets forth some explicit erotic action and still is not about sex. It is about love. (1958, 364)

Trilling[1] goes on to claim that in "breaking the taboo about the sexual unavailability of the very young", it is comparable with the scandal of "Tristan's relation with Iseult, or Vronsky's with Anna". (1958, 368)

In the 1960s, critics eager to avoid further controversy tended to focus on a type of close reading associated with formalist criticism. Page Stegner (1967, 110), an influential American critic, writes about "the great seduction scene at The Enchanted Hunters" and goes on to complain about the dense, unappreciative reader, one whose "inaccurate reading [...] places all the attention on Humbert's aberration and

[1] Editor's note: Lionel Trilling is the template for a character in Marilyn French's *The Women's Room* (Penguin, NYC, NY, US. 1977). French's character is a lauded education philosopher who dies—only to have his wife discover abusively exploitative material hidden in his bedside table—pornographic representations of women and girls. This may provide some insight into Trilling's reflections on and justification of both Humbert Humbert's obsession and Nabokov's perspective of the inhumane (and surely unforgivable) use and abuse of Dolores.

neglects his suffering and his comedy". The implication is that the intelligent reader is capable of sympathetic identification with Humbert's story; after all: "Lolita is in reality a rather common, unwashed little girl whose interests are entirely plebian, though in certain respects, precocious". (1967, 114)

Julia Bader (1972) heralded a critical change by drawing attention to the problematic over-emphasis on the aesthetic aspects of the text at the expense of the realistic:

> The questions tackled by Lolita are artistic, or aesthetic, and the "moral" dilemma is treated in aesthetic terms. Humbert's "vice" is the inexpert artist's brutal treatment of a tantalizingly undeveloped subject, whose fragile soul [he] has violated. (1972, 80)

Following Nabokov's death in 1977, there was an effort to restore his credentials as an ethical writer, in the light of his repeated claims that his sympathies in the novel rest with the child. Richard Rorty (1989, 141) points out that *Lolita* is in fact about "the blindness of a certain kind of person to the pain of another kind of person"; and that Humbert dramatises "the particular form of cruelty about which Nabokov worried most—incuriosity" (1989, 158). Although he does concede that Humbert is both noticing and heartless, in that he is selectively curious, making him an obsessive, "as sensitive as he is callous" (1989, 157). Whatever Nabokov's intent, the general perception that he is indifferent to Humbert's crime persists, with some critics commenting on the monstrous similarities between Humbert and his creator.

The issue of child abuse refuses to go away, as does the crucial element of sex/gender—that this is a girl child whom Humbert treats as a woman: he "owns" Dolores just as he asserts ownership of her mother's house. Linda Kauffman (1989, 132–133) dismisses questions of "aesthetic bliss" advocated by Nabokov in his "Afterword". She points out that psychiatrist John Ray Jr's lugubrious foreword "acts as an injunction against the kind of reading that foregrounds social issues like child abuse". She goes on to assert that Nabokov's "wry disclaimer" in terms of a moral agenda "is a sham because put simply [it] extends the Humbertian aesthetic manifesto" and "since Ray is the butt of parody, readers will go to any length to avoid being identified with him" (1989, 132). She appeals to readers and critics to resist this insidious seduction by having the courage "to analyse the horror of incest by re-inscribing the material body of the child Lolita in the text" (1989, 133).

Madness and Unreliability

Lars Bernaerts (2008) examines the concept of the "*fou raisonnant*" as a self-conscious mad person who uses his or her intellectual powers to justify dubious behaviour, as opposed to the "*fou imaginant*" who is prey to hallucinations and presents "the imagined world as if it were the textual actual world" (2008, 186). The "*fou raisonnant*" is a type of "mad monologist" whose "misleading rhetoric" is "characterized by justification and contradiction" (2008, 192). These narrators, according to Bernaerts, see themselves as outsiders, but at the same time long for understanding and recognition, and will manipulate the reader in an attempt to elicit sympathy for their warped perspective. He goes on to point out that "their discourse embodies deviations and contradictions they deny in the story of their life" (2008, 192) and in this way they fall prey to self-incrimination and accusations of unreliability.

Whether or not Nabokov's Humbert Humbert, self-confessed paedophile and murderer, is insane, his account of his relationship with Dolores is clearly unreliable. But then why does his creator go to such lengths to persuade the reader to take his side? Although admittedly, most first-person narrators, whether they mean to or not, tend to justify their behaviour:

> They are subjective, at the mercy of their feelings, and to a certain extent fallible; some much more so than others. They range from "unacknowledged bias" to extreme, devious unreliability at the other end of the scale. (Fludernik 2006, 153)

In most cases, the reader wants to trust the narrator and starts out prepared to give him or her the benefit of the doubt, but often an uneasiness creeps in, and the further the reader moves into the story, the more the narrator's credibility slips, until he or she is revealed as dishonest, deluded, naïve, and sometimes downright mad. The reader will have realised long before reaching this point that the narrator's worldview clashes with that of the implied author; a gap has opened up and the reader quickly learns to read between the lines, becoming watchful, vigilant, no longer prepared to take the narrator's account of events at face value. The reader, in short, has become suspicious.

The concept of the unreliable narrator was initially formulated by Booth in 1961: "I have called a narrator reliable when he speaks for or acts in accordance with the norms of the work (which is to say the implied author's norms), unreliable when he does not". (2nd edn., 1983, 158–159)

Once the reader's suspicions are aroused, a conviction grows that the author has created someone who cannot be trusted, and a covert communication between author and reader is established behind the narrator's back. For the most part, it is not the author's intention to make the narrator look ridiculous, it is more a subtle process of unravelling, in that he or she is unmasked through clues that a mindful reader will pick up from the text. The author's "second self", the conscious or unconscious presentation of themselves that is inserted into the text in myriad disguised ways, conjures up an idealised implied author - with Nabokov, he is a playful, provocative, a multilingual European wedded to the Old World. The reader absorbs the author's second self by a process of often-unconscious osmosis. In recognising this osmosis we are more able to identify the widening gap between the implied author and the narrator. And it is here Nabokov runs into trouble, as this rift, vital for a novel with such a contentious subject matter, is so well disguised, that many doubt its existence.

Booth's investigation in this area led him to consider the version of him or herself that the author constructs in writing the narrative. Much depends on the way in which the narrator chooses to tell their story, and whether the narrator's evaluating of a given situation is "endorsed by the implied author" (Phelan 2006, 299). Booth's concern in this respect is the ethically suspect first-person narrator. Drawing the reader's attention to the unintentional side effects of Nabokov's brilliant prose, he questions the ethics of encouraging readers to collude with a self-confessed paedophile. Aside from the moral question, he points out the risks of encouraging the reader to override the usual authorial danger signals. Once the reader is trapped in "a vicious centre of consciousness presented with all the seductive self-justification of skilful rhetoric", the implied author is in trouble, as "most of his readers [...] identify Humbert with the author more than Nabokov intends" (1983, 391).

Bonding and Estranging Unreliability

As demonstrated by Parker's 1958 review for *The New Yorker*, some readers were prepared to allow themselves to be seduced by Humbert. His knowing, sophisticated irony, his disdain for all things American, his vast knowledge of highbrow culture, his multilingual accomplishments, his exotic childhood, all have a certain snobbish appeal. As observed, earlier readers, particularly in the 1950s and 1960s, influenced by prevailing critical opinion, tended to identify with Humbert, interpreting his verbal virtuosity and erudition as an extension of the implied author, thereby misreading the novel as a plea for, if not clemency for, at least an understanding of his monstrous creation. The twenty-first-century reader, in contrast, approaches the novel in a very different ideological and critical climate, and is forewarned that they will be meeting one of the most famous paedophiles in literary history.

Leland de la Durantaye (2007, 84) talks of Humbert's "freakish and acidic irony" in his account of the death of his childhood sweetheart Annabel, a traumatic event which he would have the reader believe explains his fixation on girls the same age as Annabel when she died. Annabel's death was preceded by the loss of his mother, struck down by a bolt of lightning. All of this is told with a "merciless self-parody" (2007, 84) that leaves the reader unsure what to make of him. At this early stage in the novel some readers might be prepared to give him the benefit of the doubt and interpret the mocking tone as a way of protecting himself from unbearable pain. But as de la Durantaye (2007, 86–87) points out, he is soon waxing lyrical about the "nymphet", asking the reader to judge his paedophilia as an aesthetic activity, accessible to the discerning few: the "artist" and the "mad man" (Nabokov, 2015, 17). He then goes on to present his Lolita as a perfection of this type, a piece of art, encouraging the reader to believe that he genuinely fell in love with her. He uses his "learning" as a means of hoodwinking the reader; for example, his reference to Dante's Beatrice only serves to give a bogus legitimacy to his aesthetic appreciation of what he terms "the nymphet". What he doesn't tell us is that Dante was ten years old when he fell in love with his eight-year-old Beatrice.

Phelan (2008, 8), in attempting to address the problematic issues raised for the contemporary reader, discusses "the difficult problem of the relation between technique and ethics in *Lolita*". He notes the polarisation of readers' responses, which he divides into two main groups, those, most common in 1961, taken in by Humbert's "rhetorical appeal", and those far more common today, who are thoroughly resistant. To this end Phelan (2008, 9) sets out to redefine the concept of the unreliable narrator, distinguishing between what he calls "estranging unreliability", a type of unreliable narrating that increases the distance between narrator and reader, and "bonding unreliability", by which the distance is reduced. He notes that the relationship between the implied author and the implied narrator shifts across a wide spectrum. At one end there is what he calls "mask narration" (2008, 9) in which the narrator is a mouthpiece for the author: "Indeed, the implied author employs the mask of the character as a means to increase the appeal and persuasiveness of the ideas expressed" (2008, 9–10).

On the other end is the totally unreliable narrator, who deceives us on all accounts by "underreporting, misreporting, misevaluating, underregarding" and "under evaluating" (2008, 10)—and might be added "misrepresenting". The sliding scale of unreliability is very helpful, as it implies that some narrators are only moderately unreliable and are consequently far more difficult to spot. Estranging unreliability is more obvious, as the narrator's worldview is distinct from what we know of the author. Bonding unreliability is in one sense more complex and much more problematic because, as Phelan points out:

> … although the authorial audience recognizes the narrator's unreliability, that unreliability includes some communication that the implied author – and thus the authorial audience – endorses. (2008, 11)

In the case of Nabokov, his bond with his narrator Humbert is a shared virtuosity with language, an artistic soul, and an old-world European heritage. In the opening paragraph of his confession, Humbert says "you can always count on a murderer for a fancy prose style" (2015, 9). Here Nabokov is warning the reader: he might sound like me, he might share certain similarities, love of literature, high art etc., but he is not me. Nevertheless, there is a danger that his warning won't be heeded, especially as John Ray Jr, the psychiatrist presenting the case for the prosecution in the Foreword, comes across as rather dim-witted and speaks in platitudes. Nabokov is playing a dangerous game here: his cunning narrator, following on after the psychiatrist's introduction to Humbert as the accused, makes an appeal to the reader's vanity; in contrast to John Ray Jr, he is articulate, refined, and steeped in the world of high culture, so the temptation to bond with him on a snobbish level is strong.

Hindsight

Part II of the novel describes Humbert's abduction of Dolores and their road trip across the States. Although his crazed rhapsodies don't abate, the "bonding unreliability" spoken of by Phelan begins to crumble as the narrator suffers occasional lapses, and moments of hindsight break through. Phelan (2013, 298) points out that Part I ends with a sentence indicating a slight but significant shift in the narrative, hinting at the narrator's difficulty, now that he has achieved his heart's desire, to hold fast to his delusional self:

> At the hotel we had separate rooms, but in the middle of the night she came sobbing into mine, and we made it up very gently. You see, she had absolutely nowhere else to go (Nabokov 2015, 142)

The first sentence is focalised through Humbert, the character's perspective, "we made it up very gently" (2015, 142), which is in line with the deluded perspective that permeates most of the novel; whereas the second sentence is told from the perspective of Humbert the narrator, looking back on the experience from his prison cell: "You see, she had absolutely nowhere else to go" (2015, 142). The two sentences fight against one another, betraying the narrator's torment, and indicate that on some level he knows exactly what he is doing. Phelan notes that these instances of dual focalisation, as flashes of hindsight break through, happen more and more frequently in Part II in Humbert's asides to the reader.

Some weeks after he and Dolores have embarked on the road trip and are staying in seedy motels, Humbert (thus Nabokov) lets the reader know about "her sobs in the night—every night—the moment I feigned sleep" (2015, 176): again, the narrative conveys that it is she who is responsible for her own despair. And much later, after he has exhausted the road and settled with his "daughter" in the sleepy fictional town of Beardsley, knowing that Dolores is desperate to escape and participate in ordinary schoolgirl life, he allows her to earn cash, which he steals back from her, trapping her in a hideous endless cycle: "by that time I had brought the prices down drastically by having her earn the hard and nauseous way permission to participate in the school's theatrical program" (2015, 184–185).

These bald accounts of his depravity are unambiguous, whereas in Part I, before he has actually had sex with Dolores (in other words, and more accurately, raped Dolores), although he alludes to himself as "a vampire", a "monster", "a hideous spider", his descriptions are somehow amorphous and seem to let him off the hook. His perception of himself as an "inflated pale" spider in the "middle of a luminous web" is poetic, on one level enchanting, all part of his seductive toolkit. But when the reader is given the vile, hard little details such as her sobs every night, the "wincing bleeding child" (2015, 135), the "hard and nauseous way" (2015, 185) he gets her to earn her permission to participate in ordinary school life, he has given up exonerating himself and is admitting to the harm he has done Dolores. Phelan sees Humbert's partial self-realisation as evidence of how far he has travelled from rationalising his paedophilia at the start of the novel, and that this change is indicative of "Nabokov's increased use of bonding unreliability through partial progress towards the authorial norm" (2008, 25).

Perhaps Humbert reaches a partial (albeit extraordinarily dim) realisation of the evil he has visited on Dolores by the end of his confession? In Chapter 20, in the role of concerned ambitious father, he reflects on Dolores' ruined potential when she loses interest in playing tennis, a sport she excelled in:

> … yet I insist that had not something within her been broken by me – not that I realised it then! – she would have had on the top of her perfect form the will to win, and would have become a real girl champion. (2015, 232)

In the penultimate paragraph of the book, he says: "Had I come before myself, I would have given Humbert at least five years for rape and dismissed the rest of the charges". (2015, 308)

Phelan makes the point that for the first time he is able to use the word "rape", and this in itself is an indication of remorse, although some readers see his admission as "an insincere ploy, just one more move in Humbert's attempt to win the sympathy of his narratee". (2008, 26)

Pathological Blindness

Humbert's story is a refusal to think from the standpoint of someone else; de la Durantaye (2007) points to a passage early in Humbert's confession when he turns to the reader and says: "my story has reached a point where I can cease insulting Charlotte [Dolores' mother] for the sake of retrospective verisimilitude" (2015, 71). Here he is telling the reader that he has placed a restraint on himself when writing his confession so as to ensure he is a "conscientious recorder" (2015, 72) of events. De la Durantaye (2007, 92–93) notes that he wants to present a record of himself as he was at the time, without recourse to hindsight. But in the absence of regret, this is just another ploy to skirt around his pathological inability to see anything from Dolores' perspective. He has left her out of the account and now, at the last moment, he has found a sneaky ruse to explain why she is missing. In representing himself as an author of truth, he represents and misrepresents Dolores' reality which, after all, is the one truth that the reader ought to see.

In a peculiar way, Humbert is disconcertingly truthful about actual events; it is his pathological determination to seduce the reader into seeing things from his demented viewpoint that is typical of the "mad monologist" discussed previously. This desire to convince others of the rightness of a warped vision is a marked tendency with psychopaths; in fact it can become an obsession. What they all share in common is a longing to end their loneliness and find allies.

Nabokov's Humbert might well score very highly on the Hare Psychopathy Checklist, invented years after the novel was written. The Checklist is a screening test for potential psychopaths consisting of twenty criteria, such as "grandiose sense of self-worth, pathological lying, a lack of remorse or guilt". The scores rank from zero to forty, and those who score above thirty are considered to have strong psychopathic traits. Humbert's confession does not seek to evade what is coming to him, he doesn't seem to care whether he lives or dies; but this is because his concern is something far more integral: he wants the reader to be like him, to see things through his eyes. Humbert, like most certified psychopaths, is completely incapable of seeing things from another person's perspective. Soon after Dolores escapes him, he muses:

> … it struck me […] that I simply did not know a thing about my darling and that quite possibly, behind the juvenile clichés, there was in her a garden and a twilight, and a palace gate – dim and adorable regions which happened to be lucidly and absolutely forbidden to me. (2015, 284)

It is as if it has only just occurred to him that she might have an independent life of her own, with thoughts and feelings that are not filtered through his lens. Yet he continues to see her as his property and to discount her humanity through an unchallenged endearment: "my darling".

Years later, Humbert tracks Dolores down to the dusty shack in the middle of nowhere. Michael Wood (1995, 136–137) gives an acutely described analysis of their final meeting:

> Much of the power of this chapter of the novel […] rests on [Dolores'] sheer ruined ordinariness […] Life with Humbert was a cage, a travelling prison, a dreary round of sexual duty. Quilty […] turned out to be only quirky Sadeian games. Even so Lolita regards Quilty as "full of fun"

> and Humbert as a remote, hardly remembered nuisance: […] she seems stunned and flattened, almost erased by the life she has led.

As far as Wood is concerned, Humbert protests too much, and is too anxious for the reader to see the change in him. Put simply, Wood (1995, 139) does not believe Humbert's remorse:

> I can't believe in his repentance because the language of his renunciation is the language of gloating – as indeed his language throughout, however guilty he feels or says he felt, is full of relished remembrance.

In support of his rejection of the notion that Humbert has seen the light, Wood cites Nabokov's recitation of Humbert's reflection:

> No matter, even if those eyes of hers would fade to myopic fish, and her nipples swell and crack, and her lovely young velvety delicate delta be tainted and torn – even then I would go mad with tenderness at the sight of your dear wan face, at the mere sound of your raucous young voice, my Lolita. (Nabokov, 2015, 278)

Even at this late stage in the narrative, Humbert still has not reached any understanding of the full extent of his crime against Dolores—or any of it? He has already let the reader know of his largesse in coming to her rescue in her hour of need by giving her a generous cheque, far more than the small amount she asked for, but (as earlier observed) what he doesn't tell the reader is that this money is from the proceeds of the sale of her mother's house, only an extremely small portion of the money that is rightfully hers—he, presumably, has pocketed the rest.

The Mocked Female Reader

This urge to retell Humbert's confession and give Dolores a voice is a powerful one, especially for the female reader faced with Humbert's lie of a dangerous, deadly female sexuality applied to a twelve-year-old child. Booth (1983, 390) points out that these types of misreading of the novel:

> … do not come from any inherent condition of the novel or any natural incompatibility between author and reader. They come from the reader's inability to dissociate himself from the vicious centre of consciousness presented to him with all the seductiveness of self- justification of skilful rhetoric.

Here Booth seems to be saying that certain male, and some female, readings are predetermined by a misogynistic culture that encourages the unwary reader to be unwittingly receptive to Humbert's "skilful rhetoric".

In his address to the female members of the jury, Humbert doesn't bother with flattery, and instead adopts a tone of sneering sarcasm. In Chapter 28 of Book One, having deposited Dolores in room 342 of The Enchanted Hunters Hotel, already drugged and prepped for rape, he opens with the lines: "Gentlewomen of the jury! Bear with me! Allow me to take just a tiny bit of your precious time." So this was *le grand moment* (2015, 123). For the next few pages he ruminates and is forced to stall the rape when Dolores wakes from her drugged sleep. By the end of Chapter 29, early in the morning, he finally summons up the courage to destroy her:

> Frigid gentlewomen of the jury! I had thought that months, perhaps years, would elapse before I dared to reveal myself to Dolores Haze; but by six she was wide awake, and by six fifteen we were technically lovers. I am going to tell you something very strange: it was she who seduced me. (2015, 132)

The implied threat is that if the reader dares to object to his version of events, she is frigid, wrong-headed, dumb, ignorant, petty, prudish; no different from the majority of the adult females in this book. Kauffman (1989) appeals to readers and critics to resist Humbert's bullying, mocking address, pointing out the impossible position in which the female reader is placed: "… feminist readers have the choice of either participating in their own 'emasculation' by endorsing aesthetic bliss, or demonstrating their humorlessness and frigidity" (1989, 135).

Humbert views women with gleeful contempt. His first wife Valerie is described as plump and inarticulate: "… she waddled by my side, and began to shake her poodle head vigorously without saying a word" (2015,

27). His second wife, Dolores' mother, whom he refers to throughout as "the Haze woman", doesn't fare much better. He sums her up as "one of those women whose polished words may reflect a book club or bridge club, or any other deadly conventionality, but never her soul" (2015, 37). The adult female is either as shallow and humourless as Charlotte, or hideous. "Pratt", the headmistress of Dolores' school in Beardsley, calls Humbert in to talk about her concerns for his daughter, who is not flourishing. His description of her is devastating: "A huge woman, grey-haired, and frowsy with a broad flat nose, and small eyes behind black framed glasses" (2015, 193). A few lines on, he describes her "liver spotted hands" noticing that "the smoke she exhaled from her nostrils was like a pair of tusks" (2015, 194). Her suggestion that Dolores should be seen by the school doctor so enrages him that he briefly thinks of turning her into that despised figure—the wife. "Should I marry Pratt and strangle her?" (2015, 197). In a later chapter, a nurse, suspecting something is awry when Dolores is taken to hospital with a raging fever, refuses to allow him access to see his "daughter", yet (predictably) is vilified:

> At one point, I was rather dreadfully rude to a very young and very cheeky nurse with overdeveloped gluteal parts and blazing black eyes – Basque descent, as I learned. Her father was an imported shepherd, a trainer of sheep dogs. (2015, 241)

Humbert invites the susceptible reader to collude with him in mocking the enemy. Kauffman (1989, 135) quotes Judith Fetterly:

> ...the female reader is co-opted into participation in an experience from which she is explicitly excluded; she is asked to identify with a selfhood that defines itself in opposition to her; and is required to identify against herself.

Humbert's damning, invalidating descriptions of the various women who might have helped Dolores escape are seamlessly woven into his narrative. However, he is kinder to the unsuspecting female. He describes Mrs Holigan, the charlady whom he "inherits" when he briefly settles into 14

Thayer Street, with a grudging acceptance: "That kindly and harmless woman had, thank God, a rather bleary eye that missed details, and I became a great expert at bed making" (2015, 180). His fear of discovery sharpens his vitriol. Upon moving into Thayer Street with Dolores, he is constantly on guard:

> I often felt we lived in a lighted house of glass, and that at any moment some thin-lipped parchment face would peer through a carelessly unshaded window to obtain a free glimpse of things the most jaded *voyeur* would have paid a small fortune to watch. (2015, 180)

These neighbourhood snoops are invariably female: "… that type of haddocky spinster [whose] obscene mind was the result of considerable literary inbreeding in modern fiction" (2015, 206). How Nabokov hates his own creation. Increasingly hemmed in, Humbert lashes out at Dolores' friends at her new school, terrified that she might confide in one of them. Opal is described as "a bashful, formless, bespectacled, bepimpled creature" and Avis as "a plump lateral child with hairy legs" (2015, 190). Sarah Herbold (1999, 9) notes that the female reader is "ostracized, humiliated and condemned". Shut out of his world, she is consigned to the company of the "haddocky spinster", the "frigid gentlewomen of the jury", the "liver spotted" Pratt, and other "thin lipped, parchment faced" members. The psychiatrist John Ray Jr, he of the novel's Foreword, falls into the same camp. His account of the prisoner is lugubrious and pitted with well-worn clichés.

In the 2015 Penguin edition of *Lolita,* a black-and-white photograph on the back cover shows a middle-aged Nabokov looking out from the driver's window of his car. The image immediately recalls Humbert's six-month road trip with Dolores following her mother's death. It also carries echoes of the 1950s newspaper story that inspired the novel: the two-year ordeal of eleven-year-old Sally Horner, kidnapped by Frank La Salle. Herbold (1999, 5) points out that both Humbert and his creator lay claim to Lolita, "whom they have invented". She talks about the underlying Pygmalion theme in the novel that has led feminist critics "to ask whether there really is a woman in the text, since Lolita exists only as Humbert's representation of her" (1999, 5). She will be forever unknowable. Herbold (1999, 6) points out that it could be said:

> … that there is a woman in the text, if only in the form of a trace woman (or girl) who was – or could have been – present, but can no longer be made present, either to author, narrator, or reader.

And as there is "no objective reality" in the novel with which to measure Humbert's distorted depiction of her, Lolita as Humbert describes her is all there is to go on. What she appears to be, and what Nabokov signals to the reader in the opening chapter of the book, is a composite of a multitude of pubescent girls such that exist in Humbert's imagination.

Kauffman (1989, 138) notes that Humbert's blindness to Dolores, his inability to recognise that she has a "will or life of her own […] denies not just what is womanly in Lolita—he denies what is human" and why "he must insist that nymphets are demonic". In an intriguing signposting of intertextuality, Kauffman comments that "the myth of demonic children" ties the novel to James' *The Turn of the Screw* (1989, 138). The governess "tries to arrest the children's development; the desire to fix things indeed, is one of her motives for writing her retrospective narrative […] just as Humbert wants to 'fix the perilous magic of nymphets'":

> In both texts […] how and what you see depends on the frame: James' governess and Humbert Humbert both resort to a fancy prose style to frame a murder […] In both the governess's narrative and Humbert's, silence, exile, and cunning lie in the gap between past and present, and determine what inflection will be given to the murder of childhood. (1989, 139)

Clegg, in her critical overview of the novel, refers to the critic Ellen Pifer, who quotes Nabokov's description of Humbert as "a vain and cruel wretch who manages to appear 'touching'. That epithet, in its true, tear-iridized sense, can only apply to my poor little girl [Lolita]" (2000, 95). And yet Nabokov hands the entire narrative over to her eloquent, persuasive rapist.

Bibliography

Articles and Book Chapters

Bernaerts, Lars, 2008, "Un Fou Raisonnant et Imaginant" in E D'hoker and G Martens, eds, *Narrative Unreliability in the Twentieth Century First Person Novel,* Walter de Gruyter, Berlin, 185–200.

De la Durantaye, Leland, 2007. "Style is Matter. Humbert's Green Lane" in *The Moral Art of Vladimir Nabokov.* Ithaca. Cornel University Press, 84–100.

Herbold, Sarah, 1999. "Dolores Disparue: Reading Misogyny in Lolita. Lolita and the Woman Reader", *Nabokov Studies* 5 (1998–99) 71–98.

Kauffman, Linda, 1989. "Framing Lolita: Is There a Woman in the Text?" in Patricia Yaeger and Beth Kowaleski-Wallace, eds, *Refiguring the Father: New Feminist Readings of Patriarchy.* Carbondale. Southern Illinois University Press, 131–152.

Parker, Dorothy, 1958. "Sex – without the asterisks". *Esquire,* L, No 4 (October 1958), 102–103.

Phelan, James, 2006. "Narrative Theory, 1966–2006. A Narrative" in Robert Scholes, James Phelan and Robert Kellog, eds, *The Nature of Narrative,* Oxford University Press, Oxford, UK, 283–337.

Phelan, James, 2008. "Estranging Unreliability, Bonding Unreliability, and the Ethics of *Lolita*" in E D'hoker and G Martens, eds, *Narrative Unreliability in the Twentieth-Century First-Person Novel,* Fortieth Anniversary Edition, De Gruyter, Berlin/Boston, Germany/US, 7–27.

Rorty, Richard, 1989. "The barber of Kasbeam: Nabakov on cruelty" in *Contingency, irony and solidarity.* Richard Rorty, Cambridge University Press, Cambridge, UK, 141–167.

Nomi Tamir-Ghez, 2002. "The Art of Persuasionin Nabakov's Lolita" in Ellan Pifer, ed, *Vladimir Nabakov's Lolita – A Casebook.* Oxford Scholarship Online, The Art of Persuasion in Nabokov's Lolita | Vladimir Nabokov's Lolita: A Casebook | Oxford Academic, https://academic.oup.com/book/49042/chapter-abstract/422041803?redirectedFrom=fulltext&login=true (accessed 22 November 2024).

Books and Reports

Bader, Julia, *Crystal Land Artifice in Nabokov's English Novels,* University of California Press, CA, US, 1972.

Booth, Wayne C, *The Rhetoric of Fiction.* 2nd ed, University of Chicago Press, Chicago, Il, US, 1983.

Clegg, Christine, *Vladimir Nabokov: Lolita,* Palgrave Macmillan, London, UK, 2000.

Fludernik, Monika, *An Introduction to Narratology*. Oxford. Routledge, Oxford, UK (2006), Reprint 2009.

Nabokov, Vladimir, *Lolita,* Penguin Classics, London, UK (1955), Reprint 2015.

Phelan, James, *Reading the American Novel, 1920–2010,* Wiley-Blackwell, Malden, MA, US, 2013.

Stegner, Page, *Escape into Aesthetics: The Art of Vladimir Nabokov,* Eyre and Spottiswoode, London, UK, 1967.

Wood, Michael, *The Magician's Doubts: Nabokov and the Risks of Fiction,* London. Chatto & Windus, London, UK, 1995.

19

Living in a Pornographic World: Constraint on the Autonomy of Girls and Women

Helen Pringle

Introduction

I argue in this chapter that responses to pornography should be primarily formulated within the context of a broad-based approach that addresses different forms of discrimination and violence against women and girls (VAWG). The chapter provides an outline of how pornography works, what it does and how it is used, in regard to children and young people in particular, working with the understanding of gendered violence set out in the UN Declaration on the Elimination of Violence against Women. The main trends in access to and consumption of pornography by children and the impact on their lives, are illustrated by a selection of cases drawn from prosecutions on pornography-related charges. My references here are largely but not entirely limited to Australia; however, I believe that the conclusions apply in general terms more broadly. These cases

H. Pringle (✉)
School of Social Sciences, University of New South Wales (UNSW), Sydney, Australia
e-mail: h.pringle@unsw.edu.au

J. A. Scutt (ed.), *Women, Power and Autonomy*,
https://doi.org/10.1007/978-3-031-97958-3_19

document individual behaviour but also collective patterns of production, circulation, access and use of pornography. The cases also direct our attention to gendered patterns of violence and cruelty against girls and women, the significance of which escapes a "public health" framework as commonly recommended in understanding pornography. I conclude that a comprehensive VAWG approach that includes pornography offers a way to change the public discussion of pornography through greater receptiveness to the voices and experience of girls, rather than the acceptance of a porn aesthetic of violence and cruelty as "cool".

An entry by Marty Klein in the *International Encyclopedia of Human Sexuality* in 2015 drew attention to a striking change of emphasis in critiques of pornography, beginning around the mid-1970s, which moved away from a narrative of "immorality" to one of "public health" (2015, 567). Klein however asserted that claims about an impending "public health crisis" were "actually just a disguised moral panic", that is, the old approach in a new dress.[1] I do not share Klein's defence of pornography, but there are indeed many indications of the emergence of a framework of "public health crisis" for understanding the impact of pornography, particularly on children and young people. In 2014, for example, a governing councillor of the American Public Health Association, Pamela Luna, warned the UK Faculty of Public Health's annual conference of the urgent necessity of action on pornography and sexualization by public health doctors: "I feel we have left our kids vulnerable; as adults we've missed something, which is what is happening in the media" (Limb 2014). The head of the Australian Childhood Foundation, Dr Joe Tucci, told a symposium on "Pornography and Harm to Children and Young People", held in Sydney, Australia on 9 February 2016, that there was a "public health crisis in the making" on the scale of smoking, alcohol use, and other such issues (Kozaki 2016). Since that time, a considerable global literature has grown up around the question of pornography as a public health issue, with contributions from both sides of the scholarly "aisle". In terms of understanding pornography as a threat to public health, since 2016, a number of American states have adopted resolutions recognizing "that pornography is a public

[1] At greater length, see ABC News (2012).

health hazard leading to a broad spectrum of individual and public health impacts and societal harms" (Rothman 2021, Chapter 1).[2]

A "public health" framework offers a largely gender-neutral approach to pornography, which may yield short-term advantages in terms of political and popular persuasion. I acknowledge that pornography and associated practices do harm to boys and young men, as well as girls, and I have no wish to counsel neglect of the problem of violence against boys and young men, whether it be perpetrated by boys or girls, men or women. However, there is a need for a comprehensive strategy in terms of VAWG because of the systematically gendered patterns of sexual abuse and violence in our society, and the role of pornography and of the sex industry more generally in enacting those patterns. Pornographic objects and practices reflect, construct, normalise and even valorize violence and systemic inequality on the basis of sex.

My analysis draws on analyses of pornography in terms of gendered harm, and understands its harms in terms of violence through the broad gender-based terms of the UN *Declaration on the Elimination of Violence Against Women*, that is, "For the purposes of this Declaration, the term 'violence against women' means any act of gender-based violence that results in, or is likely to result in, physical, sexual or psychological harm or suffering to women, including threats of such acts, coercion or arbitrary deprivation of liberty, whether occurring in public or in private life".[3] I adopt this framework of subordination through violence not out of an abstract allegiance to an analysis in terms of sex and gender, but rather through an analysis of how pornography works, what it does and how it is used, in our contemporary world.

Throughout this chapter, I understand pornography not as a harmless "fantasy" but in terms of practices of subordination of women and girls, practices that in turn often lead to or are associated with other forms of "acting out" violence and abuse against them. Pornographic "objects" take different forms, and different people adopt different practices in their making, use and consumption, which do not affect everyone in

---

[2] A pro-pornography critique of the public health approach is set out in McKay et al. (2021).

[3] UN General Assembly [UNGA], *Declaration on the Elimination of Violence against Women*, 20 December 1993, A/RES/48/104, Article 1, https://digitallibrary.un.org/record/179739?ln=en (accessed 13 January 2025).

exactly the same ways. But pornographic objects and practices all find a place within a regime of the subordination of women, which enacts sex inequality. Rather than expressing choice, power and agency for women, pornography takes form as systemic gendered inequalities of power. Just as the forms it takes are varied, so also its harms range across physical, sexual and psychological areas, and its effects are not confined to "private life". The *Declaration on the Elimination of Violence against Women* adds the crucial phrase in regard to violence: "whether occurring in public or in private life".

What to do about pornography in a democracy is a serious matter involving reflection on the meaning and significance of harm, equality and freedom. However, as noted below, pornography is frequently seen as something to be laughed and joked about, rather than as raising questions about individual and collective harms of violence, abuse and subordination. Children who do not take pornography seriously, as evidenced by their laughing at it or in conversations about it, are often praised as "media savvy", as able to "see through" pornography such that it is viewed as something that is "not real". However, those children (and adults) who laugh at pornography are perhaps of most concern in our thinking about its access, consumption and use.

I begin without a set definition of pornography. In a legal sense, pornography can be usefully understood in terms of the MacKinnon/Dworkin approach as a civil rights violation (Dworkin and MacKinnon 1988, 1997), or as a form of sexual vilification, along similar lines to racial or homosexual vilification provisions set out in the Australian state of New South Wales *Anti-Discrimination Act* 1977, in which vilification is a form of discrimination.[4] In such a context of understanding, material would fit (or not) the category of "pornography" not because of what it is but of what it *does*, or what people do with it. However, for the purposes of this chapter, I use the term in a much broader way, simply put, what we encounter on the internet when we use the search term "pornography" or "porn". Again, I am less concerned with the identification and classification of pornographic *objects* than with patterns of access, use

[4] *Anti-Discrimination Act 1977* (New South Wales), Sections 20B-C (race), 38R-S (transgender), 49ZD-ZE (religion), 49ZS-ZT (homosexuality), 49ZXA-ZXB (HIV/AIDS status), https://legislation.nsw.gov.au/view/html/inforce/2024-07-01/act-1977-048 (accessed 13 January 2025).

and consumption, that is, practices of pornography in what we might call the "pornography system".

Pornography begins its work early in the lives of modern children.[5] It begins long before girls or boys have developed autonomy or even a capacity to do so. The cases cited here are not only prosecutions of individuals, but also document collective patterns of production, circulation, access and use of pornography that deeply affect the development of autonomy. Pornographic patterns of violence and cruelty against women and girls constitute what Sandra Amankavičiūtė has characterised as "coercive circumstances",[6] which are not conducive to the growth of autonomy in girls as they become women. A comprehensive VAWG approach to pornography offers a way to change the public discussion of pornography through greater receptiveness to the experience of girls, rather than being responsive to a porn aesthetic of violence, cruelty and coercion as "cool".

Trends in Accessing and Consuming Pornography by Young People

This section sketches the main patterns of young people's contact with and access to pornography, most notoriously now via the internet. Older understandings of pornography as revolving around magazines furtively bought (or "found") and used by an adolescent boy in secrecy at night as a masturbation aid continue to have some traction in our collective imagination but no longer correspond to the main patterns of access and consumption by young people, or by adults for that matter. The internet is now the most inexpensive, convenient, accessible and anonymous way to access ready-made pornography for use, especially by children who can thereby easily circumvent adult surveillance. It would be a mistake, however, to consider questions of online usage without keeping in the

---

[5] To say this is now uncontested. See these important recent reports: [France] Haut conseil à l'égalité entre les femmes et les hommes 2023; [UK] Children's Commissioner 2023a; [UK]Children's Commissioner 2023b).

[6] Sandra Amankavičiūtė, unpublished work in progress at University of New South Wales, Sydney. Please do not cite without acknowledgement.

picture, so to speak, the way in which "pornography is everywhere", as noted in the title of the 2013 report for the UK Office of the Children's Commissioner (Horvath et al. 2013). That is, pornographic materials are not only available via dedicated websites as well as through online social media such as FaceBook, Instagram and Twitter (X), but are also still accessed as more traditional objects such as men's and lads' magazines and books, as well as public outdoor advertising (Rosewarne 2007; Pringle 2010, 2014),[7] television, music videos and so on.[8] Acts and practices of sexual violence and of harassment in the street, and in workplace and recreational spaces like sporting and entertainment venues and clubs, also often take a pornographic form or use pornographic motifs (Pringle 2011a, b, c; Pringle 2015; Pringle 2013a, b). Meagan Tyler and Kaye Quek (2016) provide a useful summary of the bodies of research literature in these contexts around the concept of "pornographication", while cautioning against conflating that term with "sexualization".

Moreover, a focus on consumption of pornography by children and young people should not lose sight of the way in which pornographic materials are for the most part manufactured, distributed, and traded for profit by adults. There is no evidence that pornography commonly accessed on the internet by children and young people is substantially different from that accessed by adults. In other words, "harm" to children through or related to the consumption of pornography is not disconnected from that done to adults. However, although many writers have drawn attention to the growing market share of "amateur" pornography (Paasonen 2010; Ruberg 2016; Feona 2018; Stardust 2024), the *controllers* of pornography markets are overwhelmingly adults (mostly adult men) with connections to other parts of the sex industry. For example, the business interests of the former owner and founder of a leading Australian adult products online retailer Adultshop, Malcolm Day, spanned websites such as wickedteensluts as well as adult sex shops; Day's company Delecta also had unrealized plans to expand into the

---

[7] Classic studies of sexualized advertising in Australia include Rush and La Nauze (2006a), Rush and La Nauze (2006b).

[8] For a succinct outline of this topic, see Coy (2014). There is a significant body of work in this area which it is beyond the scope of this chapter to address in depth.

running of a mega-brothel in Sydney (Prior 2014; Cadzow 2011). So-called "amateur pornography" or "indie porn" is distributed and accessed through highly organised and profitable corporate ventures: Only Fans is a prime example of a façade of cottage-core amateurism operated by independent sole traders, behind which lie the usual suspects of corporate late capitalism.

In this context, discussions of "amateur pornography" often present its home-made quality as evidence of a greater authenticity and realness, even as evidence of an unspoiled quality—with the main "spoilers" identified as the state and law. A recent example is Zahra Stardust's portrayal of the potential of "indie porn" as including a revolutionary democratization of production and content and a global redistribution of wealth—the promise of which is claimed to be shut down by "regulatory fantasies" of law and government or, more colourfully, frustrated by "a backdrop of erotophobic regulatory paranoia" (Stardust 2024, 10). Stardust's argument situates pornography markets as pre-political, functioning in some sense as "prior" to the intervention of government. On this view, government or the state is asserted as Enemy No 1 of sexual freedom through its holding and exercise of the powers and penalties of licensing and censorship—and somehow also, of the power of creating and assigning stigma. However, markets are the creatures of government and law, and do not and cannot subsist on any other basis. "The market" more broadly functions because of laws specifying and protecting property rights, through provisions against trespass and theft for example, or through the principle of contract that agreements be kept. These underlying scaffoldings of markets are structural conditions, ensuring the very possibility of trading in pornographic materials and services as they do in other areas, and are not simply "regulatory fantasies".[9]

Young people also do not always access pornography on their own or on their own initiative. Adults are often responsible for introducing children to pornography, whether through sharing their own use of pornographic objects and practices, or through encouraging their use by

[9] This line of analysis of markets as creations of government and law owes much to Cass Sunstein's analysis of markets in speech and ideas, for example, see Sunstein (1992).

children, or simply through the casual exposure of children to pornography used by adults in the home or elsewhere. I do not refer to dysfunctional families or fathers here, but rather to families in which "normal" patterns of male entitlement and hierarchy are in place. The proceedings of the Australian Royal Commission into Institutional Responses to Child Sexual Abuse, and of other similar inquiries in Australia, indicate that risks to children of exposure to pornography are moreover posed by religious figures, teachers and other adults with the responsibility of caring for children (Prichard and Spiranovic 2014). It is not uncommon, that is, for children to access pornography through the internet or via other means through the mediation of adults in a coercive context, a context in which adults use pornography to give instruction to children on how to perform sexual acts, during what is often known as "grooming" for purposes of sexual predation (Norma 2011). It is more than perplexing, then, that many writers advocate using pornography as a form of sex education for school children (see further below).

The widespread use, citation and apparent acceptability of pornography throughout our world can be seen in this context as a form of "social grooming", where pornography and use is treated and spoken of as, with some limited exceptions, "harmless"—and as expected, cool and/ or fun (Pringle 2011a, b, c). In contrast, a primary concern that guides my approach is the need to take the question of pornography seriously. That is, pornography is no ludic pastime, existing somewhere outside of social relations and not existing in the "real world" (as its defenders often seem to imply, and as even its critics sometimes claim). It is, indeed, everywhere.

It can be difficult to accurately measure changing trends in online consumption of pornography because of different understandings and usages of the term not only by researchers but also over time. However, it is uncontested by defenders and critics of pornography alike that the pornography industry is expanding at an exponential rate, and that pornography markets are now most commonly accessed through the internet, as noted above. The traffic to the website Pornhub is illustrative of trends here. Pornhub grew to be the largest pornography site on the internet, as part of a network of video-sharing sites owned by MindGeek, which also included RedTube, Spankwire, YouPorn, etc. These sites did not for the most part require payment by users for access, and for that very reason alone were popular with young people seeking to access pornography. It should be reiterated that sites like Pornhub make no distinction between pornography for adults and pornography for children or young people. Although such sites often make a ritual nod to community sensibilities by saying that they do not support the viewing of pornography by children, they make little or no serious attempt to screen children out from access to their websites or parts of them. To pinpoint more accurately the extent of traffic by children would presuppose forms of regulation that such sites fail or refuse to perform.

At the end of each year, Pornhub provides a comprehensive set of "insights" into patterns of use, for example by geographical location, top searches, choice of favourite actors (including "most viewed amateur models") etc.[10] The themes in top searches show a striking emphasis in regard to the sexualisation of relations between family members ("step mom", "milf", "mom", "gilf", "step sister"), and an emphasis on sexualized intrusion in women's spaces and privacy ("step mom shower", "step sister caught"). Other searches of particular concern include "babysitter" and "teacher student". The *searches* on Pornhub noted in its annual tables do not of course provide a full and accurate picture of the material on the site that is accessed through those terms. A wide variety of genres of pornography is available on the site. In 2011, Abigail Bray analysed one particular genre featured on Pornhub, entitled "Passed Out Pussy: extreme videos of drunk young girls fucked to pieces and ruined for life!!" (Bray 2011).[11] This popular category and its variants featured sexual humiliation videos of intoxicated or unconscious young girls.

There is some debate about whether children are now accessing more "hardcore" material than previously, but the evidence from corporate producers of pornography themselves suggests a trend in mainstream pornography's becoming more "hardcore". Even when pornography was largely accessed via DVDs, Meagan Tyler's (2010) analysis

[10] As an example, see Year in Review 2023.

[11] The exclamation marks of the cited category's title are in the original, and the term humiliation is used unapologetically.

of the industry's leading trade magazine found that ostensibly "mainstream" video pornography became markedly more extreme and openly degrading to women (Tyler 2010). At the same time, as pornography use has become more mainstream, openly and collectively practised, mainstream pornographic "objects" or artifacts have become more hardcore. As writers like Rebecca Whisnant and Gail Dines have noted, it is no longer "your father's *Playboy*" that is in question (Whisnant 2015; Dines 2010). What boys now get off on in accessing pornography is not a glossy picture in a magazine of a blonde girl with her finger in her mouth and a faraway look in her eyes.

Part of the difficulty in making an accurate assessment of the brutality of the pornographic *material* that is accessed by children (or by adults for that matter) also lies in the use of different definitions and understandings of violence. For example, some researchers define "violence" (and "aggression") so narrowly that their research finds that there is almost none of it on pornography sites (McKee 2015; cf Pringle 2010; Bridges et al. 2016). This narrow definition of "violence" often turns not on whether acts of violence per se are done, but on whether there is a semblance of "consent" by the "actors" to that violence (or perhaps better phrased as whether there is an absence of non-consent). As noted above, I use a human rights-based understanding of violence and of its potential harms as set out in the UN Declaration on the Elimination of Violence Against Women. It is also of course the case that not all materials on sites like Pornhub are the same: people access and use pornographic objects in different ways, and users are not all affected in exactly the same way. Similar caveats can be made, say, about cigarettes or cigarette advertising without affecting the validity of a critique of the tobacco industry.

More detailed research in this area of *access* to "hardcore" pornography is needed, as also noted in the report for the UK Children's Commissioner, but the evidence we already have of what is freely available for children to access on the internet is of great concern in terms of violence against women and girls. The evidence of early and repeated direct exposure of boys, and to a lesser extent, of girls in Australia to pornography, whether softcore or hardcore, is also largely uncontested ground between defenders and critics of pornography. As early as 2007, Michael Flood provided useful empirical evidence of age of access of young people in Australia (Flood 2007; see also Crabb and Corlett 2010),[12] with the median age of first encounter with pornography being 11, and the median age of having sex with another person being 16. This means that young people today usually have sex with or via an image, that is, they "have pornography", long before they have relations of any depth of sexual intimacy with another person. Oddly, a frequent form of inquiry and report on age of exposure the age when children first "see" pornography; this peculiar way of speaking is perhaps a throwback to an age of printed pornographic material, or perhaps just an unnecessarily coy euphemism.

Pornography's Impact on Young People and Their Lives

The 2013 report commissioned by the UK Office of the Children's Commissioner as part of its inquiry into Child Sexual Exploitation in Gangs and Groups remains one of the most reliable sources for exploring the impact of pornography on children (Horvath et al. 2013). Although this report involved children in England, there is little evidence to suggest that the findings are radically different from the situation in other developed western nations like Australia or the United States. The report is cautious in its findings, but provides sufficient evidence and analysis for grave concerns about the impact of early and repeated exposure of boys in particular to pornography, and how this relates in turn to practices of sexual inequality and violence against girls and women.

My own research can add little to the kind of data collection that was undertaken for the report of the Children's Commissioner and other such reviews since that time. What I do bring to bear in terms of assessing the impact of pornography on children is research and analysis of criminal prosecutions for possession and use of pornography. The valuable evidence that prosecutions provide of pornography use by young people (and also of adults) has not been drawn on in any depth in Australian scholarly or government research. One barrier to such research is that

[12] More recent figures continue to show disturbingly early and frequent exposure.

prosecutions of minors are, appropriately, not conducted in open court or freely reported. But even so, stories of the beginnings and development of pornography use are often available through accounts given in court by adults about their childhood experiences with pornography.

One form that access to pornography associated with the internet takes among young people that is increasingly coming to judicial notice involves pornographic practices initiated and conducted by children in their everyday lives. For example, children make and circulate pornography at the edges of the global market, with sext-selfies as a kind of low-grade pornography being the most well-known and publicly controversial example of such practices. There is a growing literature on "sexting" practices and their significance among children (which I cannot address here for reasons of space), and boys from both public and private schools in Australia figure regularly in such practices. For example, in 2024, there were several reported cases of students (and teachers) whose social media photos were manipulated by AI into "deep fake" pornographic images and circulated among other schoolboys.[13]

Another practice is the making and circulation for upload, sale or swap of images and videos, usually with no semblance of agreement or consent by the subjects of the images. An example is the videotaping for the purposes of circulation on the internet and other forums of the sexual humiliation of girls and women with disabilities. In conversation with defenders of pornography, such practices have been characterised to me as "sexual assault" rather than pornography, in an apparent attempt to "save" pornography from censure. The idea that pornography might not be distinct from sexual assault, or in concert with it, is not a possibility that my interlocutors care to consider.

An illustration of this practice was a notorious incident in Werribee in the Australian state of Victoria in 2006, which involved a gang of twelve young boys calling themselves the "Teenage Kings of Werribee". The boys made a DVD entitled *Cunt: The Movie,* in which they urinated on a girl with (reputed) intellectual disabilities and set her hair on fire in the course of sexually assaulting her. In the DVD, one of the boys laughs to the camera, saying, "What the fuck, she's the ugliest thing I have ever

[13] For illustrative incidents, see *ABC News* (2024) and Ortolan and Tran (2024).

seen". The DVD also included other incidents like dropping flares on a homeless man and throwing eggs at taxi drivers. The boys then posted segments of the DVD on YouTube under the title *Pimp My Wife* (Miletic 2006a, b).[14] A detective from the Victorian Sexual Crimes Unit at the time noted of the case, "We have taken a statement from the girl and she states quite categorically that she was not a willing participant on [sic] what occurred on that particular occasion and that confirms the basis of the offence" (Miletic 2006a, b). I would however think that it is open to question what, if any, significance consent or "willing participation" bears in assessing the *wrong* of acts of ritual humiliation of others like this. In April 2007, seven of the young men involved in the Werribee incident appeared in the Melbourne Children's Court charged with assault, making child pornography and procuring sexual penetration by intimidation (Shtargot 2007). The boys' main reaction was and continued to be laughter: in 2009 one of the boys who had not been charged posted a rap song on YouTube that named the victim and laughingly reiterated the elements of the crime while criticizing the "cunts who judge us" and saying that they could all "get fucked" (Dowsley and Healey 2009).

Other cases of "home-made" humiliation videos involve collective sexual assault ("gangbangs") on unconscious or intoxicated girls, as for example the "GoPro incident" in Sydney in May 2015, involving a group of men at a party, the youngest of whom was 17, who gang-raped an unconscious girl aged 16 and filmed the assault. The incident was not immediately reported but the video was later found by police on a phone during another investigation, and the participants were charged with aggravated sexual assault (Benny-Morrison 2015; Beers et al. 2015). The video seems to fit squarely in the PornHub category of "Passed Out Pussy" noted above. The commonly-asked question of whether pornography "caused" this assault (as in the "command" model of causation in which man "sees" porn, man rapes woman) seems to miss the point: we now live in *a pornographic world*, a world in which such harms are systematically inflicted on the basis of sex.

---

[14] See also for a still broader context, Quarmby (2013).

Such cases as these I have noted indicate that some young people are not merely recording the commission of sexual assault, but are committing sexual assault at least in part *in order to* make a pornographic artifact that can be circulated or posted online. This practice is not restricted to Australia, perhaps the most notorious US example being the Steubenville incident in Ohio, involving a high school football team (Macur and Schweber 2012). These collective practices of assault as a project in the creation of pornography are very different from the archetypal pattern of access and consumption in the past noted above, in which a lone boy in a darkened room masturbates to a "men's magazine". In general, access to and use of pornography by young people is now more likely to be explicitly collective in form, a pattern that is disturbingly similar in its form to the creation and use of the Abu Ghraib torture photographs, which also were not records of torture only, but rather the *staging* of torture *in order to* circulate the images on the internet and elsewhere (Clarke 2018). The practice of pornography increasingly takes the form of public collective entertainment more than private individual titillation.

This pattern of the collective character of practices of pornography can be discerned even in cases of related prosecutions of *individuals*. The prosecution of a young university student in Australia forms an illustration here. In this case, my account is drawn from open-access court documents, available inter alia on the Australian legal research site austlii.edu.au, which record the student's conviction for possession of "child abuse materials" (child pornography).[15] Marcus Puhakka was prosecuted for crimes committed when he was a young adult, and no longer a minor, but he had begun accessing pornography on the internet by the age of 10, and at some point as a teenager he first sought out and downloaded child pornography. The material he accessed included, for example, "a cartoon of a dog having sexual intercourse with a girl apparently under the age of ten", together with videos having a COPINE rating of 10 (the highest level) such as "a baby bound and sexually assaulted, a two year old girl subjected to anal intercourse, numerous images of young girls apparently heavily sedated being sexually assaulted

[15] *Puhakka v R* [2009] NSWCCA 290, http://www.austlii.edu.au/cgi-bin/sinodisp/au/cases/nsw/NSWCCA/2009/290.html (accessed 13 January 2025), also discussed in Pringle (2011a, b, c).

and a girl under ten bound and subjected to an act of anal intercourse while crying with the pain". What attracted Puhakka in accessing pornography was not just cruelty, but sexual cruelty. The psychological report prepared for the court noted that he "displayed little insight and little affect regarding the charges", possibly because he had been viewing pornography for nearly a decade by the time he faced court.

The court psychologist indicated that Marcus Puhakka was not a pedophile in the sense that he had abused or even wanted to abuse children whom he knew. He did not "act out",[16] at least in the sense of *contact* assault of actual children. And he did not make images by recording abuse of children; he simply downloaded and viewed them. It is also the case that some of his cache of materials comprised cartoon or virtual pornography, that is, material produced without an original incident or incidents of the abuse of identifiable children (Pringle 2013a, b). Indeed, some writers argue on the basis of cases like that of Marcus Puhakka that downloading images is in some sense "victimless". In this way of thinking (which I do not share), viewing, reading, or masturbating to pornography of any kind is claimed to be not a wrong, as well as being (comparatively) harmless, because doing so does not itself harm an identifiable victim. On this basis, some influential academic and popular media accounts dispute the seriousness of downloading and possession of pornography (Adler 2001; Aviv 2013). What such accounts do is to fit cases like Puhakka's accessing of pornography into the more traditional mode of the "lone ranger" viewer of pornography rather than of the collective practices I have just noted. In other words, the young offender is portrayed as a (socially inept) loner who has accessed the "wrong type" of pornography. In order to make this individualistic picture of the "crime scene" compelling, collective practices of pornography must be bracketed out of the picture, such that access and downloading are unfortunate, but not of themselves harmful, practices in that they do no harm to identifiable persons.

Although Puhakka's case is not necessarily "typical" of access to pornography by children and young people, it is in fact not so exceptional in court records. The myth that such offending is rare is quickly

---

[16] I am very aware of the problems in using the term "act out" in this and other such cases.

dispelled by the other cases cited by Judge Blanch in terms of Marcus Puhakka's appropriate sentencing.

Two other cases, one Australian and the other from England, further illustrate this trend in pornography use. In both cases, the collective practices in which individual users are embedded become clearer. Matthew David Graham (aka "Lux") faced sentencing in Melbourne, Australia, in March 2016 for child pornography, child abuse and "hurtcore" pornography convictions.[17] While living at home with his parents in his final year as a VCE student at Epping Secondary College (high school), Matthew became a principal figure in a ring of child pornography so extreme that the sentencing judge remarked, "It is as if he is from another planet" (Johnston 2016a). Matthew had distributed through his network a video allegedly made by Peter Scully, an Australian adult man who faced murder, rape and human trafficking charges in the Philippines. The video, entitled *Daisy's Destruction*, featured the torture and rape of an Asian toddler. Judge Michael Tinney told the court, "I am very much into uncharted territory.... How any human can view [*Daisy's Destruction*] impassively ... the infant was being tortured, actual physical torture, an extremely trusting, vulnerable child who begins smiling wearing a nappy and ends a wailing physical wreck.... I have seen some shocking things over the journey of my career and I have never seen anything like that" (Johnston 2016a, b; Johnston and Bucci 2015). Another charge was related to Graham's encouragement of a British man to rape a seven year old girl with muscular dystrophy who was in his care, and to his giving advice to the man on how to conceal his identity in a video. Judge Tinney noted that a further charge of advising a Russian man on how to abduct, rape and kill a five year old girl, and film it, was unprecedented in his experience (Johnston 2016a).

Like Marcus Puhakka (although with less plausibility in my view), Matthew Graham was classified as a "non-contact offender", meaning that he did not actually assault children physically, but rather incited and/or encouraged their rape and murder by others. Matthew had told police he was not a paedophile but that he felt "power within the community"

[17] *The Queen v Graham [2016] VCC 305*. An outline of the case and charges against Graham are set out in Commonwealth Director of Public Prosecutions (2016).

through his actions; in order to gain further "respect", Matthew often assumed the online identity of an American paediatrician with access to children. He did act as a babysitter for families in his neighbourhood.

The case in England involved a secondary school student at Eton, Andrew Picard, who was found to possess on his computer over 2000 pornographic images of children as young as 2-years-old, including images of torture-rape and bestiality, some of which he had made himself.[18] At the age of 17, Picard was apprehended by an undercover officer in a Skype chatroom for teenagers when he messaged the officer, "Do you want to see pics of boys and girls your age nude?" Picard boasted of having hundreds of such images and shared with the officer indecent images of a boy aged 10, and girls aged eight and 14 (Fenton 2016).

I am not citing these cases as typical of the way young people access and use pornography on the internet. These cases I have noted could be dismissed as outliers, and their citation in discussion about pornography as misleading. However, they are indicative of emerging patterns of use of "hurtcore" and torture pornography more generally. What the different cases all illustrate is the desensitising of children and young people to cruelty and degradation through early and repeated exposure to pornography, and in particular desensitisation to sexual cruelty done to girls. The cases are now not so far from the "mainstream" as illustrations of a trend in the consumption of pornography.

I would like to draw some provisional conclusions from these two sections of the chapter. First, it is misleading to understand pornography as an individual practice of access and consumption. Even where an individual appears to be simply a solitary "end user" (as a viewer), he (or she) is embedded in collective patterns of production, circulation, access and of use. This immediately raises doubts about a "public health approach" focusing on the physical and mental health of end users (in terms of porn or internet addiction, say). Second, it is not invariably the case that the primary wrong or "harm" of pornography is best identified in terms of its being subsequently acted out in contact abuse or violence. To understand the pornography system fully, it is crucial to locate its harms

[18] I explore in depth the frequent association of possession of animal abuse and child abuse materials in an unpublished paper, on file with author.

not only in the production and acting out stages, but in the stages of circulation, access and initial use. And third, I note that the cruelty and humiliation discernible both in pornographic objects like videos and in collective usage patterns is not simply a random cruelty but is gendered in a way that fits with understandings of gender-based violence set out in the *Declaration on the Elimination of Violence against Women.* that is, cruelty is conformed into patterns of violence against women and girls.

What Are Children Learning from Pornography?

A study by David Comer Kidd and Emanuele Castano of the effects on readers of literary fiction found that spending only a few minutes reading a work of literature could increase the empathy of adults (Kidd and Castano 2013). It would be implausible then if spending only a few minutes in the company, say, of Max Hardcore did not have stunting effects on the development of empathy. By empathy here, I mean a Kantian capacity to recognize another person as an end in herself, not as a means to our own ends or as an object. The development of empathy in citizens in this respect is integral to a democracy based on recognition of the equal dignity of all regardless of their sex or gender. There is no evidence to suggest that children "learn" such values or qualities in their interactions with pornography.

Some writers argue that the greater accessibility of pornography to children and young people is not necessarily a bad thing, on the basis that pornography has long been argued to act as a form of sex education (Simon et al. 2015). There is a truth here, in that this is certainly one of the ways in which pornography works. Marcus Puhakka for example had learnt about sex from pornographic materials that he accessed on the internet. The type of material that is easy to find, or even to stumble upon, on the internet educates boys, *and* girls, about what sex is, how they should do it, what they should expect their partners to do, and what they should expect it to be like. Pornography eroticises domination over others, gives it a "kick" (MacKinnon 1993, 16). That is, when boys masturbate, individually or collectively, to pornography, they are getting off on sexual inequality. There is no question that pornography teaches—and one of its primary lessons is that inequality and dominance are natural, exciting, sexy, and cool.

Young people's understanding and experience of sex, but also their understanding of gender and sexuality more broadly, are increasingly shaped by what they or their peers observe and experience in pornography. It is not an exaggeration to say that we now live in a pornographic (porn) culture. By "porn culture", to use a term popularised by Gail Dines, is meant not simply a sexualized culture, but a culture where the way our lives are sexualized is through a porn aesthetic, in which boys are allocated a very different role from girls. Such an aesthetic *reflects* social patterns of dominance and subordination, but it also *forms* society and how we understand who we are when we live in it. Pornography is *performative* in that sense: it performs sex and it performs sex as inequality. It is *enacted* by and as inequality. Young people's expectations and practices are increasingly shaped by an image of sex that is deliberately painful or violating. A high value is not placed on respect, mutuality, communication, or tenderness in the sexual "scripts" that young people are now learning (Sun et al. 2016; Bridges et al. 2016). To emphasize again, this is not simply sexualisation, but is more accurately understood as pervasive pornographication (Tyler and Quek 2016).

Many writers who are defensive of pornography make the point that not only does it serve as a form of educating young people about sex. They argue that it can play this role because it is *harmless*, apart from certain very extreme or non-consensual forms which are allegedly few, and far from the "mainstream". The argument of such defenders of pornography is that in order to prove harm by pornography, one must show a direct, one on one, *causal* relationship between consumption of a pornographic object and the commission of an act of gross sexual violence. However, it is simply not the case that in order to ascertain the formative and performative harms of pornography, we would need to establish that kind of causal relationship on the model of a coercive command that cannot be refused. These defensive contentions about what would count as harm in the context of pornography are simply outdated. When we understand and address pornography in a human rights context, in terms of violence against women and girls, the question of harm is connected to questions of sexual violence and subordination, in a pornographic world.

A prominent defender of pornography, Alan McKee, has characterised pornography as entertainment, as if this characterisation lifted the genre, its practices and its artifacts out of the realm of critique as well as of censure (McKee 2012a, b). It is true that a common reaction, especially in collective activities, to pornography, is laughter. An example is patterns of use around a notorious video called *Two Girls One Cup*, actually a trailer for a Brazilian film called *Hungry Bitches*, which was made and posted online in 2007. After the trailer/video was posted, it became a viral practice to play it for a group of people, in order to video their reactions, with the reaction video in turn posted online. There are now millions of videos on this search term, some being remakes or parodies of the original trailer. The reaction videos have large numbers of views, more than 25 million in one case. The viewers who post their reaction videos are often very young; I have noticed videos posted by children of 5–6 years old.

This is a novel phenomenon in the consumption of pornography: the process of videoing oneself watching pornography, then posting that video on YouTube or other services. It was not technologically possible, at least as a kind of "democratic" process, until perhaps 15–20 years ago. The laughter in the reaction videos attests to an apparent refusal of young viewers to be shocked or disturbed by what they see; when viewers do react with disbelief or distaste, they are laughed at in turn by the operator of the camera. Indeed, the reaction videos tend to closely follow a script, with the common "moral" of the story being that it is not cool to stay serious, but rather, one must laugh at oneself and at others when any residual sense of shock or disturbance is manifested. The "scripted" reaction to pornography objects in this case is laughter. Far from being an individual pursuit, this practice is a rehearsal of the consumption of pornographic objects that is repeated over and over again with very little variation. There is nothing individual or even spontaneous about it.

What does this laughter signify, and why should it be of concern to us? The viewers of *Two Girls One Cup* and the viewers of their reaction do not collectively masturbate, or achieve sexual arousal from the practice (or this at any rate is not shown or referred to on screen in the reaction videos). Instead the viewers laugh—and they set in train an infinite laugh such that viewers of YouTube laugh at them laughing. This practice indicates that pornography has as much or more to do with humiliation and even cruelty than with sex *simpliciter*, and that children's laughter at this spectacle of cruelty should concern us even more perhaps than children "getting off" sexually on pornography. This example runs parallel to the making for use of amateur videos involving the sexual humiliation and assault of young girls, noted above, where the making and use are not purposed for sexual arousal and erotic satisfaction, but for the humiliation of girls through the assertion of a power explicitly figured as masculine.

The laughter of pornography by children as well as adults is at least in some cases akin to the laughter of cruelty that greets dwarfs in a circus, or the throwing of dwarfs as part of pub revels. The notion of "putting on a show" with its overt sexual overtones runs throughout the way in which a socially created deformity or disability becomes a source of mirth and a site of entertainment. When women form the spectacle in pornographic videos, they fill that space of the dwarfs, laughed at and mocked.[19] A significant implication of this is that a commonly-used "definition" of pornography as sexually explicit material intended to arouse sexual excitement seems simplistic and misleading as to what it *does*, at least in this world.

There is immense pressure in our society for people not to react to pornography as if it raises serious questions, but rather to laugh it off, and to laugh off their own reservations. Pornographic laughter is also used against those who voice concerns about any kind of demeaning treatment of women and girls, whether in entertainment, advertising or political discourse. That is, the response is that pornography is all just one big joke—and that women, in particular, need to stop taking things so seriously (Pobjie 2012). Complaints about the pornographic depiction of women become an occasion for further mocking laughter and derision at their being "stitched up", or as "man haters". Images and themes drawn

[19] The scenes in the film The Wolf of Wall Street (2013) concerning the organization of a dwarf-throwing entertainment for an office party are illustrative of the dynamic at work in such cases.

from the pornography industry are increasingly used to belittle women and denigrate their standing through making them figures of fun.

It is not surprising in this context that children often respond to questions about pornography by saying that they are not overly worried by it. A report of a 2011 study by Australian researchers found that children were largely not "bothered" by viewing pornography (Green et al. 2011). It would be surprising if a report found otherwise in a context where concern for the impact of pornography is an indication to many academic researchers, as well as more broadly, of being gripped by a "moral panic", that is, decidedly "uncool". Defenders of the pornography system often characterize opposition to or even concern about its impact as indicating a lack of a "sense of humour" or lack of comfort with "fun" as "entertainment". In this context, the claim is often made that expressed concerns for children affected by pornography is the wedge by which pornography more generally is now opposed, that is, that children are being used like "human shields" for an agenda around "a new puritanism". Robbie Swan, founder of the peak lobby for the Australian sex industry, the Eros Association, set this argument out very clearly in noting, "Most of the religious rhetoric directed at the sex industry during the 1990s concerned a loss of innocence and the 'harm' done to children by pornography and commercial sex" (Swan 2013; also Lumby and Albury 2010). Swan concluded his remarks by saying:

> … the repression of sex is decidedly unhealthy. At an individual level, *New Scientist*'s 2004 report on the sex lives of 30,000 men showed that the more frequently men ejaculated, whether through sex or masturbation, the less prostate cancer they developed in later life…. at an official and institutional level, sexual repression comes with serious consequences for the whole community. As far as human needs go, sexual desire is up there with hunger and the will to survive. When it hits a man in the groin, it easily trumps a 2000-year-old Abrahamic belief system centred somewhere in the frontal lobes of the cortex. (Swan 2013)

This risible statement as to the inevitability of an insistent male sexual desire at the heart of pornography and modern sexual practices more generally, which if frustrated leads to serious health problems for both individuals and society, is completely at odds with modern understandings of sex and sexuality as socially and historically constructed. As the *Declaration on the Elimination of Violence against Women* notes, "violence against women is a manifestation of historically unequal power relations between men and women, which have led to domination over and discrimination against women by men and to the prevention of the full advancement of women, and ... violence against women is one of the crucial social mechanisms by which women are forced into a subordinate position compared with men".[20] Pornography now presents a crisis in terms of sex and gendered violence, not a crisis of public health in which the opposing sides are puritanism and the healthy sexual life of (male) libertinism.

Conclusion

It is important to listen to what children and young people say about pornography and how they feel about it. However, it is also crucial to listen to what they *are able to say* about pornography, that is, the constraints within which they can speak and be heard with credibility and acceptance. Without a vocabulary to express one's feelings, and without a context of acceptance of those feelings, what children and others say about what they feel will differ decisively. The available vocabulary for speaking of cruelty and violence in a sexual context is very limited in terms of social acceptance, which is so crucial for a child growing towards autonomy. It is for this reason that the adoption of a VAWG approach for understanding pornography becomes an urgent task, not merely because it enables us to understand pornography and how it works today more fully and accurately. Such a strategy provides a different framework for speaking and for listening to what children, and especially in this context girls, feel about pornography and its impact

[20] UN General Assembly [UNGA], *Declaration on the Elimination of Violence Against Women*, 20 December 1993, A/RES/48/104, Article 1, https://digitallibrary.un.org/record/179739?ln=en (accessed 13 January 2025).

on their lives. And on what it means, and takes from them, to live in a pornographic world.

Responding to pornography as part of a strategy on VAWG provides an example of what it means to take pornography seriously. For example, successive formulations by the Scottish government of this strategy (Scottish government/Riaghaltas na h-Alba 2023) make links between different forms of violence against women and girls, requiring a suite of measures (and of research) across a broad front covering areas such as domestic violence, forced marriage, honour-based violence, female genital cutting, rape and other sexual offences, prostitution, and trafficking, child abuse—and pornography. Such a strategy is not oriented to achieving harm minimisation or reduction, but to reaching goals of equality and dignity among all citizens, and with respect to children and young people as they grow to adulthood.

An example of an appropriate measure formulated within this broad approach would be the establishment of a claims process for restitution on a meaningful level for sexual violence, such as has been available to victims of pornography in the US *Violence Against Women Act* of 1994, particularly in regard to the harm of child pornography (Pringle 2011a, b, c).[21] The revision of legal formulations of child pornography (or child abuse materials) and of sentencing guidelines on pornography (Mizzi et al 2010) would also be useful in terms of underlining the seriousness of questions about pornography. Penalties for the viewing, downloading and possession of pornography should be set at a high level not only in order to lead perpetrators to reconsider their actions, but also to impress upon children and others that this is a serious matter, in terms of the freedom of women and girls from violence and subordination, rather than in terms of an ungendered benchmark of public health. Such an approach around VAWG is a long-term project, but has immediate potential in terms of recalibrating the seriousness of pornography in connection with gendered violence. At stake is creating a space and a vocabulary in the public discussion of pornography that allows for

[21] The restitution provision discussed was reformulated in the *Amy, Vicky, and Andy Child Pornography Victim Assistance Act of 2018* (*AVAA*) in the wake of the case *Paroline v U.S.* 572 US 434 (2014), https://www.supremecourt.gov/opinions/boundvolumes/572BV.pdf (accessed 13 January 2025).

and hears different voices and different stories from those that fit the pornographic narrative of acceptance of cruelty and violence as "cool".

Bibliography

Reported Cases

Paroline v United States 572 US 434 (2014), https://supreme.justia.com/cases/federal/us/572/434/ (accessed 2 March 2025).

Puhakka v R [2009] NSWCCA 290, http://www.austlii.edu.au/cgi-bin/sinodisp/au/cases/nsw/NSWCCA/2009/290.html (accessed 13 January 2025).

The Queen v Graham [2016] VCC 305.

Statutes and Treaties or Conventions

Amy, Vicky, and Andy Child Pornography Victim Assistance Act of 2018 (*AVAA*), https://sentencing.typepad.com/sentencing_law_and_policy/2019/02/the-new-amy-vicky-and-andy-act-a-positive-step-towards-full-restitution-for-child-pornography-victim.html (accessed 13 January 2025).

Anti-Discrimination Act 1977 (New South Wales), sections 20B-C (race), 38R-S (transgender), 49ZD-ZE (religion), 49ZS-ZT (homosexuality), 49ZXA-ZXB (HIV/AIDS status), https://legislation.nsw.gov.au/view/html/inforce/2024-07-01/act-1977-048 (accessed 13 January 2025).

UN General Assembly [UNGA], *Declaration on the Elimination of Violence against Women*, 20 December 1993, A/RES/48/104, https://digitallibrary.un.org/record/179739?ln=en (accessed 13 January 2025).

Violence Against Women Act 1994 (US), Text - H.R.3355 - 103rd Congress (1993-1994): Violent Crime Control and Law Enforcement Act of 1994 | Congress.gov | Library of Congress (accessed 2 October 2025).

Articles and Book Chapters

ABC News (2024) "Police Investigate Fake Nude Photos of about 50 Bacchus Marsh Grammar Students Being Circulated Online," 11 June

2024, https://www.abc.net.au/news/2024-06-11/bacchus-marsh-grammar-explicit-images-ai-nude/103965298 (accessed 13 January 2025).

Adler, Amy, "The Perverse Law of Child Pornography," *Columbia Law Review* 101 (2001) 209.

Aviv, Rachel, "The Science of Sex Abuse: Is It Right to Imprison People for Heinous Crimes They Have Not Yet Committed?" *The New Yorker* 14 January 2013, http://www.newyorker.com/magazine/2013/01/14/the-science-of-sex-abuse (accessed 13 January 2025).

Beers, Lucy, Mae, Tran, Cindy and Piotrowski, Daniel, "'The Way He Gets On with Girls... Why Would He Waste His Time?': Father Defends His Son who Police Say 'Encouraged' Five Friends to Gang Rape a Girl, 16, as He Filmed on his GoPro Camera," *Mail Online* 16 October 2015, http://www.dailymail.co.uk/news/article-3274025/The-way-gets-girls-waste-time-Father-defends-son-police-say-encouraged-friends-gang-rape-unconscious-girl-16-filmed.html (accessed 13 January 2025).

Benny-Morrison, Ava, "Father Defends Son Charged over Alleged Gang-Rape of Teenage Girl Filmed on GoPro," *Sydney Morning Herald* 16 October 2015, http://www.smh.com.au/nsw/father-defends-son-charged-over-alleged-gangrape-of-teenage-girl-filmed-on-gopro-20151015-gka6ld.html (accessed 13 January 2025).

Bray, Abigail, "Merciless Doctrines: Child Pornography, Censorship, and Late Capitalism," *Signs: Journal of Women in Culture and Society* 37 (2011) 133.

Bridges, Ana J, Sun, Chyng F, Ezzell, Matthew B and Johnson, Jennifer, "Sexual Scripts and the Sexual Behavior of Men and Women Who Use Pornography," *Sexualization, Media & Society* online (2016).

Cadzow, Jane, "Sex Sells: The Business of Pleasure," *The Age* 24 October 2011, https://www.theage.com.au/business/small-business/sex-sells-the-business-of-pleasure-20111024-1mfhf.html (accessed 13 January 2025).

Clarke, DA, "Prostitution for Everyone: Feminism, Globalisation, and the 'Sex' Industry," in *Not for Sale: Feminists Resisting Prostitution and Pornography*, Christine Stark & Rebecca Whisnant, eds (North Melbourne, Australia: Spinifex Press, 2018).

Crabb, Maree and Corlett, David, "Eroticising Inequality: Technology, Pornography and Young People," *Domestic Violence Resource Centre Victoria Quarterly* 3 (2010).

Dines, Gail, "Not Your Father's Playboy," *Counterpunch*, 17 May 2010, www.counterpunch.org/2010/05/17/not-your-father-s-playboy/ (accessed 13 January 2025).

Dowsley, Anthony and Healey, Kelvin, "Werribee Sex DVD Ringleader's Hate-filled Rap Song on Web," *Herald Sun* 13 April 2009, http://web.archive.org/web/20090413190710/http://www.news.com.au/heraldsun/story/0,21985,25325367-661,00.html (accessed 13 January 2025).
Fenton, Siobhan, "Eton Pupil Andrew Picard Spared Jail after Creating and Sharing Thousands of 'Appalling' Child Abuse Images," *The Independent* 26 February 2016, http://www.independent.co.uk/news/uk/crime/eton-pupil-andrew-picard-convicted-of-creating-and-sharing-child-abuse-images-a6896966.html (accessed 13 January 2025).
Feona, Atwood, 'The Politics of Amateurism in Online Pornography' in *Photography Reframed: New Visions in Contemporary Photographic Culture*, Ben Burbridge & Annebella Pollen, ed (London: Routledge, 2018).
Flood, Michael, "Exposure to Pornography among Youth in Australia," *Journal of Sociology* 43 (2007) 45.
Green, Lelia, Brady, Danielle, Ólafsson, Kjartan, Hartley, John and Lumby, Catharine, "Risks and Safety for Australian Children on the Internet: Full Findings from the AU Kids Online Survey of 9–16 Year Olds and their Parents," *Cultural Science* 4 (2011).
Johnston, Chris, "Judge Asked to Peer into the Abyss as 'Hurtcore' Paedophile Matthew Graham Fronts Court," *The Age* 3 February 2016a, http://www.theage.com.au/victoria/judge-asked-to-peer-into-the-abyss-as-hurtcore-paedophile-matthew-graham-fronts-court-20160203-gmkm6u.html#ixzz41Z3VcvCB (accessed 13 January 2025).
Johnston, Chris, "'Lux' and the Child Pornography Crimes Too Awful to Print," *The Age* 3 February 2016b, http://www.theage.com.au/victoria/lux-and-the-child-pornography-crimes-too-awful-to-print-20160203-gmkxtr.html (accessed 13 January 2025).
Johnston, Chris, "Shocked Judge Says It Seems Pornographer Matthew Graham is 'from Another Planet'," *The Age* 18 February 2016c, http://www.theage.com.au/victoria/shocked-judge-says-it-seems-as-if-child-pornographer-matthew-graham-is-from-another-planet-20160218-gmxhwh.html#ixzz41Z2m8HHL (accessed 13 January 2025).
Johnston, Chris and Bucci, Nino, "How Matthew David Graham's 'Hurtcore' Paedophile Habit Began on the Dark Web," *The Age* 9 September 2015, https://www.theage.com.au/national/victoria/how-matthew-david-grahams-hurtcore-paedophile-habit-began-on-the-dark-web-20150908-gjhz43.html (accessed 13 January 2025).

Kidd, David Comer and Castano, Emanuele, "Reading Literary Fiction Improves Theory of Mind," *Science* 342 (2013), http://science.sciencemag.org/content/sci/early/2013/10/02/science.1239918.full.pdf (accessed 13 January 2025).

Klein, Marty, "Pornography, the Narrative of Public Health," in *The International Encyclopedia of Human Sexuality*, 3 vols, Patricia Whelehan and Anne Bolin (eds), Wiley Online Library (2015): 567.

Kozaki, Danuta, "Internet Pornography Causing Long-term Public Health Crisis amongst Australian Children, Seminar Hears," *ABC News* 9 February 2016, http://www.abc.net.au/news/2016-02-09/health-crisis-looming-over-accessibiilty-of-porn-for-children/7153016 (accessed 13 January 2025).

Limb, Matthew, "Internet Pornography is an Urgent Public Health Issue, Conference Hears," *BMJ* 349:g4475 (2014).

Lumby, Catharine and Albury, Kath, "Too Much? Too Young? The Sexualisation of Children Debate in Australia," *Media International Australia* 135 (2010).

McKay, Kimberley, Poulin, Christopher and Muñoz-Laboy, Miguel, "Claiming Public Health Crisis to Regulate Sexual Outlets: A Critique of the State of Utah's Declaration on Pornography," *Archives of Sexual Behavior* 50 (2021) 401.

McKee, Alan, "The Importance of Entertainment for Sexuality Education", *Sex Education: Sexuality, Society and Learning* 12 (2012a).

McKee, Alan, "Methodological Issues in Defining Aggression for Content Analyses of Sexually Explicit Material", *Archives of Sexual Behavior* 44 (2015).

McKee, Alan, "Pornography as Entertainment", *Continuum: Journal of Media & Cultural Studies* 26 (2012b).

Macur, Juliet and Schweber, Nate, "Rape Case Unfolds on Web and Splits City," *New York Times* 16 December 2012, http://www.nytimes.com/2012/12/17/sports/high-school-football-rape-case-unfolds-online-and-divides-steubenville-ohio.html (accessed 13 January 2025).

Miletic, Daniella, "Outcry over Teenage Girl's Assault Recorded on DVD", *The Age* 25 October 2006a, https://www.theage.com.au/national/outcry-over-teenage-girls-assault-recorded-on-dvd-20061025-ge3evq.html (accessed 13 January 2025).

Miletic, Daniella, "Rape Probe over Sex Attack DVD", *The Age* 25 October 2006b, http://www.theage.com.au/articles/2006/10/25/1161699379876.html (accessed 13 January 2025).

Norma, Caroline, "Teaching Tools and Recipe Books: Pornography and the Sexual Assault of Children," in *Big Porn, Inc: Exposing the Harms of the Global Pornography Industry*, Melinda Tankard Reist and Abigail Bray, eds (North Melbourne, Australia: Spinifex Press, 2011).

Ortolan, Mikaela and Tran, Danny, "Victorian Teachers Also Victims of Fake Explicit Images Created by Students using AI", *ABC News* 13 June 2024, https://www.abc.net.au/news/2024-06-13/ai-generated-deepfake-pornography-school-students-teachers/103969414 (accessed 13 January 2025).

Paasonen, Susanna, "Labors of Love: Netporn, Web 2.0 and the Meanings of Amateurism," *New Media and Society* 12 (2010).

Pobjie, Ben, "Porn. Don't Knock It 'til You've Tried It," *The King's Tribune* 5 January 2012, http://www.kingstribune.com/magazine-archive/january-2012/item/1419-porn-don-t-knock-it-til-you-ve-tried-it (accessed 13 January 2025).

Pringle, Helen, "Cartoon Wars: The Interpretation of Drawn Images" in *Re-mapping the Future: History, Culture and Environment in Australia and India*, Raelene Frances and Deb N Bandyopadhyay, eds (Newcastle, UK: Cambridge Scholars Publishing, 2013a).

Pringle, Helen, "Civil Justice for Victims of Child Pornography" in *Big Porn, Inc: Exposing the Harms of the Global Pornography Industry,* Melinda Tankard Reist and Abigail Bray, eds (North Melbourne, Australia: Spinifex Press, 2011a).

Pringle, Helen, "The Making of Women's Un-freedom: Sexual Harassment as Harm" in *Freedom Fallacy: The Failures of Liberal Feminism*, Miranda Kiraly and Meagan Tyler, eds (Melbourne, Australia: Connor Court, 2015).

Pringle, Helen, "The Pornification of Julia Gillard" in *Bewitched and Bedevilled: Women Write the Gillard Years,* Samantha Trenoweth, ed (Melbourne: Hardie Grant, 2013b).

Pringle, Helen, "*The Porn Report*: A Studied Indifference to Harm" in *Big Porn, Inc: Exposing the Harms of the Global Pornography Industry*, Melinda Tankard Reist and Abigail Bray, eds (North Melbourne, Australia: Spinifex Press, 2011b).

Pringle, Helen, "Pornography: Who's Sleeping with Whom?" *On Line Opinion,* 8 September 2011c, http://www.onlineopinion.com.au/view.asp?article=12579 (accessed 13 January 2025).

Pringle, Helen, "What is the Billboard Doing? Reactions to Calvin Klein," *On Line Opinion*, 24 November 2010, http://www.onlineopinion.com.au/view.asp?article=11279 (accessed 13 January 2025).

Pringle, Helen, "Wicked Slogans aren't Just Harmless Fun," *ABC The Drum* 16 July 2014, http://www.abc.net.au/news/2014-07-16/pringle-wicked-slogans-arent-just-harmless-fun/5598858/ (accessed 13 January 2025).
Prior, Neale, "Day Crew Set Up Maddox Porn Play, Court Told," *West Australian* 7 March 2014, https://au.news.yahoo.com/thewest/wa/a/21862904/day-crew-set-up-maddox-porn-play/ (accessed 13 January 2025).
Quarmby, Katharine, "Media Reporting and Disability Hate Crime" in *Disability, Hate Crime and Violence,* Alan Roulstone and Hannah Mason-Bish, eds (Oxford, UK: Routledge, 2013).
Ruberg, Bonnie, "Doing It for Free: Digital Labour and the Fantasy of Amateur Online Pornography," *Porn Studies* 3 (2016).
Scottish Government/Riaghaltas na h-Alba, *Equally Safe: Scotland's Strategy for Preventing and Eradicating Violence against Women and Girls,* December 2023, https://www.gov.scot/publications/equally-safe-scotlands-strategy-preventing-eradicating-violence-against-women-girls/ (accessed 13 January 2025).
Shtargot, Sasha, "Werribee DVD Youths Plead Guilty, Avoid Jail," The *Age* 21 July 2007, http://www.theage.com.au/news/national/werribee-dvd-youths-plead-guilty-avoid-jail/2007/07/20/1184560043673.html (accessed 13 January 2025).
Simon, Laura E, Daneback, Kristian and Ševčíková, Anna, "The Educational Dimension of Pornography: Adolescents' Use of New Media for Sexual Purposes" in *Living in the Digital Age: Self-presentation, Networking, Playing, and Participating in Politics,* Pascaline Lorentz, David Šmahel, Monika Metyková and Michelle F. Wright, eds (Brno: Muni Press, 2015).
Sun, Chyng F, Bridges, Ana J, Johnson, Jennifer A and Ezzell, Matthew B, "Pornography and the Male Sexual Script: An Analysis of Consumption and Sexual Relations", *Archives of Sexual Behavior* 45 (2016) 45: esp. 990–991.
Sunstein, Cass, "Free Speech Now," *University of Chicago Law Review 58* (1992).
Swan, Robbie, "Correspondence," *Quarterly Essay* 52 (2013): 81.
Tyler, Meagan and Quek, Kaye, "Conceptualizing Pornographication: A Lack of Clarity and Problems for Feminist Analysis". *Sexualization, Media, & Society* 2 (2016).
Tyler, Meagan, "'Now That's Pornography!' Violence and Domination in *Adult Video News*," in *Everyday Pornography*, Karen Boyle, ed (NYC, NY, US: Taylor & Francis, 2010).
Whisnant, Rebecca, "Not Your Father's *Playboy*, Not Your Mother's Feminist Movement: Feminism in Porn Culture" in *Freedom Fallacy: The Failures*

of Liberal Feminism, Miranda Kiraly and Meagan Tyler, eds (Melbourne, Australia: Connor Court, 2015).

Books, Reports and Films

Dworkin, Andrea and MacKinnon, Catharine A, *Pornography & Civil Rights: A New Day for Women's Equality* (Minneapolis MN, US: Organizing against Pornography, 1988).

Pierrette Mizzi, Tom Gotsis and Patrizia Poletti, *Sentencing Offenders Convicted of Child Pornography and Child Abuse Material Offences*, Judicial Commission of New South Wales Monograph no. 34 (2010), https://web.archive.org/web/20110217180227/https://www.judcom.nsw.gov.au/publications/research-monographs-1/research-monograph-34/Monograph34.pdf (accessed 13 January 2025).

[France] Haut conseil à l'égalité entre les femmes et les hommes, *Pornocriminalité: mettons fin à l'impunité de l'industrie pornographique!* Rapport no 2023-09-27 VIO 50, https://www.haut-conseil-egalite.gouv.fr/violences-faites-aux-femmes/travaux-du-hce/article/rapport-pornocriminalite-mettons-fin-a-l-impunite-de-l-industrie-pornographique (accessed 13 January 2025).

Horvath, Miranda AH, Alys, Llian, Masse, Kristina, Pina, Afroditi, Scally, Mia and Adler, Joana R, for the Office of the Children's Commissioner, *"Basically... Porn is Everywhere": A Rapid Evidence Assessment on the Effects that Access and Exposure to Pornography has on Children and Young People* (London, 2013), https://www.childrenscommissioner.gov.uk/resource/basically-porn-is-everywhere/ (accessed 13 January 2025).

MacKinnon, Catharine A, *Only Words* (Cambridge MA, US: Harvard University Press, 1993).

MacKinnon, Catharine A and Dworkin, Andrea, eds, *In Harm's Way: The Pornography Civil Rights Hearings* (Cambridge MA, US: Harvard University Press, 1997).

Mizzi, Pierrette, Gotsis, Tom and Poletti, Patrizia, *Sentencing Offenders Convicted of Child Pornography and Child Abuse Material Offences*, Judicial Commission of New South Wales Monograph no. 34 (2010), https://web.archive.org/web/20110217180227/https://www.judcom.nsw.gov.au/publications/research-monographs-1/research-monograph-34/Monograph34.pdf (accessed 13 January 2025).

Prichard, Jeremy and Spiranovic, Caroline, *Child Exploitation Material in the Context of Institutional Child Sexual Abuse*, Report for the Royal

Commission into Institutional Responses to Child Sexual Abuse (2014), https://www.childabuseroyalcommission.gov.au/sites/default/files/file-list/Research%20Report%20-%20Child%20Exploitation%20Material%20in%20the%20Context%20of%20Institutional%20Child%20Sexual%20Abuse%20-%20Causes.pdf (accessed 13 January 2025).

Rosewarne, Lauren, *Sex in Public: Women, Outdoor Advertising and Public Policy* (Newcastle, UK: Cambridge Scholars Publishing, 2007).

Rothman, Emily F, *Pornography and Public Health* (Oxford, UK: Oxford University Press, 2021).

Rush, Emma and La Nauze, Andrea, for the Australia Institute, *Corporate Paedophilia: Sexualisation of Children in the Media*, Australia Institute (Canberra, 2006a), https://australiainstitute.org.au/report/corporate-paedophilia-sexualisation-of-children-in-australia/ (accessed 13 January 2025).

Rush, Emma and La Nauze, Andrea, for the Australia Institute, *Letting Children Be Children: Stopping the Sexualisation of Children in Australia*, Australia Institute (Canberra, 2006b), https://australiainstitute.org.au/wp-content/uploads/2020/12/DP93_8.pdf (accessed 13 January 2025).

Stardust, Zahra, *Indie Porn: Revolution, Regulation and Resistance* (Durham NC, US: Duke University Press, 2024).

[UK] Children's Commissioner, *"A Lot of It is Actually Just Abuse": Young People and Pornography* (London, 2023a) https://assets.childrenscommissioner.gov.uk/wpuploads/2023/02/cc-a-lot-of-it-is-actually-just-abuse-young-people-and-pornography-updated.pdf (accessed 13 January 2025).

[UK] Children's Commissioner, *Evidence on Pornography's Influence on Harmful Sexual Behaviour among Children* (London, 2023b), https://assets.childrenscommissioner.gov.uk/wpuploads/2023/05/Evidence-on-pornographys-influence-on-harmful-sexual-behaviour-among-children.pdf (accessed 13 January 2025).

The Wolf of Wall Street (2013), https://www.imdb.com/title/tt0993846/ (accessed 2 March 2025).

Information Documents and Resources

2023 Year in Review of PornHub at https://archive.md/KU6oJ (accessed 13 January 2025).

Amankavičiūtė, Sandra, unpublished work in progress, University of New South Wales (UNSW), Sydney. Please do not cite without acknowledgement.

Commonwealth Director of Public Prosecutions, "Head Administrator of Child Exploitation Sites on Dark Web Gaoled for over 15 Years" 17 March 2016, https://www.cdpp.gov.au/news/head-administrator-child-exploitation-sites-dark-web-gaoled-over-15-years (accessed 13 January 2025).

Coy, Maddy, *Pornographic Performances: A Review of Research on Sexualisation and Racism in Music Videos*, Short Briefing Paper on Sexist-Racist Content in Music Videos, for EVAW Coalition, imkaan & Object (2014), https://web.archive.org/web/20160325110322/https://www.endviolenceagainstwomen.org.uk/data/files/Pornographic_Performances_FINAL_Aug_2014.pdf (accessed 13 January 2025).

Whisnant, R (2007). Not your Father's Playboy, not your Mother's Feminist Movement: Contemporary Feminism in a Porn Culture, Talk to "Pornography and Pop Culture: Re-framing Theory, Re-thinking Activism" conference, Boston, 2 March, http://www.feministes-radicales.org/wp-content/uploads/2012/05/Rebecca-Whisnant-Contempory-feminism-in-a-porn-culture.pdf (accessed 5 March 2024).

20

Barbie Meets a Very Poor Thing Silenced by the Lambs: Feminist Filmmaking (En)Counters Masculine Renditions of the Female

Jocelynne A. Scutt

Introduction

Released in 1991, *Silence of the Lambs* won Best Picture, Best Director (Jonathan Demme), Best Actor (Anthony (Tony) Hopkins), Best Actress (Jodie Foster), Best Adapted Screenplay (Ted Tally on Robert Harris' novel of the same name), missed out on editing and sound, and was the first (and so far only) horror film to win Best Picture (Awards Daily 2025). It brought Jodie Foster her second Academy Award (first for *The Accused*, 1989), with critics praising her "feminist" performance (Rotten Tomatoes nd). Yet however good her performance (and it is), Clarice Starling whom Foster plays is no movie feminist. Yes she is a woman struggling in the men's world of the FBI, surrounded by masculine figures taller, weightier, louder, more assured (at least outwardly), and

J. A. Scutt (✉)
University of New South Wales (UNSW), Sydney, NSW, Australia
e-mail: jocelynne@fraserchambers.com

Fraser Chambers, Leadenhall Building, London, United Kingdom

J. A. Scutt (ed.), *Women, Power and Autonomy*,
https://doi.org/10.1007/978-3-031-97958-3_20

wholly accepted as well-polished investigators and operatives. Nonetheless Starling's "St George and the Dragon" performance is far from encompassing feminist spirt, philosophy and action. Starling (Foster) sets out alone on her journey to undercut the male FBI detectives who are her competitors in the search to locate and capture the notorious killer who skins his victims alive. There is no sense that the captured women might collaborate in their own rescue. No notion that their lives have meaning to be tapped into by Starling so that working together with them or through their personal tragedies that culminate in flaying and death she is able to ensure the rescue of Catherine, whose life is the subject of the race against time. Absent is the idea that this rescue might come through collective effort rather than single and singular triumph: the "look what I've done, single-handed" style of a woman who has no connection with those whom she seeks to save, despite a somewhat perfunctory trip into the workplace of one of the victims, Frederika Bimmel. In imitating her male counterparts, Starling betrays the feminist ideal. However this is, perhaps, inevitable in the writing of the tale (male novelist) and the screenplay (male playwright), and its coming to the screen under the tutelage of its male director. What's more, the success that results in the saving of the victim's life and defeat of the killer comes about through the direction supplied by Hannibal Lecter, the character played by Anthony Hopkins. That Lecter is central to Starling's victory is apparent in the totality of film reviews that give far more space to Hannibal than they ever give to her, albeit his allocated screentime (16 minutes of one hour 59 minutes) is the lesser of the two (Ebert 1991; Obias 2024).[1]

The launching in 2024 of *Barbie* the film, a collaboration between the director Greta Gerwig and award-winning actor Margo Robbie (though not "award winning" or even nominated for *Barbie*), and *Poor Things*—a novel brought to the screen by director Yorgos Lanthimos with Emma Stone in the starring role, provides an opportunity to consider conflicting

[1] See Ebert (1991)—Despite "her steadiness and pluck [being] at the heart of the movie … Dr. Hannibal Lecter lurks at the heart of the story, a malevolent but somehow likable presence–likable because he likes Clarice, and helps her …" then "Lecter … is the sideshow, and Clarice is in the center ring" but still the review gives Starling no more than equal attention, if that. As to screen-time, the estimate of just under 16 minutes vies with 12 minutes or 24 minutes and 52 seconds depending upon the way the calculation is made or who makes it (Obias 2024).

views of their portrayal of women as independent owners of their own lives. What constitutes a feminist film or a feminist approach to the development of feminist consciousness in a character who is central to the story—which is her story, or is it truly hers? What does the reception of each film by The Academy say as to the appreciation of what is a woman, and what makes a performance worthy of the highest film honours? What does it say about the way in which The Academy estimates and assesses directorial ability and prowess? What does it say about valuing women's performance through the status of personhood, and what about the capacity (or incapacity) to recognise that women are actors of human dimensions rather than fodder for the male gaze. Does The Academy assess film, script, story and performance in acknowledgement that that talent exists through women's personhood rather than women in film existing in and for the minds of men?

Barbie the Backstory

On 9 March 1959 Ruth Handler's concept doll Barbie was launched onto the American market at the New York Toy Fair by her and her husband's company Mattel. Unbeknownst to parents who were to gift the doll, generation after generation, to their daughters (and sometimes sons), Barbie was styled on German doll Lily. Lily was not a doll for a child. Lilly was and remains a fetish doll sold to men in German bars and gentlemen's (or not so gentlemanly) establishments. Girls and women's response to Barbie the doll was mixed. Barbie herself was and is a complex mixture identified in the mainstream principally by her shape—slim-bodied, bust disproportionately curvy above an all-too-slender waist, long-legged, feet curved as if shod permanently in high-heels. Yet simultaneously Barbie is independent, unwed, financially secure, career-orientated. This is recounted so well in a vignette provided by MG Lord in Barbie's "unauthorised biography", *Forever Barbie* (2005). Lord writes of Barbie at 45 years of age, observing that "despite that body, Barbie has become a traditional toy—not a bad girl, but 'Miss Smarty-pants', as" (notes Lord), "one nine-year-old recently called her" (Lord 2005, vii). Lord describes an episode where she watched the girl and her friends "play with the 2003 Christmas season's must-have dolls". These were not Barbies but "a street-smart bunch called Bratz". Bratz were not a Mattel product, yet (Lord 2005, vii):

> … as soon as there was trouble – one of the Bratz got sick – Dr. Barbie was summoned. She was a professional, an authority figure, the girls gave her an English accent...

Lord goes on to relate her doubt that "any new doll will ever eclipse" Barbie: her "mutability" is pivotal. Surprisingly, given the degree of publicity and public attention devoted to Barbie the doll, even when Barbie soared in sales, Lord recalls, she was "the salutorian, not valedictorian, of the toy market" (2005, vii). That is, her changeability, her (her makers' and designers') ability to flex into the moment, to adapt by adopting the zeitgeist year by year, decade by decade, Barbie held her own against each new doll's arrival onto the market. Despite, in so doing, Barbie "came in second at the holidays to the latest flash in the pan", Barbie was king of the walk, Barbie the indefatigable, Barbie the unstoppable. Why this longevity—which continues today?

From a feminist perspective, Barbie the doll harbours contradictions. At a time when women of the 1950s have been recounted traditionally as moving out of the paid workforce and back into the home when their jobs were reclaimed by soldiers returning from World War II,[2] dolls remained traditional, too. Baby dolls, with chubby pre-toddler legs, plump baby-bodies, rounded rosy cheeks, their eye-lashed blue eyes opening and closing as the girl-owner, playing mother, lifts the baby-replica to pat its back or place it in a crib or pram; these alone were the girl-child's fare. Baby dolls swarmed onto the market with internal voice boxes squawking, sobbing, and uttering "Mama, Mama", turning girls into mothers before their time. These dolls provided girls with one road ahead, and one road only—wife, mother and, though not pressed so as

---

[2] This portrayal is mythical as despite legislation to remove married women from paid employment, or to limit women's job opportunities, women (married and single) continued to work outside the home as well as inside it, although some middle-class women were able to conform to the notion that the man should be the earner, the woman the homemaker. See Scutt (2024), particularly Chapter 9, "A Decade of Darkness—Or Into the Light? The Struggles and Successes of 1950s Women", on the 1950s decade.

to be obvious, inexorably grandmother. Nothing else. No other vision. No other life.

Then—along came Barbie. Yes, the body did generate body-anxiety or add to it for some girls. Although—was Barbie responsible or simply feeding into a notion of slender-body-with-curves (in all the right places) that was already there—even entrenched. Some girls "hated" Barbie along with their mothers or resisted Barbie when the doll was imposed upon them by mothers seeking to feminise their daughters. Some mothers refused to buy Barbie and, when pressed, purchased her offsider, Hispanic friend Midge, or sister Skipper, these the most purchased of Barbie's relatives (she has at least two sisters, one of whom has a twin brother, along with a cousin as well as African American friends joining the Hispanic cohort)—to the great distress of daughters who wanted the real thing.[3] Feminists denounced Barbie the doll as not only promoting body image fixation but prompting unhealthy dieting, bulimic vomiting, or the sometimes hidden starvation of anorexia nervosa. The 6 September 1968 Miss America protest in Atlantic City, New Jersey, run by Women's Liberationists (Gay 2018) depositing bras and other female-identified products into a rubbish bin (contrary to popular belief nothing was burned—the boardwalk was hot, dry timber and fire was too risky) and unfurling a huge "Women's Liberation" protest banner inside the convention centre, Boardwalk Hall, is sometimes depicted as an anti-Barbie event (Tanenbaum and Engler). But was this the way all girls envisioned the doll? Was this the only meaning or influence ... and was it the influence at all?

What Do Girls Want?

In *Reviving Ophelia*, Mary Pipher and Sara Pipher Gilliam (2019) write of the lives and visions of girls growing up in the 1950s and '60s and '70s—then into the 1990s and 2000s and on to the present. Their

[3] Biographer Lord (2005) undertook interviews with women who owned Barbie dolls or purchased them for their daughters, finding varying views of the dolls' impact on her interviewees' lives and aspirations or career choices: *Forever Barbie*, particularly Chapters 8, 9 and 11.

book discloses a multifaceted vision of young American girls growing into women, with myriad influences dictating their life-potential. Whilst some succumb, some resist orthodox demands to be still, comply with traditional notions of "what is a 'real' woman"—knight-in-shining-armour sweeps delicate damsel off to what? The implication is wife, mother … and that's the end (the typical fairy story told in "The Sleeping Beauty" and "Cinderella" or their modern versions "Frozen" and other Disneyfied tales). No life after Prince Charming enters it. As well, there are many who straddle varying visions in navigating a world where discrimination and sexism continue to govern their universe. Although comprising one example only, the notion that Barbie generates eating disorders is renounced in a mother and daughter interview conducted as research for the book. Prudence "wants to lose weight, but can't". She's "embarrassed to have bulimia" for "it's such a preppy disease …" Her mother, Marvallene, intercedes—saying "it's all her (Marvallene's) fault" as she's "always on diets". Maybe a mother's influence outweighs that of a doll, however "perfect" in conventional terms the doll's shape and image (Pipher and Gilliam 2019, 209).

In the Prudence-Marvallene discussion, Barbie does crest the horizon. Prudence says of her school mates that they're committed to wearing "designer clothes", enhanced by their "beautiful hair" and "straight white teeth". Dressed in her "somewhat unconventional outfit" (defiantly non-designer), she renounces this approach, saying (Pipher and Gilliam 2019, 209):

> When I first went [to the school], all the girls looked alike to me. It took a while to learn to tell them apart. I refuse to play the designer-clothes game. I'm not a Barbie doll.

Mattie Kahn, in *Young and Restless—The Girls Who Sparked America's Revolutions,* promotes a positive picture of young women growing up in relating the "untold story of the people who have helped spark America's most transformative social movements throughout history: teenage girls". There are teenage girls standing up to misplaced authority, campaigners for race rights and women's rights, young women whose names are recorded in mainstream history, and young women who have been forgotten to all but their inner-circle, until excavated by Kahn in her determined effort to ensure that naming names does not preclude young women of courage and fortitude.

These books meld well with *Forever Barbie* to provide an insight into what motivates girls. Kahn even references a doll as playing an influential role in her own growth and intellectual development. She dedicates *Young and Restless* to her parents (Khan 2023):

> What wild and unearned luck to have been born to parents who believed that there were no limits to what a girl could do and who once let me shop for a coveted and overpriced Madame Alexander doll in feverish haze.

She concludes with the message of being "so grateful" to them "on both counts".

The Madame Alexander doll is different in body and facial construction from Barbie: no slim legs, clinched waist, or disproportionate bustiness there. Yet the doll (albeit more of the conventional baby-shape) does assume adult poses and roles, most often appearing as a bride doll, but taking on characters such as Cinderella, Miss Poland, and Cruella da Ville. None of these enters the Barbie professional field, however—unlike "team Barbie" there appear to be no Madame Alexander lawyers, pilots, astronauts, athletes or media stars.

Race and the Doll—Enter, Barbie

On the frontispiece of her book, Kahn quotes Maya Angelou and Harry Styles. Angelou declares her "love" for seeing "a young girl go out and grab the world by the lapels", for "life's a bitch" and one must "go out and kick ass". This surely is Barbie, and certainly not Madame Alexander. As for Styles, whether he or his publicity agent made it up, the words resonate with Barbie's world, too:

> How can you say young girls don't get it? They're our future. Our future doctors, lawyers, mothers, presidents, they kind of keep the world going.

Five years before the Barbie doll was launched by Mattel, *Brown v The Board of Education of Topeka* saw the United States Supreme Court declare unanimously (nine to zero) that "separate is not equal".[4] In the action brought by her father, Oliver, Linda Brown was one of the pupils at the heart of the decision that racial segregation in schools violates the Fourteenth Amendment to the United States Constitution—the equal protection clause. Children from Kansas, Delaware, South Caroline and Virginia, five in all, had their rights to equal access to education untrammelled by racist school boundaries adjudicated in *Brown*, and won. Barbara Johns, who led a school strike and march out of the school yard and along the high street, was party (through her father) to *Davis v County School Board of Prince Edward County*, one of cases making up the five consolidated and heard in *Brown*. Another student was represented in *Briggs v Elliott*, it one of those five going on appeal in *Brown*, where dolls figured significantly in expert evidence given by social scientists, Mamie Clark and her husband Kenneth Clark (Khan 2023, 70–73). African American children aged three to seven years were quizzed under "the doll test" set around four dolls, two brown, two white. "Give me the doll that looks bad", and "choose a doll that looks 'nice'" ran the prompts. For "most Black children" (Khan 2023, 70–73), the result was "an unmistakeable preference for the white doll and a rejection of the brown doll" (Khan 2023, 70–73). All this was happening before Barbie the doll appeared on the market, and in the late 1960s Mattel introduced the Black and Hispanic doll friends for Barbie, with "Black Barbie" appearing in 1980 (Lord 2005, 108–109). Tellingly, Lord titles Chapter 8, addressing this issue in detail, "Barbie Like Me" (Lord 2005, 158–178). Mattel established and financially supported, under the direct control of African American team Lou Smith and Robert Hall, the company Shindana launched in 1969 with the sole mission of producing dolls for African American children, by African American designers directed by an all-African American management (Lord 2005, 166–167).

---

[4] *Brown v. Board of Education of Topeka* | 347 U.S. 483 (1954) | Justia U.S. Supreme Court Center, https://supreme.justia.com/cases/federal/us/347/483/ (accessed 3 January 2025).

This is the time of Betty Freidan and "the problem that has no name". For Friedan, many of the middle-class women with a college education who matched her lifestyle (a specific cohort: not "all" American women) were at home, frustrated and being denied a life outside the domestic sphere. *The Feminine Mystique* was published in 1963,[5] to become a critical work generating women's 1970s and onward activism (Blake-Churchill nd). It predated Germaine Greer's *The Female Eunuch* which hit the bookshop shelves in 1970, gaining plaudits and historical referencing at 50 years in 2020 (Nelson 2020). Ironically, Barbie the doll represented in many respects the freedom and career aspirations which Freidan complained were denied to her and other women in her position. Barbie's iconoclasm in respect to her independence, denial of a need to be coupled—Ken featured in Barbie's social circle and in one sense was a partner but in no way hampered her engagement with the world as a doll in her own right—and her ability to generate her own income through the many trades and professions she embraced. Barbie the lawyer, Barbie the tradie, Barbie the ambassador, the astronaut, the astronomer, the nurse, the inventor, and even Barbie the activist … mirrored the woman who renounced Greer's eunuch.

Barbie Makes It to the Screen

The reception of onscreen Barbie was dynamic. Mothers and daughters went together; wives and husbands, girlfriends in groups, couples of all ages lined up. Queues snaked through the streets and around corners outside cinemas, whilst box offices were inundated with requests for tickets by phone, online and in person, seemingly the world over. The colour pink exploded in unprecedented ways, suffering a revival that stormed into cinemas that were decorated in varying shades of pink. Women and girls wore pink frocks, pink sneakers, sandals, pumps or court shoes, tied pink bows or clips in their hair, carried pink handbags

[5] Now a "modern classic", notably an original hard copy (second hand) is publicised today as valued at £414.45 (DividingLine nd); whilst another site sets it at £996.40 (AbeBooks 1996–2025).

or wallets, adopted and adapted pink, pink, pink as an item of clothing to meet the spirit of the audience and the film. Pink was "in". In the first weekend of August 2023 *Barbie* passed the $1b mark, becoming the year's second highest-grossing film of the year and in money terms surpassing *Harry Potter and the Philosopher's Stone* and *The Dark Knight*, with Greta Gerwig becoming the first "solo female director" to make the $b list (Gregory 2023).

Not all the world did, however, see *Barbie*. By August 2023 (Hassan 2023) the film was banned in Lebanon, Kuwait, Pakistan, Saudi Arabia, United Arab Emirates (UAE), Algeria, Viet Nam and the Philippines. Kuwait's Under Secretary for Press and Publication designated the film as promoting "ideas and beliefs" alien to Kuwaiti society and "public order" whilst Algeria and Lebanon saw *Barbie* as a prompt for "homosexuality and sexual transformation" or "other Western deviances" conflicting with the respective country's "faith and morality" in "belittling the family unit" (Kuwait) or non-compliant with "religious and cultural beliefs" (Algeria). Yet Viet Nam's position was wholly based in nation-state politics: a world map shown in the movie depicted the China Sea as compliant with "the nine-dash line" consistent with China's territorial claims which Viet Nam contests (Hassan 2023).

It is difficult to fathom the "homosexuality" objection underpinning the Algeria/Lebanon ban, for Barbie in *Barbie* appears to be set in the heterosexual mould, and engaging with female friends in debate and discussion with political and social content surely cannot be taken as evidencing intimate same-sex relationships. This would be ironic in that polygamy—bringing women together to live in a common household where debate and discussion amongst them is a given, despite personal disputes that may arise amongst them—is legal in Lebanon for Muslim men (Sunni and Shia) (Musawa nd) and men in Algeria are lawfully entitled to take up to four wives (World Population Review 2025), again creating women-centred indoor households. As for the male characters in *Barbie*, their main activity in Barbieland appears to be outdoors, in full public view, and once alerted to patriarchy in "our" world, Ken's aim is clearly to emulate it. Yet the charges as to "public order" and "other Western deviances" along with "belittling the family unit" may be more readily understood, though ironically so when one considers the critique that was launched against Barbie the doll during the 1970s. Then, the proposition was that the narrow-waisted, large-bosomed Barbie portrayed a stereotype that undermined women's reality and denied the body types of real women: few if any women could conform to the exaggerated female form favoured by Mattel. Yet returning to other features of Barbie-as-doll, predating *Barbie* the movie "public order" was challenged in Barbie's depiction as an independent career-orientated woman rather than a stay-at-home mum. Where society demands conformity to a categorisation of women as home bodies, Barbie—even before the film—is anathema, and perhaps the family unit is "belittled" where Barbie remains unmarried and childless without marriage or maternity in prospect. Kuwait and Algeria are, it would seem, more tuned in to the challenge to patriarchal society embodied in Barbie the doll and her live counterpart as unveiled in *Barbie* than the traditional critique of Barbie. Can *Barbie* remake—or affirm—Barbie the doll as feminist icon?

Barbie the film does harbour elements running counter to a vision of Barbie the character as equal to men, in charge, possessed of power, strong, capable, competent and effective in running Barbieland. The image appearing early in the film of her feet, unshod, yet fashioned to fit her abandoned high-heels rather than sneakers, flat-heeled shoes or Doc Martens—Barbie standing on tiptoes sans the pumps—conjures up the warnings women receive of hammer toes, ingrown toe nails, planta fasciitis, bunions, corns, calluses on soles and heels, cramped muscles, truncated tendons, poor posture, hip and back problems eventuating from regular wearing of cramping, high-heeled footwear, or ankle injuries resulting from regular or occasional wear (APMA 2025; *Nassau Guardian* 2025; Scutt 2020; *PR NewsWire* 2014; Howell 2011). Her focus on pink as colour-of-choice for her clothing, whether gingham or monochromatic, monotone or flat-pink generates thoughts of a Disneyfied world rather than one of "independent Barbie". Yet is this way of regarding, or disregarding, pink justified? What of the contention that "pink is powerful" (Scutt 2012; Paoletti 2012)? After all, if girls wear the colour, and girls "can do anything" why decry their choice?

Barbieland vs Ourland

Ironically, despite contentions that Barbie the doll undermines women's status or claims to equality, Barbie is in charge in Barbie's world. In "our" world women are most definitely not in charge. Certainly today women world leaders are comparatively common contrasted against the time of political scientist Christine de Pizan (September 1364–c1430) and philosopher Mary Wollstonecraft (April 1759–September 1797) or later when in the nineteenth and early twentieth centuries women were classed non-persons in law (Bodichon 1854; Butler 1868; Scutt 2016),[6] gaining personhood according to law only in 1929 (Scutt 1985, 2016).[7] Entry into trades and professions is no longer formally denied,[8] despite barriers based in idiomatic assumptions about women's skills, qualifications, capacities and capabilities identified by Game and Pringle (1984) and Burton (1985, 1991) remaining into this century. It is equally certain that in spite of women's achievements in the public world of politics and business (notwithstanding unequal pay (Scutt 2024)), and (conflicting) advances in the private sphere of home and domesticity (Scutt and Graham 1984)[9], the world of women today is a vast remove from *Barbie*'s women (Fine 2010; Sieghart 2021; Washington et al. 2024;

[6] This occurred in relation to voting, entry into the House of Lords, appointment to the Canadian Upper House (the Senate), access to university, admission to professions including the law and medicine … *Bebb v Law Society* [1914] 1 Ch 286, 83 LJ Ch 363; *Beresford-Hope v Sandhurst (Lady)* (1889) 23 QBD 79, 58 LJQB 316; *Chorlton v Lings* (1868) LR 4 CP 374, 38 LJCP 25; *De Souza v Cobden* [1891] 1 QB 687, 60 LJQB 533; (1873) 11 M 784; Olive v Ingram (1738) 7 Mod 263, 2 Str 1114; Reg v Harrold (1872) LR 7 QB 361, 41 LJQB 173; Rex v Stubbs (1788) 2 Term R 395, 1 RR 503; *Viscountess Rhondda's Claim* [1922] 2 AC 339, 38 TLR 759.

[7] *Edwards v AG of Canada (Reference re the Meaning of the Word "Persons" in Sect. 24 of the British North America Act)* [1928] SCR 276; *Edwards v AG of Canada* [1929] UKPC 86; [1930] AC 143, *Edwards v AG of Canada* [1930] AC 128 http://www.bailii.org/uk/cases/UKPC/1929/1929_86.html (accessed 2 March 2025).

[8] For a recitation of the struggle to have women accepted into the iron and steel industry in Wollongong, Australia, see Janne Ellen Swift, Chapter 5, "Forging the Right to Work with Metal – Women and the Struggle for Work in Wollongong", this volume.

[9] See Anna Kerr, Chapter 2, "A Mother of a Job – The Control and Commodification of Women's Reproduction", this volume; Patricia Branco and Paula Casaleiro, "The Daughters of the Carnation Revolution: 50 Years of Women's Rights in Portugal", this volume; Chapter 4, Wandoo Grace Aibngbee, "Widows: Denial of Rights and Respect in Southern Nigeria", this volume.

Baxter 2025; Man Who Has It All 2025). *Barbie*'s women are running their world, with Kens populating it by disporting themselves on the beach as "men's men" enjoying beach volleyball and other outdoor activities, or otherwise depicting representatives of males in a non-patriarchal society. In the 1970s when Barbie was under attack as purportedly occupying a place antithetical to women's striving for equality, Barbie was gaining ground in non-traditional trades and professions. In 1970s women's world, feminists were asserting the right to transcend the traditional role of women, and lobbying for anti-discrimination and equal opportunity laws domestically and international treaties,[10] whilst Barbie was more and more appearing on toy shelves as already there. As Joyce Stevens said in a 1970s statement that was to become a poster, a song and an anthem for women's rights:

> Because woman's work is never done and is underpaid or unpaid or boring or repetitious and we're the first to get fired and what we look like is more important than what we do and if we get raped it's our fault and if we get beaten we must have provoked it and if we raise our voices we're nagging bitches and if we enjoy sex we're nymphos and if we don't we're frigid and if we love women it's because we can't get a "real" man and if we ask our doctor too many questions we're neurotic and/or pushy and if we expect childcare we're selfish and if we stand up for our rights we're aggressive and "unfeminine" and if we don't we're typical weak females and if we want to get married we're out to trap a man and if we don't we're unnatural and because we still can't get an adequate safe contraceptive but men can walk on the moon and if we can't cope or don't want a pregnancy we're made to feel guilty about abortion and ...

[10] Anti-*Discrimination Act* 1977 (NSW), View—NSW legislation, https://legislation.nsw.gov.au/view/whole/html/inforce/current/act-1977-048 (accessed 2 March 2025); *Equal Opportunity Act* 1977 (Victoria), Equal Opportunity Act 2010 | legislation.vic.gov.au, https://www.legislation.vic.gov.au/in-force/acts/equal-opportunity-act-2010/020 (accessed 2 March 2025); *Equal Pay Act* 1970 (UK), *Equal Pay Act* 1970, https://www.legislation.gov.uk/ukpga/1970/41/enacted (accessed 2 March 2025), now incorporated into the *Equality Act* 2010 (UK), Equality Act 2010, https://www.legislation.gov.uk/ukpga/2010/15/contents (accessed 2 March 2025); CEDAW (the *Convention on the Elimination of All Forms of Discrimination Against Women*), Convention on the Elimination of All Forms of Discrimination against Women New York, 18 December 1979 | OHCHR, https://www.ohchr.org/en/instruments-mechanisms/instruments/convention-elimination-all-forms-discrimination-against-women (accessed 2 March 2025).

> for lots and lots of other reasons we are part of the women's liberation movement ...

This lament is echoed in *Barbie* when Gloria (played by America Ferrara) declares, to Barbie's horror, that in the human world she's intent on exploring—or even joining, it's "literally impossible to be a woman" (Caldwell 2023). Rather, women must always "be extraordinary" yet every woman finds to her chagrin that she's "always doing it wrong". To be thin is the aim—yet it must not be "too thin" nor can she articulate the slender form as an aim. Health must be sacrificed on the altar of slimness, yet health must be women's aspiration, too. Money is essential, yet a woman is disentitled from asking for it—"that's crass". Women must aspire to being bosses, but the "mean boss" is outlawed for women—and any woman who is a boss runs the inevitable risk that whatever she does—as leader in the office, or the armed forces, in the sporting field or government department, in the private sector or public realm—she'll be classed as "mean" and the rightful target of undermining from above and mobbing from below. Being a leader requires taking the initiative, yet embracing the ideas of others is required for fear of being classed as wrongfully squashing them. Talking about your children "all the damn time" is a no, no, yet every woman is "supposed to love being a mother". Being a career woman is critical, yet "always ... looking out for other people" is deemed fundamental. The contradictions, Gloria advises Barbie, are endless.

As Barbie grows more and more distressed, at first disbelieving, then mystified, half-accepting yet still reluctantly resistant, whilst the women around them encourage Gloria onward, a woman must "answer for men's bad behaviour" Gloria declaims (classing this as madness) yet observing that if a woman draws attention to this insanity she's "accused of complaining" (Caldwell 2023). Meanwhile, the diktat is that every woman must "stay pretty for men", but simultaneously the rule is "not so pretty" that the men are "tempted too much" or that other women are threatened—because, in the end, "you're supposed to be a part of the sisterhood". A woman must "always stand out", "always be grateful" but never overlook the fact that the system "is rigged". Women are obligated, too, to acknowledge the biased set-up of the system, yet equally required, again, to "always be grateful" nonetheless. Confronting these contradictions that make living as a woman under patriarchy "too hard!" no woman receives a thank you or a medal as in the end the truth is that she's not only "doing everything wrong, but also everything is [her] fault" (Caldwell 2023).

Concluding that she is "just so tired," Gloria describes "watching [herself] and every single other woman tie herself into knots so that people will like us." And, she adds, "if all of that is also true for a doll just representing women, then I don't even know."

Greta Gerwig records that the set was awash with tears as Ferraro's Gloria delivered this monologue (Caldwell 2023). Cinema audiences were similarly transfixed, albeit criticisms found their way to popular media outlets, one contention being that the speech was insufficiently complex in addressing women's condition today, or as one male Twitter/X commentator twittered: "#Barbie is a two hour woke-a-thon brimming with feminist lectures and nuclear-level rage against men" (Caldwell 2023). As Gloria's is the only contribution that could be titled a "feminist lecture", and as "nuclear-level rage" of any description or directed at or against any *Barbie* character is difficult to detect, it seems unlikely that the movie had been watched by the twitterer rather than the comment coming from formulaic assumptions and presumptions about feminists and feminism. It certainly says something about Barbie as more than a frivolous doll to be dismissed as insignificant or inconsequential, trivial or trifling. The very concept of Barbie as the star of a major feature film filling cinema seats appears to have hit a nerve. In any event, many male cinema goers did not agree, happily attending with their partners or wives and applauding along with them. Yet it didn't make it with The Academy. What, then, the prospects for *Poor Things*?

The Academy Promotes I

Dominated by middle-aged white men, in 2012 The Academy came under fire. *The Los Angeles Times* reported on the composition of the award-granting institution, noting that Oscar voters were 94 per cent white and 77 per cent male. In a 2016 follow-up, *The Times* observed that "scant progress" had been made towards diversification: Oscar voters were 91 per cent white and 76 per cent male. Keegan et al. (2016) said this meant:

> Blacks are about 3% of the academy, up from 2%; Asians and Latinos are each just over 2%, with both groups up slightly. The academy has invited more women and minority group members over the last four years, but with its 6,261 voting members appointed for life, the organization's ranks were on track to remain overwhelmingly white and male for decades.

The article went on to note that the nomination of "an all-white slate of actors for two years in a row", and one might ask for how many years prior to that with few breaks in the colour-map, led to a January 2016 avowal "to double the number of women and minority members by 2020" and adoption of "controversial new rules" authorising voting rights to be removed from "inactive members". Academy president Cheryl Boone Isaacs was reported by Keegan et al. (2016) as confirming the goal of ensuring "we are active in bringing in different voices regardless of gender or race or sexual orientation" with "inclusiveness [as] our goal".[11]

Keegan et al. (2016) nonetheless doubted that the "doubling [of] the number of women and minority members over the next four years" could be anything other than "daunting":

> The academy has about 1,500 women and 535 nonwhite people who are eligible to vote on the Oscars, according to Times estimates. Based on those findings, doubling their numbers would require inviting at least 375 women and more than 130 people of color each year.

This would "demand a dramatic shift in admissions given that the academy's latest class—touted as the largest and most diverse in its history—was only 322 people, most of them white men". Former Academy president Hawk Koch declared "flatly" that such targets were "impossible" due to the Academy's "stringent membership requirements

[11] For a detailed analysis of race as factor in (no or few) awards by the Academy, see Reise (2024).

and the underrepresentation of women and minorities in the entertainment industry". Requisite numbers of "qualified people, period, of any race or gender" are lacking so as to make up the number of invitations necessary each year. Boone Isaacs disagreed: "the goals are attainable", there are "enough qualified people" and Academy leaders will "do everything in our power to meet our goals because we know that this is the right thing to do. We're going to make it happen."

Yet the 2016 raft of nominations announced in January that year resulted in "all 20 nominees in acting categories were white", generating "a firestorm of criticism" together with "calls for boycotts of the awards telecast". Director Spike Lee commented that fault lay more with "gatekeepers in Hollywood who control what films are greenlighted for production". This led to a conclusion (Keegan et al. 2016) that the branches of the Academy holding "most power" over the Oscar season "are the least diverse":

> The executive branch, which finances the movies and determines what films warrant an awards campaign, is 98% white. The public relations branch, which strategizes those awards campaigns, is 95% white. Other branches reflect the entrenched nature of certain hiring patterns in Hollywood crafts, such as visual effects, which is 98% male, and cinematography, which is 95% male.

The outcry led to action on the part of the telecast producers, who immediately "booked more than a dozen black presenters and performers, including Morgan Freeman, John Legend, Kevin Hart, Whoopi Goldberg and Quincy Jones"—notably one lone woman in that line-up, signifying a misogynistic blindness on their part. This is replicated in the "inclusion crisis" detailed by the USC Annenberg School for Communication and Journalism in its finding that 97 per cent of film directors "are male and 87% are white, where women hold just 21% of top executive positions and nonwhite actors garner just 27% of speaking roles" (Smith et al. 2018). Older members then began complaining of "ageism" with "lowering standards" coming into the mix, both of which take direct aim at women, for discrimination against women's entry into the moving picture professions are likely to mean that they gain credits in directing, production and other elements later than do men, and whenever women move into any male-dominated field the question of their "qualification" to do so inevitably arise. Not so with men (Sieghart 2021; Scutt 1997).

The Academy Promotes II

What did all this mean for *Poor Things* and *Barbie*? The outcome for *Barbie*, its director and principal actress is (as noted earlier) readily observed. As for *Poor Things* it is instructive to read the book of the same name upon which it is based (Gray 1992, 2002), published under the (some may consider) pretentious title: *Poor Things—Episodes from the Early Life of Archibald McCandless M.D. Scottish Public Health Officer—Edited by Alasdair Gray*. The main characters are Godwin Baxter, Archie McCandless, Wedderburn (Bella's "Wedder") and Bella (or Victoria—a name by which the central character is also known—the story not worth including here)—whose body is manipulated by Baxter's having removed her brain to be replaced by that of the foetus to whom she would have given birth had she not endeavoured to end her life through suicide. The drowned Bella/Victoria has her body rescued by the loch-keeper whose job it is to keep a watch for suicides. Dead, her body is placed in the care of the medico (Baxter) who is responsible for reviving those who immerse themselves in the river in the hope of ending their lives. Where revival is impossible, Baxter's job is to conduct the legally required autopsy before burial as a criminal—*felo de se*, the crime having taken their own life, in accordance with *Hales v Petit* [1562] (Rooney 2023), accepted law at the time. At that time, a non-consecrated graveyard and denial of a Christian burial were stipulated by cannon law (Wright 2017), though the *Burial of Suicide Act* 1823 (UK) permitted graveyard burial without the sometimes-earlier approach of a stake through the heart and interment at a fork in the highway (Wright 2017).[12] Yet neither stake nor graveyard are to be Bella/Victoria's fate. Possessed of her foetus' brain,

[12] *Burial of Suicide Act* 1823—UK Non-devolved—Legislation—VLEX 808320921, https://vlex.co.uk/vid/burial-of-suicide-act-808320921 (accessed 2 March 2025); Burial of Suicide Act 1823—Legislation—VLEX 861232135, https://vlex.co.uk/vid/burial-of-suicide-act-861232135 (accessed 2 March 2025).

years later upon death by "a cerebral stroke on 3 December 1946" (Gray 2002, 317) she is recorded as possessing two different lifespans, one for the body, one for the brain. Autopsied in the Human Society's mortuary on Glasgow Green, her age according to the brain is 66 years, dating from 18 February 1880 (the date of her foetus' extraction from Bella/Victoria's womb by Baxter, and the date of her suicide—and revival by Baxter). According to the body, so calculated from 1854, the date of her (body's) birth "in a Manchester slum" (Gray 2002, 317) her age of death is ninety-two.

The book's differences from the film, and the acknowledgement at its heart that Bella has the brain of a three-year-old (Gray 1992, 101) are illuminating. The latter is horrifying in its revelation that, as with the film, Bella is the victim of paedophilia. How else can one classify adult men engaging in sexual activity with a child of three? That she is possessed of an adult body surely cannot sweep away the exploitation inherent in the adult sexual interplay between the three-year-old and adults (plural).[13] The brain, its capacity for comprehension, its ability decide for itself and to make informed choices (according to child psychology a state not achieved completely until the early twenties (O'Reilly et al. 2013)) must be the determinant of whether one is adult—and an adult—or not. In any event, the age of consent to intimate sexual activity is, in Scotland where the story is based, 16 years, which is a vast distance from the age of Bella/Victoria's (baby's) brain (University Health nd; *Mental Capacity Act* 2005 (UK)).[14] The pity of all this is that Emma Stone, in playing Bella/Victoria, imitates babyness and presumably the Oscar for best actress was awarded at least partly for this facility. Yet she plays the baby and continues to do so with graphic vigour when she is already engaged in the sexual relationship with Wedderburn, the first of her sexual "partners".

[13] The reproductions of Bella's purported communications bears this out—see for example Gray (2022, 56, 145–150), where the exaggeratedly scrawled writing or printing signifies the hand of an extremely young child.

[14] *Mental Capacity Act* 2005 (UK), Mental Capacity Act 2005, https://www.legislation.gov.uk/ukpga/2005/9/contents (accessed 2 March 2025).

The late-in-the day intervention, in the film, of "book learning" by Bella is telling in its incorporation of sexual activity into the educational process: Bella's education is conducted in a brothel, the instruction provided by another prostituted woman with whom Bella is engaged in a sexual relationship. This is a vast departure from the book, the film-maker evidently of the view that sex, sex and more sex (with a child) will garner the attention of cinema audiences or at least that of the critics. Director Lanthimos did, as it proved (he read the Academy and other film prize-giving bodies so well), reap rewards from the change. Yet again it raises questions of mental capacity and the age of consent. A person in a position of authority, a teacher, for example, is governed by rules going to power and the capacity to exploit it (*Sexual Offences Act* 2003 (UK)).[15] The prostituted woman who instructs Bella/Victoria whilst simultaneously in a sexual relationship with her is not in a formal teacher position, and the women working in the brothel were, by Gray in the book, acknowledged as subject to coercive control and exploitation. As Bella/Victoria says in Chapter 18 "Paris to Glasgow: The Return" of the role, she is "no longer a parasite" as for less than half a week she has "earned a wage by doing a job as well and fast as possible, not for pleasure but cash like most people do", going on to add that each morning she "sinks into slumber, glad to have knocked off forty and earned four hundred and eighty francs … " (Gray 2002, 180). Then comes the episode with the medical practitioner "employed by the municipality to enforce public health regulations". It'll be "over in a jiffy" she's told and takes the prospect of the examination seriously, as if it is directed at the women's health. This charitable conviction is rudely displaced when she confronts the sight of an "ugly little man with a ferocious scowl who was barking 'Wider! Wider!' at poor Toinette like a bad-tempered

[15] Sections 16–20 relate to sexual activity in abuse of a position of trust: *Sexual Offences Act* 2003, https://www.legislation.gov.uk/ukpga/2003/42/part/1/crossheading/abuse-of-position-of-trust (accessed 2 March 2025), applying equally in Scotland, England, Wales and Northern Ireland. Although the prostituted woman who instructs Bella/Victoria whilst simultaneously in a sexual relationship with her is not in a formal teacher position, clearly such considerations as capacity, authority, power, learning and the role of an educator was far from the minds of the makers of *Poor Things* or, indeed, the actors. In light of the imminence of the #MeToo movement this is indicative of a failure to comprehend sexual rights and the exploitation inherent in the film script.

drill-sergeant" (Gray 2002, 182). Toinette, meanwhile, lies "with her legs apart on a padded table" whilst the beast of a man presses "a thing like a spoon into her loving groove or vagina (as the *Latins* call it) while nearly sticking his nose and heavy moustache in after it". The episode concludes with Bella/Victoria asserting she will not be poked about in this way, the man's attention being focused solely upon "the only part of women he cared about", and she being screamed at by Millie the brothel keeper that she is putting the establishment's licence at risk. Roaring "Insanity!" the doctor joins in, observing: "She willingly accommodates any quantity of verminous male appendages, but recoils from a clinical spatula in the hands of an impersonal scientist." As Bella/Victoria declares she is no longer in Millie's employ, leaving the doctor and his instrument, the madam and the brothel behind, whilst acknowledging it is thus that she "learned about venereal disease", she's met with the doctor's deciding she is not mad but, being English, "has something to hide" (Gray 2002, 183).

Notwithstanding the nature of the relationship between prostituted woman and owners of the industry, clearly such considerations as capacity, authority, power, manipulation, and instruction, learning and the role of an educator (Bella's same-sex "partner" and teacher) was far from the minds of the makers of *Poor Things* or, indeed, the actors. In light of the imminence of the #MeToo movement this too is indicative of a failure to comprehend sexual rights and the exploitation inherent in the film script. Or perhaps it confirms an understanding on the part of those making *Poor Things* of those very elements in its making and their likelihood of having the film stand out amongst its competitors in the race for awards.

Imitating the Classics?

In *Poor Things* (the book) Gray at various times seeks to call upon Mary Shelley's *Frankenstein* and Robert Louis Stevenson's *Jekyll and Mr Hyde* (Gray 2002, 272, 273, 290). In this his focus on sex with a minor strays far from the text or the philosophical discourse at the heart of both Shelley's and Stevenson's work. Gray's Bella/Victoria turns sex-mad rather than (as Dr Frankenstein's creation and Dr Jekyll's Mr Hyde) serial killer (Scutt 2025).[16] As well, Gray's replication of Shelley in introducing the novel with a story-teller (Shelley's letters from R Walton to his sister Mrs Saville, Gray's setting himself up as "editor" of the *Poor Things* manuscript and Archie McCandless as the story-teller) is mere imitation of form, overlooking Shelley's deliberate congruence between the character and stories of Frankenstein and Walton. Shelley's Walton plays a major role in duplicating her philosophical theme, that the "St George and the Dragon" approach to saving the world as exemplified by Frankenstein's mistaken creation of a creature whose life is misbegotten, and by Walton's drive to conquer inclement weather in his wish to single-handed (as he envisages it) discover a passage through the North Pole, is mistaken. Frankenstein sets at its heart the recognition that collective action, working together (the captain and sailors crewing Walton's north-bound expedition and demanding he turn back), is worth honouring (Scutt 2025). Frankenstein and Walton, ego-driven in wanting to "go it alone" in search of veneration and glory, bring about ruin (of Frankenstein's family through the murderous acts of his creation) or almost ruin (potential wreckage of Walton's ship and a frozen death of himself and the crew through his desire to continue the journey against falling temperatures, hardening ice, and wintry squalls).

Gray does at least promote the desire in Bella/Victoria for book-learning and an expanded education in history, geography, politics and philosophy. More than the film, *Poor Things* the book focuses on "educating Bella/Victoria" as a theme absent the need for a sexual partner to do the educating. Chapter 14 "Glasgow to Odessa: The Gamblers", through Chapters 15 "Odessa to Alexandria: The Missionaries", 16 "Alexandria to Gibraltar: Astley's Bitter Wisdom", and 17 "Gibraltar to Paris: Wedderburn's Last Flight", recounting Bella/Victoria's travels with Wedderburn and attributed to Bella/Victoria ("Bella Baxter's Letter: Making a Conscience"), is extraordinarily boring until it comes to the Russian gambler and more particularly discussion between Dr Hooker (Dr. H.) and Mr Astley (Mr. A.). These two "argue tremendously"

---

[16] Jocelynne A Scutt, "Serial Killers or Science Fiction Prototypes for a New and Better World? Revisiting Dr Frankenstein and "'the Creature', Dr Jekyll and Mr Hyde", 2024, *Synergies*, pp 1-21.

(Gray 2002, 133) about the Chinese and the Spaniards, Confucius and Lao-Tze, Roman Emperors, the Christian Bible, God, Socialism vs Communism, Napolean Bonaparte and the contended "Benefits of War", "Unemployment", "Freedom", "Free Trade", "Empire", "Self-Government", and "World Improvers" (Gray 2002, 157–163), plus "The Last Days of Pompeii", with the revellation that Bella/Victoria has read the latter along with "Uncle Tom's Cabin" and "Wuthering Heights" long before she ends up in the Paris brothel being instructed (per *Poor Things*—the film) by the fellow prostituted woman.

The book's recitation matches Frankenstein's creature's relentless drive to educate himself. He listens in to the DeLacy family occupying his neighbouring hovel, as they teach French to Safie, the son's betrothed, and teaches himself English by reading *Paradise Lost* and other works found by chance on his roaming through the countryside. Unlike Lanthimos and *Poor Things* the film, neither Gray nor Shelley finds any urge to situate this learning in a brothel. Nor does either author juxtapose philosophical or political teaching with sexual antics, as if "learning" inevitably engages sexuality or intellectual engagement allies with erotic gymnastics.

In the discussion on the Academy, its overload with white, middle-aged men, and the need for expanding its aesthetic, educated and informed membership, Keegan et al. (2016) report former Academy president Koch as saying: "This year will tell a lot ... We're not going to lower our standards. That's what keeps the Oscars the Oscars." The result in 2024, *Poor Things*, Lanthimos and Stone winning out over *Barbie*, Gerwig and Robbie affirms Koch in his assertion. Standards no lower, quite right. The best director is a man, the best actress is sex personified, the "standards" are maintained, the male gaze remains triumphant. The Oscars remain the Oscars.

The Academy and the Woman

Confirming Koch in his 2016 assertion, ten years on, standards do appear to have remained the same. The Academy's awards for *Poor Things*, its ignoring *Barbie* then, in 2025 bestowing six nominations on *Anora* and granting five: Best Picture, Best Director (Sean Baker), Best Actress (Mikey Madison), Best Original Screenplay, and Best Film Editing. Consistent with the male director history, *Anora* also affirmed the Academy's male-dominated view of what makes a great acting role for a woman. *Anora* is a film that begins in a strip-club, the main female character slinking about pandering to male purchasers of woman-as-object. Although the film purports to elevate the prostituted woman into a position of strength and capability, the world of sleaze and male domination in which the story plays out simply confirms the traditional male gaze as paramount. Actresses have won for portraying real women of power … Bette Davis, Joan Crawford,[17] Meryl Streep, Katherine Hepburn, Ingrid Bergman. But the male gaze is ever lurking or predominating: Julia Roberts and *Pretty Woman* resonates—again the prostituted woman depicted as a "winner" when the story is a nonsense of a "fairy" tale where the fairy is a woman-exploited and required by the film to engage in paid-for sexual acts as if this is a ticket to high society. And as for women directors, they remain scarce when it comes to award nominations. Undoubtedly it can and will be argued that they are an extreme minority in the world of filmmaking—as a justification (sic) for their absence from Academy nominations or awards. Yet this simply confirms the bias in the industry and the barriers women face in getting into it.

From 1929 when the Oscars were established, it took just short of fifty years for the first nomination of a woman (Lina Wertmüller for *Seven Beauties*) for Best Director in 1977 (Academy of Motion Pictures 2025). Almost twenty years elapsed before the second nomination (Jane Campion in 1993 for *The Piano*—anti-feminist, again in the guise of empowerment: a woman sexually manipulated by a lascivious neighbour, subjected to criminal assault at home, and said to profit when her finger is axed by her husband and "replaced by a better one" composed of metal—perhaps an all-too-apt allegory for her transfer from physically abusive husband to sexually exploitive neighbour). Twenty more years elapse and its Sofia Coppola for *Lost in Translation*—2003, nomination, no win. Then the miraculous break-through—six years only, this time,

[17] Though Joan Crawford in her early years was pressed into "male gaze" roles involving skimpy dressing and desperate dance: Quirk and Crawford (1968).

and in 2009 it is actual awards (plural): Best Director *plus* Best Film goes to Kathryn Bigelow for *The Hurt Locker* ... and there's an irony here, for she beats her former husband James Cameron who's nominated yet loses for the white supremacist *Avatar* (an indigenous tribe must be rescued by a "white" man harbouring a disability at that), and overall it's six Oscars to Bigelow and *The Hurt Locker*, to three for Cameron and *Avatar*. Next, come to 2017 (an hiatus of eight years) and Greta Gerwig herself is nominated for *Lady Bird*—no win. Then another break-through, a mere three years elapsing for Chloé Zhao, director of *Nomadland* and billed as "first woman of colour to be nominated and win for Best Director". Even more astounding, Zhao is not the only woman in the line-up. Same year, 2020, Emerald Fennell is nominated for *Promising Young Woman* but the double does not extend to the award. Women now appear to be on a roll, for not only is Jane Campion nominated again—2021, the very next year, but she's the first woman with multiple Best Director nominations—and wins for *The Power of the Dog*. And now they're coming thick and fast—nominations that is, not wins: 2023 and its Justine Triet for *Anatomy of a Fall*, then 2024 and Coralie Fargeat for *The Substance*, but 2025 and its back to neither nomination nor win. And, notably in that line-up its once only that more than one woman has been nominated in one year. Yet of course multiple men are nominated in the Best Director category year after year after year, with one of them winning overwhelmingly often.

But women have played a longtime and long-term role in the film industry, right from the beginning. Some have been written out of history and recovered only by being discovered through serendipity, or have been written into history as existing solely for and at the mercy of the male gaze. Naming names ever runs the risk of omitting them, yet not naming continues the cover-up or denial of scope of their work and careers. Canadian Mary Pickford (1882–1979) film actress, producer, screenwriter, co-founder of United Artists (UA) and in at the creation of the Academy and the Oscars (A&E 2021). First woman film director and first director to film a narrative story, Alice Guy Blaché (1873–1968) born Paris, France, died New Jersy, US, producer who established her own production company (Buczynski-Lee 2007, 2016). Lottie Lyell (1890–1925), Australian film actress, theatre actress, filmmaker, director, scenario writer, scriptwriter, editor, art director, producer, stunt woman (on her own films), title writer, and joint owner of production company (Nash 2015a, b; Nash nd; Wright 1985).

Then in the 1950s actress, intellectual, businesswoman, comedienne, dramaturge Marilyn Monroe founding her own film production company (MMP—Marilyn Monroe Productions, a partnership), joining some fifty unrecognised and too often undocumented film industry women who, following Mary Pickford, similarly established filmmaking companies (VeVea 2021; Lenker 2022). Hence the failure to honour women directors, women in film production is not because the women are not there.

Conclusion

The *Barbie* oversight by the Academy in 2024 is instructive in its having explicitly included in the award nominations—as noted—both the "Ken song" and the "Barbie song", and nominations for Best Supporting Actress and Best Supporting Actor. Ryan Gosling's response to his Ken-role inclusion was perceptive. Appearing in *Time Magazine*, his full statement (Ewe 2024) acknowledged the honour, whilst affirming that there is "no Ken without Barbie, and … no Barbie movie without Greta Gerwig and Margo Robbie", they being "the two people most responsible for this history-making, globally-celebrated film". He was "so happy for America Ferrara and the other incredible artists who contributed their talents to making this such a groundbreaking film." At the same time, no one on the film would possibly be recognised "without Gerwig and Robbie's talent, grit and genius". It was an "understatement" to say he was "disappointed that they are not nominated …". Their work "should be recognized along with the other very deserving nominees", the two having made actors, crew and audiences "laugh, … break their hearts, … [whilst] pushing the culture and … making history …". Then, being "on … the top layer of '[not] even believing it [was] real'", America Ferrera (Ewe 2024) similarly expressed "incredible disappointment" of the failure to nominate Gerwig and Robbie. Gerwig had, she said "done just about everything a director could do to deserve it" in creating Barbie world, "something that had no inherent value to most people and making it a global phenomenon". As for Robbie, she surmised that people may have been "fooled into thinking that the work seems easy", but Robbie "is a magician as an actress ... pulling off the amazing performance [bringing] so much heart and humour and depth and joy and fun to the character. In my book, she's a master."

Yet is it a surprise that Robbie missed out? In *Barbie* (and the role Barbie) she's a woman playing a role affirming vulnerability and the fortitude of women living in a patriarchal world, contending with making their mark in a patriarchal film world—and joking as women do about the lives they lead in escaping the role women are expected to play in the real world along with the film world. Is it a surprise that Gerwig was passed over? In conceiving and pressing on with the film-in-concept and bringing it to the screen, she turned patriarchy on its head. In answer, the Academy reinstated it firmly in the body of Ken—the doll whom the Academy dominated by white, middle-aged men put back in control. Patriarchy must be taken seriously.

Ultimately, however, Barbie/*Barbie* has the last laugh. The film's success bespeaks its winning status and that of its director and principal actress. It continues to play in cinemas and is listed prominently on the entertainment lists provided to aeroplane passengers on long-haul and medium-haul flights. *Poor Things* has sunk like a stone—impossible to find in a cinema and absent on those aeroplane lists.[18] The contrast too in the ending of each film cannot go unremarked. *Poor Things* the film ends with another young woman being exploited by the self-styled genius Baxter—with Bella/Victoria joining him in this through her admiration of his professed medical brilliance. *Barbie* ends with the most poignant scene of the movie, one with which all women in viewing it will empathise. Off she goes, proudly and gleefully towards the gynaecologist's clinic, to affirm her existence as a real woman living in the real

[18] The author looked in vain for *Poor Things* having viewed it on a flight from Sydney to Singapore immediately after its gaining the Oscar, then unable to find it again on any cinema or flight entertainment list in Australia, England or New York or on flights to or from those locations.

world we, the cinema-goers, inhabit. We smile with mingled joy for her joy, and sympathy for the hopefully warmed, but riskily cold, instrument that we've all experienced as women—the speculum that bears witness to our womanhood. And so we leave Barbie, we who would never ever wish to be anyone other than who we are, women claiming our rights and fighting hard for them. The conundrum that lies with being a woman writ large, Greta Gerwig and Margo Robbie bringing us all to the screen.

Bibliography

Reported Cases

Bebb v Law Society [1914] 1 Ch 286, 83 LJ Ch 363.
Beresford-Hope v Sandhurst (Lady) (1889) 23 QBD 79, 58 LJQB 316.
Brown v Board of Education of Topeka 347 US 483 (1954), *Brown v. Board of Education of Topeka* | 347 U.S. 483 (1954) | Justia U.S. Supreme Court Center, https://supreme.justia.com/cases/federal/us/347/483/ (accessed 3 January 2025).
Chorlton v Lings (1868) LR 4 CP 374, 38 LJCP 25.
De Souza v Cobden [1891] 1 QB 687, 60 LJQB 533.
Edwards v AG of Canada (Reference re the Meaning of the Word "Persons" in Section 24 of the British North America Act) [1928] SCR 276.
Edwards v AG of Canada [1929] UKPC 86; [1930] AC 143, *Edwards v AG of Canada* [1930] AC 128 http://www.bailii.org/uk/cases/UKPC/1929/1929_86.html (accessed 2 March 2025).
Jex-Blake v Senatus of University of Edinburgh (1873) 11 M 784.
Olive v Ingram (1738) 7 Mod 263, 2 Str 1114.
Reg v Harrold (1872) LR 7 QB 361, 41 LJQB 173.
Rex v Stubbs (1788) 2 Term R 395, 1 RR 503.
Viscountess Rhondda's Claim [1922] 2 AC 339, 38 TLR 759.

Statutes, International Treaties or Conventions

Anti-Discrimination Act (1977) (NSW), View - NSW legislation, https://legislation.nsw.gov.au/view/whole/html/inforce/current/act-1977-048 (accessed 2 March 2025).

Burial of Suicide Act (1823) - Legislation - VLEX 861232135, https://vlex.co.uk/vid/burial-of-suicide-act-861232135 (accessed 2 March 2025).

Burial of Suicide Act 1823 - UK Non-devolved - Legislation - VLEX 808320921, https://vlex.co.uk/vid/burial-of-suicide-act-808320921 (accessed 2 March 2025).

CEDAW (*Convention on the Elimination of All Forms of Discrimination Against Women*), Convention on the Elimination of All Forms of Discrimination against Women New York, 18 December 1979 | OHCHR, https://www.ohchr.org/en/instruments-mechanisms/instruments/convention-elimination-all-forms-discrimination-against-women (accessed 2 March 2025).

Equal Opportunity Act 1977 (Victoria), Equal Opportunity Act 2010 | legislation.vic.gov.au, https://www.legislation.vic.gov.au/in-force/acts/equal-opportunity-act-2010/020 (accessed 2 March 2025).

Equal Pay Act 1970 (UK), Equal Pay Act 1970, https://www.legislation.gov.uk/ukpga/1970/41/enacted (accessed 2 March 2025).

Equality Act 2010 (UK), Equality Act 2010, https://www.legislation.gov.uk/ukpga/2010/15/contents (accessed 2 March 2025).

Mental Capacity Act 2005 (UK), Mental Capacity Act 2005, https://www.legislation.gov.uk/ukpga/2005/9/contents (accessed 2 March 2025).

Sexual Offences Act 2003 (UK), Sexual Offences Act 2003, https://www.legislation.gov.uk/ukpga/2003/42/part/1/crossheading/abuse-of-position-of-trust (accessed 2 March 2025).

Articles and Book Chapters

A&E, "Who Was Mary Pickford", *Biography – Mary Pickford (1892–1979)*, Mary Pickford - Movies, Spouse & Facts, https://www.biography.com/actors/mary-pickford (accessed 2 March 2025).

APMA (American Podiatric Medical Association), *Edge Research*, 2025, Brand Assessment and Re-development, https://www.apma.org/apmamain/document-server/?cfp=/apmamain/assets/file/public/studies/apma2014todayspodiatristsurveyhighheelfindings.pdf (accessed 25 March 2025).

Abe Books, 1996–2025, Feminine Mystique. by FRIEDAN, Betty.: Very Good Hardcover (1963) | Grendel Books, ABAA/ILAB, https://www.abe

books.co.uk/servlet/BookDetailsPL?bi=31128582425&dest=gbr&ref_=ps_ms_391300534&cm_mmc=msn-_-uk_shopp_used-_-naa-_-naa&msclkid=bba6ed59fd3c160a03048ab8bb6d0e5b (accessed 22 March 2025).

Academy of Motion Pictures, Arts and Sciences (AMPAS), *Love the Oscars*, 2025, Oscars.org | Academy of Motion Picture Arts and Sciences, https://www.oscars.org/ (accessed 2 March 2025).

Awards Daily, "95 Years of Oscars …", 2025, 95 Years of Oscars: Ranking The Best Picture Winners Part Four – #25–1 – Awardsdaily, https://www.awardsdaily.com/2023/06/08/95-years-of-oscars-ranking-the-best-picture-winners-part-four-25-1/ (accessed 3 January 2025).

Baxter, Janeen, "Despite some key milestones since 2000 …", *The Conversation*, 23 March 2025, Despite some key milestones since 2000, Australia still has a long way to go on gender equality, https://theconversation.com/despite-some-key-milestones-since-2000-australia-still-has-a-long-way-to-go-on-gender-equality-250250#:~:text=Despite%20social%2C%20economic%20and%20political%20reform%20aimed%20at,among%20146%20countries%2C%20down%20from%2015th%20in%202006 (accessed 23 March 2025).

Blake-Churchill, Lindsey, "The Feminine Mystique …", nd, The Feminine Mystique | Summary, Significance, & Facts | Britannica, https://www.britannica.com/topic/The-Feminine-Mystique (accessed 3 January 2025).

Buczynski-Lee, Karen, Chapter 7, "Woman as Cabbage to Women as Prime Ministers and Presidents: Demanding Women's Rightful Space in the Film and Television Industry" in JA Scutt (ed), *Women, Law and Culture – Conformity, Contradiction and Conflict,* Palgrave Macmillan, London, 2016, 109–126.

Buczynski-Lee, Karen, "Celluloid Gardens in the Time of Consumption", *Synergies*, vol 1, 2020, 45–62, Celluloid Gardens in the Time of Consumption | Synergies: A Journal of English Literatures and Cultures, https://www.journal.edizioniets.eu/index.php/synergies/article/view/370 (accessed 2 March 2025).

Caldwell, Sophie, "Read America Ferrera's 'Barbie' monologue that provoked such an emotional reaction among viewers. Raise your hand if you cried", *Today*, 2 August 2023, Read America Ferrera's Barbie Monologue, Which Left People 'In Tears', https://www.today.com/popculture/movies/america-ferrara-barbie-monologue-full-text-reaction-rcna96237 (accessed 25 November 2024).

DividingLine, nd, *DividingLine*, The Feminine Mystique by Friedan, Betty: Very Good Hardcover (1963) 1st Edition | Dividing Line Books, https://

www.abebooks.co.uk/servlet/BookDetailsPL?bi=31313118189&dest=gbr&ref_=ps_ms_391300534&cm_mmc=msn-_-uk_shopp_used-_-naa-_-naa&msclkid=476ce3ce62701adbfe2a84529d26a7e4 (accessed 3 January 2025).

Ebert, Roger, "The Silence of the Lambs ...", *RogerEbert.com*, 14 February 1991, The Silence of the Lambs movie review (1991) | Roger Ebert, https://www.rogerebert.com/reviews/the-silence-of-the-lambs-1991#google_vignette (accessed 3 January 2025).

Ewe, Koh, "'No Ken without Barbie': Ryan Gosling Reacts to Oscars Nominations and Colleagues' Snubs", 23 January 2024, Ryan Gosling's Full Statement on Oscars Nomination | TIME, https://time.com/6576771/ryan-gosling-oscar-nominations-barbie-statement-gerwig-robbie-ferrera/ (accessed 2 March 2025).

Gay, Roxanne, "Fifty Years Ago, Protesters Took on the Miss America Pageant and Electrified the Feminist Movement, Miss America pageant is under new leadership after a sexist email scandal. But the pageant has a long history of controversy—including the 1968 protests", *Smithsonian Magazine*, January 2018, Fifty Years Ago, Protesters Took on the Miss America Pageant and Electrified the Feminist Movement | Smithsonian, https://www.smithsonianmag.com/history/fifty-years-ago-protestors-took-on-miss-america-pageant-electrified-feminist-movement-180967504/ (accessed 3 January 2025).

Gregory, Elizabeth, "Barbie hits $1 billion ...", *The Standard*, 7 August 2023, Barbie hits $1 billion: What are the other films in the billion club? | The Standard (accessed 2 September 2023).

Hassan, Beril Naz, "All the countries that have banned ...", *The Standard*, 18 August 2023, All the countries that have banned the Barbie movie | The Standard (accessed 2 September 2023).

Howell, Damien, "Differentiating the soleus from the gastrocnemius ...", *Journal of Orthopaedic and Sports Physical Therapy*, vol 41 (12), 985–986, December 2011, https://www.researchgate.net/publication/221764736_Differentiating_the_soleus_from_the_gastrocnemius_with_the_heel_raise_test (accessed 2 September 2023).

Keegan, Rebecca, Poindexter, Sandra and Whipp, Glenn, "Movies 91% white. 76% male. Changing who votes on Oscar won't be easy", *The Los Angeles Times*, 26 February 2016, 91% white. 76% male. Changing who votes on Oscar won't be easy. - Los Angeles Times, https://www.latimes.com/entertainment/movies/la-et-mn-academy-membership-20160226-story.html (accessed 2 March 2025), *Times staff writers Kevin Crust, Marisa Gerber, Taylor Goldenstein, Ben Welsh, Amy Kaufman and Josh Rottenberg contributed to this report.*

Lenker, Maureen Lee, "How Marilyn Monroe founded her own production company", *Entertainment Weekly,* 28 September 2022, How Marilyn Monroe founded her own production company, https://ew.com/movies/how-marilyn-monroe-founded-her-own-production-company/ (accessed 2 March 2025).

Musawa, "Campaign for Justice in Muslim Family Laws", nd, Lebanon - Campaign for Justice in Muslim Family Laws, https://campaignforjustice.musawah.org/repository/lebanon/#:~:text=Family%20laws%20in%20Lebanon%20allow%20polygamy%20for%20Muslim,by%20the%20rights%20of%20the%20second%20wife.%20%5B5%5D (accessed 2 March 2025).

Nash, Margot, "Lottie Lyell" in Jane Gaines, Radha Vatsal, and Monica Dall'Asta (eds), *Women Film Pioneers Project*, Columbia University Libraries, New York, NY, 2018 https://doi.org/10.7916/d8-82dq-w121 (accessed 2 March 2025).

Nash, Margot, "The Silent Work of Australian Women Scenario Writers" in Jill Nelmes and Julie Selbo (eds), *Women Screenwriters: An International Guide*, Palgrave Macmillan, London, 2015b, 169-179.

Nassau Guardian, "High Heels and your feet ...", 2025, High heels and your feet | Foot Health, https://www.thenassauguardian.com/lifestyles/foot-health/high-heels-and-your-feet/article_319977b5-8615-4405-8b22-207ac87ae09b.html (accessed 25 March 2025).

Nelson, Camilla, "The Female Eunuch at 50 ...", *The Conversation*, 8 October 2020, Friday essay: The Female Eunuch at 50, Germaine Greer's fearless, feminist masterpiece, https://theconversation.com/friday-essay-the-female-eunuch-at-50-germaine-greers-fearless-feminist-masterpiece-147437 (accessed 3 January 2025).

Obias, Rudy, "12 Actors ...", *Mental Floss*, 11 March 2024, 12 Actors Who Earned Oscar Nods for Less Than 20 Minutes of Screen Time, https://www.mentalfloss.com/article/73865/12-actors-who-earned-oscar-nods-less-20-minutes-screen-time#:~:text=%EE%80%80Screen%20time:16%20minutes%EE%80%81%20Though%20the%20final (accessed 3 January 2025).

O'Reilly, Michelle, Ronzoni, Pablo and Dogra, Nisha, "Children's Capacity to Make Decisions", *Sage Publications*, 2013, 2018, Sage Research Methods - Research with Children: Theory & Practice, https://methods.sagepub.com/book/mono/research-with-children/toc (accessed 2 March 2025).

PR NewsWire, "Bringing the Dark Side of High Heels ...", *Beverly Hills Physicians*, 28 July 2014, Bringing the Dark Side of High Heels to Light (accessed 2 September 2023).

Reise, "Film – Movie Features – Race and Appropriation ...", *as autostraddle*, 13 March 2024, Race and Appropriation at the Academy Awards: A 96 Year History | Autostraddle, https://www.autostraddle.com/2016-oscars-so-so-so-white-329290/ (accessed 2 March 2025).

Rooney, Lauren, "Grave Consequences: The societal rationale behind the medicalisation and secularisation of suicide as reflected in the burial of those who died by suicide in Ireland and England in the 19th century", *University College Dublin Law Review*, 1 April 2023, Grave Consequences: The societal rationale behind the medicalisation and secularisation of suicide as reflected in the burial of those who died by suicide in Ireland and England in the 19th century. – UCD Law Review, https://theucdlawreview.com/2023/04/01/grave-consequences-the-societal-rationale-behind-the-medicalisation-and-secularisation-of-suicide-as-reflected-in-the-burial-of-those-who-died-by-suicide-in-ireland-and-england-in-the-19th-centu/ (accessed 2 March 2025).

Scutt, Jocelynne A, "Credentials, Skills and Merit – Women and the Economics of Power" in JA Scutt, *The Incredible Woman – Power and Sexual Politics*, vol 2, Artemis Publishing, Melbourne, Australia, 1997, 59–72.

Scutt, Jocelynne A, "Pink is powerful ...", 27 January 2012, Pink is powerful - On Line Opinion - 27/1/2012 Scutt, *OnLine Opinion* 27 January 2012, https://www.onlineopinion.com.au/view.asp?article=13171&page=1 (accessed 2 March 2025).

Scutt, Jocelynne A, "Sexism in Legal Language", *Australian Law Journal*, 1985, vol 59, 10, 163–174.

Scutt, Jocelynne A, "Science Fiction Prototypes to Promote a New and Better World? Dr Frankenstein and 'the Creature', Dr Jekyll and Mr Hyde, and Yanis Varoufacis' *Another Now*", Synergies, 2025, 1–21.

Rotten Tomatoes, "The Silence ... What there is to Know", nd, The Silence of the Lambs | Rotten Tomatoes, https://www.rottentomatoes.com/m/silence_of_the_lambs (accessed 3 January 2025).

Tanenbaum, Laura and Engler, Mark, "No More Miss America …", *Dissent*, 7 September 2018, No More Miss America: A Collective Memory of Liberatory Action - Dissent Magazine, https://www.dissentmagazine.org/online_articles/no-more-miss-america-1968-pageant-protest-oral-history-women-liberation/ (accessed 3 January 2025).

Vevea, April, "Women Who Started their Own Production Companies before Marilyn Monroe", 5 September 2021, Women Who Started Their Own Production Companies Before Marilyn Monroe – Classic Blondes, https://classicblondes.com/2021/09/05/women-who-started-their-own-production-companies-before-marilyn-monroe/ (accessed 2 March 2025).

Washington, Lynette, Beer, Andrew and Kulik, Carol T, "Gender, place, leadership and levelling up across regions", *Journal of the Academy of Social Sciences*, vol 19, 2024, published online 16 December 2024, Full article: Gender, place leadership and levelling up across regions, https://www.tandfonline.com/doi/full/https://doi.org/10.1080/21582041.2024.2441856#abstract (accessed 21 March 2025).

World Population Review, "Countries Where Polygamy is Legal 2025", 2025, Countries Where Polygamy Is Legal 2025, https://worldpopulationreview.com/country-rankings/countries-where-polygamy-is-legal (accessed 2 March 2025).

Wright, Charlotte L, "The English Canon Law …", *Ecclesiastical Law Journal*, vol 19, 2, 2 May 2017, 193–211,The English Canon Law Relating to Suicide Victims | Ecclesiastical Law Journal | Cambridge Core, https://www.cambridge.org/core/journals/ecclesiastical-law-journal/article/abs/english-canon-law-relating-to-suicide-victims/A4D08D1CE33EF8C076DF607DA9050EAD (accessed 2 March 2025).

Books, Reports and Films

Bodichon, Barbara Leigh Smith, *A Brief Summary in Plain Language of the Most Important Laws Concerning Women …*, John Chapman, London, 1854, A Brief Summary in Plain Language of the Most Important Laws Concerning Women; Together with a Few Observations Thereon, https://webapp1.dlib.indiana.edu/vwwp/view?docId=VAB7030.xml (accessed 2 March 2025).

Burton, Clare, *The Promise and the Price: The Struggle for Equal Opportunity in Women's Employment*, Allen & Unwin, North Sydney, Australia, 1991.

Burton, Clare, *Subordination – Feminism and Social Theory*, Allen & Unwin, North Sydney, Australia, 1985.

Butler, Josephine, *The Education and Employment of Women*, T Brakell, Printer, Cook Street, Liverpool, UK, 1868, The Education and Employment of Women, https://webapp1.dlib.indiana.edu/vwwp/view?docId=VAB7056.xml (accessed 2 March 2025).

Fine, Cordelia, *Delusions of Gender – The Real Science behind Sex Differences*, Icon Books, NY, US, 2010.

Friedan, Betty, *The Feminine Mystique*, WW Norton, NYC, NY, US, 1963.

Game, Ann and Pringle, Rosemary, *Gender at Work*, Pluto Press, Sydney/London, UK, 1984.

Gray, Alasdair, *Poor Things – Episodes From the Early Life of Archibald McCandless M.D. Scottish Public health Officer – Edited by Alasdair* Gray, Bloomsbury, London, UK, 1992, 2002.

Greer, Germaine, *The Female Eunuch*, MacGibbon & Kee, London, UK, 1970.

Khan, Mattie, *Young and Restless: The Girls Who Sparked America's Revolutions*, Viking, NYC, NY, 2023.

Lord, MG, *Forever Barbie – The Unauthorized Biography of a Real Doll*, Walker and Company, New York, NY, US, 1994, 1995, 2005.

Man Who Has it All, Man Who Has it All, *Flipping Patriarchy – Imagining a gender-swapped world*, Unbound/Boundless, London, 2025, https://doi.org/10.1080/21582041.2024.2441856 (accessed 2 March 2025).

Paoletti, Jo B, *Pink and Blue: Telling the Boys from Girls in America*, Indiana University Press, Bloomington, IA, 2012.

Pipher, Mary and Gilliam, Sara Pipher, *Reviving Ophelia*, Riverhead Books, NYC, NY, US, 2019.

Scutt, Jocelynne A, *Magna Carta – A Treaty for Rights or Wrongs*, Palgrave Macmillan, London, UK, 2016.

Scutt, Jocelynne A, *Beauty, Women's Bodies and the Law – Performances in Plastic*, Palgrave Macmillan, London, UK, 2020.

Scutt, Jocelynne A, *Wage Rage for Equal Pay – Australia's Long, Long Struggle*, Palgrave Macmillan, London, UK, 2024.

Sieghart, Mary Ann, *The Authority Gap – Why Women are Still Taken Less Seriously than Men*, Doubleday, London, UK, 2021.

Smith, Dr Stacy L, Choueiti, Marc and Pieper, Dr Katherine, *Inclusion in the Director's Chair? Gender, Race & Age of Directors across 1,100 Films from 2007–2017*, Annenberg Inclusion Initiative, Annenberg Foundation/USC Annenberg, January 2018, Inclusion in the Director's Chair 2007 to

2017, https://assets.uscannenberg.org/docs/inclusion-in-the-directors-chair-2007-2017.pdf (accessed 2 March 2025).
Andrée Wright, *Don't Call Me Girlie* (film), 1985, Sydney, Australia.

Information Documents and Resources

Buczynski-Lee, Karen, Mourning becomes electric, Vida Goldstein takes on Politics and when Vida met the President – a Documentary Drama Film Script, MA Research Thesis, University of Melbourne VCA, 2007.

Nash, Margot, "Lottie Lyell: The Silent Work of an Early Australian Scenario Writer", *Screening the Past* 40. Special Dossier: Women and Silent Screen (2015a), http://www.screeningthepast.com/2015/08/lottie-lyell-the-silent-work-of-an-early-australian-scenario-writer/ (accessed 2 March 2025).

Nash, Margot, *Lottie Lyell – Women Film Pioneers Project*, nd, Lottie Lyell – Women Film Pioneers Project, https://wfpp.columbia.edu/pioneer/lottie-lyell/ (accessed 2 March 2025).

Quirk, Lawrence J and Crawford, Joan, *The Films of Joan Crawford*, Citadel, New York, NY, 1968.

University Health and Social Care, *Sex and the Law – Young People – Lanarkshire Sexual Health*, nd, Sex and the Law – Young People - Lanarkshire Sexual Health, https://www.lanarkshiresexualhealth.org/sex-and-the-law-yp/ (accessed 2 March 2025).

Part IV

Conclusion

Each time a woman stands up for herself, Without claiming it. Possibly without knowing it. She stands up for all women.

—Maya Angelou (1928–2014) American Medal of Freedom, 2011.

21

Conclusion: Parsing Women's Rights, Respect and Representation in Law and Society

Jocelynne A. Scutt

Introduction

What matters to women is too often seen as isolated from what matters to the rest of the world, as if women's concerns are restricted to "women's issues", sequestered from the broad spectrum of global concerns. As women are a majority in the world, and as what happens in the world happens to women as well as to men, it is odd that "women's issues" should be seen as a specialist category divorced from matters that matter to men. This "othering" has consequences.

Traditionally, women—when elected to parliaments and promoted into portfolios and at last elevated into cabinet—have been allocated "soft" areas of responsibility such as education, culture, media and arts, children and care, sport or equalities. Treasury, business and trade or

J. A. Scutt (✉)
Sydney, Australia
e-mail: jocelynne@fraserchambers.com

School of Social Sciences, Faculty of Arts, Design and Architecture, UNSW (University of New South Wales), Sydney, Australia

J. A. Scutt (ed.), *Women, Power and Autonomy*,
https://doi.org/10.1007/978-3-031-97958-3_21

defence, energy and security are seen as "hard" and generally outside women's ambit. Women have also been sidelined by being offered "honorary" posts without power though in cabinet. This happened with Enid Lyons, one of the first two women to be elected to the Australian Parliament: she and Dorothy Tangney were voted into the Senate in the 1943 federal election. In government, Lyons spoke on child endowment (for), the Queensland miners' strike (against), and the proposed 1945 amendments to the Australian Constitution to give the federal government powers in areas such as national health, family allowances, and foreign investment for a defined period post-war (against).[1] When elevated to cabinet it was to an office she pronounced "toothless", vice president of the executive council (Lyons 1972; also 1965, 1969; Buczynski-Lee and Scutt 2002). This sidelining happened to Australian senator Susan Ryan, who had served as minister for education (March 1983–July 1987) and minister assisting the prime minister for the status of women (March 1983–January 1988) in the Hawke government then, falling into disfavour, was given a cabinet post as special minister of state (July 1987–January 1988) (Ryan 1999).

There are exceptions. In the US, Frances Perkins became first woman in cabinet and first woman serving as secretary for labour (Martin 1976; Cobble 1988; Stussy 2023; Potts and Potts nd)—a post the then president recognised as crucial to his 1930s recovery plan to lift the country out of the Great Depression. But then the president was Franklin D Roosevelt who was not marching to the sound of conventional drums. Under Bill Clinton as president, Madelaine Albright became first woman secretary of state for the United States (1993–1997) (Albright 2013; Albright (with Woodward) 2020), to be followed by Hillary Clinton as secretary of state (2009–2013) appointed by Barack Obama. (Extraordinarily well-qualified for the role, this may however be seen as a "second prize" appointment to someone who ought to have been first woman president (Clinton 2016, 2017). At one time Bronwyn Bishop, an Australian politician serving in the Senate (1987–1994) and the House

[1] The referendum on "Post-war Reconstruction and Democratic Rights", aiming to grant Commonwealth legislative power (for five years) on 14 matters, including "the people of the Aboriginal race", family allowances, ex-servicemen's rehabilitation, and national health, failed: AEC (2008).

of Representatives (1994–2016), was allocated defence as minister for defence industry, science and personnel (1996–1998), however was then reverted to the "soft" portfolio of minister for aged care (1998–2001) (Parliament of Australia nd). That the "hard" field appointments are exceptions is confirmed by the media reception and constant public pronouncements as to their oddity, as exemplified by the standard iteration in the UK of "first", for chancellor of the exchequer Rachel Reeves, appointed to the post in the Starmer government in 2024 (Gov.UK nd).

Of course the division of portfolios into "soft" and "hard" simply confirms bias in the system where women are in government and a government field of endeavour looms. That education, children and care are labelled soft is a measure of their downgrading in value, not at all an indicator of their complexity and the difficulty confronting leaders in those ministries. Little doubt that this is related to women's being the principal workforce in each area, with the intelligent and resourceful labour involved not being recognised in wages, salaries and remuneration, or indeed at all under patriarchal designations of worth, whilst being downgraded when contrasted against incomes and benefits flowing to traditional male industries—for example, defence, mining, construction (Burton 1987, 1988; Scutt 1997, 2024). Education, too, is a key area when it comes to power relationships and imbalances, albeit this is not overtly acknowledged. This is exemplified by the fact that when conservative governments come to power one of the first areas of attack, if not the first target, is the education system: shifting power relationships and imbalances, as education of the masses will inevitably do, is antithetical to the principles by which these governments abide. The dismantling of the Department of Education embarked upon in 2025 in the United States at the hand of the second Trump administration (Hernholm 2025; Tonness 2025) starkly attests to this.

The distortion of economics with its focus on statistics, graphs and theoretical notions directing its options and outcomes is another example of the nonsense hard/soft categorisation. When developed by Harriet Martineau (1802–1876) through her work on political economy, economics was based in principles of human engagement in finance, business and the polity and their impact on society—comprising human beings (Martineau 1832–1834; The Martineau Society 2025). It did not isolate economic principles or their application from a necessary interface with human lives and well-being. Had this focus remained, economics would no doubt today be classified as soft. "Soft" appears to be the appellation given to disciplines and areas of endeavour that recognise humanity and the world of nature are at the heart, or should be at the heart, of decision-making, planning, and development.

Women, Power and Autonomy recognises this and the overlap in the areas of law and society where rights, respect and representation are notable in their absence or by their undermining. Wandoo Grace Aibangbee's "Widows …" crystalises the want of respect lying in the dearth of widows' rights in Southern Nigeria, in the failure to acknowledge women as persons with full human entitlements, their contribution to family, husband and children, land and property, and the denial of their identity and property rights and child custody because the husband is dead. A lack of identity and denial of rights to property and the importance of alerting women (in this case, young women) to this is replicated in Robin Joyce's literary review "Women and Property …" considering the way writers of teenage novels drew their readers' attention to property ownership and denial of it, through stories with which they could identify. A lack of respect is implicit in the lack of rights to property and independent ownership of resources. Contentions that girls and women should be and would be catered for sufficiently through provision by a father first, then a husband, overlooks the human right to housing, the respect (not to mention safety, security and sustenance) that comes with a roof over one's head and a bed under one's body as an irrefutable entitlement—and that in one's own name, not the name of another. Anna Kerr's "A Mother of a Job …", reviewing the position now confronting women under Australian law despite legal reforms, practical gains, and women's advances in law and society generally, together with Patricia Branco and Paula Casaleiro's "The Daughters of the Carnation Revolution …" on women under laws framed through revolution and reform in Portugal, show clearly that although there may be stark differences in the customs to which Southern Nigerian women are subjected, and in the position of women in the period reflected in the novels-for-girls, today's women under European laws and their offshoots are simply at one remove.

Are rights and respect gained by movement into non-traditional fields of work, into finance and business, and into gaining a political voice and parliamentary representation? Analysis of advances by women in the corporate world and the polity through positions on boards, management, in parliament and in government through Natalie Turney's "Demanding the Right of Representation for Women …", Ameena Zia's "Representation …", Karen Dacy's "'Thieving Rorters' …", and in Janne Ellen Swift's "Forging the Right to Work with Metal …" recounting the historically grand assault on a male industry simply so that women could work, stand as testament to the interaction of law, rights, respect and representation. Here again the linkage between the claim for rights in order to gain respect, the need for respect in order to gain rights, and the cross-over with the importance of representation is evident. Without occupying places and representation in the corporation, the more difficult it is for women to be seen and accepted as qualified or even entitled to jobs in industry—any industry. Yet lacking the right to parliamentary places, government posts, and representation in legislatures, the laws required to support women's propulsion by right into positions generating momentum at all societal levels are less likely to be introduced, much less passed. Yes, the vote was won when majorities of male parliaments recognised women's right to suffrage: if women were to gain the vote there was no other option. Still, that would never have occurred had women not demanded this basic right—some more, some less politely. Glen Tomasetti's 1970s women's anthem "Don't Be Too Polite Girls" (Tomasetti 1969) begins in the revolutionary claims of union women for equal pay and builds on the demands of the suffragettes for voting rights, who in turn built on the women before them. The women who would not be quiet and be still.

Anne Thacker's "Criminal Court Links to a Better Life …" and Jessica K Williams' "Lobbying for Change …" dovetail in the overlap of rights and respect in the criminal justice system which in their lack expose women to violence imposed by the state, when the crimes with which they are charged too often arise from that same cause, or the impact of violence and control imposed by intimate partners. Where change comes through the introduction of non-generic, women-centred programs, the chances for women may become real. Yes, as Baljit Banga's

"State Violence, Women's Safety and the Funding Cliff Edge …" emphasises, the need for funding to enable such programs to be established and to be sustained in essence and maintained at length is fundamental. This follows, as Banga recounts, for all women's services and particularly for those designed to serve the interests and needs of Black and minoritised women. But is the funding there? Are the programs secure? Must women and women's organisations continue to be required to jump hoops, writing submissions, pleading for grants, lobbying ministers whose priorities are directed elsewhere, or who simply do not comprehend that these interests and needs are equally important as those being pressed by others, or even more so. Without this recognition, women's vulnerability to manipulation, mistreatment, pain and peril remain, and the omission in ignorance of their rights and right to respect leaves them open to predatory hurt.

Prostituting women and pornographying them, together with subjecting them in childhood and young womanhood to paedophiliac conduct explicit in sexual use, misuse and abuse, denies them rights and respect, compounded by their (mis)representation as fully compliant, consenting and readily participating in that exploitation or even precociously "leading on" innocent men. These elements are explored in Simone Watson and Helen Pringle's "The Prostitution System as the Wreckage of Women's Autonomy …", Shabina Begum's "Informed Consent and Preventing Loss of Innocence …", Judy Forshaw's "Lolita …", Helen Pringle's "Living in a Pornographic World …", and Jocelynne A Scutt's "Barbie Meets a Very Poor Thing …". Maja von Bolton's "Surrogacy …", considering that the nature of rights and an assertion of rights can undercut realities of exploitation where women's bodies are represented and claimed as vehicles for gestation and giving birth, raises parallel issues.

Abortion lies at the heart of denial to women of rights and respect, with women's lack of membership of or representation in positions of power, particularly the judiciary and parliament, a key. This is surveyed in Kerr's "A Mother of a Job …", Branco and Casaleiro's "The Daughters of the Carnation Revolution …" and Scutt's "When a Woman's Body is Not Her Own …". Rianka Roy, Bandana Purkayastha and Anjana Narayan's "Between Legal and Non-Legal Terrains" in addressing conflicts for women flanked by law and potentially trapped in contradictions and discord generated by fundamentalist religious diktat links into the clash of law and religion encountered by women seeking only the right to health through rights and respect for their decisions, their decision-making capacity, and their entitlement. "Our bodies, ourselves" was a plea for this autonomy voiced from the end of the 1960s and through the 1970s, illustrating the importance of women's words as designating worth (Boston Women's Health Book Collective 1968). Women saw irrefutably that the language of rights, respect and representation is central to women's demands for them, and underpins whether their demands can or will be met.

Women's Rights in Language

> For lawyers language has a special interest because it is the greatest instrument of social control. Lawyers are perhaps apt to regard law as the sole, or chief, means of social control, forgetting that the law is only a special department of language and that, whereas the application of law is limited, language is all pervasive ...
>
> Glanville Williams, "Language and the Law", *Law Quarterly Review*, 1945, vol 61, 71.

For decades, common law lawyers and judges were tutored in the jurisprudence of Glanville Williams, Cambridge don, prolific author and, sadly, a Cambridge professor of law firmly fixed in the tradition of chief justice Matthew Hale and his *Pleas of the Crown.* On the matter of rape and consent, Williams' *Text Book of Criminal Law* (1983) resorts to quoting Byron, the reputed "mad, bad and dangerous to know" poet, and states without equivocation that "some women enjoy fantasies of being raped is well authenticated", for women "may, to some extent, welcome a masterful advance while putting up a token resistance" (1983, 238):

> A little still she strove, and much repented,
> And whispering "I will ne'er consent" – consented.

Nonetheless, or perhaps consistent with this, Williams' contention as to the power of language is embedded in feminist theory and practice. Catharine A MacKinnon's *Only Words* (1983) affirms this in her critique of US law and the application of the First Amendment to harms imposed on women which are labelled "speech" by the US Supreme Court to take them out of the category where they would be actionable.[2] Rape (if proven) is a recognised and theoretically penalised harm—a crime. When it occurs as pornography, however, it is decreed jurisprudentially as no longer an act defined as a crime, but speech that is non-actionable. Here, MacKinnon instances hate speech, and racial and sexual harassment constituting acts of discrimination, intimidation, subordination, and terrorism. The action that is pornography ought be so classified in law, opening makers, publishers and purveyors (not victim/survivors) to prosecution for the damage they inflict on women (and, though less often, men). This is revealed in *The Lasting Harm*, Lucia Osborne-Crowley's treatise (2024) written in "witnessing the trial of Ghislaine Maxwell", at trial's conclusion convicted in her complicity with Jeffrey Epstein's exploitative crimes against numerous young women and girls. Osborne-Crowley observes that the story of one of the four principal prosecution witnesses "perfectly encapsulates the way that trauma in childhood" alters utterly the women's life path, leaving women "vulnerable to addiction, self-loathing and more trauma". Women are snared "in a cycle of violence and shame, the way it refuses to let [women] go" (2024, 3).

The predatory conduct to which girls and young and old and older and any-aged women are subjected by men who impose their power and authority and, sadly, as in the instance of Epstein/Maxwell, engage other women to advance their manoeuvres, must be named. Yet how to recognise in legal language the harm and its initiation? The language of the law is studiously deficient in finding, for women, the words to say it.

---

2 *Roth v United States* 354 US 476 (1957), Roth v. United States | 354 U.S. 476 (1957) | Justia U.S. Supreme Court Center, https://supreme.justia.com/cases/federal/us/354/476/ (accessed 2 March 2025); *Miller v California* 413 US 15, https://en.wikipedia.org/wiki/Miller_v._California (1973), Miller v. California | 413 U.S. 15 (1973) | Justia U.S. Supreme Court Center, https://supreme.justia.com/cases/federal/us/413/15/ (accessed 2 March 2025); *Jacobellis v Ohio* 378 US 184 (1964), Jacobellis v. Ohio | 378 U.S. 184 (1964) | Justia U.S. Supreme Court Center, https://supreme.justia.com/cases/federal/us/378/184/ (accessed 2 March 2025).

This striving for naming is replicated through the trial system, where women are explicitly rendered invisible by the law itself. Throughout what became known as "the Stanford rape trial", Chanel Miller went by the name "Emily Doe", a legal fiction appearing in court documents, media reports, and circulating in gossip whilst the gossipers speculated on "who" she "really" was. In September 2019 Miller's book *Know My Name: A Memoir* was published. Miller's victim impact statement, made to the court during (the minimal) sentencing of the man convicted, had become a viral sensation, encapsulating the experience of so many other women raped, reporting or not reporting, going on trial (as rape victim/survivors live out the prosecution process) or not. Miller wanted to stand steady by her statement, speaking for herself as who she was, Chanel Miller.

Nonetheless, in the name of (purportedly) advancing the rights of rape victims through anonymising them when (even so rarely) a prosecution takes place, laws have decreed that the name of the principal witness (the woman victim/survivor) cannot be published or publicised, those defying this being at risk of prosecution. Unless laws are amended, this follows even where the party wishing to be acknowledged by name is a principal witness whom such a law is supposed to "protect".[3] This squarely raises the meaning of "protection". What is the rationale here that contends concealing a victim/survivor's name can or will do this, promoting the notion that a woman raped should be shrouded as if she is shamed and should feel ashamed of having been attacked and physically, psychologically and personally violated. In Tasmania, Australia, victim/survivor of child sexual abuse (abused at 15 years by her then 58-year-old teacher) Grace Tame took the issue to court (Tame 2022; Funnell 2019), winning the right to name her own name. Previously she had been "Jane Doe", just had been so for Chanel Miller and women in such cases in so

[3] Department of Justice (nd) contains a table of evidence provisions in each Australian jurisdiction where they prohibit publication, indicating those jurisdictions where publication of the principal witness (victim/survivor) is permitted in stipulated circumstances – for example, "permission", "consent" or court order, or as a defence to prosecution for contempt. Notably all jurisdictions bar Tasmania had such a provision as a result of campaigns against the suppression of a victim/survivor's right over publication of her own name. Note: the paper precedes amendment to section 194 of the *Evidence* Act 2001 (Tas) which now provides for such a defence.

many jurisdictions (Tasmania Law Reform Institute 2013; Department of Justice nd). Subsequently section 194 of the *Evidence* Act 2001 (Tas)[4] was amended to incorporate the victim/survivor's consent to having her name publicly known as a defence. This gives her (some) control over her own story.

Nonetheless, the use of words that are deceptive and concealing of the realities of women's lives and wellbeing are in constant use. Baljit Banga observes this phenomenon in the terminology of the *Domestic Abuse Act* 2021 (UK).[5] When in 2009 monies directed to the "Support People Programme" (SP) were no longer ring-fenced or quarantined, the UK government focus changedb from violence against women to "domestic abuse".[6] Violence against women and domestic abuse services were set in competition with one another, with domestic abuse being an amorphous category failing to recognise women and children as the main victims (and hopefully survivors) hence requiring a skewering of resources to serve their needs. The very naming of the Act itself renders invisible the major targets of this violence, effectively concealing the truth from view. Even "violence against women" misses the mark. Whose violence? Whose violence against women? Why are women (and children) the major target and why is it men who engage in it? No one denies that women can be violent. Women can be collusive (as Osborne-Crowley 2024 records). But saying this as if it were an answer to the phenomenon that constitutes violence against women is itself a denial (Natarajan 2025; Smith 2022; Radford and Russell 1992). Domestic and other violence targetting women must be named as violence committed against women, principally (and too often) by the men in their lives.

Contrary to the circumstance where the words to say it are there, but go unused, sometimes the conduct is there, but no words to say it. This arose with sexual harassment—a term coined by Lin Farley (1978) and

---

[4] EVIDENCE ACT 2001 - SECT 194 K Publication of certain identifying particulars prohibited, https://www5.austlii.edu.au/au/legis/tas/consol_act/ea200180/s194k.html (accessed 2 March 2025).

[5] *Domestic Abuse Act* 2021 (UK), Domestic Abuse Act 2021, https://www.legislation.gov.uk/ukpga/2021/17/contents (accessed 2 March 2025).

[6] Baljit Banga, Chapter 16 "Structural Inequality, Women's Safety and the Funding Cliff Edge: The Impact of the New Funding Policy in Meeting the Needs of Black and Minoritised Women", this volume.

Catharine MacKinnon (1978). Sometimes, as with "domestic abuse" and even "violence against women", the words are there but fail. As Helen Pringle says in referring to a court psychologist's report on a defendant prosecuted for possession and downloading of child pornography, the use of the term "act out" is problematic "in this and other such cases":

> The court psychologist indicated that Marcus Puhakka was not a peadophile in the sense that he had abused or even wanted to abuse children whom he knew. He did not "act out", at least in the sense of *contact* assault of actual children. And he did not make images by recording abuse of children; he simply downloaded and viewed them ...[7]

The gross oversight of injury caused is both embedded and covered up in this language, which tends to turn on its head the acceptance of who is the victim here. "Acting out" in psychology is generally applied to the patient in therapy who "acts out" to come to terms with (for example) childhood trauma (Satow 2022). But the offender in the courtroom is not a patient.[8] He is a man who has actively participated in the violation of every child who has come into his possession through the images he has downloaded. He has actively encouraged and collaborated in the making of the images which would not be there, were there no market for them, no one desiring to download them, no one to view them in their graphic confirmation of the damage done to children. This ignorance of the complicity in which those accused and convicted of these crimes engage is striking. It is abidingly present in the decisions of judges who, in sentencing for possession of pornographic images, do not appear to recognise that real children are being subjected to damage in the making of them. This fundamental fact should be incorporated unswervingly in sentencing centred in recognition of the fundamentally abusive conduct

[7] Helen Pringle, Chapter 19 "Living in a Pornographic World: Constraint on the Autonomy of Girls and Women", this volume.

[8] Nor is he a victim of any crime or violation of his person. If it were the case that in the past he had been (for example) sexually abused, that cannot excuse the crimes with which he is charged and for which he is being sentenced. The victims are the children subjected to rape and other forms of sexual abuse, and to photographing and recording for the miserable delectation of predatory offenders. The tenor of the sentencing judgment is indeed concerning, or more than concerning.

engaged in by the accused. The accused is complicit in the making of these images and hence in the impairment of the child's psychological and physical health, their right to the life of joy and happiness to which every human being is entitled. The lasting harm that results from both the maker's and the user's conduct is real. These are not simply "images" or "pictures". They are evidence—concrete, explicit confirmation—of inexcusable and horrifying harm.

This cover up is replicated in the use of the term "grooming" which fails to encapsulate the truth of the conduct it is said to portray. "Grooming" is defined by the UK Metropolitan Police (2025) as "… when a person builds a relationship with a child, young person or an adult who's at risk so they can abuse them and manipulate them into doing things." The definition is that the abuse "is usually sexual or financial, but it can also include other illegal acts". Section 21(15) of the *Sexual Offences Act* 2003 (UK) headlines the offence as **Meeting a child following sexual grooming, etc.**[9] The entire tenor of the provision, both implicitly and explicitly, is that grooming is a *precursor* to harm and it is only what follows the "grooming" that is criminal and hence open to prosecution. Just as the word "grooming" fails to recognise that harm itself lies in the process that is designated "grooming", the word "grooming" fails to recognise that harm is intrinsic to the conduct that goes under that inappropriately designated title.

The best illustration of the problem is the provision itself. Section 21(15) states:

15 Meeting a child following sexual grooming etc.

(1) A person aged 18 or over (A) commits an offence if—
  (a) A has met or communicated with another person (B) on one or more occasions and subsequently—
    (i) A intentionally meets B,
    (ii) A travels with the intention of meeting B in any part of the world or arranges to meet B in any part of the world, or

[9] *Sexual Offences Act* 2003 (UK), Sexual Offences Act 2003, https://www.legislation.gov.uk/ukpga/2003/42/section/15 (accessed 2 March 2025).

(iii) B travels with the intention of meeting A in any part of the world,

(b) A intends to do anything to or in respect of B, during or after the meeting mentioned in paragraph (a)(i) to (iii) and in any part of the world, which if done will involve the commission by A of a relevant offence,

(c) B is under 16, and

(d) A does not reasonably believe that B is 16 or over.

(2) In subsection (1)—

(a) the reference to A having met or communicated with B is a reference to A having met B in any part of the world or having communicated with B by any means from, to or in any part of the world;

(b) "relevant offence" means—

(i) an offence under this Part,

(ii) ...

(iii) anything done outside England and Wales ... which is not an offence within sub-paragraph (i) ... but would be an offence within sub-paragraph (i) if done in England and Wales.

(3) ...

(4) A person guilty of an offence under this section is liable—

(a) on summary conviction, to imprisonment for a term not exceeding 6 months or a fine not exceeding the statutory maximum or both;

(b) on conviction on indictment, to imprisonment for a term not exceeding 10 years.

All is framed on action *after* the "grooming". No provision exists under the title "grooming" itself. That is, the provision is drafted as if "grooming" in itself is not a crime, but employing it to engage in future crime—meeting up or communicating to meet up with the child or young person *is*. But what constitutes "grooming"?

As Osborne-Crowley makes explicit in *The Lasting Harm* (2024), the damage done, lives impaired, futures impoverished result not just from meeting up to impose, and imposing, sexual or sexually charged activity on the young women and girls exploited. It lies, too, in the abuse and violation innate in the lead up to this. Maxwell and Epstein, like others who engage in this predatory conduct, led their victims and sometime survivors to believe they were valued for themselves, as prized human beings, as entitled through that value and talent to be encouraged with wisdom to accomplish the levels of aptitude, expertise and flair with which they were endow and for which they were prepared to strive to attain. Yet the truth was and is that this constituted a gross breach of trust: to believe one is respected and esteemed for oneself—for one's inherent value as a human being—when this is not so, is an abuse and violation in itself. As Scutt (2024, 417–418) observes:

> The breach of trust in leading a person to believe that she is valued for herself, as a human being, as someone talented, with capability to be nurtured, with ability to be mentored, with intrinsic worth – when truth is, there is no such valuing [by the predators], no such assumption or belief in worth or talent or capability or ability or even the right to a life well-lived. The young women and girls in the Maxwell story were regarded as subhuman or not human at all. Their lives were not equal to the lives of those who used them for and to their own self-indulgent ends. "Grooming" implies "leading up to". Not the reality of what it constitutes, and is. It must be replaced by the truth-telling that is required in what happened here and elsewhere, everywhere: "predatory injury", "predatory abuse", "predatory conduct", "predatory imposition", "predatory exploitation", "predatory use", "predatory maltreatment", "predatory harm", or "predatory hurt". Yes, the crimes committed once this end was accomplished were and are real. But the conduct leading up to them was equally heinous in its essence and substance, its reality and impact. It is what, in the end, not only leads to lasting harm. It is lasting harm.

Women's Rights in Law

> I fear there is little reason to pay a compliment to our laws for their respect and favour to the female sex.
>
> Edward Christian, *Blackstone's Commentaries on the Laws of England*, 1753, 1793 edn, vol 1, 445fn

Edward Christian wrote in the time of coverture, where women were presumed advantaged by their personhood having been subsumed in that of their husbands. The notion was that if they (for example) accrued debts or committed acts classed criminal they would not be held liable for the debts or for their criminal acts. Rather, liability civil and criminal would fall upon their husbands. The reality was otherwise. Husbands could declare themselves not responsible for their wives' debts, whether the purpose of the debt was to furnish the household and family (including him) with the capacity to live at the level of sustenance their class afforded them.[10] Husbands could escape criminal liability for their wives' conduct, and wives had little or no protection from a husband's conduct. Marital rape was deemed by the revered Hale as both impossible and not criminal, by reason of the woman's consent to marriage. A husband could fritter away his wife's inheritance, property, income—any monies she owned or accrued in her own right, for she had no right or entitlement to any property or income. Even upon betrothal the intended husband had rights: any property she might give away during this period could be reclaimed by the husband once the two were wed. The lie "all my worldly goods I upon thee endow", stated as part of the traditional marriage ceremony and magnificent in its perfidy, was precisely the opposite of the reality. It was the woman who gave up all her goods—including those possessed at the time of the marriage and any accrued after it. Christian was, of course, right in his renunciation.

The continuing challenge to women's rights in law is laid bare in the contributions to *Women, Power and Autonomy*, as is the past and continuing struggle by women—sometimes with the support of men who recognise injustice when it stares them in the face—to claim rights and entitlements that should be theirs. Gains are made. Laws are reformed. International conventions and treaties are signed, ratified; optional protocols entered into.[11] Yet practicing lawyers and judges are

[10] "Necessaries" can too readily be reconstituted as "trivial" expenditure on fashion, hair, and clothing, an obsession with tribunals and courts charged with the responsibility of assessing women's wages (Scutt 2024).

[11] For example CEDAW (*Convention on the Elimination of All Forms of Discrimination Against Women)*, Convention on the Elimination of All Forms of Discrimination against Women

often well-versed in the law prior to the reforms, so unless compulsory education is incorporated as a requirement in each new statute relating to women's rights,[12] the new law runs the risk of being interpreted against the backdrop of the old, despite the legislature's intent. How many current judges, for example, were lectured in the *Sexual Offences Act* 2003 (UK)[13]; how many in changes to the *Homicide Act* 1957 (UK) through the *Coroners and Justice Act* 2009 (UK)?[14] How many were at law school when these changes were proposed and introduced, to become a part of the university curriculum. This means, almost inevitably, that such reforms run the risk of being undermined or overturned. This is starkly evident in the UK case *R v Clinton* [2012] addressing male murder of women, or femicide.[15]

Traditionally provocation law favoured men. The typical instances where provocation could lessen murder to manslaughter were where the offender was called impotent by the victim. Where the offender was called a dwarf by the victim. Where the offender came home to see his wife in flagrante delicto: that is she is caught in the act of committing adultery. Albeit adultery was not a crime in British law (in the United

New York, 18 December 1979 | OHCHR, https://www.ohchr.org/en/instruments-mechanisms/instruments/convention-elimination-all-forms-discrimination-against-women (accessed 2 March 2025); *Istanbul Convention – Council of Europe Convention on Preventing and combating Violence Against Women and DomesticViolence*, Home - Istanbul Convention Action against violence against women and domestic violence, https://www.coe.int/en/web/istanbul-convention (accessed 2 March 2025).

12 Although generally, nowadays, judicial education is accepted as essential in terms of regular or semi-regular seminars, etc. this will not serve to overcome traditional learning or socialization. The Women's Electoral Lobby (WEL) Draft Bill on Rape and Other Sexual Offences proposed provisions in reformed sexual offences laws, to require compulsory judicial education and training in the field, with prosecutors and defence counsel obligated to undertake training, too, in order to be qualified to practice in the area: *WEL Draft Bill* … in "Appendix", *Supplementary Report on Reform of Rape Laws*, NSW Department of the Attorney-General and Minister for Justice, NSW Attorney-General, Sydney, NSW, 1978.

13 *Sexual Offences Act* 2003 (UK), Sexual Offences Act 2003, https://www.legislation.gov.uk/ukpga/2003/42/contents (accessed 2 March 2025).

14 *Homicide* Act 1957 (UK), Homicide Act 1957, https://www.legislation.gov.uk/ukpga/Eliz2/5-6/11/contents (accessed 2 March 2025); *Coroners and Justice Act* 2009 (UK), Coroners and Justice Act 2009, https://www.legislation.gov.uk/ukpga/2009/25/contents.

15 *R v Clinton, R v Parker, R v Evans* (Case No: 2011/04258/C3 (1) 2011/03081/D1 (2) 2011/03115/C3 (3)); *R v Clinton* [2012] EWCA Crim 2, [2012] Crim LR 539, R -v- Clinton, Parker and Evans - judgment, https://www.judiciary.uk/wp-content/uploads/JCO/Documents/Judgments/r-v-clinton-parker-and-evans-judgment.pdf (accessed 2 March 2025).

States many states, particularly on the east coast, made it one), flagrante delicto was applied to this happening, albeit in law it means "caught in the act of committing a crime" (Legal Dictionary 2019).[16] Lobbying by women and women's groups in the United Kingdom led to abolition of provocation as a partial defence to murder, introducing "loss of control" as its replacement. Sections 54 and 55 of the *Coroners and Justice Act* 2009 (UK) defined this new defence. Section 54 provides, amongst other matters,[17] that evidence of a "qualifying trigger" substantiating loss of control is required to enable the defence to be put to the jury for its consideration as to whether manslaughter should be their verdict rather than murder. Once that evidence is before the jury, the onus lies on the prosecution to prove beyond a reasonable doubt that the defence is not substantiated. Section 55(6) rules out certain matters as triggers that can support loss of control, meaning that these matters cannot be adduced to support the accused's contention that s/he suffered a loss of control "justifying" the killing as manslaughter, not murder:

> (6) In determining whether a loss of self-control had a qualifying trigger—
>
> (a) D's fear of serious violence is to be disregarded to the extent that it was caused by a thing which D incited to be done or said for the purpose of providing an excuse to use violence;

---

16 This is not an isolated instance of a woman being classed together with criminals when that is an obvious misnomer. The corroboration rule in rape at common law, requiring a warning to be given to jurors that they must carefully scrutinize the evidence of the principal witness (complainant), put her into the same camp as a co-conspirator in a criminal prosecution for conspiracy or an accomplice; see Scutt (1979, 1980).

17 Extraordinarily problematic, section 55(3) is an additional concern. It is regressive in placing women in a position where, should the defence in reality be self-defence – killing in circumstances of the fear of being killed, the implication is that this is *not* self-defence but a ground for a reduction of murder to manslaughter only. It provides that a trigger for loss of control can be "attributable to D's fear of serious violence from V against D or another identified person". As women not infrequently kill a partner or former partner in precisely these circumstances, the defence of self-defence should apply ("… fear of serious violence" surely is what is fear of being killed) so that the woman is acquitted, not guilty on the basis of murder reduced to manslaughter. Unfortunately, in the UK a focus on reduction of murder to manslaughter where women are defendants in prosecutions for husband killing is a misdirection which auspiciously has not been followed in, for example, South Africa, Aotearoa/New Zealand or, in some instances, Australia. This was clearly the case in a conference held at City University, London, in 2024 (City St George's University of London 2024).

(b) a sense of being seriously wronged by a thing done or said is not justifiable if D incited the thing to be done or said for the purpose of providing an excuse to use violence;
(c) the fact that a thing done or said constituted sexual infidelity is to be disregarded.

R v Clinton addressed the application of section 55(6)(c). Here, three defendants (male) appealed against their convictions for murder where the wife of each was the target and victim. Jon-Jacques Clinton won his appeal. The others failed. It is the decision in relation to him that requires attention, the appellate court saying that the trial judge, as was her role under these provisions, allowed the partial defence of diminished responsibility (which the jury rejected) and disallowed that of loss of control on the basis that the evidence was insufficient for it to go to the jury. Was this disallowance correct in law?

The matters put by the defence in the trial were that Dawn Clinton, 33 years old, was killed by Mr Clinton, two years older. The immediate circumstances of the killing were:

> [54] The deceased had been beaten about the head with a wooden baton, strangled with a belt, and then a piece of rope had been tightened around her neck with the aid of the wooden baton. There were defensive injuries. The cause of death was head injury and asphyxia caused by a ligature compression of the neck. After he had killed her the appellant removed most of her clothes and having put her body into a number of different poses, took photographs of it and then sent text messages to Mr Montgomery, the man with whom she was having a relationship.

These are the matters, apart from issues relating to "infidelity" that were put to support the defence of loss of control:

> [75] He heard her kind of snigger. He was not looking at her and she was not looking at him. He heard her snigger and "sought [sic] of almost like laugh", and then she said "you haven't got the fucking bollocks". I thought "what?" so I turned round and looked. "She'd gone on to one of the pages I'd minimised, suicide sites, the hanging rope". She then went on "it would have been easier if you had, for all of us". He never ever seen "my Dawnie like that". He felt "useless, awful, confused and fearful. And then she became very angry saying that she'd done her bit with the

> children. She said "I didn't fucking sign up for this. You have them. You look after them". He said it was horrible. His wife was a different person "it was like she was somebody else". With that the walls and the ceiling just seemed to close in. She was talking but he could not hear what she was saying. He could see her mouth opening and closing. He could hear a noise, like the distant sea. He wanted everything to stop. He wanted everything to slow down. He then reached out and grabbed the piece of wood. The attack on her followed.

So the defence hung upon Mr Clinton's evidence of his wife (a) "sniggering" about his researching suicide methods, and (b) saying he would have to take care of the children. This was the evidence the trial judge said was insufficient to support putting loss of control to the jury. The appellate court, however, reconstructed section 55(6)(c) so as to reverse the trial judge, albeit agreeing that had infidelity stood alone (without the matters set out in para [75]), then loss of control would not have been available to the defendant.

Despite the clear words of section 55(6)(c) that in "determining whether a loss of self-control had a qualifying trigger ... the fact that a thing done or said constituted sexual infidelity is to be disregarded" the appeal judges reinterpreted it to find that sexual infidelity was *not* to be "disregarded". Rather it could and should be taken into account. This conclusion was constructed on the basis that "remarks allegedly made by the wife, challenged about her infidelity, to the effect that she had intercourse with five men were [not] to be ignored [as] the totality of the matters relied on as a qualifying trigger ["sniggering" about searching methods of suicide, and saying to the father of the children that he should take responsibility for them], evaluated in the context of the evidence relating to the wife's sexual infidelity, and examined as a whole, were of sufficient weight to put to the jury" [paras 76–77]. Thus the Court of Appeal reversed the meaning and intention of the parliament in seeking to eliminate from consideration a defence based in allegations of (a wife's) infidelity.

Amongst other matters, the very fact that the sniggering and statement that a father had a responsibility to care for his children were ruled out by the trial judge as lacking the quality required by section 55(4)(a) and (b) namely: "circumstances of an extremely grave character" and "causing [the defendant] to have a justifiable sense of being seriously wronged", an assessment it is difficult to find any argument against (and indeed the Court of Appeal could not) means, in any logical assessment, that provocation is reinstated by judicial edict.[18] That is, if sniggering and a statement of childcare responsibility cannot stand alone, it is clear that infidelity is the only matter to be put (as a part of "the context of evidence") that could be accepted as a trigger for loss of control, reinstating provocation despite the legislature and legislation's clear intention.

The Court of Appeal's interpretation is inconsistent with any known rules of legislative interpretation, or can be rendered consistent only by reference to the very propositions or "principles" upon which the common law provocation defence was based, which the new law intended to render obsolete.

The *literal rule* of interpretation is that words of a statutory provision mean what they say and say what they mean—here, infidelity ruled out of consideration in the loss of control defence. The *mischief rule* applies to a statutory provision designed to correct a "mischief"—here, the mischief of enabling men who kill their wives because they object to their wife's independent decision to engage in sexual relations with a person other than themselves; or the mischief of men who kill their wives inventing stories of their wife's infidelity or her making statements such as she had "slept with five other men" or "with every man in the street".[19] The *rule of harmonious construction*, being interpretation to ensure harmonious consistency with other laws—this is dependent upon which other laws one might reference. Perhaps the *Istanbul Convention*, drafted April 2011, signed 11 May 2011 and, although not effective

[18] See further on this analysis in Jocelynne A Scutt, *Woman as Property—Law, Society and the Challenge to Women's Rights as Human* (in progress) and Jocelynne A Scutt (ed), *Finance, Feminism and Fortune – Living in a Monetarised World* (in progress).

[19] As the woman is dead, she cannot speak to whether she did make such a statement or not, but it is a common contention by husbands charged with femicide to put such declarations forward as made by their wives before they (the husbands) ended their (the wives) lives. Numerous cases can be cited here – see for example *Moffa v the Queen* [1977] HCA 14, Moffa v R [1977] HCA 14; (1977) 138 CLR 601 (4 March 1977), https://www.austlii.edu.au/cgi-bin/viewdoc/au/cases/cth/HCA/1977/14.html and see Morgan (1997).

until 1 August 2014, taken properly to be considered in that the debate on abolition of provocation law was centred around the safety and well-being of women subjected to criminal assault at home and other forms of domestic violence precipitating their death at a husband's hands (Council of Europe 2025; Wells 2000; Scutt 1980, 2016). That leaves, then, the *golden rule* requiring application of a reasonable interpretation avoiding absurd or unjust results.

Two possible contentions as to "reasonableness" of interpretation and "absurd or unjust results" arise here. One is that of the traditional lawyer schooled in provocation law and its rightful (sic) support for men who kill wives who have committed adultery—or husbands who say that their wives confessed this, lawyers whose criminal law teaching included Hale and Glanville Williams whether in lectures or as a backdrop. These lawyers will contend that reasonableness lies in a construction that enables infidelity to be considered as relevant to loss of control and otherwise absurd or unjust results accrue to the defendant (now widower by his own hand). This follows, so long as (by sleight of hand) some other elements can be latched upon that provide the requisite "context". Against this is the other possible contention, that of the lawyer schooled in jurisprudential critique based in the realisation that women have a right to live, too, and that men should not be encouraged in a belief that marriage is based in ownership, possession and the right to control the women who married them, so that matters such as "sniggering" or concluding that a father has responsibilities toward his children cannot be elevated into a "context" justifying the effective rewriting back into law of "infidelity" as justifying murder.[20]

Unfortunately, the first now dictates how the law is read and to be applied in the UK, unless the parliament once again endeavours to make explicit the intention to oust provocation as a defence, firmly consigning the "she said she slept with every available man" justification to the realms of history as parliament originally intended.

[20] The Court of Appeal does attempt an argument that killing one's wife she having "confessed" or allegedly confessed to infidelity lies not only in "'rights' that the (sic) one may believe that he or she has over the other and often stems from a sense of betrayal and heartbreak, and crushed dreams"[16] but this is, with respect, unconvincing (see Scutt (n18)).

Women's Rights in Society

The contributions and contributors to this volume attest to the continuing scholarship of women determined to ensure women's rights as human are affirmed and embedded in society globally. Despite the barriers and the obstacles, women's determination spurs them on. This determination comes from support from other women and, sometimes, from good men. It remains possible because not only do women stand on the shoulders of those before them, but are pushed and pressed forward by the hands and raised up by the arms of women of the past, resolute that everything for which they fought, and what they won, will never be turned back or, if it is, the women who follow will demand restoration, will regain it and retain it, and more. Women stand, souls golden, knowing the past, alive with the present, and determined for the future.

Women, Souls Golden

I have seen women with their faces infused by the sun
Golden
Women whose souls have shone in the struggle to the top of the ramparts
Women winning the right to stand
With their arms stretched out
to the wind.

I have seen women whose personal lives
Have met the political burden of the patriarchy
And come through

With strength and with courage
Not
Given in.

Women with a strength and a courage
Unique
to women

A strength and a courage
That resists the lure

of patriarchal
power
Denies the lure of the patriarchy
to join in
join with them
join them.

Women whose dreams have taken them to the top of the mountain
Where they stand
Faces to the wind
Faces infused by the sun
Golden.

Souls strong in the strength of the knowledge
That women have been here before
At the top of the mountain
High on the ramparts
Conquering the battlements
The sun on their faces
Their hands to the wind
Free.

This struggle's not ended.
This battle's not won.
Yet these women stand in the face of the sun
Golden.
Free in the sun with the wind through their hands
Knowing this can't be taken from them
Ever again.

I have seen women with their faces infused by the sun
Golden
Women whose souls have shone in the struggle to the top of the mountain.
Women winning the right to stand
On the ramparts
With their arms stretched out
To the sun
Golden

arms stretched out to the wind.

I have seen women who have confronted the political burden of the patriarchy
sloughing it off
saying "no more"
reaching the ramparts
strong on the battlements
high at the top of the mountain

Golden
conquering
winning
Free.

'though knowing the battle's not over
Knowing the struggle's not won

Yet
golden
in the face of the sun
Strengthened.

With freedom unique
courage inspired
Faces infused
Golden
Free in the sun with the wind through their hands
Knowing this can't be taken from them
Ever again.
Jocelynne A Scutt © 2000.

Bibliography

Reported Cases

R v Clinton, R v Parker, R v Evans (Case No: 2011/04258/C3 (1) 2011/03081/D1 (2) 2011/03115/C3 (3)); *R v Clinton* [2012] EWCA

Crim 2, [2012] Crim LR 539, R -v- Clinton, Parker and Evans - judgment, https://www.judiciary.uk/wp-content/uploads/JCO/Documents/Judgments/r-v-clinton-parker-and-evans-judgment.pdf (accessed 2 March 2025).

Jacobellis v Ohio 378 US 184 (1964), Jacobellis v. Ohio | 378 U.S. 184 (1964) | Justia U.S. Supreme Court Center, https://supreme.justia.com/cases/federal/us/378/184/ (accessed 2 March 2025).

Miller v California 413 US 15, https://en.wikipedia.org/wiki/Miller_v._California (1973), Miller v. California | 413 U.S. 15 (1973) | Justia U.S. Supreme Court Center, https://supreme.justia.com/cases/federal/us/413/15/ (accessed 2 March 2025).

Moffa v R [1977] HCA 14, *Moffa v R* [1977] HCA 14; (1977) 138 CLR 601 (4 March 1977), Moffa v R [1977] HCA 14, https://www.austlii.edu.au/cgi-bin/viewdoc/au/cases/cth/HCA/1977/14.html (accessed 2 March 2025).

Roth v United States 354 US 476 (1957), Roth v. United States | 354 U.S. 476 (1957) | Justia U.S. Supreme Court Center, https://supreme.justia.com/cases/federal/us/354/476/ (accessed 2 March 2025).

Statutes and Conventions or Treaties

CEDAW (*Convention on the Elimination of All Forms of Discrimination Against Women*), Convention on the Elimination of All Forms of Discrimination against Women New York, 18 December 1979 | OHCHR, https://www.ohchr.org/en/instruments-mechanisms/instruments/convention-elimination-all-forms-discrimination-against-women (accessed 2 March 2025).

Coroners and Justice Act 2009 (UK), https://www.legislation.gov.uk/ukpga/2009/25/contents (accessed 2 March 2025).

Domestic Abuse Act 2021 (UK), https://www.legislation.gov.uk/ukpga/2021/17/contents (accessed 2 March 2025).

Evidence Act 2001 (Tas), View - Tasmanian Legislation Online, https://www.legislation.tas.gov.au/view/html/inforce/current/act-2001-076 (accessed 2 March 2025).

Homicide Act 1957 (UK), https://www.legislation.gov.uk/ukpga/Eliz2/5-6/11/contents (accessed 2 March 2025).

Istanbul Convention – Council of Europe Convention on Preventing and Combating Violence Against Women and DomesticViolence, Home - Istanbul

Convention Action against violence against women and domestic violence, https://www.coe.int/en/web/istanbul-convention (accessed 2 March 2025).
Sexual Offences Act 2003 (UK), https://www.legislation.gov.uk/ukpga/2003/42/contents (accessed 2 March 2025).

Articles and Book Chapters

Baljit Banga, Chapter 16 "Structural Inequality, Women's Safety and the Funding Cliff Edge: The Impact of the New Funding Policy in Meeting the Needs of Black and Minoritised Women", this volume.
Cobble, Dorothy S, "A Self-Possessed Woman: A View of F.D.R.'s Secretary of Labor, Madame Perkins", *Labor History*, vol 29 (February) 1988, 225–229.
Funnell, Nina, "Grace Tame Was Banned From Sharing Her Teacher's Sexual Abuse. Now She's Talking", *Body+Soul*, *news.com.au*, 12 August 2019, Let Her Speak: Grace Tame Speaks On Her Teacher's Sexual Abuse | body+soul, https://www.bodyandsoul.com.au/wellness/grace-tames-repulsive-schoolgirl-sexual-abuse-ordeal-revealed/news-story/8e4717ca9eae060a3ff685c388df204a (accessed 2 March 2025).
Hernholm, Sarah, "Trump Orders Department of Education Closure …?" *Forbes*, 26 March 2025, Trump Orders Department Of Education Closure: What Happens Next, https://www.forbes.com/sites/sarahhernholm/2025/03/26/trump-orders-department-of-education-closure-what-happens-next/ (accessed 26 March 2025).
Morgan, Jenny, "Critique and Comment – Provocation Law and Facts: Dead Women Tell No Tales, Tales Are Told About Them", *Melbourne University Law Review*, vol 21, 1997, 237–276, imageREAL Capture, https://classic.austlii.edu.au/au/journals/MelbULawRw/1997/6.pdf (accessed 2 March 2025).
Pringle, Helen, Chapter 19 "Living in a Pornographic World: Constraint on the Autonomy of Girls and Women", this volume.
Satow, Roberta, "*Trauma* What Is Acting Out? Some people try to master unprocessed past experiences by recreating them", *Psychology Today*, 16 June 2022, What Is Acting Out? | Psychology Today, https://www.psychologytoday.com/us/blog/life-after-50/202206/what-is-acting-out?msockid=12ff2003749a674e082b352875056688 (accessed 2 March 2025).
Scutt, Jocelynne A, "Admissibility of Sexual History Evidence and Allegations in Rape Cases", *Australian Law Journal*, 1979, vol 52, 817-828.

Scutt, Jocelynne A, "Book Review – Title: *Women and Crime – Three Essays*, Title: *Virginia Guiffre – The Extraordinary Life Story of the 'Playtoy' who Pursued and Ended the Crimes of Millionaires Ghislaine Maxwell and Jeffrey Epstein*, Title: *The Lasting Harm – Witnessing the Trial of Ghislaine Maxwell*", *Denning Law Journal*, vol 33, 2024, 399–420, Book Review | The Denning Law Journal, https://www.ubplj.org/index.php/dlj/article/view/2362 (accessed 2 March 2025).

Scutt, Jocelynne A, "Evidence and the Role of the Jury in Trials for Rape" in *Rape Law Reform*, JA Scutt, ed, Australian Institute of Criminology (AIC), Canberra, ACT 90–114, 1980.

Scutt, Jocelynne A, "Sexism in Criminal Law" in Satyanshu K Mukherjee and Jocelynne A Scutt, eds, *Women and Crime*, Allen & Unwin, Sydney, Australia, 1981, reprinted Routledge Library Editions, Oxford, UK, 2016, 2–21.

Stussy, Susan A, "Perkins Becomes First Woman Secretary of Labour", EBSCO, 2023, Perkins Becomes First Woman Secretary of Labor | EBSCO Research Starters, https://www.ebsco.com/research-starters/history/perkins-becomes-first-woman-secretary-labor (accessed 2 March 2025).

Tonness, Bianca Vázquez, "The Education Department was created to ensure equal access. Who would do that in its absence?" *AP*, 20 March 2025, Why was the Education Department created, and what if it closes? | AP News, https://apnews.com/article/trump-education-department-layoffs-closure-c7cddd1dbf310dadcd70e003d62a6df0 (accessed 20 March 2025).

Wells, Celia, "Chapter 4 – Provocation: The Case for Abolition" in Andrew Ashworth and Barry Mitchell, eds, *Rethinking English Homicide Law*, Oxford Academic, Oxford, UK, 2000, Provocation: The Case for Abolition | Rethinking English Homicide Law | Oxford Academic, https://academic.oup.com/book/10444/chapter-abstract/158289251?redirectedFrom=fulltext (accessed 2 March 2025).

Williams, Glanville, "Language and the Law", *Law Quarterly Review,* vol 61,71–86, 179–195, 293–406, 1945.

Books, Reports and Films/Songs

Albright, Madeleine, *Madam Secretary: A Memoir*, 2nd edn, HarperPerennial, New York, NY, USA, 2013.

Albright, Madeleine (with Woodward, Bob), *Hell and Other Destinations – A 21st Century Memoir*, HarperCollins, New York, NY, USA, 2020).

Boston Women's Health Book Collective, *Our Bodies, Ourselves – A Book by and for Women*, Simon & Schuster, New York, NY, USA, 1968.
Buczynski-Lee, Karen and Scutt, Jocelynne A, *The Incredible Woman*, The Incredible Woman Productions, Hobart, Australia, 2002.
Burton, Clare, *Redefining Merit – The Struggle for Equal Opportunity in Women's Employment*, AGPS, Canberra, ACT, Australia, 1988.
Burton, Clare, Raven Hag and Gay Thompson, *Women's Worth – Pay Equity and Job Evaluation in Australia*, AGPS, Canberra, ACT, Australia,1987.
Cardinal, Marie, *The Words to Say It* (*Les Mots our le dire*), 1976 in French, trns by Pat Goodheart, Van Vactor & Goodhart, Cambridge, MA, USA, 1983.
Clinton, Hillary Rodham, *Hard Choices*, Simon & Schuster, New York, NY, USA, 2016.
Clinton, Hillary Rodham, *What Happened*, Simon & Schuster, New York, NY, USA, 2017.
Farley, Lin, *Sexual Shakedown – Sexual Harassment of Women on the Job*, McGraw-Hill, New York, NY, USA, 1978.
Lyons, Enid, *Among the Carrion Crows*, Rigby, Sydney, Australia, 1972.
Lyons, Enid, *So We Take Comfort*, Heinemann, Melbourne, Australia, 1965.
Lyons, Enid, *The Old Haggis*, Heinemann, Melbourne, Australia, 1969.
MacKinnon, Catharine A, *Only Words*, Harvard University Press, Harvard, MA, USA, 1993.
MacKinnon, Catharine A, *Sexual Harassment of Working Women: A Case of Sex Discrimination*, Yale University Press, New Haven, CT, USA, 1978.
Martin, George, *Madam Secretary, Frances Perkins*, Houghton Mifflin, New York, NY, USA, 1976.
Martineau, Harriet, *Illustrations of Political Economy*, 9 vols, orign publication 1832–1834, printed Cosimo Classics, London, UK, 2009.
Miller, Chanel, *Know My Name: A Memoir*, Viking, New York, NY, USA, 2019.
Natarajan, Nalini (ed), *Confronting Femicide – Multidisciplinary Perspectives From Puerto Rico*, Palgrave Macmillan, London, UK, 2025.
Osborne-Crowley, Lucia, *The Lasting Harm – Witnessing the Trial of Ghislaine Maxwell*, 4th Estate/HarperCollins, London, UK, 2024.
Potts, Marjory and Robert, *You May Call Her Madam Secretary*, Public Resource Org, nd (excerpt), You May Call Her Madam Secretary, https://www.youtube.com/watch?v=V_nVctSlIHs (accessed 22 March 2025).
Radford, Jill and Russell Diana EH, *Femicide – The Politics of Woman Killing*, Twayne Publishers, Woodbridge, CT, USA,1992.

Ryan, Susan, *Catching the Waves – Life in and out of politics*, HarperCollins, Sydney, Australia, 1999.
Scutt, Jocelynne A, *The Incredible Woman – Power and Sexual Politics*, 2 vols, Artemis Publishing, Melbourne, Australia, 1997.
Scutt, Jocelynne A, *Wage Rage for Equal Pay – Australia's Long, Long Struggle*, Palgrave Macmillan, London, UK, 2024.
Tame, Grace, *The Ninth Life of a Diamond Miner: A memoir*, Macmillan Australia, Melbourne, Australia, 2022.
Tasmania Law Reform Institute, *Protecting the Anonymity of Victims of Sexual Crimes – Final Report*, November 2013, https://www.utas.edu.au/__data/assets/pdf_file/0005/461768/S194k_Final_05_A4.pdf (accessed 22 March 2025).
Tomasetti, Glen, *Don't Be Too Polite, Girls*, Melbourne, Australia, 1969 (published in *Songs From A Seat In The Carriage*, 1970, Don't Be Too Polite Girls), https://unionsong.com/u263.html (accessed 2 March 2025).
Williams, Glanville, *Text Book of Criminal Law*, Stevens, London, UK, 1979 first edn, 1983.

Information Documents and Resources

AEC, *2008 Parliamentary Handbook. Parliamentary Library*, "Past referendum fact sheet, last updated 7 November 2023, Referendum dates and results - Australian Electoral Commission, https://www.aec.gov.au/Elections/referendums/Referendum_Dates_and_Results.htm (accessed 2 March 2025).
City St George's University of London, *International Feminist Legal Network Conference ...*, 31 July 2024, International Feminist Legal Network Conference tackles violence against women • City St George's, University of London (accessed 2 March 2025).
Council of Europe, *Action Against Violence Against Women ...*, 2025, Home - Istanbul Convention Action against violence against women and domestic violence, https://www.citystgeorges.ac.uk/news-and-events/news/2024/july/international-feminist-legal-network-conference-tackles-violence-against-women
Department of Justice, *Discussion Paper ...*, Department of Justice, Tasmania, nd, Discussion-Paper-section-194K-Evidence-Act-2001-version_2.pdf, https://www.justice.tas.gov.au/__data/assets/pdf_file/0004/466033/Discussion-Paper-section-194K-Evidence-Act-2001-version_2.pdf (accessed 22 March 2025).

Gov.UK, *Home: Chancellor of the Exchequer – The Rt Hon Rachel Reeves MP*, nd, The Rt Hon Rachel Reeves MP - GOV.UK, https://www.gov.uk/government/people/rachel-reeves (accessed 2 March 2025).

Legal Dictionary, *FLAGRANTE DELICTO*, 23 March 2019, Flagrante Delicto - Definition, Examples, Cases, Processes, https://legaldictionary.net/flagrante-delicto/ (accessed 22 March 2025).

Metropolitan Police, *Grooming*, 2025, Grooming | Metropolitan Police, https://www.met.police.uk/advice/advice-and-information/gr/grooming/ (accessed 22 March 2025).

Parliament of Australia, *Senators and Members: Hon Bronwyn Bishop AO*, nd, Hon Bronwyn Bishop AO – Parliament of Australia, https://www.aph.gov.au/Senators_and_Members/Parliamentarian?MPID=SE4 (accessed 2 March 2025).

Smith, Karen Ingala, *Counting Dead Women*, 3 January 2024, Karen Ingala Smith | As I see it, https://kareningalasmith.com/page/2/ (accessed 22 March 225).

The Martineau Society, *Harriet Martineau (1802–76)*, 2025, Harriet Martineau (1802–76) – Martineau Society, https://martineausociety.co.uk/the-martineaus/harriet-martineau/ (accessed 2 March 2025).

Statutes, Conventions and Treaties

Aotearoa/New Zealand

Human Assisted Reproductive Technology Act 2004 (Aotearoa/New Zealand), Human Assisted Reproductive Technology Act 2004 No 92 (as at 01 July 2023), Public Act – New Zealand Legislation, https://legislation.govt.nz/act/public/2004/0092/latest/whole.html (accessed 2 March 2025).

Australia

Abortion Law Reform Act 2019 (NSW), View - NSW legislation, https://legislation.nsw.gov.au/view/whole/pdf/inforce/2024-12-02/act-2019-011 (accessed 22 November 2024).

Abortion Law Reform Act 2019 No 11 - NSW Legislation, https://legislation.nsw.gov.au/view/html/inforce/current/act-2019-011 (accessed 22 November 2024).

Abortion Law Reform Act 2008 (Victoria), https://www.legislation.vic.gov.au/in-force/acts/abortion-law-reform-act-2008 (accessed 2 October 2025).

Abortion Legislation Reform Act 2023 (WA), https://www5.austlii.edu.au/au/legis/wa/num_act/alra202320o2023334/ (accessed 2 October 2025).

J. A. Scutt (ed.), *Women, Power and Autonomy*,
https://doi.org/10.1007/978-3-031-97958-3

Abortion Regulations 1970 (SA), https://www.legislation.sa.gov.au/__legislation/lz/c/r/abortion%20regulations%201970/1996.08.31_(1991.07.18)/1970.-.pdf (accessed 2 November 2024).

Abortion (Northern Ireland) Regulations 2020 (NI), The Abortion (Northern Ireland) Regulations 2020, https://www.legislation.gov.uk/uksi/2020/345/contents/made (accessed 22 November 2024).

Acts Amendment (Abortion) Act 1998 (WA), https://www.legislation.wa.gov.au/legislation/statutes.nsf/main_mrtitle_2880_homepage.html (accessed 2 October 2025)

Anti-Discrimination Act 1977 - As at 1 July 2024 - Act 48 of 1977, https://classic.austlii.edu.au/au/legis/nsw/consol_act/aa1977204/ (accessed 1 November 2024).

Anti-Discrimination Act 1977 (New South Wales), sections 20B-C (race), 38R-S (transgender), 49ZD-ZE (religion), 49ZS-ZT (homosexuality), 49ZXA-ZXB (HIV/AIDS status), https://legislation.nsw.gov.au/view/html/inforce/2024-07-01/act-1977-048 (accessed 13 January 2025), Anti-Discrimination Act 1977 No 48 - NSW Legislation, https://legislation.nsw.gov.au/view/html/inforce/current/act-1977-048 (accessed 19 August 2024).

Bail Act 1980 (Qld), https://www.legislation.qld.gov.au/view/html/inforce/current/act-1980-035 (accessed 2 February 2025).

Correctional Services Act 1982 (SA), Correctional Services Act 1982 | South Australian Legislation, https://www.legislation.sa.gov.au/lz?path=%2FC%2FA%2FCORRECTIONAL%20SERVICES%20ACT%201982 (accessed 22 March 2025).

Crimes Act 1900 (ACT), Crimes Act 1900 | Acts, https://www.legislation.act.gov.au/a/1900-40/ (accessed 2 March 2025).

Crimes Act 1900 (NSW), Crimes Act 1900 No 40 - NSW Legislation, https://legislation.nsw.gov.au/view/html/inforce/current/act-1900-040 (accessed 2 March 2025), https://legislation.nsw.gov.au/view/html/inforce/current/act-1900-040 (accessed 13 January 2025).

Crimes Act 1900 (NSW), sections 83, 84, https://legislation.nsw.gov.au/view/html/inforce/current/act-1900-040 (accessed 2 October 2025).

Crimes Act 1958 (Victoria), https://www.legislation.vic.gov.au/in-force/acts/crimes-act-1958 (accessed 2 October 2025).

Crimes Legislation Amendment (Sexual Consent Reforms) Act 2021 (NSW), 3.10.1A, https://legislation.nsw.gov.au/view/html/inforce/current/act-1900-040#pt.3-div.10-sdiv.1A (accessed 13 January 2025).

Criminal Code Act 1995 (Cth), Division 271, https://www.legislation.gov.au/Details/C2021C00183/Html/Volume_2. Section 271.11 (accessed 13 January 2025).

Criminal Code Act 1995 (Cth), 271.11B (Offences against Division 271—no defence of victim consent or acquiescence), https://www.legislation.gov.au/Details/C2021C00183/Html/Volume_2. Section 271.11 (accessed 13 January 2025).

Criminal Code Act 1983 (NT), https://legislation.nt.gov.au/en/Legislation/CRIMINAL-CODE-ACT-1983 (accessed 2 October 2025).

Criminal Code 1899 (Qld), https://www.legislation.qld.gov.au/view/pdf/inforce/current/act-1899-009 (accessed 2 October 2025).

Criminal Code Act 1924 (Tasmania), https://www.legislation.tas.gov.au/view/html/inforce/current/act-1924-069 (accessed 2 October 2025).

Criminal Code Compilation Act 1913 (WA), WALW - Criminal Code Act Compilation Act 1913 - Home PageCriminal Code Act Compilation Act 1913 - [00–00–00].pdf, https://www.legislation.wa.gov.au/legislation/prod/filestore.nsf/FileURL/mrdoc_13659.pdf/$FILE/Criminal%20Code%20Act%20Compilation%20Act%201913%20-%20%5B00-00-00%5D.pdf?OpenElement (accessed 22 November 2024).

Criminal Justice Bill 2024 (UK), https://publications.parliament.uk/pa/bills/cbill/58-04/0155/230155.pdf (accessed 2 November 2024).

Criminal Justice Bill - Parliamentary Bills - UK Parliament 2024 (UK), https://bills.parliament.uk/bills/3511 (accessed 2 November 2024).

Criminal Law Amendment Act 1968–69 (Canada), https://recherche-collection-search.bac-lac.gc.ca/eng/Home/Record?app=fonandcol&IdNumber=4496481&q=RULE@copy= (accessed 2 October 2025).

Criminal Law Consolidation Act 1935 (SA)

Criminal Law Consolidation Act 1935–1969 (South Australia), https://www.legislation.sa.gov.au/__legislation/lz/c/a/criminal%20law%20consolidation%20act%201935/1992.01.15/1935.2252.pdf (accessed 2 November 2024).

Criminal Code 1899 (Qld), sections 224, 225 and 226, https://www.legislation.qld.gov.au/view/pdf/inforce/current/act-1899-009 (accessed 2 October 2025).

Criminal Law (Coercive Control …) Act 2024 (Qld), *Criminal Law (Coercive Control and Affirmative Consent) and Other Legislation Amendment Act 2024* (accessed 2 February 2025).

Equal Opportunity Act 1977 (Victoria), Equal Opportunity Act 2010, https://www.legislation.vic.gov.au/in-force/acts/equal-opportunity-act-2010/020 (accessed 2 March 2025).

Evidence Act 2001 (Tas), View - Tasmanian Legislation Online, https://www.legislation.tas.gov.au/view/html/inforce/current/act-2001-076 (accessed 2 March 2025).

Family Law Act 1975 (Cth) sections 43 (1)(a), 43(1)(b), 43(1)(c)(ca)(d), 60CC(2)(a), 61DA, . https://www.alrc.gov.au/publications/4.%20Purposes%20of%20Laws%20Relevant%20to%20Family%20Violence/family-law#_ftnref67 (accessed 14 August 2024).

Family Law Amendment Act 2023 (Cth), https://classic.austlii.edu.au/au/legis/cth/num_act/flaa2023194/ (accessed 2 October 2025).

Family Law Amendment (Shared Parental Responsibility) Act 2006 (Cth), Family Law Amendment (Shared Parental Responsibility) Act 2006, https://classic.austlii.edu.au/au/legis/cth/consol_act/flapra2006500/ (accessed 2 March 2025).

Family Law Legislation Amendment (Family Violence and Other Measures) Act 2011 (Cth), https://www.legislation.gov.au/C2011A00189/asmade/text (accessed 2 October 2025).

Health (Miscellaneous Provisions) Act 1911 (WA), Abortion, https://wnhs.health.wa.gov.au/~/media/HSPs/NMHS/Hospitals/WNHS/Documents/Professionals/Abortion---Information-and-legal-obligations-for-medical-practitioners.pdf (accessed 22 November 2024).

Law Enforcement (Powers and Responsibilities) Act 2002 (NSW), Law Enforcement (Powers and Responsibilities) Act 2002, https://classic.austlii.edu.au/au/legis/nsw/consol_act/leara2002451/ (accessed 22 March 2025).

Legislative Standards Act 1992 (Qld), https://www.legislation.qld.gov.au/view/html/inforce/current/act-1992-04 (accessed 2 February 2025).

Making Queensland Safe Act 2024 (Qld), Making Queensland Safer Act 2024 - Queensland Legislation - Queensland Government, https://www.legislation.qld.gov.au/view/whole/html/asmade/act-2024-054 (accessed 2 February 2025).

Medical Practitioners (Maternal Health) Amendment Act 2002 (ACT)

Medical Services Act 1982 (NT), Northern Territory Legislation, https://legislation.nt.gov.au/Legislation/MEDICAL-SERVICES-ACT-1982 (accessed 2 November 2024).

Mental Health Act 2016 (Qld), https://www.legislation.qld.gov.au/view/pdf/inforce/2021-03-08/act-2016-005 (accessed 2 February 2025).

Penalties and Sentences Act 1992 Qld) Penalties and Sentences Act 1992, https://www.legislation.qld.gov.au/view/pdf/inforce/current/act-1992-048 (accessed 2 February 2025).

Reproductive Health (Access to Terminations) Act 2013 (Tas), https://www.legislation.tas.gov.au/view/html/inforce/current/act-2013-072 (accessed 2 October 2025).

Sex Discrimination Act 1984 (Cth), Federal Register of Legislation - Sex Discrimination Act 1984, https://www.legislation.gov.au/C2004A02868/latest/text (accessed 1 November 2024).

Termination of Pregnancy Act 2021 (SA), South Australia: Medical termination of pregnancy, https://www.consciencelaws.org/law/laws/australia003.aspx (accessed 2 November 2024).

Termination of Pregnancy Act 2018 (Qld), Termination of Pregnancy Act 2018, https://www.legislation.qld.gov.au/view/pdf/inforce/current/act-2018-023 (accessed 22 November 2024).

Termination of Pregnancy Law Reform Act 2017 (NT), https://legislation.nt.gov.au/en/Legislation/TERMINATION-OF-PREGNANCY-LAW-REFORM-ACT-2017 (accessed 2 October 2025).

Termination of Pregnancy Law Reform Legislation Amendment Act 2021 (NT), https://legislation.nt.gov.au/en/Bills/Termination-of-Pregnancy-Law-Reform-Legislation-Amendment-Bill-2021-S35?format=assented (accessed 2 October 2025).

View - NSW legislation, https://legislation.nsw.gov.au/view/whole/html/inforce/current/act-1977-048 (accessed 1 November 2024).

Youth Justice Act 1992 (Qld), Youth Justice Act 1992, https://www.legislation.qld.gov.au/view/pdf/inforce/2024-11-03/act-1992-044 (accessed 2 February 2025).

Work Health and Safety Amendment (Industrial Manslaughter) Bill 2024 (nsw.gov.au), https://www.parliament.nsw.gov.au/bills/Pages/bill-details.aspx?pk=18597 (accessed 19 August 2024).

Europe (inc France)

European Parliament Resolution of 26 February 2014, Sexual Exploitation and Prostitution and its Impact on Gender Equality, https://www.europarl.europa.eu/doceo/document/TA-7-2014-0162_EN.html?redirect (accessed 13 January 2025).

European Parliament Resolution of 14 September 2023, Regulation of Prostitution in the EU: Its Cross-border Implications and Impact on Gender Equality and Women's Rights, https://www.europarl.europa.eu/doceo/document/TA-9-2023-0328_EN.html (accessed 13 January 2025).

European Parliament Resolution of 26 February 2014, Sexual Exploitation and Prostitution and its Impact on Gender Equality, s. B, https://www.europarl.europa.eu/doceo/document/TA-7-2014-0162_EN.html?redirect (accessed 13 January 2025).

French Loi n° 2016-444 du 13 avril 2016, *visant à renforcer la lutte contre le système prostitutionnel et à accompagner les personnes prostituées*, https://www.legifrance.gouv.fr/jorf/id/JORFTEXT000032396046 (accessed 13 January 2025).

Parliamentary Assembly of the Council of Europe (PACE) Resolution 1983 of 8 April 2014, Prostitution, Trafficking and Modern Slavery in Europe 2012, https://assembly.coe.int/nw/xml/XRef/Xref-XML2HTML-en.asp?fileid=20716 (accessed 13 January 2025).

Nigeria

African (Banjul) Charter On Human and Peoples' Rights, https://www.african-court.org/wpafc/wp-content/uploads/2020/04/AFRICAN-BANJUL-CHARTER-ON-HUMAN-AND-PEOPLES-RIGHTS.pdf (accessed 1 November 2024).

Centre for Laws of Nigeria, Criminal Code Act - Law Nigeria, https://lawnigeria.com/2025/01/28/criminal-code-act/ (accessed 1 November 2024).

Constitution of the Federal Republic of Nigeria, 1999, https://nhrc.gov.ng/files/publications/1999%20CONSTITUTION%20OF%20THE%20FRN.pdf (accessed 1 November 2024).

Constitution of the Federal Republic of Nigeria, Chapter 4 of the 1999 Constitution (Sections 34 (1), 33–46)

Criminal Code Act in Nigeria 2024, https://jurist.ng/act/criminal_code_act (accessed 1 November 2024)

Jurist.ng, Section 33 of the Constitution of the Federal Republic of Nigeria. https://jurist.ng/constitution/sec-33- 46 (accessed 29 July 2024).

Lagos Administration of Estates Law, Lagos State Administration Of Estates Law - Law Nigeria section 49(5), https://lawnigeria.com/laws/2018/02/26/administration-of-estates-law/

Marriage Act (Nigerian Legislation), Chapter 218, Law of the Federation of Nigeria 1900, Marriage Act, http://www.commonlii.org/ng/legis/num_act/ma85/ (accessed 1 November 2024), M6.pdf, https://www.lawsofnigeria.placng.org/laws/M6.pdf (accessed 1 November 2024).

Maputo Protocol on the Rights of Women in Africa: Commemorating 20 Years. | African Union, https://au.int/en/newsevents/20230705/maputo-protocol-20-years (accessed 1 November 2024).

Matrimonial Causes Act, http://www.commonlii.org/ng/legis/num_act/mca197/ (accessed 1 November 2024)

The Nigerian Constitution, https://nigerian-constitution.com/chapter-4-section-44-compulsory-acquisition-of-property (accessed 19 August 2024).

Nigeria: Violence Against Persons (Prohibition) Act, 2015 (VAPP) | Refworld, https://www.refworld.org/legal/legislation/natlegbod/2015/en/105106 (accessed 1 November 2024).

Universal Declaration of Human Rights | United Nations, https://www.un.org/en/about-us/universal-declaration-of-human-rights (accessed 1 November 2024).

Violence Against Persons (Prohibition) Act 2015, https://www.refworld.org/legal/legislation/natlegbod/2015/en/105106 (accessed 1 November 2024).

Portugal

Decree No 1 of 1910 of 25 December, https://files.dre.pt/1s/1910/12/07000/09370938.pdf (accessed 28 June 2024).

Decree-Law no 485/77 of 17 November, https://diariodarepublica.pt/dr/detalhe/decreto-lei/485-280540 (accessed 28 June 2024).

Decree-Law no 496/77 of 25 November, https://diariodarepublica.pt/dr/detalhe/decreto-lei/496-1977-300030 (accessed 28 June 2024).

Decree-Law no 392/79 of 20 September, https://diariodarepublica.pt/dr/detalhe/decreto-lei/392-1979-369814> (accessed 28 June 2024).

Law no 6/84 of 11 May, https://diariodarepublica.pt/dr/detalhe/lei/6-1984-385266 (accessed 28 June 2024).

Law no 7/2000 of 27 May, https://diariodarepublica.pt/dr/detalhe/lei/7-2000-291937 (accessed 28 June 2024).

Law no 16/2007 of 17 April, https://diariodarepublica.pt/dr/detalhe/lei/16-2007-519464 (accessed 28 June 2024).

Law no 59/2007 of 4 September, <https://diariodarepublica.pt/dr/detalhe/lei/59-2007-640142> (accessed 28 June 2024).

Law no 61/2008 of 30 November, <https://diariodarepublica.pt/dr/detalhe/lei/61-2008-439097> (accessed 28 June 2024).

Law No 104/2009 of 14 September, <https://diariodarepublica.pt/dr/detalhe/lei/104-2009-489757> (accessed 28 June 2024).

Law No 112/2009 of 16 September, <https://diariodarepublica.pt/dr/detalhe/lei/112-2009-490247> (accessed 28 June 2024).

Law no 134/2015 of 7 September, <https://diariodarepublica.pt/dr/detalhe/lei/134-2015-70196961> (accessed 28 June 2024).

Law no 136/2015 of 7 September, <https://diariodarepublica.pt/dr/detalhe/lei/136-2015-70196963> (accessed 28 June 2024).

Law no 44/2018 of 9 August, <https://diariodarepublica.pt/dr/detalhe/lei/44-2018-115946549> (accessed 28 June 2024).

Ordinance No 741-A/2007 of 21 June, https://diariodarepublica.pt/dr/detalhe/portaria/741-a-2007-442119 (accessed 28 June 2024).

Portugal 1976 (rev 2005) *Constitution - Constitute*, Portugal 1976 (rev. 2005) Constitution - Constitute, https://www.constituteproject.org/constitution/Portugal_2005 (accessed 2 April 2025).

Penal Code – Portugal, https://wfrtds.org/wp-content/uploads/2021/02/Portugal-Criminal-Code-2006-EN.pdf (accessed 1 November 2024).

United Kingdom

Abortion Act 1967 (UK) Abortion Act 1967, https://www.legislation.gov.uk/ukpga/1967/87/contents (accessed 2 November 2024).

Burial of Suicide Act 1823 (UK), Burial of Suicide Act 1823 - Legislation - VLEX 861232135, https://vlex.co.uk/vid/burial-of-suicide-act-861232135 (accessed 2 March 2025).

Burial of Suicide Act 1823 (UK), Burial of Suicide Act 1823 - UK Non-devolved - Legislation - VLEX 808320921, https://vlex.co.uk/vid/burial-of-suicide-act-808320921 (accessed 2 March 2025).

Companies Act 2006 (UK), sections 170, 172, 173.

Contagious Diseases Act 1864 (UK), The Contagious Diseases Act | Policy Navigator, https://navigator.health.org.uk/theme/contagious-diseases-act#:~:text=The%20Contagious%20Diseases%20Act%20was%20first%20passed%20in,transmitted%20diseases%20within%20the%20British%20army%20and%20navy (accessed 2 March 2025).

Contagious Diseases Act 1866 (UK), The Contagious Diseases Act | Policy Navigator, https://navigator.health.org.uk/theme/contagious-diseases-act#:~:text=The%20Contagious%20Diseases%20Act%20was%20first%20passed%20in,transmitted%20diseases%20within%20the%20British%20army%20and%20navy (accessed 2 March 2025).

Contagious Diseases Act 1868 (UK), The Contagious Diseases Act | Policy Navigator, https://navigator.health.org.uk/theme/contagious-diseases-act#:~:text=The%20Contagious%20Diseases%20Act%20was%20first%20passed%20in,transmitted%20diseases%20within%20the%20British%20army%20and%20navy (accessed 2 March 2025).

Contagious Diseases Act 1869 (Ireland), The Contagious Diseases Act | Policy Navigator, https://navigator.health.org.uk/theme/contagious-diseases-act#:~:text=The%20Contagious%20Diseases%20Act%20was%20first%20passed%20in,transmitted%20diseases%20within%20the%20British%20army%20and%20navy (accessed 2 March 2025).

Coroners and Justice Act 2009 (UK), Coroners and Justice Act 2009, https://www.legislation.gov.uk/ukpga/2009/25/contents (accessed 2 March 2025).

Custody of Infants Act 1839 (UK), 1839: 2 & 3 Victoria c.54: Custody of Infants | The Statutes Project, https://statutes.org.uk/site/the-statutes/nineteenth-century/1839-2-3-victoria-c-54-custody-of-infants/ (accessed 2 March 2025).

Domestic Abuse Act 2021, Domestic Abuse Act 2021, https://www.legislation.gov.uk/ukpga/2021/17/contents (accessed 2 March 2025).

Equal Pay Act 1970 (UK), Equal Pay Act 1970, https://www.legislation.gov.uk/ukpga/1970/41/enacted (accessed 2 March 2025).

Equality Act 2010 (UK), Equality Act 2010, https://www.legislation.gov.uk/ukpga/2010/15/contents (accessed 2 March 2025).

Freedom of Information Act 2000 (UK), Freedom of Information Act 2000, https://www.legislation.gov.uk/ukpga/2000/36/contents (accessed 2 February 2025).

Health (Regulation of Termination of Pregnancy) Act 2018 (NI), Health (Regulation of Termination of Pregnancy) Act 2018, https://www.irishstatutebook.ie/eli/2018/act/31 (accessed 2 February 2025).

Homicide Act 1957 (UK), Homicide Act 1957, https://www.legislation.gov.uk/ukpga/Eliz2/5-6/11/contents (accessed 2 March 2025).

Infant Life (Preservation) Act 1929 (UK), Infant Life (Preservation) Act 1929, https://www.legislation.gov.uk/ukpga/Geo5/19-20/34/section/1 (accessed 2 November 2024).

Marriage and Civil Partnership (Minimum Age) Act 2022 (England and Wales), Marriage and Civil Partnership (Minimum Age) Act 2022, https://www.legislation.gov.uk/ukpga/2022/28/enacted (accessed 2 March 2025); Marriage and Civil Partnership (Minimum Age) Act 2022 (legislation.gov.uk), https://www.legislation.gov.uk/ukpga/2022/28 (accessed 27 August 2024).

Married Women's Property Act 1870 (UK), 1870: 33 & 34 Victoria c.93: Married Women's Property Act | The Statutes Project, https://statutes.org.uk/site/the-statutes/nineteenth-century/1870-33-34-victoria/1870-33-34-victoria-c-93-married-womens-property-act/ (accessed 2 March 2025).

Matrimonial Causes Act 1857 (UK), Matrimonial Causes Act 1857 - UK Non-devolved - Legislation - VLEX 808408569, https://vlex.co.uk/vid/matrimonial-causes-act-1857-808408569 (accessed 2 March 2025).

Matrimonial Causes Act 1878 (UK), Matrimonial Causes Act - Oxford Reference, https://www.oxfordreference.com/display/10.1093/oi/authority.20110803100140335 (accessed 2 March 2025).

Matrimonial Causes Act 1878 (UK), The Matrimonial Causes Act of 1878 | COVE, https://editions.covecollective.org/chronologies/matrimonial-causes-act-1878-0#:~:text=As%20a%20result%2C%20the%20Matrimonial%20Causes%20act%20of,opportunity%20to%20separate%20from%20their%20physically%20abusive%20husbands. (accessed 2 March 2025).

Mental Capacity Act 2005 (UK), Mental Capacity Act 2005, https://www.legislation.gov.uk/ukpga/2005/9/contents (accessed 2 March 2025).

Public Health Act 2016, Public Health Act 2016 - SECT 324, https://classic.austlii.edu.au/au/legis/wa/consol_act/pha2016126/s324.html (accessed 22 November 2024).

Public Health Amendment (Safe Access to Reproductive Health Clinics) Act 2018, https://legislation.nsw.gov.au/view/pdf/asmade/act-2018-26 (accessed 22 November 2024).

Sexual Offences Act 2003 (UK), Sexual Offences Act 2003, https://www.legislation.gov.uk/ukpga/2003/42/part/1/crossheading/abuse-of-position-of-trust (accessed 2 March 2025).

Trade Union Act 1871 (UK), 1871 Trade Union Act, https://spartacus-educational.com/Ltrade.htm (accessed 1 November 2024).

Trade Union Act 1871 (UK), Trade-Union Act | United Kingdom [1871] | Britannica, https://www.britannica.com/topic/Trade-Union-Act-United-Kingdom-1871 (accessed 1 November 2024).

United States

Amy, Vicky, and Andy Child Pornography Victim Assistance Act of 2018 (*AVAA*) in the wake of the case *Paroline v U.S.* 572 US 434 (2014), https://www.supremecourt.gov/opinions/boundvolumes/572BV.pdf (accessed 13 January 2025).

Chinese Exclusion Act 1882 (US), Chinese Exclusion Act (1882) | National Archives, https://www.archives.gov/milestone-documents/chinese-exclusion-act (accessed 10 November 2024).

Florida Senate Bill 140 (2018), Senate Bill 140 (2018) - The Florida Senate, https://www.flsenate.gov/Session/Bill/2018/140 (accessed 2 March 2025).

Va. Code Ann, § 20-48, § 20-48. Minimum age of marriage, https://law.lis.virginia.gov/vacode/title20/chapter5/section20-48/ (accessed 2 March 2025).

Illinois General Assembly, 740 ILCS 128/ Trafficking Victims Protection Act [formerly Predator Accountability Act], http://www.ilga.gov/legislation/ilcs/ilcs3.asp?ActID=2812&ChapterID=57 (accessed 13 January 2025).

Illinois General Assembly, 740 ILCS 128/ Predator Accountability Act, http://www.ilga.gov/legislation/ilcs/ilcs3.asp?ActID=2812&ChapterID=57 (accessed 13 January 2025).

Immigration Act 1917 (Barred Zone Act) (US), Immigration Act of 1917 (Barred Zone Act) - Immigration History, https://immigrationhistory.org/item/1917-barred-zone-act/ (accessed 10 November 2024).

Immigration and Nationality Act 1965 (US), Text of H.R. 2580 (89th): An Act to amend the Immigration and Nationality Act, and for other purposes (Passed Congress version) - GovTrack.us COMPS-1376.pdf, https://www.govinfo.gov/content/pkg/COMPS-1376/pdf/COMPS-1376.pdf (accessed 2 March 2025).

Page Act 1875 (US), The Page Act of 1875 (Immigration Act), https://loveman.sdsu.edu/docs/1875Immigration%20Act.pdf (accessed 10 November 2024).

Texas Senate Bill No 1705, 85(R) SB 1705 - Enrolled version, https://capitol.texas.gov/tlodocs/85R/billtext/pdf/SB01705F.pdf (accessed 2 March 2025).

International

CEDAW, UN Treaty Body Data Base, tbinternet.ohchr.org/_layouts/15/TreatyBodyExternal/Treaty.aspx?Treaty=CEDAW, https://tbinternet.ohchr.org/_layouts/15/TreatyBodyExternal/Treaty.aspx?Treaty=CEDAW (accessed 1 November 2024).

Convention on the Elimination of All Forms of Discrimination Against Women (CEDAW), Convention on the Elimination of All Forms of Discrimination against Women, https://www.un.org/womenwatch/daw/cedaw/ (accessed 1 November 2024).

CEDAW (*Convention on the Elimination of All Forms of Discrimination Against Women,* Convention on the Elimination of All Forms of Discrimination against Women New York, 18 December 1979 | OHCHR, https://www.ohchr.org/en/instruments-mechanisms/instruments/convention-elimination-all-forms-discrimination-against-women (accessed 2 March 2025).

Convention on the Elimination of All Forms of Discrimination Against Women, (CEDAW) Article 16.

Convention on the Rights of the Child, Article 3, Convention on the Rights of the Child | OHCHR, https://www.ohchr.org/en/instruments-mechanisms/instruments/convention-rights-child (accessed 14 August 2024).

Convention on the Rights of the Child, Article 1, 1989, Convention on the Rights of the Child text | UNICEF, https://www.unicef.org/child-rights-convention/convention-text (accessed 2 February 2025).

Convention on the Rights of the Child, Article 24(3), 1989, Convention on the Rights of the Child text | UNICEF, https://www.unicef.org/child-rights-convention/convention-text (accessed 2 February 2025).

Geneva Conventions – Third Geneva Convention, IHL Treaties - Geneva Convention (III) on Prisoners of War, 1949, https://ihl-databases.icrc.org/en/ihl-treaties/gciii-1949 (accessed 2 March 2025).

Geneva Conventions – Fourth Geneva Convention, IHL Treaties - Geneva Convention (IV) on Civilians, 1949, https://ihl-databases.icrc.org/en/ihl-treaties/gciv-1949 (accessed 2 March 2025).

International Covenant on Civil and Political Rights (ICCPR), Background to the International Covenant on Civil and Political Rights and Optional Protocols | OHCHR, https://www.ohchr.org/en/treaty-bodies/ccpr/background-international-covenant-civil-and-political-rights-and-optional-protocols (accessed 2 March 2025).

International Covenant on Civil and Political Rights, Article 23.1, International Covenant on Civil and Political Rights | OHCHR, https://www.ohchr.org/en/instruments-mechanisms/instruments/international-covenant-civil-and-political-rights (accessed 2 March 2025)..

Istanbul Convention – Council of Europe Convention on Preventing and Combating Violence Against Women and DomesticViolence, Home - Istanbul Convention Action against violence against women and domestic violence, https://www.coe.int/en/web/istanbul-convention (accessed 2 March 2025), https://www.coe.int/en/web/istanbul-convention (accessed 14 August 2024).

UN General Assembly, *Convention on the Elimination of All Forms of Discrimination Against Women*, 18 December 1979, UNTS, vol. 1249, p. 13,

Art 1, https://treaties.un.org/pages/viewdetails.aspx?src=treaty&mtdsg_no=iv-8&chapter=4&clang=_en (accessed 13 January 2025).

UN General Assembly, *Convention for the Suppression of the Traffic in Persons and of the Exploitation of the Prostitution of Others*, 2 December 1949, U.N.T.S., vol. 96, p. 271, https://treaties.un.org/pages/viewdetails.aspx?src=ind&mtdsg_no=vii-11-a&chapter=7&clang=_en (accessed 13 January 2025).

UN General Assembly, *Declaration on the Elimination of Violence against Women*, 20 December 1993, A/RES/48/104, https://digitallibrary.un.org/record/179739?ln=en (accessed 13 January 2025).

UN General Assembly, *Protocol to Prevent, Suppress and Punish Trafficking in Persons, Especially Women and Children, Supplementing the United Nations Convention against Transnational Organized Crime* (Palermo Protocol), 15 November 2000, Article 3, https://treaties.un.org/Pages/ViewDetails.aspx?src=ind&mtdsg_no=XVIII-12-a&chapter=18&clang=_en (accessed 13 January 2025).

United Nations Rules for the Treatment of Women Prisoners and Non-custodial Measures for Women Offenders (the Bangkok Rules) (BGR), United Nations Rules for the Treatment of Women Prisoners and Non-custodial Measures for Women Offenders (the Bangkok Rules) | OHCHR, https://www.ohchr.org/en/instruments-mechanisms/instruments/united-nations-rules-treatment-women-prisoners-and-non-custodial (accessed 2 March 2025).

United Nations Standard Minimum Rules for the Treatment of Prisoners (the Nelson Mandela Rules) (NMR), Nelson Mandela Rules (NMR, Rule 11), The United Nations Standard Minimum Rules for the Treatment of Prisoners, https://www.unodc.org/documents/justice-and-prison-reform/Nelson_Mandela_Rules-E-ebook.pdf (accessed 2 March).

Universal Declaration on Human Rights (UDHR), Universal Declaration of Human Rights | United Nations, https://www.un.org/en/about-us/universal-declaration-of-human-rights (accessed 2 March 2025).

Index

J. A. Scutt (ed.), *Women, Power and Autonomy*,
https://doi.org/10.1007/978-3-031-97958-3

H

9783031979576